American Children's Literature and the Construction of Childhood

Twayne's History of American Childhood Series

Series Editors
Joseph M. Hawes, University of Memphis
N. Ray Hiner, University of Kansas

American Children's Literature and the Construction of Childhood

Gail Schmunk Murray

Twayne Publishers

An Imprint of Simon & Schuster Macmillan • *New York*

Prentice Hall International

London • *Mexico City* • *New Delhi* • *Singapore* • *Sydney* • *Toronto*

American Children's Literature and the Construction of Childhood
Gail Schmunk Murray

Copyright © 1998 by Gail S. Murray

Twayne Publishers
An Imprint of Simon & Schuster Macmillan
1633 Broadway
New York, NY 10019

Library of Congress Cataloging-in-Publication Data

Murray, Gail Schmunk.
    American children's literature and the construction of childhood /
Gail Schmunk Murray.
        p.   cm. — (Twayne's history of American childhood series)
    Includes bibliographical references and index.
    ISBN 0-8057-4107-0 (alk. paper)
    1. Children's literature, American—History and criticism.
2. Children—United States—Books and reading.   3. Children in
literature.   I. Title.   II. Series.
PS490.M85   1998
810.9′9282—dc21   98-27647
                                                      CIP

This paper meets the requirements of ANSI/NISO Z3948-1992 (Permanence of Paper).

10 9 8 7 6 5 4 3 2 1

Printed in the United States of America

For Joe, for remembering what childhood was like;
for Kristen, Greg, and Erin, for sharing theirs with me

A — In ADAM'S Fall
We finned all.

B — Heaven to find,
The Bible Mind.

C — Chriſt crucify'd
For ſinners dy'd.

D — The Deluge drown'd
The Earth around.

E — ELIJAH hid
By Ravens fed.

F — The judgment made
FELIX afraid.

New England Primer, 1777, reprint edition, 1843,
courtesy of Special Collection, Burrow Library, Rhodes College.

Contents

Illustrations

Series Editors' Note

The history of children is coming of age. What began in the 1960s as a spontaneous response by some historians to the highly visible and sometimes unsettling effects of the baby boom has emerged as a vigorous and broad-based inquiry into the lives of American children in all generations. As this series on American childhood attests, this new field is robust and includes the work of scholars from a variety of disciplines.

Our goal for this series is to introduce this rich and expanding field to academics and general readers interested in children and their place in history. All of the books provide important insight into the changing shape and character of children's lives in America. Finally, this series demonstrates very clearly that children are and always have been influential historical actors in their own right. Children play an essential role in the American story that this series is designed to illuminate.

In this volume, Professor Murray focuses on children's literature, an important part of the process by which American adults sought to shape childhood to reflect their aspirations for their children and their society. She gives special attention to those works in which adult messages to children were most clearly expressed. Although some children's literature challenged traditional attitudes, the values of the dominant culture were normally paramount. As Professor Murray makes abundantly clear, children's literature provides a window into the heart of American culture and illuminates the role that the education of children played in its evolution.

Scholars who write on the history of children's literature often stress literary issues and do little to assess the social and cultural origins or significance of this literature. Professor Murray places children's literature in its proper social and political context and provides a balanced assessment of both its literary and historical significance. She also includes valuable discussions of how African-American and Native American children were portrayed in children's literature over time as well as an insightful analysis of the recent influence of multiculturalism. Professor Murray's successful integration of literary and historical perspectives represents a significant contribution to this field.

N. Ray Hiner
University of Kansas

Joseph M. Hawes
University of Memphis

Acknowledgments

This book began as an essay, an exercise in using primary documents to understand the socialization of children in early America. When I quickly discovered, as historians of children's literature always do, that children's books don't reveal much about the lives of real children, I began to look for indications that parents, clergy, teachers, and authors used this medium to teach acceptable social mores and behaviors. From that short paper some 10 years ago, and several years of seeking organizing themes for my course on the history of childhood in America, came the desire to use children's literature to examine the social constructions of childhood.

I am most appreciative to colleagues and former colleagues, already overburdened with their own research, who took time to read all or parts of this manuscript; I am particularly grateful to Jennifer Brady at Rhodes College and to Kenneth Goings at the University of Memphis. I received unfailing assistance from the reference staffs at the libraries of the University of Virginia, the College of William and Mary, the University of Kansas, the University of Michigan, the University of Memphis, Vanderbilt University, and especially Rhodes College. For access to rare children's books, I am indebted to the Rockefeller Collection at Colonial Williamsburg, the Spencer Collection at the University of Kansas, and the Mississippi Valley Collection, University of Memphis. I owe an enormous debt of thanks to Annette Cates of the Inner-Library Loan Office at Rhodes College for saving me many research trips. A Faculty Development Grant from Rhodes College enabled me to devote one summer to research, and a National Endowment for the Humanities summer institute, "Educating a Citizenry: School and Society in Jefferson's America," provided six weeks of stimulating discussions, intense readings, and enough humid weather to last several years. To Bob Gross and Peter Onuf, who directed that institute, thanks.

As one trained to research and write about early American history, I am especially appreciative of many new friends in the fields of cultural studies and children's literature. Ideas from chapters 2 and 3 have previously been presented at various history and children's literature conferences. My students in the History of Childhood program at Rhodes shared in fruitful debate over Alcott, Alger, and Harris and provided helpful "reader response" to the writings of Blume, Fitzhugh, Klein, and L'Engle.

I'm most appreciative of the faith that Ray Hiner, an editor of the Twayne Series on the History of Childhood in America, had in a historian's ability to articulate the significance of children's literature within its historical context. He helped me stay the course when the demands of teaching American history seemed all-consuming. When those demands became too heavy, I retreated with a stack of children's books: what better way to relax!

Introduction

So the children's books told the truth, as they mostly do. It was not the whole truth; it never is . . . but it is the kind of truth difficult to extract from more objectively complete histories.
—Anne Scott MacLeod, *American Childhood*

Few of the many fine surveys of children's literature seek to understand the critical connection between the creative work of fiction and the cultural and social reality of which the author is a part. No story is developed in a historical vacuum; the nexus between any children's book and its time is crucial to understanding the book's importance. Children's literature provides insights into the social milieu in which the work was developed and uncovers the values that society hopes to transmit to its children. Children's books often tell us much more about the image of the ideal child that society would like to produce than they do about real children. Cultures have many ways to socialize the young, and Western cultures have relied heavily on books to transmit certain social values and to cast aspersions on other cultures.

American Children's Literature and the Construction of Childhood argues that the meaning of childhood is socially constructed and that its meaning has changed over time. Of course, society has never spoken with one voice, but in every era, except perhaps the present one, a dominant culture has prevailed. Books written for children reveal this dominant culture, reflect its behavioral standards, and reinforce its gender-role expectations. This is not to deny that certain works attempted to subvert traditional values: *Huckleberry Finn* is a prime example. Yet as iconoclastic as he was, Samuel Clemens still mirrors such conventional attitudes in his work as the inherent "goodness" of the renegades Tom and Huck. For the most part, the canon of children's litera-ture adults have promoted has had particular social conventions to uphold.

On the whole, children's literature is a conservative medium. Clergy, teachers, parents, and writers have all used it to shape morals, control infor-mation, model proper behavior, delineate gender roles, and reinforce class, race, and ethnic separation. Historically, children's fiction has not encour-aged creativity, exploration of behaviors, or self-expression. In this study, I have tried conscientiously to evaluate literature in terms of the cultural work it was designed to do within each historical period rather than argue whether a particular piece constitutes a "good" children's book. I have chosen those children's books that most reflect American culture as a whole and in which the adult messages to children are most explicit. Also, in the interest of limit-ing materials, I have excluded poetry, science fiction, folktales, and nonfic-tion (with the exception of primers), and I have limited authors after the colonial period to those born in the United States. An annotated bibliography found at the end of the text will lead the interested reader to more detailed critical studies on historical periods and children's authors.

The organization of *American Children's Literature and the Construction of Childhood* is chronological with the exception of chapter 5, which extracts the issue of minority culture from three eras to consider that theme as a whole. The story begins with the British settlers to North America and the books they imported for their children. Although not growing out of colonial culture, the sentiments of British catechisms, books of manners, and tradi-tional tales helped reinforce the Anglo-American culture. I have given partic-ular stress to primers and catechisms written by dissenting Englishmen and colonial Puritans because of their clear delineation of the meaning of child-hood as a time of preparation for adult religious discernment, and for their emphasis on acquiring literacy. John Newbery's influence on the entertain-ment value of children's stories is aligned with John Locke's educational the-ories, both of which found ready acceptance in the British colonies.

Chapter 2 examines the uses to which the Revolutionary generation put British tales that emphasized such republican virtues as self-sacrifice, honesty, dependability, charity, and thrift. It explains how the memory of George Washington was molded into a moral tale, and how secular didactic stories and Protestant Sunday school literature combined to create a secular set of behavioral standards for children, standards that reflected the country's con-cern that only self-sacrificing citizens could make republican government work. Society's construction of childhood underwent significant change in the late eighteenth century as children came to be seen as rational beings capable of moral decision making as soon as they had received some instruction. The tales of Peter Parley and the Rollo stories of Jacob Abbott introduced a truly American literature for American children before 1850, and the new phenom-enon of juvenile magazines vastly expanded the child-reader audience.

The middle half of the nineteenth century saw an explosion in children's literature and brought to attention numerous authors who have since been considered canonical: Lydia Maria Child, Louisa May Alcott, Horatio Alger, and Mark Twain. Chapter 3 pays particular attention to the gender construction of Victorian America and the "bad boy, good girl" themes it produced. The popular female domestic-fiction writers are portrayed not as Hawthorne's "scribbling women" but as canny presenters of those values society honored. Childhood became a romantic period in which the goodness and innocence of the child, male or female, could transform the curmudgeonly folks around them. Horatio Alger's plethora of books portrays a society at once attracted by the excitement of urbanization but also frightened by the potential loss of personal integrity and face-to-face relationships in the city. While both Alcott and Twain are presented as products of their generation, they also created subversive texts. Although dime novels began as reading for the urban working class, their dramatic plots and fast-paced action soon affected writing for children, much to the consternation of the professional gatekeepers in education and of the newly organized American Library Association.

Popular series books, especially those created by Edwin Stratemeyer and his syndicate, continued this controversy in the world of children's literature. Innovations in printing made inexpensive books possible, and the syndicates reduced costs even further by commissioning authors who were paid only per manuscript, with no royalties. Sports stories, boarding school stories, mysteries, and career girl adventures all found their niche in series. In addition, female writers continued to create Victorian sagas of orphaned girls redeeming the faulty world around them. In the late nineteenth and early twentieth centuries, childhood innocence remained a mainstay, but children more actively created better situations. It was not their goodness alone but the good they *did* that transformed others.

In Chapter 5, we take a step back to consider how the dominant white, middle-class arbiters of what children should read have systematically stereotyped people of color and non-Americans. Beginning with Alcott and Harriet Beecher Stowe and continuing through the series books, the powerful messages about race and class emerge. Included are the complex stories Joel Chandler Harris crafted. His "story within a story" reveals a rich collection of African-American folktales that compose the "inner story." Harris sets this folktale into an "outer story" full of Old South mythology and the stereotyping of emancipated African-Americans. W.E.B. Du Bois's efforts to create a periodical for black children, the *Brownies' Book*, and Mary Ovington White's rendition of an African-American protagonist without negative stereotyping are considered.

The period between the two world wars saw enormous changes in American society that had tremendous impact on children. Child labor, public schools, clubs and youth groups, and public entertainment changed radically. Children were no longer viewed as innocent redeemers; their fears and hopes were more realistically portrayed. But childhood itself was a protected, separated time in which children could revel until they had to face adulthood. Series books continued to introduce teenagers and young adults to adventure. Although such adventure stories were carefree and middle class, they valued resourcefulness in solving problems, courage, and cleverness. For the younger child, the nuclear family existed to shape, protect, and isolate the child from the frightening world. Stories in which a single child protagonist explored his or her limited and protected world, enjoyed friends, and experienced some interesting adventures predominated in the hands of such authors as Elizabeth Enright and Eleanor Estes. Life of a sort—small town, carefree, protected— was realistically portrayed. Laura Ingalls Wilder incorporated a highly idealized image of frontier life in her Little House series, an image that revealed her distaste for New Deal programs of economic assistance for farmers. A few authors sought to introduce minority or working-class children into their stories, but for the most part this was a "Dick and Jane" book culture.

Little changed in the construction of childhood following World War II. Just as solid patriotism and constant vigilance were seen as ideological weapons in the Cold War, the nuclear family was idealized as the seedbed of democratic values and lauded as the expression of woman's proper place. The ugly theme of death was reintroduced into children's literature in *Charlotte's Web* but in the familiar guise of both a family story and a coming-of-age story. Of all the mid-century authors, Dr. Seuss (whose real name was Theodor Geisel) seems most to step outside of time with his fantastical stories and whimsical illustrations. But even he gives voice to direct attacks on contemporary life in both *The Cat in the Hat* and *Horton Hears a Who*.

And then the cataclysm hit. Beginning in the 1960s, children's literature took a dramatic turn away from the family story and the series mysteries to embrace the "problem novel." Chapter 7 explains how J. D. Salinger's *Catcher in the Rye* became the touchstone for adolescent fiction in the 1960s. Authors imitated his first-person narrative style, his alienated teenage protagonist, his vernacular language and clipped dialogues; their novels focused on a specific problem that impeded the protagonist's development, whether an alcoholic parent, a divorce, a mental health problem, the death of a sibling, an unwanted pregnancy, gang rumbles, or abuse. Stories for younger children, too, often revolved around the type of childhood crisis heretofore not discussed openly: divorce, masturbation, voyeurism, deliberate lying, menstruation, and sexual activity. Given the social dislocation in America society at large, manifested in public sentiment about Vietnam, civil rights, and the counterculture, the altered literary themes of the 1960s and 1970s should come as no surprise. The social construction of childhood inherent in these two decades of writing for children reveals a different purpose for childhood.

Firmly steeped in contemporary therapy and self-help philosophies, adults believed that children had the inner resources to handle emotional pain; they believed that some suffering would prove helpful in adulthood. In this construction, children are neither sinful nor innocent but survivors. As in the social construction of childhood in colonial America, the lines between what children know and do, and what adults experience, have been considerably blurred.

Also beginning in the 1970s, some teachers and parents began to demand that children's books reflect the ethnic and racial diversity of their urban classrooms. Critics demanded more than just a recoloring of skin tones; they wanted strong, resourceful minority protagonists. Publishers, aware of new trends in immigration that brought large numbers of Hispanic and Asian peoples to America in the 1980s, grew more open to cultural diversity. Authors of children's literature found themselves caught up in the larger so-called culture wars of the 1980s in which some critics judged books only on the basis of whether racist and sexist assumptions were present. By the 1990s, much of the adolescent buying public rejected themes of cultural diversity and social action in favor of bland romance novels. Younger children, too, consumed new adventure and thriller series books, along with character stories mass-marketed and targeted at them through TV and the movies. The popularity of Dr. Seuss and Maurice Sendak with adult buyers suggests that a nostalgia for a romanticized vision of childhood, or at least a childhood in retreat of adult themes, is currently underway.

1

The Sinful Child:
Anglo-American Colonial
Children's Literature, 1690–1810

In 1691 a small advertisement appeared in Henry Newman's
Almanac:

> There is now in the Press, and will suddenly be extant, a Second Impression of the
> New England Primer enlarged to which is added, more Directions for Spelling; the
> Prayer of K. Edward the 6th, and Verses made by Mr. Rogers the Martyr, left as a
> Legacy to his Children.[1]

This advertisement comprises the earliest information extant on the best-
known children's book of the entire British colonial era in North America,
the *New England Primer*. Historians calculate that the original primer first
appeared sometime between 1687 and 1690, although no copies of it have
survived; the earliest surviving edition dates from 1727. Over its 150-year
publication history, six million copies were sold, attesting to its enduring
power even into the years of the new American republic.[2] In addition to the
primers that taught children to read and provided them with their first exercises, children in colonial America could read works on proper behavior,
folktales, Puritan hymns and catechisms, and a few didactic, child-directed
stories. In the seventeenth century, few families could afford to purchase children's books, but by the mid-eighteenth century children's books became a
symbol of affluence and reflected parents' aspirations for their youngsters.

Although none of these books resembles the entertaining illustrated stories available today, the role of children's books in colonial society was not
much different than the role children's literature assumes now. Literature for

1

children was produced by and sold to adults to teach, persuade, convince, and solidify social values and establish mores for the rising generation. If we bear in mind that children's literature of any era is much more apt to reflect the ideals to which adults want children, families, and society to aspire than it is to reflect *actual* children, families, and societies, then children's literature can serve as a window into a culture. Because the material is written for young people with limited knowledge of the world and of relationships, its values are often distilled, simplified, and readily apparent. In Western culture, children's literature has been one of the chief sources through which adults could teach, persuade, and elevate particular values and social mores for the next generation. As a window into cultural values, then, children's literature provides insight into society's goals, gender expectations, and ideals. Literature for children can help reveal a society's current construction of childhood. This chapter will present a view of childhood through an examination of the children's literature that was available in British North America.

Colonial Children

A glance at the portrait paintings from colonial America would lead an observer to think that colonial children were treated, and expected to behave, like miniature adults. Infants and toddlers, regardless of gender, wore long shifts. After a child became ambulatory, he or she would add robes and collars to the decorative petticoat. Around age six, children assumed clothing similar in style to adults' and therefore specifically gendered. In the seventeenth century this meant that young boys donned breeches and loose shirts at six or seven; girls continued to wear long petticoats, with overskirts, bodices, aprons, and caps, just like their mothers. Children in portraits appear stiff and overdressed, posed in formal surroundings with perhaps one small toy clutched in their hands. The colonial child appears unlikely to run and play, to sass his parents, or even to get dirty. Parents did not want children crawling about on the floor in what appeared to them to be animalistic and primitive behavior. Rather, they provided children with "standing chairs" to keep them in an upright (human) position. Corsets and tight wraps were designed to keep the child's growing body stiff because adults believed that immature bones were easily misshapen. Thus, from a physical perspective, adults wanted children to look like adults.[3]

From an economic perspective, most seventeenth-century families found that all hands could benefit the household in some way. From the age of three or four, children could run small errands, feed the chickens and ducks, gather eggs or kindling, tend the baby, and churn butter. By age 8 or 10, young boys already worked most of the day either with their father or another male relative, or alternatively they began an apprenticeship at a local artisan's shop.

Young women mastered the full range of domestic chores—food preparation, spinning and weaving, sewing and mending, laundry, cleaning, gardening, butchery—with their mothers or as assistants to other relatives and neighbors. This "placing out" eased the burden of too many children in the home and provided essential labor to individuals without children. Most children received enough schooling to master reading, writing, and ciphering (arithmetic), although their education might well have taken place at home under parental tutorship rather than in an organized school.[4]

Because colonial children dressed like adults, worked in the fields and the home, and had little time for playing with peers, they have often been depicted historically as miniature adults. The reality of colonial childhood defies such simple categorization, however. Scholars have discovered that colonial law recognized the special status of childhood and protected that status with laws governing the obligations of parents to educate their children in the tenets of Christianity, the obligation of masters to educate and train apprentices, and the protection of children from physical abuse. The Body of Liberties, passed in Massachusetts Bay Colony in 1641, recognized age 16 as the age at which a child became accountable to the law.[5] The journals and autobiographies of Puritan families reveal that there were "clear distinctions between adults and children [who were] well into their teens" in such areas as the kind of discipline used, the expectations for labor, and the attendance at various communal gatherings. Church records show that children were catechized separately and somewhat differently than were young adults. Parents and clergy wrote lovingly and frequently about the joy their children brought and indicated a clear awareness of their immature state and their difference from adults.[6] Even though colonial children dressed like adults and worked with them in the fields and homes, colonialists did conceptualize childhood as a unique and separate stage of development.

Colonial Children's Books

Few colonials had time to pen works for children, and those who did faced great challenges in acquiring the technology and royal permission required to have the works printed. Well into the eighteenth century, most children's literature was imported directly from England. The mercantile economy of Great Britain dictated that the monarch control the number and location of printing presses through licensure. Since the purpose of the colonies was to supply raw materials to the mother country and provide her with new markets for the sale of manufactured items, the Crown saw little reason to license printers in the colonies themselves. Massachusetts Bay Colony obtained permission to set up one print shop in 1638 to facilitate routine colonial business and to print necessary legal forms. The colonies of Pennsylvania and New

York each received permission for a printery later in the century, and Virginia opened a print shop and bookstore in Williamsburg in 1703. Since each line of type was hand set and each page printed singly, books were time consuming to print. Most colonists and booksellers placed orders for desired books directly with a London printer until the eighteenth century, when colonial printing became more common.[7]

In the seventeenth century, children could expect little in the way of printed material written especially for them. Such folktales as *King Arthur and His Knights of the Round Table* constituted one source of children's literature. Particularly in the eighteenth century, as colonial life on the eastern seaboard approximated British gentry culture, so-called courtesy literature became extremely popular. Essentially advice manuals, such books prepared young men and women to enter into genteel society with all the social graces appropriate to their age and gender. Young children were advised in *The School of Good Manners:* "Bite not thy Bread but break it; but not with slovenly Fingers, nor with the same wherewith thou takest up thy Meat. . . . Drink not nor speak with anything in thy mouth." This popular advice manual is usually attributed to the colonial printer Eleazer Moody, for many copies were sold under his imprint. Scholar Jane Bingham, however, has illustrated that it was clearly pirated from the well-known British work *The School of Manners* (4th edition, 1685).[8]

Older children found more gender-specific advice. Young women were admonished to cultivate "one of the chief beauties in a female character, that modest reserve, that retiring delicacy, which avoids the public eye" in *A Father's Legacy to His Daughters* by one Dr. Gregory. Gregory also urged young women to steer clear of religious controversy. Lord Halifax first published *The Lady's Gift, or Advice to a Daughter* in 1688 for his own daughter. This work, which went through 15 editions before 1765, was especially popular in the Chesapeake colonies. A confirmed Anglican, Halifax urged his daughter to avoid the sour Puritans and to view religion as a comfort, not something to fear. Young men received instruction on how to secure the best education, suitable travel, exercise, and the art of graceful conversation. Other popular titles included *Principles of Politeness, and of Knowing the World* (1775) by Philip Dormer Stanhope (Lord Chesterfield), *Compleat Gentleman* (1622) by Henry Peacham, and *The Complete English Tradesman* (1725–1727) by Daniel Defoe. A very few women wrote courtesy books for genteel ladies, most notably Mrs. Leigh, who wrote *The Mother's Blessing* (1616). Advice manuals designed to ensure the hierarchical and patriarchal functioning of the economically secure household included Benjamin Wadsworth's *The Family Well-Ordered* (1712) and Isaac Ambrose's *The Well-Ordered Family* (1762).[9]

Older children read fiction written for adults, such as Daniel Defoe's *Robinson Crusoe,* John Bunyan's *Pilgrim's Progress,* and Jonathan Swift's *Gul-*

liver's Travels, rather than literature designed specifically for children. First sold as imports, these books were eventually reproduced by American printers in the early eighteenth century, sometimes in simplified and bowdlerized versions, and were readily available.[10] By far the best-selling children's works produced in the American colonies were the primers and catechisms (aids to learning religious doctrine) of the various separatist groups that had settled around Massachusetts Bay. Every family constituted a potential market for these texts, even the more middling classes. The primers embody the pedagogical philosophy and moral values of the era as well as set forth the doctrinal positions of the dissenting sects.

The Pilgrims who migrated from Scrooby, England, to Holland and finally to the New World landed far north of their intended destination of Virginia. Jamestown and other outposts on the Chesapeake were established by gentlemen and adventurers for their own and their investors' profit. The Pilgrims of "Plimouth Plantation" came as families, bringing their children with them. They also brought some books, although given the stringency of these children's early years, we cannot know to what extent they read them.[11]

Within a decade, a better educated and more financially secure company of religious dissenters arrived in Massachusetts Bay with 11 ships, 700 passengers, and substantial belongings. Under the direction of John Winthrop, these families set out to establish a "City on a Hill," their version of a Christian community in which both business and religious life were directed by a body of "saints" or church members.[12] With the establishment of these "dissenting communities" came a dedication to scriptural authority and literacy that would have wide repercussions for the New World. As disaffected English continued migrating during the 1630s, "New England" came to include five separate colonies: the original Plymouth and Massachusetts Bay Colonies, Connecticut, New Haven, and Rhode Island.[13] Not all inhabitants were Puritans, but in the "orthodox" colonies of Massachusetts Bay, Connecticut, and New Haven, the clergy maintained clear authority and placed much emphasis on creating well-ordered Christian communities of likeminded citizens. Convinced that the very survival of their holy experiment depended upon strict obedience to both God's word and civil magistrates, the clergy insisted upon the biblical literacy of the young.

One of the most respected divines in Massachusetts Bay, the Reverend John Cotton (1584–1652), produced a child's introduction to Puritanism in 1646 called *Spiritual Milk for Boston Babes; in either England: Drawn out of the breasts of both Testaments for their Souls nourishments: But may be of like use to any Children.* Although published abroad, this was undoubtedly the first children's book written in the American colonies.[14] The title reflected life in Cotton's former pastorate, Boston in Lincolnshire, as well as in his current residence, Massachusetts Bay Colony. Similar catechisms were common in England, both in the Church of England and among dissenting sects. Calvinists had produced several catechisms, the most popular being the *Westminster Catechism*. However, *Spiritual Milk for Boston Babes* was the shortest and simplest Puritan catechism yet devised. Some catechisms posed over 100 questions for the catechumens to memorize. Cotton pared the questions to just 64, many of which could be answered in only one sentence. *Spiritual Milk for Boston Babes* could be both understood and memorized by children.

> Q. What hath God done for you?
> A. God hath made me, He keepeth me, and He can save me. . . .
> Q. How did God make you?
> A. I was conceived in sin and born in iniquity. . . .
> Q. What is prayer?
> A. It is calling upon God in the name of Christ by the Help of the Holy Spirit, according to the will of God.[15]

In 1660 Cotton's congregation in Boston voted "that Mr. Cotton's Catechism should be used in families for teaching children, so that they might be prepared for public catechizing in the Congregation."[16] By 1684, New England printers began reproducing *Spiritual Milk for Boston Babes* for a colonial audience.

That same year at least 60 copies of another enormously popular Puritan work made their way to America. James Janeway's (1636?–1674) *A Token for Children, Being an Exact Account of the Conversion, Holy and Exemplary Lives and Joyful Deaths of Several Young Children* had first appeared in England in 1671 and recounted in vivid detail how 13 children faced their imminent death with confessions of faith and convictions of salvation. Speaking directly to the parents who had purchased the book, Janeway urged them to

> pray, pray, pray, and live holily before them, and take time daily to speak a little to your Children one by one, about their miserable Condition by Nature. . . . Put your Children upon learning their Catechism, and the Scriptures, and getting to pray and weep by themselves after Christ.[17]

The Boston cleric Cotton Mather (grandson of John Cotton) found such inspiration in *The Token* that he too collected childhood "deathbed accounts" from Massachusetts Bay Colony. He subsequently published his accounts in 1700 as an addendum to the first colonial printing of Janeway's work. Mather entitled his contributions "A Token for the Children of New England; or Some Examples of Children in Whom the Fear of God Was Remarkably Budding Before They Dyed."[18]

We cannot know exactly what meaning these pious and somber accounts held for the seventeenth-century child. However, their popularity with parents can be explained by recourse to both Puritan theology and the actual cir-

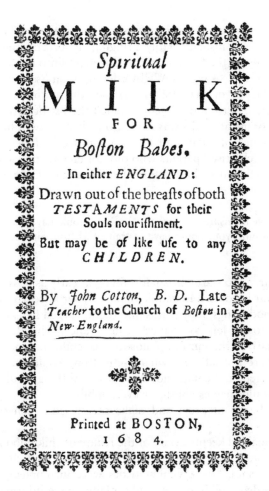

John Cotton, *Spiritual Milk for Boston Babes* (1646, reprinted 1684)

cumstances of life in seventeenth-century New England. Puritan theology firmly held that individuals could not effect or cause their own salvation; God's grace alone achieved that. However, parents were obliged to raise their children in accord with biblical precepts, in particular "Train up a child in the way he should go: and when he is old, he will not depart from it" (Proverbs 22:6). They believed such religious guidance would prepare the child to recognize God's saving call and receive the grace of salvation when it came. As adults, these former children would give a public testimony in which they confessed their state of sin and indicated their desire to be fully reconciled to God. The congregation would then examine the individual's motives and behaviors and "test" the strength of his or her conversion. Puritan parents held it to be their greatest obligation to educate their children in the tenets of the faith and prepare them for this "conversion experience." As the Reverend Peter Bulkeley admonished, "Holy bringing up of children is one special meanes of conveying the blessing of the Covenant unto them."

Cotton Mather's "A Family Well-Ordered, or an Essay to Render Parents and Children Happy in one another" stressed the mutual obligations of parents and children. "Promoting piety" headed the list of parental obligations. To remain ignorant of God's ways and God's history with his people was to invite the presence of Satan and his temptations. In *Farewell Exhortation*, Richard Mather chastised parents who did not take their teaching obligations seriously. He depicted a child before the "Heavenly Throne" criticizing his parents:

> All this that we here suffer is through you: You should have taught us the things of God, and did not; you should have restrained us from Sin and corrected us, and you did not.[19]

Parents were urged to start Christian training as early as possible: "While you lay them in your bosoms, and dandle them on your knees, try by little and little to infuse good things, holy truths into them," urged Benjamin Wadsworth. Nothing was to be left to chance or ignorance. The Reverend Timothy Dwight summarized the Puritan philosophy of child training when he wrote, "If children were not advised; what useful thing could they know? If they were not exhorted, and commanded; what useful thing would they do; what useful habit would they establish, or even imbibe? . . . They would evidently become mere beasts of prey; and make the world a den of violence and slaughter."[20]

Parents remained keenly aware of the reality of childhood mortality in the seventeenth century as well. Exact figures on infant and child mortality are impossible to obtain, "since vital statistics were incomplete, stillbirths were often not recorded, children, especially infants, were informally buried, and the high frequency of such deaths made their occurrence unremarkable."[21] In New England, infant mortality averaged about 10 percent, while in the Chesapeake, disease and infection killed 25 to 30 percent of all infants. When all New World colonies are averaged together, one in every four infants could expect to die before adulthood. The unpredictability and suddenness with which an illness could carry away a child, was an ever-present and frightening reality. In addition, accidents, poisons, and especially fires were notorious for claiming young lives.[22] Cotton Mather reminded parents of this harsh reality in his *Right Thoughts in Sad Hours* when he wrote, "A dead child is a sight no more surprising than a broken pitcher, or a blasted flower." Having seen several grandchildren die, the poet Anne Bradstreet mourned:

> No sooner came, but gone, and fall'n asleep,
> Acquaintance short, yet parting caused us weep;

Three flowers, two scarcely blown, the last i' th' bud,
Cropt by th' Almighty's hand; yet is He good.[23]

All colonists lived under the shadow of death and believed that God alone controlled all destinies: God sent healing and death alike. Children learned early on to accept God's ways with humans, including the possibility of untimely death. Thus the earliest books for children presented both the realities of human existence and the correct theological understanding of it. Death was never considered too macabre or frightening for children to hear about or witness.

Primacy of Literacy

Because Puritans took religious education of the young so seriously, it is not surprising to find early legislation mandating it. "The Word Written and Preacht is the ordinary Medium of Conversion and Sanctification," explained Thomas Foxcroft in Boston.[24] "Now in order to obtaining these Benefits by the Word, it is requisite, that Persons be diligent in Reading and Hearing of it." England had no such mandates. But Puritan clergy and laymen knew their noble experiment in creating the City on a Hill depended on a pious and educated following. Exposure of common people to the biblical text was a relatively new phenomenon: although Coverdale had translated the Bible into English in 1535, the authorized King James version (1611) was the principal Puritan text brought to America.

Primary responsibility for literacy training was assigned to parents. In 1642 Massachusetts Bay Colony required the selectmen of each town "to take account from time to time of all parents and masters, and of their children, concerning their . . . ability to read and understand the principles of religion."[25] Parents taught the alphabet and the recognition of simple words at home so that by the time a child started school, he or she could recite the alphabet, recognize the letters, and read short words and sentences. Parents unable or unwilling to provide basic instruction often sought out a local woman, frequently a widow, who held an informal "school" in her kitchen. Known as "dame schools," these institutions flourished throughout the colonial era. If children were apprenticed out, as they often were by age 10, the responsibility for further education fell upon the master instead of the family of origin.

Whether through ignorance or overwork, some families must have been derelict in their duties, because in 1647 the Massachusetts Assembly passed the first colonial law requiring that children become literate. In the words of the law itself, "[O]ne chief project of the ould deluder, Satan, [is] to keepe men from the knowledge of the Scriptures." However, "great neglect in many parents and masters in training up their children in learning, and labor" had resulted.[26] The law declared that every township of over 50 householders had to provide a school, which could be financed publicly or privately.[27] In the scattered settlements in the rest of New England and especially in the Chesapeake, many children learned basic reading at home with the use of primers (such as the *New England Primer,* described previously) but had little opportunity for further education. Basic literacy prepared them to read stories like those found in *The Token for Children* and, because they were already so familiar with its contents, to read the Bible. Much that passed for reading may have been recitation of memorized lines rather than reading with comprehension. But to the seventeenth-century parent, such recitation was purposeful. *The Christian Directory* of 1673 admonished parents, "Cause your younger children to learn the words, though they be not yet capable of understanding the matter. . . . A child of five or six years old can learn the words of a Catechism or Scripture, before they are capable of understanding them."[28]

Such at least was the "prescriptive literature" on religious education in Puritan New England. What a society prescribes identifies its ideals and what it considers essential to its cultural survival. How successful were the colonists in achieving the biblical literacy and theological knowledge they so desired? Kenneth Lockridge's seminal essay on colonial reading, *Literacy in Colonial New England,* argued that the ability to sign one's name was an indication of literacy because penmanship and arithmetic ("ciphering") were taught after reading skills had been mastered. Thus Lockridge took any evidence of personal signatures as evidence that that person had achieved reading competency.[29]

However, literacy involves many different combinations of skills; "some people [were] able to read printed books but not handwriting, and still others able to read everything, as well as write themselves," whereas some could probably read adequately but not write at all, not even to sign their names. When Lockridge argued that colonial literacy reached about 70 percent by the beginning of the eighteenth century, he based his figures on the ability to sign legal documents. This analysis is particularly problematic when assessing literacy of girls, as the scholarship of Jennifer Monaghan has shown. Many girls attended school long enough to become quite accomplished in reading but did not go to the grammar schools or take private penmanship courses because society considered this skill necessary only for those who would hold public roles (that is, for men). Whereas reading was a requisite for *all* children in a Puritan community, writing was perceived as a function of governance and employment. Thus New England laws usually required that children be taught to read but rarely to write. Monaghan argued for a much higher literacy rate for girls than had Lockridge. Certainly functional literacy—the ability to read simple children's books—was much higher. When the Massachusetts General Court asked towns to provide a list "of the youth from the age of nine years and upward, who cannot read," the town of Beverly reported that "[we] doe not find any youth of the age of nine years or exceeding it that cannot read: or that are not Endeavoring to learn."[30] Given the overstatement to which political officials are prone, the Beverly report indicates a serious effort to provide basic literacy skills.

Whether early education fell to parents or to dame schools, the basic tool they used was the primer, and the *New England Primer* was probably their preferred choice. Building on the features of the old English hornbook, a piece of horn on which were carved the alphabet and one-word syllables, the *New England Primer* added simple rhymes, biblical proverbs and sayings, and some form of catechism. Thus it became the principal schoolbook, religious text, and book for home instruction in colonial America. Its popularity spread well outside the Puritan settlements, for Benjamin Franklin recorded selling 37,000 copies of the *New England Primer* in Philadelphia alone between 1749 and 1766. As many as six million to eight million new copies found their way into children's hands, not counting those that were handed down from older to younger children.[31]

Pedagogically the *New England Primer* introduced children to several progressive levels of instruction. Although the *Primer* underwent many revisions through the decades, its pedagogical outline remained constant. The text first introduced children to the printed alphabet (without illustrations), which they may have already been able to recite orally. Children then learned lists of consonant and vowel sounds, mastered syllables, and finally learned a list of one-syllable words. Gradually children worked through two- and three-syllable words unrelated by sound or theme. Whether they simply memorized a word's appearance or whether they attempted to sound out the words cannot be determined from the text itself. After mastering lists of three-syllable words, children moved on to rhyming verses, which remain the best-known section of the *Primer:*

In *Adam's* Fall, We sinned All
This *Book* attend, Thy Life to mend
The *Cat* does play, And after slay
The *Dog* doth bite, a Thief at Night.[32]

This memorization aid and teaching device was followed by an "Alphabet of Lessons": proverbs and morally instructive sentences taken from the Bible and arranged so each sentence began with a successive letter of the alphabet. For example, "*A* wise son maketh a glad Father, but a foolish son is the heaviness of his Mother. *Better* is a little with the fear of the Lord, than great treasure and trouble therewith." Additional religious materials including the Lord's Prayer, the Apostle's Creed, and a catechism followed. Earliest editions of the *Primer* used the Westminster Assembly's "Shorter Catechism" with its 107 questions and answers that ranged from 8 to 100 words each. Other editions contained John Cotton's shorter *Spiritual Milk for Boston Babes* instead; the 1775 edition contained both catechisms as well as several hymns for children by Isaac Watts. Many editions also included a poem called "A Dialogue between Christ, Youth and the Devil" and an account of one John Rogers, an English Puritan martyr of 1554.[33] Having mastered the *New England Primer,* the colonial child was then able to make his or her way through the Psalter and the Bible.

The evolution of the *New England Primer* presents in itself a brief history of both the religious and political experiences of the northern American colonies. The religious enthusiasm of the Great Awakening, which spread throughout the colonies from the late 1730s through the 1770s, found its way into the *Primer* as well. The simple alphabet rhyming verses, which had featured "cat," "dog," and "eagle," became instead verses about Christ, the "deluge," and Elijah. Biblical verses replaced simple, secular rhymes. Changing politics was also accommodated. "King Charles the Good, No Man of Blood" was replaced in 1727 by "King William's Dead / and left the throne / To Ann our Queen / of great Renown." Frequent changes must have been frustrating to printers, who next adopted "Our King the good / No man of blood," which held until the colonies began to chafe under British restrictions. A colonial printer then devised "Kings *should* be good / Not men of Blood." After independence both the "K" and "Q" verses were altered to read "The British King / Lost States thirteen" and "Queens and Kings / Are gaudy things."[34]

Although the most popular early book of instruction, the *New England Primer* had competition. Not all parents, especially outside of Puritan New England, wished their children exposed to "dissenting" theology. In 1750 the English printer John Newbery composed the more secular *Royal Primer,* which sold quite well in American cities. The Quaker clergyman John Woolman produced *A First Book for Children* in 1766, in which simple sentences, unrhymed, were presented for the beginning reader: "The Lark will fly in the Field / The Cat doth run after the Mouse, / The Chub swims in the Brook, / And the Good boy will do good in his place."[35] *Tom Thumb's Play Book: To Teach Children Their Letters as Soon as They Can Speack, Being a New and Pleasant Method to Allure Little Ones in the First Principles of Learning* appeared in 1771. A 3-by-2-inch "toy book," the Tom Thumb text resembled the secular alphabet book of modern times: "A, an Archer who shot at a Frog." Rhymes helped children memorize and remember their letters.[36] *The American Primer,* published in Boston in 1776, attempted to capitalize on the strike for independence but actually differed little from the *New England Primer.* Later editions even used the woodcut that had been labeled "George III" and titled it "the Honorable John Hancock, esq."[37]

Chesapeake Colonies

Much less is known about reading habits, printing, and publishing in the southern colonies than in the northeastern ones. Although initial settlement occurred somewhat earlier than that of New England (Jamestown, for instance, was settled in 1607), population growth was very slow due to the low ratio of females to males, the relatively late age of marriage, and the high death rate for both adults and infants.[38] Business adventurers founded the "Virginia Plantation" with the goal of profit for the joint-stock company. The idea of a permanent settlement, the immigration of whole families, and the establishment of community life occurred much later than it had in New England. The Chesapeake colonies did not pass laws regarding literacy or the establishment of schools. Even printing was an eighteenth-century phenomenon in the southern colonies. Although some official government printing was done earlier, the first tracts known to have been produced in Virginia or Maryland date from at least 1700; printers turned out sermons, laws, speeches, or newspapers, not principally books.[39] A survey of Richard Beale Davis's extensive discussion of early southern printers reveals no production of children's books; however, Davis may have ignored them as insignificant for his purposes, or most books for children may have been imported from England. Advertisements in such southern newspapers as the *Virginia Gazette* and the *Virginia Almanac* indicate "various sorts of small Books for Children." The account books from a Williamsburg, Virginia, bookstore between the years 1750 and 1752, and 1764 and 1766 reveal that chapbooks (short, inexpensive English stories for children) and conduct manuals/advice books were popular sellers.[40]

By the early eighteenth century, a native-born, or Creole, majority began to control the economic and social life of Virginia. This Chesapeake elite established a more cohesive society, modeled on the rural English gentry, and built grand brick homes in the urban centers of Williamsburg and Annapolis as well as in the surrounding countryside. They filled their gracious homes with luxury items from England, including books. Their children, particularly sons, received a formal classical education of the type appropriate for an English gentleman.[41] Planters usually hired a tutor to provide instruction right in the home. Philip Fithian's diary concerning his employment as a tutor to the Robert Carter family provides considerable insight into planter families.

In towns such as Williamsburg, private schools run by either men or women were available. Newspaper advertisements for teachers and for pupils attest to the availability of schooling, at least for those who could pay. Citizens of Williamsburg also established a "free school" for the poor in 1706 to teach basic reading, writing and arithmetic. Virginia law required masters to provide for the education of their apprentices but did not make provisions for public schooling.[42] Planters tended to expend more money and effort in planning for the education of sons than of daughters, although most did realize that a woman's household management demanded a good basic education. Following a general knowledge of reading, Scripture, and handwriting, young women were directed toward music, dancing, needlework, and other more "refined" skills.[43]

Like his New England counterpart, the southern colonist was most likely to own books of a religious or theological nature, but whether or not this zeal was transferred to catechisms and religion-based primers for children is simply unknown. In-home teaching of basic reading was just as common as in New England, but the text used might have been Dilworth's popular English work *New Guide to the English Tongue*. In the Prentiss Family Library Collection (housed at Colonial Williamsburg), a 1699 edition of *English Examples to Lily's Grammar Rules for Children's Latin Exercises* and Clarke's *The Rational Spelling Books: or, an easy Method of Initiating Youth into the Rudiments of the English Tongue* (Dublin, 1796) speak to the nature of imported works for children in the South.[44]

Throughout the American colonies, whether a book purchased was imported from England or printed in the United States made little difference. The Crown controlled printing, but once a craftsman had obtained a license to set up a print shop he could print whatever he chose. Authors could not prohibit the reprinting of their work. Such prominent colonial authors as Noah Webster and Jeremy Belknap lobbied with Parliament for copyright protection. Not until after the Revolution did some states pass copyright laws. Finally, in 1790 federal legislation gave authors "the sole Liberty of printing, publishing and vending" any book of their creation for 14 years.[45]

With the maturing of colonial settlements throughout the New World and their rapid population growth came the expansion of towns into entrepôts, cultural centers, and seats of considerable wealth. One British naval officer, after visiting New York City for the first time in 1756, wrote, "The nobleness of the town surprized me more than the fertile appearance of the country. I had no idea of finding a place in America, consisting of near 2,000 houses, elegantly built of brick, raised on an eminence and the streets paved and spacious, . . . but such is this city that very few in England can rival it in its show." From 1650 to 1750, colonial population grew from 330,000 to one million.[46] With this growth came an expansion of printeries, a greater variety of children's literature, and more disposable income with which to purchase it. Joining the popularity of religious catechisms, stories of holy children, and primers came more secular books, stories designed to entertain as well as to teach.

Influence of John Locke and John Newbery

John Newbery (1713–1767) pioneered this new kind of children's literature from his print shop and bookstore at St. Paul's Churchyard, London. Beginning in 1744 Newbery printed and sold a steady stream of children's books, some of which he probably authored himself. His good friends, such as Oliver Goldsmith, wrote others, and some titles were simply reworkings of popular folktales. Newbery's most popular book, *A History of Little Goody Two-Shoes* (1765), which he claimed was "from a manuscript found in the Vatican with illustrations by Michael Angelo," has actually been attributed to Goldsmith.[47] Newbery's fame as the first children's book author stems from his production of books meant for the pleasure and entertainment of children, with instruction as a secondary by-product.

Newbery's ability to entertain and morally instruct is perhaps best understood by examining *Goody Two-Shoes*. The principal characters are two orphaned children, Margery Meanwell and her brother. The children, who live from hand to mouth, are the stereotypical "poor but good" children who would populate much of child fiction for the next century. They are taken in and cared for by Mr. Smith, a kindly clergyman, who gives Margery a pair of shoes; Margery then cries out with joy, "[T]wo shoes, two shoes," hence her nickname. When Mr. Smith can no longer care for the orphans, the brother is apprenticed at sea and Margery seeks employment as a nursemaid for a wealthy English gentleman. As governess and teacher, she is so accomplished and modest that her employer falls in love with her and proposes marriage.[48] Her new status provides her with the title "Goodwife" or "Goody," but her earlier nickname follows her as well. Newbery used these child characters to model such virtues as charity, industriousness, kindness, obedience, and gratitude as well as to reflect the prevailing class structure as assailable by virtue rather than by the accumulation of wealth alone.

Unlike in the Puritan tales of pious children, the reward for good and moral lives in Newbery's books was not a holy death or the promise of heaven but achieving respect and material well-being. Margery became an established English housewife and her brother, a successful businessman. The emphasis on proper social behavior, hard work, and reward persuaded historian Nancy Cott that "Newbery single-handedly created (or discovered) the children's book market. . . . [His books] do nothing less than idolize, as they help define, middle-class values."[49] No wonder this book, as well as most of the Newbery collection, was so often reprinted in the colonies, where almost everyone considered himself or herself upwardly mobile.

Newbery himself stands as a model of entrepreneurship. Not only was his approach to writing for children new but the whole idea of publishing *pri-*

THE HISTORY OF

GOODY TWO SHOES.

Sir Charles Jones with his Lady Goody Two Shoes Visiting the Poor of the Village.

Ash & Mason N.º 139 Chesnut St.Philad.ª

Goody Two-Shoes as reproduced in A. S. W. Rosenbach,
Early American Children's Books (Portland, Maine, 1933)

marily for children was predicated on a belief that parents would spend money to indulge as well as to educate their offspring. He conceived the idea of collecting stories, riddles, maxims, and behavioral instructions into small books, such as *The Circle of the Sciences* and *Be Merry and Wise*.[50] He by no means abandoned the belief that children's books should teach good conduct and religion. *A Little Pretty Pocketbook* (1744) resembled the older courtesy literature that genteel parents had always purchased. For example, the book offered the following instructions: "Behaviour when at Home. 1. Make a Bow always when you come Home, and be instantly uncovered. 2. Be never covered at Home, especially before thy Parents or Strangers." But Newbery, unlike his predecessors, surrounded the advice with more entertaining pieces.[51] In *The Museum: A Private Tutor for Little Masters and Misses*, basic alphabet and reading instruction led to instructive descriptions of the "Seven Wonders of the World, Westminster Abbey, St. Paul's, and the Tower of London" as well as some specific rules for behavior. This was followed by the almost obligatory religious material: passages of Scripture and the "Dying Words of Great Men when just Quitting the Stage of Life."[52] Soon after Newbery's books appeared in London, printers Hugh Gaine in New York City and Isaiah Thomas in Boston were printing American editions of Newbery's works.[53]

John Newbery became one of the principal vehicles through which philosopher John Locke's ideas about child rearing and the psychology of learning were introduced in America. With Locke's Enlightenment philosophy, a whole new construction of childhood emerged that redefined the nature of the child and his or her proper role in society. In *Some Thoughts Concerning Education* (1693), Locke had emphasized the innate capacities of the child's mind and the reasoning abilities he believed parents could encourage by proper instruction. In contrast to Puritan dogma, Locke did not view children as burdened by original sin but rather as empty vessels awaiting instruction. By describing a child's mind as a *tabula rasa*, he argued that early education was critical in character formation. For Locke, a child's moral sense was embryonic. "I imagine the Minds of Children as easily turned this or that way, as Water itself. . . . They are Travellers newly arrived in a strange Country, of which they know nothing. . . . They love to be treated as rational creatures sooner than is imagined," Locke wrote.[54] This theory of the malleability of the child persisted well into the nineteenth century, when it was co-opted by the romantic movement to produce the idea of a wholly innocent child (see chapter 4). Locke embraced not innocence but pliability. His construction of childhood viewed human rationality as the greatest of God's creations and the goal toward which the maturing child moved.

Locke also believed children should enjoy learning, not find it burdensome; they "are not taught by Rules," which they readily forget, but by "repetition and habit-formation," he argued. Through Locke, Newbery came to understand that children learned best when the lesson or moral was presented in an entertaining manner rather than when they were afraid of punishment or hell. Thus the modeling and explaining of acceptable and unacceptable behavior could produce the desired behavior in the child. Locke advocated presenting new information only as it related to the child's natural curiosity. He would teach the alphabet not by printed lists of letters, syllables, and words but through games, dice, and picture books.[55] John Ely, an American imitator of Newbery, wrote in the preface to *The Child's Instructor,* "The mind is the noblest work of God and capable of infinite improvement. . . . As we prize our own happiness, as we regard the welfare of society, as we love our children, let us attend to their instruction."[56]

Newbery often introduced his books with short essays admonishing parents to follow Lockean precepts, as in *A Little Pretty Pocket-book*. Many of his books were not stories at all but dialogues between parent and child, in which the child posed a question and the parent responded with a didactic explanation. A child's curiosity about a raisin, for example, produced an explanation of grape growing, harvesting, and drying. He even went so far as to attempt to instruct young people in physics in *The Newtonian System of Philosophy, Adopted to the Capacities of Young Gentlemen and Ladies . . .* , which he published under the name Tom Telescope.[57]

This emphasis on rational thought and instructive literature prompted Newbery and children's authors who followed to criticize the use of fairy tales, ghost stories, and other fantasies for children. Locke had urged foregoing discussions of "evil spirits" until children were of an advanced age. He reasoned that little children might confuse the "fantasies of goblins, spectres, and apparitions" with the "true notion of God."[58] Before long, writers for children came to distrust "fairies, enchanted castles, hobgoblins, romances," and the like "because they filled the child's mind with "improper ideas" and were indeed "baneful poisens."[59] Fantasy had no place in shaping the minds needed to lead a practical and rational New World society. Instead, children's books were designed to present useful information. *False Stories Corrected* devoted itself to explaining the impossibility of the existence of ghosts, mermaids, fairies, harpies, and even Jack Frost. The author explained the pelican's eating habits thoroughly and presented an engraving so the reader might be disabused of the old wives' tale that pelicans pulled live fish from their stomachs.[60]

Perhaps the most extreme case of this preoccupation with rationality is the retelling of the popular Aesop fable "The Lion and the Mouse." In the preface, children learned about actual lions: their hunting behavior and their ferocity. They learned that in reality, a lion would devour a mouse, not befriend it, as happens in Aesop's fable. The fable was an old favorite, probably reprinted because of its instructive moral that charity will receive a reward. However, an anonymous author or printer deemed that a realistic explanation was necessary to prevent children from being misled.[61]

John Locke believed that habits set down early in life led to established behaviors and high moral character. Parents were encouraged to teach such habits as industriousness, honesty, meekness, and obedience through both example and illustration. Children's books could certainly provide that illustration—and would, from the mid-eighteenth through the early twentieth century. The encouragement to be good differed, however, from the same instructions presented in the Puritan literature a century earlier. In a 1699 work Cotton Mather had insisted on a child's good behavior because "if by Undutifulness to your Parents, you incur the Curse of God, it won't be long before you go down into Obscure Darkness."[62]

Inherent in Newbery's formula—and part of Lockean educational theory as well—was the belief that eighteenth-century society could be reformed and improved through the moral education and elevation of the child. Like much of Enlightenment thought, Locke's views were implicitly optimistic. Indeed, this made them well suited for the exuberance and optimism of late-eighteenth-century America. As the British social historian Lawrence Stone has noted, this didactic literature appealed to upwardly mobile persons who valued "thrift, hard work, and moral self-righteousness," whether those persons were in London or Boston.[63] Children in the newer stories behaved well because they were rewarded with friends, success, and material possessions: middle-class rewards.

John Newbery's understanding of the rational capacity of the child and of the potential market for children's literature coincided with another major intellectual and political movement of mid-eighteenth-century America: republicanism. Republican ideals had their genesis in two traditions. First was the classical political tradition of Aristotle, who defined man as a "political animal" and who emphasized the necessity of virtuous, propertied men participating in government to protect it from selfish self-interest. Second were the writings of the British Whigs, who emphasized the necessity for elected citizens (Parliament) to limit the power of the monarch and his court.[64] Only men who were willing to put personal gain aside to work for the betterment of the state were considered worthy to rule. When powerful men abandoned virtue and rationality, as many colonials believed the British government was doing, evil, greed, and tyranny could result.

As colonial spokesmen moved into and through the American Revolution, the need to strengthen morality, rationality, and education helped shape the kind of literature they wanted the rising generation to read. Children's literature in the early Republic reflected republican ideals and emphasized virtuous and rational behavior through instructive texts. Although the Americans would continue to borrow British stories for their children, they would modify them to fit America's geographical location and American republican sentiments. Secular stories were sometimes tempered with providential explanations. For example, a Philadelphia publisher pirated Newbery's *History of Little King Pippin* in 1786. But in the story of a poor boy whose good behavior won him accolades from his peers while "Naughty George Graceless" was disgraced, the American publisher condemned George to death, although George was eventually saved by another boy's prayers.[65]

Domestic Fiction and Gender Issues

The influence of both Johns—Locke and Newbery—permeated British and American writing for children toward the end of the eighteenth century. A cadre of British women created popular nursery stories that combined didactic instruction with genteel domestic settings. Among those most read in America were Anna Letetia Aiken Barbauld (1743–1824), Maria Edgeworth

(1767–1849), Mary Butt Sherwood (1775–1851), and Sarah Trimmer (1741–1810). These authors brought a softer tone to the rather sterile discourses that had passed for children's literature before Newbery and, consciously or not, embodied the prevailing ideology of middle-class domesticity. With the popularity of stories written specifically for children and printed in small, easily held volumes, a small market for specific children's literature emerged on both sides of the Atlantic. Motivated in part by conceptions of the malleable child—ideas given prominence by continental philosophers John Locke and Jean Jacques Rousseau—these English women began writing instructive and entertaining stories for children, most of which were equally popular in America. They infused their stories with Protestant aphorisms and moral injunctions. Built largely on dialogues between a child and an adult, their didactic purposes were readily apparent. These authors domesticated and enlarged on Newbery and created a realistic though genteel home setting where curious, well-mannered children served as the catalysts for the instruction that followed. Their emphasis on moral character and early education had direct appeal to parents in the early American republic.

Anna Laetitia Barbauld wrote *Easy Lessons for Children* (1778) for her nephew Charles, presenting simple stories of preschool activities occurring in a proper middle-class British home. Manners, behavior, piety, and simple facts about nature were presented in short, simple sentences. *Easy Lessons* was printed in Philadelphia in 1788, followed by *Lessons for Children* (1807); both were written for an older child, and both found an eager market among urban middle-lass families on the eastern seaboard. *Evenings at Home* (1792), a collaboration between Barbauld and her brother, Dr. John Aikin, contained stories that could conveniently be read aloud in the evenings, a practice typical of the genteel eighteenth-century family. As a testament to the stories' popularity, 21 different American publishers reprinted the Barbaulds' *Evenings at Home*. According to the historian of British children's literature Gillian Avery, Barbauld may have been especially popular in America because of her dissenting religious views and her denial of aristocratic privilege in favor of moral hierarchies. Such ideas appealed to Americans of the Revolutionary era.[66]

Sarah Trimmer, a mother of 12 who always published under the name Mrs. Trimmer, became active in the British Sunday school movement and filled her children's stories with pious youngsters and readily solved moral dilemmas. Her best-known work in America, *Fabulous Histories* (1786), used a robin family to exemplify tranquil and self-giving domestic virtues. Worried that the decorum and deference of British society was on the wane, she attempted to inculcate the young with piety and self-sacrifice. Mrs. Sherwood was the pen name of Martha Mary Butt Sherwood, a prolific writer for the Sunday School Union and for the schools she established while living with her husband in India. In *The Fairchild Family* (1818–1847), a didactic four-part series set in her native England, Lucy, Emily, and Henry learn obedience, patience, and similar virtues from their ever-patient mother.[67] Mrs. Sherwood was tremendously popular in America.

The most controversial personality of this British pantheon was Maria Edgeworth. Working with her educator-father Richard Edgeworth, she promulgated John Locke's educational philosophy through the enormously popular *Parent's Assistant* (1796) and *Practical Education* (1798), both aimed at introducing parents to Lockean theories of learning. *The Parent's Assistant* was so popular in America that it was still being reprinted a century after it first appeared. Maria Edgeworth authored some 20 books on her own, including the popular novel *Castle Rackrent,* but her children's books were her most popular in America. *Early Lessons,* which appeared in 1801, eventually contained six volumes of similar titles and took children from beginning to advanced reading. These stories featured a brother and sister, Harry and Lucy, and seem to have been read by almost every nineteenth-century writer who mentions his or her childhood reading! In the second volume, *Harry and Lucy: A Series of Tales for the Young* (1813), Edgeworth explained her philosophy of teaching through her stories: "Much that would be tiresome and insufferable to young people, if offered by preceptors in a didactic tone, will be eagerly accepted when suggested in conversation, especially in conversations between themselves." Thus Harry often brings home bits of information from school lessons to share with his younger sister, who occasionally provides some comic relief by misunderstanding the lesson.[68]

British female authors fueled and shaped the development of American children's literature in fundamental ways. They assumed that all experience was premised on moral choices and that the socialization of the young into a morally correct social order was a female responsibility. With the decline of a Puritan hegemony in education, children's literature assumed the role of inculcating morals and defining behavioral principles. The language of these works helped shape and reshape the ethos of female domesticity and motherhood throughout the nineteenth century. American parents, regardless of their country of origin, loved these instructive children's stories. Even a collection called *American Popular Lessons* (1820) by Eliza Robbins was subtitled "Chiefly selected from the writing of Mrs. Barbauld, Miss Edgeworth and other approved authors."[69]

Because the gendering of children's literature emerges as a major theme in nineteenth-century criticism, we might ask what gender messages were implicit in seventeenth- and eighteenth-century writing for children. Certainly colonial society defined most economic roles, and all political roles, by gender. Males held all positions of religious authority except among the Quakers. The length and quality of schooling differed for boys and girls. However, the basic messages of children's primers and religious texts were not gender-specific. All children needed knowledge of Scripture and all were to live a pious life, dedicated to God, becoming church members when so moved by their conscience and voted by their peers. Boys usually received more schooling, as mathematical and handwriting skills were necessary for employment, participating in government, and doing business. Advice manuals were gender-specific, for they dealt with the roles individuals would play in both public and private life.

The families in which the stories are set are very gender-defined: boys skate, farm, chase animals, and become sailors while girls work in the home and seldom venture far from it. Certainly children did not need to turn to printed material to gain an understanding of gender roles in the preindustrial world of colonial America. Effective knowledge did not depend on experiences with books but on participation in a female circle. Girls learned domestic skills, which were also production skills, from their daily participation in the household routine, either their own or that of the household to which they were apprenticed.[70] In the instructive dialogues and moral tales of Newbery and his many female followers, however, both boys and girls were admonished to cultivate the same set of virtues: honesty, piety, industry, frugality, and patience. Noble and righteous character depended not on gender but on correct behavior. In the eighteenth-century didactic story, both male and female characters provided advice, explanations, and instructions to children. Both boys and girls listened and obeyed.

2

Virtues for the New Republic, 1790–1850

As a political event, the American Revolution (1776–1783) marked a pivotal divide in the diplomatic and economic history of the country. Historians disagree over whether ideas about self-government in local politics combined with radical Protestant theology to create this climate of revolution or whether the political break itself caused a reordering of traditional hierarchy and privilege in social relationships, family structure, educational opportunity, and institutional organization. The effect of the American Revolution on the writing and dissemination of children's literature, however, was anything but dramatic. In the tumultuous years of the Revolution itself, printers concerned themselves primarily with political tracts and newspapers. Importation of reading materials from Europe slowed, and the disastrous effects of war dramatically interrupted formal schooling. But the Revolution produced no great rush to produce American-made books for American children.

In the years immediately following the Revolution, patriotic fervor was tempered by anxieties that this noble experiment in republican government might not succeed. New Americans saw dangers within if republican sentiment were lost, and they saw dangers without in the presence of British, Spanish, and French traders and settlers in North America. Consequently many civic leaders regarded universal education as the most successful antidote to European political influence. Statesmen and clergymen began to advocate more democratic access to schooling. Additionally, American authors began to fashion a variety of didactic, instructional works for children, based on popular British models of instructional stories. A few authors were also infused with American nationalism; most emphasized a generic Protestant piety along with a rational Enlightenment-influenced description of the natural world. Books became more physically attractive, and new periodicals designed solely for young people introduced thousands of children to this new literature of civic virtue.

But at the same time that these expositions of middle-class virtues and the cultivation of a well-defined set of sound habits found their way into children's literature, so did another set of equally powerful didactic suppositions. A wave of emotional biblical Protestantism swept through all of the new United States between about 1800 and 1820, bringing renewed interest in church member-ship in established communities and spreading Protestant precepts and conver-sions among the newer frontier settlements from Pennsylvania down through Alabama. This "Second Great Awakening," as it was called by later historians, also contributed to a national desire to provide children with suitable indige-nous writings. The Sunday School Union, created in 1824, produced thou-sands of children's tracts, imbued with conversion motifs and highly idealized children performing daily tasks. These two strains—republican virtue and Protestant evangelicalism—would be combined by such perceptive early Amer-ican children's authors as Jacob Abbott and William Holmes McGuffey to develop a unique, indigenous American literature.

The expansion of the franchise to include men without property added thousands of new voters to the rolls and enabled the creation of grassroots political parties. A rapidly expanding population, both indigenous and immi-grant, turned villages into towns and towns into cities, and added nine states to the Union between 1820 and 1850. The evangelical revival produced not only a diversity of Protestant sects but also a plethora of missionary, educa-tional, and charitable institutions. Newly "awakened" Christians sought moral perfection not only in their own lives but in the larger society as well. Many of them worked tirelessly to create or improve such social institutions as schools, benevolent societies, prisons, and asylums. The French aristocrat Alec de Tocqueville, visiting the United States to examine prisons, concluded that Americans were inordinately devoted to voluntary associations and social improvement. Beginning with individual moral reformation—whether that meant abstinence from strong drink or denouncing slave-owning—and mov-ing to such societal reforms as free public schools, savings banks for laborers, Sunday schools, and relief for the poor during recessions and epidemics, the so-called Benevolent Empire moved forward. Although the genesis of this reforming zeal had originated in denominational revivals, its moral suasion soon moved outside narrow church confines into large national interdenomi-national organizations like the American Tract Society, the American Sunday School Union, and the American Temperance Society. The creation of a morally responsible society fueled by individual acts of charity seemed within the grasp of the reformers.

American culture, too, seemed destined to progress and gain wider recog-nition. In 1837 Ralph Waldo Emerson called for American independence from the cultural hegemony of Great Britain. "Our day of dependence, our long apprenticeship to the learning of other lands, draws to a close," Emerson announced in his address "The American Scholar." "[Let] the single man plant himself indomitably on his instincts and there abide, [and] the huge world will come round to him."[1] Emerson articulated what so many Americans already felt: the country needed an identifiable American culture for American citizens. A small part of that desired cultural nationalism occurred in the literature written especially for children after 1820.

Universal Education

Victory in the war against England suggested to some that the colonists' superior resolve and high rate of literacy (at least in New England) had led to their military success. Leaders of the Revolution believed firmly that the continued success of this experiment in republican government depended upon the education and virtue of all its citizenry. "Where the common people are ignorant," wrote Benjamin Rush, "a nation, and above all, a *republican* nation, can never long be free and happy."[2] In his First Message to Congress in 1790, President George Washington emphasized that "Knowledge is in every country the surest basis of public happiness. In one in which the measures of government receive their impression so immediately from the sense of the community, as in ours, it is proportionably *essential*."[3] For many, an educated citizenry was possible only through free access to schooling. By the end of his eight years in office, Washington was still enamored of the same idea: only public schools could create unanimity and patriotism. In his "Farewell Address" he argued that "The more homogeneous our citizens can be made, the greater our prospects of permanent union."[4] Learned Americans truly feared for the survival of the Republic without a dedication to universal education. Noah Webster argued that education would "implant in the minds of the American youth, the principles of virtue and liberty; and inspire them with just and liberal ideas of government, and with an inviolate attachment to their own country." A thorough education in Scripture, reading, law, commerce, and government were "necessary for the yeomanry of a *republican* State."[5]

However, the confederation government fashioned in 1777 to unite the colonies and sustain their rebellion was barely a national government at all. Individual states and their representatives centered their unity almost exclusively on simply ousting the British from those colonies declaring independence. Further than that, few wanted to put any significant powers in the hands of a national government. The greater energy for creating a new nation lay within the state legislative bodies, not the Confederation Congress. The only significant way the Confederation government committed itself to public education was through its organization of the western territory it had acquired from various state accessions at the end of the war. In 1785 the Confederation Congress surveyed and organized the territory that lay north of the Ohio River—some 160 million acres the new states had acceded to the federal government. Designating this region the Northwest Territory, Congress created townships six miles square. Congress required that one lot (640 acres) of each township platted in this vast territory be reserved for income that would help maintain a township school.[6]

When state political leaders realized that the very limited powers of the Confederation did not serve the economic or defensive interests of the United States, they led a movement to create a more federally powerful government under a new Constitution. Yet even the Philadelphia Constitution officially adopted by the states in 1789 did not give the federal government authority over education. John Adams, in his *Defense of the Constitution,* wrote that "there should not be a district of one mile square without a school in it, not [one] founded by a charitable individual, but maintained at the public expense of the people themselves."[7] States, he implored, must create a viable, accessible educational system. His state, Massachusetts, had already required town schools during its status as a colony, and it continued to do so in its new state Constitution.[8] At least six of the other state legislatures followed Adams's advice and devised proposals for expanding education. In Pennsylvania, Benjamin Rush recognized the implicit educational demands of a democratic society. "We have changed our forms of government, but it remains yet to effect a revolution in principles, opinions, and manners so as to accommodate them to the forms of government we have adopted," he wrote.[9] He advocated a public education that included primary school through college. His free grammar schools would educate both boys and girls in the basics of reading and penmanship and theology; in addition, girls would add domestic skills, whereas boys would follow the traditional curriculum of the eighteenth-century British academy.[10] Speaking of creating "Republican machines," Rush argued that American schools would "homogenize" the people and "thereby fit them more easily for uniform and peaceable government."[11]

Thomas Jefferson, proposing a system of publicly funded schools for the new state of Virginia, submitted to the legislature a "Bill for the More General Diffusion of Knowledge." Like many of the Founding Fathers, he worried that without education, citizens would be ripe for demagoguery and tyranny. They might not "know ambition under all its shapes, . . . [nor] exert their natural powers to defeat its purposes."[12] To preserve the Republic, his proposal required the state to provide schooling "for the term of three years, and as much longer, at their private expense, as [children's] parents, guardians or friends, shall think proper."[13] Jefferson's proposal was far less generous than it might at first appear, as after three years only one child per school could advance at public expense to an academy. Georgia legislators also attempted to establish public schools in the flush of the Revolution.[14] To the dismay of many young republicans, many states (including Virginia and Georgia) were unwilling to tax their citizens to support public schools, no matter how logical the plan. Conceding the centrality of education in the

Republic, statesmen still considered schooling a parental responsibility and therefore a familial expense.

Every president from George Washington through Andrew Jackson heralded the advantages of a national university that would rival the best universities of Europe. Washington and Madison even included the topic in important federal addresses. At his death, Washington willed 50 shares of stock toward the creation of a national university, but the project never received enough financial support from Congress to proceed with construction. By 1830 this lofty idea was lifeless.[15] Institutions of higher education would remain the responsibility of private benefactors, religious institutions, or state governments.

Almost all the voices for public education included pleas for female education as well. Not that the founders visualized political or social equality for women; rather, they postulated that a mother's formative influence over her children meant that she should be properly steeped in republican virtues and moral principles herself. Such an argument meant that female education would have to include more than simply domestic duties. In an address to the students of John Poor's Young Ladies' Academy in Philadelphia, Dr. Benjamin Rush urged that when women married, they should "be qualified . . . by a peculiar and suitable education, to concur in instructing their sons in the principles of liberty and government" and so ought to be educated in history, geography, natural philosophy, and Christianity.[16] Equally adamant about the necessity of women's education, Abigail Adams, wife of the nation's first ambassador to England and second president, wrote,

> If we are to have Heroes, Statesmen and Philosophers, we should have learned women. . . . If much depends as is allowed upon the early Education of youth and the first principles which are instilled take the deepest root, great benefit must arise from literary accomplishments in women.[17]

Abigail Adams's articulation of what later historians would call "Republican Motherhood" demanded that women have an education that included more than basic literacy for biblical reading; as mothers of future voters and statesmen, women needed unassailable moral and literary credentials. Although they would exercise their influence only in the private sphere, women found in this ideology considerable support for female education.

In the Northeast, girls had mastered reading at home or in Dame schools throughout the colonial era, and some village grammar schools had admitted them as well (although often at separate times from boys.) By 1789, Massachusetts law prohibited its town schools from excluding girls at the elementary level.[18] A few women founded private academies for girls from gentry families, like Emma Willard's famous Academy for Women in Troy, New York (1821), Catherine Beecher's Hartford Female Seminary (1823), and the

Mt. Holyoke School (1837). Such ideas even found their way into children's literature. In an early "Harry and Lucy" story, Maria Edgeworth presented a defense of female education when the mother in the story rebuked a gentlemen who said that girls don't need to know science. The mother gently chided him and explained that only when women "show off their knowledge" are they "abhorrent," but the "unaffected and unassuming" educated girl is a treasure to her husband and family.[19]

Schooling for both genders largely depended on parental status: when a child's labor was needed in the home, shop, or farm, then his or her schooling remained primitive. In none of the proposals were African-Americans, whether slaves or free citizens, included as subjects for a republican education. As is often the case, the rhetoric of political leaders far outstripped the willingness of the public to fund schools. Most American children in the early Republic acquired a rudimentary schooling of basic literacy, writing, and elementary arithmetic; only the elite received more.

Texts for a New Nation

Given the exalted position of education in the new Republic, one would assume statesmen rushed to produce textbooks and other reading materials for children that would reflect the principles of republican government and the selfless virtues the founders claimed such government demanded. The first such text printed was *The History of America, Abridged for the Use of Children of all Denominations,* published in Philadelphia in 1795. The text contained biographies, descriptions of exploration and founding, and brief histories of the 15 states, perhaps cribbed together from other adult reading matter.[20] But the Revolution brought no major reorganization of schools or of texts. Few made the step from theory to practice, from advocating schooling to writing books for these schools to use.

Only Noah Webster translated his revolutionary rhetoric into school textbooks. "America must be as independent in literature as she is in politics, as famous for arts as for arms," Webster wrote to his friend John Canfield in 1783.[21] With the *American Spelling Book* (1783), Webster launched the first of a progressive set of volumes designed to carry the student from learning the letters and sounds of the alphabet through sophisticated reading material by classical and contemporary authors and statesmen. Webster carefully expunged all aristocratic and monarchical discourses. At every level, Webster intended that the reading material be instructive in Republican virtues and morals. He dropped the biblical aphorisms of early New England primers and introduced students to American history, standardized American spelling, proper behavior, and his own brand of evangelical Christianity, all at the same time. He rejected the Bible as suitable reading for children, although his opposition differed from John Locke's (see chapter 1). Whereas Locke found the Bible too complex and even frightening for young minds, Webster believed that its constant reading *trivialized* the power of Christianity. "Nothing has a greater tendency to lessen the reverence which mankind ought to have for the Supreme Being, [because of] . . . careless repetition of His name upon every trifling occasion. Let *sacred things* be appropriated to *sacred purposes.*"[22] Webster sought instead to appropriate the *moral* teachings of the Bible, much as Jefferson did in his "Life and Morals of Jesus of Nazareth." What Webster urged was no less than the infusion of republicanism with Protestant morality. "How little of our peace and security depends on REASON and how much on *religion and government,*" he wrote.[23]

The American Spelling Book (later called *The Elementary Spelling Book*) became a standard American reader; it was commonly referred to as "Old Blue-back" because of its binding. The speller was basically a primer, a first reader based on the same pedagogy that had been in use in the colonies for 200 years. Students began by memorizing the alphabet and the sounds each letter made, then moved on to syllables and short words, building new words from these. A "table," which was a list of words organized alphabetically, was followed by a "lesson," a one-paragraph story. Children had to be able to spell aloud all the words in the table before starting the reading lesson. Thus spelling was mastered, not as a separate subject but as an integral part of learning to read.[24]

A few years later Webster brought out *The Little Reader's Assistant* (1790) for children who had gained fluency through the speller. In accord with his conviction that men must know their origins to participate in the republic, this work included considerable reading on American history. Webster also devised a "Federal Catechism" to instruct students in the principals of republican government:

Q: What is a constitution of government?

A: A constitution of government, or a political constitution, consists in certain standing rules or ordinances, agreed upon by a nation or state, determining the manner in which the supreme power shall be exercised over that nation or state, or rather how the legislative body shall be formed. . . .

Q: What objections are there to aristocracy?

A: In an aristocracy, where a few rich men govern, the poor may be oppressed, the nobles may make laws to suit themselves and ruin the common people. Besides, the nobles, having equal power with one another, may quarrel and throw the state into confusion; in this case there is no person of superior power to settle the dispute.

Q: What are the defects of democracy?

A: In democracy, where the people all meet for the purpose of making laws, there are commonly tumults and disorders. A small city may

sometimes be governed in this manner; but if the citizens are numerous, their assemblies make a crowd or mob, where debates cannot be
carried on with coolness and candor, nor can arguments be heard:
Therefore a pure democracy is generally a very bad government. It is
often the most tyrannical government on earth; for a multitude is often
rash, and will not hear reason.

Q: Is there another and better form of government than any of these?

A: There is. A *representative republic,* in which the people freely choose
deputies to make laws for them, is much the best form of government
hitherto invented.[25]

Webster went on to issue numerous readers, spellers, geographies, and
his well-known *American Dictionary of the English Language* (1828). Again,
his goal was to create distinctly American forms, so that his source for
spelling and grammar was the *spoken* language of Americans as it was evolv-
ing in the new Republic. In Webster's works, one can see the amalgamation
of rational Republican thought with traditional Christian precepts. Both
merged with a recitation of colonial resistance to England to produce inspirational stories for the young reader. Webster frequently talked of "the national
character" he hoped to form through his writings. His brand of history was
designed to inspire young citizens by example and to provide models for life.
In this way, Noah Webster set the tone for generations of early texts and histories.

A Boston schoolteacher, Caleb Bingham, presented Webster with some
early competition in textbook sales and also revealed the ambivalence of
American authors to limit their reading of British authors. Bingham compiled
a popular reader called the *American Preceptor* (1794), in which he declared,
"[A] preference has been given to the productions of American genius. . . .
[However, my work] has not been wholly confined to America; but has
extracted from approved writers of different ages and countries." British
sources such as Pitt, Pope, and Addison definitely predominated, even though
Bingham gave a nationalistic twist to the title of the collection.[26]

Read almost as commonly as the schoolbooks of the early Republic was
Mason Locke Weems, better known as "Parson Weems," whose *Life and
Memorable Actions of George Washington* (1800) captivated the new nation.
Weems was born in Maryland in 1759, served briefly as an Anglican clergyman, then turned to book publishing and sales. But he also tried his hand at
writing in a shrewd calculation of popular mood in post-Revolutionary America. In 1799 he wrote to a friend, "I've something to whisper in your lug.
Washington, you know, is gone! Millions are gaping to read something about
him. I am very nearly primd and cockd for 'em. Six months ago I set myself to
collect anecdotes of him. My plan! . . . [I] show that his unparreled [*sic*] rise
& elevation were due to his Great Virtues." The letter goes on to list Weems's

analysis of Washington's character, including "Religion, patriotism, magninmity [*sic*], industry, temperance, and justice."[27]

Thus did Weems begin the idealization of Washington's character, as well as the laudatory style with which Americans would compose political biographies for decades to come. Weems met immediate criticism for his exploitation of the Washington story. One reviewer called Weems "an author, a peddlar, and a preacher" who hawked books after he preached a sermon. Certainly there was some of the charlatan in Weems, for the author did promote himself as "Former Rector of Mount Vernon," which was absolutely not true: he was a former rector, but not of Mount Vernon, for there was no such parish; Washington might have heard him preach once at Truro! But Weems apparently knew his audience, one hungry for the exploits (true or not) of a great man who also embodied both the rustic and republican virtues that many Americans idealized. For a nation with a very short history, Weems wrote the American *Aeneid* with his reformulation of the founding story of America, complete with Revolutionary origins and heroes.

The expanded edition of this work (*The Life of Washington the Great,* 1806) became the most famous of the parson's works, containing as it does both the cherry tree story and a foretelling by George's father of a divine purpose for young George when cabbage plants he had planted grew to spell out GEORGE WASHINGTON! Although respectable historians did not repeat Weems's tales, the stories continued to appear in children's literature. Anna Reed composed an 1829 biography of Washington for the American Sunday School Union in which she attributed the general's finest characteristics to the influence of his pious mother. Peter Parley's *Life of George Washington* (1832) continued several of the myths, as did William Holmes McGuffey's popular readers.[28]

Fascinating and lucrative as the success of Parson Weems's history lessons might have been, schoolchildren in the New Republic also continued to use British texts and to read British essayists in American schools. The British textbook *English Reader* (1799) by Lindley Murray continued to outstrip both Caleb Bingham and Noah Webster in sales. As late as 1849, American teachers were complaining about the reprinting and use of Murray's British textbooks.[29]

The perceived British New England bias in the early republic's texts for children led the Cincinnati publishers Truman and Smith to seek a set of schoolbooks they believed would better reflect the agricultural, small-town atmosphere of Ohio. They first asked Catherine Beecher to write them; she had moved to Cincinnati with her clergyman father and opened a girls' school there. When she declined, they turned to a former schoolteacher and current professor in Ohio, William Holmes McGuffey, to try his hand at "western books for western people."[30] In his writing, McGuffey modified the pedagogy of reading education as well.

Because McGuffey had taught in the short-term, poorly attended small grammar schools of Ohio, he understood the necessity of making literacy acquisition a faster process. If farm children were to learn to read, they would have to be able to do so quickly. Instead of drilling students with lists of words that must be spelled aloud, McGuffey went straight from the alphabet to short sentences. He introduced shorter paragraphs and more illustrations into his texts and kept the books quite short. A graduated collection of titles slowly introduced the reader to more complex thoughts and more difficult reading. The first and second readers had 85 lessons each of spelling and reading. The third reader gave rules for reading aloud and featured short stories. In the fourth reader, McGuffey presented poetry and a wider range of subjects in essay form. Because so many German and other ethnic families had settled on the frontier, McGuffey included word pronunciations, as well as lists of frequently mispronounced words, such as "lows" for "allows" and "childers" for "children" and "keer" for "care." When Truman and Smith published his first set of readers, they advertised them as "especially adaptable for western schools."[31]

McGuffey's readers differed from Webster's "Blue-back" speller in several ways. Their method of reading instruction was new; they quoted Scripture even less frequently than Webster had; and they were more inclined to present short, pithy moral and ethical dilemmas. Most of the lessons dealt with morality rather than republicanism. Like the Sunday school materials to be discussed later in this chapter, great men rose in esteem not by courageous deeds but by pious or benevolent behavior. In the advanced readers, students were less likely to pore over solely British authors. The expansion of the American literary scene in the 1820s and 1830s meant that McGuffey's fourth reader (1837) could include essays by Lyman and Catherine Beecher, Lydia Sigourney, and William Ellery Channing. In fact, 40 percent of the 235 lessons came from American authors.[32]

"Peter Parley"

Samuel Goodrich (1793–1860), better known by his pen name Peter Parley, did more than any other American up to his day to develop children's literature as a separate genre. To be sure, the didacticism and moralisms of earlier authors remained. But Goodrich developed a more personal style to convey his instruction. As he was to reflect later, "I imagined myself on the floor with a group of boys and girls, and I wrote to them as I would have spoken to them." Goodrich, who began as a printer and publisher in Boston, brought out his first book, *Tales of Peter Parley about America,* pseudonymously in 1827. Like "Parson Weems," he wished to instruct about the American past while inculcating virtuous behavior. This book, as would Parley's later ones, began with discussion of Parley himself: "Here I am! My name is Peter Parley! I am an old man. I am very gray and lame. But I have seen a great many things, and had a great many adventures, and I love to talk about them." This contrived narrative allowed description of numerous events from America's past, including stories of Native Americans, early European settlements, and Revolutionary battles; frequent illustrations complimented the text. This pattern of the personal and genial old storyteller was repeated in each of the many Parley books that followed.[33]

In *Stories about Captain John Smith* . . . Goodrich used Smith's fanciful autobiography to illustrate not only "bad" behavior but also proper moral attitudes. Describing how young Smith ran away from the master to whom he was apprenticed in England, he wrote,

> This was a wicked step. He felt guilty. . . . Now little boy, you have just such a heart as he had. I do not mean that you *act* as wickedly—I hope you never will. . . . [But] if you feel it as you ought to do, it will make you *humble*. . . . To be happy, one must be good and be useful. We know . . . that Cpt. Smith was not happy. . . . How much more useful, and honorable, and happy would he have been, had he stayed at home—had he been sober and industrious, and especially had he assisted his mother! How much evil would he have escaped![34]

Whether writing a reader, a travelogue of Europe, an American history text, or a biography of Benjamin Franklin, Goodrich employed the same techniques of speaking directly to the reader, explaining events or describing sights in simple, direct language, and highlighting moral principles. Like the writers of other didactic stories discussed later, he voiced disdain for fairy tales, fantasy, and other "atrocious books," claiming that he drew his inspiration from the British domestic writer Hannah More. A few of his works appear to have been directed at an adult audience, such as the unusual *Lives of Celebrated Women* (1848), which included a two-page argument for the recognition of female talent. In all, Goodrich authored 107 titles and left an indelible track on the landscape of children's literature.[35] He was no gifted expositor; his genius lay in his recognition of a growing market for an American children's literature, one that recognized the necessity for early learning, achievement, and moral exactitude.

The American Didactic Story

By the 1830s, then, America had developed its own particular school texts through Noah Webster and William McGuffey. America had found a consummate storyteller and hero-creator in Samuel Goodrich. So it is not surprising that it also found a bevy of local authors to rival the popularity of the British domestic-story authors, like Maria Edgeworth, Anna Barbauld, and Sarah Trimmer, discussed in chapter 1. Their American counterparts shared similar didactic and moralistic goals but eliminated the British nursery nanny, male tutor, and afternoon tea parties.

Catharine Sedgwick (1789–1867), Lydia Maria Child (1802–1880), Lydia Sigourney (1791–1865), and Jacob Abbott (1803–1879) certainly borrowed from the British didactic tradition, adding their own distinctive American flavors to produce a viable American children's literature. Their ability to conflate a nondenominational Christian moral theology into behavioral instructions, couched in story form, became the hallmark of most literature for children in the early Republic. Their construction of childhood still posited Locke's rational child, but they also incorporated a generic Protestant moral code into everything they taught. Good behavior received its just rewards; naughty children got lost in the woods, drowned, were attacked by wild animals, or fell ill.

Fantasy and imagination remained suspect. As one scholar has noted, "The child who opened an Edgeworth or an Abbott story entered a family-centered world, presided over by preternaturally calm and rational parents. . . . Magic, sentiment, and high adventure had no place amid this pervasive, didactic reasonableness."[36] Like the early textbooks, this literature served to allay fears that the Republic might disintegrate because of moral laxity or simple ineptitude and confirmed for parents that the moral backbone of American culture remained firm.

Catharine Sedgwick and Lydia Sigourney epitomized the ideal of American womanhood as constructed by nineteenth-century culture. As classically defined by historian Nancy Cott, women of the middling and upper classes were identified and praised solely for their domestic virtues. Within this private sphere, set off from the public realm of male work and politics, women were expected to nurture husbands, rear children, practice piety, and make their home a buffer and retreat from the public realm. Sedgwick wrote both children's and adult domestic novels. Her *Moral of Manners; or Hints for our Young People* typified bourgeois advice on work habits, cleanliness, demeanor, and virtue. Sigourney had written stories and poetry as a young woman, but after her marriage she published her work anonymously. Her husband, Charles, objected to women having a public role, and she herself wrote that "woman should keep in her own sphere and not attempt to fill men's place."[37] Sigourney not only obliquely modeled this role, she prescribed it in her popular advice books *Letters to Young Ladies* (1835) and *Letters to Mothers* (1839). In *The Girl's Book* she described the "perfect" wife and mother, supposedly as an inspiration to young women, and castigated those with domestic flaws, such as being "neglectful of their children," "too fashionable" or given to vanity, or too "fretful and shallow." Her sentimental, domestic verses ran for years in such popular juvenile periodicals as *Juvenile Miscellany*.[38]

Lydia Maria Child (1802–1880) was already a published author when she married, and unlike many nineteenth-century female authors, she continued to write and publish under her own name throughout her marriage; in fact, she was the principal breadwinner during much of David Child's fervent but ill-paying abolitionist activities. She acknowledged her authorial debts to Laetitia Barbauld and Maria Edgeworth, even as she complained in the introduction to her first children's book that wonderful as their works were, they were "emphatically *English*." She sought instead to provide the same moral instruction in a distinctively American setting. Instead of a British tutor as the information source, Child used an aunt or mother to supply information in *Evenings in New England* (1824). Using the popular didactic formula of children posing questions, the female authority figure had the opportunity to discuss battles of the American Revolution, life on the Indian frontier, and games played in the American nursery.[39]

Such a narrative format provided numerous opportunities for Child to express both democratic sentiments and Christian morality. For example, when the aunt tells little Lucy that "our happiness depends very little upon wealth" but rather on one's ability to do "what we know and feel to be right," we sense both value systems at work. Invoking what will become a theme in American children's literature throughout the century, the aunt upholds the potential for upward mobility. "[D]estitute widows and orphans typically succeed through persevering hard work in earning the respect and charity of the rich and thereby climbing up to the plateau of middle-class prosperity," she intoned.[40] To the emerging middle class, both the aristocracy and the lower classes were profligate, wasteful, and disorderly. Both set a bad example for middle-class youth.

Sunday School Literature

The rise of the Sunday school movement in early America produced a voluminous literature for children and left indelible impressions on secular children's literature as well. In fact, the evolution of children's literature from the republicanism and didacticism of Noah Webster to the moral tales of William Taylor or Horatio Alger cannot be understood without reckoning with the powerful impact of evangelicalism.

The first American Sunday schools began in several East Coast cities around 1790. Like their British progenitors, the earliest Sunday schools targeted working children who could not attend common schools during the regular sessions. In 1790 Benjamin Rush and other Philadelphia elites founded the First Day Society, designed to instruct the "offspring of indigent parents" in reading and writing on Sunday mornings, using the Bible as their sole text. In the afternoon, teachers encouraged the children to attend services at the church of their choice. For a decade, the First Day Schools flourished.[41]

But unlike in Great Britain, Sunday schools did not remain principally a vehicle for literacy education. By the 1820s the focus of the Sunday school had shifted away from providing basic literacy to purveying a decidedly evangelical Christian message. Literacy, if taught at all, was used as a means of evangelizing the child, and through him or her perhaps the entire family would embrace Christianity. Soon Sunday schools enrolled children of church members along with any others they might persuade with prizes and picnics. The Sunday schools provided organizers the opportunity to teach morals and basic Christian doctrine at a time when doctrinal issues were no longer a part of secular education. At the same time, teachers used the Sunday school to introduce middle-class manners and concepts of discipline into working-class families.[42]

This new direction in Sunday school education can be traced to the Reverend Robert May of London. May advocated conversion over literacy training, and the children of his congregation were rewarded for regular attendance and for reciting Bible passages with tickets that could be redeemed for such prizes as Bibles and books. The British publication *A Sunday School Teacher's Guide* recommended that children be "awakened . . . [b]y all that is awful and all that is pathetic in religion." In 1811, Reverend May brought his technique to Philadelphia, where it was warmly received by the many evangelicals created by the Second Great Awakening. The converts precipitated by these revivals were predominately women. Many of them became Sunday school teachers, although men continued to serve as heads, or "superintendents," of the Sunday school. Larger cities like Philadelphia organized citywide Sunday school unions to coordinate their missions and training schools and to publish reading materials. At first, most of their lessons were reprinted from British Sunday school materials. Officials found some of it too classbased or hierarchical and thus edited portions of stories before printing them. By 1820, the Philadelphia union was publishing 45,000 tracts a year.[43]

In 1824, when supporters from several denominations created the American Sunday School Union, over 720 separate Sunday schools came under its umbrella. The movement spread during the next two decades, reaching thousands of American children, enculturating them in evangelical Christianity while spreading middle-class values like punctuality, obedience, cleanliness, and self-motivation. The American Sunday School Union also began its own publishing operation. Authors contracted to produce the usual morally explicit tale, but one that also featured a conversion experience, often followed by "the beneficent influence of that child on family or friends."[44] The child-death scene remained a popular device to exemplify faith, trust, and piety, reflecting a renewed zeal for emotional Christianity. *The Dairyman's Daughter,* the most popular book in the American Sunday school medley, embodied both of these themes, for the dairyman's daughter's death served as the catalyst for converting other family members and creating a moral reawakening in the family's youngest daughter. This saccharine work sold over a half-million copies in the United States and England and was published in at least 19 different languages.[45]

Hundreds of children's books authorized by the Sunday School Union appeared in the next 20 years, usually authored anonymously, unless a particularly well-known individual like Jacob Abbott or Mary Butt Sherwood consented to devise a story. These were hardcover, pocket-size books designed to be read quickly and easily. Plots were formulaic. The publishers warned potential contributors to stay away from fantasy or fairy-tale stories and to concentrate on "facts." They preferred the recounting of actual events, that is, moral dilemmas that real people, especially children, faced.[46]

In small towns without a public library, the Sunday school library often provided the only reading material available for whole families, thus dramatically increasing the dissemination of the evangelical message. One researcher found that in 1835, three Sunday school libraries housing a total of almost one thousand volumes provided her town's only books for borrowing. As a shrewd marketing device, the American Sunday School Union offered "complete libraries" for sale to public schools as well as to churches; an advertisement in 1851 offered a list of 100 volumes for only $10. Small sets were available to families for $2. A "Child's Cabinet Library" of 50 leather-bound books could be had for a somewhat larger sum. Like secular publishers of the early antebellum era, the Sunday School Union also developed its own juvenile periodicals. The A.S.S.U. inaugurated the *Youth's Friend and Scholar's Magazine*, which began publication 1823, and *Infant's Magazine* for younger children, which was published from 1829 to 1834; each carried stories, poems and Scripture verses and could be purchased by subscription.[47]

Joanna Gillespie, who has studied Sunday school literature extensively, argues that the books had two major messages: they taught that "any problem, secular or spiritual, could be broken into manageable components and mastered" and also that a "serious effort would equal success." Those who strove for improvement, whether moral, spiritual, or material, would probably be successful.[48] Attaching "scriptural authority" to moral improvement remained a significant influence of this evangelical genre.

Needless to say, the stories upheld and authorized the acceptable gender distinctions inherent in nineteenth-century America. Boys in these stories tended to be active, to seek adventure, and to learn their lesson from honest mistakes. Girls involved themselves in domestic tasks, played daintily, and usually exhibited concern for others without having to learn a lesson first.[49] In short, these stories attempted to anchor youngsters in the moral certitudes of their elders, elders who must have looked at the mobility, geographical expansion, and social reform of the 1820s and 1830s with considerable apprehension.

Jacob Abbott and the Confluence of Two Streams

Between 1790 and 1850 the population of the United States expanded from just under 4 million to over 23 million, and more families began to achieve a financially comfortable status that allowed for the purchase of playthings and books for their children. In this diversifying economy, family structure slowly altered as more men found work outside the farm and women played a less direct role in family production. The entire family no longer functioned as one economic unit, thus leaving women and children more leisure for such activities as schooling and reading. This expanded market of readers allowed authors like Lydia Child and Jacob Abbott to write specifically for children.

Samuel Goodrich and Lydia Child had made the didactic story into more engaging fiction with expanded story lines and sympathetic child characters. Meanwhile the Sunday School Union sought to ensure morally uplifting stories in the hands of young readers. New England clergyman, math professor, and headmaster Jacob Abbott (1803–1879) succeeded in joining these two temperaments of children's literature—entertaining didacticism and Protestant morality—with his series about Rollo, who very well may have been "the first truly American child character in literature." In addition to the usual devotional writings expected of nineteenth-century clergymen, Abbott's reputation as something of a specialist on children grew out of his parenting manual *The Young Christian* (1832). He expressed his conviction that religion was "caught, not taught" when children observed adult behaviors. A Boston publisher who liked his ideas had a collection of engravings he had not used for other publications, and he asked Abbott if he might write a story around the pictures. The result was *Rollo Learning to Talk* (1834), designed to be read to a very young child. *Rollo Learning to Read* followed, as did 13 more Rollo books in this first series (1834–1843). (Abbott returned to the character Rollo in 1853 and composed another 10 volumes.)

According to the well-known children's literature specialist Cornelia Meigs, Jacob Abbott showed considerable awareness of what we call child development today. The progression of the Rollo series from *Rollo Learning to Talk* and *Rollo at Play* to *Rollo Learning to Read* and the Rollo travel series revealed the protagonist passing through normal developmental stages, mastering new physical and intellectual challenges, and progressing through different "moral stages."[50] Abbott explained his pedagogical strategy in the introduction to *Rollo Learning to Read:*

> The difficulty with most books intended for children just learning to read, is, that the writers make so much effort to confine themselves to *words of one syllable*, that the style is quaint and uninteresting, and often far more unintelligible than the usual language would be. The author's design here has been, first to interest the little reader, hoping, by this interest, to allure him on to the encounter of the difficulties in the language, and to the conquest of them.[51]

While providing adventures and common domestic settings, Abbott consistently made sure that his readers "had been exposed to the rudiments of Christian morality. They had learned with Rollo *how* to live" their appropriately middle-class, Protestant values. Abbott wrote, "These books are intended to exhibit some of the temptations, the trials, the difficulties, and the duties, which all children experience in circumstances similar."[52]

Abbott reflected the common middle-class assumptions that the country was solidly Protestant and that cultural values were dependent upon upholding Christian beliefs upon which most citizens could agree. He listed these commonly shared assumptions in his instructions to beginning teachers:

God exists
Humans are responsible to God
The human soul is immortal
Mankind has been given a revelation of God in the Bible
Personal knowledge of God is essential to the salvation of each Soul
Belief in Jesus as Savior is necessary for the forgiveness of past sins

If teachers stress these concepts they can do "vast amounts of good" without offending anyone's particular doctrine, said Abbott.[53] Christian piety clearly underlay all of Abbott's work.

Abbott usually provided a "bad boy" as a foil for Rollo's morally superior or better-reasoned decisions.[54] However, unlike Samuel Goodrich, he did not use the authorial voice to lecture the reader about moral choices but rather led the reader to draw his or her own conclusions, based on the situation. For example, in *Rollo's Vacation* (1839) an older boy, Jonas, who is employed by Rollo's father, teaches Rollo how to carve a jack-o'-lantern. Having taught the reader a probable new skill, Abbott has Rollo leave the jack-o'-lantern out on a woodpile. Jonas reminds him to put up his tools and put the project in a safe place, but Rollo dallies and soon discovers that a cow has eaten his new prized possession. Abbott allows Rollo to show his anger and threaten to stone the cow but has Jonas realize his error:

"I don't think the cow is to blame," said Jonas; "but I tell you who is."
"Who?" said Rollo.
"Somebody that let her get at your Jack-o-Lantern. If you stone anybody, you had better stone him, if you can catch him."
"Who was it?" said Rollo.
"The boy that left the Jack-o-Lantern on the log."[55]

With similar moral didacticism, Abbott eventually authored over 100 fictional titles in numerous series, as well as about 80 purely religious texts or schoolbooks. The "Lucy" books feature a female protagonist, who, though tempted otherwise, always makes the morally correct choice; the "Jonas" books feature the young man in the dialogue just quoted. Many consider the

"Franconia" stories to represent Abbott's best work. The hero, Phonny, gets into considerable mischief; he daydreams, but he accepts the logical punishment, which is moderately and instructively meted out. Beechnut, a 12-year-old companion, serves as the authorial voice, the one who helps Phonny straighten out messes and make decisions.[56]

But one comes away from the text strongly suspecting that Abbott is really speaking to parents, showing them how much influence they can have over their children by modeling just and upright behavior. In his books one finds affirmation of Lockean precepts of the openness and susceptibility of the child's mind. The emphasis on child nurture and the careful formation of personal and moral habits is clearly aligned to Enlightenment thought. Parents and schools are challenged to provide environments conducive to modeling and habit formation. For example,

The development of the moral sentiments in the human heart, in early life,—and everything in fact which relates to the formation of character,—is determined by

THE FUNERAL.

Jacob Abbott, *Rodolphus* (New York: Harper & Bros., 1852)
Courtesy of the Mississippi Valley Collection, University of Memphis Libraries

formal precepts and didactic instruction. . . . Thus growing up in the right atmosphere, rather than the receiving of the right instruction, is the condition which is most important to secure in plans for forming the characters of children.[57]

On the opening page of the story *Rodolphus,* Abbott admonished parents, "The manner in which indulgence and caprice on the part of the parent lead to the demoralization and ruin of the child is illustrated by the history of Rodolphus." Abbott developed these same ideas fully in his book for parents, *Gentle Measures in the Management and Training of the Young* (1871), and in his book for beginning teachers, *The Teacher: or Moral Influences* (1836). Using his own school at Mount Vernon as a model, Abbott provided strikingly modern advice on classroom management while emphasizing the Christian nature of the entire enterprise of teaching. Always referring to the student as "he" even though Mount Vernon was a girls' school, he advocated some class decision-making and more positive than negative reinforcement, and concentrated on the positive gains each individual student made.[58]

There is an immediacy in Abbott's stories that prefigures such realistic boys' stories as Thomas B. Aldrich's *Story of a Bad Boy* (1869) or Samuel Clemens's *Tom Sawyer* (1871). There is also a pious, generic, cultural Christianity that very much locates the Rollo stories in time and place to early-nineteenth-century America.

American Nationalism

Following the War of 1812, sometimes referred to as America's "Second War for Independence," American nationalism leapt forward. Internal markets had greatly expanded in the years just preceding the war when trans-Atlantic trade was hindered by the Napoleonic Wars. As settlers continued to move westward across the Appalachians, new markets were created as well. With the military victory over Great Britain in 1812, American self-confidence flourished, as did the effort to define an American identity. Fiction writers began to create a distinctive culture that was more than just a derivative of British gentry and manners. In particular, Washington Irving (1783–1859) and James Fenimore Cooper (1789–1851) invented a self-conscious—if romantic—American identity with diverse regional roots. Irving's setting of German folktales in the Catskills of upstate New York and Cooper's fanciful descriptions of American Indian and British colonial conflict on the late-eighteenth-century frontier were written for adult audiences. But older children soon appropriated this adventure-filled literature for themselves, drawn to it by the thrill of mystery and escapade and the colorful regional settings. Irving's *The Sketch Book* (1819) featured both British and American "sketches," including the two short stories that became child favorites: "Rip Van Winkle" and "The Legend of Sleepy Hollow."[59]

J. Fenimore Cooper's romantic portraits of frontiersmen and American Indians shaped the American mind for generations and created myths that resurfaced in children's literature and dime novels. His Leatherstocking Tales began with the novel *The Pioneers* in 1823, then went backward in time to sketch Native American life during the French and Indian War in 1757 in *The Last of the Mohicans* (1826). Other tales included in the series were *The Prairie* (1827) and *The Deerslayer* (1841). Cooper was the "first American professional author, one who earned his living by writing."[60] Although he had no intention of writing for children, his colorful characters and vivid (for their day) plots appealed to adolescent readers. Because many Americans assumed that his portraits of eighteenth-century Cooperstown, New York, Natty Bumpo's frontier explorations, and the Mohican attack on Ft. Henry during the French and Indian War were all historically accurate, teachers began to recommend Cooper's novels to young readers as well.

In fact, Cooper knew nothing empirically about Native American life. He depended heavily on the accounts of missionaries and travelers, especially a Reverend John Heckewelder, who had lived with the Delawares. They became the "good" Mohicans in his novels, while their enemies the Iroquois were depicted as the villains. Although the clash between Anglos and Natives was set in the pre-Revolutionary colonies, the metaphor of the inevitable conquest of red by white represented Cooper's view of antebellum America: the native, though intelligent and sophisticated, was doomed.[61] A few years after the main Leatherstocking Tales appeared, Congress debated the fate of over 100,000 Indians still living east of the Mississippi. After a heated debate in which many argued that the native population could never survive unless it was protected from the advances of civilization, the Indian Removal Bill of 1830 was passed. Even though Chief Justice John Marshall ruled that the Cherokees had a right to their land and to its protection against the claims of the state of Georgia, President Andrew Jackson proceeded with their ousting. Through forced treaties and land purchase and under threat from federal troops, the last of the southeastern tribes were removed by 1838.

Social Reform Activity: Temperance and Abolition

The very forces that drew Americans toward a national identity also spun the nation centrifugally outward to address a wide range of new social institutions, organized movements for social reform, and utopian communal experiments. The rapid expansion westward, the gradual development of factories to replace artisanal production of clothing and tools, the increasing distinctions between worker and capitalist, and the apparent increase of poverty and crime in cities led many Americans to question the "progress" of the early nineteenth century. The rapidity of change in communities and in families within two generations increased fears about a stable future. The self-improvement or "moral perfectionism" inherent in popular evangelical religion led its followers to target institutions and relationships, as well as individuals, for perfectionist reform. In a burst of collective initiative, American men and women created organizations to evangelize the unchurched, dispense temporary aid to the ill and unemployed, urge abstinence from distilled spirits, create free public schools, advocate property rights and political roles for women, experiment with communal living, and agitate for the abolition of slavery. Those caught up in social reform frequently worked in two or more causes, although adherents of one (for example, relief for the poor) could be vigorous opponents of another (like women's rights.)

Almost all reform advocates were white, middle class, and Protestant; the objects of their reform were often people of color, working class, and unchurched or Catholic. (Most black abolitionists and temperance advocates organized separately from their white counterparts, whose racism often colored their goals.) Whole communities like Rochester, New York, experienced evangelical upheavals and outpourings of benevolent activity. Rural southern communities remained virtually untouched by the reformers except in urban temperance crusades.

Appeals for reform found their way into the popular journals and novels of the day and formed the basis of new media entirely. The experimental Oneida Community published its own newspaper to disseminate its social and theological ideas; Elizabeth Cady Stanton began a women's-rights newspaper; Harriet Beecher Stowe immortalized abolitionist sentiment in *Uncle Tom's Cabin*. Children too were the targets of some reformers' zeal. The public-school movement drew its energy from the efforts of Horace Mann, Henry Barnard, and George Peabody. Even the South, which had generally consigned education to the private sector, saw the rise of common-school movements in cities like Charleston, South Carolina, and New Orleans. Not surprisingly, the push for public schools, as well as the more nurturing (or Pestalozzian) teaching methods advocated by educational reformers, found expression in children's periodicals. An education was often portrayed as the route to success in life, and over a dozen magazines emerged to advocate common schools and educational reform.[62] The reformers' sway also fell heavily on children of the poor, as agencies sought to distinguish the "worthy poor" from those considered simply lazy and to provide for the upkeep of the former. Abandoned or widowed mothers often resorted to an orphanage to care for their children while they worked. Many children, as Horatio Alger's novels later revealed, fended for themselves in the cities.

But how much did middle-class children learn from their books and magazines about this reform ferment in American society? Since children's literature remained devoted to moral uplift, one might expect that only those reform themes defined as morally improving would be discussed. In fact, advocation of peace over war, temperance over drunkenness, and abolition over slavery were the chief social reforms to appear frequently in children's literature.[63]

The American Peace Society, organized by William Ladd in 1828, grew out of local peace societies formed by Christian pacifists in the Northeast during the previous decade. United by their vision of Christ as a peacemaker and by their belief in the efficacy of moral regeneration, they contended over questions of personal self-defense, defensive wars, and violence for the sake of abolition.[64] In children's literature, authors defined the early national period in marked contrast to the revolutionary era, a time in which war was "briefly necessary" to create the Republic. In this later period of enlightened Christianity and benevolent activity,

> There is another warfare, boy, and other foes to slay
> Than where to spill their followers' blood, men throw their own away,
> It is a warfare fierce and long; the foes are all within
> And there they battle and are strong, this conflict is with sin.[65]

Reformers linked pacifism with other personal and social traits needing purifying if heaven was to be brought to earth. Writers did not negate America's Revolutionary heritage but implied that society now had the opportunity to strive for higher goals. The peace crusade became more visible within children's literature during the Mexican War (1845–1848) when many New Englanders authors opposed what they saw as slave owners' grab for Texas and possibly even more territory. Numerous children's stories turned on the ruin and pain of a youngster who joined the army, such as "The Farmer Turned Soldier" in an 1846 edition of *Youth's Companion.*

Even more compelling in the minds of its supporters was the temperance message: drinking brought about financial ruin, family strife, physical debility, and spiritual loss. It led directly to lives of poverty and crime. In children's literature, this road to ruin often began with "confections (sugarplums, raisins, figs and candy), proceeding to cordials and winding up at the grog shop." In *The Glass of Whiskey* (1825) young Hugh first tastes liquor, sprinkled with sugar and nutmeg, at age six. This unfortunate taste cultivation results in an early death when he downs an entire jug of rum found in the closet. The Cold Water Army, a temperance organization for young people, produced its own periodical. The American Sunday School Union published many of the antidrinking stories, including *The Glass of Whiskey,* which attempted a quasi-medical explanation of the "poisonousness" of alcohol and its addiction-creating nature. *The Reformed Family* (1835) portrayed the business losses and want produced by the father's drinking, which led the mother to seek solace in alcohol as well until a religious conversion led the parents to recovery. A school text written in 1835 by Lyman Cobb appeared to be a fairly typical primer but included numerous sentences about the effects of alcoholic beverages, followed by essays on intemperance, including one entitled "The Effects of Intemperance Upon a Republick." The popular periodical *The Youth's Companion* carried frequent stories in which a drunkard came to no good end; in the summer of 1831 an editorial series was published even on the horrors of "D. Ts."[66]

According to many reformers, just as the greatest threat to individuals lay within, in temptations to alcohol and criminal activity, so the greatest threat to the nation's character also lay within: the evil of slavery. Abolitionism, however, constituted the most potentially divisive and costly advocacy of any of the reform movements. As a Christian principle or benevolent ideal, support for abolition seemed clear, but as a topic sure to result in declining book sales in both the North and the South, abolitionism presented serious problems for publishers. The two major political parties of the antebellum era, the Democrats and the Whigs, found antislavery to be their most divisive issue and spent much of their energies trying to keep this sectional issue from splitting their parties. Antislavery proponents generally turned to their own publications to perpetuate their views. Authors for children faced the same dilemmas.

Personally, Samuel Goodrich and Jacob Abbott both expressed sympathy for abolitionism, but in their children's fiction they either ignored the subject entirely or presented a cautious critique of slavery. For example, in *The Tales of Peter Parley About Africa,* Goodrich wrote,

> I do not, by this, mean to blame every person who keeps slaves. But slavery is a bad system; it always brings great evils along with it. Instead, therefore, of defending slavery every good person should condemn it, and use his efforts, on all proper occasions, to hasten the time when there shall be no slavery in the land.[67]

Some of the textbooks, including McGuffey's readers, included a few sentences about the evils and degradation of the slave trade. But since the trade had been declared illegal by the U.S. Congress in 1808, faulting its practice was hardly a bold stance. For most writers, criticisms of the ownership of slaves, without advocating immediate abolition, was the more common route. Many writers portrayed the *concept* of slavery as being at odds with American principles of liberty and freedom.

The American Anti-Slavery Society, founded by William Lloyd Garrison in 1833, turned some effort toward the child audience. It published *The Slave's Friend* for two years, beginning in 1836; the work used the popular dialogue style, as well as stories, to provide information about the sale, trade, work, and abuse of slaves in America.[68] These highly sentimentalized portrayals stopped short of advocating political solutions but dwelt instead on the moral corruption of anyone involved in the institution of slavery. The Oberlin (Ohio) Youth's Abolitionist Society published *Youth's Emancipator* during 1842 and 1843, placing a great emphasis on the ability of young people to effect social change. Author Eliza Follen in *The Liberty Cap* (1846) focuses on the moral agency of the child in one story in which the young boy tells his mother, "I think that if the men don't do something about slavery soon, we boys had better see what we can do, for it is all too wicked." In *Little Laura: The Kentucky Abolitionist* the local printer's shop is burned for publishing an abolitionist newspaper, and Laura speaks from her deathbed about the importance of the abolitionist's work.[69] Other authors urged children to speak out against slavery, aid fugitives, boycott products made by slaves, and contribute money to antislavery causes, as the following poem illustrates:

> LISTEN, little children, all,
> Listen to our earnest call:
> You are very young 'tis true,
> But there's much that you can do.
> Even you can plead with men
> That they buy not slaves again,
> And that those they have may be
> Quickly set at liberty. . . .
> Sometimes when from school you walk,
> You can with your playmates talk,
> Tell them of the slave child's fate,
> Motherless and desolate.
> And you can refuse to take
> Candy, sweetmeat, pie or cake,
> Saying "no" unless 'tis free—
> The slave shall not work for me.[70]

Lydia Maria Child took an aggressive and consistent stance against slavery, which resulted in her removal as editor of *The Youth's Companion* after eight years. But her progression to that position was gradual. She condemned slavery as early as 1824 but also suggested how difficult it would be to abolish it. Reflecting concepts of both racial inferiority and some of the assumptions of the Colonization Society, Child wrote,

> The negroes are very numerous, and they have been so unused to liberty, that they would become licentious and abandoned if left to themselves. Therefore, all that a good man can do, at present, is to make all the slaves in his power as comfortable as possible, to instruct their children to give freedom to those who deserve it, to use all his personal influence to remove the evil, and to wait patiently till the curse of slavery can be entirely and safely removed from the land.[71]

Child's view reflected popular thought in much of the North and South: slavery would eventually die out after the moral conversion of enough slave owners. In her story "Jumbo and Zairee," published in *Juvenile Miscellany* in 1831, Child questioned assumptions about inherent racial inferiority; she attributed African-Americans' limitations to the servitude in which they were held, not to lack of innate abilities. And yet at the end of the story, the two black children, having lived with and been educated by a white family, are sent back to Africa to live "more happily" with an African family. Here Child seems to argue for the position of the American Colonization Society, whose solution to the slavery question was to relocate all African-Americans and restore America to "whiteness."[72]

By the time "Mary French and Susan Easton" appeared in her periodical in 1834, Child had openly confronted race prejudice and probably assured her own dismissal from the magazine. In the story, set on the frontier, an unscrupulous peddlar captures two girls, one an emancipated slave and one the daughter of a white settler. The latter has her face blackened by the kidnapper, and both girls are sold into slavery in the South. Child thus illustrated how the evil of slavery touched both white and black. Upon revealing her true identity to the slave owners, Mary is of course treated well and restored to her family, whereas Susan, also a free person, is held in slavery. Revealing the ambivalence of white America, Mary does not plead Susan's case too strongly, lest her own freedom be jeopardized.[73] In retrospect, Child's abolitionism hardly seems radical and her own assumptions about the potential for "savagery" in blacks hardly progressive. But by addressing a child audience about the realities of the slave trade, the human emotions of those in bondage, and the moral toll slavery exacted from white America, she did more than any other author except Harriet Beecher Stowe (see chapter 4) to sensitize white children to racial issues.

Also in the fold of antebellum reform movement, the national Friends of the Indian as well as various denominational societies worked not only to stem the tide of westward removal but also to bring schooling, health care, and Christianity to native settlements. In *Evenings in New England*, Lydia Child constructed the following exchange between young Robert and his Aunt: Robert asks, "If [Indians] were so very thick when Maine was first settled, where can they have fled?" His aunt responds that war and disease have caused many deaths. Unsatisfied, Robert queries, "But what right had we to take away their lands?" The Aunt responds that most Indians sold their land for cash, but she admits that "they are too often cruelly imposed upon by artful, dishonest men." Robert piously responds, "How I do wish something could be done to make all the Indians as happy and prosperous as we are."[74] Childs had no difficulty presenting a vexing moral dilemma to her young readers while chastising their elders in the process; no real solutions are proposed, but moral responses and "evil" are named.

One final reform issue, relief of poverty and assistance to the poor, proved equally troubling to antebellum Americans. The British distinctions between the "worthy poor" (those who by virtue of age, illness, or incapacity could not support themselves) and the "unworthy poor" (those who were unemployed without visible signs of debility) permeated American thinking in the early nineteenth century as well. Anglican parishes and Puritan communities provided support for the worthy poor if they were permanent residents; others were place in almshouses (workhouses) or sent packing. In the 1820s New York and Massachusetts undertook legislative studies of the extent of poverty and the availability of public relief. Many states began construction of new institutions to house the poor at the public's expense. Meanwhile numerous private agencies attempted to provide basic necessities to the poor in individuals' own homes while simultaneously instructing them in methods of thrift, helping them seek work, and encouraging their children to be sent to charity schools. But those who aided the poor worried about making them dependent, sapping their resolve to work, and not bringing about moral improvement in lives often touched by alcohol abuse. These conflicting ideas about aiding the poor appeared regularly in children's literature.

As part of one's thankfulness for God's blessings, children were encouraged to give to the less fortunate and to pity the sick and the handicapped. But the "unworthy poor" remained suspect in the supposed land of opportunity. Noah Webster's 1835 *Instructive and Entertaining Lessons for Youth* cautioned that "if the poor continue in poverty, it is usually for want of industry, or judgment in the management of their affairs, or for want of prudence and economy in preserving what they earn."[75] Unlike earlier children's stories, particularly those from England, poor families were no longer portrayed as upright, simple, and noble in their poverty. Rather, Americans assumed they possessed some flaw that kept them from realizing the opportunities around them.

Early Juvenile Periodicals

Nothing reveals the emergence of childhood as a distinctive and protected period in the middle-class experience like the juvenile periodicals in the antebellum period. Along with the common school, juvenile periodicals became a dependable source of instruction in the emerging middle-class value system. Children took great delight in reading about fictional characters like themselves, and existing memoirs indicate that the stories' didacticism didn't fall too heavily on readers. Caroline Healey Dall, reminiscing in 1883 about the arrival of the *Juvenile Miscellany* in her childhood, wrote, "No child who read the *Juvenile Miscellany* . . . will ever forget the excitement that the appearance of each number caused. . . . The children sat on the stone steps of their house doors all the way up and down Chestnut Street in Boston, waiting for the carrier. . . . How forlorn we were if the carrier was late!" Fifty years later, Dall could still recall the titles of many of the stories.[76]

Like other fledgling businesses of the early republic, dozens of journals began, ran a few years, and then folded. Yet a few begun in the antebellum era remained to dominate publishing as late as the thriving Gilded Age. The Sunday School Union, the American Temperance Society, and the Anti-slavery Society all used juvenile magazines to push their reform messages. As such, their audience was small and their survival short-lived.

The *Juvenile Miscellany* under Lydia Maria Child's editorship began in Boston in 1826. She enlisted the leading female writers of the day, including Lydia Sigourney, Catherine Sedgwick, Sarah J. Hale, and Eliza Leslie, although some published under pseudonyms. The magazine was designed to appeal across age and gender lines. As noted earlier, Child had become an advocate of abolition and other humanitarian reforms; she brought those reform ideals to the *Miscellany* as well. In a story called "Adventure in the Woods," which appeared in 1826 during ongoing debates over Indian removal policy, she portrays Native Americans as competent and kind, even to the extent of returning two captive children to their own home. Child's biographer notes that magazine subscriptions began to fall off even before the fateful appearance of the previously mentioned story of Mary and Susan Easton in 1834. Child announced her resignation to readers: "After conducting the *Miscellany* for eight years, I am now compelled to bid a reluctant and most affectionate farewell to my little readers." Child then began a short sermon on morals and behavior. Sarah Josephus Hale assumed editorship, but the magazine ceased publication within two years. Karcher contends that more than Child's abolitionism contributed to the periodical's demise, but its failure to stay within the bounds of conventional discourse certainly contributed to its decline: "[T]he cultural establishment . . . conceived of children's literature as a buttress for the dominant society's hierarchies of race, class, and gender—not as a site for challenging them."[77]

The longest-lasting and most influential magazine in these early years was the *Youth's Companion,* publishing continuously from 1827 to 1929. Founded by an active Boston Congregationalist, Nathaniel Willis, the magazine concentrated on stories of piety and obedience and included the didactic teaching dialogues so common in other children's stories. Authors provided suggestions on spending money, including not only contributing to missions and Sunday school but setting aside two pennies to buy the next edition of the *Youth's Companion.*[78] The four-page weekly paper, sold on a subscription basis, had many less-successful imitators.

Noting the popularity of juvenile periodicals, Samuel Goodrich saw additional possibilities for selling his children's stories, and in 1832 he introduced *Peter Parley's Magazine* but left it after only one year. Still convinced there were profits to be made, he joined *Merry's Museum for Boys and Girls* in 1841. Begun just enough later to be able to capitalize on expanding markets and transportation, this magazine lasted into the 1870s. Louisa May Alcott published the works of several well-known authors when she served as editor.[79]

By 1850 American authors could successfully compete with British authors for a small audience of child readers. But the creation of an identifi-

able American children's literature had not automatically followed the creation of an American nation. While political leaders called for free public
education and American-oriented textbooks, Noah Webster and Mason
Weems were the only authors of the Revolutionary generation who actually
wrote for children. In the nineteenth century Samuel Goodrich, writing as the
prolific Peter Parley, imagined himself conversing directly with children and
thus supplemented the growing common-school movement with his travel-
ogues and adventure stories. While pietistic conversion stories and cautionary
moral tales were successfully produced through the efforts of the American
Sunday School Union, they competed with more didactic family stories developed in the hands of predominantly female writers. Jacob Abbott's Rollo stories best typify the subtle blending of ethical and religious teachings into secular formats.

Although the antebellum period of American history saw the popularity
of numerous social reform activities, children's stories reflected few of these
adult tensions and critiques. Abolitionism and temperance did appear as
themes in some works, especially in the adventuresome periodical the *Juvenile Miscellany* under Child's editorship. The birth of the "classics" of American children's literature in the golden age of Anglo-American children's
books occurred after 1850.

3

Good Girls, Bad Boys, 1850–1890

By mid-century the United States saw itself as a fully modern nation, embodying individuality, creative energy, and a solid moral core. The industrialization of textiles, begun in New England in the 1830s, had spurred many inventive technologies, so that clothing, tools, and food-stuffs poured from small factories, reducing the cost of consumer goods, presenting new work options for young men and women, and enlarging the scope of a market-driven, capitalist economy. National markets for these factory-produced goods developed because of cheaper and wider distribution via turnpikes, canals, and railroads. Those same modes of transportation enabled rapid geographic expansion as thousands of newly arrived immigrants traveled from Boston, Charleston, New York, or New Orleans to settle on farms from Ohio to Minnesota, from Missouri to Texas. Meanwhile growing numbers of unemployed, underemployed, and transitory workers took up residence in major cities. Persons of wealth controlled larger percentages of urban property and goods than they had earlier in the century. Consumerism flourished with a burgeoning middle class. All told, disparities between economic groups increased, and the poor, more concentrated in urban centers than before, became more visible.

Disparities between regions of the country also increased in the 1840s and 1850s. Central to political and economic disputes of that generation was the expansion of slavery into the territories. The Civil War, which raged from 1861 to 1865, dramatically altered politics, the economy, regional insularity, and demographics. The devastation it created, the entry into American life of the emancipated person of color, and the slow recovery for the rest of the white South composed part of the story of America between 1850 and 1890. The rapid expansion of business and industry in the North and the hastening of westward expansion completes the story of America in this era.

Urban centers teemed with people by 1890. Immigration was nothing new to America, but in the latter part of the century non-English-speaking, non-Protestant ethnic groups constituted the largest portion of newcomers, making the easy assimilation of foreigners more difficult. They came as laborers to jobs in expanding industries; they fostered the transportation boom. Frontier towns of the early century like Louisville, Memphis, St. Louis, and Chicago became major centers of trade, shipping, and sales. Housing, city services, water supplies, and schools rarely kept up with demand. Slums and tenement housing, with their attendant health and sanitation problems, drew a new crop of reformers to attack crime, poverty, alcohol, and prostitution. Many of these new charity workers particularly targeted children of poverty and thus also became advocates of longer school terms and compulsory education. Equally part of the transformation of the city was a movement to create "green space," or parks and playgrounds and boulevards, and a visible high culture—opera houses, museums, and art galleries. The city presented a new colorful context for writers, and a growing middle class of professionals and white-collar employees provided a ready market for stories with an urban flavor.

Expansion into the frontier West brought settlers into contact with Native Americans, many of whom had been transplanted there themselves beginning with the resettlement into "Indian territory" in the 1830s. The federal government used the army and the Bureau of Indian Affairs to force tribes onto reservations and to acquiesce to federal control. Railroads and white settlers rushed into the plains and across the Rocky Mountains. Towns filled in the counties sparsely populated in the prewar states, and 13 new states entered the Union by 1890, bringing the total to 44.

After 1850 two complementary, full-fledged literary genres provided extraordinary numbers of texts for family and child audiences. One strain was the family or domestic novel, written principally by women and focused on character development and moral suasion. The other strain was adventure literature, penned mostly by male authors and concentrating more on plot and setting than on character transformation. While the two seemed to dichotomize characters in children's fiction into "good girls" and "bad boys," the genres share a tradition of didactic instruction inherited from the eighteenth century, made more entertaining by credible characters and interesting plots. Both strains drew heavily on characteristics increasingly identified with the emerging middle class: an internalized moral code, ingenuity, persistence, practicality, and independence.

By mid-century, both British and American culture came to assign to childhood a more idealized and sanctified position. Life itself might be sordid, unpredictable, dangerous. But the child had yet to be corrupted by the real world; she came directly from the hand of God (or Nature). Wordsworth best articulated this philosophy in "Intimations of Immortality":

Our birth is but a sleep and a forgetting
The soul that rises with us, our life's star,

Hath had elsewhere its setting.
  And cometh from afar:
  Not in entire forgetfulness,
  and not in utter nakedness,
But trailing clouds of glory do we come
  From God, who is our home:
Heaven lies about us in our infancy!
  Shades of the prison-house begin to close
  Upon the growing boy.[1]

This romantic construction of childhood as a brief, angelic state of innocence permeated nineteenth-century culture and allowed writers either to see children as instruments of others' redemption or to see childhood as a time of pleasure, escape, and freedom before the stultifying hand of adult responsibility changed the child's life forever. A romantic childhood fit nicely into the Victorian domestic novel for young girls and equally well into the escapist adventures for young men.

Publishers found quite an expanded family market in Victorian America. Books written especially for children became profitable. Victorian domesticity so valued shared family activities that reading aloud became common, so that children often heard stories that were far beyond their reading abilities.[2] Thus the line that separated adult and child fiction in the mid- to late nineteenth century became blurred, and British fiction was no less popular than books written for an American audience. *Pilgrim's Progress, Tom Sawyer, Little Lord Fauntleroy, Little Women, Robinson Crusoe,* and *Wide, Wide World* were known to child and adult audiences alike and were passed on to second and third generations of readers in the same family. At the same time, technical improvements in book printing and binding lowered costs appreciably. The cylinder or rotary press could print thousands of pages in an hour.[3] Improved transportation and cheaper household lighting made books accessible to even those of moderate means. Higher levels of literacy contributed to increased book sales at mid-century. When the Association of New York Publishers met at the Crystal Palace in 1855, it honored its most popular authors and toasted this dramatic increase in book sales. Speaker George Palmer Putnam declared that publishing was advancing 10 times faster than the population itself.[4] Child readers represented a sizable share of that market.

The child to whom the new stories were addressed had undergone some transformation as well. No longer did society view children as the corrupted products of original sin, redeemable only through God's ineffable grace. As Calvinism gave way to the belief in moral perfectionism (see chapter 2), many Christians held that salvation was achievable through *human* action, in conjunction with God's grace. Not only might children be saved at a young age, children in fact embodied more of God's grace than those who had had longer association with the "tainted" world. Thus the new children's literature romanticized the child's innocence and gave her or him a role in the conscious improvement of adult moral character. The construction of childhood moved from society's need to redeem the child to one in which the child became the redeemer.[5] American Victorian culture found literature written for children a convenient vehicle for the transmission of moral and behavioral standards, and at the same time it elevated the child to a powerful symbolic status within the culture.

Domestic Fiction

Girls' domestic fiction began with the unlikely novel *Wide, Wide World* by Susan Warner (1819–1885)—unlikely because, by modern standards, the characters are woodenly drawn and the plot is plodding and transparent. But its immense sales and its popularity with women and children alike encouraged a rash of female authors to use similar tropes to develop a devoted female audience. Harriet Beecher Stowe (1811–1896), Sarah Chauncy Woolsey (1835–1905), Martha Finley (1828–1909), Louisa May Alcott (1832–1888), Harriet M. Lothrop (1844–1924), and a host of others published from mid- to late century. As the term "domestic fiction" implies, this literature privileged the home and family as the best context for the character building and moral reformation writers believed must precede the improvement of the larger society. Women or girls usually served as the superior moral force, guiding others (usually male) to a reformation of their character through long-suffering devotion, acts of charity, prayer, and tears. Drawing heavily on the theology of the Sunday school movement discussed in the previous chapter, domestic fiction embodied a worldview that took children and their role seriously, not as characters to be acted upon but as ones who could transform and "save" their culture. In a work designed to rehabilitate the reputation of this domestic fiction, scholar Jane Tompkins has called *Wide, Wide World* the "summa theologica of nineteenth-century America's religion of domesticity," a religion that depended not on theological argument and sectarianism but on the saving power of acts of piety, charity, and motherly love. Tompkins argues that rather than representing a sentimental and distorted ideology, these writers accurately reflected the pervasive worldview, theology, and desire for social reformation (through individual moral reform) that characterized mainstream American culture at mid-century.[6]

These female writers had deep ties to New England, either having lived there all their lives like Warner, Lothrop, and Finley or having been sent there as girls to attend boarding school. All were steeped in Congregational, Episcopal, or Unitarian theology, with Alcott's and Stowe's fathers having been active in antebellum reform. Their stories continued the didactic tradition of Edgeworth and Barbauld, but instead of simply imparting information through exemplary children, this domestic fiction emphasized girls who occasionally failed in exemplary behavior. However, their failures were reformative and they used their heightened piety to influence others. Although many of the authors came from privileged backgrounds (all but Finley and Alcott), their heroines found their virtue tested by suffering financial losses, in geographical dislocation, or in being gravely misunderstood by family and friends. In every case, a young woman served as the catalyst for remarkable character improvement for some or all of those with whom she came in contact, and she usually saw this as her chief duty and obligation in life. This depiction of the child as a redeemer of the larger society runs consistently through the domestic literature of the last half of the nineteenth century. Not only are children portrayed as innately good and innocent but their noble intentions and loving natures are often at odds with a cruel, materialistic world. Because of their inherently good nature, children alone could serve as instruments of reformation.[7]

Susan Warner, writing under the pseudonym Elizabeth Wetherell, produced over 30 novels (although she always referred to them as "stories"), beginning with *Wide, Wide World* in 1850.[8] Warner did not start out to write children's literature; however, in creating a 10-year-old protagonist who survived the death of both her parents, was forced to move in with an unsympathetic aunt in rural New England, and then blossomed under the attentions of the local clergy family, Warner cultivated a sympathetic character for an approving adolescent audience. Her second novel, *Queechy* (1852), followed a similar pattern of orphan girl cast into poverty, only to be rescued by a wealthy Englishman captivated by her sweet nature and pious Christianity. Within a year, sales of the two books reached 104,000 and *Wide, Wide World* had had 14 printings, a remarkable popularity given that the novel as a literary genre was still suspect as salacious and corrupting in many parts of the United States and that some "authorities" urged young women to stay away from such fiction.[9]

Wide, Wide World served as a bridge between the pious and dull Sunday school stories of the 1830s and the child-centered adventure stories later in the century. It also created a paradigm that, with only a few exceptions, would dominate the family novel for the next 60 years. Foremost in this pattern is the model of the female orphan bereft and alone in the "wide, wide world," not seeking her own way but needing someone to care for her. When the reader first meets Ellen Montgomery, she is the privileged only child of an urban businessman and his pious, genteel, beautiful, frail wife. A second characteristic of this genre is that very "good" persons often succumb to fatal illnesses that have no medical explanations or cures; their inevitable deaths are preceded by long confinements during which the patient's strength gradually wastes away. Such a trope allowed other characters to recognize their own moral failings when confronted with the dying one's pious acceptance of God's will. The death of a moral innocent also imitates the sanctification of Christ's crucifixion.

Susan Warner, *The Wide Wide World,* illustrated by Frederick Dielman
(Philadelphia: Lippincott Publishers, 1892)

In Warner's novel, Mrs. Montgomery's doctor prescribes a journey to
Europe for her health while Mr. Montgomery suffers "severe financial setbacks," which require him to travel to Europe on business. Thus Warner
moves the plot along, getting rid of the parents without paying attention to
the inherent contradiction between "financial setbacks" and extensive European travel. Both parents perish abroad, leaving an orphan without an inheri-
tance who is then thrown upon relatives.

Ellen accepts without argument the plan to live at an aunt's, complies
without complaint to demands that she assist with the household chores (the
Montgomerys had had a maid), and befriends loutish locals who visit her
aunt. Ellen draws on memories of her mother's self-sacrifice in order to perfect her own moral attributes. "Though we *must* sorrow, we must not rebel,"
Mother had intoned before her overseas departure. Mrs. Montgomery had
sold a ring given her by her mother in order to buy Ellen a writing desk and a
Bible, which she gives her as "parting gifts." By this model of sacrifice, young
women like Ellen were instructed not to assert their own needs or wishes but

to wait for a protector to intervene. Ellen's innocence and inherent goodness bring out the best in a gentleman who becomes a benefactor of the family. Later, as Ellen struggles in the unhappy situation at her aunt's, the local minister's son becomes her protector and adviser. The reader is left with the clear impression that John will marry Ellen when she grows up and will provide her with the kind of genteel life for which she was destined all along by virtue of her goodness. As Tompkins makes clear, Ellen escapes from the trials of living with relatives and of being misunderstood and underappreciated by being rescued. Rather than becoming stronger or more independent through her struggles, she is reinfantilized, freed of responsibility and made entirely dependent once again of the kindness of others.[10]

The moral of the story—and it certainly has one—appears in some advice that Mother gives Ellen before her death: "God sends no trouble upon his children but in love; and though we cannot see how, he will no doubt make all this work for our good." When an unhappy Ellen saw a "deformed" child playing in the street, she immediately rejected her own unhappiness, reminded that she had little to be sad about compared to that poor unfortunate, even though one might not understand why suffering happens. Acceptance and self-sacrifice only increase moral perfection, which is the clearly understood goal of life. The lengthy story unfolds to reveal how goodness always endures and surmounts adversity.

Writers of mid-century domestic fiction targeted their novels to a middle-class acutely aware that genteel behaviors and activities brought them closer to the upper-class society they emulated. Likewise, the distance between them and common and uncultured laborers and immigrants served as a reminder of their own status. Such social distinctions were well preserved in Victorian fiction. Like the British family stories popular when Warner was a child early in the century, her stories emphasized the great social chasm between the genteel environment into which her heroines were born and the rough rural environment into which circumstances cast them. In a scene that occurs before Ellen leaves her parents, she looks out her window into the backyards of crowded urban shacks, which she describes as "ugly . . . dingy, dirty, and disagreeable—women, children, houses, and all." Even when heroines dispense charity to poorer neighbors, it is usually with an air of noblesse oblige. In Maine, Ellen is portrayed as the cultured fish out of water who finds few kindred souls in her new rural environment and who must dye her white stockings gray so as to not seem too "dainty." Not surprisingly, the only "respectable" genteel friends there are Miss Alice and her brother John, the clergyman's adult children. People of quality are immediately recognizable by their "refined speech," their "behavior," and their "Christian teachings."[11]

Much later, in London, Ellen assesses the women at a dinner party on their beauty and manners and on their soft, modulated voices; by contrast, she found the rural New Englanders loud, coarse, and uncouth. How accurately Warner captured American class sensibilities is revealed by the critical praise the novel received at the time for its attention "to social distinctions."[12] Those "proper" distinctions were not to be confused, however, with the artificial class distinctions believed to dominate European society. Ellen's removal from Aunt Fortune's rural home to live in her Scottish grandmother's elegant London home provides Warner with a wonderful opportunity to castigate the British. Dialogue among Ellen's London relatives emphasizes the cultural backwardness and political naivete of Americans. Ellen wants to defend her native country from British slurs but cannot appear improperly argumentative.

Warner's use of evangelical religious themes certainly repeats elements of eighteenth-century children's literature. Ellen's most prized possession, the Bible her mother gave her, reminds her of how she read daily from it to her mother. After her mother's death, an acquaintance explains that "God had to separate" Ellen from her mother so that Ellen might come to depend solely on God. A long dialogue in which this unnamed gentleman urges Ellen's conversion (although she already appears to be a completely devoted and obedient Christian) occupies much of the text.[13] Her neighbor Miss Alice then becomes the chief spokesperson for piety, teaching by example and conversation, self-sacrifice, Christian duty, humility, and selflessness. Alice, like Mrs. Montgomery, mysteriously becomes thinner and paler, only to die. Ellen, already exemplary in the text, determines to emulate Alice's example of putting others first. Along with Rev. Humphreys she visits the cottage of a poor family whose son is dying, and Warner is able to re-create yet another pious death scene, and the boy's last words—"Thanks be to God for his unspeakable gift"— become a motto for Ellen during future trials.[14] Even the death of her beloved mother is portrayed not as a time of grief but rather as cause for rejoicing that the loved one is "going Home," for death is only a temporary separation. Curiously, only deaths of good, angelic characters occur. Ellen's Aunt Fortune becomes quite ill and spends a week in bed, which is an opportunity for Ellen to demonstrate all her domestic skills in running the household (except for building the fires, which is clearly a man's work). Aunt Fortune, however, is anything but pious or angelic—and she recovers.

Warner's work bridged the old Puritan piety-for-salvation's-sake and the newer nineteenth-century piety-for-character-formation. In evangelical Christianity, religious devotion was not marked by church membership alone but by acts of self-sacrifice, generous deeds, and the cultivation of piety. When Ellen is urged by neighbor children to join in Sunday afternoon charades and guessing games, she declines, saying, "I think Sunday was meant to be spent in growing better and learning good things . . . and I have a kind of *feeling* that I ought not to do it." Chastising her, one of them cries, "You had better go somewhere else though, for we are going on; we have been learning to be good long enough for one day." Ellen is hurt by their exclusion and wants to retort, but remembering Alice's good example, she instead does a kindness for one of them and they "were shamed into better behavior."[15] This attention to character formation is much stronger than actual prayer or biblical study; in fact, Warner provides no descriptions of actual church attendance at all.

Evangelical Protestant beliefs became so much a part of American culture that they were assumed to be normative without their direct cultivation. In defining and describing this "cultural religion," Warner exemplifies mainstream America at mid-century. Horace Bushnell's *Christian Nurture* (1846) captivated Christian educators with the notion that "Christianity was not a matter of proof or conversion; a person should assume that he was saved and that he could make correct choices; . . . the starting point of Christian experience began with a feeling of the Spirit of God," and this spirit was best translated as love of God and of fellow humans.[16] American religion had mostly forsaken doctrinal and sectarian disputes in favor of a sentimentalized, generic, emotional Christianity. Children's literature too moved from teaching correct doctrine and theology to teaching sentimental Christian character instead.

This contrast between Locke's rational, cerebral child rearing, in which the child was treated as a rational being, and the romantic notions of childhood prevalent in Victorian fiction becomes apparent in Warner's characterizations of Ellen's parents. She describes Ellen's almost completely absent father as distant and aloof and as one who did not want to tell Ellen that she had to live with her maiden aunt. When her mother tearfully tells her that she must leave, Warner notes that "It touched even him,—and he was not readily touched by anything."[17] The mother, on the other hand, appears on almost every page until Ellen leaves, sharing her feelings with Ellen, physically touching and kissing the child constantly, and always trying to prepare her for the coming separation. It is the mother's emotional world that dominates the novel.

Warner's idealized portraits of Mrs. Montgomery, Rev. Humphreys, and Alice and John Humphreys grate in their sentimentality, their pious self-denial, and the unrealistic circumstances of their lives. Though serving a rural Maine parish, Alice does no household work; the poor cleric Humphreys employs at least one servant; John is either away at seminary or at some occupation that allows him to come home for lengthy periods. All are extremely pious. At one point John chastises Ellen for reading even the sedate *Blackwood's Magazine* and makes her promise never to read a "novel."[18] (How Susan Warner reconciles that dialogue with her own writing of novels is never clear.) Yet *Wide, Wide World* had significant impact on the reading public of the 1850s. Louisa May Alcott even featured Jo Marsh reading *Wide, Wide World* in *Little Women*. Warner's narrative serves as a bridge to the newer fiction of mid-century by continuing the didactic instruction from earlier works but minimizing the intellectual content and providing more adventuresome settings in which moral instruction can take place.

Most of the themes of Warner's fiction occur in some form in all the family stories of the late nineteenth century. The orphaned or partially orphaned protagonist recurs in almost all the stories. *Five Little Peppers and How They Grew* (1881) by Harriet Lothrop features five siblings living with their widowed mother and struggling constantly against poverty. Sarah Chauncy Woolsey wrote five stories about the Carr family, using the pen name Susan Coolidge. In *What Katy Did* (1872) and *What Katy Did at School* (1873) Woolsey depicts a widowed father trying to rear a large family with the help of his maiden sister and his eldest daughter. The Carr daughters and their moral maturation comprise the focus of the books, with Katy Carr's injury and slow, painful recovery the major teaching device of the first book. The other moral model for the girls' edification is the ailing cousin Helen, who comes to visit. Other adults, especially the girls' father, play minor roles in the stories.[19] In the Elsie Dinsmore series by Martha Finley, Elsie's mother is dead, and her father abandons her to the care of her grandfather. Even Louisa May Alcott's "little women" do without their "Papa," who served as a chaplain in the Civil War during the entire first volume of *Little Women* (1864). Only in *The Birds' Christmas Carol* (1887) by Kate Douglas Wiggin (1856–1923) does the child protagonist, Carol Bird, live within an intact family. Her "failure" to be an orphan is quickly overridden by a prolonged illness and eventual death.

A second common theme involves the pervasive awareness of class differences, the implication that, although characters who are poor are usually honest and kind, they lack the refinement and sensitivity of their social betters. In *The Birds' Christmas Carol*, the wealthy Bird family, who have provided invalid Carol with every imaginable toy and book, invite the desperately poor Irish family next door for Christmas dinner. But the meal is served not in the formal dining room, which might make them feel "uncomfortable," but up in Carol's bedroom, where the children will be more "at home." As in *Wide, Wide World,* the poor speak differently—dialects and colloquialisms are emphasized. Particularly in *Elsie Dinsmore,* all the servants (who are African-American) speak in dialect and are the only persons who befriend Elsie at her grandfather's plantation. In *Little Women,* Marmee dispenses charity cheerfully to a poor German family even when it means that the Marches go without their own Christmas breakfast, but these children never interact with the March family. Only in *The Five Little Peppers* is there nothing shameful or suspect about poverty. When the Pepper children befriend the wealthy Jason, who is visiting in the neighboring village, he treats them as equals and friends and invites one of them to visit him in the city. In fact, his father becomes the "fairy godfather" who rescues the Peppers from poverty by hiring Mrs. Pepper to be his housekeeper and moving the family into his city mansion.

Thirdly, illness frequently becomes the catalyst for either religious conversion or moral reformation. A crippling back injury forces Katy in *What*

Katy Did to acknowledge the "Great Teacher" and reorient her world around the needs of others rather than pursue her own entertainments. She learns this desired acceptance of her illness from her semi-invalid aunt Helen. Carol Bird in *The Birds' Christmas Carol* teaches the entire family the pleasure of giving to others and models the virtue of acceptance of circumstances. As Mrs. Bird tells her husband one evening,

> Donald and Paul and Hugh [Carol's brothers] were three strong, willful, boisterous boys, but now you seldom see such tenderness, devotion, thought for others, and self-denial in lads of their years. A quarrel or a hot word is almost unknown in this house, and why? Carol would hear it, and it would distress her; she is so full of love and goodness.

Mr. Bird calls Carol "an angel of the house." When she dies on Christmas Day, Wiggin does not use the term "death" but couches the reality in metaphor: "[T]he 'wee birdie' had flown to its 'home nest.' Carol had fallen asleep!" The book ends on a sentimental note: "Carol lives again in every chime of Christmas bells that peal glad tidings and in every Christmas anthem sung by childish voices."[20]

Beth March, the most idealized of the "little women," dies angelically, as does another famous fictional child, Little Eva, in Harriet Beecher Stowe's *Uncle Tom's Cabin* (1852). Susan Warner has heroine Ellen's mother, father, and mentor, Miss Alice, all succumb to death within a few years. The most dramatic death in this body of literature is not a death at all: in the sequel to *Elsie Dinsmore, Holidays at Roseland* (1868), Elsie is banished by her father for a small misdeed; she falls ill and her father believes her dead. The mourning father undergoes a religious conversion, only to have Elsie stir to life again! Martha Finley's biographer has noted that Finley never intended to create a series of Elsie books, but her initial manuscript was so long that the publisher suggested they issue it in two parts. By the second installment, it was clear that Elsie was too popular to die off.[21]

The Victorian preoccupation with death reflected a dire reality: over half of all children would not live to become adolescents. Even as improved diet and sanitation in colonial America gradually improved mortality rates, the increasing immigration and crowded urban housing of nineteenth-century America meant that infant and childhood mortality continued to be a serious reality.[22] But death served a didactic function for domestic-fiction writers just as it had for Puritan divines two centuries earlier. God's sovereignty could best be reflected through cheerful acquiescence to God's will, even in the face of death. The pure, innocent child provided the best vehicle for transmitting God's love to a wider audience. But this presence of Christian piety is neither uniform nor explicit in domestic fiction; in fact, one might construct a continuum of religious persuasions from the preoccupation of Martha Finley's character Elsie Dinsmore to Harriet Lothrop's adventuresome Pepper family, who never attend church or read Scripture. No matter; all the model characters exemplify such Christian virtues as honesty, devotion to family, helpfulness, obedience, and humility. The point is that the values upheld for children did not change much over time; how those values were transmitted did.

All children's fiction to this point addressed obedience, respect for elders, truthfulness, and trust in God. *The Wide, Wide World* and *Elsie Dinsmore* resemble eighteenth-century works in their insistence upon Bible study, prayer, personal conversion, and Sabbath keeping. In these works and those like them, evangelical Protestantism is preferred. In fact, Martha Finley wrote disparagingly of Catholicism in *Casella* (1868) and even has one of her characters refer to Catholics and Mormons as "pander[ing] to men's lust . . . ; both teach lying and murder."[23] However, *Little Women* and *The Five Little Peppers,* like the Victorian culture that produced them, show that values can be transmitted equally well without overt doctrine; goodness is simply a matter of possessing or developing self-sacrificing behavior.

Is Alcott Different?

Within this collection of mid-century female writers of domestic fiction, only one author remained a household name into the late twentieth century: Louisa May Alcott. Certainly she fits nicely into the genre: her four major children's books and hundreds of juvenile stories portray idealized childhoods, present life lessons taught by a self-sacrificing mother, describe scenes of domestic tranquillity, and use children to epitomize moral regeneration and character improvement. Even the most atypical and controversial of her children's books, *Little Women* (1868), teaches girls to "aspire to domesticity and moral goodness," to put others first, and to seek constantly to improve their character.[24] Its sequel, *Good Wives* (1869), assures Alcott's readers that there will be no rebels among the March girls: all will marry and assume the domestic roles for which their mother, Marmee, and society have prepared them. In the two works, the March family is poor, but it is a genteel and refined poverty expected only to last while Papa is away; the older girls must earn some income but not at the expense of their education. Although the girls do not fit the paradigm of orphans, their father returns from war only at the end of the book, and the girls are left alone when their mother makes a long trip to nurse him. The "child redeemer" is not the main character, Jo, but her younger sister Beth, who never misbehaves, has an ethereal kind of beauty, contracts a fatal illness while taking food to a poor German family, is unfailingly cheerful during her illness, and dies embracing her fate. Most of the marks of mid-century domestic fiction are certainly there.

Louisa May Alcott, however, is not typical of the female domestic writers of mid-century. She grew up in a much less affluent family; she was well educated but financially insecure. Her schoolteacher father, Bronson Alcott, drifted in and out of Boston's most esteemed intellectual circles, and Louisa knew well most of New England's important writers, including Ralph Waldo Emerson, who remained a lifelong friend of the family. Young Louisa was often a pupil in one of her father's schools and did not attend public school until age 14. By 16 she was teaching school herself.[25]

Alcott established herself as a writer with the novel *Moods* (1864) and with her fictionalized memoirs from her Civil War volunteer work, which she published as *Hospital Sketches* (1863). Having proven her skill as a writer, she was asked by prominent Boston publisher Thomas Niles to try her hand at a "girls' story" that would sell as well as works by the popular "boys' author" Oliver Optic (see the following section). Within six weeks she had drawn again on her personal experience to create *Little Women.* With the publication of the book, Alcott's popularity soared, and she did not hesitate to capitalize on the potential profits her March family had created. The sequel to *Little Women* (today often published as an appendage to the original) revealed Alcott's acquiescence to popular opinion. Titled *Good Wives,* this continuing story appeared the next year. In *Little Men,* published in 1871, Alcott featured some of the educational reform so dear to her father by setting the book at a school for boys that Jo March and her husband, Professor Bhaer, founded.[26] The conclusion of the series, *Jo's Boys,* appeared in 1886, shortly before Alcott's death. She had never set out to write a girls' series, but she found her characters had become too beloved, and her success too dear, to abandon the project.

Recently much controversy has swirled around interpretations of Alcott's life, the extent of her feminism, the subtexts of *Little Women,* and her anonymous sensationalized "pulp fiction." The discoveries by Madeline Stern and Leona Rostenberg of Louisa May Alcott's pseudonymous short stories revolutionized literary portraits of the "little woman" herself.[27] Many of these popular pieces are characterized by "violence, deceit, infidelity, and licentiousness," hardly themes Alcott had cultivated in her acknowledged fiction.[28] As a consequence, scholars have begun to look more closely at her children's literature and to find that all was not as romantic and ideal as was previously interpreted. In at least four areas, Alcott's writing departs from the paradigm of acceptable female behavior, which *The Wide, Wide World* had so assiduously scripted. Thus Alcott reminds us that Victorian domesticity and the separate-sphere ideology were not monolithic constructs encompassing all middle-class American women all the time.

Unlike Susan Warner, Martha Finley, and Kate Wiggin, Louisa Alcott created a protagonist with obvious gender ambiguities. Josephine March refuses to be called anything other than the masculine derivative of her name, "Jo," and in the very first chapter she declares, "I can't get over my disappointment in not being a boy." She has her beautiful long hair cut and sold to earn money for her mother, a physical assault on her femininity. Whenever the sisters perform one of Jo's plays, she always takes the male role. Her very desire to become a writer and her avowal never to marry certainly mark her as defiant of traditional gender expectations. She tells Laurie that "I don't believe I shall ever marry. I'm happy as I am, and love my liberty too well to be in any hurry to give it up for any mortal man." That her best friend refuses to go by his proper name of Theodore and prefers the feminized "Laurie" also contributes to the story's gender ambiguity. In none of the other popular American works of this period do authors so obviously flirt with acceptable role definitions.

Alcott's characters are also not the upright and well-mannered children of the earlier stories of Lydia Maria Child, Jacob Abbott, or even Susan Warner. Alcott allows her female characters to misbehave, feel resentment and envy, and disobey authority. The plot often turns on recognition of the implications of misbehavior to others: there is a personal price for selfishness, greed, and jealousy. She does not preach character or virtue overtly, yet each of the four girls and their neighbor Laurie display some character fault that they seek to eradicate by book's end, a story line that parallels their enactment of *Pilgrim's Progress* from the basement to the attic in one of Jo's melodramas. Alcott tries to portray Marmee as an enlightened parent who does not dictate behavior or punish misdeeds. Marmee even allows the girls a week's vacation from chores. She is, in fact, manipulating them into a position in which daily living becomes impossible and they see the necessity of daily household chores. The teaching may not be as didactic as that in earlier children's literature, but the moral lessons are just as clear.

Third, in terms of religious reformation, Alcott's characters have virtually no interaction with traditional religion. The Marches' father is a minister, but he is absent until the final chapter of the first volume. Alcott deliberately does not create Sunday school characters who are either always good or who suffer immediate reprisals for wrongdoing. As her alter ego, Jo, tells the others, Jo likes to write stories for children but would not "depict all her naughty boys as being eaten by bears . . . because they did not go to a particular Sabbath school, nor [would] all the good infants who did go be rewarded by every kind of bliss."[29] Since Sunday school literature and its authors continued to be popular in the 1860s, some criticized *Little Women* for secularizing Christian concepts, particularly Alcott's use of *Pilgrim's Progress* as a sort of moral epic with no religious basis. One reviewer found the book "without Christ. . . . Don't put it in your Sunday School Library."[30] The poet Amy Lowell wrote in 1919 that she had not been allowed to read Alcott as a child because "she was supposed to use very bad English and to be untrue to life," but perhaps it was the lack of piety that bothered Lowell's parents.[31] Although long sermonizing scenes are absent in Alcott's work, the generic struggles to improve one's character and behavior is the central theme of the sisters' growing up. Protestant values are so deeply embedded in *Little Women* that the author doesn't have to dwell on them at all.

Unlike writers of similar domestic stories, Alcott dares to raise the issue of female assertiveness through her characterization of Jo March. Jo's forceful personality, her outspokenness, and her chafing at the constraints of propriety kept *Little Women* popular with girls long after the Victorian age had faded away. As many scholars have noted, Jo *is* Louisa herself, and as an independent woman, the author struggled not to make Jo conform to societal expectations. Jo delights in small acts of rebellion against conventional society, like cutting her hair (although for a noble cause). And yet in *Good Wives* Alcott takes back the assertiveness Jo expressed in *Little Women,* including her decision not to marry. Almost as soon as *Little Women* appeared, Alcott claimed she was besieged with letters wanting the story of the March girls continued. Apparently Alcott did not want to conform, for she wrote to a friend:

> Jo should have remained a literary spinster but so many enthusiastic young ladies wrote to me clamorously demanding that she should marry Laurie, or somebody, that I didn't dare refuse and out of perversity went and made a funny match for her. I expect vials of wrath to be poured upon my head, but rather enjoy the prospect.[32]

When Jo turns demure and blushing around the German professor, "the reader with a good memory is incredulous," said one critic, "and what originally [was] a story of Jo's refusal to accede to a repressive feminine role now becomes a story of courtship and marriage."[33] The professor criticizes her writing, and eventually their marriage puts an end to Jo's writing career and raises the image of contented domesticity.

To sustain reader interest, Alcott was forced to build future stories around the children of the March sisters, for clearly as adults they are not very interesting characters. In *Little Men* (1871), Alcott created another rebellious girl in Nan, who wants to become a doctor. Yet like Jo Marsh, Nan too capitulates to practicality.[34] While presuming to instruct mid-century children on how to grow up, Alcott also seems to say that remaining childlike is ultimately more interesting and more satisfying. Similar to Susan Warner's earlier assessment, Alcott seems to indicate that reinfantilization is young women's only real option.

Alcott seemed to struggle with this domestic picture she had created in the final two novels, in which Jo is both a working professional (teacher and school administrator) and a wife and mother. Completing *Jo's Boys* in 1886 on the cusp of the emergence of the "new woman" in American society, Alcott becomes more adventuresome with her female adolescents. Laurie's grandfather endows a women's college where one of Jo's former students studies medicine, one niece studies art, and another becomes a professional actress. Jo tells the students that now some unmarried women "have grown famous and proved that woman isn't a half but a whole being, and she can stand alone."[35] Certainly even genteel American society could accommodate an enlarged role for women by this time. Or perhaps, as scholar Karen Halttunen has argued, "Through the character of Jo March, Alcott performed literary penance for her [own] greatest sins against the cult of domesticity: her flight to Washington [to volunteer as a nurse], her Gothic period, her consuming literary ambition, and her refusal to marry."[36] Yet even as Alcott experienced a larger role for women, she disliked having to write domestic fiction and continue the story line of the March family. As she worked on *Jo's Boys* she wrote that she would love to close the book with an "earthquake which should engulf Plumfield [School] and its environs so deeply in the bowels of the earth that no youthful Schliemann could ever find a vestige of it!"[37] However, Alcott was nobody's fool. She had salvaged the family's finances more than once with her writing, and like one of the little women, she would "do her duty."

Although Louisa Alcott grew up amid social reformers, even living briefly with her family in the utopian, experimental Fruitlands community, she never incorporated into her fiction the social issues that troubled her father. She had frequent contacts with such abolitionists as William Lloyd Garrison and Theodore Parker in her father's home; privately she verbalized strong support of abolition. But in her children's stories, she avoided addressing these subjects directly. The opening scene of *Little Women* features Marmee reading a letter from Papa, a chaplain in the Civil War, to the four daughters. Alcott fails to discuss why he volunteered for this service to the Union cause, what he might be observing on the battlefield, or any connection between this war and slavery. Unlike Lydia Maria Child, she stayed almost completely away from abolitionist commentary. Alcott utilized no African-American characters in her works, nor did she address the discriminatory practices against them in her New England hometown. In *Good Wives*, the Plumfield school Jo and her husband, Professor Bhaer, have established admits primarily outcasts, including one "merry, little quadroon," hardly nondiscriminatory language.

Stories for Younger Children

Although the biggest growth segment of children's publishing between 1850 and 1890 was probably the adolescent market, more interesting and realistic stories also began to appear for younger children. Lucretia Peabody Hale (1820–1900), who edited a newspaper with her brother Edward Everett Hale and wrote children's stories for periodicals, collected some of those stories into the entertaining *Peterkin Papers* (1880) and *The Last of the Peterkins* (1886).[38] In these amusing anecdotes, an intact family of seven stumbles through numerous misadventures without losing members to death, without its children being orphaned, and without falling into undeserved financial distress. In many ways Hale seems to poke fun at Victorian conventionality and at the overwhelming presence of family in everyone's business.

Likewise, Rebecca Sophia Clarke (1833–1906), who wrote as Sophie May, first wrote children's stories for Sunday school papers such as the *Congregationalist* and *Little Pilgrim*. The stories soon appeared as a collection about a three-year-old child, called *Little Prudy* (1863). Like Hale, Clarke utilized humor to make her toddlers more realistic and appealing and abandoned the format of exemplary children. Instead her characters misused words, using expressions like "condemned milk" and "smacked potatoes." These children scampered through funny but harmless misadventures, pranks, and visits with friends. By 1884, Clarke had 28 different titles about Prudy for her sister "Dotty Dimple," and by the end of the century she had started writing about Prudy's children.[39]

Adventures for Boys

What was it about the mid-nineteenth century that led to a distinct gender differentiation in writing for children? Certainly gender had always defined social and public roles; even within the household, colonial families divided most tasks according to gender. However, fathers worked daily on the family property—whether farm or artisan shop—and had a direct hand in the supervision and discipline of children. This transition was underway by the time of the American Revolution and continued during the geographical expansion of the nineteenth century. As men found employment at some distance from the home, mothers gradually assumed primary responsibility for child rearing and early education. Males came to be defined by skills other than working the land or taming the wilderness: entrepreneurship, business acumen, and professional skills assumed major importance. By mid-century, physical prowess, assertiveness, and business success stood as the paramount values that male authors admired, and hence these values were lifted up in the fiction they produced. Moral messages and behavioral precepts continued to appear, but only on the road to adventure, not as didactic teachings in and of themselves. Cultural scholar Karen Halttunen found that advice manuals for young men after 1850 might pay lip service to traditional values like sobriety, industry, and frugality, but they introduced much more aggressive advice about getting ahead, managing others, and boldly pursuing advantages.[40] Children's fiction would slowly follow this trend.

William Taylor Adams (1822–1897) stands as a transitional figure for these new male values. Like so many of the nineteenth-century female writers, Adams was a school teacher, administrator, and evangelical Christian. And like most of them, he chose to write under pseudonyms, Oliver Optic being the best known. The success of his early book *The Boat Club* (1854) led to several series of stories for boys, each replete with boisterous adventures, moral choices, and uplifting conclusions.[41] In Adams's books, right always triumphed, although the hero had to help it along. Religious doctrine was entirely absent, but just as in girls' domestic fiction, Protestant virtues like honesty, friendship, obedience, and trust continually characterized the heroes. Two themes important in girls' literature never permeated Adams's stories, however: self-sacrifice and the edifying characteristics of illness.

Adams wrote at least 116 series books and edited two different periodicals during his long career. Like the Peter Parley books or the Rollo stories of an earlier generation, Oliver Optic addressed his readers directly with moral imperatives, which is not surprising since Adams served as a Sunday school superintendent for much of his life and was noted for his temperance lectures.[42] To ensure that the reader did not miss the moral, Adams commented explicitly at the end of *Gold Thimble* (1862), "If you had a little friend who was very poor, but very proud, you might do something for him in such a way that he would not feel as though he was accepting a gift." This is exactly what the character proceeded to do when he recovered a stolen thimble.

In Adams's early works, an adult figure (father, coworker, older friend) stood as the role model and instructor to the protagonist, much as in earlier didactic fiction. But as the series progressed, the wise instructor figure disappeared, and the heroes appeared as boys on their own, either orphaned or supporting a widowed mother. Their adventures in the world provided self-taught lessons for which they did not need an older moral guide. In fact, sometimes the hero did not improve his character at all. As his plots gradually emphasized adventure over moral instruction, Adams joined the ranks of dime-novel authors (see chapter 4) in competition for the juvenile audience. Many teachers and critics found his stories, like those of his contemporary and friend Horatio Alger, too sensationalized, too quixotic, and too apt to provide mere escapism at the expense of good literature and exemplary moral lessons.[43]

In a similar vein, Harry Castlemon, whose real name was Charles Austin Fosdick, began a popular series with the story of *Frank the Young Naturalist* (1864). Writing for boys became a calculated enterprise for Castlemon, who once told a reporter, "Boys don't like fine writing. What they want is adventure, and the more of it you can get into 250 pages of manuscript, the better fellow you are."[44]

Harry Castlemon's and William Taylor Adams' popularity was soon overshadowed by the success of Horatio Alger's urban tales of "poor boy makes good." In the booming heyday of the Gilded Age, many saw in Alger's stories the exuberance and optimism of America itself, the unbridled leveling of democratic opportunity. Later critics assailed Alger for blind boosterism, for promoting cutthroat capitalism, unabashed materialism, and unlimited opportunity. But his name entered the American lexicon anyway, standing for "social mobility and economic opportunity, . . . [d]etermination, self-reliance, and success."[45] A 1940s pundit proclaimed: "Alger is to America what Homer was to the Greeks."[46]

Yet both his detractors and supporters failed to understand Alger's message to young men and his place in the evolution of American culture. Linking sagas like *Ragged Dick* to a belief in the unlimited opportunities of the 1870s ignores the reality of Alger's conservative and middle-class view of the world and fails to recognize the very limited financial success of any of his works. Reading Alger as an advocate of unbridled opportunism ignores his devotion to such Puritan ethics as thrift and the uplifting quality of any occupation that involved hard work and honesty.[47]

Alger, the son of a clergyman and also a Harvard graduate, grew up in limited financial circumstances but profited from the genteel life of Unitarian Boston. His circumstances were comfortable enough to allow him the obligatory grand tour of the Continent before he settled down to his clerical duties. His writing experience began during his college days with short stories, poetry, translations for Boston weeklies, and two unremarkable books. Turned down for service in the Union army because of myopia and his short stature (he was five feet two), Alger wrote ballads and poems for the Union cause before turning out his first children's book, *Frank's Campaign* (1864), which was based on a boy's war experience. Cleverly capitalizing on war interest, Alger produced a popular work. Alger would later claim that "I soon found reason to believe that I was much more likely to achieve success as a writer for boys than as a writer for adults."[48]

However, in 1864 that success was not yet assured, and Alger accepted a clerical appointment to a Unitarian Fellowship. A seemingly successful tenure there turned sour when Alger was accused of "deeds too revolting to relate" involving young men of the congregation.[49] Before formal charges could be brought, Alger resigned his church post and moved to New York City. Although the scandal continued to be stirred by some parents in Brewster, New York, it never kept publishers, including some church-related periodicals, from handling Alger's work. He spent the rest of his life as an author, capitalizing on his already-popular boys' fiction, and as a reformer dedicated to improved working conditions for city children. He worked tirelessly for Charles Loring Brace's Children's Aid Society (C.A.S.), which convinced poverty-stricken parents and homeless that children would prosper better in the country. The C.A.S. then sent these children to live with and work for farmers in the Midwest. Alger's philanthropy also promoted the Newsboy Lodging House, which provided cheap but safe rooms for "ragged dicks." Alger never married, but he adopted or provided financial assistance to numerous boys he met in the city. More than one biographer has noted his apparent expiation of guilt in this subsequent benevolent behavior.

Alger's most famous work, *Ragged Dick* (1867), first appeared, as did many of his stories, as a series in the *Student and Schoolmate* periodical. Alger continued the saga of Dick Hunter and the New York newsboys in what became known as the Ragged Dick Series: *Fame and Fortune* (1868), *Mark the Match Boy* (1869), *Rough and Ready* (1869), *Ben the Luggage Boy* (1870), and *Rufus and Rose* (1870).[50] Although over 100 children's books would follow, the themes laid down in this series remained consistent throughout his career. Like his friend William Taylor Adams, Alger did not create Sunday school heroes with no discernible faults, but their failures were superficial compared to their deeper humanitarian values. It was the heroes' honesty, compassion, and trust that allowed others to recognize their potential and thus help them out on their journey of pecuniary advancement. For example, at the beginning of *Ragged Dick,* 14-year-old Dick Hunter admits to smoking and to spending his days' earnings at the Old Bower Theater. But he was not without virtue, for "[h]e was above doing anything mean or dishonorable. He would not steal, or cheat, or impose upon younger boys, but was frank and straight-forward, manly and self-reliant." The character-improvement issue, then, which so pervaded much nineteenth-century children's fiction, was not activated for most of Alger's heroes; they were generally solid, honest persons already, although they would seek to improve some behaviors. The movement in Alger's stories, rather, is toward an improved financial situation and the acquisition of "respectability." In the last line of *Ragged Dick,* Dick signs his name "Richard Hunter, Esq.," and the reader knows that a great chasm has been bridged.[51] As Karen Halttunen has noted, "Character alone could no longer ensure success" in postbellum America; the upwardly mobile needed skills as well as character. Alger advocated assertiveness, persistence, charm, and the ability to take advantage of both situations and people.[52]

Although "rags-to-riches" has come to define Alger's message, careful examination of his heroes reveals that none of them actually becomes rich; rather, they move from being street hustlers or rural immigrants or part of the urban working class to become salaried and respectable bookkeepers or managers. In fact, no hero becomes self-employed or even particularly wealthy; they have white-collar jobs in someone else's business. Even when the hero succeeds in developing all his city smarts and assertive skills, the overwhelming odds of the capitalistic system might still be against him if it were not for another part of Alger's formula: a good measure of luck.[53] Ragged Dick discovers numerous ways to improve his situation: giving up entertainment and extravagances, saving his profits, making extra money by volunteering help, finding someone who will tutor him in grammar. But he profits even more by sheer coincidences. He gets a new wardrobe by befriending a young tourist; he gains a clerking position by rescuing the son of a prominent businessman from drowning. In each case, he shows assertiveness and bravery, but he also happens to be in the right place at the right time. In the six books of the Ragged Dick series, "not a single favorite ever secures a clerical position purely on personal initiative. . . . *Fortune's* favor is indispensable to lift poor boys out of the ditch."[54]

Contrary to popular belief, Alger's heroes do not covet great wealth; businessmen are sometimes portrayed as grasping, mean, and insensitive. Boy-heroes may help to recover lost fortunes for others through their courage and wiliness, but they do not become millionaires themselves. Neither do boys seek their fortunes in the factory or in agriculture, the predominant employment areas of the era. Instead, Alger's heroes aspire to the white-collar world of clerking, accounting, and sales that the growing urban centers offered. They simply want to permeate the chasm that separates the working-class culture from middle-class mores and respectability. The aspiring young men certainly adopt the values and morality of their benefactors and employers. No labor unions or strife between worker and owner occur.[55]

Another way in which Alger's stories departed from the more instructive adventure tales of Peter Parley or Oliver Optic is the almost complete absence of parents. Alger's children are alone in the big city. Adult figures move in and out of their lives, providing lucky breaks or instruction or simply encouragement; just as often, adults exploit children and disregard their needs in pursuit of their own success. Dismayed at the hundreds of "street Arabs" he encountered in New York, Alger turned his stories into guidebooks for boys who might venture to the city, a common enough occurrence in postbellum America. For example, in *Ragged Dick,* the hero escorts young Frank Whitney around the city and explains the various cons and ruses that a young boy might fall into, which boardinghouses are safest and cheapest, what food items typically cost, and which locations to avoid. He also frequently created characters "whose appearance was deceiving," teaching the reader how to distinguish pretense and appearance from a man's true character and thus avoid deception. Alger cared sincerely about the migration of young men to America's cities, having observed their lives carefully at the Newsboys' Lodging Home, and he wanted to provide them with both skills to negotiate the city and those moral values from which they might have been cut adrift.[56] The upwardly mobile boys about which Alger wrote cannot be made into metaphors for America in the Gilded Age. Alger held to traditional virtues like the control of passion; he had a distinct distaste for unbridled greed. The unfettered ambition modeled by America's new "robber barons" in steel, railroads, and manufacturing never became models for Alger's boys. Alger's heroes covet middle-class acceptance and respectability more than they want independence; they conform rather than rebel. "There is not," writes Anne Scott MacLeod, "a Natty Bumpo or a Huck Finn among them."[57]

Alger did not avoid female characters, but clearly he was not as comfortable writing about them, and they never claimed centerstage. *Rufus and Rose* features a seamstress employed as an "out-worker"—one who sews piecework at home—who can make only a third of the wages that newsboys make on the street. And in *Helen Ford* (1866), Alger editorialized against the sweatshop labor that provided one of the few employments for women: "the narrow choice allowed to women, who are compelled to labor . . . [l]eads to an unhealthy and disastrous competition . . . [a]nd enables employers to establish a disgracefully low scale of prices."[58] The reader again finds clear evidence that Alger has no great love for unbridled capitalism.

What, then, was Horatio Alger's view of postbellum America, and what was his message to his young readers? "Serve your employer well, learn business as rapidly as possible, don't fall into bad habits, and you'll get on," says a character in *Tom Turner's Legacy*.[59] He might have added give up bad habits, be alert to opportunities, stay honest, and hope for a stroke of luck. None of these is a new character trait; all had been lifted up by the earliest of America's didactic writers. Even though Alger's settings in urban centers represent a departure in children's literature, his choice of values does not. Alger capitalized on America's growing love of adventure and fortune stories, as epitomized by the success of dime novels, but he lauded traditional moral values, honored personal face-to-face contacts, and rewarded true friendship and loyalty. Deep down, as his hero Ragged Dick exemplifies, he believed people wanted to be good and wanted to help others. As historian Michael Zuckerman has noted, "Alger's heroes succeed, to the extent that their own attributes have anything to do with their success, because they are *good,* not because they have sharper fangs and longer claws than anyone else."[60]

These are not stories of unbridled capitalism or the lure of industrialization. Alger's stories taught moral values and respectable behavior in a new setting, with adventures bordering on the sensational, but moral values nonetheless. The stories, notes historian Joseph Hawes, "pleased two sets of readers—the newsboys who enjoyed the stories about themselves, and the respectable members of society who liked the nobility of the characters, their virtuous actions, and their invariable success."[61] Horatio Alger broke no new moral ground; rather, he introduced high adventure, suspense, and urban settings into the same moral configuration of the early nineteenth century. He disposed of the sentimental, pious child of English and American didacticism but retained a clear focus on middle-class morality. Alger's boys were *good* boys in a *bad* environment.

"Bad Boys"

This was not the case with the characters created by Samuel Clemens, who named a new literary genre when he published a satirical essay in the *Californian* in 1865. "The Story of the Bad Little Boy That Bore a Charmed Life" reversed the inimitable reward system of the popular Sunday school stories and domestic or family stories. Clemens portrayed a devilish child who lied to his mother and pulled pranks on various adults and children, yet he was neither punished nor underwent religious conversion, nor did he die. In "The Story of the Good Little Boy Who Did Not Prosper" in the *Galaxy* (1870), the well-behaved protagonist is wrongly accused of theft, unjustly punished, and unable to restore his teacher's faith in him even by martyrlike good behavior.[62] Titles that mimicked Clemens's, albeit with less effective irony, include Thomas Bailey Aldrich's autobiographical *The Story of a Bad Boy* (1869) and George W. Peck's *Peck's Bad Boy* (1883). In these and other similar tales, male writers constructed the hero as a tough, adventuresome, manly, disobedient, free-spirited boy who displayed an engaging sense of humor and an uncanny knack for exposing adult foibles.

Clemens's spoof on both children's books and conventional religiosity was penned for adult audiences. But in creating a new model of boyhood, Clemens soon found an eager audience of adolescent boys as well. Never deliberately mean nor a bully, the "bad boy" gets himself and others into continual trouble; nonetheless, he survives and flourishes. Employing irony to the fullest extent, Clemens questioned the whole premise of the child who would redeem the surrounding ugly, corrupt world, as in *Ragged Dick* and *Elsie Dinsmore.*

Suspecting that this theme struck a chord among American readers, Clemens parlayed the motif of his two satirical essays into popular novels for the burgeoning adolescent audience. Using romantic settings like the antebellum frontier of Missouri and the untamed Mississippi River, but peopling them with morally ambiguous characters like Tom Sawyer and Huck Finn, Clemens introduced a new kind of boy hero. He disconcerted the conventions of morality and of childhood found in Horatio Alger, Martha Finley, and Louisa May Alcott. Creating adults who acted like children and children who must act like adults, Clemens confused the boundaries of a self-satisfied America and its assumptions about the nature of childhood as well. In many ways, Samuel Clemens's quintessential American novels *Tom Sawyer* (1876) and *The Adventures of Huckleberry Finn* (1885) presented a new kind of child hero, a lovable bad boy. As Aunt Polly said of Tom Sawyer, "He warn't bad so to say—only mischievious. Only just giddy. . . . He never meant any harm, and he was the best-hearted boy that ever was."[63] As literary scholar Steven Mailloux has noted, the creators of the bad boy genre anticipated psychologist G. Stanley Hall's path-breaking *Adolescence: Its Psychology* when they showed that "laziness, lying, and thievery" did not mark boys for a life of crime; rather, "semicriminality [was] normal for all healthy boys."[64] Cultural critic Leslie Fiedler has argued convincingly that this new hero defined America at mid-century. "The Good Bad Boy is, of course, America's vision of itself, crude and unruly in his beginnings, but endowed by his creator with an instinctive sense of what is right."[65]

Thomas Bailey Aldrich recounted his own boyhood memories from rural New England, where he was taken to live with his grandfather; his fictional

Rivermouth is Portsmouth, New Hampshire. Aldrich's *Story of a Bad Boy* first appeared as a serial in the juvenile periodical *Our Young Folks* in 1869.[66] A serious literary figure of the Gilded Age (he edited the *Atlantic Monthly* from 1881 to 1890), Aldrich turned a not-uncommon childhood into adventuresome, descriptive narrations of rural pleasures, boyhood escapades, and interfering adults. He once commented that he *wrote* the kinds of stories he wished he could have *read* as a child. "This is the story of a bad boy," he wrote in his preface. "Well, not such a very bad, but a pretty bad boy. . . . I call my story the story of a bad boy, partly to distinguish myself from those faultless young gentlemen who generally figure in narratives of this kind. . . . I didn't want to be an angel."[67] His protagonist Tom Bailey, like all the boys of the bad boy genre, finds school tedious and boring, with arbitrary rules and spiteful schoolmasters. Church and Sunday school are even more confining, and young Tom totally rejects the available books for children. [68] Aldrich clearly intended to break with the didacticism of earlier children's literature: children need not be virtuous to become proper adults. Always the reader knows that the "naughty" boy grows into a solid, accomplished citizen.

Milwaukee journalist George W. Peck (later mayor of the city) created his bad boy for a newspaper column in 1882. His character incorporates an altogether more mischievous boy hero than Tom Bailey, but he still implies that misbehavior is a normal part of childhood. In fact, it is necessary to the development of a successfully competitive adult. One story begins with the caveat "Of course all boys are not full of tricks, but the best of them are. That is, those who are readiest to play innocent jokes, and who are continually looking for chances to make Rome howl, are the most apt to turn out to be first-class businessmen."[69] Unlike Horatio Alger's heroes, Peck's bad boys do manipulate, coerce, and deceive their way to power, even if their triumph is limited and their punishment swift and sure.

Since the stories first appeared as newspaper columns, they were no doubt intended to entertain adults and rekindle remembrances of youthful pranks. But when the collected columns appeared as books, *Peck's Bad Boy and His Pa* (1883) and *Peck's Bad Boy, Number 2* (1883), George Peck joined with Samuel Clemens in forever crossing that boundary in children's literature between contrived childhood and reality. Mischief and adventure became more sinister under Peck and included surprising sexual overtones. In the story "Boy with a Lame Back," the protagonist tricks his father into believing that a "woman of the street" wants to meet him that evening on the corner. He then tells his mother what his father is up to. The boy Hennery ends up with a "lame back" because of a severe beating by his father. In another episode, Hennery learns that his mother is about to return from a trip to Chicago. So he borrows clothing from a young woman he knows, places it strategically around the house after his father goes to bed, and then awaits the "fireworks" that occur when his mother comes home and assumes some "hussie" has been there.[70]

Far more than any of the children's fiction previously examined, George Peck's stories portrayed American urban life as it really was in the Gilded Age. Peck's settings are unromanticized in any way. For example, Hennery constantly harasses the neighborhood grocer, giving Peck the opportunity to detail unsavory business practices, including the donation of moldy crackers to a church bazaar, the sale of a basket of small potatoes with a few large ones strategically placed on top, dishonest meat weighing, and the sale of yellow lard as butter.[71] And Peck articulates the popular perception of corrupt politicians with Hennery remarking, "Pa said I was a liar, and he expected to see me wind up in congress. Say—is Congress anything like . . . Sing-Sing?"

Samuel Clemens created the term "bad boy," and it is his characters that have burned most deeply into the American psyche. As beloved and as castigated as any children's books, his two bad boy stories, *The Adventures of Tom Sawyer* and *The Adventures of Huckleberry Finn,* operate on multiple levels. When the National Endowment for the Humanities recently surveyed teachers and scholars for a list of books and documents that ought to be taught in all American high schools, *Huckleberry Finn* finished third behind Shakespeare (*Macbeth* and *Hamlet*) and the U.S. Constitution.[72] Yet Twain's books were heavily criticized in their day for being vulgar and unsuitable for children. A reviewer in the *New York World* called Twain's work "cheap and pernicious stuff" and condemned *Huckleberry Finn*'s "irreverence which makes parents, guardians and people who are at all good and proper [look] ridiculous." The Concord, Massachusetts, library banned *Huckleberry Finn,* calling it "trash of the veriest sort . . . not elevating," "coarse," and "irreverent."[73] Louisa May Alcott complained, "If Mr. Clemens cannot think of something better to tell our pure-minded lads and lasses he had better stop writing for them."[74] In the late twentieth century, attacks on *Huckleberry Finn* mainly involve Twain's portrayal of the runaway slave Jim as demeaning (see chapter 5). Other critics charge that the book reads like installment writing, lacking cohesion and a credible ending.[75] Some scholars are just as vehement in their praise of the novel. One claims it is "the nearest thing we have to a national epic . . . ; [its language] expresses our popular character, our humor, our slant." Another argues that "Huck's voice combined with Twain's satiric genius changed the shape of fiction in America."[76]

To be sure, Samuel Clemens turned the Sunday school formula of bad-behavior-brings-punishment on its head. He celebrates this Tom Sawyer, who "plays hooky, upsets church services, plagues adults with pranks, and engages in other forms of misbehavior." This devilish character found $12,000 in a cave without ever having reformed his character. Clemens particularly took on the motif of innocent children dying bravely in earlier children's fiction, for Tom Sawyer arranged to be "dead" and watched the grief-stricken funeral preparations and eulogies.[77] In the "Notice" preceding the novel, Clemens warned the reader: "Persons attempting to find a motive in this narrative will be prosecuted; persons attempting to find a moral in it will be banished; persons attempting to find a plot in it will be shot."[78] Thus spoofing traditional children's fiction, Mark Twain spoke for much of brash America as the Gilded Age emerged full upon the urban landscape.

Anne Scott MacLeod argues that by the late nineteenth century, moral certainty, that foundational ingredient of all children's literature up through Horatio Alger, was under assault. The bad boys evaded moral choices and downplayed their significance. Tom Bailey takes no responsibility for the boating death of his friend; Tom Sawyer freely lies and steals, although he does speak up to prevent the unjust conviction of Muff Potter; and Huck Finn flaunts his unconventional behavior.[79] However, the bad boy genre also romanticized American male childhood and the carefree neighborhoods that nurtured it. There is a nostalgia in Aldrich's reminiscences and Clemens's river episodes that reminds the reader that childhood is a sacred time with particular freedoms and joys. There is an encouragement in Peck's tales to engage in mischief to sharpen one's wits for the competitive future. But in none of them has the construction of childhood been dramatically altered. As critic Ann Trensky has noted, the boys in these stories don't grow up; they are "generally isolated, unchanging, perennial children of a golden age."[80]

Juvenile Periodicals

Most of the children's magazines created by the reformers and pietists of the early nineteenth century failed to survive the competition of the domestic stories and boys' adventures discussed in this chapter. Only the *Youth's Companion,* begun in 1829 under the strict editorship of Congregationalist minister Nathaniel Willis and subheaded "Sabbath School Recorder," survived and thrived in the postwar era (see chapter 2). Editorship passed in 1857 to Daniel Sharp Ford, who was able to adapt to the demand for more adventuresome, dramatic stories without giving up the strong moral flavor that *Youth's Companion* had always cultivated. Although the magazine became more of a family publication under Ford, stories for children remained an integral part of the publishing mix. Such notables as Harriet Beecher Stowe, Louisa May Alcott, and Jules Verne contributed stories. And although Ford dropped the didactic stories and sermonizing of the antebellum issues, he still kept tight reins on the content, censoring "improper" language, unpunished crime, and unhappy endings.[81]

Most of the popular children's magazines in the postbellum years were new arrivals in the publishing world. Over 130 magazines for children began between 1840 and 1870, with 105 more added by 1900. New technology and improved modes of transportation made the last half of the century a golden age for juvenile magazines. Writers of the era were quick to recognize this potential for steady income through periodical contributions. Whereas British periodicals continued to appeal to an elite and pious cadre of families, American periodicals developed wider appeal for several reasons. American business investors had overseen the laying of three thousand miles of train track by 1840, and by 1890 railroads crisscrossed America from coast to coast, hauling millions of tons of consumer goods at remarkably cheap costs. In addition, technological improvements that speeded mass circulation of reading material included rotary presses, improved engraving techniques, and machines able to produce a continuous web of paper. When postal rates declined in the 1870s, subscription magazines came well within the reach of even modest family incomes.[82]

Reader interest grew apace with expanded marketing and production. Although literacy had been high in Puritan New England, dispersion of the population into the middle colonies and then across the Appalachians loosened the Puritan hegemony over learning. The Chesapeake and southern colonies had never stressed literacy beyond the children of the elite. But the dictates of the new Republic, as detailed in chapter 2, hastened the movement to create free public schools. As immigration increased the competition for jobs in the cities after the Civil War, many states began requiring some schooling. By 1900, 31 states required school attendance of all children ages 8 to 14.[83] Education and literacy were prized by many working-class families, who saw them as opportunities for their children to escape the limitations of wage labor.

Just as American society expected public schools to take a large role in inculcating moral standards, Anglo-American culture, and a strong work ethic, so too did juvenile literature contribute to the enculturation process. Juvenile periodicals appealed to families who identified themselves as refined and genteel and who wanted to be sure that their children entered society sufficiently socialized. As Gordon Kelly concluded in his detailed analysis of postwar children's periodicals, these magazines transmitted the cultural norms of a "gentry class" who were "perpetuating . . . a definition of self and society amid the turmoil and disorder—at times it seemed to them the disintegration—of American life in the Gilded Age."[84]

Adolescent boys and girls from this bourgeois class had more leisure than their working-class counterparts and hence more opportunities to enjoy the new periodicals. Some were also involved in producing their own journals and newspapers. The "Novelty Press" first appeared in stores about 1867, and hundreds of young adults used their literary and creative talents to produce original work on their own printing presses. Eventually these youngsters created a national organization of novelty printing-press owners who shared their creative writing, discussed sales and management, and debated such contemporary social issues as the rights of African-Americans to belong to their organization and the role of young women in the organization and in society at large. Many of the participants wrote about their debt to various periodicals for infusing them with career goals, the love of reading, and a sense of control over their lives.[85]

Our Young Folks, published by Ticknor and Fields of Boston, first appeared in 1865 and set the standard for attracting notable writers. Under Lucy Larcom and John Townsend Trowbridge, the journal attracted such writers as Thomas Bailey Aldrich, Louisa May Alcott, Jane Andrews, Lydia Maria Child, Charles Dickens, Lucretia Hale, and Harriet Beecher Stowe. When that publishing house sustained financial disaster in the Boston fire of 1872, it was sold to Scribner's, and *Our Young Folks* merged with the new publication Scribner's was launching, *St. Nicholas.*[86]

William Taylor Adams (Oliver Optic) launched *Oliver Optic's Magazine* in 1867, although he left the paper after a year. The *Riverside Magazine for Young People* appeared in 1867 and was edited by Horace Scudder, another mid-century author. Scudder made no bones about his dislike of the British literature that still dominated the American juvenile market, believing it too infused with class-based stories for democratic children. In addition, he introduced more sophisticated illustrations than the usual wood cuts, employing such gifted artists as Thomas Nast, Winslow Homer, and John LaFarge. *Riverside Magazine* moved away from the didactic and moral messages standardized by *Youth's Companion.* Instead, Scudder took the genre of children's literature seriously, as his column "Books for Young People" in the first two issues testified. He advocated imagination rather than didacticism in writing for children. Innovations in both story and illustration made it more difficult to achieve financial success against the more traditional *Youth's Companion,* and *Riverside Magazine* folded in 1873. The culmination of this golden age of children's periodicals was *St. Nicholas.* Edited by author Mary Mapes Dodge, it enjoyed the enviable record of bringing stories to children for the next 70 years.[87]

Dime Novels

The same improved printing technology and increased literacy that made novels and periodicals less expensive for the American public also introduced a less welcome medium that was not endorsed by the dominant and genteel middle class. The dime novel, castigated as a blight on the literary landscape and called "pestilent stuff" by the *New York Tribune,* brought new heroes and reading excitement to a wide reading public. The term "dime novel" carries some confusion. In *Mechanic Accents,* literary scholar Michael Denning concluded that critics used the term to identify and condemn three separate kinds of popular literature of the nineteenth century. The five-cent "story paper," which began as early as 1839, had an eight-page, cheaply produced format and could be purchased weekly by subscription. Printers used pirated British novels and hurriedly written short stories, broken down into short installments, to keep customers buying the next issue. Examples included the *New York Ledger* (1855) and the *New York Weekly* (1859), which had wide appeal among the city's working class, especially those enrolled in night schools. These publications proved that fiction, cheaply priced, would sell well. When the post-office began to charge book rates for the papers, they became less of a bargain. While the majority of papers in this genre sought an adult audience, some were created with children in mind. Combining the popular juvenile magazine format with the cheap and quick production of the story paper, publishers targeted a child audience for such papers as *Frank Leslie's Boys' and Girls' Weekly,* whose installments featured the rapid action, hair's breadth escapes, and occasional violence of the story papers and dime novels.[88]

The actual dime novel began about 1845 as a five-by-$8^{1}/_{2}$-inch pamphlet that contained just one story. Within a dozen years, postal increases put most of the early publishers of these novels out of business. In 1860 Erastus F. and Irwin Beadle tried the format again, this time with a popular story by Ann S. Stephens that had been serialized some years earlier. *Malaeska, or Indian Wife of the White Hunter* (1860) thus became the first of the Beadles' popular cheap novels. The Beadles reduced the size of the format to 4 by 6, but the pamphlet form gave way to book form as page numbers increased to as many as one hundred. The novels sold for 10 cents apiece, at a time when most novels cost at least a quarter.[89]

The highly dramatic, sentimental plot of *Malaeska* set the pattern for future dime novels. It sold 300,000 copies and was translated into five languages. The Native American wife of a white hunter, Malaeska heeds her dying husband's words to return to his family in New York City. The family welcome Malaeska's baby but not her, allowing her to remain with them only as the child's nurse. Malaeska's son is not told of his heritage and becomes a rabid Indian hater. When she eventually reveals her identity to him, he commits suicide, and she dies the next day of grief.[90]

Erastus Beadle's "Beadle's Dime Novels" became the most popular title of dozens of inexpensive series. Sometimes known as "yellow-backs," Beadle's novels sold over four million copies in just five years. Imitators included Munro's Ten Cent Novels and Robert DeWitt's Ten Cent Romances. The tremendous sales of this cheap fiction persuaded a Chicago publisher to put together a series or library of short fiction printed in softcover pamphlets of 16 or 32 pages. Because such pamphlets could be mailed at low periodical rates, the books in this collection, called the Lakeside Library, could sell for only 10 or 20 cents each. Soon series titles and library marketing were standard operating procedures for Beadle & Adams (the Fireside Library), George Munro (the Seaside Library), and Street & Smith (various series). All three kinds of publications—the story paper, the dime novel, and the cheap library—featured the same kinds of improbable adventure stories, male heroes, and brushes with the law. Sometimes one story would appear serially in the story paper, then be published in its entirety as a dime novel, and then be reprinted as part of a series, like those of the hero Deadbeat Dick.[91] The plots were formulaic; crime and violence—or at least the threat of violence—were common; victims were always innocent; and the hero always emerged triumphant.[92] The most popular titles and series focused on the frontier, the romance of settling the West, and the stereotyped conflicts with the American Indian. Urban crime and the detective novel, which became more popular late in the century, were best known through the hero Nick Carter from the *Nick Carter Library* (1890). Another popular series that began as a dime novel but then took on a history of its own was the prep school and college life series that began with *Frank Meriwell* (1896). *Larry Locke, the Man of Iron* (1884) even spun off a series of stories about working women, beginning with *Leonie Locke; or The Romance of a Beautiful New York Working-Girl* (1885).[93]

Although much of the professional criticism directed at this body of literature focused on its detrimental effect on children, youngsters were not the original audience for the publications. Michael Denning has argued convincingly that the principal readership of the story-paper and of the original dime novels was young factory workers, recent immigrants, and young working-class women. With uncomplicated plots and a streamlined vocabulary, the genre was considered "realistic fiction" for working-class adults when it first appeared.[94] When young boys could borrow or scavenge copies, the thrill of reading about adult adventures tantalized them as much as it did adults. And much like violent films of today, this fiction was blamed when any youth got into trouble with the law. The public became so convinced that this cheap fiction taught lawlessness that Anthony Comstock, founder of the New York Society for the Prevention of Vice, could harangue an audience about

> the growth of vile literature. . . . Every publisher of the vile sensational papers for boys is shaping the career of the youth of our country. They glorify crime; the hero of each story is a boy who has escaped the restraints of home and entered on a life of crime.[95]

Even Tom Sawyer often reminded Huck Finn and the other boys of just how crimes should be committed, and Huck's staging of his own attack and bloody trail into the woods clearly points to the dime novel for inspiration.

Since both Oliver Optic (William Taylor Adams) and Horatio Alger had taken their heroes on exciting adventures with near escapes, what made the dime novel subject to such great critical abuse? For one thing, the protagonists were not sympathetic orphans adrift in the city. The heroes of dime novels were adults fully engaged in adult activities or older boys who had run away from home. As one scholar has observed, these heroes "patronize bars, dance halls, and gambling houses (but never brothels). . . . [They] drink freely and usually prefer hard liquor."[96] As the plots unfolded, the criminal was caught but usually not reformed; the evil that corrupted the mining camp or small town or urban neighborhood was too invasive to be extinguished in one arrest; and the heroes were not without their flaws, although they would certainly live to fight another day (and sell another book). The didactic insistence of Alger that people were basically good and could be trusted does not permeate the dime novel, nor does the romantic construction of the innocence of childhood.

The haste with which plots could be written and the efficiency with which series could be produced and sold resulted in the adjective *cheap* being used to describe both their price and their quality. The era of the dime thriller ended around 1890, probably for numerous reasons. The Panic of 1893 had seen the finances of several major publishers collapse; large-edition Sunday newspapers began to carry serials and human-interest tales, and the glossy magazines created in the 1890s made the "yellow-back" novels seem out of date and tawdry.[97] But the dime novel had grown up with America, had certainly helped moved children's writing away from domestic fiction to plot-driven adventure stories, had profound implications on the public's reception of such bad boy fiction as *Tom Sawyer* and *Huckleberry Finn,* and ensured that serial books would continue to entice young readers well into the twentieth century.

The second half of the nineteenth century saw American children's literature truly come into its own and produce some novels with worldwide appeal. More importantly for this study, these stories also reveal much about how the late Victorians regarded childhood. The typical female protagonist was innately kind, cheerful, innocent, and charitable. She provided a model of what society might become. The typical male protagonist engaged in minor misdeeds and humorous pranks but underneath was also caring, loyal, and a good citizen in the making. The literature was written by white middle-class authors for a white middle-class audience. A few novels, like *Little Women* and *Huckleberry Finn,* might work to subvert traditional roles, but only within acceptable social limits. The influence of pulp fiction and dime novels would be felt even more in the decades to come, as series books would provide inexpensive adventure stories for both boys and girls. Yet the allure of an idealized domesticity would also move into the next era to help society stave off the rapid social changes afoot.

4

Middle-Class Child Consumers, 1880–1920

A gradual transformation in society's construction of childhood occurred in the late nineteenth century that complemented and extended the romantic notions of childhood innocence. Romantic poets like William Wordsworth and William Blake had immortalized the innocence of childhood and lauded its tempering, redemptive effects on adults. Whereas the Puritan child in literature had sought to redeem adults by the child's own precocious piety, from John Cotton's *Spiritual Milk for Boston Babes* (see chapter 1) to Harriet Beecher Stowe's Little Eva (see chapter 3), the romantic paradigm presumed the child would convert adults to higher moral behavior and more lofty social goals, not to dogmatic Christianity.

In their daily lives, increasingly large numbers of children no longer participated in the production of the family's income. Children from all economic classes spent more weeks per year in school than children had earlier in the century. Many children over age 12 continued to work at least part time, but they now spent some of the money they earned on themselves rather than contributing to the family's survival. Rather than being viewed as economic assets in the household, children became valued for their social and emotional contribution to the family. Sociologist Viviana Zelizer has traced this reconstruction of the meaning of childhood in American society through a variety of sources. In an examination of the efforts to ban children from certain occupations, the monetary value of children in wrongful death lawsuits, and a rising demand for adoptable infants, Zelizer has shown that American society over time invented a "priceless" child of great emotional worth.[1]

Various social changes impacted society's reevaluation of the child. Educational reformers inspired by the ideas of Horace Mann had worked from the 1830s on to encourage state legislators to increase the length of the school day, to lengthen the school term, and to encourage students to stay in school beyond basic literacy training. Many educators worked to establish "normal schools" for the professional training of teachers, especially young women. At the same time, so-called progressive reformers began to attack child labor publicly, especially in mines and factories, as crippling children's physical and mental development. Spurred by the lobbying efforts of the National Child Labor Committee and its hundreds of local and state affiliates, some state legislatures began to limit the hours per week that children could work, to outlaw evening employment, and to set minimum ages for the children's employment. Child labor activists were often joined by labor unionists who wanted children out of the factories to open more jobs to male breadwinners. They also lobbied employers for a "family wage" so a child's earnings would not be needed to keep the family solvent.

Finally, by the 1920s, advances in technology, mass production, and communications meant that many of the unskilled jobs children had performed became obsolete. Society was determining—on many fronts—that children belonged in school and at play rather than in the workplace. The social construction of childhood that resulted from these various progressive reforms indicate society's belief in a "right to childhood" that legislation and institutions could ensure. The creation of the United States Children's Bureau in 1912, headed by former social worker Julia Lathrop, represents the pinnacle of this philosophy. The bureau "focused on reducing infant and maternal mortality, improving child health, abolishing child labor, and advocating care for children with 'special needs.' "[2]

As a result, children and young adults began to create their own culture, to expect entertainments and activities specifically designed for them, and to participate as consumers of popular culture in wider and more varied venues. Baseball, nickelodeons, penny arcades, amusement parks, and finally motion pictures all catered to young adults with a little extra money and some time to enjoy it. Advances in printing technology increased the availability of literature written for children exponentially while also lowering the price of the printed word. New concepts of advertising and marketing persuaded a burgeoning and child-centered middle class that books should fill the child's life. And children themselves, seeking entertainment, enlargement of their confining lives, and the vicarious friendship of "chums," school athletes, and young adventurers, avidly consumed the new children's literature. School and sports stories, Western and foreign adventures, mysteries, and America's first successful works of fantasy characterize this era. However, family-centered domestic novels, like *The Little Colonel* (1895) and *Pollyanna* (1913), also continued the tradition of highly gendered, pious models for girl readers.

Schooling as an experience of enculturation had changed dramatically by the latter half of the nineteenth century, at least for the child in an urban environment. The American high school came into its own, and the numbers of students enrolled in these public institutions began to outnumber those in private academies. The high school found itself under attack by many business leaders as providing irrelevant if not useless information to the aspiring factory worker or manager. They pressured the public schools to devote more time to "practical" subjects like bookkeeping, home economics, and manual arts.[3] High schools also saw the development of an extraordinary array of extracurricular activities. Sports teams, homemaker clubs, school newspapers, and bands were all designed to keep young people in school longer by appealing to their urge to socialize.

Traditional domestic roles for women gradually underwent significant redefinition as well. Media stories began to discuss the "new woman," a term first used by Sydney Grundy in an 1894 play called *The New Woman*. The media popularized the term to contrast young women of the 1890s with their mothers' generation. The new woman "rode a bicycle, played tennis or golf, showed six inches of stocking beneath her skirts, and loosened her corset."[4] She was freer in expressing opinions, likely to dress in conservative tailored suits or shirtwaists without petticoats and frills, and sought employment in a wider range of occupations than had been available to her mother or grandmother. Female activists truly believed that a new era was at hand. Lucy Stone commented that while her opportunities had been limited to sewing, teaching, factory work, and domestic chores, her daughter, a graduate of Boston University, "might do what she chose; all the professions were open to her; she could enter any line of business." Stone was overly optimistic; women were coming to dominate teaching and nursing, and they did provide much of the labor in offices and department stores. By 1900, about 20 percent of all women worked outside the home, although their employment might be episodic, depending on home or child responsibilities. Nevertheless, they continued to be excluded from traditional male professions and were routinely paid less than men doing similar work. By 1890, the new woman could vote in four states but not in any federal elections.[5]

New opportunities for higher education combined with career options opened up myriad possibilities for authors who wanted to appeal to young women. The wonders of mechanization in industry and the vast capitalistic expansion of American business introduced new themes that appealed to young men as well. As peer culture came to dictate what youngsters did in their leisure time, and middle-class comforts ensured that they had some, young Americans consumed fiction as never before. Children's literature reflected these new interests and values and became a battleground for the preservation of "high culture."

The Series Books

Building on the financial success of the dime novels and capitalizing on the efficiency of book distribution by 1900, publishers found they could successfully market children's fiction by developing ongoing series of books. Certainly books with continuing characters were not something new in children's literature. Since the mid-nineteenth century, authors like Horatio Alger, Martha Finley (Elsie Dinsmore), Louisa May Alcott, and William T. Adams (Oliver Optic) knew how to sustain buyer interest with continuing characters or settings (see chapter 3). Sometimes authors encouraged children to buy the next book in the series by blatantly advertising within the text itself. For example, in *Luck and Pluck* (1869), Horatio Alger's narrative voice interjected, "And now, kind reader, let me hope to meet you soon again with the second volume of the 'Luck and Pluck' series,—*Sink or Swim.*" Harry Castlemon's *Frank on the Prairie* (1865) ended with "These were Archie's first impressions. . . . He had adventures more than he wanted, and what they were shall be told in *Frank Among the Rancheros.*"[6] These early works with continuing characters almost always featured a single author, although the last several Horatio Alger titles were ghostwritten.

The term "series book," however, usually describes a particular genre that began in the 1890s and reached its pinnacle with the creation of the Stratemeyer Syndicate about 1905. In these cases, large publishing syndicates featured an anonymous stable of authors who filled out a very specific plot outline, using well-defined character guidelines to develop the story. Aggressive marketing by these publishing houses created and sustained public interest in their series. These new series books removed the stories' settings from the confines of the family and centered them instead on peer group activities, foreign travels, or the solving of a mystery. Thus these new series books combined new understandings of childhood with the formulaic style, production, speed, and affordability of the dime novels to capture a large segment of the juvenile reading public in the late nineteenth century.

Boarding school stories, with their emphasis on peer group experience, represent an important type of gendered series books. Edward Stratemeyer (under the pseudonym Arthur Winfield) wrote the long-lived Rover Boys series (1899–1926). The first book, *The Rover Boys at School* (1899), introduced three brothers Tom, Dick, and Sam Rover, who in the course of 30 books went from boarding school and overseas adventures to find their missing father to college and finally to marriage and fatherhood. In this series's spin-off, the Putnam Hall series, the sons of the three Rover brothers went off to boarding school themselves.[7]

Because the protagonist in a school story represents the young male preparing to enter American business and industry circles, he can exhibit very spunky behavior and even defy authority *if* a moral principle is at stake. In these stories, the hero improves the school or the situation in which he finds himself. Thus the protagonist emerges as an example of American ingenuity and determination while still upholding ethical principles and looking out for those less privileged. For example, in *The Rover Boys at School,* Tom Rover violates school policy by setting off a firecracker; he then compounds his guilt by running away to escape punishment. However, his lawyerlike rebuttal that he had not actually violated school policy because he was not yet officially enrolled in the school convinces the headmaster of his spunk and intelligence. Not only is Tom accepted into the school without punishment, but he becomes a leader in improving administration-student relations. In *The Racer Boys at Boarding School* (1912), the Racer brothers actually renovate a run-down, poorly organized academy and turn it into a fine boarding school.[8] In both cases the heroes embody the admired male characteristics of the Gilded Age: energy, cleverness, initiative, glibness, and entrepreneurship without the negative characteristics of avarice, dishonesty, and greed.

For girls, the messages and motifs of boarding school stories remain separate from those for boys. The second of Sarah Chauncey Woolsey's (Susan Coolidge) popular Katy books, called *What Katy Did at School* (1873), stands as an example of the more traditional domestic fiction (see chapter 3), which used a private-school setting for one of its stories. Thus it serves to bridge the domestic stories of mid-century with the late-century school story. The Girls at Central High series is typical of series books that are centered solely on the female school experience. Here clubs, school loyalties, snobbish cliques, and old-fashioned teachers become the stock ingredients for numerous female adventures. Unlike boys' fiction, however, much girls' fiction features the importance of true friendship along with the solving of mysteries. Parents, if they appear at all, are "shadowy and indulgent figures" who account for little in the development of the plot.[9] Hence these school stories appealed to emerging adolescents who were shaping their own age-bounded social groups and experiences.

As much as children's authors might resort to tried-and-true definitions of femininity and domesticity, many young women were entering a radically different culture by the end of the nineteenth century. By 1890, more women than men were graduating from high school. As colleges and universities proliferated, many found that they could not meet enrollment expectations without admitting women as students. Midwestern universities in Chicago and Michigan became coeducational in the 1870s. When the new University of Chicago opened in 1892, women comprised about 40 percent of its enrollment, and by 1902 the number of women on campus exceeded the number of men. Some educators feared that college was becoming feminized and that this would deter good male students from enrolling.[10]

Meanwhile, all-women colleges flourished in the Northeast and the South; Vassar enrolled its first class in 1865, vowing to prepare young women as rigorously as did any all-male college. Smith (1875), Wellesley, (1875), Bryn Mawr (1885), and Sophie Newcomb (1889) are among those female colleges that were producing outstanding graduates by the turn of the century.[11] The seriousness with which many privileged young women took their college education was not reflected in the popular fiction available to them. Jean Webster's *When Patty Went to College* (1903) features a heroine who seems to spend most of her time avoiding studying, getting ready for dates, and playing practical jokes on her friends. She is admired for her fashionable good looks and her ready repartee, not her scholarship. In 1905, a *Good Housekeeping* "College Girls' Special Edition" carried articles about the "ideal husband" and budgeting for a vacation but said little about the challenges of academic life. *Ladies' Home Journal* began a series called "College Girls' Larks and Pranks." In real life, female students competed very successfully in the academic realm, but readers would never know that from this particular school series.[12]

Some contrast can be found in the High School Girls series begun in 1910 by Jessie Graham Flower. In this series the heroine Grace Harlow eventually graduates from high school (necessitating a change in the series title), successfully completes college, and becomes a women's dormitory supervisor. In this capacity, she develops friendships with an interesting circle of female professors. Flower thus accurately reflects what an educated woman might in fact do in the early twentieth century. In *Grace Harlow's Problem* (1916), Grace finally has to choose between her job and a marriage proposal. Typically, she chooses the latter, but even then the series survives as she and her new husband volunteer in France for the duration of World War I.[13]

Another popular type of series book revolved around sports activities. Walter Evans, in an exhaustive study of boys' sports stories, characterizes one type of story as that in which a friendless boy, usually a new pupil, is "adopted" by an older and more popular student, who sees the boy's true worth and good character. A conflict develops early as the protagonist is set upon by a school bully or bullies. His physical strength, self-image, and abilities gradually improve under the tutelage of his best friend until he finally proves himself in some major crisis or game. This proving fully integrates him into the life of the school and into the prestigious clique of athletes. Usually the bully undergoes some reformation of character by the end of the story.

Another important character in this standard formula is the "outsider," usually a very intelligent but nonathletic boy who recognizes the great character of the hero, performs the role of admirer, and is included in the clique after the hero proves himself.[14] Once the hero has proven himself the formula has to change: the now-established hero can enter into other aspects of life, bringing his noble, manly, honest character to bear on all sorts of situations, or the hero can continue in athletic competitions of limited duration (one big game, one season) surrounded by various subplots and transformations of minor characters.[15]

A variation on this theme simply portrayed young men in various sports activities, always following an unwritten "sportsman's code" through which the student learns courage, leadership, and perseverance, traits that merit victories both on the playing field and in life. In this sports fiction, athletic competition is privileged over any other aspect of school life and is presented as the only adequate preparation for the future. Devotion to sports is, of course, the basic foundation of the code. But complementary features included forswearing drinking, gambling, cheating, or too much interest in girls. In addition, the hero has to take defeat bravely, compliment opponents, be modest about accomplishments, and subordinate personal success to the success of the team.[16] Sports stories published before 1930 were usually set in boarding schools or private colleges; boys were privileged, white, but not excessively wealthy. (It was often the bully who used his lavish wealth to intimidate or bribe others.) It comes as little surprise that public figures raised on this boys' literature of the early twentieth century came to describe their work and their goals as businessmen in terms of sport metaphors: "drive to the finish line," "play on a winning team," "practice makes perfect," "winners never quit."

Of all the boys' sports heroes, Frank Merriwell, created by William Gilbert Patton writing as Burt L. Standish, became the most popular. He began appearing in serialized stories in the *Tip Toy Weekly* boys' paper and continued as a stock character for 20 years. The Frank Merriwell books themselves ran from 1901 to 1916; in all, Patton produced 208 titles featuring Frank, his brother Dick, and his son Frank Jr. Frank Merriwell not only displayed all the characteristics of a fine athlete in almost every sport (to keep the series going) but he was also decent, honest, modest, and polite. Merriwell stories also ran as comic strips and as radio shows in the 1930s.[17] Almost as popular were the sports stories of Ralph Henry Barbour (1870–1944). *The Half-back: A Story of School, Football, and Golf* (1899) launched a lucrative sports series for the Appleton Publishing Co., and in 1907 Barbour created a female counterpart to his male heroes in *The Crimson Sweater*. Although the latter concept developed into only a four-volume series, it featured Harry (Harriet), an engaging, athletic, and competitive young woman. Before his career ended, Barbour had written at least 160 sports titles.[18]

The Crimson Sweater did not stand alone. Sports stories for girls came into their own during the 1890s and flourished after the turn of the century. Almost all the novels and short stories in this genre were set at the "Seven Sisters" colleges or at fictional women's schools. At its best, this genre socialized adolescent women into the college life they would encounter or at least provided fictional models of women who made physical prowess and an active lifestyle a priority. At a time when fewer than four percent of America's young women went to college, almost all the girls in the series books matriculated in college. In this milieu, authors privileged the peer group, the attraction of male companionship, and all activities independent of adult supervision. Grace Margaret Gallaher's *Vassar Stories* (1900), Anna Chapin Ray's *Sidney at College* (1908), and Jean Webster's *When Patty Went to College* not only profiled the camaraderie of female education but also emphasized the role of competitive athletics, especially women's basketball. This is hardly surprising, for almost as soon as James Naismith's new sport was introduced in 1891, college women began forming their own basketball teams to compete in intraschool games. By the turn of the century, many women's colleges had teams playing neighboring schools.[19]

But the use to which authors put athletic competition in girls' sports stories differed significantly from the purpose of sports in boys' fiction. As noted previously, sports toughened a boy into a man and prepared him for the initiative, competition, and perseverance needed to succeed in a capitalist economy. For girls, no such preparation for public roles was openly contemplated, but girls could be toughened for the moral and social reform tasks that might lie ahead. As one character says in *The Girls of Central High* (1914): "The games and exercises we have . . . are making us stronger and abler to meet the difficulties of life."[20] Also, girls' sports stories provided the opportunity for author and reader alike to reject school authority in one respect, for teachers and administrators often favored traditional calisthenics and walking over competitive team sports. Athletic college women certainly projected the image of the new woman, an image that loomed large in the early-twentieth-century debate over "woman's proper place." She harmonized both athleticism and feminism.[21]

For boys, no topic held more potential for thrills, bravery, surprise, and triumph than war, and the publishing syndicates were more than happy to reinforce contemporary notions of Anglo superiority, to illustrate American "guidance" of less-developed countries, and to capitalize on actual armed conflicts. In 1898 Edward Stratemeyer developed a story about two boys on a battleship, which he sent off to a publisher just as Admiral George Dewey steamed into Manila Harbor and sank 10 Spanish ships anchored there—the first action of the Spanish-American War. The publisher asked Stratemeyer to rewrite the story, placing it in the Philippines. *Under Dewey at Manila; of the War Fortunes of a Castaway* appeared within the year. This book began the Old Glory series, and the same cast of characters traveled to the Far East for the series Soldiers of Fortune.[22] With the eruption of World War I, series writers sought to place their characters on the front, working with the Red Cross and on the Atlantic and expressing patriotism at home. The use of fighter planes particularly intrigued series authors, who by 1959 had developed 60 different series centering on aviation alone, including four female-aviator books.[23]

The Conquest of the United States series (1916) by H. Irving Hancock highlights the theme of a potential invasion of the U.S. by the Germans. In the first book, the American military meets defeat, and the defense of the country falls to a group of teenage patriots who had military training in high school. These very political books seem directed to an adult audience, many members of which felt President Woodrow Wilson's neutrality policy and his failure to develop American war readiness posed a serious threat to U.S. security. In fact, the War Preparedness Movement and the National Security

League in the U.S. promoted armament production and universal military training.[24] *The Khaki Girls* by Edna Brooks centers on World War I adventures, and other series books for girls acknowledge the war by including a volume or two with a Red Cross or war setting.[25]

Regardless of the type of series book examined, the books' heroes seem indistinguishable from one another. In the boys' series, the protagonist was usually between 14 and 17 years of age, athletic, high spirited, courageous, self-confident, enthusiastic about new and challenging situations, pleasantly dispositioned, respectful of parents and coaches, and protective of girls and younger boys. The chief character in girls' series, like her fictional counterpart 50 years earlier, was often orphaned and making her way in life or through school by virtue of determination, good character, cleverness, compassion, and intuition. She could be assertive and ambitious, but knowledge of domestic skills and appreciation of fashion and good manners remained a part of her definition. Often female characters appeared first in a boys' series, perhaps to attract some female readership. Their role was ornamental and supportive and allowed the author to teach boy readers some social graces and manners by including social gatherings in the plot.

Strong female characters emerged more slowly. Girls' series number about half of those for boys, and the range of activities is somewhat narrower.[26] Like her male counterparts, girls in series fiction experienced great freedom from parental control and relied heavily on the peer group for identification and approval. She demonstrated her abilities on the athletic field or court, showed mastery of mechanics and technology, for example with autos and airplanes, sacrificed for others, befriended the outsider and distinguished between true and false friends, charmed adults with her manners and social graces, and managed to prove her mettle over and over. Whereas boys tended to prove themselves through sports or adventures, girls proved themselves by gaining social acceptance and maintaining a spotless reputation. Girls were less likely to fight unjust situations directly. Unlike male heroes, who helped others while also advancing their own cause, female protagonists were expected to be happy simply by virtue of their good deeds.[27] So although these adolescents' adventures strain one's credulity, the characters themselves accurately reflect the dominant values and gender definitions of their day.

Genius of the Stratemeyer Syndicate

Many of the era's most successful series books germinated under the editorial genius of Edward Stratemeyer (1862–1930). A children's author since "Victor Horton's Idea" appeared in *Golden Days* magazine in 1888, he became editor of the boys' weekly *Good News*. Stratemeyer went on to finish 3 Oliver Optic novels that W. T. Adams had begun and also completed at least

11 books under Horatio Alger's name. He continued creating boys' novels for various publishers in the 1890s and launched four series, including the Old Glory series previously mentioned, under several pseudonyms.[28] Around 1905 he created the Stratemeyer Syndicate, which perfected writing and marketing techniques that had already been used successfully by the dime novel and pulp fiction trade. Stratemeyer advertised for writers who would work for a flat fee, relinquish claim to authorship, and forego royalties. The author also agreed not to use the pseudonym he was given for any other works outside the syndicate. For a cost of about $75 the syndicate had any and all legal rights to the production and profits from that novel. When he first began publishing, Stratemeyer's books sold for the same price as other juvenile titles, about $1.00 to $1.25. But in 1906 he approached one of his publishers, Cupples and Leon, and suggested they market the Motor Boys series for just 50 cents a title. In an era of cost accounting, national advertising campaigns, and competitive marketing, Stratemeyer had found a niche. His syndicate alone produced 81 distinct series.[29]

Stratemeyer outlined the plot for each book himself, chapter by chapter, then sent these out to his stable of writers, expecting, as one writer told *Fortune* magazine, that an author could take the outline "from conception to typeset" in 40 days. As writers, both Stratemeyer and his daughter Harriet would write from 9 to 5 daily, completing about three chapters (or 7,500 words) a day.[30] He promoted a new series by issuing the first *three* titles simultaneously; he called these books the "breeders" for the rest of the series. Additional volumes followed quickly.[31] Like the early series books, Stratemeyer used a "hook" in the last chapter to set up the suspense for a sequel. For example, "Helen could not foresee that in only a few weeks she would find a mysterious bracelet and be caught up again in a mystery that would puzzle her and amaze her friends." He also promoted the series by insisting that each volume refer to events in previous volumes to increase reader interest in those. Stratemeyer carefully edited each submission to ensure that character descriptions remained consistent and that no obvious discrepancies appeared.[32] He continued to write many volumes himself—current estimates suggest 275 singly authored books written under 83 pen names, the best known being Captain Ralph Bonehill and Arthur M. Winfield. His two daughters, Edna Stratemeyer and Harriet Stratemeyer Adams, took over editorship of the literary syndicate on his death and oversaw the publication of 480 more titles before the whole operation was sold to Simon and Schuster in 1984.[33]

Of course, Stratemeyer had some failures as well. At the height of the progressive campaign to limit or ban the sale of alcohol, Stratemeyer launched a series about youngsters forming a Temperance Club called the White Ribbon Boys series. It never caught on with young consumers. Nor did a fantasy series called The Flyaways, launched in 1925.[34] But for the most part, Stratemeyer well understood the influence of the peer culture, technology, and the market at the turn of the century. In a rare personal interview in 1904, he articulated his philosophy on writing for children:

> I have no toleration for that which is namby-pamby or wishy-washy in juvenile literature. This is a strenuous age. . . . [The children] of today are clever and up-to-date and appreciate what is true to life quite as much as their elders. . . . Every story ought to have a high moral tone, but the moral ought to be *felt* rather than *mentioned.*[35]

With one brief comment, Stratemeyer captured the exuberance and optimism of the Gilded Age while simultaneously recognizing the moral zeal of Progressivism. Competition, industriousness, and cleverness—when put to good uses—brought both happiness and success. Ken Donelson, in his text on young adult fiction, has expressed the same understanding of this new era:

> Foreigners were not to be trusted. . . . The outdoor life was healthy. . . . Good manners and courtesy were essential for moving ahead. Work in and of itself was a positive good and would advance one in life. Anyone could defeat adversity, any adversity,—if that person had a good heart and soul. . . . Evil and good were clearly and easily distinguishable. And good always triumphed over evil (at least by the final chapter).[36]

Character repentance and reformation rarely surfaced as the chief plot in any Stratemeyer book. Plot always took precedence over characters, and every possible geographical setting and juvenile interest made it into some series. Outdoor adventures, career choices, technology and invention, school experiences, sports, travel, aviation, and solving mysteries comprise the chief topics the teenage heroes explored. Hunting and wilderness adventures became particularly popular in the era of Teddy Roosevelt. His robust lifestyle, his call for the creation of national wilderness areas and parks, and a general belief in America's cultural superiority combined to fuel a number of "outdoors" series.

All sorts of professional, middle-class careers are explored in the series books as well. In *A Business Boy; Or, Winning Success* (1908), a young man reported his observations of employee theft to the shop owner, who put the boy in charge of the store. His "hard work and new ideas" increased sales, enhanced appearances, and improved employee morale. The thief underwent a character transformation, but more importantly, the hero became a partner with the original owner. The Tom Swift Jr. series highlighted technology, the Moving Picture Boys and the Motion Picture Chums explored the cinema, and several series featured pilots or pilots-to-be.[37]

For the most part, adolescent activities, and hence adolescent reading, remained gendered in the series books. Stratemeyer introduced the Dorothy Dale series (1908–1924; 13 volumes) for girls, the Motor Girls (1910–1917), and the Ruth Fielding series (30 volumes) between 1913 and 1934. He hired a number of female writers to crank out the plots according to his outlines; a few, particularly in the Ruth Fielding series, actively sought to portray the possibilities open to the new woman of the twentieth century.

The Ruth Fielding series certainly suggests the emergence of this new prototype for girls. When the series begins in 1913, Ruth Fielding is an orphan who is forced to live with her miserly Uncle Jabez. She minds dutifully, but her clever recovery of his lost money box persuades him to send her off to boarding school—an opportunity she much prefers. Not only does Ruth win over the snobbish, cliquish girls at the school but she also wins plaudits from her teachers for her scholarship. On that point, the plot differs little from the other orphan-makes-good stories of Victorian domestic fiction writers. However, in later books Ruth Fielding travels to Europe during World War I. In *Ruth Fielding at Cameron Hall,* she marries her boyfriend, Tom, but keeps her own name. She continues to work as an actress (and amateur sleuth), although the conflict between being Tom's wife and being a professional woman dominates much of the action. Scholar Carol Billman describes Ruth Fielding as a "no-nonsense, unsentimental, independent, aggressive, ambitious, assertive" heroine. Authorship of the Fielding series changed hands several times, which may explain why the independent and successful character eventually decides to cease her foreign travels and "leave further adventures to her daughter."[38] Or her forthright and ambitious nature may have proved too much for a society that had grudgingly accorded women the franchise in 1920 but continued to deny them significant access to political, economic, and intellectual power.

But Progressive themes were not limited to an occasional portrayal of "the new woman." In the Do Something series, Janice Day transformed the dying village of Poketown into a prosperous commercial center. Janice convinced the locals to clean up their yards, paint their homes, build a new school with a modern curriculum, rename the town after its founder (Polk), and "join" the twentieth century.[39] Other individual books sometimes touched on the questions of women's suffrage, female sports teams, and prohibition.[40] As long as social concerns remained subservient to a tantalizing plot development, authors could reflect contemporary issues in their series books.

Although the great preponderance of serialized fiction targeted adolescents, the huge publishing empires did not overlook the younger reader. The plots of these series books emphasized misadventures and temporary unhappiness, even if the issues were no more than a lost toy or a vacation spoiled by the weather. The standard formula emphasized happy families and happy children. Most of the series books for younger children, like those for their older siblings, were gender-specific. For example, the 34-volume Honey Bunch series, which began in 1923 and ran until the mid-fifties, featured a picture-perfect little girl who led a highly idealized life with loving and doting parents. (Shirley Temple made several Honey Bunch movies.[41])

The Bobbsey Twins series marked the Stratemeyer Syndicate's first venture into younger fiction. The 115 volumes, beginning in 1904 and continuing until 1992, changed little in basic formula. According to Stratemeyer scholar Diedre Johnson, the "veneer of realism" in these stories barely covered a highly idealized family situation, steady gratification of material desires, and a consistent theme of "wish fulfillment" by the authors. By virtue of using the device of two sets of twins in one family, Stratemeyer cleverly appealed to a broad age range and both genders of readers. Flossie and Freddie, as rambunctious yet cherubic four-year-olds, helped convince the second- or third-year reader of his or her maturity, while the eight-year-old twins, Nan and Bert, provided contemporary role models of intelligent, active, yet serious youngsters. The two-parent family featured a nurturing at-home mother who managed her active family along with teaching Sunday school and volunteering for charitable causes. The family employed an African-American couple to help with the children and the household. (See chapter 5 for a discussion of the racial stereotyping of this series.) While the series did adapt somewhat to changing trends in children's literature (the twins investigated mysteries, for example), the twins had only "grown" to ages 6 and 12 by the 1960s. The white, middle-class ethos surrounding the family and all their vacations, recreational activities, and school experiences hardly reflected the turbulent years of the later twentieth century.

Professionalization and Criticism of Series Literature

Another outgrowth of Progressive reform, in addition to expanded schooling and limits on child labor, was a fixation on youthful behavior and a perception that unsupervised young people, especially boys, could become sexual deviants and criminals. Psychologist G. Stanley Hall of Clark University was one of the first to conduct research on child development; his conclusions led him to define and describe a discrete stage of human development he called "adolescence." Hall argued that individual human development recapitulates the development of humankind (civilization). Adolescence corresponded to the savage, nomadic era of development and hence was to be closely confined and controlled. However, he believed that all the restraints previous cultures had placed on its maturing young had been removed in modern America. He wrote in 1905, "Never has youth been exposed to such dangers of both perversion and arrest as in our own land and day."[42]

Hall's social Darwinist approach to child development combined too conveniently with America's growing fear of the increasingly large numbers of immigrants "flooding" into the cities. Numerous well-meaning reformers sought to channel, regulate, guide, and suppress adolescent behavior. The "youth problem," as it was sometimes called, was taken up by settlement

house workers who tried to provide recreational outlets for youth, by organizers of the Boy Scouts, Campfire Girls, and Girl Guides (later the Girl
Scouts), and by self-proclaimed critics of the popular literature that young
people were reading. Many worried about the effect of "sensationalized" stories on young minds and moral character. Just as proponents of high culture
had attacked dime novels as promoters of lawlessness and crime 20 years earlier, so the serialized children's books of the syndicates were subjected to criticism and abuse.

Critics generally attacked the series books either for a mediocre writing
style or for exaggerated, sensationalized, and overstimulating plots. A review
of the Rover Boy series in *Literary World* (February 1900) remarked that
"none of these [series] books represents the highest ranges of reading for
boys, but all approach the dime novel order."[43] The official librarian of the
Boy Scouts of America, Franklin K. Mathiews, found Scouts everywhere too
absorbed in the series books for his tastes. Mathiews complained that "in this
'mile-a-minute' fiction some inflammable tale of improbable adventure is told
. . . and when it comes to getting on in the world, the cleverness of these hustling boys is comparable only to those . . . who have made millions in a
minute." In another speech, he called the series books "explosive! Guaran-
teed to blow your boy's brains out!" Mathiews went on to become instrumen-
tal in the creation of National Book Week to promote children's reading of
classics and other "sound literature."[44] Kate Douglas Wiggin, a children's
author and a tireless advocate of progressive kindergartens, also bemoaned
the popular syndicate books. "If you find a twelve-year-old boy addicted to
juveniles you many as well give the poor little creature up. . . . His ears will
be deaf to the music of St. Paul's Epistles and the Book of Job; he will never
know the Faerie Queene or the Red Cross Knight, [or] Don Quixote," she
complained.[45] In a broad generalization, the head of the National Council of
Teachers of English pronounced in 1906 that most books written for girls
were particularly poorly conceived:

> They seem to have been written mostly by people deficient in good red blood.
> They lack invention, action, humor; they run on (or off) in a patter of endless talk
> without point and without savor. . . . The tradition seems still to hold that any-
> thing will do for girls, if only there isn't too much of it.[46]

In 1905 the *Library Journal* asked, "Shall the libraries resist the flood and
stand for a better and purer literature and art for children, or shall they 'meet
the demands of the people' by gratifying a low and lowering taste?" Editorial
writers went on to call the series books "trashy" and "tawdry." The respected
children's magazine *St. Nicholas* refused to review the series books or even
mention them by name in its columns.[47]

Such critiques of the vast numbers of stories being published for young
people reflect the decline of a common aesthetic regarding good literature.

Whereas Victorian domesticity had valued the family reading hour, during which a parent read aloud from Charles Dickens, Louisa May Alcott, James Fenimore Cooper, or other approved classic authors, now children were choosing their own books, which were targeted specifically to adolescents, not families. As a consequence, critics felt an obligation to monitor these juvenile texts more closely. School librarians and English teachers in particular began to redefine children's literature by age and difficulty and to separate it from adult fiction. By 1912, a suggested purchase list for public libraries' children's sections included few classics or adult titles.[48]

These self-proclaimed experts had tremendous authority in shaping the development of children's literature because their comments influenced book purchases by school and public libraries. These attacks on mass-produced children's literature principally emanated from newly professionalized teacher or librarian organizations. Educators, along with doctors, lawyers, dentists, and others, created professional organizations to set admission standards for their discipline, to promote their professional activities through published journals and annual meetings, to lobby legislators and the media, and to exercise influence over the standards and practices of their members. The National Education Association was created in 1857, and the American Library Association in 1876. Both organizations followed children's book publishing closely and both set standards to which they believed children's literature ought to subscribe. The latter group created the *Library Journal* in 1876 to circulate ideas about professional management and preservation of books as well as to review current literature.[49] In 1884, Columbia University established the first program in the country in Library Economy (later called Library Science) and offered its first classes in 1887.[50] Children's libraries themselves had their inception in Hartford, Connecticut, under the aegis of Caroline M. Hewins in 1875. The exemplary Children's Room of the New York Public Library followed in 1906 under Anne Carroll Moore.[51] It was Moore who began the first critical reviewing of children's books in *The Bookman* (1918) and in a weekly column called "The Three Owls" in the *New York Herald Tribune*. She used the column as a megaphone to call for books displaying "originality, beauty, spontaneous appeal, and an imaginative approach."[52]

School librarianship, which had the potential to shape children's literature, developed considerably later. The Cleveland and Newark, New Jersey, public libraries were the first in the country to establish branches in public high schools, in 1899. The early twentieth century saw the gradual funding of high school libraries. In 1918 the National Education Association issued a report on the standards for such libraries, but in general they were viewed as luxuries until after World War II.[53] School librarians then lent their voices to the criticism of much popular children's fiction. The superintendent of New York's school libraries complained that popular boys' books did not belong in the school library, even though readers loved them: "[T]he books are not immoral, but they are poorly written, their heroes are too often of the 'cheap and smart' variety, and their ideals are not always the best."[54]

The National Council of Teachers of English supported the publication in 1906 of *A Bibliography of Children's Reading* to ensure that edifying works with literary merit formed the curriculum in America's high schools. These professionals put forth an argument that has persisted throughout the history of children's literature—that it serve a moral function. "Boys are not scholars, and most of them are not even scholars in-the-making," the NCTE argued. "But they are men in the making, and good ideals are an exceedingly valuable element in the process."[55] A poll of 800 pupils and 36,000 teachers in 34 cities by the American Library Association and the Carnegie Corporation in 1926 found that the reading habits of fifth to seventh graders were largely determined by the Stratemeyer Syndicate. The students found almost "no flaws" in these books, whereas their teachers labeled the books "trashy." Consequently the ALA published the *Winnetka Graded Book List* of recommended titles for young people's reading. "Children's book people were a strong-minded lot who were certain that they knew what was good in books and good for children," commented historian Anne Scott MacLeod in an essay about turn-of-the-century reading.[56]

And how did young readers themselves influence the development of children's literature? A 1907 survey of elementary school children revealed that what they valued in books were action, lively dialogue, and prominent illustrations. Many of the children's series books followed exactly that formula in developing their stories, so that regardless of the criticism of professionals, children's reading spanned quite a variety of topics and formats.

Boys' Adventure Tales

In addition to the wildly popular series books of the late nineteenth and early twentieth centuries, more traditional authors continued to present boys with lively tales of adventure, historical fiction, and biography. Authors in the tradition of Horatio Alger wanted to spin a good story but also help young men develop such character traits as discipline, honesty, empathy, determination, and courage, which would serve them well in the highly competitive industrial world they would enter. In addition, some authors were mindful of America's growing concern with manhood: a fear that boys raised in urban environments would not reach the strength of body or character that previous generations had experienced. With more fathers working in business and industry away from home and with mothers having assumed the moral responsibility for child rearing, some Americans feared that young boys would become too feminized.

The Young Men's Christian Association (YMCA), brought to the United States from England in 1851, began as an organization that would promote comradeship, spiritual strength, and safety, one that would "uplift" young urban workers. As the organization grew it began to focus on "building" men through an emphasis on sports and citizenship. The Boy Scouts of America soon took the lead as the premier organization for shaping preadolescent boys into men. Although the national organization, established in 1910, was headed by a professional bureaucracy, local troops were led by volunteers, mostly young professional men. They sought to build character and to serve as masculine models to middle-class boys with increasing free time on their hands. Boy Scout activities emphasized physical fitness, experience in a natural environment, and serving others, all themes highlighted in the new adventure fiction for boys.[57]

Howard Pyle (1853–1911), an artist whose fame lies in book illustrating, chose classic and medieval stories for his adventure books. His first stories for children appeared in the popular juvenile magazines of the late nineteenth century, such as *Harper's Young People* and *St. Nicholas*. This led to his authoring numerous books in which he retold medieval myths or legends and illustrated them with realistic paintings and calligraphy. *The Merry Adventures of Robin Hood* (1883), *Otto of the Silver Hand* (1888), *Men of Iron* (1892), *The Story of King Arthur* (1903), and an entire series based on the Arthurian legends were among his best-selling works.[58] Pyle appealed to those with a professional interest in children's literature and those familiar with Sir Walter Scott's writing, for like Scott, Pyle drew on classical tales with mostly medieval settings. Pyle's technique was stilted, ornate, and stylized prose. A recent critic has cited Pyle's "conscious archaism" as off-putting and pretentious, but to the young adults still being schooled in heavy doses of classical languages and European history, the stories did have appeal.[59] The historian of children's literature Gillian Avery has noted that some of Pyle's stories and even some of his layouts are "close imitations" of the works of Hans Christian Anderson and Randolph Caldecott.[60]

The works of Joseph A. Altsheler also served as antidotes to the Stratemeyer series books; critics found them more historically based and better written. *The Young Trailers* (1907) portrayed vivid Indian-settler conflicts on the Kentucky frontier in the previous century and led to the Young Trailers series of eight titles. The author emphasized respect for the natural environment and the shared values of white and Indian cultures: courage, trustworthiness, and honesty. The reconciliation between warring parties in this work served as a pattern for later stories. Altsheler produced a series of titles based loosely on the French and Indian War with parallels to the work of James Fenimore Cooper. His Civil War series followed young men on both sides of the conflict and at least a dozen other titles focused on Western adventures or on World War I.[61]

Fantasy and Humor

Alongside adventure tales and the school, sport, and mystery adventures of the popular series books, American children could also sample a genre that English children had relished for decades: fantasy. In 1887 Palmer A. Cox, a Canadian plying his journalism and fiction in the United States, introduced impish little creatures called "Brownies," whose tales were based on Scottish legends. Cox believed the Brownies were so named for their hair color and weather-beaten faces, but others have suggested that the name came from the Old World tradition of leaving food for these fairy-creatures under the tradi- tional "Browny-stone" near a church.[62] Beginning with *The Brownies: Their Book* and continuing through 12 sequels, Palmer's works delighted adults along with their children. Written in verse and illustrated with pen-and-ink drawings that enter into the text, dance around it, realign the margins, and almost spill off the page, stories about the Brownies brought readers both visual and aural delight. In the opening tale, the Brownies visit a schoolhouse by night and disappear at daybreak, as was their custom, but

Palmer Cox, *The Brownies,* illustrated by Palmer Cox (1887; reprint, 1964)
"The Brownies at School," copied with permission from Dover Publications, Inc., Mineola, N.Y.

So great had been the haste to hide,
The windows were left open wide;
And scholars knew, without a doubt,
That Brownies had been thereabout.[63]

Thus Cox used realistic situations familiar to children and peopled them with these imaginary creatures. Although the Brownies principally engaged in helpful activities unseen by the "real" world, they often got into more scrapes, arguments, and injuries than was common in nineteenth-century domestic stories. Cox expected his stories to be entertaining and to teach morals as well. He once remarked that "my work for children would always have happy endings. . . . It is time enough for children when they get big to learn that a reckoning must be made with suffering and bloodshed."[64]

Palmer Cox's illustrations, as much as his verses and moral didacticism, confirmed the popularity of the Brownies books. As an illustrator, he worked for numerous national companies preparing advertisements for Ivory Soap, Lion Coffee, Clark's Spool Cotton, and Pond's Extract. Well before Walt Disney, Palmer capitalized on his fictitious creations. He marketed the Brownie characters on rubber-stamp printing sets, playing cards, puzzles, spoons, tumblers—almost an endless assortment of salable items linked to his books.[65]

Whereas Palmer Cox created mythical creatures whose adventures occurred in the real world, Frank Baum (1856–1919) went one step further. With the exception of the framing of his story in a very real Kansas, *The Wonderful Wizard of Oz* (1900) partakes wholly of an imaginary world of its own: Baum's colorful land of Oz, populated with talking animals, witches, a live scarecrow, flying monkeys, and a rusty tin man. Like Horatio Alger before him, Frank Baum came to children's literature almost by accident but found in it a lifelong career. Baum enjoyed writing and had published some poems and nonfiction as a young adult. He tried acting as a career but turned to business to support his growing family. Then as a journalist and ever-diligent student of marketing and sales, he thought he could surely produce popular children's books at least as interesting as those he saw flooding the market. He took the familiar verses of the "Mother Goose" nursery rhymes and wrote prose versions of them, and then asked the young artist Maxfield Parrish to illustrate them. Their book appeared inauspiciously in 1897. Baum himself noted that it "was not appealing to children, although adults went wild over the beautiful [Parrish] drawings."[66]

A few years later Baum approached another prominent artist and good friend, William Wallace Denslow, about illustrating some of Baum's poetry. They completed *Father Goose, His Book* in 1899, which was much more successful than his initial venture into children's publishing. Its success led Baum to plan a project that had been simmering in his mind for some time: to expand a bedtime fairy tale he had invented for his sons into a full-length children's book. He called the story "The Emerald City" and again asked

Frank Baum, *The Wonderful Wizard of Oz*, illustrated by W. W. Denslow (1900)

Denslow to supply illustrations. The interested publisher insisted upon a title change because of an old superstition that "any book with a jewel in its title was doomed to failure." Thus renamed, *The Wonderful Wizard of Oz* appeared in 1900. Critics generally liked the fantasy and often compared it to *Alice's Adventures in Wonderland*. The first printing of 10,000 copies sold within two weeks; some version of the book has been in print ever since.[67]

From its creation, critics have pondered the suggestive symbolism of Oz.[68] Baum publicly stated that he did not intend to embody a moral scheme in his writing.[69] Yet one scholar quotes Baum as saying that he wanted to write stories that "bear the stamp of our times and depict the progressive fairies of today."[70] Because Baum's characters are so clearly drawn and the plot involves so obvious a quest for self-knowledge, it is hard to forego analogies and symbolic interpretation. When a young heroine begins a quest to return from a colorful and vibrant land of make believe to her drab and impoverished home in Kansas, accompanied by characters who are seeking courage, love, and intelligence, analysis seems tempting.

Interpretations of the Oz story have been complicated by the Metro-Goldwyn-Mayer movie of the same title that appeared in 1939 starring Judy Garland and is today much better known than the novel. Some of the best-known elements of *The Wizard of Oz,* like Dorothy's ruby slippers and her famous line "There's no place like home," are inventions of the film that do not appear in the book at all.[71] Many of the current essays on *The Wizard of Oz* center on the film, not the children's text.[72] Further complications in understanding *Oz* result from Baum's 13 sequels, a score of other spin-offs, including the film *The Wiz,* featuring an African-American cast, and most recently Disney Studio's *Return to Oz.*[73]

Interpretations of this children's fantasy fall into two categories: historical and psychological. For the purposes of this study, the historical are far more significant. Henry M. Littlefield's provocative historical reading of *The Wizard of Oz* links the fictional characters and places to real persons, places, and events of late-nineteenth-century America. He argues that Baum was influenced by the political winds that swirled through the Midwest with the rise of Populism in the 1880s, and he makes much of Baum's early career in Aberdeen, South Dakota, a town undoubtedly affected by the starkness of the prairie and the dashed dreams of plains farmers caught between the vagaries of nature, the oppression of large bank loans, and the expensive consumer goods needed for survival.

Baum supported the Populist Party's platform in 1896, headed by William Jennings Bryan, to put more cash in national circulation by freely coining silver, to regulate the moneyed interests of the East Coast, and to limit the political clout of elites. Thus in Littlefield's reading, the Wicked Witch of the East, with the Munchkin people held like slaves in her control, represents the powerful financial interests in the eastern seaboard cities. The Tin Man too was under her spell, so that he chopped away his wooden parts and had them replaced with tin, just as the moneyed powers "dehumanized a simple laborer so that . . . he became a kind of [heartless] machine."[74] The Scarecrow represents the Kansas farmers who need to become strong and savvy about their weak political position. The Cowardly Lion represents candidate Bryan himself, who is impressive vocally but lacks the real courage to take on all opposition and win the campaign. Dorothy is "Everyman" in search of truth; one of the items she needs to return home is the power of the silver shoes (the coinage of silver). The Emerald City is Washington, D.C., where everyone is blinded by green, the color of money. Littlefield even compares the march to the Emerald City by Dorothy and her companions to the insurrection of Coxey's Army, which marched to the White House demanding work during the Depression of 1893–1894. Citing numerous other parallels with American life, Littlefield sees Baum's characters as being "[l]ed by naive innocence and protected by good will[;] the farmer, the laborer and the politician approach the mystic holder of national power to ask for personal fulfillment."[75]

Recently two political scientists have modified Littlefield's historical reading by suggesting that William Jennings Bryan appears in the text, not as the Cowardly Lion but as Dorothy Gale herself, intent on a journey to the White House as a presidential candidate in both 1896 and 1900. Dorothy's adventures in Oz thus represent allegorically the various obstacles Bryan faced in his campaigns, including wicked eastern bankers and his well-financed Republican opponent. The Cowardly Lion in this interpretation is the Populist Party itself, a third-party coalition of farmers, laborers, and reformers who were unsuccessful nationally in 1892 and 1896. So in 1899 they joined forces with the Democratic Party to run Bryan for president. Thus Dorothy (W. J. Bryan), the Tin Man (industrial workers), the Scarecrow (farmers), and the Lion (the Populist Party) travel the "yellow brick road" (campaign trail) seeking the Wizard, who will grant them success (election). The Wizard refuses, just as the voters turned down Bryan in his bid for the presidency. The optimism in the fairy tale reveals that Baum still held out hope in 1899 that Bryan and his "silver platform" might prevail.[76]

The Oz fantasy also works as a metaphorical description of the United States at the turn of the century. The Winkies live in the West in a wild and unsettled region full of prairie wolves; the Munchkins of the East somewhat resemble the so-called Pennsylvania Dutch settlers; the China People to the south are genteel and fragile; and the Wizard's kingdom is in the center of Oz, not unlike Chicago, where Baum was living when he wrote the novel.[77]

Finally, the saga of Dorothy and her friends on the yellow brick road works as a modern-day *Pilgrim's Progress,* in which the characters seek to find something they do not think they possess but that turns out to be internal rather than external after all. The Scarecrow sets out to find a brain but discovers he can already think very well; the Tin Man wants a heart in his mechanical body but learns he already can give compassion and love; the Lion wants courage but finds he has plenty of it when he must defend his friends; and Dorothy wants to find her way back to her family in Kansas, but Witch Glinda tells her, "Your Silver Shoes will carry you over the desert. . . . If you had known their power you could have gone back to your Aunt Em the very first day you came to this country."[78] None of the characters is able to make his or her self-discovery without the companionship of the others, another Baum moralism.

Unlike all the other American children's fiction of the period—series books, boys' adventure tales, girls' domestic novels—the Oz stories appealed to both boys and girls. In Dorothy Gale, Baum created a female protagonist who embodied both feminine virtues (compassion, kindness, acceptance of those different from herself, concern for others' feelings) and masculine attributes (rationality, assertiveness, single-mindedness, courage, persever-ance). By surrounding Dorothy with nonhuman characters and creatures, he avoided the troublesome issues of sexual attraction. By creating the magical land of Oz, Baum avoided such overtly controversial arenas as religion, race, and social problems.

The only other successful humorous and fantastical children's work of lasting merit came from poet Carl Sandburg (1878–1967). His *Rootabaga Stories* (1922), *Rootabaga Pigeons* (1923), and *Potato Face* (1930) are collec-tions of stories that he created for his daughters. That the era's favorite poet and Lincoln scholar should write imaginative children's stories may not be well known, and many Sandburg scholars ignore his children's works. But the wordplay and use of idiom and colorful metaphor are pure Sandburg. Liter-ary critic Joanne Lynn has called the *Rootabaga Stories* "tales that are deeply rooted in the physical realities of the American Midwest, its geography, its economy, its folkways, its language." (The poet also produced at least two collections of poems for children, a topic not covered in this study.) Maud and Miska Petersham contributed the fanciful pen-and-ink illustrations.[79]

These short tales barely contain a plot but base their attraction on aural pleasure. Sandburg plays with words; he invents sounds. Although a few of the tales, like "How the Animals Lost Their Tails and Got Them Back," resemble Rudyard Kipling's "Just So" stories, the language and rhythm of the prose strikes one as pure Americana. Often the titles suggest an explanation, but the story never actually produces it. At the time of publication, these "bedtime stories," as Sandburg himself referred to them, met with serious criticism from some reviewers. "What shall the intelligent child make of this?" queried one skeptic. The stories are built around zany names for char-acters—Gimme the Ax, Potator Face Blind Man, Bozo the Button Buster, and for places—the Village of Cream Puffs. Some of the stories resemble folktales in plot and structure; others depict magical feats and fantasy lands; some sim-ply play with words and sounds. Certainly all are meant to be read aloud. Scholar Agnes Perkins believes that at least two of his stories, "The Spink Bug and the Hunk" and "How Two Sweetheart Dippies Sat in the Moonlight," are antiwar fables.[80]

Victorian Domesticity's Continued Popularity

The exploits of adolescents on foreign adventurers, young women at college, or fantastical characters in the Emerald City did not deter girls from a contin-ued fascination with female characters caught in difficult domestic situations and triumphing in their circumscribed and gendered worlds. Such fictional characters as Lloyd Sherman (*The Little Colonel*, 1895), Sara Crews (*The Secret Garden*, 1911), and Pollyanna (*Pollyanna*, 1913) became national heroines for both girls and their mothers. While the child's universe was expanding rapidly at the turn of the century, many genteel women were intent upon preserving the morals and manners of the Victorian era.

Between 1895 and 1912 Annie Fellows Johnston completed a 12-volume series of Little Colonel books. Directed at the same female audience that had adored *Little Women,* the Elsie Dinsmore books, and the Katy series (see chapter 3), Johnston's protagonist Lloyd Sherman is nicknamed "the Little Colonel" because her temper resembles that of her grandfather, an irascible former Confederate officer. But in all other aspects, Lloyd's behavior reflects Victorian propriety: she is well mannered, compassionate to those less fortunate, sociable and popular with her friends, mature and "lady-like" with adults, and unfailingly cheerful. Set in Kentucky, the series also reflects turn-of-the-century racial stereotyping, with the African-American employees on Colonel Sherman's estate exhibiting characteristics of the "happy darky" (see the discussion of Johnston in chapter 5). As the series progressed, Lloyd moved from little girl to bride; to expand the series, Johnston created spin-offs featuring Lloyd's best friends, Betty and Mary, who participated in various school and travel adventures.

Both the author and the publisher sought to capitalize on the enormous popularity of the Little Colonel series through a number of strategies. When hundreds of girls wrote to Annie Fellows Johnston relating how Mary Ware's journal keeping had inspired them to record their own daily activities and concerns, the L. C. Page Company produced *The Little Colonel Good Times Book,* a calendar-journal for just that purpose, which sold well nationally. All around the country, girls formed "Little Colonel Clubs" to encourage each other to emulate the activities and moral qualities of Lloyd Sherman and her friends. They unfailingly staged plays and circuses to raise money for the poor, visited elderly neighbors, and took food to the ill. After Shirley Temple starred in a 1935 movie version of the first book in the series, Macy's department store opened a Little Colonel Shop, and several designers marketed the frilly sorts of dresses, hairbows, and other accessories that Temple had worn in the film.[81]

Lloyd Sherman and her friends perpetuated waning Victorian values of femininity in their domestic pursuits, charitable activities, and discussions of eligible young men. Lloyd's mother, Mrs. Sherman, was highly idealized, and mothering was frequently suggested as the best "career" for a girl. *Little Colonel's Hero* (1902) finds the Shermans on a European holiday during which Lloyd befriends the Sattawhite children, who are staying in the same hotel. Their pronounced bad manners, mischievousness, and disobedience to staff and parents are attributed to the inattention of their mother. Mrs. Sattawhite is portrayed as being more interested in attending society functions than in nurturing her children. She devotes much more lavish attention on her French poodle than on her children. In the final book of the series, *Mary Ware's Promised Land* (1912), one character wonders if "association with a woman like Mrs. B. . . . who made addresses in public" might not lead to "strong-minded women's rights notions [that would] detract from her feminine charm." One might expect that such conservatism about the new woman and the futures of their daughters would have made the series particularly popular with adults. Many mothers and grandmothers wrote to the author, praising her for these antifeminist sentiments.[82]

Professional educators and librarians often criticized the Little Colonel series, just as they had attacked other series books. They accused Johnston of writing too much about dances, boys, and "heart-throbs." In both Boston and Pittsburgh, the Little Colonel books were removed from library shelves as unsuitable for young girls. However, the books' popularity in other libraries and in bookstores across the country demonstrated the nation's remarkable penchant for domestic girls' stories.[83]

Several other American women joined Annie Fellows Johnston around the turn of the century in replicating the Victorian sentiments and female protagonists that had been popular in the previous generation. Like *Little Women* and *The Wide, Wide World* (see chapter 3), the later novels idealized family life, saw the exemplary heroine transform the moral character of those around her, modeled Christian charity and compassion while maintaining class awareness, and used accidents and illness to teach compassion and discipline. These authors continue that construction of childhood that romanticizes the innocence of children, especially girls, and keeps their protagonists operating at a juvenile (presexual) level even as they get older. The innocent child serves as a redeemer for some older, usually unmarried and lonely adult; she might also serve as a model of self-sacrifice and empathic understanding for other children. Romantic childhood implies that the child, though she may make mistakes and learn from them, is essentially good and pure. By contrast, adults have been corrupted by the world and have become either scheming and manipulative (usually males) or crabby, loveless, and bitter (usually females).

The twentieth-century domestic novels differ little from their nineteenth-century counterparts, except that the young heroines are likely to travel farther, encounter a more disparate environment, and be more outspoken. As mentioned earlier, women's and children's novels diverged from each other as the former became more realistic and urbane, while the latter continued to emphasize pious, self-sacrificing accommodation. A few best-sellers, like Kate Douglas Wiggin's *Rebecca of Sunnybrook Farm* (1903) and Eleanor Porter's *Pollyanna* (1913), continued to appeal to a wide-ranging adult audience. Other popular works of girls' domestic fiction in this era included Lucy Maud Montgomery's *Anne of Green Gables* (1908), Gene Stratton Porter's *A Girl of the Limberlost* (1909), and Jean Webster's *Daddy Long-Legs* (1912).[84]

Portrayals of girls did become more complex in these later domestic stories. Young women like Rebecca of Sunnybrook might chafe at the limitations placed on young girls: "Boys always do the nice splendid things, and girls can

'DON'T BE KIND, MR. ALADDIN'

Kate Douglas Wiggin, *Rebecca of Sunnybrook Farm*, illustrated by Helen Grose
(Boston: Houghton-Mifflin, 1931)

only do the dull nasty ones that get left over. They can't climb so high, or go out so far, or stay out so late, or run so fast, or anything," she laments.[85] Though Rebecca is far more complex than her fictional colleagues a half-century earlier, she still epitomizes domesticity when she relies on men for protection and advice and eventually marries.

For all her resourcefulness, Rebecca is aided, supported, and rescued in various points in the plot by a handsome neighbor, Adam Ladd, whom she calls "Mr. Aladdin," thus emphasizing his rescuing role. Ladd seems likely to become her suitor when Rebecca is older (she is only 17 when the book ends). In fact, at her school graduation at the end of the novel, Ladd comments that "[I am] glad I met the child; proud I know the girl; longing to meet the woman."[86] As the real world was learning to accommodate the new woman with her shorter skirts, bicycles, and attendance at colleges, girls' domestic fiction paradoxically eliminated any suggestions of sexual maturation or inclination. Wiggin remained steadfast on Rebecca's innocent nonsexuality. Although the reader may detect Mr. Ladd's growing interest in the developing Rebecca, Wiggin has the heroine warn him off. "I know what you are thinking, Mr. Aladdin,—that my dress is an inch longer than last year, and my hair different; but I'm not nearly a young lady yet; truly I'm not."[87]

Even though the book's enormous popularity led to repeated pleas from readers for a sequel to *Rebecca,* Wiggin would not take Rebecca beyond her 17th year. Finally, in 1907 she published *New Chronicles of Rebecca,* which was not a sequel that forced Rebecca to grow up but rather a compilation of stories designed to flesh out the first book and to fit chronologically *between* the chapters of the original work.[88] So Rebecca remained frozen on the brink of womanhood, virginal and guileless.

Wiggin also relied heavily on idealized portraits of happy, nurturing families in both *The Birds' Christmas Carol* (1887) and *Mother Carey's Chickens* (1911). In the latter, the mother is a "happy, contented, active woman," while the father is "gay, gallant . . . [with a] kind smile and the jolly little sparkles of fun in his eyes. [He was] splendid as the gods." This emphasis on the importance of the psychologically healthy family unit stems from Wiggin's immersion in Frederick Froebel's philosophy of early childhood education (kindergartens) as ideally replicating the loving, familial environment. Wiggin herself set up some of the first kindergartens in California and used some of the money she made from her writings to continue to support the kindergarten movement.[89]

Rebecca bears other similarities to female protagonists of this genre. She is a semi-orphan when the story begins. With her father dead, her mother cannot afford to care for all her children at the marginal Sunnybrook Farm, so Rebecca is sent to live with two maiden aunts in Maine. Her caregivers are dutiful and correct in what they provide but have no understanding of the needs and interests of children. In this small Maine village, the child-redeemer can work to enhance or transform the lives of adults around her. Rebecca's future is secured when Aunt Miranda wills her the lovely home and farm; Rebecca knows she can go to college and become the teacher she has always wanted to be. Kate Douglas Wiggin's own devotion to the formative influence of early education, her Rousseauian belief in the goodness of the natural child, and her interest in teacher training can all be seen in the Rebecca books. (See the bibliographical information for chapter 3.)

The redeeming capabilities of the innocent orphan emerge conspicuously in *Pollyanna* as well, with its many parallels to both *Rebecca* and *Anne of*

Green Gables. In all three novels, the orphaned protagonists are reared by unsupportive relatives who experience personal reawakenings because of the girls' natural charms, goodness, patience, and insight. Pollyanna transforms not only her spartan Aunt Polly but also the sickly Mrs. Snow, the town curmudgeon Mr. Pendleton, the lethargic Reverend Mr. Ford, and the friendly but sad Dr. Chilton. Porter also utilizes the trope of the moral influence of an injured or dying young woman, as had Susan Warner in *Wide, Wide World,* Kate Douglas Wiggin in *The Birds' Christmas Carol,* and Louisa May Alcott in *Little Women* (see chapter 3). Late in the book, Pollyanna is injured in an auto accident and spends months in bed with paralyzed legs. This tragedy works transforming powers on her friend Jimmy, Aunt Polly, and several villagers and leads to the reconciliation of long-separated lovers Dr. Chilton and Aunt Polly.

Children's accidental injury and death had become a major Progressive concern by 1910, a year in which car accidents were the leading cause of death for children between ages 5 and 14. Reformers organized the Playground Association of America to provide play spaces outside of city streets, while others agitated for additional safety devices on automobiles.[90] Porter's intent was not to promote reform, however; she used the accident only as a device to complete the transforming power of Pollyanna's positive thinking. In Porter's hands, the suffering caused by the accident does not bring redemption in and of itself, but it multiplies the number of persons drawn into "the glad game" as they seek to comprehend the tragedy that has befallen the heroine.

Well before the Reverend Norman Vincent Peale's preaching and message of overcoming disappointment with "positive thinking" captivated American popular culture, Porter's heroine was promoting the same idea in the glad game: whenever one felt disappointed or unhappy, one should find something positive about the situation and concentrate on that. In the text, Pollyanna explains how she had been wanting a doll, but when her widowed father received a box of items from the Ladies Missionary Society, it included an old pair of crutches rather than the doll she was anticipating. She at first was disappointed, but then she concentrated on being "glad" that she didn't need crutches.[91] Not only does Pollyanna introduce a great variety of individuals in the novel to this psychological ploy, but so commonplace did her name become that *Pollyanna* began to appear in official lexicons as "a person able to find apparent cause for happiness in the most disastrous situations; a person who is unduly optimistic."[92] Thousands of readers established "Glad Clubs." A silent movie, a Shirley Temple film, and a 1960 Disney Studio film were all based on Porter's story.[93] Eleanor Porter wrote a sequel, *Pollyanna Grows Up* (1914), which was also enormously popular. Several ghostwritten sequels were arranged by Porter's publisher after her death in 1920.[94]

Most contemporary critics have savaged *Pollyanna* as the worst of the cloying, improbable girl-orphan novels. British scholars Mary Cadogan and

Patricia Craig have called the heroine "stupid . . . tactless and infuriating"; she cannot "comprehend reality" and has the vocabulary "of a four-year-old." They seem almost delighted when, at plot's end, Pollyanna "needs those little crutches after all."[95] Literary scholar Jerry Griswold points out, however, that Pollyanna was anything but the blind and naive optimist that the term *Pollyanna* has come to imply. Using a Freudian paradigm, he illustrates how cleverly Pollyanna saw through the patterns adults use to perpetuate their power and keep others at a distance. Once she understands their "game," she diffuses it cleverly and turns these very patterns on their heads, typically through invoking the glad game. For example, Aunt Polly finds her typical child behavior and exuberance upsetting and punishes Pollyanna for it. When Pollyanna is late for dinner, Aunt Polly decrees only bread and milk for supper, but Pollyanna claims to love bread and milk. When Pollyanna opens her bedroom windows for cool air and lets flies indoors, Aunt Polly sends her to her room to read about the diseases borne by insects. Pollyanna thanks her for the interesting reading materials. When Pollyanna seeks to escape her hot bedroom to sleep on the porch, Aunt Polly punishes her by confining her to that same porch, which Pollyanna finds delightful. "For the third time since Pollyanna's arrival, Miss Polly was punishing Pollyanna—and for the third time she was being confronted with the amazing fact that her punishment was being taken as a special reward of merit. No wonder Miss Polly was feeling curiously helpless." Similar incidents result in Pollyanna's receiving a nicer bedroom, a new wardrobe, and considerable freedom over her home schooling. Griswold argues that this "reverse psychology" provides Pollyanna with considerable influence over her environment.[96]

Gene Stratton Porter (1863–1924) put a slight spin on the orphan theme in *A Girl of the Limberlost* (1909), for Elnora is not an orphan sent to live with an unloving relative but a bereft child who is born on the night her father drowns in the swamp. Her mother has never forgiven her, for it was her labor pains that kept her from rescuing her husband. Porter presents in the mental cruelty inflicted on Elnora a case of what would be considered certifiable child abuse by modern standards. She also goes much further into sexual territory than do the creators of the virginal Rebecca or the always-innocent Pollyanna. The heroine of *Limberlost* is observed getting ready for bed by a peeping Tom: "He could see the throb of her breast under its thin covering and smell the fragrance of the tossing hair. . . . He gripped the limb above that on which he stood, licked his lips and breathed through his throat to be sure he was making no sound." Nothing more ensues, of course. By the end of the novel, Elnora's sweet disposition has brought healing to her mother and to her intended husband.[97]

One more early-century book deserves discussion in light of the social concerns of the Progressive era. Alice Hegan Rice (1870–1942), a native Kentuckian, set her story *Mrs. Wiggs of the Cabbage Patch* (1901) in a Louisville slum characteristic of similar poor neighborhoods in all America's burgeoning cities. The story realistically portrays both the marginal existence of single-parent families without any government assistance and the unconscious paternalism and classism present in the efforts of the "charity ladies" who eventually come to Mrs. Wiggs's assistance. Rice knew both worlds well, for she was one of those privileged southern women who engaged in benevolence work and founded a settlement house in Louisville's Cabbage Patch slum.[98]

Rice reflects the nascent sociological understanding of 1900 that the poor were neither shiftless nor immoral but lacked the education, opportunity, and refinement to succeed in middle-class pursuits. Mrs. Wiggs cannot find a job when the book opens, and her oldest son, Jimmy, does unskilled labor when he can find it. Of her late husband, Mrs. Wiggs reports that he "travelled to eternity by the alcohol route," so one suspects the family was no better off when he was alive. They live a hand-to-mouth existence in the Cabbage Patch neighborhood, so named because the "ramshackle cottages played hop-scotch over the railroad tracks."[99] Pride inhibits their asking anyone for assistance; when a nearby church sends a Christmas basket of food, Mrs. Wiggs refuses to admit that the family has no coal for the winter. But when her oldest son dies from pneumonia she relents and asks a "society lady" for help.

The family's integrity also attracts the attention of a local newspaper magnate, who treats them all to the theater. Rice attempts to keep this obvious tale from becoming too maudlin and sentimental by treating almost every event with humor, but the jokes are derived from the Wiggs' dialect (their ethnicity is never named) and from their lack of education. The children are named Europena, Asia, and Australia because the only book in the house is an atlas. They attempt to leave the theater after the first act because they believe the play is over. The message seems to be that, although the poor talk and act very differently from the bourgeois class, they are good people just the same. There is no indication that the family will ever escape poverty, although one of the sons secures a promising job. More important to the author is the determination, good humor, and practicality of the family. Mrs. Wiggs's final words resonate perfectly with all the girl heroines in domestic fiction: "Looks like ever'thing in the world comes right, if we jes' wait long enough!"[100]

Burnett and American Values

Frances Hodgson Burnett (1849–1924) was born in England and set her most popular children's stories there as well. She qualifies for this study, however, because she lived in the United States for extended periods of time and married an American, and because her best-known novel, *Little Lord Fauntleroy* (1886), features an American child protagonist. Frances Hodgson led a comfortable middle-class life in Manchester, England, until the American Civil War caused the textile mills to fail, plunging the family into dire straits. They emigrated to Knoxville, Tennessee, where Hodgson turned her writing hobby into a supplementary income by sending off short pieces to women's magazines. She continued to write even after marrying Dr. Swan Burnett, with whom she had two sons. After meeting Mary Mapes Dodge and Louisa May Alcott, Hodgson began writing children's stories and published three of them in Dodge's *St. Nicholas*. The story "Little Lord Fauntleroy" was serialized in *St. Nicholas* in 1885 before it appeared in book form. By 1893, only *Ben Hur* was held by more libraries than *Little Lord Fauntleroy*.[101] Burnett continued writing for children; *A Little Princess* (1908) and *The Secret Garden* (1911) remain her most popular after *Fauntleroy*.

Unlike the female child redeemers in much late-Victorian domestic fiction, *Little Lord Fauntleroy* offers up a feisty, polite, articulate American boy as the agent of change for an older curmudgeonly relative and other stuffy English characters. Like Rebecca or Pollyanna, Cedric appears from the outset to be clever and mature beyond his years. But whereas Wiggin and Porter based their characterizations on the romantic notion of childhood innocence and its inherently redemptive powers, Burnett drew on the theme of the superior qualities of those with aristocratic blood, which neither circumstance nor environment can destroy. Cedric's father was disinherited when he married a young American woman; the father's premature death has left the mother and son living in modest circumstances in America. When the dour Earl of Dorincourt, Cedric's grandfather, summons him to England to be educated as the aristocrat he is, the stage is set not only for Cedric to transform the earl into a compassionate and benevolent landlord but also to highlight that Cedric's American notions of equality and integrity of the poor provide needed ballast to the aristocratic and class-based notions of English society. *Little Lord Fauntleroy* is more than a male Cinderella tale, for Cedric's reversal of fortune is not due to magical powers or beauty. Nor is *Little Lord Fauntleroy* a new twist on Horatio Alger's theme of hard work and good luck meriting social advancement. Cedric becomes wealthy because he was *born* to aristocracy. He already possesses all those qualities necessary to be an extraordinary leader and gentlemen. This is not a novel about social mobility.[102]

Cedric can also work wonders on his grandfather's self-indulgent and critical nature because Cedric represents the best of both his parents, and hence the best of both nations. His mother has imbued him with a democratic, leveling spirit, as seen in his friendship with the corner grocer at the beginning of the story, and with his championing of better living conditions for the laborers on his grandfather's estate. His father bequeaths him a noble bearing, good looks, and an inquisitive mind. Lord Fauntleroy epitomizes an ideal harmony between the two nations that Burnett loved and implies that each has something to give to the other. Just before he leaves America to take up residence in England, Cedric comments, "If there is ever to be another war with America, I shall try to stop it."[103]

Like *Pollyanna*, *Fauntleroy* has entered into the English lexicon in a way the author never intended: it has come to mean a "gentle-mannered or elaborately dressed boy," implying something of a sissy.[104] Ironically, the well-known children's book collector and historian F. J. Harvey Darton referred to the book's popularity as "a sickly fever [that] ran through England" and called the hero that "odious little prig in the lace collar."[105] This narrowing of Burnett's characterization of Cedric to an overdressed, feminine prissy probably contributed to the book's rapid decline in popularity by the 1930s. As such, Burnett's emphasis on the deficiencies of both American and British values, and what each could teach the other, was lost on an American reading public that frankly found little it wished to emulate in British society by the post–World War I era.

Burnett also serialized *A Little Princess* in *St. Nicholas* as the story "Sara Crewe" (1887) before she expanded it into a full novel in 1905. Again, Burnett fashioned a Cinderella-like fairy tale with a twist. Sara is the privileged daughter of Captain Crewe, who places her in an exclusive girls' school in England before being sent to South Africa in the Boer War. When he is reported missing in action and no payments arrive for Sara's tuition, she becomes the "Cinderella" of the school, living in the servants' quarters and working for her tuition. She is unable to redeem the harsh director of the school, but her inherent goodness and trusting nature win the attention of another adult, a reclusive friend of her father's, who accomplishes the rescue of the "little princess" and restores her father's full estate to her. As a clever and inventive young lady, Sara Crewe is much less interesting than either Rebecca of Sunnybrook or Pollyanna; while these two young women have to make their way in a hostile world, Sara is born to wealth and privilege. Like Burnett's Cedric, she must only continue to exhibit the true virtues of her class to triumph.

A Little Princess provided yet another venue for Shirley Temple to play an engaging child hero on film. However, the script writers altered the story so that Sara not only has her father's fortune restored but finds him alive (he temporarily lost his memory) in a nearby veterans' hospital—a cloying addition to an already fantastical plot

The Secret Garden ostensibly features the familiar girl redeemer at the outset but soon becomes the story of two protagonists, neither of whom is very likable or worthy of emulation. Redemption must occur first within themselves and then can be extended to adults.[106] The two cousins, Mary Lennox and Colin Craven, both suffer from illness and have been abandoned by adults. The ill child is a trope with a long tradition in romantic notions of childhood innocence; the theme recurs in *Elsie Dinsmore, The Birds' Christmas Carol, Pollyanna,* and *What Katy Did* and is even spoofed in Huck's staged funeral in *Huckleberry Finn*. In *The Secret Garden*, Colin is confined to bed by an unnamed illness whose genesis seems to have been his father's exiling him to one room of the estate because his birth caused his mother's death. Whether Colin's illnesses are real or imagined is unclear; Burnett writes that he "shut himself in his room and thought only of his fears and weakness." Burnett's own 15-year-old son, Lionel, died of consumption, and some of Colin's symptoms mimic those of consumption. Mary, an orphan brought from India to live with her uncle in Yorkshire, also suffers from health problems, with her digestion and her liver. She discovers the invalid Colin and a hidden and overgrown garden on her uncle's estate.

In this plot, Burnett is able to invoke the civilizing and healing power of the natural world in the garden, a theme that has intrigued numerous critics. The setting follows a long history of pastoral literature; in this instance the garden has fallen into despair because of Mr. Craven's pain at the death of his wife. But as in much romantic literature, this sacred natural spot brings healing and peace to those who participate in its beauty.[107] *The Secret Garden* also employs the motif of the redeeming qualities of the female heroine, whose interest in Colin and devotion to restoring the garden revive Colin's good health.

Burnett's adoption of Christian Science beliefs probably undergirds the novel's emphasis that Colin must believe himself able to walk before he can do so. Two years later the same "power of positive thinking" emerged in Porter's *Pollyanna*. But the characters experience more than a moral reformation: they also go through a process of socialization in learning what it is to be fully human, to enter into relationship with others.[108] Both Mary and Colin have been emotionally, as well as physically, crippled, and their prepubescent discovery of each other initiates them into another level of maturity. As in the other novels previously discussed, the author seemed intrigued by class distinctions yet perfectly comfortable with them. Once Mary discovers the garden, she forms a threesome with Colin and the gardener's son Dickon to restore it to its original beauty. Together they enjoy this Edenic spot as they delight in each other's company. However, when the garden restoration is complete and Colon has relearned how to walk, Dickon loses his usefulness as a companion and must return to his mundane chores on the estate.[109]

In her autobiography, Frances Burnett recalled the extensive reading she had done as a child as consisting mostly of "horrid little books . . . containing memoirs of dreadful children who died early of complicated diseases, whose lingering developments they enlivened by giving unlimited moral advice and instruction." Yet Burnett too wrote of exemplary children, blessed not so much with evangelical piety as with an inherent goodness or innocence, a trust of others, and the ability to convert unredeemed adults to their own romantic visions.[110]

Juvenile Periodicals

The appetite and appreciation for monthly children's publications that emerged just before mid-century continued to grow, maturing into several long-running periodicals. Developed from the foundations of the earlier successful *Our Young Folks* and *Riverside Magazine,* author Mary Mapes Dodge (*Hans Brinker; or The Silver Skates,* 1865) launched *St. Nicholas* in 1873 as an adjunct to the adult periodical *Scribner's Monthly.* Dodge served as editor for its first 30 years; her trademark was making reading a pleasure and delight for children in much the way Scudder had tried to do earlier in *Youth's Companion* (see chapter 3). Dodge had a keen eye for good fiction; numerous classics first appeared as serialized stories in *St. Nicholas:* Alcott's *Eight Cousins,* Thomas Nelson Page's *Two Little Confederates,* Mark Twain's *Tom Sawyer Abroad,* Rudyard Kipling's *Just So Stories,* Frances Hodgson Burnett's *Little Lord Fauntleroy,* and Joel Chandler Harris's *Daddy Jakes the Runaway.*[111] The journal garnered an English-language readership worldwide, as evidenced by letters to the magazine in 1896 from Austria, France, Germany, Italy, Scotland, China, and Latin America.[112] Forty-eight pages long and lavishly illustrated, *St. Nicholas* epitomized an affluent, literate, and bourgeois America in which children were free to enjoy leisure. The St. Nicholas League awarded gold and silver badges to young authors whose poems and prose were accepted for publication in the magazine; the award went to such future famous writers as Ring Lardner, Stephen Benet, Cornelia Otis Skinner, and Edmund Wilson.[113] Other authors who wrote for *St. Nicholas* included Kate Douglas Wiggin, Thomas Bailey Aldrich, Rudyard Kipling, Frances Hodgson Burnett, Robert Louis Stevenson, Howard Pyle, and Teddy Roosevelt.[114] Other major publishers ventured into children's periodicals and capitalized on the middle-class market as well. *Harper's Young People* (later changed to *Harper's Round Table*) successfully circulated between 1879 and 1899. Dozens of other magazines came and went through the period, appealing to a growing number of young middle-class readers who sensed in this medium a lightness of spirit that mirrored their own ebullience as the twentieth century matured.[115]

America's growing involvement in the world community and the growing tensions in Europe over colonial holdings and competing national identities fostered a spirit of interest in world cooperation, a spirit that would be so strong after World War I that it would foster both isolationism and pacifism among some. The progressive spirit, too, fostered a belief that better knowledge of foreign nations and culture would result in improved methods of assimilating immigrants to America's shores. Thus some children's literature set out to teach children about other cultures. Lucy Fitch Perkins (1865–1937) produced an extensive collection of works for young children from different cultures and historical periods. Between 1911 and 1935 she wrote and illustrated over two dozen "twin" books, including those about the Irish twins, the Spartan twins, the Pioneer twins, and the Spanish twins. The formula to which she wrote confined her ability to develop creative plots; the cultures and traditions portrayed appear stereotyped and shallow by today's standards. For example, The *Pickaninny Twins* (1931) depicts southern African-American sharecroppers' children as dirty, ignorant, and lazy.

Even though children's literature, in both novels and periodicals, had become a flourishing business by the 1920s, the America that these stories reflected was culturally, ethnically, religiously, and racially extremely narrow. The original inhabitants of America and all people of color appeared in children's fiction only as stereotypically hostile Indians, as slaves, or as black laborers or domestics. The stories also taught specific behavioral mores, gender roles, class attitudes, values, and manners, all of these reflecting prevailing white middle-class standards. Although a few subversive subtexts might be extracted from children's literature after 1850, just how thoroughly and deeply American books taught race and class distinctions can be seen in chapter 5.

5

Race, Ethnicity, and Region, 1850–1930

By the late nineteenth century American literature for children had come into its own. Although British works continued to sell well to an American upper middle class still clinging to Victorian sensibilities, such distinctly American characters as Huckleberry Finn, Jo March, and Lloyd Sherman (the Little Colonel) soon created their own devoted following. As in the British literature it had so long imitated, American child fiction most commonly featured an Anglo, genteel, domestic scene designed consciously to socialize American children into particular middle-class mores. At the same time, Americans mythologized the freedom and adventuresomeness of American children vis-à-vis their English counterparts. That the Victorian setting of children's literature excluded the majority of children in many parts of the United States mattered not at all to the creators of this idealized childhood. Americans too privileged the autonomous middle-class family, bourgeois standards of morality, and a benign paternalism toward nonwhite groups. Within this larger parameter, American children's literature began to feature regional stereotyping, particularly with reference to racial distinctions. Because nineteenth-century authors for children continued both to view literature as a way of shaping moral character and to image children as innocent guides in a corrupt world, they constructed settings and dialogues that conformed to America's growing preoccupation with a whiteness reinforced by racial and ethnic hierarchies. Thus mainstream children's literature played a vital role in defining America's vision of itself.

A visitor to the United States in 1860 would have found over four million African-Americans being held as slaves and another half-million free people of color. In all, African-Americans represented nearly 15 percent of the country's population. Whether slaves or free, all persons of color suffered under the historic rationalizations that had created New World slavery in the seventeenth century. Historian Winthrop Jordan has traced degrading attitudes toward people of color—regarding their mental abilities, their physical appearance, their sexuality—back to Renaissance England. Jordan found that English travelers habitually described Africans as "black," regardless of the myriad skin tones they encountered, "which in itself suggests that the Negro's complexion had powerful impact upon their perceptions." And with the epithet "black" came the literary associations of darkness, evil, corruption, and sinfulness.

Christian Europeans justified African slavery through exegesis of passages in Genesis in which Noah casts out his son Ham and declares that Ham's son Canaan should serve all the other brothers forever. Associations of Canaan with Africa led to the acceptance of Africans as perpetual servants. Although slavery was not practiced in England proper, British colonists in North America, Africa, and the Caribbean had no qualms about creating a color-defined basis for slave-holding in their settlements, a practice much like that of the Spanish and Portuguese invaders. The Portuguese first sold Africans to some Virginia colonists in 1619, but their status as slaves cannot be confirmed before specific slave codes were passed by the Virginia House of Burgesses in 1660. Even if Africans came to Virginia only as indentured laborers, their permanent bondage was assured within 40 years.[1] Slavery was practiced in all the New World colonies, including New England, the Middle Colonies, Spanish Florida, the Caribbean, and South America. The vast majority of bond labor went to tobacco, sugarcane, and rice planters for use in labor-intensive agriculture, principally in semitropical British and Spanish colonies.

In New England and the Mid-Atlantic, whites used slaves in artisans' shops, in domestic employment, and for unskilled labor jobs rather than as large gangs of agricultural workers. With continued white immigration to the growing colonial coastal cities, these northern colonies used proportionally many fewer slaves than did the Chesapeake and the Deep South. At the time of the American Revolution, the slave population of Massachusetts was about 3 percent, while in New York, 15 percent, but in the southern states, 30 to 35 percent of the population was enslaved. As Leon Litwack illustrated in his 1961 study *North of Slavery*, multiple and overlapping explanations account for the difference in slave-holding between regions. Certainly the Revolutionary rhetoric about the tyranny of George III and the natural-rights language of freedom and equality alerted some colonists to the hypocrisy of slave-holding. But the economics of plantation agriculture, which depended on a large, affordable workforce in ways that smaller farms, commerce, and business in New England did not, could override ideological argument. But different agricultural practices alone cannot account for the fewer numbers of slaves in the northern colonies. Litwack illustrates how free white laborers made northern slave owners uncomfortable by modeling independent wage earning to a slave population.[2]

Service in the Revolutionary cause earned freedom for many northern slaves. Many of the new state constitutions of the original 13 colonies outlawed slavery directly, and other state legislatures developed plans for gradual emancipation. In Massachusetts, a lawsuit filed by some slaves resulted in an end to legal slavery there. By 1800, one out of every nine Africans was technically free of slavery, most of them in the northern states. By 1830, only 3,568 northern blacks, mostly in New Jersey, were still enslaved. However, free African-Americans found political and social equality proscribed at every turn. Many states, including Pennsylvania and Rhode Island, instituted race-based voting restrictions early in the nineteenth century, even for black property holders. Everywhere people of color had limited access to schooling, jobs, and such public facilities as hospitals and almshouses.

The imaging of the dark-skinned person as a radically different kind of human being drew strength and popularity from the so-called scientific views of race first promulgated in the early nineteenth century. The roots of pseudoscientific racism go back to Thomas Jefferson's *Notes on the State of Virginia* (1785), in which he analyzed many aspects of his native state in response to questions posed by the Frenchman François Marbois. Jefferson wanted Virginians to gradually abolish slavery and to "colonize" the freed blacks in some distant location so that no race mixing might occur in the United States. He could not imagine blacks and whites coexisting in Virginia after their shared history of slavery. Jefferson also held that African-Americans were qualitatively and inherently different from whites. They had a "strong disagreeable odor," they lacked "forethought," they were "more ardent" but less logical than whites, and "in imagination, they are dull, tasteless, and anomalous." Observing their behavior on his plantation, Jefferson deduced that slaves needed less sleep, grieved less deeply over loss, and lacked the ability to be deeply reflective.[3]

From these unscientific and misguided assumptions, later so-called scientists elaborated complex theories of racial characteristics. This "science" of racial difference paralleled the growing defense of slavery and was being articulated by southern intellectuals as a beneficent and positive economic system. George Fredrickson, in *The Black Image in the White Mind* (1971), has demonstrated the powerful influence these apologists wielded for racial subordination. They claimed to prove that physiological differences determined inferior intellectual abilities in all descendants of African peoples. (Exceptions like surveyor and mathematician Benjamin Banneker were explained as the consequence of a white ancestor.) Other spokesmen argued that the "historic" triumph of Anglo-Saxons in the development of Western civilization evidenced white superiority. In an 1850 speech, Dr. Josiah C. Nott, a leading scientific racist, told his audience that Caucasians "in all ages [have] been the rulers. . . . [I]t is written in man's nature by the hand of his creator." For Nott, all races fell along a continuum of capabilities, with the African-American at the lowest end. Another writer in 1860 felt comfortable asserting that it was "well established [that] the negro is an inferior species, or at least a variety of the human race. . . . [B]y himself he would never emerge from barbarism, and even when partly civilized under the control of the white man, he speedily returns to the same state if emancipated."[4]

Children's literature duly absorbed pseudoscientific racism, albeit in a curious form. A collection of stories produced for the Christmas trade by Appleton Publishing Company in 1869 included what authors claimed was an "old Seminole story" but was actually part of the nineteenth-century construction of racial hierarchies. In this tale, after God created the first black man "He soon saw He had bungled; so He determined to try his hand again. He did so, and made the red man. He liked him much better than the black man, but still he was not exactly what He wanted. So He tried once more, and made the white man; and then He was satisfied." In case the acceptable hierarchy remained unclear to children, God then brought three boxes to the men and let the white man choose one first. He chose the box containing "books and papers." The red man chose next and took the box with "bows and arrows." The box that remained for the black man (he had no choice in the matter) contained shovels, hoes, and other tools. "From this it is clear that the Great Spirit intended" for each race to remain within the vocational sphere and social space with which that race was already identified.[5]

Thus in elaborate pseudoscientific works, in the popular imagination, and in children's literature, a hierarchy of racial types dictated and guided culture, behavior, and politics. National political activity after 1830 became increasingly divisive; both major parties, the Whigs and the Democrats, tried to hold on to their slavery supporters and to antislavery proponents as well. Those who believed in slavery's worth and argued that its spread into unsettled territories was essential for the nation's economic prosperity contended with those who believed slavery's deleterious effects on free labor must be contained within the old South. A small but vocal third contingent argued for the complete and immediate abolition of slavery everywhere. Rooted in the imperative of the moral perfectionism that grew out of early-nineteenth-century evangelicalism, radical abolitionism (often called Immediatism) saw the slavery controversy not as essentially economic or humanitarian but as moral. The salvation of individuals as well as the moral health of the nation depended upon the extermination of slave-holding. So powerful did this division become after the Mexican War in 1848 (some called it "the Slaveowner's War") that the nation remained politically paralyzed and internally divided until the end of the Civil War. But even white abolitionists could support emancipation while still advocating a paternal, benevolent, gradual "improvement" of people of color.

Contributing to white America's distorted impressions of African-Americans were the minstrel shows that began in the 1840s in New York City. The "darky" played by a white actor in blackface soon became a stock theater character. Most of the humor of the minstrel turned on making fun of the black man in some way. One stock character was the tattered field hand, with his foolish grin, his shuffling walk, his southern speech, and his love of watermelon. Another common stereotype portrayed in the minstrel shows was the northern urban dandy dressed in bright-colored but poorly fitting clothes, trying to sound impressive but misusing or mispronouncing words and hustling money or shooting craps on the street.[6]

White Americans carried these and other stereotypes of inferiority long after slavery was abolished by the Thirteenth Amendment in 1865. Significant outmigrations after the Civil War still found the African-American population concentrated in the southern states. The war and emancipation did increase opportunities for property ownership, voting, and other legal rights for blacks. Some historians have argued that under the protection of reconstructionist federal policies, southern race relations actually improved between 1865 and 1877.[7] Those gains, however, were checked by the resurgence of southern white political power after reconstruction ended in 1877. While some southerners looked backward nostalgically to an idealized and beneficent plantation society, other proponents of the "New South" sought to minimize racial conflict and war bitterness by substituting a vision of racial and social unity. They wanted the South to embark upon an industrial and market-oriented future. In this vision, African-Americans were expected to provide gratefully the heavy industrial and agricultural labor needed to jump-start the economy. In return, the white South would supply education for both races, albeit separately, and the brutalities and "unpleasantness" of the past would be set aside. Thus "reconstructed," the South ideally would join in a spirit of unity and cooperation with the North.

A system of racial segregation developed throughout America to reinforce attitudes of white superiority and to effectively limit social and economic opportunities for anyone classified as nonwhite. Perhaps because this segregation was legalized in southern states and was de facto in housing patterns and schooling in the rest of the country, common black issues of equal access became fragmented and localized rather than national in scope. African-American voices were limited to a few spokespersons with differing goals, a situation historian Joel Williamson has called "the feudalization of black life."[8] The National Association for the Advancement of Colored People, founded in 1910 in New York by members of the black Niagara Movement and some white race liberals, represented one of the few eloquent voices on behalf of social, cultural, political, and economic equality for African-Americans. Booker T. Washington, advocating a different vision and speaking to a different audience, advanced technological training to equip the black citizen for full economic participation in an industrializing South. White America succeeded in blunting the power of these civic, religious, and educational leaders by ignoring specific black contributions and creating instead a hegemonic portrayal of a uniform and inferior black culture.

Mainstream white culture continued to utilize racial stereotyping to perpetuate its superior image, and it also propagated racial separation to ensure that few meaningful encounters across racial lines would occur. Between 1880 and 1890, white southern attitudes became nationalized views, a perspective readily identifiable in the literature written for children.

Middle Class Visions and Race

The most influential American novels dealing with race and childhood after 1850 were not works specifically aimed at a child audience, yet they soon became classics: Uncle Tom's Cabin (1852) and The Adventures of Huckleberry Finn (1885). Both books are set in antebellum slave-holding states, and in very different ways, each book calls into question America's racial attitudes. Harriet Beecher Stowe (1811–1896) attacked slavery so directly in Uncle Tom's Cabin that President Abraham Lincoln called her "the little woman who wrote the book that started this great war."[9] Yet she embodied the ambivalent attitude toward blacks' capabilities that was common among antebellum abolitionists. Samuel Clemens (1835–1910), writing after slavery had ended, reflected reconstruction-era acceptance of racial stereotyping in his portrayal of Jim yet called into question the baseness of discriminatory practices. Both authors attacked the worst abuses of discrimination, but in other respects their novels reflect the conventions of their own cultures.

In 1850, as Congress faced the task of governing the new southwestern territory acceded by Mexico after the Mexican War, politicians executed a series of political moves designed to dampen sectional antagonisms over slavery. Instead, the Compromise of 1850 actually exacerbated tensions. Among its many provisions was Congress's right to tighten the Fugitive Slave Law that had been on the books since 1793 in return for southern support of the admission of California to the Union as a nonslave-holding state. Under the provisions of the Fugitive Slave Law, an African-American anywhere could be enslaved merely on the testimony of a claimant that the person had been owned by the claimant; the law also authorized and paid federal marshals to hunt down suspected runaways. Free blacks unable to produce documentation of their status were enslaved without being allowed to give testimony on their own behalf.

Two years after this legislation passed, Harriet Beecher Stowe's Uncle Tom's Cabin rekindled the slavery debate that the Compromise of 1850 had failed to forestall. Initially subtitled "The Man Who Was a Thing," Stowe's novel drew much more popular attention to the fate of the millions of African-Americans held in bondage than any abolitionist activity had been able to muster. Using the emotional formulas perfected by other writers of domestic fiction, Stowe portrays a religious, hardworking slave family torn apart by the sale of the father (Uncle Tom). Remaining obedient, honest, and devout despite his fate, the noble Tom rescues a white child (Eva) from drowning while being taken downriver to be sold. In appreciation for his deed, Eva's grateful father (St. Clare) buys Tom and takes him to their luxurious home in New Orleans. St. Clare proves a kind if detached master, but following his untimely death, his widow sells Tom to the cruel Simon Legree. Legree succeeds in destroying Tom's spirit by beating him to death, a crime Stowe depicts as so devastating that Legree's soul is "past repentance, past prayer, past hope."[10]

Uncle Tom's Cabin became a vehicle for numerous abolitionist agendas. Through the breaking up of Tom's family by his sale to a slave trader and the pursuit of Eliza and George by slave captors, Stowe illustrates the inhumanity and barbarous nature of human bondage. In the character of Simon Legree, Stowe has the perfect examples of the depravity and corruption that ownership of other humans produces. On the other hand, Little Eva and her father represent benevolent slave-holding, which nonetheless cannot alter slavery's basic invasive powers. Stowe reveals her assurance in the efficacy of evangelical religion by using the death of the innocent and saintly Eva to redeem the orphaned Topsy. This member of the St. Clare household symbolizes the most fallen of creatures; she is ragged, dirty, and ill behaved. Her reformation into an obedient Christian slave shows Stowe's assurance in the power of evangelical Christianity. It was common for abolitionist writers to feature racial harmony between children as the ideal to which society could move. Stowe's novel clearly reflected the abolitionist faith in "immediatism": the instantaneous freeing of one's slaves served as a pure Christian act of the highest order, which would save the slave owner from moral depravity and everlasting damnation and provide the slave with the opportunity to become a wage-earning Christian. Stowe's stereotyped docile slaves (or reformed recalcitrants, as in the case of Topsy) were designed to counteract white fears of racial violence and upheaval if slavery was abolished.[11]

Uncle Tom's Cabin: or, Life Among the Lowly originally appeared in serialized form between June 5, 1851, and April 1, 1852, in the *National Era* with Stowe writing furiously between the publication of segments to complete the saga. When the book appeared later in 1852, it became an instant success, selling about 1.5 million copies in its first year. A *London Times* review of the book noted that Stowe had earned "the largest sum of money ever received by any author, either American or European, from the sale of a single work in so short a period of time." A dramatized version of the story found an even larger audience, especially among the white working class, who were generally hostile to abolitionism until outraged by Legree's monstrous behavior.[12]

Although certainly not intended as children's literature, the novel was undoubtedly read by and to children, as were many Victorian novels during the family reading hour in the evening.[13] The final segment of the original serialization of *Uncle Tom's Cabin* included a paragraph directed specifically to children in which Stowe urged them to remember to pity the poor and oppressed. "Never if you can help it, let a colored child be shut out from school or treated with neglect and contempt on account of his color. Remember the sweet example of little Eva. . . . [W]hen you grow up, I hope the foolish and unchristian prejudice against people merely on account of their complexion will be done away with."[14] Stowe also crafted a child's edition of the novel, *Pictures and Stories from Uncle Tom's Cabin,* with a simplified text; however, it did not sell well. In England, a publisher produced an inexpensive Sunday school edition of the original book that reached thousands of British children. What Lydia Maria Child had been unable to do for abolitionism in her children's stories in the *Juvenile Miscellany* (see chapter 2), Stowe certainly achieved 20 years later.[15]

The popularity of *Uncle Tom's Cabin* was met by an equally strong critique, not only in the South but also by those in the North who found the abolitionist agenda threatening. They charged that the characters and scenes were inaccurately drawn and were exaggerated for emotional effect. They attacked Stowe's purpose and integrity, condemning her as a tool of radicals. Stowe readily admitted that she had never lived in the Deep South and had visited a border state only briefly, but because she asked the abolitionist speaker Frederick Douglass, as well as her own domestic servants, for descriptive information about plantation life, she argued that her settings and characterizations were accurate. Stowe also relied heavily on escape narratives, especially those of Josiah Henson and Henry Bibb, both of whom had come to Cincinnati. Because Stowe found herself so much on the defensive, she crafted a second book to prove the accuracy of her fictionalized settings, the plausibility of her plot, and the treatment of slaves in the contemporary South. She amassed a "mountain of materials" that convinced her that "as much as I thought I knew before, I had not *begun* to measure the depth of the abyss." This documentary evidence, drawn largely from published reports by slave-owners themselves, provided the basis for *A Key to Uncle Tom's Cabin,* published in 1853.[16]

But like almost all white Americans of her time, including many abolitionists, Harriet Beecher Stowe unwittingly perpetuated certain racial stereotypes. According to one critic, she "portrayed only light-skinned blacks as aggressive and intelligent," as in the cunning escape over the frozen Ohio river by Eliza and her child. Meanwhile dark-skinned blacks such as Uncle Tom and Topsy are portrayed as docile and submissive, or as capable of being made so through love and attention. It might have been Tom's devotion to evangelical theology that allowed Stowe to make his character noble rather than merely passive. Stowe saw herself as speaking for the inarticulate fugitive as well as the enslaved, but when one of those fugitives, Harriet Jacobs, sought Mrs. Stowe's advice on publishing her memoirs, Stowe refused to respond to her letters. Apparently Stowe wanted to appropriate Jacobs's story for her own use, or give no help at all. Jacobs eventually managed to publish her account, *Memoirs of a Slave Girl,* under the pseudonym Linda Brent.[17]

When black characters appear in children's fiction in the latter half of the nineteenth century, they are rarely distinguished from the slaves of the old South. Like other Americans, children's writers participated in the construction of the myth of the familial nature of black and white relationships in the old South, and they perpetuated these stereotypes in the new South as well. They portrayed African-Americans only in subservient roles, in which their docility, simple-mindedness, and penchant for having a good time bolstered their creator's own confidence in the racial hierarchies they embraced. The portrayal of a new South in which the evil of slavery had been replaced by a benevolent and constructive working relationship between the races became a mainstay of the literature produced in both the North and the South. Visual representations of people of color featured exaggerated physical characteristics, such as enlarged red lips, kinky hair, very dark skin, and women with particularly large breasts. In *The Image of the Black in Children's Fiction* (1973), Dorothy Broderick identified seven common stereotypical black characters: the contented slave, the wretched freedman, the comic Negro, the brute, the tragic mulatto, the local-color darky, and the exotic primitive.[18] She might also have mentioned the devoted freed person who chooses not to leave the plantation. So complete are these stereotypes that in some works, the reader cannot even tell whether the African-American is working as a servant or serving as a slave.

Martha Finley's *Elsie Dinsmore* (1867) portrayed a remarkably pious white child living with her grandfather on a southern plantation before the Civil War. The stock black characters, slaves on Roselands plantation, appear as solicitous, meek, and pious domestic servants, for they are never referred to as slaves. Neither her absent father nor her disinterested grandfather (her mother is dead) understands Elsie; her only comfort comes from the house slave "Aunt Chloe," as Elsie calls her. Finley portrays Chloe as docile, jolly, and ever-obedient, one "never willing to leave her nursling, but [who] watched over her night and day with the most devoted affection, and slept in a cot bed in one corner."[19] In the span of numerous sequels, Finley follows Elsie through adolescence, her marriage to her father's best friend, Mr. Travilla, and her life with seven children and a granddaughter who is her namesake. Elsie and her husband travel abroad during the Civil War so that Finley need not include any grim reminders of that bloody affair. Upon their return to Roselands and to Travilla's estate, The Oaks, the couple finds the emancipated slaves still working on the old plantation, where they remain content and happy.[20] The clear message to children involves both the paternal care of whites for blacks and the lack of black initiative or discontent with the existing economic and social system, exactly the prevailing white cultural motif.

One of the most popular apologists for the benefits of slavery and the old "southern way of life" was lawyer and novelist Thomas Nelson Page (1853–1922). Raised on a plantation in Hanover County, Virginia, Page spoke for a generation of southerners who believed their way of life had been destroyed by the war and emancipation. In *The Negro: The Southerner's Problem* (1904) he presented a skewed history of American slavery as a beneficent institution for blacks and whites alike, and he defended the postreconstruction disenfranchisement of the African-American male. His novels and local-color vignettes made him a spokesman for those in the New South who lamented the passing of a romanticized southern culture. Venturing into juvenile fiction, Page wrote *Two Little Confederates* (1888), which is loosely based on his childhood memories of the Civil War. Two young boys who initially view the war as exciting and full of adventure narrate the story. In the opening scene Page minimizes the horrors of slavery by referring to "Old Balla," the senior slave on the plantation, as "their boon comrade and adviser." In thus drawing on the stereotype of a protective male version of the mammy, Page ignores Balla's lifelong bondage. His further description—"He lived alone (for his wife had been set free years before, and lived in Philadelphia)"—again implies that slavery is not so bad; separation is a minor inconvenience. Later an escaped Union soldier gets into the plantation henhouse and falls asleep, drunk, inside. The boy Willy tries to "guard him," but then Uncle Balla comes and ties the door shut, bragging to himself that "Willy jes' gwi' let you get 'way, but a *man* got you now." Since the prisoner escapes easily through the roof, the slave becomes an object of ridicule. A great comic incident is made over the prisoner's escape through the roof, a laugh produced by mimicking the slave's pretense of cleverness.

As Union soldiers advance toward Richmond and the Oakland plantation, the mistress tells Balla and the house slaves that they may leave, "but if you go, you can never come back," to which Balla replies, "[W]har is I got to go? I wuz born on dis place n' I 'spec' to die here. . . .Y'all sticks by us, and we'll stick by you." At the end of the war, the slaves do leave the plantation since there is no work there. Later, when the white family's fortunes return, so do their former slaves, happy to be back at their old plantation home.[21] Page simply used children's fiction to reiterate his unreconstructed interpretation of southern history.

Francis Boyd Calhoun wrote only one children's book, *Miss Minerva and William Green Hill* (1909), but her tales of a white orphan who goes to live with his unmarried Aunt Minerva became almost a classic among postbellum southerners. After Calhoun died suddenly the year after the book appeared, the publishers, Reilly and Lee, found another southern writer, Emma Speed Sampson, to turn Billy and Miss Minerva's tales into a profitable series of children's books. Sampson produced 10 Minerva titles between 1918 and 1939 and introduced into them a set of African-American characters who completely reiterated for children the southern—and by then national—stereotypes of people of color. Miss Minerva's cook, Aunt Cindy, is a fat, docile, motherly character with a shiftless and lazy husband, Jimmy-Jawed Jupiter. All the male characters are deficient in one way or another. All have pejorative or comical names: Admiral Farragut Moses, First Thessalonians and his twin, Second Thessalonians, Wilkes Booth Lincoln, Oleander Magnolia Althea. All the black characters speak an almost unintelligible dialect (one can hardly imagine children being able to read it), and all accept their low position in the racial hierarchy of the community. Sampson describes Aunt Cindy as a "strong stickler for social inequality between the races [who] had no idea of permitting the colored children for whom she was responsible to get notions above their heads." As in Thomas Nelson Page's writing, the reader cannot tell if these people of color are slaves or free domestic servants. One child reports, "I comed up from the plantation to b'long to Josephime." Although the later books in the series dropped some of the dialect, shortened the original offensive names, and introduced a cultured, middle-class black cousin to the children, the series remained clearly a product of a racially hierarchical society.[22]

Annie Fellows Johnston (1863–1931) perpetuated romantic notions of an idealized South in her Little Colonel series. Loosely basing Lloyd Sherman on acquaintances she met during a brief stay in Kentucky, Johnston created a spunky female character whose irascible grandfather, Colonel Lloyd, had rejected the girl's mother for marrying a "Yankee." It is his granddaughter and namesake, Lloyd Sherman, who is the "Little Colonel" of the series's titles. Johnston added conventionally acceptable, stereotyped African-Americans to most of the plots. Although the stories have postbellum settings, the servants might as well be slaves. All of them serve as domestic help or field laborers, live in servants' cabins behind Colonel Sherman's lovely home, enjoy music, dress in calico and bright colors, and are devoted to the colonel and his once-estranged family. In *Little Colonel's Christmas Vacation,* Lloyd's mother says of her cook, "If she were not such a superior cook, I wouldn't put up with her whims, but in these days, when everybody is having so much trouble with servants, we'll have to humor her. She's a faithful old creature." In one brief speech, Johnston confirms the popular assumptions that African-Americans were always loyal to, and appreciative of, their white employers, while as employees they were childish and unpredictable. Johnston (and numerous others) habitually use the pejorative "pickaninnies" for all black children. In *Little Colonel's Hero,* Lloyd Sherman so captivates the heart of a retired German colonel that he gives her his beloved Saint Bernard. When Lloyd brings the dog back to her Kentucky home and introduces the dog to the black domestics on her plantation, he growls menacingly at them. When she instructs the dog to "shake hands" with the "pickaninnies," he "did not seem to relish this part of his introduction to Kentucky." Then she sends them all to fetch something for the dog, saying, "If you all fly around and wait on him right good, he'll like you lots bettah."[23]

Johnston's children's books became one of the most popular series of the early twentieth century (see chapter 4); fans wrote from across the nation, not just the South, in praise of the "inspiring" character of Little Colonel. With each new reader, Johnston perpetuated demeaning racial stereotypes, consciously or not. Not until the creation of *Crisis* magazine and the publication of *Hazel* could readers find positive examples of black family life, work ethic, and cultural contributions in American literature for children.

Race and the "Great American Novel"

For all the praise and scorn that has been heaped upon Mark Twain's *Adventures of Huckleberry Finn* (1885) as the quintessential American novel, most of the late-twentieth-century critique has focused on Twain's portrayal of race. Scholars argue over whether Samuel Clemens (1835–1910) sought to criticize the racial stereotyping of the 1880s by using heavy satire or whether, instead, his writing attacks postreconstruction prejudice directly. A recent collection of critical essays on *Huckleberry Finn* is devoted solely to "the race question" in the novel. Defenders of Clemens as an enlightened critic of discrimination argue that by featuring a warm friendship between Huck and Jim, Twain was deliberately passing critical judgment on the racial divisions of postreconstruction America, and that his use of the word "nigger" over 200 times is both an accurate reflection of antebellum language and a thrust at the continuing stereotyping of blacks in the 1880s. Critics of Twain argue that his portrait of Jim mimics the stereotype perpetuated by the minstrel show: Jim is childlike, simple, superstitious, and deferential.[24]

In creating two characters, Huckleberry Finn and Miss Polly's slave Jim, who for very different reasons seek to escape the "sivilization" of American society, Twain may have been criticizing American culture at several levels. When *Huck Finn* appeared in 1885, America's social experiment with "reconstructing" plantation society had ended without significant social change; African-Americans found themselves disenfranchised again, this time by exclusionary state voting regulations. The "Negro question" no longer loomed as the most compelling intellectual issue, legislation legalizing separation of the races based on assumed innate differences was all but in place, and Anglo-Saxon superiority was assumed. Most Anglo-Americans encountered African-Americans either as low-paid laborers and domestic workers or as characters in the hugely popular minstrel shows that traveled to even small-town America. Samuel Clemens's language, his several black characters who harbor exaggerated fears of ghosts, and the way Huck and Tom play with Jim's freedom can also be read as statements in support of Jim Crow America.[25]

While Clemens's position on race relations and the abilities of African-Americans seems ambivalent at best, his novel is so shot through with irony that the reader cannot always discern his narrative intent. For example, when Huck attempts to use a logical argument about the wisdom of the biblical King Solomon with Jim, Jim succeeds in convincing Huck that Solomon was at *all* wise. As Jim leads Huck through a logical exercise of his own, he demonstrates the absurdity of using pure logic in all situations and reveals his own cleverness. Stung by Jim's ability, Huck responds with a straightforward racial put-down characteristic of American thought in 1885: "I see it warn't no use wasting words—you can't learn a nigger to argue. So I quit."[26]

Although Jim fits some stereotypes of slaves, such as being superstitious and believing in ghosts, Twain also portrays him as thoughtful, cautious, considerate, wise, self-sacrificing, and shrewd. Huck's "Pap," a confirmed alcoholic, would not vote once he learned that a free black man could vote too, highlighting the assumed superiority of whites. The reader cannot escape the absurdity of a white drunk feeling superior to a hardworking black man.[27] Twain's ambiguous portrayal of race is also seen in the riverboat accident. The explosion did not hurt anybody, says Huck, it just "killed a nigger." Aunt Sally emphasizes this common devaluing of blacks by replying, "Well, it's lucky; because sometimes people do get hurt." Is she articulating popular opinions of blacks as less than full human beings, or does she serve to emphasize the absurdity of racist beliefs?

Toward the end of the novel, when Jim is willing to risk recapture rather than see Tom Sawyer go without a doctor for his gunshot wound, Huck comments that Jim is "white inside." Such an assessment also operates at several levels. Readers could conclude that Huck has shown that friendship knows no color bounds, or they could hear Huck professing white superiority even as he ostensibly compliments Jim. If Clemens intended a double satire, the reader would realize no one would want to be "white inside" if white represents most whites in this novel. When the doctor praises Jim for the way he stayed with the injured Tom, the reader expects the crowd to give up their plans to hold Jim captive as a runaway slave, thus rewarding him with citizenship for his outstanding bravery. Instead, the crowd rewards Jim by promising that "they wouldn't cuss him no more." Is Clemens disgusted by slavery and using irony to highlight that, or does he merely reflect the society in which he lives? The boys' treatment of Jim in the latter part of the novel parallels the way white society played with and manipulated people of color in postbellum America. As Neil Schmitz has written, "Jim's situation at the end of *Huckleberry Finn* reflects that of the Negro in the Reconstruction, free at last and thoroughly impotent, the object of devious schemes and a hapless victim of constant brutality."[28]

Many critics argue that Clemens carefully and accurately captured black vernacular dialect in Jim's voice. Certainly other nineteenth-century authors had African-American characters speak in dialect as well, but in many cases, such speech was a code for other physical and behavioral stereotypes. Because of these assumed characteristics, the use of dialect alone could identify a speaker as black and no other descriptors were needed. Thus African-Americans became interchangeable stereotypes, as in the stories by Annie Fellows Johnston or Harriet Beecher Stowe (discussed previously). Shelley Fishkin argues that Twain perfected his use of dialect in earlier short stories and then used it most carefully with Jim. She argues that evidence from the manuscript of *Huckleberry Finn* shows Twain's conscious decision to eliminate dialect from Jim's speech in places where Jim expressed strong emotion, wherever Twain did not want the reader to labor over words and miss the impact of the feelings expressed. According to Fishkin, Twain returned to dialect as a way to enhance Jim's character, not as a substitute for creating one.[29]

Clemens's use of irony and satire, his attacks on conventional religiosity, and his romanticizing of escape from "sivilization" attracted critical attention in his day; however, his ambiguous stance on race relations did not. What children may have found in *Huck Finn* was a boy-centered adventure tale, tantalizing in its rule breaking and exciting in its plot-driven narration, reflective of the dime novel tradition. In Jim they most likely saw the docile, compassionate, slow-of-speech black stereotype that surrounded them in popular culture, in books, and at minstrel shows. Jim's freedom at the end of the book carries little weight with children for whom slavery is not even a memory.

Uncle Remus and the "New South"

On first encounter, Joel Chandler Harris's (1848–1908) *Uncle Remus, His Songs and Sayings* (1880) seems to be yet another stereotype of African-American males, in this case the "benevolent darky," fondly caring for his white "family" and expressing disdain for the freedmen who have left their plantations and are roaming through the Georgia countryside. In "A Story of the War," Uncle Remus talks about those "sunshine niggers," the migrating blacks in search of work and family connections. Harris puts typical southern white attitudes into Remus's mouth: "Dey begs my terbacker, en borrys my tools, en steals my vittles, en hit's done come ter dat pass dat I gotter pack up en go." Or "You slap de law onter a nigger a time er two, an' larn 'im dat he's got fer to look after his own rashuns an' keep out 'n udder fokes's chick'n-coops, an' sorter coax 'im inter de idee dat h's got ter feed 'is own chilluns, an' I be blessed ef you ain't got 'im on risin' groun.' "[30] As a consequence of such portrayals of freed peoples, the Uncle Remus books have been castigated by some critics as not-so-subtle racist propaganda that perpetuates demeaning stereotypes of African-Americans. Some libraries have removed the books from circulation; schools have dropped them from reading lists; and the stories have been rewritten to eliminate the character of Uncle Remus the story-teller while preserving the animal folktales he tells.

Harris's stories originally appeared in the *Atlanta Constitution*, edited by Henry Grady, a leading spokesman for the New South. Grady urged southerners to look to the future, to industrialize, to diversify their economy, and to heal their animosities toward the North. As part of that reunification effort, the old South was reconstituted in memory as a place of benevolent slave

UNCLE REMUS

HIS SONGS AND HIS SAYINGS

THE FOLK-LORE OF THE OLD PLANTATION

By JOEL CHANDLER HARRIS

*WITH ILLUSTRATIONS BY FREDERICK S. CHURCH AND
JAMES H. MOSER*

Cherokee Publishing Company
Atlanta, Georgia
1981

"Uncle Remus," from Joel Chandler Harris, *Uncle Remus: His Songs and His Sayings*
(1880; reprint, Atlanta: Cherokee Publishing, 1981)

owners, happy slaves, and their peaceful coexistence. Any measures the new South might take to ensure white supremacy were seen as a restatement of a social system that had worked well and could continue to do so; assumptions about black inferiority and docility were widely held in the North as well.

Harris's first short sketches for the newspaper appeared in 1879, continuing a column that already featured the black "Uncle Si," which used dialect to make fun of uneducated blacks, much like the popular minstrel shows of the postwar era. Gradually, however, Harris evolved the Uncle Remus character into a more nuanced and dignified man who told colorful African-based folktales. His first Uncle Remus story featured "Mr. Rabbit" (who soon became the Brer Rabbit of later stories) and the Tar Baby. The verbal description of Uncle Remus does not necessarily suggest the postbellum stereotype of ebony skin and exaggerated features. But the title page of the original volume portrays a comical character, quite in line with other contemporary illustrations of African-Americans. Harris himself may have deplored the illustrator's depiction, for in 1887 he wrote to the editor about to publish *Free Joe*, "[G]ive the old negro man some dignity." Harris's appeal regarding illustrations, however, had little impact on the production and marketing of his books.[31]

These multilayered stories present a much more complex picture of the new South and the place of emancipated peoples in that landscape than a superficial reading might disclose. Most Uncle Remus tales harbor both an inner story, the animal tale, and an outer story, the interplay between Uncle Remus and the white child, who is never named. In the outer story, Harris seems to be giving his postbellum audience what they want to believe about the new South. He portrays a patient elderly retainer fondly entertaining an admiring child. Sometimes they conspire against the adults and share stolen pastries or leftovers from dinner, thus infantilizing the elder Remus. Harris evokes the pastoral setting of the plantation for each story, as in the opening story of the 1880 collection, where Miss Sally sees "the child sitting by Uncle Remus. His head rested against the old man's arm, and he was gazing with an expression of the most intense interest into the rough, weather-beaten face that beamed so kindly upon him." In another idyllic scene, Uncle Remus takes the boy "on his knee, and stroking the child's hair thoughtfully and caressingly," proceeds to spin a folktale. The portrait of the little boy on the old man's lap evokes "a picture of utter confidence and trust, . . . of pastoral innocence and peace."[32]

But the inner story is something quite different than this commonplace stereotyping suggests. After the idyllic introduction, Uncle Remus tells the boy one of the many folktales Harris himself had heard from plantation slaves when he worked as a printer's assistant in rural Georgia. Folklorists have been unable to sort out which of the tales may have originated in Africa and which might have grown out of the American experience of slavery itself.[33] Most of these folktales, which evoke themes of trickery and evasion, feature the triumph of the weaker animal over the more powerful. Folklorists and critics read the tales as representing the struggle of the slave to survive the dehumanization of slavery, to outwit his superiors, and to enjoy the devilish tricks played by the weak on the more powerful. As written by Harris in the 1880s and '90s, these tales can also represent a subtle support for the freedman's struggle against white oppression in the new South.

Bernard Wolfe first defined the subversive nature of the character of Brer Rabbit in a 1949 essay, "Uncle Remus and the Malevolent Rabbit." He interpreted Brer Rabbit as a "symbol of covert resistance to white power" and read the tales as patent instructions on survival within the system. He noted that many of the stories involved subterfuge to escape work: Brer Rabbit feigns an injury or leaves work early on the pretext that his wife is very ill. Other stories seem "obsessed with images of food" and often portray the animals hunting or fishing to augment their food supplies. In many tales, Brer Rabbit succeeds in outwitting or outmaneuvering either Brer Fox or Brer Bear. Still others represent alternative routes to survival. Brer Possum plays dead, illustrating that a direct assault on white supremacy would be futile. Brer Terrapin triumphs by virtue of his endurance as well as his clever strategies. Taken altogether, these stories present an amazing array of "beatings, tortures, savage assaults, and deadly ambushes," wrote one critic. "They reproduce," in other words, "the emotional universe of the slave."[34]

Was Joel Chandler Harris aware of the covert meaning of these African-American folktales? Can the same person who constructed the reactionary outer story be aware of the subversive nature of the inner story? Harris himself indicated that he understood why the rabbit was favored by the black storytellers. He wrote, "[H]e selects as his hero the weakest and most harmless of all animals, and brings him out victorious in contests. . . . It is not *virtue* that triumphs, but *helplessness;* it is not *malice,* but *mischievousness.*"[35] Although living in the Jim Crow South, Harris may have identified with the repression of the African-American and used the seemingly innocuous avenue of children's stories to underscore and preserve African-American culture. A recent revisionist interpretation argues for Harris's growing awareness of white bigotry and repression, his eventual rejection of new South values, and his complete disillusionment with racial categories. Thus, if Harris understood the subtext of his animal tales, he used the character of Uncle Remus to guard against the power of that subtext because of the virulent racism that surrounded him. "To neglect the Brer Rabbit tales because a white man was the first to write them down," argues another defender, "is to betray the black man's folk tradition."[36]

No doubt the subversive nature of the Uncle Remus stories was lost on white children, and we cannot presume that many black children in late-nineteenth-century America were reading them either. Instead, white children probably saw in the Uncle Remus stories and their illustrations what society was already teaching them about African-Americans and the need to marginalize people of color within society. Children probably heard in the animal tales entertaining stories that gave them some sense of satisfaction that small creatures can after all get the better of larger ones.

Racial Stereotyping after 1900

Well into the twentieth century, almost no children's stories featured African-Americans in any kind of positive roles. When people of color did appear, the characters continued to be limited to laborers or domestic servants who spoke ungrammatically and in dialect. Scholar J. B. Dobkin searched through eight thousand "nickel library" titles and found *no* black heroes at all; he could identify about 50 persons of color who figured in the story lines in some way. In *Black Tom, the Negro,* a detective fiction, the reader discovers at the end of the story that the hero was actually a white man in disguise.[37] Two popular picture books that relied heavily on demeaning illustrations perpetuating racial stereotypes were *Little Black Sambo* (1899) and *Watermelon Pete and Other Stories* (1914).

Helen Bannerman, a Scotswoman living in India with her family, wrote and illustrated *Little Black Sambo* for her own children but was persuaded by the London publisher Grant Richards to relinquish all rights to both the text and illustrations when it published the book in 1899. Though not technically an American work, it is included here because of the many editions brought out by publishers in the United States, some of which strongly reflect American stereotypes of African-American children. How did a tale set in India come to feature African-derived names (Sambo, Jumbo, Mumbo), and why did Bannerman portray the characters with exaggerated facial features, black skin, and curly hair? Scholar Phyliss Yuill has gathered evidence of multiple explanations: Bannerman might have been influenced by the popular minstrel shows playing British cities during her frequent visits there; her illustrations reveal an uncanny similarity to the popular German picture book *Der Struwwelpeter* (*The Black-a-Moor*); or she may have been influenced by nineteenth-century American fiction featuring black servants and substituted those images in her mind for her own Indian servants.[38]

Whatever her inspiration, the book gained almost immediate popularity in the United States, appearing in editions by Frederick Stokes (1900), Reilly and Britton (1905), Cupples and Leon (1917) and in the extremely popular A. Whitman and Co. edition of 1925. J. B. Lippincott reissued the original Stokes edition in 1941, while other companies continued to bring out the text with various illustrators well into the 1970s. The original Stokes edition features Bannerman's illustrations, but later editions reflect distinctly American stereotypes. American illustrators set the tale in Africa or the U.S. South. The Reilly edition features characters with "grossly exaggerated lips, eyes, and hair," with Sambo's mother appearing as a typical mammy figure. The Cupples edition's illustrations portray minstrel-type figures with black faces and large white mouths. Not only do the illustrations fit the American stereotype of African-Americans, but the colorful, mismatched clothes the text describes Sambo wearing emphasize the white belief that people of color chose outlandish colors. The family's devouring of stacks of pancakes at the end of the story reiterates white beliefs that African-Americans were gluttonous and greedy.[39]

The same prejudicial themes can be found in the 1914 *Watermelon Pete and Other Stories,* published by Rand McNally (no author given). This picture book with several short stories features a boy described as having a mouth "just the shape of a big slice of ripe watermelon." This moral tale about the ill effects of eating watermelons from his neighbor's garden ends with Pete sitting down to a huge breakfast of pancakes with the neighbor and his wife, a clear reprise of the *Little Black Sambo* motif.[40]

In the very popular *Penrod* (1914) by Boothe Tarkington (1869–1946), the hero encounters two black boys named Herman and Verman, the latter a none-too-subtle pejorative word play on the homonym *vermin*. One of the boys is missing two fingers because he was curious about what "would happen if he used a knife on his hand." The boys speak in such a thick dialect that neither Penrod nor the child reader could possibly understand them. Penrod's friend makes a joke about the difference between those "coons" (the black children) and the raccoon they keep as their only pet. Not only are the children stereotyped as "pickaninnies," their father is portrayed as a "lawless brute," another popular African-American stereotype. During the story, he serves jail time for fighting and wounding another black man with a knife. Even the children embody this lawlessness when they threaten a white boy with the warning "[We'll] cut out your gizzard."[41]

The popular series books of the early twentieth century, such as The Bobbsey Twins, Nancy Drew, The Hardy Boys, and Tom Swift, included stereotyped black characters that changed little from the earliest series, in about 1900, until the 1950s, when public opinion demanded a "clean-up." The white, middle-class Bobbsey Twins interact with their household servants Sam and Dinah, whose speech is written in heavy dialect and who appear accepting of their subordinate positions. Dinah serves as both cook and nanny to the children, while her husband, Sam, labors in the house and yard and works as the family chauffeur. Both speak in a heavy southern dialect: "What's a dish yeah I heah Nan say?" By 1950, the black couple are still working happily in the Bobbsey household; however, their dialect is gone. (The Stratemeyer Syndicate reissued early Bobbsey Twin stories in the 1950s with updated illustrations and with all black dialect eliminated.[42])

The speech of African-Americans implied an inferior education or intelligence, and their occupations certainly denoted an inferior social and economic status. Physical characteristics remained exaggerated into the twentieth century as well. Most black women in the series books are obese; the Bobbsey family's servants have "kinky heads" and love watermelon. When black characters appear in the Nancy Drew or Hardy Boys books, they do so as yardmen, servants, or perpetrators of some dishonest scheme. The Rover family's black servant, Alexander Pop, never loses his black dialect during the decades of Rover Boy stories, despite the fact that these stories are set in the Northeast. For example, in *The Rover Boys in the Mountains* (1902), servant Aleck remarks, "[Y]o' is a sight fo' soah eyes, deed yo' is." The Tom Swift series also includes a token black with a most demeaning name: Eradicate Andrew Jackson Abraham Lincoln Sampson. His name, his southern dialect, and his mangled grammar serve to devalue everything about this character.[43] For thousands of children, their first exposure to people of color was through stereotyped and prejudicial fictional presentations.

Two major efforts to counteract the negative stereotyping and minimizing of the black experience had links to the National Association for the Advancement of Colored People (NAACP), created in 1909 in New York City through the merger of the Niagara Movement, an organization of black men emphasizing racial pride, and a number of white lawyers and activists. By 1914 the organization had offices, permanent staff, and a membership of six thousand. Its first president was Oswald Garrison Villard, grandson of the white abolitionist leader William Lloyd Garrison. The NAACP began its own journal, the *Crisis*, which ran from 1910 to 1934 and was brilliantly edited by W.E.B. Du Bois. In 1912 he introduced readers to an annual children's issue, devoted to the problems of rearing African-American children in a white-majority, often hostile environment. He worried that too many parents tried to shield their children from the realities of discrimination and lynching and that parents failed to talk openly about segregation and the subtle behaviors that black children must learn to survive insults. In a 1919 issue of *Crisis,* he wrote that "to seek to raise [African-American children] in ignorance of their racial identity and peculiar situation is inadvisable—and impossible." Instead, Du Bois sought to expose children to the history of their race, the achievements of people of color in America, and "the delicate code of honor and action in their relations with white children." He recognized that traditional children's books provided none of the information that black children needed. Rather, the stereotyping of African-Americans imprinted harmful images in children's minds. Notably, when the *Crisis* children's issue in 1912 published a list of recommended children's books, it omitted such "classics" as *Little Black Sambo, Elsie Dinsmore, Two Little Confederates,* and the entire Little Colonel series.[44]

Acknowledging that this annual issue was "easily the most popular number of the year," Du Bois toyed with the idea of starting a separate juvenile periodical for black children themselves. In 1919, not long after the death of his own young son, who was denied critical health care because of his race, Du Bois launched the children's magazine the *Brownies' Book* and recruited the former Philadelphia teacher, writer, and literary editor of the *Crisis* Jessie Fauset to assist him. Although no accurate records have survived, Du Bois's papers suggest that subscriptions for the periodical averaged about five thousand a year over its 24 issues, never enough to provide adequate financial support for the magazine. When it folded, some of its more popular columns continued in the *Crisis*. The *Brownies' Book* was the only publication designed for African-American children until *Ebony, Jr.* appeared in 1973.[45]

Black authors contributed 98 percent of the content in *Brownies'*, and the magazine's consistent philosophy highlighted black achievement in many areas. Every issue contained biographies of African-Americans. Authors also stressed pride in mastering middle-class, "cultured" behaviors, the cultivation of unreproachable morals, and duty to the race. When illustrations accompanied stories, they featured blacks in realistic activities, and drawings lacked the exaggerated physical characteristics prevalent in mainstream magazines. Du Bois insisted that each issue provide children with information about world events and acquaint them with the cultures of other peoples.[46]

One of the regular columns in the *Brownies' Book*, "The Judge," featured an elderly man presiding over a Court of Children in which "the law is old and musty and needs sadly to be changed." Eventually, he mused, "the children will change it." But meanwhile, "refined colored persons" must follow this acceptable code of behavior. Another column, "Little People of the Month," highlighted photos and stories of real African-American children involved in exemplary activities. Violet Harris analyzed the content of all the fiction that appeared in the *Brownies' Book* and found none that featured a comic black figure or a stereotypical mammy or "happy darky." Characters never referred to another black as a "nigger," nor were any black characters described as physically ugly. Racial characteristics, when described, covered the whole range of skin tones, hair types, and facial features. Black characters spoke standard English, not dialect, and they held various jobs at all levels of society, not just laboring or domestic ones. The slave past was always described "as a tribulation and unending misery."[47]

Another influential member of the NAACP, white activist Mary White Ovington, tried her hand at juvenile fiction with a pointed racial message. In 1913 she published *Hazel*, the story of a middle-class African-American girl living in Boston with her widowed mother. Following her father's death, Hazel and her mother move to a poor section of the city where the mother's domestic labor supports them. Because of frail health, Hazel spends the winter with her paternal grandmother in rural Alabama, where she encounters racial discrimination and different codes of behavior than she had known in New England. Well aware of the stereotypical portrayal of black children in mainstream literature, Ovington expresses her didactic authorial motive in

Hazel

"Hazel," from Mary White Ovington, *Hazel* (1913)
Copied with permission from Ayer Company Publishers, Inc., North Stratford, N.H.

the preface: "[C]olored children in the United States might also like to have their . . . books telling of happenings that were like their own."[48] The illustrator, Harry Roseland, created an African-American heroine with classical features, long, gently curled black hair, and fashionable though simple clothing.

Mary Ovington refused to write in dialect, instead conveying southern speech through syntax, grammar, and regional expressions. Ovington's portrait of Hazel's grandmother bears some resemblance to the stereotypical mammy who is "dressed as though she had come out of a rich story book. On her head was a turban of a rich, deep red, and about her neck was a gay ban-

Granny

"Granny," from Mary White Ovington, *Hazel* (1913)
Copied with permission from Ayer Company Publishers, Inc., North Stratford, N.H.

danna." This woman does not take care of white children, however, but supports herself independently on a small farm.[49] Hazel's best friend in Alabama, Scipio, has an alcoholic and abusive father, but other black males in both Boston and Alabama are principled, hardworking, devoted family men.

Following the philosophy of Du Bois and Fauset at the *Crisis,* Ovington believed black children should know about life under slavery, segregation, discrimination, and lynchings, and thus included them all—softened for a child audience—in *Hazel.* Grandmother doesn't know her birth date and explains how she was sold away from her mother as a young child; Hazel can enter the "white" train car only if she pretends to be the maid of the white teacher who is taking her back home to Boston; Scipio tells about a lynching he witnessed. The simple plot structure allows Ovington to portray both the culture of educated, professional, integrated middle-class black life in Boston and the poor, rural, uneducated sharecropping rural existence of blacks in Alabama. Class and education separate Hazel's two worlds, and both are oversimplified, yet their realism far exceeded anything else in print for children in the early twentieth century.

Ethnicity in America, 1850–1920

Just as American popular culture moved very slowly to portray people of color accurately in the portrait of American life, so too were persons of foreign birth or with identifiable ethnic speech often the objects of humor in children's stories. Foreign immigration to the United States after 1830 dispelled the image of the U.S. as a homogeneous nation. During the 1840s and 1850s, four million immigrants took up residence in the United States, so that foreign-born citizens accounted for about 17 percent of the total population. Needing immediate employment and seeking cultural familiarity, many immigrants remained in the ethnic enclaves rapidly developing in urban seaboard areas. Others, especially those with money for transportation, traveled to the Midwest, homesteading land in Minnesota, Michigan, and Iowa. By 1860, German and Irish immigrants composed over 60 percent of the population of St. Louis and nearly half of the populations of New York City, Chicago, Cincinnati, Milwaukee, Detroit, and San Francisco. Baltimore and New Orleans had significant ethnic concentrations—up to 30 percent—as well as large numbers of African-Americans. Between 1860 and 1890 another 10 million northern European immigrants flooded into the United States, to be joined by 8 million French Canadians, southern Europeans, and Asians. By 1890, in New York City alone, four out of every five people had been born abroad or were children of foreign-born parents. Between 1900 and 1917, more than 17 million immigrants arrived in the United States.[50]

As it had during the peak immigration decade of the 1850s, opposition to foreign immigration developed serious, articulate, and powerful support in the late nineteenth and early twentieth centuries. Immigrants came to represent to many Americans the worst features of urban society: crime, government corruption, illiteracy, intoxication, and poverty. The Boston Immigration Restriction League called for literacy tests for immigrants in 1894, and in 1896 and repeatedly throughout the next decade, Henry Cabot Lodge sponsored such legislation in Congress. Although it had been vetoed continually by a succession of presidents, a strict immigration restriction law took effect over President Wilson's veto in 1917.[51]

A few of the dime novel series featured immigrant adult heroes. To attract ethnic sales, the Ten Cent Irish Novel series and the Die Deutsche Library series appeared. Yet the vast majority of the literature marketed specifically to children continued to feature white, middle-class youngsters and to speak patronizingly or disparagingly of any outside this mainstream. *Peck's Bad Boy* (1883) by George W. Peck features a mischievous urban youngster in Minneapolis. His language reflects ethnic slurs common to the Gilded Age. He continually teases the neighborhood Polish grocer, whom he calls the "Polacker." On another occasion he refers to the firecrackers he set off in his neighborhood as "niggerchasers."[52]

But it was really the syndicated series literature for children that thrived on ethnic stereotypes, white superiority, and an imperialistic view of Americans' ingenuity. Whether in his own country or in the United States, the "foreigner" never measured up to the standards of the Anglo-Saxon hero of the syndicated series books. Just as we have seen repeated references to the limited ability of African-Americans, so were other people of color set apart as inferior by virtue of race. In the 1911 book by Frank Patchin, *The Battleship Boys' First Step Upward*, two brown-skinned Hawaiian crewmen leave the ship at a critical time, and the protagonist comments, "[B]lack goes all the way through; I'll bet they're black clear to the bone." Race seems the only logical explanation for why anyone would fear potential combat. In *Young Volunteer in Cuba*, an American boy comments, "[They] could raise [extra produce] if they tried. But the average Cuban . . . is rather lazy . . . and consequently he doesn't grow any more than he actually needs [to eat]." Americans in foreign locations frequently display their superiority in mining, in farming, and in anything technological. When a Mexican pilot meets the American "flying ace Ted Scott," the Mexican pilot shows "awe" with an "almost dog-like devotion in this eyes." In Borneo (*Boy Explorers in Borneo*, 1922) the natives are so awed by rifles that they make the American one of their gods. Americans consistently reveal disdain for local customs, whether cooking in Puerto Rico, cockfighting in the Philippines, or native religious practices in Hawaii.[53]

People of Asian descent emerge from children's fiction as backward, superstitious, and heathen. Chinese men invariably wear a pigtail. In a popular series by Eleanor H. Porter, a decidedly "modern" girl named Billy (who defies, in a few ways, Victorian stereotypes of domesticity) is getting married. Her disgruntled sister-in-law writes home about the wedding and about the Chinese cook who insists on delivering a gift to the honored couple. According to that letter, "Ding Dong, or whatever his name is," left a gift for Billy and said Billy would "heap plenty velly good luckee" if he opened the gift before she got "mallied." His name, his gift, and his accent are dispatched and disparaged in one paragraph. In contrast to the Chinese, the Japanese in pre–World War II stories usually were viewed as industrious, clean, hardworking, and imitators of American ingenuity because of their "progressive" farming and conservation of resources.[54]

With some exceptions, America's own native peoples did not fare well in children's literature either. In one of the Stratemeyer series books, *For the Liberty of Texas*, westerners refer to American Indians as "sneaking comanches," "treacherous," "savage and lawless," "bloodthirsty," and "dirty." In *With Washington in the West*, the settlers shoot retreating natives in the back because "they need the lesson." Exceptions to this stereotyping include author George Bird Grinell, who spent considerable time in the West and reflected native traditions quite accurately in *Pawnee Hero Stories and Folk Tales* (1889) and *By Cheyenne Campfires* (1926). Helen Hunt Jackson, well known for her crusade on behalf of Native American rights, accurately portrayed the West in *Nelly's Silver Mine* (1878).[55]

The beginning of the Great War in 1914 soon plunged the world of children's literature into stories set all around the world, often with xenophobic results. Formerly fellow Anglo-Saxons, people of German extraction found themselves referred to as "Heinies," "Teutons," "Fritzies," "Hun baby-killers," "German madmen," and "savage dogs." In *Dave Darrin and the German Sub* (1919), native Germans are "stupid looking." Boys' adventure books took readers on submarines (*Boy Scouts on a Submarine*, 1918; *Dave Darrin and the German Submarines*, 1919), to the European front (*Army Boys Marching into Germany*, 1920), and onto the Atlantic Ocean (*Uncle Sam's Navy Boys with the Marines*, 1919). In short, writes Frederick MacDonald, the Germans emerge from the series books as "barbarians who wasted land, ruined homes, orphaned and mutilated little children, and butchered old people."[56]

Curiously, gypsies represent the ethnic group—if they can be called that—most often targeted as villainous in early-twentieth-century children's writing. Their appearance always made them stand out: they were portrayed as dark, swarthy, wild, "foreign-looking" in a rather generic but frightening sense. Gypsies turn up in the title of at least a half-dozen of the girls' series books (for example, *Ruth Fielding and the Gypsies*, 1915, and *The Corner House Girls among the Gypsies*, 1915) and appear as important characters in many more, such as *The Clue in the Old Album* (1947), featuring girl sleuth Nancy Drew. In the absence of any discussion of immigration at all, the gypsy stands for all foreigners.

Gypsies seemed to pose a special threat to young girls because of their propensity to kidnap young girls and force them into their alien lifestyle. They were rootless, lawless, and did no regular work, making them the perfect villain for the Anglo-Saxon, Protestant focus of children's literature. Since gypsies both attracted and frightened young white protagonists, they represented not only fear of the immigrant but fear of and attraction to the many other changes in early-twentieth-century mores, like the emergence of the "modern woman." "Like other marginal groups, the alien gypsy becomes the 'other' in order that white middle-class women might define themselves" in ways that are both domestic and protected yet also adventuresome and independent.[57]

Any sort of race mixing that found Anglo-Americans marrying with African-Americans, Native Americans, or other "foreigners" received unequivocal disparagement. William Baker wrote in *The Boy Ranchers* (1934) that the Yagui Indians of Mexico "have blended with negroes, *degenerate* Spaniards and Mexicans until it is almost an insult to apply the name 'Indian' to them." They "live like beasts" and have "lost the ideals of their race, a dragged out remnant steeped in crime."[58]

Regionalism in Children's Literature

If American authors were not quick to recognize the unique cultural contributions of different ethnic groups to American life, they did enjoy highlighting the regional differences found within the country. So-called local color stories affirming America's regional diversity began appearing in children's literature in the latter half of the nineteenth century. However, well before this regional genre emerged, southerners upheld regional distinctiveness to the point of calling for southern books for southern children. The best-known journal of the old South, *DeBow's Review*, called for "southern school books" in a September 1852 edition. Current schoolbooks, it contended, "devote *two* pages to Connecticut onions and broomcorn and less than ten lines to Louisiana sugar." In particular, the editor resented disparaging remarks about slavery, "poor negroes," and "abolitionist poems." In addition, DeBow wished to promote southern industry, and book publishing seemed a lucrative possibility. The secessionist-minded economic conferences held in Memphis and in Charleston in the late 1850s also called for books written and published in the South.[59] Quite a few Confederate children's books did emerge during this brief period, although over 70 percent of them were textbooks, including the *Dixie Primer, The First Dixie Reader,* and *The Geographical Reader for the Dixie Children* (1863). Another small group of publications were catechisms and hymnbooks, but very little juvenile fiction emerged. *The Boys' and Girls' Stories of the War* (n.d.) consisted of five poorly written defenses of the Confederacy. A book of very sentimental poetry did include this rhyme:

> D is for Davis, oh, wide as the sea
> Shall the fame of our glorious President be
> And L stands for Lincoln,
> Oh, woe to his crown!
> "King Cotton," "King Cotton" is trampling him down.
> And U's for the Union
> A wreck on the sea!
> And V's for our Victory
> Bright as the sun,
> And W for Washington
> Soon to be won![60]

Following the Confederate surrender and the reestablishment of the Union, proponents of the New South anxiously sought to bind up, heal, and obliterate those distinctions between the regions. Both North and South found the period of reconstruction too difficult, and each region retreated from a commitment to healthy economics and politics in its own way. Joel Chandler Harris's *Uncle Remus* (discussed earlier) contributed to a sense that blacks and whites got along well in the new South and represents a southern attempt to put the war out of view. Popular juvenile author Joseph Altsheler typified the northern perspective that the war be best forgotten in *Before the Dawn: The Story of the Fall of Richmond* (1903). The two main characters, Confederate soldiers, meet on the road to Richmond at the end of the war. One applauds Grant's behavior after Appomattox: "[He] did everything he promised General Lee. He's the right sort all through—so is the Yankee army. I've got nothing against it. They never insulted us with a single word." Although they are saddened by the defeat of their forces, they hold no bitterness and even make a joke about the last days of the Confederacy.[61]

As authors began to remark that regional variations could be healthily contained within the national spirit, children's heroes expanded beyond a middle-class, town-based, familial environment. Characteristics of this genre include the use of dialect and the importance of the particularized setting for the plot. The frontier West became the most popular regional setting, although nostalgia persisted for a mythic old South. Noah Brooks popularized crossing the plains in *The Boy Emigrants* (1877), and Edward Eggleston set his popular story, *The Hoosier School Boy* (1883), in rural Indiana.[62] Such themes as bringing civilization to the frontier and "taming the wilderness" fit nicely with America's sense of cultural superiority and inventiveness. Likewise, these themes upheld the racial hierarchy that defined whiteness, whether middle class or struggling rural, as superior in the hierarchy of race that continued to define the United States into the twentieth century.

6

Idealized Realism, 1920–1950

It is hard to find a more turbulent era in American history than the three decades bracketed in this chapter. The Revolutionary era lent itself to more mythmaking; the Civil War era strengthened sectional divisions not yet fully healed. But the three decades after the World War I Armistice in 1918 ran the gamut of experience and were fraught with contradiction. Even to contemporaries, the twenties were heralded as the decade of prosperity: except for a brief recession in 1921, the economy grew rapidly throughout the decade, and family consumerism increased accordingly. Mass-circulation magazines and cheap novels flourished; even hardcover book sales increased through the efforts of the new Book-of-the-Month Club and the Literary Guild. All had to compete with the popularity of commercial radio and the mass distribution of films, but books sales remained strong. Seventy years of argument and agitation by women's rights advocates finally achieved the vote for women in 1920. The concept of the "new woman" that had emerged in the previous generation evolved into a boyish, fun-loving "flapper," and women continued to finish high school at higher rates than men; some earned college degrees and were able to enter a few professions.[1]

Yet the Roaring Twenties also saw some of the darkest aspects of American history. Plummeting agricultural prices devastated farmers, and the period between 1927 and 1929 saw both drought and then floods destroy thousands of acres of crops. Before the Great Depression hit the rest of the country, rural Americans faced foreclosures and evictions on a steady basis. Meanwhile, white southerners continued to enforce segregation; everywhere African-Americans were denied equal education, kept out of skilled laboring jobs, and bypassed for professional work. A steady diet of World War I propaganda had heightened American ethnocentrism to the extent that Congress set quotas on most immigration and excluded Asians altogether. President Calvin Coolidge signed the immigration restriction law, commenting that "America must be kept American." Articulating these nativist and racist ideas, a new version of the Ku Klux Klan organized at Stone Mountain, Georgia; it claimed five million members by the mid-twenties.[2]

The thirties brought problems of its own. Like the rest of the industrialized world, the United States spun into a major economic depression that spanned the entire decade. Franklin D. Roosevelt's various efforts to shore up business, restore employment, and keep people from literally starving certainly met with success, but unemployment never fell below 14 percent the entire decade; for minorities the figure topped 50 percent in certain regions. Children suffered nutritional deficits, and teenagers dropped out of school if any kind of work presented itself. Marriages and childbearing were postponed. Schools remained open in some cases only because teachers accepted vouchers or simply went without pay. With the coming of World War II in 1939 and America's entry in December 1941, the economy turned sharply upward, and soon almost anyone seeking work could find it (although women and minorities still endured wage discrimination). One horror had been exchanged for another.

Writing for children never ceased during this tumultuous time; rather, heightened professional interest led to the establishment of important new prizes in children's literature. The American Booksellers Association spearheaded the creation of Children's Book Week to encourage the sales of children's literature. To promote works of literary merit, in 1922 the Newbery Medal, named for the eighteenth-century publisher John Newbery, was created to honor the best American children's book. In 1937 a similar award named in honor of Randolph Caldecott was given for the best children's book illustrations. Mindful of consumer interest and disposable income, publishing companies established separate divisions for children's books to handle the volume of new titles produced. The *Horn Book Magazine* was founded in 1924 by Bertha Mahony solely to review children's books for librarians, teachers, and parents.[3] Anne Carroll Moore, head of the children's department of the New York Public Library, headed a movement to see that books written for children were critiqued with the same rigor previously reserved for adult fiction. This professional cadre of editors, librarians, and teachers argued for more literarily crafted works for young people while serving as gatekeepers on just what constituted quality fiction. They bolstered the prevailing ideology that childhood was a sacred time for children to enjoy life while still maintaining that basic character and values must be encouraged.

The construction of childhood that emerged in the early twentieth century no longer posited a naturally innocent child who would serve as a redeemer for a fallen world. But childhood, and particularly the nuclear family that nurtured children, was idealized and modeled with unceasing repetition in children's books. It was almost as if authors consciously sought to remove any unpleasantness of real life—whether discrimination against minorities, suffering and death, the consumerism of the twenties, or the effects of the Great Depression. In the face of an increasingly pluralistic culture, authors of children's books emphasized nostalgia and dominant-culture, middle-class themes. World War II rarely turned up as a subject for traditional children's literature until well after that traumatic event had passed. This is not to say that children's literature of the 1920s and 1930s sought to re-create the romanticized and sentimental world of Pollyanna or even Rebecca of Sunnybrook Farm. New authors sought to create more realistic settings, whether in the past or in a specific American region, such as a Wyoming ranch or a Florida swamp. They strove for exacting physical detail and attempted to realistically portray children's abilities and emotions. Yet the family setting into which this more realistic child was placed remained highly idealized. To create such a setting, authors employed several strategies.

Retreat to Another Era

In the somber reality of the Great Depression, two authors in particular sought to return their readers to earlier—and by implication, simpler and happier—times. Laura Ingalls Wilder (1867–1957) reconstructed her childhood memories into eight novels and produced one book about her husband's boyhood. Wilder had been a rural school teacher and a farm wife; she did some journalistic writing at the urging of her daughter. However, she was 65 years old and struggling financially when her first book, *The Little House in the Big Woods* (1932), was published. The Little House series loosely traces the Ingalls family's migrations from Wisconsin to Kansas, to Minnesota, and finally the Dakota Territory as Laura's father sought livelihood in various occupations across the Great Plains. Wilder believed that the personal character traits she learned growing up on the frontier were the same ones necessary to survive the ordeal of the Depression: resourcefulness, courage, frugality, integrity, and dependence on family.[4] *Little House on the Prairie* (1935) continued these themes, with Pa's restlessness determining the family's moves, even to the Indian Territory, where white settlers were not supposed to homestead. In *The Banks of Plum Creek* (1937), the Ingallses settle in Minnesota; here the challenges are not the weather and Indians but the more familiar fictional themes of sibling rivalry and school. *By the Shores of Silver Lake* (1939) introduces dramatic tension into the Ingallses' lives with a bout of scarlet fever that leaves Laura's sister Mary blind. Laura begins to teach school to bolster the family income. The Ingallses' financial fortunes—like those of the country as a whole—do not improve dramatically in the series.[5]

Several critics have compared the available historical record of the Ingalls family with Laura Wilder's reconstruction of it in her children's stories. She claimed her stories were "nothing but the truth," and many teachers and admirers have believed them to be accurate portrayals of frontier life. However, recent scholarship has found Wilder's construction of frontier life skewed to conform to the "frontier myth" that historian Frederick Jackson Turner used to hypothesize the American spirit of conquest, adventure, and individualism at the end of the nineteenth century. Scholar Anita Fellman argues that Wilder used her writing to "recast her past" by making herself the dominant personality in a family in which she "had played second fiddle to a smart, good, beautiful sister." She also elevated her financially plagued father into a paragon of patience, wisdom, and success.[6]

Both Fellman and William Holtz have illuminated the intricacies and depths of the working relationship between Laura Wilder and her daughter, Rose Wilder Lane. The latter was a professional journalist and author who guided her mother to produce her earliest publications, articles about being a farm wife. Rose rewrote one article "from beginning to end. . . . She revised the lead, cut out detail and reorganized the development." When her mother complained that it had become Rose's article, Rose said she was simply "teaching her mother how to write for a national audience." The article was accepted for publication. Holtz has brought scholarly attention to the extent to which Rose Wilder Lane helped create the Little House series, using Lane's published writing as well as her personal diaries as evidence. Lane encouraged her mother to put her memories into a story; "[I]f you find it easier to write it in the first person, write that way," she wrote to her mother. "I will change it to the third person, later." Rose promised not to tell anyone that she had "run the manuscript through my own typewriter," and it was she who successfully marketed the finished copy to Harper Brothers. The following year, Laura Wilder sent her daughter another manuscript she had written about her husband's New York boyhood. It had been rejected earlier; Rose Lane reworked it into a more idyllic story and got it accepted as *Farmer Boy* (1933). Several years later Lane wrote a synopsis for a short story set on the frontier called "The Hard Winter." Essentially the same plot appeared later in Wilder's Little House series in *The Long Winter*.[7]

Rose Wilder Lane wrote for several popular American magazines, including the *Saturday Evening Post, Harper's Monthly,* and the *Ladies' Home Journal;* she also wrote some novels, including a best-seller, *Let the Hurricane Roar* (1933). Based on frontier stories she had heard from Wilder, the book was both a paean to rugged individualism and a critique of New Deal economic policies. *Publisher's Weekly* advertised it as "the book that makes you proud to be an American!" (Lane intended an adult readership, but after about six months, Longmans began to advertise it as one of their "Junior Books."[8]) Like her mother, Lane was ideologically opposed to F.D.R's recovery programs. Both women painted the government as a meddling irritant in their fiction and stressed the importance of individual effort, both contemporaneously and in the past. Although one of Wilder's handwritten manuscripts details how the U.S. government offered to pay for her sister's tuition at the Iowa School for the Blind while the Wilders lived in the Dakota Territory, Rose Lane reconstructed this incident in *Little Town on the Prairie* to have

Laura take a job as a teacher to help pay for Mary's schooling. No matter how dire the family's straits became in the stories, Pa always managed to provide. The government didn't help. When Roosevelt approved agricultural subsidies during the Depression, Wilder quit the Democratic Party in protest. Years later, in 1993, Rose Lane claimed that her mother's books were intended as a criticism of the New Deal.[9]

As preoccupation with the New Deal gave way to America's entry into World War II, the rugged individualism and family isolation of Wilder's early books gave way to a heightened cooperation between neighbors, more communal activities, and outright expressions of patriotism. In *The Little Town on the Prairie* (1941), Wilder presents her own version of American history. She recounts a Fourth of July oration that relates in some detail how "a few barefoot Americans" had to fight the whole British army "and their hired Hessians and the murdering scalping redskinned savages that those fine gold-laced aristocrats turned loose on our settlements." At the public school exhibition, Wilder's part of the program covers American history only up to 1825, allowing her to forego discussion of Indian Removal, the Mexican-American War, the Civil War and reconstruction, and segregation. However, even limited to early history, Laura leaves out slavery, attacks on Indians, and other unpleasantness from her narrative.[10] Once again, Wilder fit her childhood memories to her—and the nation's—political ideology.

By setting her stories two generations in the past, Wilder could avoid the troublesome question of emerging feminism. The child Laura experiences some conflict with her mother over "lady-like behavior," but her crime is never more serious than riding bareback or refusing to wear a sunbonnet. In *These Happy Golden Years* (1945), as Laura plans her wedding to Almonzo Wilder, she says she will not "promise to obey." He asks her if she favors "women's rights," and she responds that she does not favor the vote for women. Her only objection to the word *obey* is that by using it she might forgo the right to use her own good judgment on some future occasion. To young readers in post–World War II America, Wilder implied that women need have no political interests.[11]

Although Wilder created far more interesting characters than had the early-nineteenth-century didactic writers, her message was little different from that of Lydia Maria Child or Jacob Abbott. After hearing a Fourth of July program, Laura ponders to herself:

> God is America's king. Americans won't obey any king on earth. Americans are free. That means they have to obey their own consciences. No king bosses Pa; he has to boss himself. Why . . . when I am a little older, Pa and Ma will stop telling me what to do. . . . I will have to make myself be good.[12]

Nor could Wilder escape some of the baser ethnocentric thinking of the 1930s, which in her children's novels manifests as hostility toward Native

Americans. When Laura first sees Indians in *Little House on the Prairie,* she describes them as "bold and fierce and terrible," and she later calls them "wild men." At another point, she portrays one visiting Indian as friendly and dignified but another as "dirty and scowling and mean." In the Dakota Territory, the settlers (including her father) assume they have a right to the land even though the government had set it aside for the natives. A neighbor of the Ingallses' comments, "Treaties or no treaties, the land belongs to folks that'll farm it. . . . They never do anything with this country themselves. . . . That's only common sense and justice."[13] Though perhaps accurately conveying the views of many settlers in 1870, Wilder does nothing in 1935 to correct these misconstructions of the reality of Indian land claims. While claiming to have truthfully presented her life in the Midwest in the late nineteenth century, Laura Ingalls Wilder, with the guiding collusion of her daughter, Rose Lane,

"Indians at the General Store," from Laura Ingalls Wilder, *The Long Winter,*
illustrated by Garth Williams (Harper, 1953)
*Pictures © 1953 by Garth Williams, renewed 1981; used by permission of
HarperCollins Publishers. This selection may not be re-illustrated.*

perpetuated and enhanced the myths of American individualism and exceptionalism while reinforcing a dying Victorian domesticity.

Carol Ryrie Brink (1895–1981) introduced a similar frontier heroine in the namesake of *Caddie Woodlawn* (1935). Like Laura Wilder, Brink drew on her memories of life in Idaho and on the shared memories of the Wisconsin aunt with whom she lived after age eight.[14] Brink's protagonist, however, takes a kinder view of the original inhabitants of Wisconsin. From the beginning of the book, Caddie and her brothers interact with the Indians and develop a particular friendship with one of them. When Caddie overhears neighbors talk of a surprise attack on the Indian village, she secretly rides out to warn them.[15] Here Brink seems to reflect a significant aspect of the 1930s, the time in which she wrote. A federal investigation of government policies toward Native American peoples, the Merriam Report of 1928, had found dire poverty and ineffectual boarding schools on the reservations. Reformers called for congressional action, resulting in the Indian Reorganization Act of 1934, also dubbed the "Indians' New Deal" because it recognized the validity of Native American traditions and culture.[16] Brink reflects this appreciation of natives and their culture.

Brink forced the gender-role question sharply by depicting Caddie as an 11-year-old tomboy engaging in a variety of humorous and dangerous activities with her two brothers. She fumes against her Boston-reared mother's attempts to make her more ladylike. The contrast between Caddie and her cousin Annabelle, a "delicate apparition" with "tiny buttoned shoes . . . tiny hat . . . velvet streamers floating out behind," proves too much for Caddie, and she takes the cousin on a hair-raising horseback ride during which Annabelle falls into the hay. Although her father always encouraged Caddie's outdoor activities, believing they would improve her frail health, this time she is severely reprimanded. Soon afterward, her father delivers one of the most famous lectures in children's literature, explaining that Caddie must act more like a lady. It is women, he intones,

> "who keep the world sweet and beautiful. Women's task is to teach men and boys gentleness and courtesy and love and kindness. It's a big task, too, Caddie. . . . A woman's work is something fine and noble to grow up to, and it is just as important as a man's. . . . No man could ever do it so well. . . . How about it Caddie? Have we run with the colts long enough?"[17]

Like Wilder, once Brink has set the disparity of roles before the reader, she reifies the dying Victorian sentiment that supported such dichotomized gender distinctions and has Caddie acquiesce to her father's dictum.

Both Wilder and Brink failed to give credence to the reality of female life on the frontier, a reality that saw many women performing male tasks with competence and satisfaction. Frontier women may have taken their pianos and sofas west with them, but they did not live in isolated Victorian parlors.

They could make soap and brand cattle, kill rabbits and mend fences, and still see themselves as ladies. But the expanded vision of frontier femininity remains largely unexplored by these authors.

Unlike Wilder and Brink, Marjorie Rawlings (1896–1953) did not set her novel in the 1870s to idealize the past. Rather, the starkly realistic setting for *The Yearling* (1938) keeps this adolescent novel from being saccharine. Rawlings lived much of her life at Cross Creek, a region she described as a community of seven families, five white and two black, living amid the rivers, swamps, clearings, and scrub of north Florida. Her editor Maxwell Perkins suggested that she write about a boy living in such a place, for "the best part of a man is a boy." She eventually took his idea to heart but wrote him that the book was definitely "*not* a story for boys, though some of them might enjoy it. It will be a story *about* a boy—a brief and tragic idyll of boyhood. . . . [I]t is important that no announcement ever be made, anywhere, that the book is a 'juvenile.' "[18] *The Yearling* came out in 1938 to much critical acclaim and won a Pulitzer Prize in 1939.

The setting of *The Yearling* reflects the austerity of Depression America, even though the story takes place on the Florida frontier in the 1870s. The plot centers on Jody Baxter, a boy living on an isolated Florida farm with his undemonstrative mother, Ora, and his financially struggling father, Penny, who becomes an invalid. Jody's pleasures increase dramatically with the adoption of a wild fawn. However, when the fawn grows up (and becomes a yearling), it ravages the family's crops. Penny Baxter orders his wife to shoot the deer; when she only wounds it, Jody must finish the job. He then lashes out angrily at his father and runs away. *The Yearling* works as a coming-of-age novel as Jody realizes that he must return to the farm and its painful memories.

Rawlings had perfected the local color genre in several sketches she had published in *Scribner's Magazine,* and these same powerful descriptions and her carefully wrought dialect enhance *The Yearling*'s power. In an essay she wrote for *College English,* Rawlings rejected the term "regional literature" and argued that she simply intended to write compelling stories: the setting was mere backdrop.[19] Because she knew and loved the scrub country and respected the poor whites who eked out a living there, Rawlings didn't need to idealize her characters. She let their foibles and strengths stand alone. Jody's idyllic boyhood is well tempered with death, pain, and loss—much more so than in either Wilder's or Brink's frontier stories.

More Realistic Family Stories

The family story, that quintessential Victorian genre, hung on into the twentieth century in more guises than merely stories set on the frontier by Wilder or Brink. The turmoil of the period between the two World Wars seemed to attract numerous writers who wanted to situate childhood experiences in the safe confines of a supportive family. Anne MacLeod has argued that the family stories of the 1920s did little to alter the Victorian ethos. They continued to stress Victorian values and domestic gentility; "poor but worthy 'naturally genteel' children were adopted or befriended by affluent gentlefolk." Sports stories and school stories also continued to promote the values of hard work and personal integrity. Both boys and girls learned independence and self-reliance in more realistic ways than earlier Victorian fiction had presented.[20]

In this sense, Dorothy Canfield Fisher's (1879–1958) *Understood Betsy* (1916) was ahead of its time. Fisher was already a successful writer for adults when this story of an orphan girl's maturation first appeared as a serial in *St. Nicholas* magazine. Fisher called her novel "a real juvenile, but one which perhaps might interest grown-ups," perhaps in the way that *Rebecca of Sunnybrook Farm* and *Pollyanna* were read across generational lines. Although the story of 10-year-old Elizabeth, her two maiden aunts in the Midwest, and her move to a warmer, more nurturing home with cousins in Vermont is narrated by Elizabeth herself, the message of the book is directed at parents. Fisher advocated a Montessori philosophy in teaching and parenting and had published two books on the subject. *Understood Betsy* provided a fictional vehicle to illustrate the transformation that supportive, child-centered parenting that taught self-reliance could produce. "Betsy's development from help-lessness and dependency to independence and responsibility" is chronicled in her physical move from one household to another.[21] In making the idealized family an adopted one, Fisher's plotting resembles the work of Kate Douglas Wiggin in *Rebecca of Sunnybrook Farm* (see chapter 4). Both women became activists on behalf of reformed parenting and schooling.

However, Wiggin and Fisher were exceptions. Most family stories of the late Victorian period through the 1920s featured a solid middle-American family who struggled to ensure their children a carefree childhood while still maintaining control over the inculcation of such virtues as discipline, honesty, and responsibility. By the 1930s, authors began to introduce greater realism into their stories through attention to detail, particularly regional settings. Characters, too, were drawn with far more realistic childlike attributes, language, and interests than earlier. Authors shifted the focus from children who had to triumph over adversity to the strength of relationships within the family. Stories narrowed to a constricted time frame: one year, one summer, one friendship.[22]

Even when authors broadened their perspectives to write about families in other countries, they stressed similarities to the American ideal, not differences, as in Kate Seredy's *The Good Master* (1935), set in Hungary, and Hilda Van Stockum's *The Cottage at Bantry Bay* (1938), about an Irish family.[23] Nonetheless, the idealization of the happy, industrious, understanding family was largely the same as in Louisa May Alcott's depiction 70 years earlier of the March family.

Actual family life in the years between the wars was as diverse as the burgeoning population of any major city: there were single-parent families, extended families, and homeless children; Protestant, Catholic, Jewish, and agnostic families; blacks, Native Americans, Italians, Mexicans, old New Englanders, and Germans, among others. Few families were untouched in some way by the Depression, not only in terms of reduced financial circumstances but also in having to relocate, having extended family move in, or foregoing college or even high school to work. Yet children's fiction portrayed family life almost exclusively as solvent, white, middle class, small town, and well adjusted.

Elizabeth Enright (1909–1968), niece of Frank Lloyd Wright and daughter of a cartoonist and an illustrator, was one of the few children's authors before World War II to illustrate her own books. Much of the delight of her stories lies in the graceful, simple drawings that accompany each book. Well published as an adult novelist and essayist, Enright is probably best remembered for her family stories for children. *Thimble Summer* (1938), *The Sea All around Us* (1940), the Melendy family series, and the Gone-Away books comprise her best-known children's works; *Thimble Summer* won the Newbery Award for 1939. The effects of the Depression are hinted at in this story of nine-year old Garnet Linden. She knows that her father sits up late in the kitchen, worrying about the drought's effect on his crops; she dreads bringing in the mail when she sees that it consists mostly of bills. Yet principally the story revolves around Garnet's various escapades, from being accidentally locked in the town library overnight to running away briefly to the nearest city when she feels unappreciated. Her anger is short lived, for she spends most of her time in the city buying presents for her family and having to hitchhike home for lack of cash. The overarching theme of the story is revealed early on as Garnet muses, " 'I have a nice mother. . . . I have a nice family.' It made her feel safe and warm to know she belonged to them and they to her."[24] Although both she and her brother feel confined by life on the farm, by the end of the book she has begun to treasure her discoveries there, and another youngster has moved in with the family who intends to become a farmer himself.

The Saturdays (1941) was the first of three books featuring the Melendy family: four children, their father, and their housekeeper who spend the summer holiday inventively. Enright consciously attempted to create realistic children, although she admitted in an essay that they might be "a little more reasonable and ingenious than live children are apt to be."[25] For example, the children pool their individual allowances so that once a month, each child can have $1.60 with which to do exactly what he or she wants, whether going to the circus or visiting the art museum. In *Then There Were Five* (1944), the Melendys take an orphan boy living with a problematic relative into the family circle. All of Enright's works but *The*

Saturdays have rural, idyllic settings in which children lead lives quite independent of adult interference. The care and support of family members and siblings is usually constantly evident; often the child develops a particularly strong bond with an older neighbor or relative. Each novel has a small focus: one child or one summer or one discovery, insulated from external reality, in which Depression or war are ever-present. The same ideals that permeate the frontier stories suffuse Enright's books: reliance on family for emotional support, inventiveness, honesty, and resilience. In Enright's idealized childhood, fears are present, but the overall message is that childhood should be a time of security, happiness, and exploration of the natural world. The most memorable Enright characters are girls: Garnet in *Thimble Summer,* Mab in *The Sea around Us,* the Melendy daughters. But they spend their time in activities similar to boys': games, explorations, and chores.[26] The reader encounters normal, well-adjusted, carefree children in Enright's work without either the Depression or the war intruding.

Eleanor Estes (1906–1988), children's librarian and author, created another ideal family, the Moffats, and set them in the small New England town of Cranbury. The Moffat series began in 1941, although the stories are set just before and during World War I. No hint of homefront activities, dislocation, or enlistments intrudes into the narrative until the final volume. Rather, it is the aura of the Depression that pervades the tone of Estes's works. Mrs. Moffat, a widow who takes in sewing to support her four children, cannot afford to keep the family home, and they are forced to move into smaller quarters. Nevertheless, she appears as the epitome of the perfect mother, never complaining, never losing patience with the children's misadventures (like their losing the purse on the way to buy coal on a winter's day), and seeing the humor in even the most trying circumstances. She always has time to hear about the children's activities, even if she cannot stop sewing to attend their schooltime functions. Estes reiterated the theme that happiness is to be found in simple pleasures and family activities; she set her kind of experiential wealth against the family's actual financial poverty. Unlike in earlier stories featuring poor families (such as *The Five Peppers and How They Grew*), no wealthy patron rescues the family from poverty; no lost fortune is recovered. Yet class differences, so apparent in the stories of the late nineteenth century, such as *Pollyanna,* do not figure into stories written after the Depression. For example, in *The Middle Mofatt* (1942) Jane plays constantly with the girl across the back fence; these neighbors are well-to-do, if their personal maid and fine furniture are any indication. Yet this class difference does not affect the girls' relationship.[27] Certainly the real financial upheavals many families experienced in the 1930s kept middle-class Americans from hasty judgment of others' poverty.

In an oft-cited passage, Estes describes Jane Moffat hanging by her knees "to look at things from between her legs, upside down. Everything had a different look altogether, a much cleaner, brighter look."[28] Compared to the world in 1942, the Moffat books certainly did present a "much cleaner and brighter look." It was this idealized world where children were protected from realities like death and war that most writers sought to convey. In *Rufus M* (1943), Estes makes wartime more visible: Sylvie, the older sister, works for the Red Cross, a trainload of soldiers leaves town, and the family starts a Victory garden.[29] But the war evokes no real emotions from the children or their mother.

Estes continued writing family stories after World War II. *Ginger Pye,* a 1952 Newbery winner based on Estes's own dog, Ginger, and *Pinky Pye* (1958) revolved around another middle-class family in Cranbury; *The Alley* (1964) centered on a whole neighborhood's escapades rather than on one family's. Like those of Enright, Estes's characters develop and act like real children; they are believable. But their family and small-town experiences set up an idealized set of relationships that isolate both the fictional children and the reader from the real world outside the family.

The two authors who attempted to represent American life more realistically between the wars did so through extensive and conscientious study of American regions and minority populations. Lois Lenski (1893–1974) wrote and illustrated almost 100 books, ranging from picture books for preschoolers to historical fiction to regional stories for different elementary-school ages. She also illustrated over 50 books written by such well-known writers as Kenneth Grahame and Cornelia Meigs. She won Newbery Honors several times, but her books were also criticized and censored. Her writing spanned the Great Depression through the 1970s.[30]

Lenski came of age just as America's exuberance, which had carried it into World War I, was then shattered, and people became disillusioned about the goodness of humanity and the innate superiority of democracy. While many writers made this disillusionment with humanity their theme, many other Americans adopted a "one-world" stance and worked for better international cooperation and understanding. Progressive thought, which always held that education was the key to social improvement, continued to influence public school reformers. Lenski too believed that education could produce sensitive and tolerant citizens and nations. In much of Lenski's juvenile fiction, this belief that as children learn about each other, they will appreciate those different from themselves takes precedence over any other message. Lenski's credo is reflected in a piece she wrote for the *Wilson Library Bulletin:*

> Before we can hope to understand foreign nations and live at peace with them, we must understand our own country and the different kinds of people who live in it. . . . I believe that children should be constructively taught a sympathetic approach to the strange person . . . by that I mean any person different from themselves in race, color, creed or background. Without such teaching, children are apt

to follow the crowd like sheep; they think in herds, because they haven't the courage for independent thinking and action. They are thoughtless—they can torture a newcomer . . . who is different. . . . It is these racial and regional differences that make our country unique.[31]

Lenski's didactic purpose in writing children's books is evident even in her historical fiction. *Phebe Fairchild: Her Book* (1936) follows a young girl who negotiates between the "frugal, self-sufficient rural life of northwestern Connecticut" and the more sophisticated and fashionable "social scene" of New Haven in about 1830. Implicit in the story is a message about understanding and accepting the manners and mores of different social groups. In another historical fiction, Lenski used a real historical event—the capture of Mary Jemison by the Seneca Indians in 1758—to create a sensitive portrayal of Native Americans and white settlers. Captive Mary Jemison settled into Seneca life and became a "white Indian," refusing to be "redeemed" back to her village, a sensational occurrence at the time. Lenski used *Indian Captive* (1937) to illustrate cultural adaptation and tolerance. Both books reflect an author highly concerned with how different groups understand each other and how far an individual can go to empathize with another culture. Taimi Ranta points out that *Indian Captive* was only a runner-up for the Newbery Medal; the award that year went instead to *Matchlock Gun,* a frontier story in which Indians are the stereotypical "painted, war-whooping, tomahawk-throwing savages" with which American historical writing for children was already resplendent.[32]

Lenski also wrote and illustrated two series that concentrated on different ethnic and regional cultures within the United States. Her Round-about-America books were designed as easy readers for younger children; the more difficult Regional series had slightly older children in mind. The latter began with *Bayou Suzette* (1943); by the time Lenski had finished the series two decades later, she had written stories set in rural north Florida, the North Carolina mountains, the Arkansas delta, farms in South Dakota and Iowa, Oklahoma oil fields, and San Francisco's Chinatown, among others.[33] Each book begins with an author's preface in which Lenski gives a brief history of the region or ethnic group she is portraying. Lenski took great pride in having personally visited all the locations she depicted, spending weeks talking with families, making notes on their speech patterns and expressions, and sketching them engaged in their daily activities. She then used her information to create fictional characters and fictional plots. Lois Kuznets has termed this method "faction": using facts to write fiction.[34] Unlike the historian, however, Lenski chose from available facts to make her plots work didactically. Most of her characters are poor, white, and not well educated, but Lenski does not turn them into victims. Children almost always reside in an intact, nuclear family and, even if working in the cotton fields or harvesting vegetables, enjoy outdoor games and family-centered activities.

Lenski was criticized for taking her realism too far, as in her 1945 work *Strawberry Girl*. The plot of this story involves the Boyer family, recently settled on a small farm in the Florida panhandle, planning to raise strawberries as a cash crop. The Slaters are squatters on neighboring land who graze their cattle on open land, resulting in continual run-ins with the Boyers. The children attempt to be friends, but Mrs. Slater resents the Boyers' finer possessions, and Mr. Slater's alcoholism embarrasses his children and deprives the family of needed cash. Lenski was criticized for including an alcoholic in a children's book. Yet Lenski introduces a visiting evangelist toward the end of the story, and Mr. Slater is converted to sobriety.

Lenski's own value system intrudes into her portrayals in other ways as well. The Slaters display every imaginable stereotypical image of the Florida "cracker": they are lazy, dirty people with uncombed hair; unpainted houses; boys who refuse to go to school. The Boyers, on the other hand, although poor, labor hard in the fields and save their cash for a new cookstove and an organ; the children excel at school, and Mrs. Boyer nurses the ill Mrs. Slater back to health despite being unwelcome in her house. In *Cotton in My Sack* (1949), Lenski focuses on a white sharecropping family who is told by the landowner that if they will only work hard, they can at least become tenants. Schooling is presented as the way to a better life, and the schoolteacher takes it upon herself to visit Joanda's family and give them flower seeds: " 'You'd have a pretty yard, if you'd clean it up and plant some flower beds,' Miss Fenton went on. . . . 'Why don't you rake up these tin cans and bottles and make your yard look nice?' " The economic inequities of the system, the realities of substandard housing, and little leisure time do not seem to have captured Lenski's attention.[35] The middle-class educator's voice intrudes into the fictional story.

Florence Crannell Means (1891–1980) grew up in a Baptist minister's family in which she was frequently exposed to people of other races and cultures and in which the unity of humankind was stressed. Her earliest books, written for young children, stressed Christian ethics as the undergirding principle of a democratic society. Beginning in 1929 with *Rafael and Consuelo,* she chose Mexican-American families, migrant workers, Asians in a small Colorado town, and Jewish families as her focal points. As she began writing for older children, her stories became more complex but continued to stress the diverse experiences of American children; they explored, in some fashion, the need for social acceptance of those who were different by virtue of race, class, ethnicity, or education. That Means was able to construct believable children from other cultures and make them interesting to a mainstream, middle-class, white readership without becoming preachy or didactic is a tribute to her writing and her research.

Means wrote of African-Americans in *Shuttered Windows* (1938) after visiting the Mather School for black girls in South Carolina. So insistent was she that she not misrepresent their feelings and goals that she went back to the school and read her chapters aloud to the senior English classes for their comments and suggestions. She also engaged in a lengthy exchange of letters with African-American author Arna Bontemps (discussed later) to talk about black dialect and to ask which black college might serve as the best setting for a future novel.[36] She traveled to the former Amache Assembly Center in Colorado to learn firsthand how the interned Japanese-Americans had lived; she interviewed many of the detainees and the staff of the center before completing her story of the Ohara family's experience in *The Moved-Outers* (1945). Several stays among the Navaho and Hopi peoples contributed to her descriptions of the mesas, the everyday lives of Indian women, and the sacred practices described in *Our Cup Is Broken* (1969), one of her later works.[37]

Florence Means situated her young protagonists in the middle of their families (except for some, who were portrayed in school settings). But her goal was not to idealize the womblike protection the family can provide from life's insults and wounds. Means was far more intent on portraying the diversity present within any ethnic or cultural group and on inviting the reader to recognize the shared humanity that crosses class and racial lines. Sarah in *Our Cup Is Broken* experiences the blossoming of first love like any teenage protagonist in the postwar era, but the young couple is separated by disapproving parents on both sides, for reasons of both race (she is Hopi, he is white) and class. The African-American students in *Shuttered Windows* come in all shades of skin tone, have varied cultural and educational backgrounds, and display a wide variety of speech patterns, hobbies, and talents. Other novels deal equally forthrightly with the lives of migrant workers (*Knock at the Door*) and Chicano families (*The House under the Hill* and *Teresita of the Valley*). In addition to being one of the first to consider diversity an important theme for children, Means wrote more evocatively about the Depression than any other author of the thirties. *A Penny for Luck* (1935) is set in a small, impoverished, played-out mining town in Colorado.[38]

By contemporary standards for writing about ethnic and racial groups, Means would be limited in her understanding of the pervasiveness of prejudice and naive in her "can't-we-all-get-along" philosophy. But when her works are put into the historical context of the 1930s and 1940s—a time of blatant discrimination against Mexican-Americans in the Southwest, institutionalized poverty on Indian reservations, legal segregation in the South, and flagrant disregard for Constitutional rights during the internment of Japanese-Americans—then her writing displays courage and prescience.

Young Children

Two picture books for young children deserve mention as reflections of the American mind during the Depression. Mabel Caroline Bragg (1870–1945), writing as Watty Piper, crafted the immortal *Little Engine That Could* (1930), which reflects the optimism with which Herbert Hoover and most business-men entered the Depression. Their initial reaction to plummeting employ-ment was to encourage individuals to be thrifty, to try hard to find other work, and to assist the needy by contributing to such philanthropic agencies as the Red Cross. They saw nothing basically wrong with the economic sys-tem. Like the Hoover administration, the Little Engine pulls slowly but steadily toward his goal, even over the most difficult terrain, doing what he has always done in a determined and steadfast manner.

The Little House (1942), written and illustrated by Virginia Lee Burton, who won a Caldecott Medal for her drawings, tells the story of urban encroachment from the perspective of a little house who witnessed all the changes. As the peaceful countryside gradually gave way to highways, hous-ing, and industry, the little house was moved further out so it could be in the countryside again. That house, wrote one critic, "represents something more than just rural life [under threat]. The house stands for a whole civilization and perhaps also, for the American Constitution," which some considered threatened first by Roosevelt's New Deal programs and then by the repres-sion of certain civil liberties during World War II. Certainly Americans did adapt to sprawling urbanization by moving to the suburbs.[39]

Syndicate Books

By the 1920s, the Stratemeyer Syndicate already had a successful track record in both appealing to a juvenile audience and reflecting the cultural changes in American society. Not driven by the critical approbation of the professionals in children's literature, Stratemeyer and his publisher were driven by their perceptions of the market. They rightly concluded that older children and adolescents wanted to read about believable peers in exciting situations. They also continued the nineteenth-century tradition of targeting books by gender. What was new by the early twentieth century were girls having adventures or careers, or solving mysteries.

The Ruth Fielding series, which had been introduced in 1913, presented young women with a new role model: someone who enjoyed her acting career. In mid-series, when Ruth marries her longtime boyfriend, she com-bines a professional career and a successful marriage. However, this new woman of the decade after 1910 experienced growing ambivalence about her dual role as the series continued. Scholar Carol Billman finds the heroine's behavior developing "to almost grotesque proportions at times in these last novels" to become "borderline schizophrenic." Fielding seems passionate about her profession yet acts increasingly subservient to her husband. The series ends in the midst of the Depression (1934), with Ruth declaring, "This time I'm home never more to roam," a typically dramatic statement for her but one that conveys society's ambivalence toward working women.[40] Female employment actually increased during the Depression, and it certainly sky-rocketed during World War II. But in either case, many women and almost all men perceived female work efforts as temporary solutions, either to boost family income or to bolster the war effort. When women married and had children in the years between the wars, social convention still dictated that they leave the workplace.

Nothing changed life in the twenties quite like the automobile. Freeing young people from the confines of courting in the parlor, the automobile truly brought dating into its own.[41] For the affluent young woman, it also provided the freedom of movement that only boys had experienced earlier. The allure of the automobile found its way into series books early. The Auto-mobile Girls series and the Motor Girls series both began in 1910; these books showed girls using technological know-how, exhibiting independence, and escaping domesticity for their own private peer-group experiences. And yet the stories did not suggest that the adventuresome girl reader throw off traditional role expectations. The series characters almost always had a romantic interest during their adventures, and they clearly desired nothing more than the "perfect marriage." One of the ads for the Motor Girls series read "Their adventure is exciting enough for the veriest tomboy, [but] the dis-tinctive feminine appeal is not lacking. . . . They design clothes, they shop for the newest hats, and they give marvelously clever parties." The role model and the message for girl readers seems at odds with itself—greater freedom but continued subordination. Indeed, that was the social construct girls' adventure fiction provided.[42] The Overland Riders series began in 1920, written by Grace Harlowe (a pseudonym). Here young married couples trav-eled the country on adventures, but the husbands seemed to have by far the most adventures; women derived their satisfaction from assisting them and from the coupled relationship itself.[43]

In 1927 the Stratemeyer Syndicate introduced the mystery genre via the Hardy Boys, which was soon followed by the even more popular Nancy Drew. Leslie McFarlane was the ghostwriter for most of the first 25 Hardy Boys books, the best titles of the series. The two Hardy brothers—tall, dark-haired, 16-year-old Frank and blond, curly-haired, younger brother Joe—solved mysteries that baffled even their father, a professional detective. Although one could be sure the boys would solve the mystery in the end, the Hardy Boys books contained multilevel plots with intriguing interconnected-ness. While this series was one of the first to concentrate on solving mysteries, there was still enough outdoor action and escape from threatening situations to qualify it as an adventure series as well.[44]

Best known of all the mystery solvers, of course, is Nancy Drew: pert, assertive, brilliant, and driving a blue roadster, no girl heroine has ever quite taken her place. The series, written pseudononymously by Carolyn Keene, began with *The Secret of the Old Clock* in 1930. Stratemeyer always kept the identities of his writers a secret, and for some time historians and critics believed that his daughter, Harriet Stratemeyer Adams, had created Nancy Drew. But a lawsuit in 1980 over the rights to previously published titles between Grosset and Dunlap (the original publisher) and Simon and Schuster (which bought the syndicate) revealed conclusively that journalist Mildred Wirt Benson had written 23 of the first thirty Nancy Drew titles. As she explained at a press conference some time later, all the authors who wrote for the Syndicate signed over their rights to the material, including the claim of authorship. So for stories that sold thousands of copies over dozens of years, Benson received a flat $125 for each book she wrote.[45] Benson also claimed that Stratemeyer did not like the way she developed the character of Nancy Drew, that he felt she was too "flip" and independent. But because the publishers did like it, she was asked to write more. When she left the syndicate, various authors drafted the books, based on outlines prepared by Stratemeyer or his daughter, Harriet.[46]

Nancy Drew quickly became the "reigning queen of the juvenile formula fiction world," outselling every other children's book title on the market by 1934.[47] The popularity and long-lasting appeal of this character have intrigued popular-culture students. On the one hand, Drew embodies the kind of privilege and unfettered femininity that young women envied: she wore fashionable clothes, employed polished manners at parties and dances, had a steady boyfriend, drove her own convertible wherever she wished, didn't have to work, and never performed household chores because her family employed a housekeeper.[48] In addition, although she had two bosom "chums" and a boyfriend, she didn't attend school. On the other hand, she embodied a whole host of characteristics usually associated with males: intellect, logical reasoning, tenacity, sports accomplishments, high-speed driving skills, and even the ability to throw a punch when necessary. She was so competent that her lawyer father sometimes asked for her advice, saying that "she was a more helpful partner to him in his work than any man he could pick from the legal talent of the country."[49] The role reversal in which she engages applies only to Nancy Drew; her girlfriends display all the traditional female attributes. Even her boyfriend, Ned, intones, "You tell me what to do and I'll obey orders with no questions asked." Anne Scott MacLeod concludes that Drew's appeal was based on her autonomy and her "largely inadvertent feminism." That is, she "countered every stereotype of 'feminine' weakness, including such standard fictional attributes as frivolity, vanity, squeamishness, and irrationality, quite as much as dependence and incompetence."[50]

The syndicate had found a formula that worked; Nancy Drew plots changed little through the decades, with three exceptions. First, several scholars have noted that Stratemeyer's original outline and character sketch called for a more traditional female hero. In the first book, Nancy is locked in a closet by the crook, and she is "too frightened to think logically. She beat frantically upon the door with her fists. . . . At last, exhausted . . . , she fell down upon the floor, a dejected, crushed little figure."[51] That was the first and last time Nancy Drew exhibited defeat, although she had many close calls with danger. Mildred Wirt Benson created a more self-confident if less realistic heroine after that. When Harriet Adams took over outlining the plots, she said she found Nancy "too bold and bossy" and tried to tone down her independence, producing some conflict with Benson. Adams enlarged the role of the housekeeper, Mrs. Gruen, and introduced Nancy's two female friends. Benson was later to say of Adams, "She was . . . refined. I was a rough-and-tumble newspaper person. . . . We just had two different Nancys [in mind]."[52]

Second, in 1959 the publishers undertook major revisions of 34 of the series books to eliminate racial and ethnic slurs and stereotyping that by then had become offensive to many readers. The Nancy Drew books often contain one African-American caretaker, laborer, or porter. In *The Secret of the Old Clock,* the black caretaker at a cottage Nancy visits is stereotypically portrayed as drunk, lying, and unreliable. He has a police record; he "rolls his eyes" and speaks in thick dialect; he refers to himself as a "black boy," belying his middle-age status. In *The Hidden Staircase* (1930), Nancy describes a black woman: "I never saw a more surly looking creature. She looks positively vicious." The writer also portrays the woman as fat and slovenly and as speaking in dialect.[53] Chapter 5 discussed the frequent use of gypsies in series books to stand for that which is alien, foreign, and evil. In *The Clue in the Old Album* (1947), Nancy is kidnapped by a band of gypsies as she is tracking a handbag thief with "mottled complexion and piercing black eyes." The evilness of these gypsies even includes an arranged marriage for a 14-year-old girl.[54] As these and other stereotypes disappeared from later books, the earlier stories were rewritten, although not to describe racial and ethnic minorities as contributors to mainstream America; they were simply eliminated altogether. The African-American caretaker just described was turned into a white working-class custodian who helped Nancy solve the crime.[55]

These 1959 revisions also simplified and streamlined the plots. Diana Beeson and Bonnie Brennan agree that in the process of updating the plots, "Nancy's independent character is softened and . . . she relies much more heavily upon others for help and guidance." Originally Nancy had solved most mysteries virtually on her own and went to the police only to have the criminal apprehended; in the rewritten books, Nancy relies on advice from her housekeeper and works much more closely with police to track down criminals. By 1959, it had become unacceptable for her to work "outside the law" or to be so completely independent minded.[56]

The quality of the mysteries Nancy Drew solves also contributes to the immense popularity of these books. Although she herself is not a romantic or "feminine" character, the plots ooze romanticism. As Deidre Johnson has observed, even "her 'clues' are dainty mementos—scarlet slippers, ivory charms, and the like." Her sleuthing takes place in a very feminine world of Victorian mansions, dances and dinner parties, old estates, and tea shops. She is often restoring heirlooms, rescuing women's purses or possessions, and generally maintaining the status quo.[57]

Nancy Drew, "girl sleuth," spawned numerous imitators, almost all built on the same formula of independent, attractive, clever girls tracking criminals, thwarting danger, and yet never giving up their visible feminine attributes. The Stratemeyer Syndicate even spun out its own imitators, the Kay Tacey books (1934–1942) and the Dana Girls series (1934–1980s). Judy Bolton, less glamorous than Nancy Drew, moved from age 15 in the first book (1932) through age 22 (1967), solving mysteries through perseverance and intelligence. Unlike Nancy Drew, she aged and married, although her husband worked for the F.B.I. and frequently crossed paths with Judy as she was unraveling a mystery. Unlike the earlier Ruth Fielding series, marriage did not present insurmountable difficulties to the professional woman in this later series.[58] In a perceptive essay entitled "Nancy Drew and Her Rivals— No Contest," Anne Scott MacLeod analyzes why the imitators never succeeded in displacing the popularity of the Drew novels and concludes that

> Nancy Drew is the very embodiment of every girl's deepest yearning. As an image that combines the fundamental impulse of feminism with utter conventionality, she represents a wish that . . . is . . . felt at some level by every woman faced with the disadvantages of her sex.[59]

African-Americans

The Depression and World War II brought little respite from the stereotypical portrayal of African-Americans described in chapter 5. It was not as if white writers were unaware of the bigotry and employment discrimination that faced people of color. Early in the 1930s the Urban League organized boycotts in major American cities under the slogan "Don't Shop Where You Can't Work." As America geared up for possible war in 1941, A. Philip Randolph, president of the Brotherhood of Sleeping Car Porters, prepared to stage a massive protest march on Washington, D.C., if President Roosevelt did not act to prohibit racial discrimination in the military and in the defense industry.[60] Thousands of black sharecroppers and tenant farmers left southern plantations for higher wages in urban centers, especially St. Louis, Detroit, and West Coast cities. Meanwhile a handful of African-Americans educated at elite ivy-league universities, as well as the many graduates of such historically black schools as Fisk University, Howard University, Meharry Medical College, and many others, helped create a flourishing black professional class in America's cities. W.E.B. Du Bois's *Crisis* brought the best African-American poets and essayists to public view.

Yet children's fiction carried on as if all persons of African descent worked in the fields or as domestic servants and spoke with a thick dialect infused with humorous slang. When the Bobbsey twins embarked on a southern vacation, Flossie commented on the "cute" former-slave cabins still inhabited by black sharecroppers. The twins joined the "pickaninnies" in the cotton fields, and Bert won the prize for picking the most cotton (presumably cotton-picking took no skill, and besides, blacks were lazy). " 'They must like their work,' said Nan. 'They seem so happy.' 'Cotton picking is healthful exercise,' smiled the plantation owner."[61] In the Nancy Drew series, there are 17 African-Americans in the first 18 books; all work as servants in white families. When Nancy traveled to the South, the novel perpetuated a *Gone with the Wind* myth; one southern man says of the family's cook, "Beulah's a rare person. She sort of lives in the past, and is very much like her mother, who worked for my mother. She imitates her in everything." In another book, *The Mystery at Lilac Inn,* Nancy set out to interview candidates for housekeeper. The only person sent by the employment agency was black: "She was dirty and slovenly in appearance and had an unpleasant way of shuffling her feet when she walked."

Racially offensive matter was not limited to series books. The 1946 Caldecott Medal winner, *The Rooster Crows: A Book of American Rhymes and Jingles,* with illustrations by Maud and Miska Petersham, featured "cherubic" white children throughout the entire text, and four pages of illustrations were devoted to deformed-looking black children sitting by a "dilapidated cabin with a black, gun-toting barefoot adult." (After 18 years of complaints, the publisher decided to eliminate, not improve, the illustrations of black children.[62]) *Little Brown Koko* (1940), written by Blanche Seale Hunt, related some 22 stories about a small African-American child, most of which centered on his voracious appetite and his penchant for avoiding the chores his mother assigned. The accompanying illustrations feature her as a stereotypical mammy, and Koko has the oversize lips and kinky hair common in works created early in the century.

Ever since NAACP official Mary White Ovington had written *Hazel* (1913) and W.E.B. Du Bois had begun the *Brownies' Book* magazine (1919), thoughtful African-Americans sought avenues to create children's literature that would be read by black and white children alike. Both groups could profit from seeing the rich varieties of black family experience and from learning about high-achieving African-American men and women and their contributions to American life. Black authors had difficulty finding publishers; Carter G. Woodson even formed his own publishing company so authentic stories and histories of African-Americans would be available. A few major companies, such as Alfred E. Knopf and Harper and Brothers, began to publish some of the popular writers who emerged during the Harlem Renaissance.[63]

The Harlem Renaissance, with its ebullient outpouring of literature based on the black American experience by such authors as James Weldon Johnson,

Langston Hughes, and Claude McKay, influenced a small stream of writing for children as well. Arna Bontemps (1902–1973) was taken by his father from his native Louisiana to grow up "less southern and less Negro" in California. After college he moved to Harlem during the twenties to teach and write, and he later penned his memoirs and combined them with essays in *The Harlem Renaissance Remembered* (1972). His most popular adult novel, *Black Thunder* (1936), is based on Gabriel Prosser's famous slave rebellion in Virginia in 1800. Bontemps left Harlem during the Depression to teach in Alabama and began a 42-year correspondence with Langston Hughes.

Of his Harlem days, Bontemps wrote that "I began to suspect that it was fruitless for a Negro in the United States to address serious writing to my generation, and I began to consider the alternative of trying to reach young readers not yet hardened or grown insensitive to man's inhumanity to man." He and Hughes collaborated on *Popo and Fifina: Children of Haiti* (1932). The book was well received critically; an early review in the *New York Times* lamented that "Popo and Fifina prompt us to wish that all our travel books for children might be written by poets." In the story, which follows the children on their daily activities, contains "rich descriptive passages" and strong black characters who interact with the children.[64]

Three children's books that grew out of Bontemps's Alabama experiences are worth noting, for they each attempt to portray poor southern black children in a nonstereotypical, realistic way. *You Can't Pet a Possum* (1934) is about Shine Boy and his attempt to convince his grandmother to allow him to keep a stray dog. Bontemps captures the warmth as well as the misery of sharecropping families, and although he uses slang expressions to convey their southern setting, his use of dialect is minimal, just enough to indicate southernness, if not race. *Sad-Faced Boy* (1937) is notable for its evocation of southerners' feelings of being lost and overwhelmed in Harlem; *Lonesome Boy* (1955) is the coming-of-age story of a black boy in New Orleans who wants to become a jazz trumpeter. Bubber's Grandpa is the wise adult whose counsel is rejected as Bubber goes his own way. "You better mind how you blow that horn, sonny boy. You better mind," Grandpa warns him, and in a fantasy/dream sequence, Bubber finds himself playing for the devil. That experience dissuades him from seeking fame, and he returns home.[65]

Because Bontemps chose southern settings and poor farm families, he didn't depart from stereotyping as much as one wishes. His children are often barefoot and love to eat, and in the latter two books the protagonists play musical instruments quite naturally. These are stories written principally for a white audience; black culture is not misrepresented, but it is presented in a familiar and nonthreatening form. Middle-class white children just might recognize in these characters the same worries and struggles that they themselves experience. For example, in *The Sad-Faced Boy*, three Alabama boys hop a freight train to New York to visit their uncle in Harlem. In the midst of getting lost and several other adventures, they form a band (the Dozier Brothers), which performs in office buildings for small change. When one of the boys gets sick, the other two draft an unwilling neighbor, Abe Bergman, and blacken his face, minstrel-style, so they can continue their music making. No one mentions that he is white and Jewish, only that "he don't look like a Dozier Brother."[66] Bontemps evoked an image—the minstrel—that whites understood, but he used it in his own construction of humor.

Like many African-Americans, Bontemps believed that America's fight for the ideals of freedom and democracy in World War II would open up educational and vocational opportunities for people of color. Consequently he devoted considerable energy to also producing biographies and nonfiction designed to inform and inspire *black* youth. In addition to individual biographies on noted black Americans, he published two collections in which more ordinary African-Americans excel in their chosen vocations: *We Have Tomorrow* (1945) and *100 Years of Negro Freedom* (1961).

World War II and the Holocaust

Nothing in the first half of the twentieth century has shattered idealism and destroyed innocence quite like World War II. The philosophical, psychological, and sociological implications of the war set into place a new construction of childhood in America and changed dramatically the nature of children's literature. But none of that happened *during* the war, only after it. The war years themselves were barely reflected in the children's literature of the time, as evidenced by the popular works of Elizabeth Enright and Eleanor Estes, discussed previously. Most children's stories took place as if nothing were very different. Scholar Caroline Hunt has suggested that some authors "turn[ed] to fantasy in their resolute exclusion of wartime reality. . . . [Others] retain[ed] an uneasy normalcy but still exclude[d] actual mention of the war."[67] In escape to fantasy, Hunt has in mind such animal stories as Walter Farley's *The Black Stallion* (1941) and its sequels and Mary O'Hara's *My Friend Flicka* (1943). One might also include the Curious George books for young readers, introduced by H. A. Rey (1898–1977) and Margret Rey (1906–) in 1942. Although the Reys were refugees from Nazi Germany, their popular books ignored the war; each book focused on a single adventure of George, who was a "good little monkey, but he was always curious." Adults merely reacted to his escapades, and his owner was known only as "the man."

Some stories that evade any discussion of the looming war have already been discussed: the Moffat series and the Melendy family stories. In addition, the high school story, usually featuring an adolescent's struggle with popularity, dating, and personal issues, became very popular with older children and teenagers. Maureen Daly (1922–) was a sophomore in college when she wrote *Seventeenth Summer* (1942), a sensitive story about one young woman's struggle to discover "true love." The story is engaging and carefully written, but the fantasy quality of this one "eternal summer" precludes the possibility of anything so ugly as war intruding. Even though her male acquaintances are 18, there is no mention of the draft; even a Fourth of July parade fails to include anyone in uniform.[68]

Not the war itself but the ideological principals of democracy and fair play pervade many of the adolescent sports stories of John Tunis (1889–1975). A fear of fascism permeated American society in the 1930s, and American educators lauded the value of civics or government courses as antidotes. Tunis held firmly to the conviction that athletics, especially team sports, formed character, responsibility, cooperation, and democratic spirit. Like the war, sports were democratically based on merit and demanded teamwork and courage. Tunis built his plots more around the inner struggles of athletes to "do the right thing" rather than on the fitness the games promoted. His first major success, *Iron Duke* (1938), was intended as an adult novel about a first-year college athlete. Editors at Harcourt, Brace persuaded him to let them market it as a "juvenile," and his career as a children's writer took root.[69]

Read today, John Tunis's adolescent novels are more valuable for the microscope Tunis trains on discrimination, bigotry, and prejudice than for their sports action. Whether Tunis realized it or not, the war focused attention on the same social issues, which became the defining issues of the 1950s and 1960s. In *The All-American* (1942), Tunis presents these concerns in two ways. The hero feels ashamed and guilty for deliberately injuring a football opponent who is Jewish. Later in the story, after the hero has transferred to another school and team, he rallies his teammates to decline to play a game against a southern school for which they must temporarily banish their African-American player. When *The All-American* appeared, the president was attempting, through Executive Order 8802, to eliminate discrimination in the military and defense plants. *The Keystone Kids* (1943) featured a Jewish baseball catcher who suffered such slurs as "Buglenose" and "yellow kike"; the team's young manager felt compelled to stand up for the catcher against all the other players, including his brother. Tunis emphasized the importance of rules and fairness in the 1944 *Yea! Wildcats,* in which a basketball coach had to dismiss key players for breaking training, even though parents and townspeople sought to override his decision. In an indirect slap at totalitarianism and mob rule, the coach prevails and shapes a competitive team without any star players.[70] Tunis's concern for the fair and equitable treatment of all citizens reflects America's overriding ideology about its participation in the war. (Well after the war, Tunis wrote several excellent World War II novels, including *Silence over Dunkerque,* 1962.)

Children were shielded from the reality of war in children's fiction but had no such protection in real life. Of course, American children did not view the war firsthand, as did their European and Asian counterparts. But historian

William Tuttle, who collected thousands of remembrances from persons who were children during the war, found that these individuals retained lifelong impressions of violence, death, disfigurement, and starvation from seeing newsreels at local movie theaters, looking at the photographs in *Life* magazine, and listening intently to the radio.[71]

Hunt theorizes that adults hoped the war would be short lived and that it would not intrude too directly on children's lives. By 1943 or 1944 that optimism was probably no longer tenable, and war themes became apparent in a few works. *Johnny Tremain* (1944) is the fictional story of a boy apprentice drawn into support for the American Revolution. This historical setting

Illustration by Lynd Ward from *Johnny Tremain* by Esther Forbes © 1943 by Esther Forbes Hoskins, © renewed 1971 by Linwood M. Erskine, Jr., Executor of the Estate of Esther Forbes Hoskins. Reprinted by permission of Houghton Mifflin Co. All rights reserved.

allowed author Esther Forbes to create a subtheme of patriotism and to reiterate the need for "common people" to take up the cause of liberty even as she described the places and emotions of a much earlier conflict. Forbes recreated 1770s Boston and peopled it with real historical personages, including James Otis and Samuel Adams, using the extensive historical research she collected for her Pulitzer Prize–winning adult work, *Paul Revere and the World He Lived In.* A few years after *Johnny Tremain,* Forbes wrote a children's biography of Paul Revere.[72]

Forbes indicated that originally she had planned for Johnny to be a neutral observer of the fight for independence, but when the Japanese bombed Pearl Harbor in 1941, she concluded that there was no such thing as neutrality in wartime. Consequently she restructured the plot so that Johnny became a patriot, and the subtext becomes clear. Johnny's adventures, acquaintances, and daily activities share the stage with a pervasive call to principles and patriotism. He suffers a severe injury to his hand that cuts short his hopes of becoming a craftsman, but he finds he can still aid the war effort. Late in the book, as he lies in bed on Sunday morning listening to the peal of church bells, Johnny muses,

> He had heard them clanging furiously for fire, crying fiercely to call out the Sons of Liberty. He had heard them toll for the dead, rejoice when some unpopular act had been repealed, and shudder with bronze rage at tyranny. . . . but he had never loved them more than on Lord's Days when . . . the soft bells said "We are at peace."[73]

Such were America's deepest hopes in 1944 as well. Johnny's message to young readers during the war was twofold: just as he had survived a critical injury, they too would survive and overcome the war, but the cause justified giving up one's life if that became necessary.

Forbes's interpretation of the Revolution reflects the ideological slant of a much earlier generation of historians. The so-called Whig school of thought believed that the Revolution was based on the principles of Enlightenment philosophy, that is, the inherent natural rights of human beings and the "social contract" they make among themselves to create a government. For example, in *Johnny Tremain,* James Otis presides over a meeting of the Sons of Liberty. He rhetorically asks, "For what will we fight?" only to have Samuel Adams reply, "[W]e will fight for the rights of America. England cannot take our money away by taxes." "No, no. For something more important than the pocketbooks of our American citizens. . . . There shall be no more tyranny. . . . A man shall choose who it is shall rule over him."[74] By the time Forbes wrote *Johnny Tremain,* in 1942, professional historians had moved beyond this ideological explanation of the conflict to a more nuanced and multidimensional understanding of the causes of the Revolution. Progressive historians had examined the economic vested interests of Revolutionary leaders, and historians of the imperialist school had shown the logic of Parliament's decrees and the sympathy toward the Crown that prevailed in much of the colonies. Though acknowledging that such sentiment might have existed, as in Sam Adams's comment just quoted, Forbes held firmly to the Whig patriotic stance. Leonard Wibberly argues that *Johnny Tremain* "keeps alive the American myth that . . . our Revolution established certain inalienable rights for people, which if preserved would protect mankind from tyranny in all the centuries ahead."[75]

Current historical thought finds such blatant oversimplification of the causes of the Revolution not only disturbing for its prowar stance but false and misleading as well. It ignores the indifference on the part of a great many colonists regarding the break with England and fails to see the very unrevolutionary social consequences of independence, such as the continuation of franchise restrictions, slavery, and the slave trade. Forbes's interpretation of the Revolution makes sense as a statement about patriotism only in 1942. It is ahistorical in understanding the Revolution but quite contemporary in reflecting American enthusiasm for the current war.

Florence Crannell Means's regional fiction (discussed previously) contained one momentous World War II topic: the incarceration of both Japanese citizens residing in America (Issei) and American citizens of Japanese heritage (Nisei) in "processing centers" and "internment camps" for the duration of the war. At the beginning of *The Moved-Outers* (1945), Sue Ohara appears to be any California teenager, discussing school activities with her friends and writing to her brother, in the U.S. Army. But after Pearl Harbor, her life is drastically altered. Because of the Oharas' Japanese ancestry, Sue's father is immediately imprisoned by the F.B.I., and she and her brother leave their high school for a detention center, all their belongings hurriedly put into storage. Hopes for college, managing the family nursery business, and other trappings of middle-class life are put on hold for the duration of the war. Because of her on-site research and personal interviews, Florence Means convincingly conveyed the primitive conditions at Santa Anna detention center, hastily created at the famous California racecourse. The bare-bones housing in former stables, the mix of all economic classes and educational levels in the camps, the energy with which the detainees set up schools, activity centers, and musical performances, and the steadfast American patriotism of most of the inhabitants permeates the novel. Means keeps the novel from being too dark with Mr. Ohara's release from detention to rejoin the family and by having Sue leave the camp to take a job on the "outside" and attend college. Yet the depiction of Sue as a typical teenager intensifies the disruption of the camp experience; the oldest brother is killed in action; Kim enters the army in an all-Nisei unit; and the parents do not know when they can resume a normal life. Unlike most children's fiction, there is no happy ending for *The Moved-Outers*.[76]

Means's depiction of the country's constitutionally questionable actions was evenhanded. She never criticized the removal decision but merely highlighted the suffering it caused for so many innocent civilians. She shows Kim tempted by the anti-American "gang" at Amache Center but has him shed his bitterness and resume his "Americanism." The book appeared at about the time the United States was closing its detention camps, although the war continued. Powerful voices lobbied Congress to keep Japanese-Americans off the West Coast; hiring discrimination against Asians persisted. *The Moved-Outers* was not universally praised, and some libraries refused to buy it. Means's reminder of this tragedy came far ahead of the time when Americans would feel guilty over this issue of internment; in 1983 a class-action suit by survivors of these camps resulted in monetary restitution for their losses.[77]

Equally surprising in its forthright theme of discrimination is Eleanor Estes's *The Hundred Dresses* (1944). In this simply told, simply illustrated (by Louis Slobodkin) tale, a poor Polish girl, Wanda Petronski, is the butt of much teasing by the other girls in Miss Mason's class because she wears the same faded dress to school each day. Yet Wanda claims that she has "a hundred dresses" at home in her closet, which causes the girls to ridicule her even more. When Miss Mason announces a contest for the best drawings in the class (girls are to draw dresses, while boys draw motor boats), Peggy, the most popular girl in the class and the leader of Wanda's persecution, is sure she will win. But Wanda, who submits 100 drawings to the contest, each remarkably colorful and original, wins the medal. The winner cannot receive her prize, however, for her father has removed her from school, sending a note that says in part, "We move away to big city. No more holler Polack. No more ask why funny name."[78] The offending girls seek to make amends by going to the Petronski home, only to find that the family has indeed moved. They decide to write Wanda a letter, telling her about the prize, marking a large "Forward" on the envelope. Some weeks later they receive a reply. Wanda asks that each girl be given one of her drawings, drawings that replicate their features precisely. Maddie comes to realize that, through all the exclusion and teasing, Wanda liked the girls anyway. The book ends without any explicitly stated moral but with Maddie having gained a clear understanding of how cruel she has been.

The discrimination that children often practice against someone who is different, who is outside the clique, is presented without comment. Unlike earlier fiction, no adult intervenes to lecture the persecutors on their Christian duty of kindness or on the moral imperative of friendship. When Maddie feels real remorse, it is too late to make any difference, and the book ends with her wondering if she will feel guilty "forever." Wanda Petronski is described by Estes as "very quiet," with feet "usually caked with dry mud." She sat in the back of the room, "where the rough boys who did not make good marks . . . sat." She lived in the poorest part of town, and she "didn't have any friends. She came to school alone and went home alone."[79]

The one descriptor that is never used for Wanda is "Jewish," and yet that subtext is an obvious one in a book that appeared in 1944. Americans were aware of the Nazis' systematic efforts to ghettoize and then to deport Jews from the mid-1930s on. By late 1942, the U.S. State Department acknowledged what many Jewish-Americans had been claiming: that the systematic elimination of Jews was being carried out in gas ovens at the so-called work camps. Meanwhile, anti-Semitic hiring and housing practices were prevalent in American cities.[80] Like American guilt over the Holocaust and over those Jews who managed to escape Germany but were refused entrance into the United States, the offending classmates had no way to apologize or retract their exclusion of Wanda. The one person who had the power to stop Wanda's persecution, Miss Mason, did nothing. When she receives Mr. Petronski's letter, she tells the class, "[T]his is a very unfortunate thing to have happen. Unfortunate and sad, both. And I want you all to think about it." Like Maddie, who "felt sad because she knew she would never see the little tight-lipped Polish girl again and couldn't ever really make things right between them," so too the United States would have to live with its guilt "forever."[81] It had failed to act when it could have. Estes's social commentary in a "simple" children's book is amazing.

Henry Gregor Felsen (1916–) wrote several adventure books for children tied much more closely to the war, such as *Navy Diver* (1942) and *Submarine Sailor* (1943). But his most unusual war story was *Struggle Is Our Brother* (1945), set in the Ukraine. Other books about the suffering and dislocation of European children during wartime did not appear for several decades. Felsen's propagandistic dedication was to "the boys and girls in the countries invaded by the Nazis, who have given their lives that boys and girls who read this book might live." In addition, a few nonfiction war stories appeared for children, although for the most part these books belonged to the Landmark Book series, which began in 1955.

The only other children's books to address World War II directly during wartime were some of the Syndicate or pulp books. Like their predecessors, the series books about World War II relied heavily on formulaic situations, heavy patriotism, and stereotyping of the enemy. R. Sidney Bowen (a pseudonym) took his teenage protagonist Dave Dawson through a whole series of adventures set in almost all the various important battles of the war: Dunkirk, Libya, Singapore, the Russian Front, Gaudalcanal, and the air war over Britain.[82] Every book ends with an Allied victory after daring and courageous efforts by the young patriots. Dawson not only disdained the enemy (whichever one he was fighting at the time) but he also disparaged them. Of course, Asians made an easier target for contempt than Germans, who were also Anglo-Saxon and not so easily stereotyped by race. In Singapore, he found the Chinese cowardly and asserted that "men who once had claimed kinship with the white races but had sunk so low . . . were no longer any part of a white man's world." At another point, he referred to "hordes and hordes of little brown rats [who] were going to spring savagely at white men's throats."[83] Because his stereotyping fit exactly with public prejudices, Dave Dawson was immensely popular during the war.

Likewise, the Cherry Ames, Nurse series brought the patriotism of wartime to a young female audience. Helen Wells was hired by Grosset and Dunlap to create a career "girl" who solved mysteries and could incorporate the homefront enthusiasm to win the war into the plot. *Cherry Ames, Army Nurse* (1944) left her "own gay little room" to do her part for the war. "If thousands of men were to be healed and returned to battle . . . *if we were to win,* Cherry wished she could cry out to other girls . . . how desperately nurses were needed." Helen Wells's character meshed nicely with the efforts of the U.S. government to get women into factories, hospitals, and supply stations. Even though working women seemed to be a large and expanding market during wartime, the series writers were careful to preserve traditional gender-role distinctions. Cherry consistently defers to medical doctors, noting that "any nurse who tries to play doctor isn't a very responsible nurse."[84] After the war, the Cherry Ames series continued to follow her nursing career until she married a doctor whom she met in the first book of the series.

In the years between the wars, American children's fiction viewed the child as participant in a special, protected, happy stage of life into which the realities of war, discrimination, poverty, and dislocation should not enter. Family-centered stories predominated, whether set nostalgically in the past or set in the present. Series books from the Stratemeyer Syndicate introduced mysteries, travel adventure, and sports into their plots, but they portrayed only a white, privileged culture. A few writers, both African-American and white, broadened the spectrum of protagonists to include children of color, of poverty, and of minority populations. Culturally America did not change radically after the war, as it had in 1918 after World War I. Children's literature continued to focus on the family as the central force in children's lives, while adolescent fiction centered almost exclusively on high school activities, sports, and cars. The real impact of war on American culture came not with World War II but with Vietnam.

7

Child Liberation, 1950–1990

World War II set in motion the powerful political and cultural determinants that came to be known as the Cold War. In 1946, the American diplomat in Moscow, George F. Kennan, sent a 16-page telegram to President Truman outlining his belief that the United States must engage in "long-term, patient, but firm and vigilant containment of Russian expansive tendencies." The following week, former British prime minister Winston Churchill used the term "Iron Curtain" to describe the Soviet Union's attempt to control eastern Europe.[1] The Cold War had begun, and it reverberated on the American cultural scene for decades.

Of course, children's literature did not concern itself directly with diplomacy, air-raid shelters, McCarthyism, or Sputnik. But according to social historian Elaine Tyler May, the international Cold War bolstered an ideological cold war within America that depended on protecting traditional gender roles and the isolated nuclear family. If women could be confined to domestic and supportive roles, their sexuality and power could be contained in the same way the democratic forces needed to contain Communism and keep it from extending.[2] The Cold War presented internal as well as external dangers, from perceived threats of socialistic government programs to subversive books, from uppity blacks to progressive education.

A particularly gnawing worry was that accepted gender roles might be altered by the influence of socialism, in which men and women workers presumably were treated equally. Thus women who had worked in factories and businesses during World War II found themselves rushed back to domesticity, not only to create job openings for veterans (some of whom were also women) but also to ensure a more traditional role for women. What domestic promoters overlooked, however, was that women had been entering the paid workforce in steadily increasing numbers since the beginning of the century. It was the redomestication of women in the fifties that marked a departure from the trend, not the reverse. As part of the renewed emphasis on domesticity, society sought to redefine chores for women in light of the technological advances that lessened the time it took to keep house. In the fifties women experienced higher demands on their home-decorating abilities, creative and attractive meal presentation, sewing and fashion sense, and volunteer activities. Homemaking was glamorized by the women's magazines so that teenage girls would consider it more attractive than a mere dead-end job in the workplace.

Additionally, ever since mothers had begun working on the homefront during World War II, social critics had identified an upswing in "juvenile delinquency." They blamed working mothers, comic books, movies like *The Blackboard Jungle,* movie stars like James Dean, and rock and roll for a perceived defiance of authority and intensified peer identification among the nation's young people.[3] Meanwhile, in the "other America," which Michael Harrington described in his book of the same title in 1962, African-Americans vocally and visibly protested their second-class status, the urban poor became increasingly ghettoized, and people in Appalachia, on Indian reservations, and in the borderlands of the Southwest experienced greater poverty than ever before. The affluence and consumerism of the dominant culture exacerbated their sense of isolation from the American dream those in the "other America" were free to pursue.

The authors of children's literature responded to these perceived threats and to the Cold War mentality by focusing on the nuclear family and togetherness as protection from the ills of the external world. The family became the "air-raid shelter," protecting the child from the "nuclear threats" of delinquency, socialism, and irresponsibility. The children's fiction of the fifties, according to scholar Anne Scott MacLeod, was "remarkable for its silences and was exceptionally unrevealing about the anxieties of its time."[4] In the fifties, society constructed childhood as a time of complete dependence on adult providers, of socialization by schools, clubs, and peer activities, and of freedom from any responsibility before age 18. Experts believed that being a child should be a wonderful experience in which children were carefree, protected, and supervised and had lots of fresh air and competitive activities. If children's literature was to play its traditional role of reiterating acceptable social mores and teaching traditional values, it would have to emphasize the protected aura of childhood and address adults' fears about the threats of the external environment.

The Nuclear Family

Numerous authors contributed to the idealization of the nuclear family and the perpetuation of almost Victorian gender roles. The Stratemeyer Syndicate launched the Happy Hollisters series in 1953 as adventure-stories-cum-mysteries that perpetuated the same ideal-family motif made so popular in the Bobbsey Twins. The Hollisters included two older siblings, Pete (age 12) and Pam (age 10), and three younger ones, Ricky (7), Holly (6), and Sue (4), along with two typically cheerful parents, a dog, a cat, and five kittens. In her study of the Stratemeyer Syndicate, Diedre Johnson found the Hollisters the "happiest" and the most idealized family of all the children's series, something like "a cross between a 1950s television show and a display model for an advertiser's version of the ideal American family."[5]

At the same time, teen girls were fed a steady diet of high school romance novels, such as *Junior Miss* (1947), *Going Steady* (1950), and *Going on Sixteen* (1946). The teenage protagonist, usually from an intact, happy nuclear family, struggled with popularity, dating (though not much overt sexual activity), and self-image. Author Beverly Cleary (1916–) produced more thoughtful and literary works, such as *Fifteen* (1956) and *Sister of the Bride* (1963), but they still reinforced the message that women are incomplete without men, that if relationships aren't working, it must be the woman's fault, and that fitting in is more desirable than standing out in a career. Adults tended to give wise advice when asked, and with the exception of an occasional pout, teens seemed appreciative of parental support. Popular with girls and professional reviewers alike, most of these books simply continued the high school story themes of the 1930s.[6]

Whereas "career books" had targeted young women in the 1930s and 1940s and perhaps engendered plans for a career, by the 1950s the career story was almost dead. Adolescent girls found no new fictional models to inspire them toward independence; self-awareness and feminism did not fare well in the fifties. The one career series that was popular in the fifties, the Connie Blair mystery series, features a beautiful young blond working in a highly glamorized ad agency. The stories present her as more concerned about her appearance and her clothes than about her work; she seems to gain needed information or advance her career chiefly by playing up her femininity rather than through her competence. Betsy Allen, the author, was actually the pseudonym of Betty Cavanna, a popular writer of high school romances, the most popular fictional genre for girls.[7] The Connie Blair series implies that even a working woman needs to know how to catch a man. The three most popular girls' series books of the 1940s and 1950s featured heroines who never went to college, even though six times as many American women were attending college in 1950 as had matriculated in 1910. Nancy Drew was frozen in postgraduation status, Cherry Ames went to nursing school, and Vicki Barr dropped out of college to become an airline hostess.[8] Given the culture of the 1950s, such female roles appealed to young female consumers.

Postwar affluence meant that middle-class children had allowance money to spend on movies, plastic toys, and books; advertisers began to target them directly as consumers. Paperbacks hit the popular market in 1939 with the

Pocket Books edition of Pearl Buck's *The Good Earth;* several other companies launched paperback subsidiaries within a year or two. By 1951, annual sales of paperbacks reached 230 million. Adolescents' books, and to a lesser extent children's books, became part of that burgeoning market. If libraries and schools did not have the books young people wanted to read, readers simply bought their own. The Scholastic Book Club, as well as several other clubs, promoted inexpensive children's books through the schools. Children themselves created the demand for such hot items as Davy Crockett hats (1955), Hoola Hoops (1958), and Barbie Dolls (1959).[9] The world of children's books in general had become but another of the many items mass-marketed to the child consumer.

The number of children's book titles reached staggering proportions by the 1950s: histories, biographies, picture books, books by foreign authors, family stories, fantasies, science fiction, series mysteries, romances, and sports stories constituted the chief varieties.[10] Reviews of children's books by major authors began to appear in the *New York Times* as well as in myriad journals designed for teachers and librarians. Children's television programs like *Captain Kangaroo* presented award-winning children's books on the air. A brief sampling of the great variety of books available reveals America's optimism in the 1950s.

Theodor S. Geisel, better known as Dr. Seuss (1904–1991), certainly cannot be identified with just one decade in American history, but some of his themes provide a critique of the 1950s. His prolific stories, poems, and beginning readers charmed the public for over half a century. At his death, he had sold over 200 million books; as recently as 1990, his *Oh, the Places You'll Go!* was listed on the *New York Times* best-seller list for a record number of weeks.[11] But his greatest impact on children's literature came in the 1950s.

Geisel claims that the rhyme "And that is a story that no one can beat, / And to think that I saw it on Mulberry Street" came to him on board an ocean liner, and he couldn't get the rhythm or the rhyme out of his head. When his wife suggested that he write a story around it, he penned and illustrated *And to Think That I Saw It on Mulberry Street,* which was rejected by 28 publishers before it was accepted by Vanguard Press and published in 1937.[12] His texts have varied between rhymes and prose, and the illustrations, all of which are his creations, vary from charcoal drawings to pencil sketches with the odd color used for emphasis. He told author Jonathan Cott that "my style of drawing animals derives from the fact that I don't know how to draw. I began drawing pictures as a child . . . trying, let's say, to get as close to a lion as possible; people would laugh, so I decided to go for the laugh." As poet Karla Kuskin has observed of his characters, they have "slightly batty, oval eyes and a smile you might find on the Mona Lisa after her first martini."[13]

The popularity of Geisel's books is probably overdetermined: the relentless rhythm of the text, the fantastical creatures that cavort through the pages, the sheer exuberance and playfulness of the story line, the appeal children find in flouting traditional authority figures. One critic laid his appeal to "the unflagging momentum, feeling of breathlessness, and swiftness of pace, all together acting as the motor for Dr. Seuss's pullulating image machine." Dr. Seuss can be iconoclastic, moving, irreverent, and sentimental; he delivers biting social commentary in seemingly nonsense verse. Geisel told an interviewer that *Yertle the Turtle* (1958), about a turtle who sits on the backs of all his subject turtles, was modeled on the rise of Hitler in the thirties. *The Lorax* (1971) is an impassioned plea for conservation of the natural environment.[14]

Two of his dozens of books can serve as icons for the fifties: *Horton Hears a Who* (1956) and *The Cat in the Hat* (1957). Both are hilariously illustrated, cleverly rhymed, and enormously entertaining; both comment on American society as well. *Horton Hears a Who* continues the saga of the elephant with butterflylike ears introduced in *Horton Hatches the Egg* (1940). In *Horton Hears a Who,* the elephant hears voices coming from a speck of dust, which infuriates those around him. The merciless teasing comes principally from Vlad Vladikoff, a perhaps Russian "black-bottomed eagle," and several authoritarian kangaroos, one with a "me too" child in her pocket. Horton has discovered a microscopic world peopled by the Whos, and he takes it upon himself to try and save Who-ville from extinction by the other, unhearing animals. Horton's mantra to anyone who will listen becomes "a person's a person, no matter how small." The animals try to lock Horton up, however, because of his "unreasonable" behavior. To prove their existence, he asks all the tiny persons in Who-ville to make all the noise they can so the animals can hear them. Not until every last man, woman, and child participates do they grab the attention of the kangaroos; Who-ville is saved. Besides being a rollicking good rhyme, *Horton* stands as a twentieth-century moral tale. Horton's persistence in what he knows to be true, and his fidelity to the seemingly insignificant, is finally rewarded.[15] The story is also a commentary on the mindless conformity of suburbia, where no room exists for the unusual and unique.

After Geisel had written a dozen successful children's books, his editor, William Spaulding, at Houghton Mifflin, suggested he write a primer for beginning readers and sent him a list of 300 words he could use to write it. The task seemed too daunting, and Geisel was about to quit when he decided he would start with a title drawn from the first two words on the list that rhymed and go from there. The words happened to be *hat* and *cat*. From that beginning, it still took him nine months to work out a plot from the word list. *The Cat in the Hat,* with its nonconformist protagonist in a striped stovepipe hat, was born. Although the publisher had a hard time selling it to schools wedded to their Dick and Jane readers, it was an immediate success on the popular market; gradually schools too began to use the book. Random House then began a Beginner Books series featuring several more Dr. Seuss titles.[16]

The plot of *The Cat in the Hat* involves two bored children left home alone on a rainy day, hardly an acceptable setting for a typical family story. Completely uninvited, a strange-looking, human-acting, cat appears and entices the children to play all kinds of games. A talkative goldfish (whom Seuss likened to a modern-day Cotton Mather) cautions the children, "No! No! Make that cat go away! / Tell that Cat in the Hat / You do NOT want to play. / He should not be here. / He should not be about. / He should not be here / When your mother is out!" The cat introduces the children to two friends, Thing One and Thing Two, who wreak havoc in the house until the goldfish spots Mother coming up the sidewalk. In a fantastical suspension of time, the cat cleans up all the mess, restoring the room to pristine loveliness and leaving before Mother enters the room. When she asks the children what they have done all day, of course the reader expects them to tell the truth. Instead, Seuss writes, "And Sally and I did not know / what to say. / Should we tell her / The things that went on there that day? / Should we tell her about it? / Now, what SHOULD we do? / Well . . . / What would YOU do / If your mother asked YOU?"[17] This flouting of parental authority and societal mores, writes Selma Lanes in *Down the Rabbit Hole,* brings children genuine pleasure. The suspense that builds and builds as the Things destroy the house produces vicarious anxiety and then brings enormous relief when no punishment follows and everything is as it should be.[18] To posit a situation in which parents are not in control and children skirt the truth unpunished directly contradicts the conventionalities of the 1950s.

While Dr. Seuss portrayed the fifties by questioning the complacency and conformity of the decade, E. B. White (1899–1985) created in *Charlotte's Web* (1952) a timeless animal fable that stresses the power of friendship, the unity of the family of mankind, and the inevitable cycles of birth and death. White had accumulated a national reputation as a columnist and essayist for the *New Yorker* magazine and as the reviser of Strunk and White's perennially useful *Elements of Style* before he ever entered into children's fiction. He favored the animal fable as a way to probe deep human feelings; each book was extensively researched to ensure that the animals realistically adhered to the traits and behaviors of their particular species. *Stuart Little* (1945) features a tiny mouse on a quest for the beautiful bird Margalo, a search White said was everyone's search for "the perfect and unattainable." His last book, *The Trumpet of the Swan* (1970), relates the adventures of a mute trumpeter swan who learns to play the trumpet to overcome his handicap.[19] But *Charlotte's Web* remains his greatest achievement. When *Publisher's Weekly* conducted an informal public poll to find the best children's book written between 1930 and 1960, *Charlotte* won overwhelmingly. For America's bicentennial, they polled teachers, librarians, and publishers to find the 10 best children's books since 1776, and again White's book emerged as the top choice.[20]

E. B. White, *Charlotte's Web*, illustrated by Garth Williams (New York: Harper & Row, 1952)
Illustrations copyright renewed © 1980 by Garth Williams.
Used by permission of HarperCollins Publishers.

White's empathy with the natural world, his astute powers of observation of animal behavior, and his experiences on his Maine farm were already apparent in his 1948 essay "Death of a Pig," published in the *Atlantic Monthly*. Two years later, as he was tending his animals, he observed a large spider spinning an egg sac. So intrigued was he by the process that when he left the farm a few days later, he cut down the egg sack and took it to New York City with him. Having placed it in a dresser drawer, he avidly watched the tiny spiders hatch. Soon afterward, he began to draft the story of a pig (Wilbur) and his spider friend (Charlotte). To describe spider behavior exactly, he even corresponded with arachnid expert Willis Gertsch of the American Museum of Natural History.[21]

In this fable, Wilbur finds himself twice spared from death. As the novel opens, young Fern Arable saves the runt pig from her father's ax and nurses him to strength. When Wilbur is sold to Mr. Zuckerman, he loses Fern's companionship as well as that of his siblings. Friendless, lonely, and bored, Wilbur exclaims, "I'm less than two months old and I'm tired of living." But when he finds out that Zuckerman intends to butcher him in the spring, Wilbur finds he is terrified of death as well. Wilbur learns to deal with his loneliness and fears when he is befriended by Charlotte. After teaching him much about life, she saves him from becoming sausage by weaving extraordinary words into her webs and making Wilbur the chief attraction at the state fair, guaranteeing that Zuckerman will keep him around for "all the rest of his days." As one critic put it, Wilbur is "a small Everyman [who] survives and triumphs over the pathos of being alone."[22]

But Wilbur's two brushes with death do not exhaust White's statement. Unlike Wilbur, Charlotte is no youngster; following her instincts, she spins an egg sac, deposits her eggs, and prepares to die. Wilbur, however, has learned much about the cycles of life and about the beauty of the barnyard, and although he "will never forget Charlotte," the reader knows that because of her, he will never feel afraid and alone again. Paralleling Wilbur's maturing, Fern too evolves from a playful child to a young woman more interested in Freddie and the amusements at the fair than in animals. This story faces frankly some of childhood's basic fears—abandonment and death—and suggests that someone older and wiser will always be there to protect a child from harm. In the process, death is tamed, so that it becomes a natural part of the life cycle: for the child, "dying in season evokes no terrors," writes John Griffith. Thus White's story speaks both to the situation in which every child finds herself or himself, that existential realization that one is insignificant in the grand scheme of the universe, and to the universal "answers" human beings have given as antidotes to that aloneness, or friendship and love.[23]

Some critics have faulted White's labored construction of the novel, the interfacing of reality (Fern, Zuckerman, the fair) with fantasy (talking animals, word-spelling spiders). Others claim his structure of Fern's rescue of Wilbur blunts the more interesting rescue by Charlotte and her barnyard assistants later. However, few fail to delight in White's lyrically poetic language, his evocative descriptions of various settings, and his animal characters who, acting like humans, never lose the particular characteristics of, for example, rodents, geese, pigs, or spiders. The farm and the barnyard are a pastoral idyll, the barn full of such peaceful smells, "as though nothing bad could happen ever again in the world."[24] Such was the optimism and confidence of America after World War II up through the "Camelot" years of John F. Kennedy's administration.

Social Dislocation and Protest: The Sixties

Depending on one's political persuasion and social consciousness, the 1960s represent either the nadir of foreign policy, internal harmony, and traditional values or the pinnacle of a much-needed protest against imperialistic foreign encroachments, new visions of social and economic equality, and a release from oppressive moralisms. Deep divisions over U.S. policy manifested themselves most visibly in two arenas: the civil rights movement and the armed conflict in Vietnam.

The roots of the civil rights movement go well back into the nineteenth century, to the boycotts and editorials of Ida B. Wells Barnett, and into the twentieth-century black nationalism of Marcus Garvey, the local efforts against job discrimination by the Congress on Racial Equality (CORE), and successful lawsuits against all-white professional schools in the 1930s led by the NAACP. African-Americans filed the lawsuits that culminated in the *Brown v. Board of Education of Topeka* ruling in 1954, and they organized the Montgomery bus boycott in 1955. Federal legislation, like the Civil Rights Act of 1964 and the Voting Rights Act of 1965, recognized the constitutional correctness of the movement's goals, but those who actually accomplished desegregation and voter registration were not congressmen, federal judges, or the Supreme Court; they were the thousands of ordinary African-Americans and few white supporters who consistently and persistently risked jobs, respectability, and personal safety to protest the lack of equal opportunity. Their witness to principle was not lost on other groups dissatisfied with some aspect of American society; by the 1970s organized protest movements found voice among sensitized women, Hispanics, Native Americans, and teenagers.

By the early sixties, many Americans also began to doubt the wisdom of the country's growing involvement in what was essentially a civil war in Vietnam. Following Mao Zedong's successful nationalist revolution in China in 1949, the United States viewed Indochina as a critical strategic stronghold against encroaching Communism and hence part of the Cold War policy of containment. The United States assisted France financially as it sought to maintain colonial control in southeast Asia and to stem a nationalist movement by Ho Chi Minh. President Eisenhower refused, however, to commit American land forces to the French effort; after a major French defeat at Dienbienphu in 1954, an international conference divided the country of Vietnam at the 17th parallel until the United Nations could oversee elections. Fearing a possible Communist victory if elections took place, the United States colluded with South Vietnamese leader Diem to prevent those elections, hoping to deny the Communists a voice and unite the country by force in 1955. From that point on, United States advisers, trainers, equipment, and finally soldiers became increasingly involved in assisting the South Vietnamese government against Communist troops. When Lyndon B. Johnson assumed the presidency upon the assassination of John F. Kennedy in November 1963, some Americans had already begun to question the U.S. presence in Vietnam. Much of the most visible protest against U.S. military actions took place on college campuses.

College student radicalism, although always limited to a minority of students, consistently garnered media headlines. Students conducted antiwar rallies and "teach-ins" and disrupted recruitment activities on campuses across the country. Others joined the Student Nonviolent Coordinating Committee (SNCC) to lead voter registration drives, summer educational projects, and protest marches against discrimination across the South. The "student movement" also agitated for expanded curricula and greater personal freedoms on campus; some moved off campus and into communities, trying to organize poor neighborhoods for a voice in local politics.

These calls for radical social change came from well-educated, affluent students who often challenged mainstream culture in other ways, such as experimenting with sexual freedom, drugs, or "acid rock" music. Although student radicals were not always culturally radical hippies, and few youths devoted to drugs or alternative lifestyles committed themselves to long-term social change, the public conflated the two groups into one. Historian Theodore Roszak labeled the resulting phenomenon the "counterculture."[25] High school and even junior high students adopted the dress, hairstyles, music, and antiauthority trappings of this so-called counterculture or youth movement. As the products of America's productivity, affluence, and suburban lifestyles, children of the 1960s evidenced a reaction against the 1950s optimism and confidence of their parents. Affluent young people who did not hold down jobs and spent only part of their day in school found both the time and the money to create their own subculture, a subculture whose main purpose was to differentiate its members from traditional society. Music, films, adolescent novels, clothing, gangs, and haircuts all served as cultural icons of separation from, and disaffection with, adult society. For perhaps the first time in American history, writers of young adult literature had to choose between creating stories mirroring traditional values and showing the consequences of antisocial behavior. Another challenge was to produce stories that accepted the teen subculture at face value and challenged adult prohibitions and mores.

Meanwhile, secondary education incurred increasing attacks by the media and the general public, particularly after the Soviet Union launched the first artificial earth satellite, *Sputnik,* in 1957. The baby boom had already strained capacity in many school districts, and then the Russian scientific leap forward brought intense scrutiny to math and science programs in American high schools. In 1958, *Life* magazine launched a series entitled "The Crisis in Education," which argued for making the schools a battleground in winning the Cold War by intensifying studies in history and democracy as well.[26] Many experts feared teen culture not only because it so differentiated itself from adult values but because they feared it led students away from the disciplined education necessary to "defeat the Russians" in science, in space, and in the court of world opinion.

The New Construction of Childhood

Most scholars seem to agree that J. D. Salinger's *Catcher in the Rye* (1951) became the prototype of the problem novels that dominated juvenile writing in the 1960s and 1970s, although few of the imitators achieved the stylistic quality Salinger did. Salinger (1919–) did not write for children; his short stories appeared mostly in the *New Yorker* during the fifties, and he has been in seclusion ever since. (In 1997 the publishing world heralded the publication of *Hapworth 16, 1924*, although it turned out to be not a new Salinger creation but a reproduction in hardcover of a short story he had published in the 1960s.) Older teens began reading Salinger's *Catcher* and collected short stories because he described the feelings of alienation from society that many of them also experienced. Salinger's protagonists were teenagers trying hard to grow up amid great disillusionment with American society: Holden Caulfield from *Catcher*, and "Franny" (1955) and "Zooey" (1957) from his short stories of the same names. High school teachers began to assign Salinger's novel because of its brilliant characterizations, its frankness about adolescent anomie, and its clarity of style. *Catcher in the Rye* also included frank colloquial language, an encounter with a prostitute, a young man in therapy, and a persistent defiance of school authorities that provoked public outrage across the country. *Catcher* became the most widely censored book in American schools and libraries.[27]

The altered construction of childhood that would permeate American culture by the end of the 1960s can already be discerned in Salinger's classic. Holden Caulfield's dream is to become the "catcher in the rye," who saves all the children who innocently run through the grain fields and fall over the edge of the cliff. He fears a loss of innocence and feels responsible for its preservation. But the world as he knows it is so full of "phoniness" that innocence cannot survive. Reality (which includes the death of his beloved brother) is so painful that Holden loses touch with himself; he relates his rejection of adult society in first-person narratives with his psychiatrist. He desires to become an adult without adopting the values of a world that seems artificial, corrupt, and hypocritical.

Originally Salinger's view of adolescence opened the way for a more frank discussion of teenage feelings and problems than had ever existed before. Writers embraced a new realism for a young adult audience, which publishers identified as readers between 13 and 20. However, this realism began to enter into the stories designed for preteen children as well, which featured protagonists from ages 8 to 12. Consequently, a new construction of childhood emerged during the 1960s. It recognized that children could not always be protected from the dangers and sorrows of real life; they might be better prepared to cope with pain if adults did not try to protect them from it. "Experts" held up the child's inner emotional and psychological strength as evidence that children could handle reality. The boundaries that had protected children and adolescents from adult responsibilities throughout the nineteenth century and the first half of the twentieth century became much more permeable. Such previously defined adult issues as sexuality and suffering entered the realm of childhood.

In addition to refocusing their understanding of the state of childhood, Salinger's work influenced the style, language, structure, and themes of writers for children and young adults. Sheila Egoff, in her comprehensive analysis of children's literature of the 1960s and 1970s, delineates the characteristics of the new problem novel:

—The protagonist is alienated from the adult world, and often from peers as well.
—The author uses a first-person narrative.
—The style of writing is clipped, colloquial, and confessional; dialogue predominates; vocabulary is limited and relies heavily on the vernacular and slang.
—The settings are urban, usually in New York or California.
—Sexuality is openly and frequently discussed.
—Parents are absent, either physically or emotionally.[28]

We can add to that list that the family is rarely important to the construction of the main character's identity; the family often produces the crises with which the young protagonist must cope. The production of problem novels dramatically escalated during the turbulent sixties; almost no social convention or personal problem remained exempt from treatment by some author. The titles of these novels alone seem to have been designed to outrage or annoy adults who did not accept the "anything goes" philosophy of writing. Examples include *The Pigman* (1968), *I'll Get There: It Better Be Worth the Trip* (1969), *Dinky Hocker Shoots Smack!* (1972), *Confessions of an Only Child* (1974), and *My Name Is Davey: I'm an Alcoholic* (1977).

Such contemporary-issue stories constituted by far the largest number of titles published for children each year during the seventies. Those who track children's reading habits note that those books publishers considered young adult novels no longer were the purview of adolescents only; although they featured teenage protagonists, their simplified language and enticing themes made them popular among 8- to 10-year-old readers.[29] Their intended audience, however, was the adolescent, and as such their characters led lives supposedly reflective of their audience.

Many commentators consider S. E. Hinton and Paul Zindel to be the first to take up the Salinger banner and realistically re-create the often dismal world of teenagers. Susan Hinton (1950–) writes principally about, and through the voice of, adolescent boys; perhaps that is why her publisher chose the moniker S. E. Hinton for all her books. She wrote her first novel,

The Outsiders (1967), at the age of 16, apparently inspired by her own experiences at a Tulsa, Oklahoma, high school. Articulating the painfully acute sense of isolation many of her contemporaries possessed, this first novel critiques the artificial social and class divisions that separate the "greasers," the working-class boys who live on the east side of town, from the socially prominent, affluent "socs" on the other side of town. The two groups' mutual distrust erupts into violence; one of the socs is stabbed to death, a prelude to additional violence, another death, and a gang rumble. Teens in both social groups are alienated from their families and place little trust in adults. *The Outsiders* also functions as a coming-of-age novel for the protagonist Pony Boy, who begins to reflect on his painful maturation through writing about it. This first effort previews the themes of her later works, *That Was Then, This Is Now* (1971), *Rumble Fish* (1975), and *Tex* (1979). They all revolve around male-bonding activities: participating in teenage gangs and motorcycle clubs and breaking wild horses. Adolescent girls find no voice in these early works; they remain incidental to the action, stereotyped and trivialized, except in *Tex,* in which the protagonist falls in love with the strong, outspoken Jamie.

The insulation the nuclear family of the 1950s provided is completely absent in Hinton's novels. The parents of the chief protagonist and his two brothers in *The Outsiders* were killed in a car crash before the story opens; the father in *Rumble Fish* is an alcoholic ex-lawyer who simply doesn't care what happens to his children, which perhaps explains why the "hero" Rusty-James slashes his wrists toward the end of the novel. In *Tex,* the book's namesake and his brother live with their father, who seldom appears in the novel. For Hinton, peers (especially the male gang) provide the emotional support that the maturing adolescent needs and gives a purpose to life that the family does not.[30]

Like J. D. Salinger, Paul Zindel (1936–) came to prominence not as a children's writer but as a novelist (and also as a Pulitzer Prize–winning playwright). But with his unforgettable creation of Mr. Pignati in *The Pigman* (1968) began a successful career writing for teenagers. Two adolescent voices, those of John and Lorraine, alternately narrate this story of their unconventional friendship with Mr. Pignati, a lonely widower they meet while playing pranks on the telephone. He serves as their guide through the trials of adolescence, while they provide him with the family and connection to the outside world he lacks. At the same time, Zindel reverses conventional roles as Pignati indulges in childlike games and romps through the zoo, while the two children become the worried adults and caretakers after his heart attack. They even play-act at being adults, moving into his house and throwing a disastrous party. This novel provides a good example of the new construction of childhood, for Zindel effectively dismantles the boundaries between childhood and adulthood. A sequel about the same two protagonists, *The Pigman's Legacy* (1980), replays a too-similar plot.[31]

John and Lorraine experience alienation from their families, whose lives seem completely unconnected to theirs. One critic has found that the teens in Zindel's many books routinely possess wretched parents, which she describes as "drunkards, bullies, slatterns, dolts, and drearies." Zindel has responded to such criticisms by stating that "Kids don't like to admit how strong an influence parents have on them, and it's natural to have to reject them . . . in order to find themselves."[32]

Zindel's *My Darling, My Hamburger* (1969) shocked the establishment of children's literature almost as much as the *Catcher in the Rye* had 18 years earlier. The parents in this novel are particularly dismal and unfeeling; one couple whose son's girlfriend has just broken their date for the senior prom lectures him on the proper way to take out the garbage. When beautiful and popular high school senior Liz becomes pregnant by her boyfriend, she can find no way to tell her parents. She has a surreptitious and messy abortion; her boyfriend deserts her, partly because of the advice from his insensitive father; she does not finish high school. Using characters at the beginning of the novel similar to those of the high school romance genre, Zindel turns them into dismal parodies of carefree teenagers. In something like a modern moral tale, their futures are irreparably doomed because of their sexual liaison. In *I Never Loved Your Mind* (1970) the couple represent the opposite type of teen from the popular Liz and Sean of *My Darling*. These protagonists—a beer-drinking cynic and an idealistic environmentalist—who have dropped out of high school and work in the same hospital call up all one's associations of the counterculture. Their short-lived love affair is transforming for Dewey, but Yvette is a literal flower child who leaves Dewey to travel with a rock group in hopes of establishing a commune in the Southwest. The book ends without the resolution of anyone's future; the strength here is in Zindel's characterizations and in his evocation of the counter culture.[33]

Although parents appear as vapidly deficient if not clinically sick in Zindel's work, usually at least one sympathetic adult (although perhaps needy himself, as in the case of Mr. Pignati) befriends a confused teenager in each novel, providing at least a small measure of hope to the reader that the anomie of adolescence can be surmounted. Zindel's writing, especially the four early works already cited, has been repeatedly lauded for its ability to capture what one critic called "the bright hyperbolic sheen of teenage language accurately and with humor." Ten years as a high school chemistry teacher in New York no doubt accounts for some of this ability. His later children's fiction, such as *Pardon Me, You're Stepping on My Eyeball!* (1976), *Confessions of a Teenage Baboon* (1978), and *The Amazing and Death-Defying Diary of Eugene Dingman* (1987) do little to update his facility with the vernacular or to introduce new themes. His contributions to articulating a new genre of literature, the young adult novel, lie with his first three works.

By the 1970s, the so-called problem novel dominated writing for ages 12 and up, and no topic lay outside the bounds. Nat Hentoff (1925–) introduced the controversial topic of draft evasion in his 1968 novel *I'm Really Dragged but Nothing Gets Me Down,* and John Donovan (1928–1992) introduced the homosexual attraction of two lonely young men in *I'll Get There. It Better Be Worth the Trip* (1969). The most creatively gifted and stylistically accomplished writer for young adults was probably Robert Cormier (1925–). No adolescent writer weaves a complex story more adroitly nor leaves the reader with such a sense of utter despair and futility. The young protagonist Jerry in *The Chocolate War* (1974) experiences brutal physical punishment when he tries out for the football team at a private Catholic high school. Jerry courageously and individualistically tries to protest against a compulsory chocolate candy sale and consequently suffers emotional coercion from Brother Leon and a physical battering from the Virgils, a high school gang. The story is shot through with religious symbolism and references, making Jerry's annihilation all the more sinister. Surrounded by Catholic brothers, Jerry can find no resolution to his predicament at the school, no redemption for the emotional and physical pain he has suffered. He is crippled to the point of resignation. "They don't want you to do your thing, not unless it happens to be *their* thing, too," he tells his only friend. "Don't disturb the universe, no matter what the posters say."[34]

The despair found in *The Chocolate War* parallels the lingering death of American idealism that occurred in the jungles of Vietnam. War heroes came back to a society that showed little interest in—and considerable distaste for—their experiences "in country." Whether they could regain the optimism and confidence to take back their emotional lives was uncertain. So it is for Jerry at the end of the novel. Life no longer provided answers for a whole generation of children, nor did their literature.

The final contributor to the young adult novel genre under consideration here is a writer who straddles the imprecise boundary between young adult literature and children's literature, having achieved success in both. Like the three writers just discussed, Judy Blume (1938–) has provoked considerable controversy and censure for her themes. Although all her works center on childhood problems, either perceived or real, one book, *Forever . . .* (1975), is particularly addressed to a teen audience. Given the topics already taken up by Hinton, Zindel, and Cormier, Blume's story of a teenage love affair full of tenderness and passion may at first seem tame. The narrator, Katherine, however, does not become pregnant during her passionate encounter with her boyfriend and thus is not punished for premarital sex. She simply moves on with her life, which includes falling in love with someone else. Critics found in *Forever . . .* not only a condoning of teenage sexual activity but also a virtual how-to manual for making love.[35]

Without a doubt, the young adult novels of the 1960s and 1970s opened new themes for children's writers, utilized the first-person narrative almost exclusively, failed to state moral standards and mores even implicitly, let alone explicitly, and broke all language taboos with the liberal use of slang and formerly censored four-letter words. Author and commentator Daniel Pinkwater provided the ultimate capstone of the young adult problem novel in 1982 with, appropriately, *Young Adult Novel,* which Michael Cart calls "a hilarious takeoff on a genre . . . that had always taken itself far too seriously."[36]

The "New Realism"

The same barriers would be breached when writing for the younger child as well. The "new realism" of 1960s children's literature differed significantly from the family stories by Eleanor Estes or the colorful regional stories of Marjorie Rawlings, which had been considered realistic in the 1930s (see chapter 6). Although earlier authors sometimes confronted such difficult issues as social ostracism, injury, or even death, obvious consequences always followed antisocial behavior, and significant learnings often grew from painful events. Not so after Louise Fitzhugh (1928–1974) broke new ground in 1964 with her book *Harriet the Spy.* This charming first-person narrative by a privileged 11-year-old New Yorker challenged critics for younger audiences, just as Zindel and Hinton had done for older youth. *Harriet* was acclaimed as "a watershed," "satirical and astringent," "honest and complex"; it was also criticized for being full of "disagreeable people and situations" and being totally "unsuitable for children." Precocious Harriet has few friends except for her quotation-spouting nanny, Ole Golly; to learn more about life, she records observations of her peers, and of the privileged society around her, in a notebook. When those observations fall into the hands of her classmates, Harriet has to learn to interact with the world as a person, not as an impersonal spy. Her ability to do so is limited and imperfect and includes some serious prevaricating. Neither Harriet nor her classmates are childlike or innocent in the traditional sense: they are self-absorbed, cruel, and judgmental. Their growth, both personally and socially, makes them every bit as interesting as characters in a well-developed adult novel, but it also meant that *Harriet* produced considerable outcry from parents and teachers.[37]

Fitzhugh unleashes a strong social commentary through Harriet's notebooks as well. Harriet lives surrounded by adults who are devoted to material gain and seem ignorant of their needs and feelings, let alone the needs of the children they encounter. Only Ole Golly loves and understands Harriet, but she too is completely fallible, almost a parody of a role model. Fitzhugh certainly implies that the modern family is a poor place in which to raise a child. A later work, *Nobody's Family Is Going to Change* (1974), published posthumously after the author's untimely death at age 46, stands as an even more radical critique of a culture where upward mobility takes precedence over parental understanding of a child's inner needs. This narrator is an African-

American feminist whose father ridicules her ambition to become a lawyer in the same unfeeling way that he disparages his son's desire to become a professional dancer. The reader understands the well-meaning position of this father, a self-made man who feels the weight of obligation to "uplift the race." Both children, but especially Emma, come to realize that one has power only over oneself and not over others. "They're not going to change, I have to change" represents Fitzhugh's resolution of this generational conflict.[38] Here again, adults do not make the world better or safer for children; children themselves shoulder the responsibility for learning how the world works and then finding a way to adapt to it. The child has become parent to herself.

Louise Fitzhugh, *Nobody's Family Is Going to Change* (New York: Farrar, Straus, Giroux, 1974) Copyright 1974 by Louise Fitzhugh. Reprinted by permission of Farrar, Straus, and Giroux, Inc.

Because Louise Fitzhugh encouraged her good friend Marijane Meaker to turn from writing adult novels to writing for children, another contributor to the genre emerged. Under the pen name M. E. Kerr, Meaker (1927–) created the unforgettable characters Dinky Hocker, obese and unhappy, who is carted off to Europe by her parents so that she will stick to her diet (*Dinky Hocker Shoots Smack!*, 1972), and the eccentric but brilliant teacher Miss Blue, who can change lives but cannot keep her job (*Is That You, Miss Blue?*, 1975), Kerr has a particular affinity for portraying the loner and outsider, even in the exclusive girls' boarding school of the latter novel. In her own way, each of the main student characters provides a commentary on the failure of modern society to nurture its children.

Judy Blume's contemporary realism principally addresses this younger reader as well (her protagonists generally are 10 to 12 years old), yet she writes with the same forthrightness that she uses in adolescent fiction. In interviews, she has consistently stated her desire to candidly address the anxieties, real and imagined, that modern children face. Several critics have argued that Blume starts not with a character but with a problem and develops the plot from the situation. In some dozen books, Blume manages to build stories around menstruation, masturbation, voyeurism, kissing, obesity, and scoliosis, as well as parental arguments, divorce, being the middle child, peer pressure, minor theft, lying, poor self-image, and religious beliefs. The child narrators in Blume's works may or may not have intact families, but it is the peer group that exerts the dominant influence in their daily lives. Almost total self-absorption defines her protagonists; they are usually precocious and inquisitive without being particularly insightful. Nevertheless, Blume's novels generate huge sales.

In *Are You There God? It's Me, Margaret* (1970), Blume reveals the normal maturation anxieties of a 12-year-old, including her preoccupation with her developing breasts, menstruation, and boys. Her quest for meaningful religious and philosophical explanations of causation and power in the universe remains unresolved in the novel, but Blume's failure to provide religious certainty met with far less criticism than did her frank discussions of physiology.[39] Much of Blume's attraction lies in her use of simple language and snappy dialogue, making the books an unchallenging easy read. Her success is also built on the humor she infuses into the mundane daily activities of children, like Margaret and her friends talking to their breasts to help them develop or Peter's constant harassment by his two-year-old brother, Fudge, in *Tales of a Fourth-Grade Nothing* (1972) and *Superfudge* (1980).

Blume's works do not tread into the dark emotional recesses that Zindel's do, nor do her characterizations evolve as complexly as Fitzhugh's. Even with her frank vernacular, her characters are mainstream, suburban, middle-class kids. They are likely to solve their own problems, or mature enough to gain perspective on them, so that she can conclude the books without undo trauma. She presents conflict within families, including divorce in *It's Not the End of the World* (1972), and within one's self, as in Tony's watching his female neighbor undress through his binoculars in *Then Again, Maybe I Won't* (1971). But Blume's characters are almost never engaged in social issues or caught up in any kind of social conflict. One cannot imagine one of her creations joining the Children's Army, as does Emma in *Nobody's Family,* and espousing the creed "If the decision makers were forced to make decisions that would be good for *children,* there would only be good decisions made."[40]

Norma Klein (1938–1989) is yet another author who wrote successfully for both children and adults. Her best-known children's book, *Mom, the Wolfman, and Me* (1972), is told by 11-year-old Brett, who lives with her mother in a New York City apartment. Brett's mother is the sixties liberated woman: a professional photographer with a live-in boyfriend, whom Brett initially detests (and calls "wolfman"). Brett acts more like her mother's confidant and partner in running the household than like a daughter. Their open discussions of Brett's illegitimacy, her mother's sexual relationship, and Brett's fears of her mother becoming conventional and boring all work to draw Brett into an adult world while she is still trying to sort out childhood. Klein depicts the mother's ambivalence about marriage to her boyfriend and models a gender-role reversal with the photographer mother and the bread-baking boyfriend in true 1960s fashion.[41]

It may appear that all children's fiction is set in East Coast cities and involves precocious daughters, but not so. Although Fitzhugh, Kerr, Blume, and Klein fit that paradigm, many other authors have taken their realistic fiction to other shores. Bill Cleaver (1920–1981) and Vera Cleaver (1919–) invented many memorable child heroes over a long career. Vera has continued to produce similar works since her husband's death. Particularly notable among their creations are Mary Luther Call in *Where the Lilies Bloom* (1969) and Grover Ezell in *Grover* (1970). Fourteen-year-old Mary Luther keeps her orphaned siblings together in poverty-stricken Appalachia; Grover copes with the suicide of his terminally ill mother and his father's subsequent slide into depression, learning to share his grief with his two close friends. Here again are children undergoing adultlike tests of character and stamina and shouldering adult responsibilities. The Cleavers develop characters of depth and insight who often live in economically deprived regions like Appalachia, South Dakota, or small-town Florida. Their lack of financial privilege and sophisticated urbanity does not keep the Cleavers' characters from tackling difficult personal and social problems. Their first book, *Ellen Grae* (1967), finds Ellen "carrying an insupportable burden of knowledge about the deaths" of the parents of her best friend; *Me Too* (1973) shows the emotional strain that a mentally handicapped daughter has on her parents and on her twin sister, who must finally accept that she cannot change her sister or the way society views her. John Rowe Townsend accurately notes that "endurance" emerges as the key descriptor of the Cleavers' protagonists.[42]

This new realism in children's literature moved to posit a new construction of childhood: children are neither innocent nor sinful. They should not be protected from reality, because they can develop the ego strength to overcome alienation and pain. Experiencing life is the best preparation for adulthood. As in colonial times, modern society has blurred distinctions between childhood and adulthood. In children's fiction, children recognize that adults either do not have their best interests at heart or are powerless against the emotional pain modern culture inflicts. Authors posit great faith in their characters—and in the human spirit—to survive distressing and painful assaults.

It would be a mistake to conclude that *all* families are absent or ineffectual in contemporary realistic fiction. One exception is certainly the stories of author Mildred Taylor (1943–), set in racially tense, Depression-era Mississippi. Her saga about the Logan family begins with *Song of the Trees* (1975), followed by the Newbery winner *Roll of Thunder, Hear My Cry* (1976), *Let the Circle Be Unbroken* (1982), *The Friendship* (1987), and *The Road to Memphis* (1990). Drawing heavily on her father's tough-minded character and the reminiscences he shared, Taylor's young protagonist Cassie Logan is also based on a spunky young African-American girl Taylor knew. The books reveal the determination and pride that allowed black families to survive the vestiges of Jim Crow segregation, while not minimizing the toll that bigotry and racial violence took. Stories with southern blacks as characters usually portrayed them as uneducated share-croppers; in Taylor's hands, the Logans farmed land which they had owned for generations. Mrs. Logan is a schoolteacher. Some of the tension and violence which occurs in the novels results from class hatred as well as from racial prejudice.[43]

When Taylor's work first appeared in the mid-seventies, people of color had reason to feel optimistic about their inclusion in the political process, improved race relations, and greater economic opportunity. The 24th Amendment (1964) had outlawed the poll tax in federal elections, and the Voting Rights Act of 1965 brought federal supervisors into the registration process in the South. In Mississippi, the proportion of registered black voters went from 7 to 59 percent. Rural school districts found their "freedom of choice" registration plans did not keep courageous blacks from enrolling in formerly all-white schools.[44] Taylor's emphasis on the strength of the black family and the integrity by which the previous generation lived fit with the black pride that was enhanced by, and reactive to, the civil rights effort. By the late 1980s, when her later works appeared, African-American spokespersons were less optimistic about the achievements of integration and were acutely aware that people of color disproportionally appeared on the lists of the unemployed, the murderers, and the imprisoned. Whereas discrimination might have hardened the resolve and endurance of some, it had victimized others and the casualties continued.

Vietnam and the Reconstruction of War

The United States' involvement in the internal struggle for control of Vietnam left America demoralized and divided. Richard M. Nixon won reelection to a second term in 1972 with a promise that he would end U.S. involvement in the war that had raged in southeast Asia since 1950. Agreements signed early in 1973 ended hostilities between the U.S. and North Vietnam but did not bind the South Vietnamese to accept a peaceable resolution of the conflict. American troops began returning home, but the South Vietnamese continued to fight until their final defeat in 1975.

"America's longest war," as historian George C. Herring dubbed it, had cost the U.S. at least $150 billion, taken over 58,000 American lives, and sent home at least 10,000 paraplegics.[45] Both veterans and those who had followed the war only on television divided into two camps. There were those who believed the U.S. had a moral responsibility to fight for democracy and could have won the war had we escalated it to include the Chinese Communists and perhaps even used nuclear weapons. By pulling out, they argued, too many men and women had died for no reason. The other group believed that the U.S. should not police the politics of the world, and that protests, by challenging the government's militaristic policies, had been responsible for ending the war. As a consequence, some began to reexamine America's foreign policy, including the rationales for past wars.

Adult fiction and films, such as *The Deer Hunter* and *Coming Home,* began to rework the meaning of Vietnam in the national psyche.[46] Literature for children steered clear of the Vietnam conflict but produced some serious reinterpretation of earlier American conflicts. *My Brother Sam Is Dead* (1974), by the brothers James (1928–) and Christopher Collier (1930–), relates the adventures of two brothers during the American Revolution. Unlike *Johnny Tremain* (see chapter 6), with which it is often compared, the Colliers' book does not champion the patriot position as the only plausible or moral stance that might have been taken in 1776. The Meeker family tries to remain neutral in the conflict but finds it impossible to do so. The authors portray the moral ambiguity in the Revolutionary era when the protagonist Sam, having chosen the patriot side, is executed by the patriots on trumped-up charges of cattle stealing. Long after the war, Sam's brother Tim reflects, "I keep thinking that there might have been another way, besides war, to achieve the same end." Patriot and Tory emerge as very human, befuddled, self-interested players in a largely confusing drama. One of the authors was a college professor of history, and the stance of *My Brother Sam* reflects the then-current historiographical position that the Revolution had multiple causes and served multiple ends. The Colliers' refusal to drape the conflict in patriotic bunting provoked some criticism, however, and some parents saw this as a reason to get the book removed from local libraries.[47]

So too did Vietnam pave the way for stories about World War II. A German youth coming of age in Nazi Germany would have evoked little sympathy from readers in 1944, but in 1966, *Darkness over the Land,* written by Martha Stiles, considered his situation empathetically. James Forman's *The Survivor* (1972) graphically relates the trials of a Dutch family working in the resistance movement. Bette Greene (1934–) turned a Nazi soldier who escaped from his Arkansas POW camp into a compassionate, empathetic, memorable character in *The Summer of My German Soldier* (1973). This first-person narrative of Patty Bergen's unhappy existence in a small Arkansas town, with an appearance-conscious mother and an abusive father, is a typical problem novel, but the setting in the World War II homefront brings a sharp critique to that often-sentimentalized era. Only Anton, the escapee, and Ruth, the black housekeeper, understand Patty's need for nurture and self-esteem. The novel does not set out to examine the morality of war, but the wholly likable Anton forces the reader to question the government's consistent portrayal of Germans as crazed butchers and, by extension, to question government propaganda in general. Even the prolific Judy Blume used a World War II homefront setting for *Starring Sally J. Freedman as Herself* (1977). Sally views the events around her as if all of life were war propaganda—evil or good. Part of her maturation is her discovery that life is much more complex.[48]

Varieties of Contemporary Fiction

Of course, solid historical fiction for children appeared outside the theme of war as well. Scott O'Dell's (1898–1989) first novel for young adults makes a powerful statement about the wisdom, inner strength, and attachment to the natural environment of its protagonist, Karena. The *Island of the Blue Dolphin* (1960) tells the story of a sister and brother left behind when their tribe leaves a South Sea home island. Loosely based on some "sketchy information" about a girl left on an island off the coast of California for 18 years, O'Dell uses Karena's voice to relate her brother's death at the hands of a wild dog, her attempt to kill the dog, only to nurse it back to health as her only companion, and her reluctant reunion with tribal peoples who return to the island.

O'Dell's *Sing Down the Moon* (1970) brings the same kind of detailed empathetic treatment to one of the darkest episodes in United States history, the forced relocation of native peoples during the Great Plains Wars of the 1860s and 1870s. He focuses specifically on the Navaho's 300-mile march to Fort Sumner, New Mexico, as prisoners of the U.S. Army. The sparse dialogue and syntax capture Navaho speech patterns, and the spare, matter-of-fact description of how native peoples survived this ordeal reflects their stoical acceptance of what they cannot change. Perry Nodelman has observed that O'Dell withholds the narrator's name until almost the end of the book, for she is consistently treated by the whites as a nonperson. "The name eventually revealed is an ironic comment on those dark hours in Navaho history: Bright Morning." The novel follows Bright Morning from age 14, when the Navahos lived peaceably on the land, through the Long Walk and her escape from the soldiers as a young wife and mother. Sheila Egoff calls Bright Morning "one of the most sensitive and spirited heroines in modern children's literature."[49]

The horrors of the colonial slave trade provided Paula Fox (1923–) with the context for her Newbery Award–winning *Slave Dancer* (1973). Winner of awards from the Guggenheim Foundation and the National Endowment for the Arts, Fox has written adults novels and traditional children's fiction, as well as this historical tale of Jessie Boller's kidnapping and "enslavement" as a flute player on board an American ship carrying actual slaves for sale.[50] Her straightforward, graphic descriptions of the conditions on board the slave ship and the inhumanity of the white sailors resonate with the tremendous increase in scholarship during the 1970s about the slave trade and the racism in which it was rooted. Jessie is described as a "creole," which in his New Orleans home signifies mixed-race parentage, born in the U.S. Several black writers and scholars have attacked Fox for trying to portray (as all writers of fiction must) feelings and racial identity she hasn't experienced.[51] Some readers found the following passage particularly disparaging of Africans: "I hated the slaves! I hated their shuffling, their howling, their very sufferings. . . . Oh, God! I wished them all dead! Not to hear them! Not to smell them!" One can argue, however, that rather than disdaining blacks, Fox re-creates the horrible reality of the slave ship, the corrupting and depressive influence it has on everyone aboard.

Fantasy as a genre has been excluded from the scope of this study because its themes are by and large outside the "real time" that links fiction writing to the historical circumstances from which it grows (although certainly science fiction and the "evil enemy" of the Cold War are closely related). However, two contemporary authors deserve mention here, for their quasi-fantasy stories encompass broad concerns of the post–World War II era. Madeleine L'Engle (1918–), author of nearly 20 children's books, presented a trilogy that introduces Evil as a concrete entity (somewhat reminiscent of the C. S. Lewis Narnia series), time travel, modern physics, and a strong dose of Western Christian theology. In *A Wrinkle in Time* (1962), physicist Mr. Murry is missing; his daughter, Meg, a friend, Calvin, and Meg's younger brother Charles Wallace travel through time and space to find him. Three Wise Women lead Meg on her journey through time and space, teaching her how to "tesser," or "wrinkle," through time. Meg locates her father, who is being held captive on the planet Camazotz by a disembodied brain known only as IT. With definite parallels to Cold War anxieties about the power of Commu-

nism and its use of brainwashing to win adherents, the inhabitants of Camazotz are described as blindly obeying IT's wishes. They exist as mindless con-
formists. Meg and her father manage to escape the planet, but brother
Charles Wallace is taken in by IT's logic. Meg discovers that only the power
of love is strong enough to overwhelm Evil and free Charles Wallace.

Meg's journey is both an excursion to reclaim her father and a journey to
self-discovery; her risk taking and philosophic probing have given her the
self-confidence and self-love she lacked when the story began. L'Engle constructs Evil as a real presence that thrives wherever human love and individual personality are lacking. (She doesn't seem to admit that evil comes from
within the human psyche.) Mr. Murry had joined a group on Camazotz
known as the "fighters," who sought to beat back Evil and its promise of carefree living; they included such persons as Jesus, Gandhi, Einstein, Bach, and
St. Francis. L'Engle continued the Murry family's encounters with Good and
Evil, otherworldly helpers and guides, and time and space travel in *A Wind in
the Door* (1973) and *A Swiftly Tilting Planet* (1978).[52]

Justice and Her Brothers (1978) by writer Virginia Hamilton (1936–)
also concentrates on the development of latent psychic powers, in this case by
the heroine Justice. She too has a "wise woman" to initiate her into such mysterious powers, ones her twin brothers Thomas and Levi also share. Hamilton
already had a string of successful children's stories and African folktales to
her credit before embarking on fantasy. Completing the Justice trilogy are
Dustland (1980) and *The Gathering* (1981). Critic Sheila Egoff believes Virginia Hamilton sees children as embodying a transforming power that can
impact some of the sickness of humanity, the despair of the problem novel-
ists. "Our place isn't here. . . . Our time isn't now, but in the future," muses
Justice on behalf of all children.[53]

For those who grew tired of the realistic problem novels and found the
philosophical overlays of fantasy too difficult to manage, the 1980s presented
a new, revised version of the 1950s high school romance stories. Just as the
politics of the Reagan years repudiated much of the social activism of the previous two decades, so the new romance novels retreated from social problems
to gendered, comfortable, feel-good topics. The Sweet Valley books began
the trend, followed by the Sweet Valley High and Sweet Valley Twins series,
and for younger readers, the Sweet Valley Kids. Sold directly as paperbacks,
these series did for young readers in the eighties what the Rover Boys and the
Bobbsey Twins had accomplished earlier: they developed a devoted following
of buyers and unleashed the bile of librarians and teachers. The plots are virtually interchangeable from one novel to the next, as are the characters. Critics have called them "escapist" and "grown-up nostalgia repackaged for the
young" and "emotionally recidivist." But publishers understood the market;
many teens either were wearied by unsolvable problems or simply did not see
themselves reflected in the dysfunctional families often portrayed. Market
researchers knew that romance sold to adults; it also worked in the youth

market. By the end of the 1980s, there were 34 million Sweet Valley High books in print.[54]

Author-Illustrators

Finally, a brief look at two contemporary author-illustrators whose works present a banquet of visual delights: William Steig and Maurice Sendak. Steig (1907–) was a successful cartoonist, illustrator, and sculptor before embarking on his first children's book at age 60. His chief characters are animals, like Sylvester in *Sylvester and the Magic Pebble* (1969), dogs in *Dominic* (1972), and mice in *Abel's Island* (1976.) He illustrates all his own works, some with full-color painting, others with pen-and-ink line drawings. When asked why this penchant for animal protagonists, Steig told an interviewer, "I think using animals emphasizes the fact that the story is symbolic—about human behavior." One can hardly imagine more engaging protagonists. Dominic, with piccolo, bandanna, and hats in his hand, starts off on his life's journey, only to meet a wise witch (an alligator): "That road there on the right goes nowhere. There's not a bit of magic up that road, no adventure, no surprise,

William Steig, *Dominic,* illustrated by William Steig (New York: Farrar, Straus, Giroux, 1972) Copyright 1972 by William Steig. Reprinted by permission of Farrar, Straus, and Giroux, Inc.

nothing to discover or wonder at. Even the scenery is humdrum. . . . [A]fter a while, you'd reach a dead end and you'd have to come all that dreary way back to right here where we're standing now." So instead, Dominic takes the other path, full of tribulation, danger, needy people, love, illness—everything that makes life worth living. Such is Steig's unbounded enthusiasm for life, the unfettered enthusiasm of childhood as he understands it. Steig once told an interviewer, "The child is the hope of humanity. If they are going to change the world, they have to start off optimistically. I wouldn't consider writing a depressing book for children."

Despite this defense, Steig's stories are neither sentimental nor dull but are more like fairy tales in their universal appeal. The fairy-tale quality failed to register with the Illinois Police Association, however, which alerted all law enforcement officials in the state to the illustrations in *Sylvester and the Magic Pebble,* which depict the helpful policemen as pigs. "This most certainly must mold the minds of our youngsters to think of police as pigs, rather than as their good friends," they wrote, and they urged local police associations to get the book removed from public and school libraries.[55]

Maurice Sendak (1928–) remains perhaps the most controversial writer for young children, even into the 1990s. Before he began to write for children, he provided the illustrations for almost 50 well-known children's books, so he knew the field intimately. When he turned to writing the stories as well as illustrating them, he created a sensation almost immediately. His *Where the Wild Things Are* (1963) remains—even 35 years later—a must-have book for every child under the age of six. This picture book contains few sentences and many full-page color drawings, so that much of the story comes not from words but images. The plot is seemingly simple and psychologically complex. Young Max becomes angry with his mother and tells her, "I'll eat you up!" She banishes him to his bedroom, which, in his isolation, is transformed into a lush tropical forest, populated with monsters of all shapes and sizes who make him their king. When he tires of playing with them, he sails back home and into his room. In a statement of recognition of all he has done and of ultimate forgiveness for it, he finds his dinner waiting for him, "and it was still hot."

Critics attacked the book for presenting monsters who "gnashed their terrible teeth" and "rolled there terrible eyes" to young children who might have nightmares from them.[56] According to Sendak and others, the critics overlooked three critical aspects to the story. One is that children need to express their anger at adults, as Max does to his mother for calling him a "wild thing." Another is that children are loved regardless of their behavior, as exhibited by her provision of a hot supper, even in the midst of his punishment. And most importantly, in the story Max has the power to tame the wild beasts he meets and to win their accolades and friendship. *Where the Wild Things Are* empowers children to own their feelings and to trust their inner strengths, even in frightening situations. Sendak himself said that there are "games children must conjure up to combat an awful fact of childhood: the fact of their vulnerability to fear, anger, hate, frustration—all the emotions that are an ordinary part of their lives. . . . To master these forces, children turn to fantasy." It is through fantasy that Max deals with his fears and his isolation, and then can peacefully go to sleep.[57]

Sendak's later books have taken an even deeper psychological twist. Many are bewildered by his Brueghel-like drawings of vacant-eyed, gnarled children, oftentimes naked, in *In the Night Kitchen* (1970) and *Outside Over There* (1981). Both of these fairy-tale-like picture books use surrealistic illustrations that seem fraught with issues of the dark side of childhood dreams and fantasy, including Freudian allusions to overt sexuality. *Outside over There* is particularly disturbing because the child Ida, instructed to look after her little sister, momentarily ignores her, only to find that goblins have come and stolen the baby away. Certainly Sendak has captured the ambivalent feelings most children have toward their siblings, and he suggests that fantasy is the best way to resolve those feelings. But others find this wish fulfillment too frightening for young children. Because Sendak's books operate at different levels, he has developed quite an adult following. *Outside over There* was consequently issued simultaneously as both a child and an adult book. In probing his deepest unconscious for what childhood fantasies and images are all about, Sendak may, as one critic suggests, "be leaving the child behind."[58]

The Culture Wars

When African-American critics early this century began to alert the children's book world that stories presenting people of color in active, responsible, creative roles were absent from the canon of children's literature, little notice was taken. Committed reformers such as Mary White Ovington, W.E.B. Du Bois, Arna Bontemps, and Langston Hughes began to publish a few children's stories and books but tended to concentrate on nonfiction as the better medium to supply role models for black children (see chapters 5 and 6). After the civil rights activity of the 1950s and early sixties, more literature featuring African-American and Native American protagonists appeared at all levels, from picture books to young adult novels. Illustrator Ezra Jack Keats (1916–1983) used a nameless black boy as the only character in *The Snowy Day* (1962) and then went on to produce a number of easy books in which the child, eventually named Peter, does everyday sorts of things—learns to whistle, adopts a stray cat. William Armstrong's (1914–) first children's book, *Sounder* (1969), relates the story of a black sharecropper who steals a ham for his hungry family. The arrival of the sheriff to arrest the man prompts the dog Sounder to attack him, and he shoots the dog. Sounder limps away wounded while the father goes to jail, leaving the young son to grow up mostly on his own. Paula Fox, discussed earlier, wrote of a 10-year-old black boy who is kidnapped by a gang of youths and forced to accompany them on a crime spree in *How Many Miles to Babylon?* (1967). Keats was awarded a Caldecott Medal for his artistry, Armstrong won a Newbery Medal, and Fox's book also garnered honors. In all three cases, white authors told stories of black children, which caused a sometimes bitter debate over who can and should write about "the black experience."

Julius Lester, author of many folktales and the nonfiction children's book *To Be a Slave* (1968), wrote a well-publicized letter to the children's book editor of the *New York Times* in 1970. In it, he argued that only African-Americans can truly understand and write about the black experience. "When I review a book about blacks (no matter the race of the author), I ask two questions," he wrote. " 'Does it accurately present the black perspective?' 'Will it be relevant to black children?' The possibility of a book by a white answering these questions affirmatively is almost nil."[59] Much debate ensued, many critics arguing that a book should be judged on nothing but its literary merits; good stories should be published, regardless of the race of the author. However, many black authors, teachers, and librarians argued that even well-meaning white authors stereotyped minority peoples in their works. Whites could not write about black children, they said, because they had not shared a history of prejudice and didn't understand the complex social codes black children learned to survive. They blamed a white-controlled publishing world for not encouraging black authors with legitimate stories to tell. In the Armstrong story cited previously, for example, whereas white reviewers found a moving tale of the suffering of a poor black family, Albert Schwartz contended that *Sounder* failed on several counts. It did not adequately indict the racist system under which the sharecroppers lived; Armstrong didn't assign anyone in the family a name, which dehumanized and impersonalized them; the mother was uncaring about her child's pain and hunger, which is a white misconception about black families; and the message of the book is that if blacks are patient, things will turn out all right.

Such critics certainly had a long history of demeaning and unfair portrayals of black characters on which to base their argument. And they had some important learnings to share with the dominant culture. The Council on Interracial Books for Children (CIBC) organized in the late 1960s and began publishing a bulletin in 1968 that reviewed current books (and some earlier "classics") on the basis of their accurate portrayal of minority peoples and women. Provocative, helpful, and enlightening, the *Bulletin* could also be harsh and shrill. Certainly the CIBC stirred the debate over feminist and multicultural perspectives in other journals, as well as at children's literature conferences, and taught non-African-Americans how to examine certain assumptions about the goals of integration and racial harmony.

After decades of black pride, affirmative action, and sensitivity training, some of the early efforts in developing African-American protagonists now seem to have been designed to please a white audience first. As Judith Thompson explained it in an essay in the *Wilson Library Bulletin*, such themes in children's books "tend to reinforce the very attitudes they are trying to dispel. In too many of these books the white child dominates the story. . . . The black child . . . is the passive character. He is the problem which causes the white child to act."[60] But reviewers could point to some works that moved beyond showing blacks struggling for acceptance to a straightforward assertion of a strong black culture. For example, Virginia Hamilton's first novel, *Zeely* (1967), features a tall, regal African-American (Zeely) whom the neighbor girl Geeter first thinks is a night traveler and then an African queen imprisoned on a hog farm against her will. The beautiful relationship that develops between these two young black women creates its own world without the intrusion of white sensibilities. When Geeter's uncle tells her that anyone can be a night traveler, anyone who "want(s) to walk tall. . . . [I]t is the free spirit in any of us breaking loose," African-American culture stands tall as well. In *M. C. Higgins, the Great* (1974), Hamilton creates the strong black family in which M. C. comes to know his own mind and appreciate his rural home, which had been in the family since his great-grandmother escaped from slavery there, without sentimentality or the promise of a happy ending. *Stevie* (1969), by illustrator and author John Steptoe (1950–1989), depicts an inner-city black child and uses black dialect for the first time in a book for young children.[61]

But African-American writers could also stir controversy for their portrayals of poor blacks. Alice Childress (1920–1994) told the story of a 13-year-old black heroin user in *A Hero Ain't Nothin' but a Sandwich* (1973), using "black English" in a contemporary urban setting. Other books include *Those Other People* (1989), which concerns rape, blackmail, suicide, and racism, and *Rainbow Jordan* (1981), with three black female narrators.[62]

Literature about African-Americans was soon caught up in the much larger debate over "multiculturalism" and "diversity," which became buzzwords of the 1980s. Historically, there are two probable roots for the growing awareness of the country's multicultural population. The civil rights movement, and the growth of black pride in its wake, did much to mobilize sensitivities of other groups of minority peoples in the United States. The American Indian Movement (AIM) began with the Chippewa peoples in Minnesota and led to demands for the return of tribal lands, as well as to a call for the reclamation and preservation of native skills, traditions, and beliefs. Their militancy led to the Indian Self-Determination Act of 1974, which allowed tribes the right to control the federal-aid programs to their reservations and to oversee their own schools. Native American teachers ensured the perpetuation of native culture and spirituality. Young Mexican-Americans in high schools and colleges worked for Chicano studies programs and urged that Mexican-American children not be forced into English-only schools.[63] Heightened awareness and militancy among all these groups called attention to their rightful inclusion in the definition of "American" and indicated the necessity of their historical experiences and cultural values being included in the literary and artistic representations of the United States.

The second historical influence on multiculturalism was the new pattern of immigration that developed after 1970. The population of the country had grown from a little over 200 million in 1970 to 250 million in 1990, and the fastest-growing immigrant group was from Central and South America, followed by Asia. In 1990, Hispanic people comprised a quarter of the populations of California and Texas.[64] But unlike immigrants in the nineteenth century, recent immigrants have not yielded as readily to the "melting pot" dictum. With radio stations, movies, music, and newspapers in their native languages, Mexican-Americans and Asian-Americans have been able to preserve much of their own culture as they adapt to living in the United States. The analogy of the "tossed salad" or the "stir-fry" has replaced the "melting pot" as a culinary descriptor of modern America's cultural mix.

The call of multiculturalists to define America as a collection of various cultures instead of a unified set of cultural assumptions triggered a heated reaction, from talk-radio programs to curricular debates at prestigious universities. At the core of this debate lie two critical questions: what does it mean to be an American? And who "owns" American history? On campus after campus, debates developed over how much to broaden the scope of traditional American history to include more on the experiences of non-Anglo, Protestant settlers and their descendants. In an angry response to those who sought to teach a more pluralistic culture, the distinguished historian Arthur M. Schlesinger Jr. argued that a shared history created a national identity that was essential for the survival of the nation. He called the emphasis on multicultural education "a cult" that "threatens to become a counter-revolution against the original theory of America as 'one people.' "[65] A related debate developed among professional historians about who should teach and write ethnic histories. White scholars of African-American history found themselves under attack because they wrote from outside the black experience, an argument known as "essentialism." Debates ensued over what it meant to investigate history from the "outside," and although most concluded that theoretically all scholars operate from this position unless they are writing autobiography, minority scholars argued for "essential" insight. Most multiculturalists did not argue for essentialism in the writing or teaching of minority history, only that historians broaden their inclusion of information and seek to present that information in ways sensitive to the culture that produced it.

Essentialist arguments made their way into the writing of children's literature as well. As noted earlier, at the height of the "culture wars," non-African-American authors were attacked for any portrayal they attempted outside their own racial identity. The CIBC contended that such portrayals would inescapably reflect racist assumptions. The 1989 book *Children of the*

River by Linda Crew, an Anglo, relates the experiences of Sundara, a Cambodian immigrant to the U.S. Crew perpetuates two myths about Asians, claims writer Ai-Ling Louie. Sundara is an academic overachiever, which is *not* typical of most Asian immigrants, and she is also extremely beautiful and sexy, a modern "Suzy Wong." Both stereotypes work to make the Cambodian more acceptable to the dominant Anglo culture.[66] Susan Jeffer's (1942–) *Brother Eagle, Sister Sky* (1991) was written from outside the Native American experience and has been faulted for portraying the northwest Indian people it describes as if they were nineteenth-century Plains Indian warriors.

Author Jane Yolen vehemently argued against essentialism in a recent *Horn Book* essay. "What we are seeing now in children's books is an increasing push toward what I can only call the 'Balkanization' of literature. We are drawing rigid borders across the world of story, demanding that people tell only their own stories. . . . [That] would mean that no stories at all could be told about some peoples or cultures until such time as a powerful voice from within that culture emerges." And professor Kay Vandergrift has noted that were children's literature only written by "insiders," the field would not exist, for children do not write it.[67]

Historically, the absence of voices from within a culture might reflect discrimination by the publishing world, or just an absence of voices. For example, in the 1950s the major authors writing about native peoples were Florence Crannell Means (see chapter 6) and Ann Nolan Clark (1896–). Both were Anglos who achieved remarkable insight into Native American cultures by living on reservations and understood how hard it was to translate a worldview from one culture to another. "I believe there are four Indian group concepts that differ greatly from concepts in our [Anglo] group patterns," Clark wrote in 1969. "These are the Indian feelings about land, about work, about time, and about the spiritual life." She tried to honor those concepts in several stories about Native American children, which appeared in the 1940s. *Secret of the Andes* (1952) tells the story of the boy Cusi and his friendship with an older herder, revealing in the process much about the Inca's history and spirituality. *Santiago* (1955) traces the story of one child's anguish at being caught between parallel cultures in Guatemala.[68]

Because of the movement for multicultural inclusion, more authors from within minority traditions began to publish. Lawrence Yep (1948–) portrayed Chinese culture vividly in *The Serpent's Children* (1984) and *The Rainbow People* (1989). In *Dragonwings* (1975) he used reminiscences of Chinese-Americans during the 1906 earthquake as the basis of his novel. Japanese-American experiences dominate the stories of Yoshiko Uchida, including *Samurai of Gold Hill* (1972), *A Jar of Dreams* (1981), and several others. The picture book *Grandpa's Town* (1991) even features a bilingual text.[69] Among Native Americans, Jamake Highwater's (1942–) first novel, *Anpao: An American Indian Odyssey* (1977), was a Newbery Honor book. A later quartet of Ghost Horse stories traces three generations of a Plains Indian family, including the loss and regaining of one family's cultural heritage.

Portrayals of Chicano children are not as common as one would expect, particularly given the large increase of Hispanic population within the United States in the past twenty years. Joseph Krumgold (1908–1980) wrote . . . *And Now Miguel* in 1953, which stood alone for some time. The Council on Interracial Books for Children surveyed the field in the early 1970s and found most Mexican-American characters were migrant workers, illiterate, passive, and always very poor. In the past decade, Mexican-America Gary Soto (1952–) has published several short stories about teenagers and children living in California, including *Baseball in April and Other Stories* (1990) and *Taking Sides* (1991). The latter relates the racism a Chicano baseball player encounters on an otherwise all-Anglo team. His stories are laced with Spanish words and phrases and include glossaries to identify unknown words. Critic Michael Cart believes that in the years to come, more bilingual children's books will be available for children for whom English is a second language.[70]

Any cause is bound to elicit parody and satire, and so it was with multiculturalism. James F. Garner (1960–), a Chicago actor, concocted *Politically Correct Bedtime Stories* (1994), a rewriting of familiar fairy tales to eliminate any expressions or activities that might be considered "sexist, racist, culturalist, nationalist, regionalist, ageist, lookist, ableist, sizeist, speciesist, intellectualist, socioeconomicist, ethnocentrist, phallocentrist, [or] heteropatriarchalist." Consequently, Little Red Riding Hood's trip to Grandmother's house is not assigned her because she is a girl, grandmother is not old, the wolf is merely "an outcast from society." Further, Red Riding Hood stopped the woodchopper from perpetrating a "speciesist" act, and she and Grandma and the wolf "felt a certain commonality of purpose" and "set up an alternative household based on mutual respect and cooperation."[71] The genuine problems of what kinds of messages and models children's literature presented to girls, to people of color, and to those of mixed race can more easily be pushed aside with satire than by addressing the root concerns.

Issues of gender-role stereotyping and girls as active protagonists is a case in point. A rash of attention to gender-role stereotyping and the lack of female heroines in children's fiction coincided with the renewed feminism of the 1960s. In the 1970s, the Interracial Council on Books for Children reviewed many new books and published several essays about sexism in child fiction. In recent years, the issue has all but been ignored in critiques of children's literature. The extensive *Children's Books and Their Creators* (1995) contains an encyclopedic collection of essays on authors and illustrators of twentieth-century children's works, as well as longer essays on particular literary genres. Great attention is paid to essays on multicultural literature, but "sexism" is indexed only once for the 712-page text. After a spate of career books for girls in the 1970s, authors now assume that the career playing field is level for both men and women and thus ignore the particular obstacles young women face from elementary school to the workplace. Girls' coming-of-age stories remain far less common than boys' coming-of-age experiences. The traits frequently associated with females, such as compassion, nurturing, bonding, empathy, and caregiving, not only continue to be associated principally with girls (or female animals) but are valued less than characteristics usually associated with boys: independence, assertiveness, self-actualization, self-sufficiency, and defiance of authority. Another gifted author, Australian Mem Fox, related her stunned awareness that readers of her book *Possum Magic* (1990) transposed the gender of the invisible main character "Hush" from female to male when they talked about the story, because a male protagonist is what they expected.[72] Until the "female experience is held up as authentic and important" in and of itself, sexism will still define the growing-up experience.[73]

Children's literature since 1950 has grown and changed more than in any other period in American history. Having stated the obvious, it is more difficult to say what those changes mean. The growing affluence of Americans in general, a population that increasingly learns English as a second language, and books with a heightened realism centered on personal and family problems have come to characterize the post–baby boom generation. Long-maintained silences about children and drugs, sexual expression, crime, violence, and abuse have been broken. Children of both genders and from all races, ethnicities, economic levels, and regions of the country now take center stage in books for children and young adults. Fiction is often manufactured to certain specifications: race, gender, television programs, new movie releases. Books for children continue to reveal the truths about American culture while disclosing the anxieties and pleasures of real children as well. Both racial assumptions and gender assumptions remain deeply entrenched in society and are reflected in children's literature just as pervasively as they are anywhere else.

Epilogue: Into the Twenty-first Century

Historians generally don't write about the present, let alone the future, not because they don't care about what happens but because their training restrains opinion without a factual, evidential base. What appears to be a new development in the short term may be nothing more than a brief blip in a long-term trend. Only the creative artists themselves know where they want to take the field of children's literature. The economics of the publishing world, the critics, and the buying public will determine if authors get to set that agenda. Who controls society's voice at this juncture, and what do they (we) believe children should know and experience?

Interest in multicultural themes and diverse childhood experiences has waned since the early 1980s. After a flurry of activity in the 1970s, the percentage of books about and by minorities has leveled off. A 1990 survey of the five thousand children's books published that year found that only 51 were written by black authors. That could change with some of the new African-American-owned publishing houses, like Just Us Books (Orange, New Jersey) and Black Butterfly Children's Books (New York City).[1] The titles these publishers produce present African-Americans from all walks of life, living in inner cities, suburbia, and on southern farms. Mary Hoffman's (1943–) *Amazing Grace* (1991) is particularly notable, as are works by the African-American illustrators Jerry Pinkney (1939–) and Tom Feelings (1933–). Because of the growth of the Latino population, books for and about Latino children surely will increase dramatically. But in general, the drive for multiculturalism has been hampered by an old American theme: the call for immigration restriction. This time, that theme has been bolstered with attempts to make English as the official language of the country and with budgetary cuts that seriously impede school districts from teaching elementary students in their primary language.

The 1990s have seen radical changes within the publishing industry. Mergers, buyouts, downsizing, and multimedia corporations have reorganized many of the major publishers. Today movies and television programs are produced by the same companies that publish children's books, so what is produced may have more to do with the other enterprises the corporation owns than with what an editor considers a good children's book. Corporations are more interested in marketing potential with tie-ins than with quality of literature. The reverse is also true; children's books that sell well are being made into films or television shows. A recent movie was based on James Marshall's *The Stupids Die* (1981), and the popular *Babysitter's Club* (1982) by Ann Martin was scheduled for movie production in 1995. The television networks Showtime and Nickelodeon recently began an animated series called *The Busy World of Richard Scarry,* based on his popular preschool books.[2] This incestuous relationship between the various media alters significantly the kinds of literature that emerge for children.

During the 1980s, children's publishing was a hot industry. Jerry Griswold has noted that between 1982 and 1990, sales of children's books quadrupled in the United States, while the number of children ages 5 to 13 actually declined. In the same period, other areas of the publishing industry faced declining sales and staff reductions. The figures are a little less promising in the 1990s but still impressive. The fiscal 1993 figures indicated that the profits of the largest-grossing children's publisher, Western Publishing, actually declined 3 percent, but the second-largest company, Random House, gained over 8 percent. The much smaller Scholastic Publishing Company increased a whopping 59 percent over the previous year, partially due to the phenomenal success of the Goosebumps series (discussed later). Book sales of children's literature are forecast to increase 16.6 percent over the next five years to a total of 397.5 million books by the year 2000.[3]

It is the sale of paperbacks that has fueled the profits in children's publishing in the last 10 to 15 years. Consumer spending on paperbacks is expected to rise 48.7 percent over the next five years, largely because of tie-ins with television and movies. The marketing of children's books has also changed dramatically during the last few years. At Simon and Schuster, for example, management established a separate children's book division with its own sales force in 1993. At that time, 10 percent of sales went to mass-market distributors: wholesale food chains, department stores, pet shops, and office-supply stores. In 1996, almost a quarter of sales went to similar outlets. Children's books are no longer limited to traditional book stores or toy stores. A survey by *Publisher's Weekly* found that independent and chain bookstores account for only 15 percent of the total consumer market for children's books, while discount stores sell almost 30 percent and book clubs account for another 18 percent. Marketing to the nonbook stores often means that books must have a tie-in to another product (such as clothing or toys) or garner instant recognition by reflecting a popular TV show or movie.[4]

Many publishers bank heavily on series books, usually issued in both hardcover and paperback, to ensure a steady consumer base. Scholastic introduced the Goosebumps series for 8- to 12-year-olds in 1992. Taking the 1930s mysteries a step further, Goosebumps books are horror stories with limited ghoulishness and a happy resolution to the adventure. Panned by many critics, the series has increased sales dramatically for Scholastic. Random House competes with a series called Supermodels of the World, Simon and Schuster has the Fear Street series for 12- to 15-year-olds, and Pleasant Company has made the American Girls series almost a household name with its stories about girls living all over the country and in different historic periods. Pleasant Company's American Girl Library also publishes complementary books that suggest craft and party ideas and provide grooming advice.[5]

Finally, the production and marketing of children's books has also been affected by the trend toward middle schools in public education. So-called young-adult literature used to be targeted to 13- to 18-year-olds. The reorganization of many school districts has resulted in middle schools for grades six through eight (ages 11 to 13) rather than junior highs with grades seven through nine. Thus the ages to which adolescent literature was directed have moved downward to include younger children and thus increase sales to middle schools and their libraries.[6]

The political phrase "family values" surfaced during the Reagan campaigns as a catchword used by politicians seeking the conservative vote and by Protestant religious groups attacking mothers in the workforce, gay and lesbian unions, and abortion rights. The Reverend Pat Robertson organized the Christian Coalition to further his own presidential ambitions as well as to pressure the traditional political parties to adopt conservative planks in their platforms in 1992. Candidate Bill Clinton's wife, Hillary, was even drawn into a "cookie-baking debate" by Republican image makers seeking to disparage her role as political adviser and confidante. When the off-year elections in 1994 saw a Republican majority elected to Congress on an avowedly conservative agenda, family values again played a major role in their articulation of what was wrong with America. The term seemed to stand for school prayer, nuclear families for raising children, mothers at home with young children, antiabortion, antipornography, antifeminism, and antigovernment social programs.

Critical to conservatives' understanding of childhood was a 1950s image of the two-parent, financially secure nuclear family in which children remained protected from the disturbing images of poverty, crime, disabilities, and suffering. Such an image severely limits where families might live, where children might go to school, and who has the right to be a parent. The opposition, not to be seen as somehow antifamily, saw the publication of Hillary Rodham Clinton's It Takes a Village (1995), a paean to the small-town, Protestant values she believes shaped both her and Bill Clinton's childhoods. Her philosophy recognizes that not all children experience such caring parents; thus she advocates fuller governmental protection of children's rights. The term "family values" is not about the reality of childhood experiences, of course, but about nostalgia for a hypothetical time when at least children, if no one else, could be protected from life's harshness.

The concerns of political figures complement some child development specialists who began to articulate the notion of "the disappearance of childhood," the title of a 1982 book by Neil Postman. Marie Winn's 1983 book *Children without Childhood* and Dr. David Elkind's *The Hurried Child* (1981) reiterate that theme: that children in the late twentieth century cannot enjoy being a child, either because middle-class parental pressure to achieve starts before kindergarten or because the adult world of sex, violence, suffering, and death is constantly foisted upon children.[7] All imply that a return to a real era of childhood is necessary to prevent social disintegration. Literature critic Jerry Griswold sees the contemporary interest in children's literature as yet another manifestation of adult nostalgia for childhood. He concludes that adults are buying children's books for themselves and notes that Harper and Row marketed Maurice Sendak's *Outside Over There* (1981) and *We Are All in the Dumps with Jack and Guy* (1993) to both children and adults.[8]

However, Griswold fails to note that the Sendak titles are anything but comforting or nostalgic. *Outside Over There* is a modern-day fairy tale about baby-snatching, and *All in the Dumps* depicts the plight of homeless children in picture book format. Much closer to the mark of books for the new nostalgia is William J. Bennett's collected *Book of Virtues: A Treasury of Great Moral Stories* (1993), in which former U.S. Secretary of Education and former chair of the National Endowment for the Humanities resurrects some didactic folktales, sanitizes some fairy tales and classical epics, and tries to find a lesson in other poems and stories for children, even if that lesson seems not to be part of the original work. The collection is arranged by theme, such as "Honesty," "Self-Discipline," "Loyalty," and "Faith."

This attempt to provide parents with moral stories complements the work of another cultural warrior, E. D. Hirsch Jr., in *Cultural Literacy: What Every American Needs to Know* (1987). Hirsch developed an entire schema to teach the so-called basic tenets of Western civilization at every grade level so Americans would possess a "shared knowledge" and hence a uniform culture. Bennett's collection implies that works of fiction, poetry, and folk wisdom did not grow out of any particular historical circumstances—and yet his very attempt to produce such a collection in 1993 definitely reflects his personal position in the family values debate. It is a collection that fits perfectly with the didactic literature of the early nineteenth century. This very long collection of stories and poems (818 pages) must not have been too popular with children, for it was reissued with fewer selections and lavish illustrations.[9]

Just what construction of childhood do Americans hold at the end of the millennium? Clearly, a white, middle-class voice is not the only one heard at this juncture. What recent immigrants from Laos want for their children, and what values they hope to inculcate, will differ dramatically from those of a ranching family in Wyoming, a Puerto Rican family in New York City, or a wealthy African-American family in Atlanta. Most children appear to live their lives more completely within their peer orbits and to draw much of their culture from movies and TV than ever before, but even the media culture is not homogeneous. Stories for children will no doubt continue to portray children solving their own problems, using their inner strength and their friends to work out solutions. Millions of adults, whether they have children or not, will mentor children through what they write, say, and do and thus continue to perpetuate the cultural values that matter to them. There is no consensus on what those values are. Even within the political power structure that usually speaks for the dominant culture, opinion is divided or ambivalent. Children and childhood have become the pawns in an ideological war between those who advocate individual responsibility for families and social problems and those who would give governments and institutions broad powers over what happens to children.

Minorities in the United States—whether racial, ethnic, religious, or regional—have always struggled to preserve and transmit their values in the face of a dominant cultural ethos. That these minorities are being heard more directly and their values being shared more widely with others may be very good for the construction of a new understanding of childhood.

Chronology

1845   The dime novel is inaugurated with *Malaeska, or Indian Wife of the White Hunter*

1850   Susan Warner's *Wide, Wide World* launches a rash of Victorian domestic fiction in the United States

1852   *Uncle Tom's Cabin* by Harriet Beecher Stowe

1854   The Oliver Optic series by William Taylor Adams begins

1864   Horatio Alger publishes his first book for boys after being dismissed as a clergyman

1868   Louisa May Alcott's *Little Women* is published, followed by *Little Men* in 1871

1872   The juvenile periodical *St. Nicholas* begins

1876   *Tom Sawyer* is introduced by Samuel Clemens under the pseudonym Mark Twain

1882   George W. Peck introduces "Peck's Bad Boy" in a Milwaukee newspaper column

1885   Twain's *Adventures of Huckleberry Finn*

1886   Frances Hodgson Burnett's *Little Lord Fauntleroy* creates a hero and a new fashion in boys' clothing

1880   Joel Chandler Harris creates Uncle Remus and uses him to retell African folktales in *Uncle Remus, His Songs and Sayings*

1890s   The "new woman" is touted by the press

1895   Annie Fellows Johnston introduces the "Little Colonel" books

1899   Edward Stratemeyer launches the Rover Boy series, which runs until 1926

1900   Helen Bannerman's *Little Black Sambo* is published in the U.S. one year after it appears in England

The Wonderful Wizard of Oz by Frank Baum

1901   The first work of the Frank Merriwell series by William Gilbert Patton is published

1903   Kindergarten proponent Kate Douglas Wiggin writes *Rebecca of Sunnybrook Farm*

1904   Stratemeyer Syndicate introduces the Bobbsey Twins series

The National Child Labor Committee is organized to work for protective legislation for child employees

1910   The Boy Scouts of America is organized

1911   Burnett's *The Secret Garden*

1912   Congress establishes the United States Children's Bureau

1913   The Ruth Fielding series, another Stratemeyer creation, begins

        Eleanor Porter's *Pollyanna* sets a behavioral norm

1914   *Penrod* by Boothe Tarkington appears

1919   W.E.B. Du Bois launches the *Brownies' Book,* a periodical for African-American children

1922   Creation of the Newbery Medal for the best American children's book

1924   The *Horn Book Magazine* is established to review children's literature

1927   The Hardy Boys series of mysteries is brought out by the Stratemeyer Syndicate

1930   The first book about detective Nancy Drew appears, written under the pseudonym Carolyn Keene

        Watty Piper crafts the immortal *Little Engine That Could*

1932   *The Little House in the Big Woods* inaugurates the series by Laura Ingalls Wilder

1934   Arna Bontemps writes *You Can't Pet a Possum* to realistically portray African-American childhood experiences

1937   Dr. Seuss books are introduced by Theodor Geisel with *And to Think That I Saw It on Mulberry Street*

        The Caldecott Award is established to honor exceptional illustration of American children's books

1940s   The popular horse novels by Walter Farley and Mary O'Hara appear

1941   Eleanor Estes's series The Moffats begins

1943   Lois Lenski's Regional series begins with *Bayou Suzette*

1944   *Johnny Tremain* by Esther Forbes invokes patriotism

        Eleanor Estes's *The Hundred Dresses* illuminates discrimination

1945   Florence Crannell Means's *The Moved-Outers* presents the reality of Japanese-American relocation camps

1946   Beginning of the Cold War

1951   J. D. Salinger's *Catcher in the Rye* directs young adult literature toward first-person introspection

1952   E. B. White creates Zuckerman's famous pig in *Charlotte's Web*

1954   *Brown v. Board of Education of Topeka Kansas* begins the slow process of school integration

1957   *The Cat in the Hat* by Dr. Seuss launches Random House's Beginner Reader series

1959	The Stratemeyer Syndicate "updates" its remaining series books to eliminate ethnic and racial slurs and stereotypes
1962	Madeleine L'Engle begins a series of time-travel fantasies with *A Wrinkle in Time*
1963	Maurice Sendak's *Where the Wild Things Are*
1964	*Harriet the Spy* by Louise Fitzhugh leads the trend to greater realism and first-person narration in children's fiction
1967	*The Outsiders* by S. E. Hinton
1968	Interracial Council on Book for Children creates a *Bulletin* to evaluate books for racism and sexism
1970	Debate in the *New York Times* over who is qualified to write fiction about the African-American experience
1974	*My Brother Sam Is Dead* questions the necessity of war during the Vietnam conflict
1975	Judy Blume's *Forever* frankly discusses teenage sexual encounters
	Mildred Taylor introduces the sagas of the Logan family in *Song of the Trees*
1980s	The Sweet Valley High series and its spin-offs
1970s and 1980s	Children's literature begins to respond to needs of parents and teachers for multicultural novels
1982	Neil Postman's *The Disappearance of Childhood*
1992	The Goosebumps series introduces horror stories to children
1993	William Bennett's *Book of Virtues: A Treasury of Great Moral Stories* appears

Notes

Chapter 1

1. This advertisement is reprinted on the first page of a facsimile edition of the 1777 *New England Primer Improved for the More Easy Attaining the True Reading of English* (Boston: Ira Webster, 1843).

2. Paul Leicester Ford, ed., *The "New England Primer": A History of Its Origin and Development* (New York: Dodd, Mead, & Co., 1897), 17; E. Jennifer Monaghan, "Literacy Instruction and Gender in Colonial New England," *American Quarterly* 40.1 (March 1988): 20.

3. Karin Calvert, *Children in the House: The Material Culture of Early Childhood, 1600–1900* (Boston: Northeastern University Press, 1992), 39–47.

4. Ross W. Beales Jr., "The Child in Seventeenth-Century America," in Joseph M. Hawes and N. Ray Hiner, eds., *American Childhood: A Research Guide and Historical Handbook* (Westport, Conn.: Greenwood Press, 1985), 15–56.

5. Joseph M. Hawes, *The Children's Rights Movement: A History of Advocacy and Protection* (Boston: Twayne, 1991), 4–5.

6. As quoted in Ross W. Beales, "In Search of the Historical Child: Miniature Adulthood and Youth in Colonial New England," in N. Ray Hiner and Joseph M. Hawes, eds., *Growing Up in America: Children in Historical Perspective* (Urbana: University of Illinois Press, 1985), 10, 14; David Stannard, "Death and the Puritan Child," *American Quarterly* 26 (1974): 456–76.

7. Jane Bingham and Grayce Scholt, eds., *Children's Literature: An Annotated Chronology of British and American Works in Historical Context* (Westport, Conn.: Greenwood Press, 1980), 87.

8. Eleazer Moody, *The School of Good Manners,* as quoted in Monica Kiefer, *American Children through Their Books, 1700–1835* (Philadel-

phia: University of Pennsylvania Press, 1948), 75; William Sloane, *Children's Books in England and America in the Seventeenth Century* (New York: Kings's Crown Press, 1955), 30.

9. Kiefer, ibid., 79; Daniel Blake Smith, *Inside the Great House: Planter Family Life in Eighteenth-Century Chesapeake Society* (Ithaca, N.Y.: Cornell University Press, 1980), 66–67; Mary Lystad, *At Home in America as Seen through Its Books for Children* (Cambridge, Mass.: Schenkman Publishing, 1984), 17; Sloane, *Children's Books,* 37; Ruth K. MacDonald, *Literature for Children in England and America from 1646–1774* (Troy, N.Y.: Whitston Publishing Co., 1982), 68–70.

10. Bingham and Scholt, eds., *Fifteen Centuries,* 108.

11. John Demos, *A Little Commonwealth: Family Life in Plymouth Colony* (Oxford: Oxford University Press, 1970), 22.

12. Paul S. Boyer et al., *The Enduring Vision: A History of the American People,* vol. 1, 2d ed. (Lexington, Mass.: D. C. Heath & Co., 1993), 57.

13. Jack P. Greene, *Pursuits of Happiness: The Social Development of Early Modern British Colonies and the Formation of American Culture* (Chapel Hill: University of North Carolina Press, 1988), 21.

14. Elizabeth A. Francis, "American Children's Literature," in Hawes, *American Childhood,* 190.

15. *New England Primer,* 1777 edition, Webster facsimile.

16. James Axtell, *The School upon a Hill: Education and Society in Colonial New England* (New York: W. W. Norton, 1974), 26.

17. Sloane, *Children's Books,* 44; quote, 50.

18. Ibid., 50–53; A.S.W. Rosenbach, *Early American Children's Books* (1933; rpt., New York: Kraus Reprint Corp., 1966), 18–19.

19. Rosenbach, ibid., 3–4; Edmund S. Morgan, *The Puritan Family: Religion and Domestic Relations in Seventeenth-Century New England* (New York: Harper & Row, 1944; Harper Torchbook edition, 1966), 91–92.

20. The Wadsworth quote is from Morgan, *The Puritan Family,* 96; the Dwight quote may be found in Peter Gregg Slater, *Children in the New England Mind: In Death and in Life* (Hamden, Conn.: Archon Books, 1977), 132.

21. Charles R. King, *Children's Health in America: A History* (New York: Twayne Publishers, 1993), 3.

22. Beales, "The Child in Seventeenth-Century America," 27; King, *Children's Health,* 3–6.

23. The Mather quote is from Slater, *Children in New England,* 93; Jeannine Hensley, ed., *The Works of Anne Bradstreet* (Cambridge, Mass.: Belknap Press, 1967), 237.

24. Axtell, *The School upon a Hill,* 13.

25. Lawrence A. Cremin, *American Education: The Colonial Experience, 1607–1782* (New York: Harper & Row, 1970), 124–25.

26. David D. Hall, *Worlds of Wonder, Days of Judgment: Popular Religious Belief in Early New England* (New York: Alfred A. Knopf, 1989), 38; Axtell, *The School upon a Hill*, 22.

27. Cremin, *American Education*, 181.

28. As quoted in Hall, *Worlds of Wonder*, 37.

29. Kenneth A. Lockridge, *Literacy in Colonial New England: An Enquiry into the Social Context of Literacy in the Early Modern West* (New York: W. W. Norton, 1974), 73.

30. Hall, *Worlds of Wonder*, 32–34; Monaghan, "Literacy Instruction," 24–28, 33–34.

31. Ford, ed., *The "New England Primer": A History*, 19–20; Monaghan, "Literacy Instruction," 20.

32. Ford, ibid., 37–38. The alphabet probably was not illustrated in the first editions, but woodcuts appear by the 1725 edition. Rosalie V. Halsey, *Forgotten Books of the American Nursery: A History of the Development of the American Story-Book* (Boston: Charles Goodspeed & Co., 1911; Detroit: Singing Tree Press, 1969), 14–15.

33. Ford, ibid., 24–43. The "shorter" in the Westminster title distinguished it from Herbert's catechism, which contained over 1,200 questions and answers. Webster, ed., *New England Primer* (1843).

34. *New England Primer*, 1762 edition, as reprinted in Ford, 25, 27, 29–30. Emphasis mine.

35. Charles F. Heartman, *Non–New England Primers* (Highland Park, N.J.: Harry B. Weiss, 1935), xii–xiv; Cornelia Meigs et al., *A Critical History of Children's Literature*, rev. ed. (New York: Macmillan Co., 1969), 117.

36. Lystad, *Family*, 5–6.

37. Heartman, *Non–New England Primers*, 23.

38. Greene, *Pursuits of Happiness*, 81.

39. Richard Beale Davis, *Intellectual Life in the Colonial South, 1585–1763*, vol. 2 (Knoxville: University of Tennessee Press, 1978), 492, 595–98.

40. *Virginia Gazette* (22 April 1757) and *Virginia Almanac* (1762, no issue number), as quoted in Mary Stephenson, "Child-Life in Virginia: Eighteenth Century and Early Nineteenth Century," Colonial Williamsburg Foundation Research Report, 1969, 1–2; Gregory A. Stiverson and Cynthia Z. Stiverson, "Books Both Useful and Entertaining: A Study of Book Purchases and Reading Habits of Virginians in the Mid-Eighteenth Century" (Williamsburg, Va.: Colonial Williamsburg Foundation Research Report, 1977), n.p.

41. Greene, *Pursuits of Happiness*, 85, 93.

42. Edmund Morgan, *Virginians at Home* (Williamsburg, Va.: Colonial Williamsburg, 1952), 15–17; Robert C. Gerling, "The Educational Opportunities of Children in Colonial Virginia" (Williamsburg, Va.: Colonial Williamsburg Foundation Research Report 295, typescript), 4–6, 7–9. See also his unnumbered appendix for the reproduction of newspaper advertisements for schools and tutors.

43. Smith, *Inside the Great House,* 62–65.

44. Meigs, *Critical History,* 1953 ed., 132; "Child's Play? Children's Books in Early America: An Exhibition from the Collections of the Colonial Williamsburg Foundation for the 22nd Congress of the International Board on Books for Young People" (n.p., 1990), 2.

45. John Tebbel, *A History of Book Publishing in the United States,* vol. 1 (New York: R. R. Bowker, 1972), 138–39.

46. Boyer, *Enduring Vision,* 114, 104.

47. Meigs, *Critical History,* 1969 ed., 62; Kiefer, *American Children,* 12.

48. Meigs, ibid.; Lystad, *At Home,* 20, 28–29.

49. Nancy Cott, "Notes toward an Interpretation of Antebellum Childrearing," *Psychohistory Review* 7 (1977–1978): 5–6.

50. Meigs, *Critical History,* rev. ed., 58, 61.

51. A page from this work is reproduced in Halsey, *Forgotten Books,* opposite p. 49.

52. Ibid., 61.

53. Meigs, *Critical History,* rev. ed., 122–23.

54. James Axtell, ed., *The Educational Writings of John Locke* (Cambridge, England: Cambridge University Press, 1968), 115, 230, 181.

55. Ibid., 158, 172–73, 228–30, 255–59.

56. [John Ely], *The Child's Instructor* (New York: Burtus, 1818); A.S.W. Rosenbach, *Early American Children's Books,* identifies the anonymous author, 71.

57. Tom Telescope, *The Newtonian System of Philosophy,* 4th ed. (London: Newbery, 1770).

58. Locke, *Educational Writings,* 303, 241.

59. Maria Edgeworth, *Practical Education,* vol. 1, 2d American ed. (Boston: n.p., 1815), 4–5.

60. Anonymous, *False Stories Corrected: Learn to Unlearn What You Have Learned Amiss* (New York: S. Wood & Sons, 1814), 5, 20–21, 25–26, 28, 37–39.

61. Anonymous, *The Happy Family; or, Winter Evenings' Employment* (New York: J. C. Totten, 1815). For additional examples of rationality in children's books, see Gail S. Murray, "Rational Thought and Republican Virtues: Children's Literature, 1789–1820," *Journal of the Early Republic* 8 (Summer 1988): 159–77.

62. Cotton Mather, "A Family Well-Ordered, or an Essay to Render Parents and Children Happy in One Another" (Boston: n.p., 1699), as

quoted in Rosenbach, *Early American,* 4.

63. As quoted in Jacqueline S. Reinier, "Rearing the Republican Child: Attitudes and Practices in Post-Revolutionary Philadelphia," *William and Mary Quarterly* 39.1 (January 1982): 154.

64. For the importance of republican ideals in understanding the values of Revolutionary and Jeffersonian America, see Robert E. Shalhope, "Republicanism and Early American Historiography," *William and Mary Quarterly* 39 (April 1982): 334–56; Lance Banning, "Jeffersonian Ideology Revisited: Liberal and Classical Ideas in the New American Republic," *William and Mary Quarterly* 43 (January 1986): 3–19; Joyce Appleby, "Republicanism in Old and New Contexts," ibid., 20–34.

65. Reinier, "Rearing the Republican Child," 155.

66. Jacqueline S. Reinier, *From Virtue to Character: American Childhood, 1775–1850* (New York: Twayne Publishers, 1996), 34–35; Betty P. Goldstone, *Lessons to Be Learned: A Study of Eighteenth-Century English Didactic Children's Literature* (New York: Peter Lange Co., 1994), 107–11; Gillian Avery, *Behold the Child: American Children and Their Books, 1621–1922* (Baltimore: Johns Hopkins University Press, 1994), 46.

67. Judith St. John, "Mrs. Trimmer—Guardian of Education," *Horn Book Magazine* 46 (February 1970): 21–23; Meigs, *Critical History,* 70–71, 77–81.

68. James Newcomer, *Maria Edgeworth* (Lewisburg, Penn.: Bucknell University Press, 1973), 15–19; Daniel T. Rodgers, *The Work Ethic in Industrial America, 1850–1920* (Chicago: University of Chicago Press, 1974), 129; Maria Edgeworth, *Harry and Lucy: A Series of Tales for the Young,* vol. 2 (Baltimore: Kelly and Tiet, 1868), v.

69. Sarah Robbins, "*Lessons for Children* and Teaching Mothers: Mrs. Barbauld's Primer for the Textual Construction of Middle-Class Domestic Pedagogy," *The Lion and the Unicorn* 17.2 (December 1993): 136; Avery, *Behold the Child,* 65.

70. For a similar argument about books and young women in New England, see Richard D. Brown, *Knowledge Is Power: The Diffusion of Information in Early America, 1700–1865* (New York: Oxford University Press, 1989), 160–67.

Chapter 2

1. As quoted in Paul S. Boyer et al., *The Enduring Vision: A History of the American People,* vol. 1, 2d ed. (Lexington, Mass.: D. C. Heath & Co., 1993), 367.

2. As quoted in David Hawke, *Benjamin Rush, Revolutionary Gadfly* (New York: Bobbs-Merrill Co., 1971), 332. Emphasis mine.

3. As quoted in Monica Kiefer, *American Children through Their Books, 1700–1835* (Philadelphia: University of Pennsylvania Press, 1948), 133. Emphasis mine.
4. As quoted in Jean H. Baker, *Affairs of Party: The Political Culture of Northern Democrats in the Mid-Nineteenth Century* (Ithaca, N.Y.: Cornell University Press, 1983), 73.
5. As quoted in E. Jennifer Monaghan, *A Common Heritage: Noah Webster's Blue-Back Speller* (Hamden, Conn.: Archon Press, 1983), 13.
6. Boyer, *Enduring Vision,* vol. 1, 194.
7. As quoted in Lorraine Smith Pangle and Thomas L. Pangle, *The Learning of Liberty: The Educational Ideas of the American Founders* (Lawrence: University of Kansas Press), 96.
8. Rush Welter, *Popular Education and Democratic Thought in America* (New York: Columbia University Press, 1962), 24.
9. As quoted in Baker, *Affairs of Party,* 72.
10. Hawke, *Benjamin Rush,* 331–34.
11. Baker, *Affairs of Party,* 76.
12. Thomas Jefferson, *Writings,* ed. Merrill D. Peterson (New York: Library of America, 1984), 365.
13. Ibid., 367.
14. Keith Whitescarver, "Creating Citizens for the Republic: Education in Georgia, 1776–1810," *Journal of the Early Republic* 13 (Winter 1993): 455–79.
15. Baker, *Affairs of Party,* 75–76; Welter, *Popular Education,* 26.
16. As quoted in Jacqueline S. Reinier, "Rearing the Republican Child: Attitudes and Practices in Post-Revolutionary Philadelphia," *William and Mary Quarterly* 39.1 (January 1982): 158.
17. Abigail Adams to John Adams, 14 August 1776, in *Adams Family Correspondence,* vol. 2, L. H. Butterfield et al., eds. (Cambridge, Mass.: Harvard University Press, 1963), 94.
18. Boyer, *Enduring Vision,* 187.
19. Maria Edgeworth, *Harry and Lucy* (Poughkeepsie, N.Y.: Poetters, 1815), 12–13.
20. John Tebbel, *A History of Book Publishing in the United States,* vol. 1 (New York: R. R. Bowker, 1972), 193.
21. As quoted in Alan K. Synder, *Mind and Morals in the Early Republic* (Lanham, Md.: University Presses of America, 1990), 52.
22. Noah Webster, *The Grammatical Institute,* 12, as quoted in Synder, *Mind and Morals,* 59–60.
23. Thomas Jefferson, *The Jefferson Bible,* ed. F. Forrester Church (Boston: Beacon Press, 1989); Noah Webster, *An American Selection of Lessons,* 147, as quoted in Ruth Elston, *Guardians of Tradition: American Schoolbooks of the Nineteenth Century* (Lincoln: University of Nebraska Press, 1964), 225.

24. Monaghan, *Common Heritage,* 14, 33.

25. This edition of the "Federal Catechism" appeared in *The American Spelling Book* (Boston: 1798), 154.

26. Caleb Bingham, *The American Preceptor; Being a New Selection of Lessons for Reading and Speaking* (New York: Evert Duyckinck, 1815). Bingham was one of the few early authors who was not a Federalist. He included Jefferson along with Washington, Adams, and Franklin in the American selections. His second collection, *The Columbian Orator* (1797), also sounded much more American than it was.

27. Mason L. Weems, *The Life of Washington,* ed. Marcus Cunliffe (Cambridge, Mass.: Belknap Press, 1962), ix–xi, xiii, xv.

28. Cunliffe, ed., ibid., xxxi–xvi, xxi; Jane Bingham and Grayce Scholt, eds., *Children's Literature: An Annotated Chronology of British and American Works in Historical Context* (Westport, Conn.: Greenwood Press, 1980), 162; Jacqueline Reinier, *From Virtue to Character: American Childhood, 1775–1850* (New York: Twayne Publishers, 1996), 96.

29. Charles Carpenter, *History of American Schoolbooks* (Philadelphia: University of Pennsylvania Press, 1963), 63; Elston, *Guardians of Tradition,* 6.

30. Harvey C. Minnich, *William Holmes McGuffey and His Readers* (1936; rpt., Detroit: Gale Research Co., 1975), 24, 31–32.

31. Ibid., 27–30, 60–63; Tebbel, *History of Book Publishing,* 552.

32. Minnich, ibid., 38–43.

33. Samuel G. Goodrich, *Peter Parley's Own Story, From the Personal Narrative of the Late Samuel G. Goodrich* (New York: Sheldon & Co., 1864), 238; Helen S. Canfield, "Peter Parley, II," *Horn Book Magazine* 46 (June 1970): 276–77.

34. Samuel G. Goodrich, *Stories about Captain John Smith, of Virginia; for the Instruction and Amusement of Children* (Hartford, Conn.: H. & F. J. Huntington, 1829), 95.

35. Cornelia Meigs et al., *A Critical History of Children's Literature* (New York: Macmillan and Co., 1953), 142–44; Samuel G. Goodrich, *Lives of Celebrated Women* (Boston: C. H. Peirce, 1848).

36. Daniel T. Rodgers, *The Work Ethic in Industrial America, 1850–1920* (Chicago: University of Chicago Press, 1974), 129.

37. Nancy Cott, *The Bonds of Womanhood: "Woman's Sphere" in New England, 1780–1830* (New Haven, Conn.: Yale University Press, 1977); Avery, *Behold the Child,* 85–86; Carol Gay, "Lydia Sigourney," *Dictionary of Literary Biography,* vol. 42, ed. Glenn E. Estes (Detroit: Gale Research, 1985), 324–25, 327.

38. Anne Scott MacLeod, *A Moral Tale: Children's Fiction and American Culture, 1820–1860* (Hamden, Conn.: Archon Books, 1975), 51–52; Avery, *Behold the Child,* 84.

39. Carolyn L. Karcher, *The First Woman in the Republic: A Cultural Biography of Lydia Maria Child* (Durham, S.C.: Duke University Press, 1994), 60–62.
40. Lydia Maria Child, *Evenings in New England*, 58, as quoted in Karcher, 62–63.
41. "Constitution of the First Day Society," as quoted in Reinier, *From Virtue to Character*, 79.
42. Ann Boylan, *Sunday School: The Formation of an American Institution, 1790–1880* (New Haven, Conn.: Yale University Press, 1988), 6–9.
43. Reinier, *From Virtue to Character*, 80–81, 89; Boylan, *Sunday School*, 10.
44. Boylan, *Sunday School*, 10–11, 33, 38, 46; Joanna Gillespie, "Schooling through Fiction," *Children's Literature* 14 (1986): 62–63.
45. Alice B. Cushman, "A Nineteenth-Century Plan for Reading: The American Sunday School Movement," *Horn Book Magazine* (February 1957): 67.
46. Ibid., 66–67; Joanna Bowen Gillespie, "An Almost Irresistible Enginery: Five Decades of Nineteenth-Century Methodist Sunday School Library Books," *Phaedrus* (Spring–Summer 1980): 9.
47. Boylan, *Sunday School*, 48–49; Cuchman, "Sunday School Movement," 61, 64, 67–69. The Child's Cabinet Library is pictured in Boylan, 51.
48. Gillespie, "Schooling," 64.
49. Mary Lystad, *At Home in America as Seen through Its Books for Children* (Cambridge, Mass.: Schenkman Publishing, 1984), 9.
50. John B. Boles, "Jacob Abbott and the Rollo Books: New England Culture for Children," *Journal of Popular Culture* 4 (Winter 1972): 509, 511, 513, 518; Meigs, *Critical History*, 147.
51. Abbott, *Rollo Learning to Read*, v–vi, as quoted in Boles, "Jacob Abbott," 514.
52. As quoted in Boles, 519, 517.
53. Jacob Abbott, *The Teacher: or Moral Influences Employed in the Instruction and Government of the Young* (Boston: William Peirce, 1836), 157–61.
54. Bernard Wishy, *The Child and the Republic: The Dawn of Modern American Child Nurture* (Philadelphia: University of Pennsylvania Press, 1968), 58–61.
55. As quoted in Boles, "Jacob Abbott," 517.
56. Meigs, *Critical History*, 149–50; Boles, "Jacob Abbott," 512.
57. Jacob Abbott, *Rodolphus, a Franconia Story* (New York: Harper & Bros., 1852), v–vi.
58. Ibid., 10; Abbott, *The Teacher*.
59. Jean V. Matthews, *Toward a New Society: American Thought and Culture, 1800–1830* (Boston: Twayne Publishers, 1991), 67.
60. Meigs, *Critical History*, 128–29; J. Bingham, *Writers for Children*, 148–49; Matthews, *New Society*, 67–68.

61. J. Bingham, *Writers for Children,* 149; Matthews, *New Society,* 91.

62. Carl R. Kaestle, *Pillars of the Republic: Common Schools and American Society, 1780–1860* (New York: Hill and Wang, 1983); R. Gordon Kelly, *Mother Was a Lady: Self and Society in Selected American Children's Periodicals, 1865–1890* (Westport, Conn.: Greenwood, 1974), 6.

63. John C. Crandall, "Patriotism and Humanitarian Reform in Children's Literature, 1825–1860," *American Quarterly* 21 (Spring 1969): 3–17.

64. Valarie H. Ziegler, *The Advocates of Peace in Antebellum America* (Bloomington: Indiana University Press, 1992), 3, 10–12.

65. "The Little Soldiers," *Youth's Casket* (1856), as quoted in Crandall, "Humanitarianism," 12.

66. Crandall, "Humanitarianism," 9–10; Mary Lystad, *At Home in America as Seen through Its Books for Children* (Cambridge, Mass.: Schenkman Publishing Co., 1984), 37, 48, 62; Lyman Cobb, *Juvenile Reader,* 1, 2, and 3 (Dansville, N.Y.: A. Stevens, 1835).

67. As quoted in Crandall, "Humanitarianism," 13.

68. Arnold Arnold, *Pictures and Stories from Forgotten Children's Books* (New York: Dover Publications, 1969), 52; Holly Keller, "Juvenile Antislavery Narrative and Notions of Childhood," *Children's Literature* 24 (1996): 99.

69. Violet Joyce Harris, "The Brownies' Book: Challenge to the Selective Tradition in Children's Literature" (Ph.D. diss., University of Georgia, 1986), 92; Keller, "Juvenile Antislavery Narratives," 91–92.

70. Keller, ibid., 87; poem from *The Slave's Friend* 4, as quoted in Keller, 95.

71. Lydia Maria Child, *Evenings in New England* (1824), as quoted in Karcher, *First Woman,* 64.

72. Hanley Kanar, "Abolition Ambiguity, Fictive Blacks, and Drawing of White/Black Social Boundaries," paper delivered at the "Modern Critical Approaches to Children's Literature" conference, Nashville, April 1995.

73. Karcher, *First Woman,* 165–69.

74. Ibid., 64.

75. As quoted in Elston, *Guardians of Tradition,* 280.

76. Karcher, *First Woman,* 58.

77. Ibid., 57, 66–67, 151, 153–54, 169.

78. Avery, *Behold the Child,* 82–83.

79. Canfield, "Peter Parley," II:280, III:416; Meigs, *Critical History,* 145.

Chapter 3

1. William Wordsworth, "Ode: Intimations of Immortality from Recollections of Early Childhood," in Douglas Hunt, ed., *The Riverside Anthology of Literature* (Boston: Houghton Mifflin Co., 1988), 767.

2. Anne Scott MacLeod, *American Childhood: Essays on Children's Literature in the Nineteenth and Twentieth Centuries* (Athens: University of Georgia Press, 1994), 114–16.

3. John Tebbel, *A History of Book Publishing in the United States*, vol. 1 (New York: R. R. Bowker, 1972), 258–59.

4. Ronald J. Zboray, "Antebellum Reading and the Ironies of Technological Innovation," *American Quarterly* 40 (March 1988): 65–67.

5. Bernard Wishy uses the heading "The child redeemable" to discuss child rearing manuals and children's literature between 1830 and 1860 and "The child redeemer" to describe similar materials written between 1860 and 1890. See *The Child and the Republic: The Dawn of Modern American Child Nurture* (Philadelphia: University of Pennsylvania Press, 1968).

6. Jane Tompkins, *Sensational Designs: The Cultural Work of American Fiction, 1790–1860* (New York: Oxford University Press, 1985), especially chapters 5 and 6; quote is from page 125.

7. Wishy, *The Child and the Republic*, 81–104.

8. Gillian Avery, *Behold the Child: American Children and Their Books, 1621–1922* (Baltimore: Johns Hopkins University Press, 1994), 114.

9. Glenn E. Estes, ed., *Dictionary of Literary Biography*, vol. 42 (Detroit: Gale Research Co., 1985), 363, 365; Jane Tompkins, afterword, in Tompkins, ed., *The Wide, Wide World* (New York: Feminist Press, 1987), 584.

10. Tompkins, ibid., 601.

11. Susan Warner, *The Wide, Wide World* (1850; rpt., Philadelphia: Lippincott Publishers, 1892), 16, 240, 12, 26–31.

12. Estes, *Dictionary*, 366.

13. Warner, *The Wide, Wide World*, 70–74.

14. Ibid., 278.

15. Ibid., 307, 310, 314.

16. Russel Nye, *Society and Culture in America, 1830–1860* (New York: Harper & Row, 1974), 301–02.

17. Warner, *The Wide, Wide World*, 61.

18. Avery, *Behold the Child*, 114.

19. Shirley Foster and Judy Simons, *What Katy Read: Feminist Re-Readings of "Classic" Stories for Girls* (Iowa City: University of Iowa Press, 1995), 107–13.

20. Ibid., 64–65; Kate Douglas Wiggin, *The Birds' Christmas Carol* (Boston: Houghton Mifflin Co., 1886; rpt., 1941), 16–17.

21. Estes, *Dictionary*, 181.

22. Charles R. King, *Children's Health in America* (New York: Twayne Publishers, 1993), x, 106–09.

23. Estes, *Dictionary*, 183.

24. Beverly Lyon Clark, "A Portrait of the Artist as a Little Woman," *Children's Literature* 17 (1989): 82.

25. Cornelia Meigs, Anne Thaxter Eaton, Elizabeth Nesbitt, and Ruth Hill Viguers, *A Critical History of Children's Literature,* rev. ed. (New York: Macmillan and Co., 1969), 227–28.

26. Ruth MacDonald, *Louisa May Alcott* (Boston: Twayne, 1983), 13, 29–30; Judith Fetterly, "Little Women: Alcott's Civil War," ed. Madeline Stern, in *Critical Essays on Louisa May Alcott* (Boston: G. K. Hall, 1984), 140.

27. For new Freudian and feminist interpretations of Alcott, see Stern, ibid., and Martha Saxton, *Louisa May* (Boston: Houghton Mifflin, 1977). The most recently published Alcott "thriller" is *A Long Fatal Love Chase* (New York: Random House, 1995). Other so-called sensational stories can be found in Madeline B. Stern, ed., *Behind the Mask: The Unknown Thrillers of Louisa May Alcott* (New York: Morrow, 1975); *Plots and Counterplots: More Unknown Thrillers of Louisa May Alcott* (New York: Morrow, 1976); and *A Double Life: Newly Discovered Thrillers of Louisa May Alcott* (Boston: Little, Brown, 1988).

28. Angela M. Estes and Kathleen Margaret Lant, "Dismembering the Text: The Horror of Louisa May Alcott's *Little Women,*" *Children's Literature* 17 (1989): 99. Judith Fetterly argues that Alcott "uses the mask of femininity and the persona of a 'little woman' to enact a devastatingly successful power struggle with a series of men" in her sensational story "Behind the Mask," in Fetterly, "Little Women," 141.

29. From *Little Women,* as quoted in MacDonald, *Louisa May Alcott,* 15; Estes and Lant, "Dismembering," 104–5, 109.

30. Jerry Griswold, *Audacious Kids: Coming of Age in America's Classic Children's Books* (New York: Oxford University Press, 1992), 262, n. 16.

31. The Lowell piece is reprinted in Stern, *Critical Essays,* 216.

32. Estes and Lant, "Dismembering," 104.

33. Ibid., 115.

34. Elizabeth Lennox Keysar, *Whispers in the Dark: The Fiction of Louisa May Alcott* (Knoxville: University of Tennessee Press, 1993), 85–86.

35. As quoted in MacDonald, *Alcott,* 42–43.

36. As quoted in Beverly Lyon Clark, "A Portrait of the Artist as a Little Woman," *Children's Literature* 17 (1989): 95, n. 6.

37. As quoted in MacDonald, *Louisa May Alcott,* 140.

38. Jane M. Bingham, ed. *Writers for Children: Critical Studies of Major Authors Since the Seventeenth Century* (New York: Scribner's Sons, 1988), 265–66.

39. Estes, *Dictionary,* 127–32.

40. Karen Halttunen, *Confidence Men and Painted Women: A Study of Middle-Class Culture in America, 1830–1870* (New Haven, Conn.: Yale University Press, 1982), 203–05.

41. Estes, *Dictionary,* 14.

42. Daniel T. Rodgers, *The Work Ethic in Industrial America, 1850–1920* (Chicago: University of Chicago Press, 1974), 137; Jane Bingham and Grayce Scholt, eds., *Fifteen Centuries of Children's Literature: An Annotated Chronology of British and American Works in Historical Context* (Westport, Conn.: Greenwood, 1980), 186.

43. Ibid., 137–43.

44. Kenneth L. Donelson and Alleen Pace Nilsen, *Literature for Today's Young Adult,* 3d ed. (Glenview, Ill.: Scott, Foresman & Co., 1989), 146.

45. Carol Nackenoff, *The Fictional Republic: Horatio Alger and American Political Discourse* (New York: Oxford University Press, 1994), 3.

46. See quote in prefatory material to Gary Scharnhorst, *The Lost Life of Horatio Alger Jr.* (Bloomington: Indiana University Press, 1985), n.p.

47. For a thorough discussion of critical approaches to Horatio Alger, see Nackenoff, *Fictional Republic,* 3–11.

48. From the introduction to *Paul Prescott's Charge,* as quoted in Scharnhorst, *Lost Life,* 63.

49. Scharnhorst, *Lost Life,* 1–3, 66–67, 70, 77, 80. The circumstances of Alger's resignation involved charges of homosexuality.

50. Michael Zuckerman, "The Nursery Tales of Horatio Alger," in *Almost Chosen People: Oblique Biographies in the American Grain* (Berkeley: University of California Press, 1993), 220.

51. Ibid., 132; Horatio Alger Jr., *Ragged Dick and Struggling Upward* (New York: Penguin Books, 1985), 7.

52. Halttunen, *Confidence Men,* 199–203.

53. Rodgers, *Work Ethic,* 142; Zuckerman, "Nursery Tales," 233.

54. Zuckerman, ibid., 230–31. Emphasis mine.

55. Nackenoff, *Fictional Republic,* 78–80, 84–88; 221–22.

56. Ibid., 33, 42–44, 53–54, 59–60.

57. MacLeod, *American Childhood,* 79.

58. As quoted in Nackenoff, *Fictional Republic,* 255.

59. Ibid., 91.

60. Zuckerman, "Nursery Tales," 225. Emphasis mine.

61. Joseph M. Hawes, *Children in Urban Society: Juvenile Delinquency in Nineteenth-Century America* (New York: Oxford University Press, 1971), 117.

62. Ann Trensky, "The Bad Boy in Nineteenth-Century American Fiction," *Georgia Review* 27.4 (Winter 1973): 505–08.

63. Ibid., 508–09; Clemens quote, 509.

64. Steven Mailloux, *Rhetorical Power* (Ithaca, N.Y.: Cornell University Press, 1989), 112. Quote is from G. Stanley Hall, *Adolescence: Its Psychology.*

65. *Love and Death in the American Novel* (New York: Criterion Books, 1960), as quoted in Avery, *Behold the Child,* 197.

66. R. Gordon Kelly, *Mother Was a Lady: Self and Society in Selected American Children's Periodicals, 1865–1890* (Westport, Conn.: Greenwood Press, 1974), 149; Estes, *Dictionary,* 43–47.

67. Thomas Bailey Aldrich, *The Story of a Bad Boy* (New York: Garland, 1976), 7.

68. MacLeod, *American Childhood,* 71–72.

69. George W. Peck, *Peck's Bad Boy and His Pa* (Chicago: Thompson & Thomas, 1883), 28.

70. Ibid., 23–27, 39–41.

71. Ibid., 214, 299.

72. James S. Leonard, Thomas A. Tenney, and Thadious M. Davis, *Satire or Evasion? Black Perspectives on Huckleberry Finn* (Durham, N.C.: Duke University Press, 1992), 1–3.

73. Mailloux, *Rhetorical Power,* 124–25.

74. Kenny J. Williams, "*Adventures of Huckleberry Finn;* or, Mark Twain's Racial Ambiguity," in Leonard, ed., *Satire or Evasion?,* 229.

75. See, for example, John H. Wallace, "The Case Against *Huck Finn,*" and Bernard W. Bell, "Twain's 'Nigger' Jim: The Tragic Face behind the Minstrel Mask," in Leonard, ed., *Satire or Evasion?*

76. First quotation is from Clifton Fadiman in Shelley Fisher Fishkin, *Was Huck Black? Mark Twain and African-American Voices* (New York: Oxford University Press, 1993), 133. Second quotation is from Fishkin, 3.

77. Ibid., 154; Griswold, *Audacious Kids,* 146.

78. Mark Twain, *The Adventures of Huckleberry Finn* (1885; rpt., New York: Bantam Books, 1965), n.p.

79. MacLeod, *American Childhood,* 74–76.

80. Trensky, "Bad Boy," 515–16.

81. Kelly, *Mother Was a Lady,* 12–13, 23; Peter Hunt, ed., *Children's Literature: An Illustrated History* (Oxford: Oxford University Press, 1995), 230.

82. Kelly, *Mother Was a Lady,* 7–9; Gillian Avery, 146; Boyer, *Enduring Vision,* vol. 1, 289.

83. Boyer, *Enduring Vision,* vol. 2, 682.

84. Kelly, *Mother Was a Lady,* xx.

85. Paula Petrick, "The Youngest Fourth Estate: The Novelty Toy Printing Press and Adolescence, 1870–1886," in *Small Worlds: Children and Adolescents in America, 1850–1950* (Lawrence: University of Kansas Press, 1992), 125–42.

86. Kelly, *Mother Was a Lady,* 23; Avery, *Behold the Child,* 146.

87. Hunt, *Children's Literature,* 230; Avery, *Behold the Child,* 146, 148–50; Kelly, *Mother Was a Lady,* 15–16.

88. Kelly, ibid., 49; Michael Denning, *Mechanic Accents: Dime Novels and Working-Class Culture in America* (New York: Verso Press, 1987), 10–11, 19, 22.

89. Denning, ibid., 11–12.

90. Donelson, *Literature for Today's Young Adult,* 471.

91. Denning, *Mechanic Accents,* 11–12; Bingham, ed., *Writers for Children,* 146–47.

92. Deidre Johnson, *Edward Stratemeyer and the Stratemeyer Syndicate* (New York: Twayne Publishers, 1993), 27–30.

93. Denning, *Mechanic Accents,* 185, 204.

94. Ibid., 13, 16–25.

95. As quoted in Mailloux, *Rhetorical Power,* 120.

96. Johnson, *Stratemeyer Syndicate,* 24.

97. Denning, *Mechanic Accents,* 12.

Chapter 4

1. Viviana A. Zelizer, *Pricing the Priceless Child: The Changing Social Value of Children* (1985; rpt., Princeton, N.J.: Princeton University Press, 1994).

2. Kriste Lindenmeyer, *"A Right to Childhood": The United States Children's Bureau and Child Welfare, 1912–1946* (Urbana: University of Illinois Press, 1997), 1.

3. Lawrence A. Cremin, *American Education: The Metropolitan Experience, 1876–1980* (New York: Harper & Row, 1988), 544–46. For a full discussion of this debate between "traditional" education and "practical" education, see David Nasaw, *Schooled to Order: A Social History of Public Schooling in the United States* (New York: Oxford University Press, 1979).

4. Rosalind Rosenberg, *Beyond Separate Spheres: Intellectual Roots of Modern Feminism* (New Haven, Conn.: Yale University Press, 1982), 54.

5. Lois Banner, *Women in Modern America,* 2d ed. (San Diego: Harcourt Brace Jovanovich, 1984), 1–2, 6–7, 21–22; Lucy Stone quotation from Sheila Rothman, *Woman's Proper Place: A History of Changing Ideals and Practices, 1879 to the Present* (New York: Basic Books, 1978), 43.

6. Faye Riter Kensinger, *Children of the Series and How They Grew* (Bowling Green, Ohio: Bowling Green State University Press, 1987), 21.

7. Deidre Johnson, *Edward Stratemeyer and the Stratemeyer Syndicate* (New York: Twayne Publishers, 1993), 94–97.

8. Ibid., 100–101.

9. Gillian Avery, *Behold the Child: American Children and Their Books, 1621–1922* (Baltimore: Johns Hopkins University Press, 1994), 169; Jane Smith, "Plucky Little Ladies and Stout-Hearted Chums: Serial Novels for Girls, 1900–1920," *Prospects: An Annual of American Cultural Studies* 3 (1977): 156.

10. Rosenberg, *Beyond Separate Spheres*, 30, 43–44; Banner, *Women in Modern America*, 5.

11. For the particular difficulties these colleges had to overcome, especially the charge that women who studied rigorously would become infertile, see Sheila Rothman, *Woman's Proper Place*.

12. Lynn D. Gordon, "The Gibson Girl Goes to College: Popular Culture and Women's Higher Education in the Progressive Era, 1890–1920," *American Quarterly* 39.2 (Summer 1987): 216–20.

13. Smith, "Plucky Little Ladies," 170–72.

14. Daniel T. Rodgers, *The Work Ethic in Industrial America, 1850–1920* (Chicago: University of Chicago Press, 1974), 145–46; Walter Evans, "The All-American Boys: A Study of Boys' Sports Fiction," *Journal of Popular Culture* 6 (1972): 107–8, 111.

15. Evans, ibid., 108–9.

16. Ibid., 113–14.

17. Kenneth L. Donelson and Alleen Pace Nilsen, *Literature for Today's Young Adult*, 3d ed. (Glenview, Ill.: Scott, Foresman & Co., 1989), 522; Evans, "All American Boys," 106.

18. Donelson, ibid., 522; Evans, ibid., 105.

19. Sherrie A. Inness, " 'It Is Pluck, But—Is It Sense?': Athletic Student Culture in Progressive-era Girls' College Fiction," in Claudia Nelson and Lynne Vallone, eds., *The Girls' Own: Cultural Histories of the Anglo-American Girl, 1930–1915* (Athens: University of Georgia Press, 1994), 236, n. 1, 240–42, 218; Smith, "Plucky Little Ladies," 166.

20. As quoted in Johnson, *Stratemeyer Syndicate*, 123.

21. Inness, "Is It Pluck," 225, 217–19; Smith, "Plucky Little Ladies," 169.

22. Donelson, *Literature for Today's Young Adults*, 510.

23. David K. Vaughn, "The Possibilities of Flight: Shaping Reader Response in American Aviation Series Books, 1909–1959," paper presented at a Library of Congress symposium on dime novels, series books, and paperbacks, June 9–10, 1995.

24. Elizabeth A. Frank, "Advocating War Preparedness," ibid.; Paul S. Boyer et al., *The Enduring Vision: A History of the American People*, vol. 2, 2d ed. (Lexington, Mass.: D. C. Heath & Co., 1993), 769.

25. Smith, "Plucky Little Ladies," 170.

26. Johnson, *Stratemeyer Syndicate*, 103–6, 110, 112.

27. Smith, "Plucky Little Ladies," 170; Johnson, *Stratemeyer Syndicate*, 119–20.

28. Donelson, *Literature for Today's Young Adults,* 510; Johnson, *Stratemeyer Syndicate,* 2–3.

29. Deidre Johnson, "From Paragraphs to Pages: The Writing and Development of the Stratemeyer Syndicate Series," in Carolyn Stewart Dyer and Nancy Tillman Romalov, eds., *Rediscovering Nancy Drew* (Iowa City: University of Iowa Press, 1995), 29; Peter A. Soderbergh, "The Stratemeyer Strain: Educators and the Juvenile Series Book, 1900–1973," *Journal of Popular Culture* 7 (Spring 1974): 865; Carol Billman, *The Secret of the Stratemeyer Syndicate* (New York: Ungar Publishing Co., 1986), 21.

30. Billman, ibid., 25.

31. Johnson, *Stratemeyer Syndicate,* 6–7; Donelson, *Literature for Today's Young Adult,* 511–12.

32. Donelson, ibid.

33. Johnson, *Stratemeyer Syndicate,* ix, 8. Sorting out pseudonyms and real authors has intrigued both collectors and scholars; see Deidre Johnson, *Stratemeyer Pseudonyms and Series Books: An Annotated Checklist of Stratemeyer and Stratemeyer Syndicate Publications* (Westport, Conn.: Greenwood Press, 1980). The Children's Literature Research Collections at the University of Minnesota Library has published *Girls' Series Books: A Checklist of Hardback Books Published 1900–1975* (1978).

34. Billman, *The Secret of the Stratemeyer Syndicate,* 25.

35. Johnson, *Stratemeyer Syndicate,* 94, 6.

36. Donelson, *Literature for Today's Young Adult,* 513.

37. Johnson, *Stratemeyer Syndicate,* 64–79, 7–9, 51–55.

38. Johnson, ibid., 112–13; Billman, *The Secret of the Stratemeyer Syndicate,* 57–63.

39. Johnson, ibid., 114.

40. Smith, "Plucky Little Ladies," 165.

41. Johnson, *Stratemeyer Syndicate,* 125–31.

42. Hall, *Adolescence: Its Psychology and Its Relations to Physiology, Anthropology, Sociology, Sex, Crime, Religion, and Education* (New York: Appleton, 1905), as quoted in David Nasaw, *Schooled to Order: A Social History of Public Schooling in the United States* (New York: Oxford University Press, 1979), 89.

43. Sonderbergh, "The Stratemeyer Syndicate," 864–65.

44. Dora Smith, *Fifty Years of Children's Books* (Chicago: National Council of Teachers of English, 1923), 5–6; Billman, *The Secret of the Stratemeyer Syndicate,* 32–33.

45. As quoted in Anne Scott MacLeod, *American Childhood: Essays on Children's Literature of the Nineteenth and Twentieth Centuries* (Athens: University of Georgia Press, 1994), 121.

46. Smith, *Fifty Years,* 25.

47. Billman, *The Secret of the Stratemeyer Syndicate*, 32–34.

48. MacLeod, *American Childhood*, 114–16, 124–25.

49. Dennis Thomison, *The History and Development of the American Library Association, 1876–1957* (Chicago: American Library Association, 1978), 1–10.

50. Donelson, *Literature for Today's Young Adult*, 488.

51. Peter Hunt, ed., *Children's Literature: An Illustrated History* (New York: Oxford University Press, 1995), 229.

52. Smith, *Fifty Years*, 23.

53. Donelson, *Literature for Today's Young Adult*, 508–9.

54. As quoted in MacLeod, *American Childhood*, 123.

55. Smith, *Fifty Years*, 25.

56. MacLeod, *American Childhood*, 122.

57. David MacLeod, "Act Your Age: Boyhood, Adolescence, and the Rise of the Boy Scouts of America," in Harvey Graff, ed., *Growing Up in America* (Detroit: Wayne State University Press, 1987), 397–413.

58. Jane M. Bingham, *Writers for Children: Critical Studies of Major Authors Since the Seventeenth Century* (New York: Scribner's, 1987), 447–49.

59. Quote is from John Rowe Townsend, *Written for Children*, 4th ed. (New York: HarperCollins, 1990), 82.

60. Avery, *Behold the Child*, 138.

61. Rodgers, *The Work Ethic in Industrial America, 1850–1920* (Chicago: University of Chicago Press, 1974), 148; Joseph A. Altsheler, *The Young Trailers: A Story of Early Kentucky* (New York: D. Appleton-Century Co., 1907), ii.

62. Roger W. Cummins, *Humorous but Wholesome: A History of Palmer Cox and the Brownies* (Watkins Glen, N.Y.: Century House Americana, 1973), 56.

63. Palmer Cox, *The Brownies: Their Book* (1887; rpt., New York: Dover Publications, 1964), 7; Hunt, *Children's Literature*, 236–37.

64. As quoted in Cummins, *Humorous but Wholesome*, 114–15.

65. Ibid. See illustrations on 141–45, 149–51, 159, 226.

66. Michael Patrick Hearn, *The Annotated Wizard of Oz* (New York: Clarkson N. Potter, 1973), 20–21.

67. Ibid., 21–30, 33.

68. See, for example, Martin Gardiner and Russel Nye, *The Wizard of Oz and Who He Was* (East Lansing: Michigan State University Press, 1957); Henry M. Littlefield, "The Wizard of Oz: Parable on Populism," *American Quarterly* 16.1 (Spring 1964); William R. Leach, ed., *The Wonderful Wizard of Oz by L. Frank Baum* (Belmont, Calif.: Wadsworth Publishing Company, 1991); Jerry Griswold, "There's No Place but Home," in Griswold, *Audacious Kids: Coming of Age in America's Classic Children's Books* (New York: Oxford University Press, 1992),

29–41; and John G. Geer and Thomas R. Rochon, "William Jennings Bryan on the Yellow Brick Road," *Journal of American Culture* 16.4 (Winter 1993): 59–63.

69. As quoted in Hearn, 39.

70. Gardiner and Nye, *The Wizard of Oz and Who He Was,* 30.

71. In the book, Dorothy receives silver slippers, and her final words are "Aunt Em! I'm so glad to be at home again!"

72. See, for example, Paul Nathanson, *Over the Rainbow: The Wizard of Oz as a Secular Myth of America* (Albany: State University of New York Press, 1991); Salman Rushdie, *The Wizard of Oz* (London: British Film Institute, 1992); Todd S. Gilman, " 'Aunt Em: Hate You! Hate Kansas! Taking the Dog. Dorothy': Conscious and Unconscious Desire in *The Wizard of Oz,*" *Children's Literature Association Quarterly* 20.4 (Winter 1995–1996): 161–67.

73. Griswold, "There's No Place but Home," 32.

74. Littlefield, "The Wizard of Oz," 49–52.

75. Ibid., 52–54, 57.

76. Geer and Rochon, "William Jennings Bryan on the Yellow Brick Road," 60–62.

77. Griswold, "There's No Place but Home," 30.

78. Hearn, *The Annotated Wizard of Oz,* 337.

79. Joanne L. Lynn, "Hyacinths and Biscuits in the Village of Liver and Onions: Sandburg's *Rootabaga Stories,*" *Children's Literature* 8 (1980): 118–19; Carl Sandburg, *Rootabaga Stories* (New York: Harcourt, Brace, and Co., 1922).

80. Lynn, ibid., 121–22; Agnes Regan Perkins, "Carl Sandburg," in Jane M. Bingham, ed., *Writers for Children: Critical Studies of Major Authors Since the Seventeenth Century* (New York: Charles Scribner's Sons, 1988), 503–10.

81. Sue Lynn McGuire, "The Little Colonel: A Phenomenon in Popular Literary Culture," *Register of the Kentucky Historical Society* (Spring 1991): 121, 134–35, 139.

82. Ibid., 130; Annie Fellows Johnston, *The Little Colonel's Hero* (Boston: L. C. Page, 1902).

83. McGuire, "The Little Colonel," 126.

84. Michael Denning, *Mechanic Accents: Dime Novels and Working-Class Culture in America* (New York: Verso Press, 1987), 187; Donelson, *Literature for Today's Young Adult,* 518–19.

85. Kate Douglas Wiggin, *Rebecca of Sunnybrook Farm* (1903; rpt., Boston: Houghton Mifflin Co., 1931), 12.

86. Ibid., 317.

87. Ibid., 273.

88. Jerry Griswold, "Spinster Aunt, Sugar-Daddy, and Child-Woman: *Rebecca of Sunnybrook Farm,*" in Griswold, ed., *Audacious Kids: Com-*

ing of Age in America's Classic Children's Books (New York: Oxford University Press, 1992), 84.

89. Bingham, ed., *Writers for Children,* 605–8.
90. Zelizer, *Pricing the Priceless Child,* 32–34, 50.
91. Eleanor H. Porter, *Pollyanna* (1913; rpt., Laurel, N.Y.: Lightyear Press, 1977), 42–43.
92. *The New Shorter Oxford English Dictionary* (Oxford: Clarendon Press, 1993).
93. Jerry Griswold, "Radical Innocence: *Pollyanna,*" in Griswold, ed., *Audacious Kids,* 215–17.
94. James J. Martine, ed., *Dictionary of Literary Biography,* vol. 9.1 (Detroit: Gale Research Co., 1981), 294.
95. Mary Cadogan and Patricia Craig, *You're a Brick, Angela! A New Look at Girls' Fiction from 1839 to 1975* (London: Victor Gollancz, 1976), 100–101.
96. Griswold, "Radical Innocence," 218–21.
97. Cadogan and Craig, *You're A Brick,* 102–4.
98. Alice Hegan Rice, *Mrs. Wiggs of the Cabbage Patch* (1901; rpt., New York: D. Appleton-Century Co., 1937), ix–xi.
99. Ibid., 4.
100. Ibid., 154.
101. Estes, ed., *Dictionary of Literary Biography,* vol. 42, 99–105.
102. MacLeod, *American Childhood,* 77–83.
103. As quoted in Jerry Griswold, "Motherland, Fatherland, or Oedipal Politics: *Little Lord Fauntleroy,*" in Griswold, ed., *Audacious Children,* 99.
104. *The New Shorter Oxford English Dictionary.*
105. As quoted in Phyllis Bixler Koppes, "Tradition and the Individual Talent of Francis Hodgson Burnett: A Generic Analysis of *Little Lord Fauntleroy, A Little Princess,* and *The Secret Garden,*" *Children's Literature* 7 (1978): 206.
106. Jerry Griswold, "Positive Thinking: *The Secret Garden,*" in Griswold, ed., *Audacious Kids,* 267, n. 9.
107. Koppes, "Tradition and the Individual Talent," 198–99.
108. Shirley Foster and Judy Simons, *What Katy Read: Feminist Re-Readings of "Classic" Stories for Girls* (Iowa City: University of Iowa Press, 1995), 185, 172; Griswold, "Positive Thinking," 204–6.
109. Foster, ibid., 189.
110. Koppes, "Tradition and the Individual Talent," 191–92. Burnett's quotation is from her autobiography, *The One I Knew Best.*
111. Hunt, ed., *Children's Literature,* 230–31; Avery, *Behold the Child,* 150–51.
112. Avery, ibid., 151.
113. Bingham, ed., *Writers for Children,* 214–15.
114. Kensinger, *Children of the Series,* 17.

115. Avery, *Behold the Child,* 150–52. The phrase "lightness of spirit" is found on 147.

Chapter 5

1. Winthrop D. Jordan, *White over Black: American Attitudes toward the Negro, 1550–1812* (New York: W. W. Norton, 1968), 5, 17–20, 27–28, 70–77. The biblical story of Noah, Ham, and Canaan is found in Genesis 9:20–27.

2. Leon Litwack, *North of Slavery: The Negro in the Free States* (Chicago: University of Chicago Press, 1961), 3–10; John B. Boles, *Black Southerners, 1619–1869* (Lexington, Ky.: University of Kentucky Press, 1984), 75. See also Leonard P. Curry, *The Free Black in Urban American, 1800–1850* (Chicago: University of Chicago Press, 1981).

3. Thomas Jefferson, *Notes on the State of Virginia,* ed. William Peden (New York: W. W. Norton and Co., 1954), 138–41.

4. George Fredrickson, *The Black Image in the White Mind: The Debate on Afro-American Character and Destiny, 1817–1914* (New York: Harper & Row, 1971), 79–83.

5. *Appletons' Juvenile Annual for 1869: A Christmas and New Year's Gift for Young People* (New York: D. Appleton and Co., 1869), 373–74.

6. Russell Nye, *The Unembarrassed Muse: The Popular Arts in America* (New York: Dial Press, 1970), 162–64.

7. See especially C. Vann Woodward, *The Strange Career of Jim Crow,* 3d rev. ed. (New York: Oxford University Press, 1974).

8. Joel Williamson, *The Crucible of Race: Black-White Relations in the American South Since Emancipation* (New York: Oxford University Press, 1984), 52–57.

9. Quote from Joan D. Hedrick, *Harriet Beecher Stowe: A Life* (New York: Oxford University Press, 1994), vii.

10. Harriet Beecher Stowe, *Uncle Tom's Cabin* (1852; rpt., New York: Penguin Books, Signet Classics, 1966). See also Jane Tompkins, *Sensational Designs: The Cultural Work of American Fiction, 1790–1860* (New York: Oxford University Press. 1985), 133.

11. Holly Keller, "Juvenile Antislavery Narrative and Notions of Childhood," *Children's Literature* 24 (1996): 86–89.

12. Hedrick, *Harriet Beecher Stowe,* 208, 223.

13. Anne Scott MacLeod makes this point in the essay "Children, Adults, and Reading at the Turn of the Century" without citing *Uncle Tom's Cabin* specifically. In *American Childhood: Essays on Children's Literature of the Nineteenth and Twentieth Centuries* (Athens: University of Georgia Press, 1994): 114–26.

14. Keller, "Juvenile Antislavery Narrative," 98.

15. Ibid.; Hedrick, *Harriet Beecher Stowe,* 233.

16. Hedrick, ibid., 211, 218–19, 230–31. The quote comes from Stowe's letter to Elizabeth Cabot Follen.

17. Paul Boyer et al., *The Enduring Vision: A History of the American People,* 2d ed. (Lexington, Mass.: D. C. Heath, 1993), 451; Hedrick, *Harriet Beecher Stowe,* 249; Harriet A. Jacobs, *Incidents in the Life of a Slave Girl* (New York: Oxford University Press, 1988).

18. Kenneth W. Goings, *Mammy and Uncle Mose: Black Collectibles and American Stereotyping* (Bloomington: Indiana University Press, 1994), 13–18; Dorothy Broderick, *Image of the Black in Children's Fiction* (New York: R. R. Bowker Co., 1973).

19. Martha Farquaharson Finley, *Elsie Dinsmore* (1867; rpt., New York: Arno Press, 1974), 32–33.

20. Jacqueline Jackson and Philip Kendall, "What Makes a Bad Book Good: *Elsie Dinsmore,*" *Children's Literature: Annual of the Modern Language Association Group on Children's Literature Association* 7 (1978): 64.

21. Thomas Nelson Page, *Two Little Confederates* (1888; rpt., New York: Charles Schribner's Sons, 1945), 4, 31, 56. See also the commentary in Violet Harris, "*The Brownies' Book:* Challenge to the Selective Tradition in Children's Literature" (Ph.D. diss., University of Georgia, 1986), 81.

22. John Scott Wilson, "Race and Manners for Southern Girls and Boys: The "Miss Minerva" Books and Race Relations in a Southern Children's Series," *Journal of American Culture* 17.3 (Fall 1994): 69–71. The quotations are from Emma Sampson, *Miss Minerva's Scallywags* (1927).

23. Sue Lynn McGuire, "The Little Colonel: A Phenomenon in Popular Literary Culture," *Register of the Kentucky Historical Society* 89 (1991): 123–25; Marilyn Kaye, "Annie Fellows Johnston," *Dictionary of Literary Biography,* vol. 42, ed. Glenn E. Estes (Detroit: Gale Research Co., 1985), 255–56; Annie Fellows Johnston, *Little Colonel's Hero* (Boston: L. C. Page, 1902), 187.

24. James S. Leonard, Thomas A. Tenney, and Thadious M. Davis, *Satire or Evasion? Black Perspectives on Huckleberry Finn* (Durham, S.C.: Duke University Press, 1992). A recent bibliography lists over 600 books and articles on *Huckleberry Finn.* See M. Thomas Inge, ed., *Huck Finn among the Critics: A Centennial Selection* (Frederick, Md.: University Publications of America, 1985).

25. Richard K. Barksdale, "History, Slavery, and Thematic Irony in *Huckleberry Finn,*" in Leonard, *Satire or Evasion?,* 49–55; Steven Mailloux, *Rhetorical Power* (Ithaca, N.Y.: Cornell University Press, 1989), 64–66; Fredrick Woodard and Donnarae MacCann, "Minstrel Shackles and Nineteenth-Century 'Liberality' in *Huck Finn,*" in Leonard, ibid., 143–45.

26. Mailloux, *Rhetorical Power,* 72–74.

27. David Smith, "Huck, Jim, and American Racial Discourse," in Leonard, *Satire or Evasion?,* 105, 112.

28. Ibid., 106, 115; Neil Schmitz, "Twain, Huckleberry Finn, and the Reconstruction," *American Studies* 12 (Spring 1971): 60.

29. Shelley Fisher Fishkin, *Was Huck Black? Mark Twain and African-American Voices* (New York: Oxford University Press, 1993), 101. The principal argument in Fishkin's study is that Huck's voice is based on a black child Clemens met, described in detail in a letter to his wife, then made a character in a *New York Times* story called "Sociable Jimmy" in 1874.

30. Joel Chandler Harris, *Uncle Remus: His Songs and His Sayings, the Folk-lore of the Old Plantation* (New York: D. Appleton, 1880; rpt., Atlanta: Cherokee Publishing Co., 1981), 178.

31. Ibid., publisher's introduction, 2; Louis D. Rubin, "Uncle Remus and the Ubiquitous Rabbit," *Critical Essays on Joel Chandler Harris,* ed. Bruce Bickley Jr. (Boston: G. K. Hall, 1981), 159, 164–65; Wayne Mixon, "The Ultimate Irrelevance of Race: Joel Chandler Harris and Uncle Remus in their Time," *Journal of Southern History* 56.3 (August 1990): 468–69.

32. Harris, ibid., 19–20, 26; Robert Bone, "The Oral Tradition," in Bickley, *Critical Essays on Joel Chandler Harris,* 138.

33. Bickley, *Critical Essays,* xxi.

34. Bone, "The Oral Tradition," 134, 138–41.

35. As quoted in Rubin, "Uncle Remus and the Ubiquitous Rabbit," 166 (emphasis his).

36. Mixon, "The Ultimate Irrelevance of Race," 476–79; Bone, "The Oral Tradition," 134.

37. Dharathula H. Millender, "Through a Glass, Darkly," in Donnarae MacCann and Gloria Woodard, eds., *The Black American in Books for Children* (Metuchen, N.J.: Scarecrow Press, 1972), 146; Michael Denning, *Mechanic Accents: Dime Novels and Working-Class Culture in America* (New York: Verso Press, 1987), 210.

38. Phyliss J. Yuill, *Little Black Sambo: A Closer Look* (New York: Council on Interracial Books for Children, 1976), 1–3, 9–10, 15–18.

39. Ibid., 10, 15, 24, 43–44.

40. John Denis Mercier, "The Evolution of the Black Image in White Consciousness, 1976–1954: A popular Culture Perspective" (Ph.D. diss., University of Pennsylvania, 1984), 19–20. The quote is from *Watermelon Pete.*

41. Violet Joyce Harris, "The *Brownies' Book:* Challenge to the Selective Tradition in Children's Literature" (Ph.D. diss., University of Georgia, 1986), 82–83.

42. Ibid., 117–19.
43. Paul C. Deane, "The Persistence of Uncle Tom: An Examination of the Image of the Negro in Children's Fiction Series," *The Black American in Books for Children: Readings in Racism,* Dannarae MacCann and Gloria Woodard, eds. (Metuchen, N.J.: Scarecrow Press, 1972), 117.
44. Joel Williamson, *The Crucible of Race: Black-White Relations in the American South Since Emancipation* (New York: Oxford, 1984), 76; Harris, "The *Brownies' Book,*" 1–3, 131. Her quotations are from the *Crisis* 18 (1919).
45. Ibid., 118, 105–6, 268, 108–9.
46. Ibid., 109–15, 121, 130, 137.
47. Ibid., 141, 208–17.
48. Mary White Ovington, *Hazel* (1913; rpt., Freeport, N.Y.: Books for Libraries Press, 1972), v.
49. Harris, "The *Brownies' Book,*" 87–88; quotation from *Hazel* (New York: Crisis Publishing Co., 1913), 55.
50. Paul S. Boyer et al., *The Enduring Vision: A History of the American People* (Lexington, Mass.: D. C. Heath and Co., 1993), 415, 628–29, 726.
51. Ibid., 741.
52. Denning, *Mechanic Accents,* 30; George W. Peck, *Peck's Bad Boy* (Chicago: Thompson & Thomas, 1883).
53. J. Frederick MacDonald, " 'The Foreigner' in Juvenile Series Fiction, 1900–1945," *Journal of Popular Culture* 81.3 (Winter 1974): 534–35, 538; Deidre Johnson, *Edward Stratemeyer and the Stratemeyer Syndicate* (New York: Twayne Publishers, 1993), 81–83.
54. MacDonald, ibid., 85–86; Eleanor H. Porter, *Billy— Married* (Boston: Page Co., 1914), 3–4; Johnson, *Stratemeyer,* 85.
55. Johnson, ibid., 86–87; Kenneth L. Donelson and Alleen Pace Nilsen, *Literature for Today's Young Adult,* 3d ed. (Glenview, Ill.: Scott, Foresman & Co., 1989), 521.
56. MacDonald, "The Foreigner," 535.
57. Jane S. Smith, "Plucky Little Ladies and Stout-Hearted Chums: Serial Novels for Girls, 1900–1920," *Prospects: An Annual of American Cultural Studies* 3 (1977): 162, 172; Nancy Tillman Romalov, "Lady and the Tramps: The Cultural Work of Gypsies in Nancy Drew and her Foremothers," *The Lion and the Unicorn* 18.1 (June 1994): 26.
58. MacDonald, "The Foreigner," 535; emphasis in the original.
59. Sarah Law Kennerly, "Confederate Juvenile Imprints: Children's Books and Periodicals Published in the Confederate States of America, 1861–1865," (Ph.D. diss., University of Michigan, 1956), 30–33, 37–38.
60. Ibid., preface, 224; quoted passage from 226–28; Mary Lystad, *At Home in America as Seen through Its Books for Children* (Cambridge, Mass.: Schenkman Publishing Co., 1984), 58.

61. Joseph A. Altsheler, *Before the Dawn: The Story of the Fall of Richmond* (New York: Doubleday, Page, & Co., 1903), 367–68.
62. Fred Erisman, "Regionalism in American Children's Literature," *Society and Children's Literature,* ed. James H. Fraser (Boston: David R. Godine, 1978), 56–57.

Chapter 6

1. Paul S. Boyer et al., *The Enduring Vision: A History of the American People,* vol. 2, 2d ed. (Lexington, Mass.: D. C. Heath & Co., 1993), 800, 803, 814–15.
2. Ibid., 823–24.
3. Anne Scott MacLeod, *American Childhood: Essays on Children's Literature of the Nineteenth and Twentieth Centuries* (Athens: University of Georgia Press, 1994), 125, 158; Sheila Egoff, "Precepts and Pleasures: Changing Emphases in the Writing and Criticism of Children's Literature," in Sheila Egoff et al., *Only Connect: Readings on Children's Literature* (New York: Oxford University Press, 1969), 444; Peter Hunt, ed., *Children's Literature: An Illustrated History* (New York: Oxford University Press, 1995), 242–43.
4. Jane M. Bingham, *Writers for Children: Critical Studies of Major Authors Since the Seventeenth Century* (New York: Scribner's, 1987), 617–18.
5. Ibid., 619–21.
6. Anita Clair Fellman, "Laura Ingalls Wilder and Rose Wilder Lane: The Politics of a Mother-Daughter Relationship," *Signs* 15.3 (1990): 550.
7. William Holtz, *The Ghost in the Little House: A Life of Rose Wilder Lane* (Columbia: University of Missouri Press, 1993), 148, 224–25, 231, 238–39.
8. Fellman, "Laura Ingalls Wilder," 537; Kenneth L. Donelson and Alleen Pace Nilsen, *Literature for Today's Young Adult,* 3d ed. (Glenview, Ill.: Scott, Foresman & Co., 1989), 513. *Let the Hurricane Roar* has been republished under the title *The Young Pioneers* (1976).
9. Fellman, "Laura Ingalls Wilder," 537, 553, 557–58; Holtz, *Ghost in the Little House,* 306–7.
10. Suzanne Rahn, "What Really Happens in *The Little Town on the Prairie,*" *Children's Literature* 24 (1996): 119–21.
11. Elizabeth Segal, "Laura Ingalls Wilder's America: An Unflinching Assessment," *Children's Literature in Education* 8.2 (Summer 1977): 65–66; Mary Lystad, *At Home in America as Seen through Its Books for Children* (Cambridge, Mass.: Schenkman Publishing Co., 1984), 85–86.
12. As quoted in Rahn, "What Really Happens," 118–19.
13. Segal, "Laura Ingalls Wilder's America," 66–68.
14. Bingham, *Writers for Children,* 85.

15. Susan Naramore Maher, "Laura Ingalls and Caddie Woodlawn: Daughters of a Border Space," *The Lion and the Unicorn* 18.2 (December 1994): 137–38.

16. Boyer, *Enduring Vision*, 875.

17. As quoted in MacLeod, *American Childhood*, 4.

18. Samuel Irving Bellman, *Marjorie Kinnan Rawlings* (New York: Twayne Publishers, 1974), 66; Bingham, *Writers for Children*, 463–64.

19. Samuel Irving Bellman, "Marjorie Kinnan Rawlings: A Solitary Sojourner in the Florida Backwoods," *Kansas Quarterly* 2.2 (Spring 1970): 79.

20. MacLeod, *American Childhood*, 158, 164.

21. Ida H. Washington, *Dorothy Canfield Fisher: A Biography* (Shelburne, Vt.: New England Press, 1982), 79–81.

22. Ibid., 166.

23. Sally Allen McNall, "American Children's Literature, 1880–Present," in Joseph M. Hawes and N. Ray Hiner, eds., *American Childhood: A Research Guide and Historical Handbook* (Westport, Conn.: Greenwood Press, 1985), 391.

24. Elizabeth Enright, *Thimble Summer* (New York: Holt, Rinehart, and Winston, 1938), 49.

25. Caroline Hunt, "Elizabeth Enright and the Family Story," *The Lion and the Unicorn* 14.2 (December 1990): 17–19. Enright quote from *Children's Literature Review*, vol. 4 (Detroit: Gale Research Co., 1976), 68.

26. Hunt, "Elizabeth Enright," 21.

27. John Rowe Townsend, *A Sense of Story: Essays on Contemporary Writers for Children* (Philadelphia: J. B. Lippincott, 1971), 79. 84; MacLeod, *American Childhood*, 169.

28. Eleanor Estes, *The Moffats* (New York: Harcourt, Brace & World, 1941), 9–10.

29. Louisa Smith, "Eleanor Estes' *The Moffats:* Through Colored Glass," in Perry Nodelman, ed., *Touchstones: Reflections on the Best in Children's Literature*, vol. 1 (West Lafayette, IN: ChLA Publishers, 1985), 68.

30. Cech, ed., *Dictionary of Literary Biography*, vol. 22, 243; Anita Silvey, ed., *Children's Books and Their Creators* (Boston: Houghton-Mifflin, 1995), 402.

31. Lois Lenski, "Regional Children's Literature," *Wilson Library Bulletin* 21 (December 1946): 289, 291.

32. Cech, ed., *Dictionary*, 246.

33. Kay E. Vandergrift, "A Feminist Perspective on Multicultural Children's Literature in the Middle Years of the Twentieth Century," *Library Trends* 41.3 (Winter 1993): 373–74.

34. Lois R. Kuznets, "Fiction, Faction, and Formula in the Regional Novels of Lois Lenski," *Proceedings of the Children's Literature Association* 9 (1982): 96.

35. Lois Lenski, *Cotton in My Sack* (Philadelphia: J. P. Lippincott, 1949).
36. Siri Andrews, "Florence Crannell Means, " *Hornbook* 22 (January 1946): 16–18; Suzanne Rahn, "Rediscovering Florence Crannell Means," *The Lion and the Unicorn* 11.1 (1987): 102; Vandergrift, "Feminist Perspective," 364–65.
37. Rahn, ibid., 109, 100.
38. Ibid., 102–4.
39. Ibid., 169–70; Ruth B. Moynihan, "Ideologies in Children's Literature: Some Preliminary Notes," in Francelia Butler, ed., *The Great Excluded,* vol. 2 (Storrs, Conn.: Children's Literature Association, 1973), 168–69.
40. Carol Billman, *The Secret of the Stratemeyer Syndicate* (New York: Ungar Publishing Co., 1986), 74, 77.
41. See Beth L. Bailey, *From Front Porch to Back Seat: Courtship in Twentieth-Century America* (Baltimore: Johns Hopkins University Press, 1988).
42. Nancy Tillman Romalov, "Mobile Heroines: Early Twentieth Century Girls' Automobile Series," *Journal of Popular Culture* 28 (Spring 1995): 231–32.
43. Jane S. Smith, "Plucky Little Ladies and Stout-Hearted Chums: Serial Novels for Girls, 1900–1920," *Prospects: An Annual of American Cultural Studies* 3 (1977): 171.
44. Deidre Johnson, *Edward Stratemeyer and the Stratemeyer Syndicate* (New York: Twayne Publishers, 1993), 141–42.
45. Nancy Tillman Romalov, editor's note, *The Lion and the Unicorn* 18.1 (June 1994):v–vii; "Press Conference," ibid., 81–82. Wirt also reported that the Depression forced the price per book down to $75.
46. Geoffrey S. Lapin, "Outline of a Ghost," ibid., 61, 63.
47. MacLeod, *American Childhood,* 30–31.
48. Kathleen Chamberlain, "The Secrets of Nancy Drew: Having Their Cake and Eating It, Too," *The Lion and the Unicorn* 18.1 (June 1994): 7.
49. As quoted in ibid., 3.
50. Ibid., 39, 43; As quoted in MacLeod, *American Childhood,* 46.
51. As quoted in ibid., 42.
52. Johnson, *Stratemeyer Syndicate,* 150; Chamberlain, "Secrets of Nancy Drew," 3, 4, 11.
53. Donnarae MacCann, "Nancy Drew and the Myth of White Supremacy," in Carolyn Stewart Dyer and Nancy Tillman Romalov, eds., *Rediscovering Nancy Drew* (Iowa City: University of Iowa Press, 1995), 132–34.
54. Nancy Tillman Romalov, "Lady and the Tramps: the Cultural Work of Gypsies in Nancy Drew and Her Foremothers," *The Lion and the Unicorn* 18.1 (June 1994): 32–33.
55. MacCann, "The Myth of White Supremacy," 133–34.

56. Diana Beeson and Bonnie Brennan, "Translating Nancy Drew from Print to Film," in *Rediscovering Nancy Drew,* 196.

57. Johnson, *Stratemeyer,* 151–52.

58. Bobbie Ann Mason, *The Girl Sleuth* (1975; rpt., Athens: University of Georgia Press, 1995), 76–89.

59. MacLeod, *American Childhood,* 30–48, quote from 47.

60. Boyer, *Enduring Vision,* 873, 915.

61. Mason, *The Girl Sleuth,* 38–39.

62. Nancy Larrick, "The All-White World of Children's Books," in Donnarae MacCann and Gloria Woodard, eds., *The Black American in Books for Children* (Metuchen, N.J.: Scarecrow Press, 1972), 160.

63. Dharathula H. Millender, "Through a Glass, Darkly," in *The Black American,* 150; Jane M. Bingham, ed., *Writers for Children,* 77.

64. Bingham, ibid., 79; James J. Martine, ed., *Dictionary of Literary Biography,* vol. 9 (Detroit: Gale Publishing Co., 1981), 112–13, 117; Trudier Harris, ed., *Dictionary of Literary Biography,* vol. 51, 16.

65. Martine, ibid., 123.

66. Arna Bontemps, *Sad-Faced Boy* (New York: Houghton-Mifflin Riverside Press, 1937), 108.

67. Caroline C. Hunt, "U.S. Children's Books about the World War II Period: From Isolationism to Internationalism, 1940–1990," *The Lion and the Unicorn,* 18.2 (December 1994): 191.

68. Ibid., 194.

69. Ibid.; John Cech, ed., *Dictionary of Literary Biography,* vol. 22 (Detroit: Gale Publishing Co., 1983), 321–23.

70. Cech, ed., *Dictionary,* 323; William M. Tuttle Jr., *Daddy's Gone to War: The Second World War in the Lives of America's Children* (New York: Oxford University Press, 1993), 157.

71. Tuttle, ibid., 150–54.

72. Cech, ed., *Dictionary,* 177–78.

73. Ibid.; M. Sarah Smedman, "Esther Forbes' *Johnny Tremain:* Authentic History Classic Fiction," in *Touchstones,* 89, 86; quote from 93.

74. As quoted in Christopher Collier, "Johnny and Sam: Old and New Approaches to the American Revolution," *Hornbook* 52 (April 1976): 137.

75. Ibid., 92, 132–38.

76. Florence Crannell Means, *The Moved-Outers* (Boston: Houghton-Mifflin Co., 1945).

77. Rahn, "Rediscovering," 109–11; Vandergrift, "Feminist Perspective," 365–69.

78. Eleanor Estes, *The Hundred Dresses* (New York: Harcourt, Brace & World, 1944), 47.

79. Ibid., 3, 10.

80. Boyer, *The Enduring Vision*, 918.
81. Quotes from Estes, *The Hundred Dresses*, 48, 76.
82. Hunt, "U.S. Children's Books," 199, 201–2.
83. J. Frederick MacDonald, " 'The Foreigner' in Juvenile Series Fiction, 1900–1945," *Journal of Popular Culture* 8.3 (Winter 1874): 535, 539.
84. Mason, *Girl Sleuth*, 108–11.

Chapter 7

1. Paul S. Boyer et al., *The Enduring Vision: A History of the American People*, vol. 2, 2d ed. (Lexington, Mass.: D. C. Heath & Co., 1993), 939.
2. Elaine Tyler May, *Homeward Bound: American Families in the Cold War Era* (New York: Basic Books, 1988), 9–11.
3. Charles E. Strickland and Andrew M. Ambrose, "The Baby Boom, Prosperity, and the Changing Worlds of Children, 1945–1963," in Joseph M. Hawes and N. Ray Hiner, eds., *American Childhood: A Research Guide and Historical Handbook* (Westport, Conn.: Greenwood Press, 1985), 560–64.
4. Anne Scott MacLeod, *American Childhood: Essays on Children's Literature of the Nineteenth and Twentieth Centuries* (Athens: University of Georgia Press, 1994), 50.
5. Deidre Johnson, *Edward Stratemeyer and the Stratemeyer Syndicate* (New York: Twayne Publishers, 1993), 156–57.
6. MacLeod, *American Childhood*, 50–56.
7. Bobbie Ann Mason, *The Girl Sleuth* (1975; rpt., Athens: University of Georgia Press, 1995), 115–18.
8. Jane Smith, "Plucky Little Ladies and Stout-Hearted Chums: Serial Novels for Girls, 1900–1920," *Prospects: An Annual of American Cultural Studies* 3 (1977): 174, n. 7.
9. Kenneth L. Donelson and Alleen Pace Nilsen, *Literature for Today's Young Adult*, 3d ed. (Glenview, Ill.: Scott, Foresman & Co., 1989), 538–39; Strickland, "Baby Boom," 558.
10. For a detailed overview of scores of titles, see Dora V. Smith, *Fifty Years of Children's Books* (Chicago: National Council of Teachers of English, 1973), 62–82.
11. Martha Parravano, "Dr. Seuss," in Anita Silvey, *Children's Books and Their Creators* (Boston: Houghton Mifflin, 1985), 591.
12. Clifton Fadiman, "Professionals and Confessionals: Dr. Seuss and Kenneth Grahame," in Sheila Egoff, G. T. Stubbs, and L. F. Ashley, eds., *Only Connect: Readings on Children's Literature* (New York: Oxford University Press, 1969), 321.
13. Jonathan Cott, *Pipers at the Gates of Dawn: The Wisdom of Children's Literature* (New York: Random House, 1981), 18; Kuskin quote, 9.

14. Ibid., 29–30, 8.

15. Ruth B. Moynihan, "Ideologies in Children's Literature: Some Preliminary Notes," in Francelia Butler, ed., *The Great Excluded,* vol. 2 (Storrs, Conn.: Children's Literature Association, 1973), 170–71; Dr. Seuss, *Horton Hears a Who* (New York: Random House, 1954), unpaginated.

16. Cott, *Pipers,* 25.

17. "Cotton Mather," in ibid., 26; Dr. Seuss, *The Cat in the Hat* (Boston: Houghton Mifflin, 1957), 11, 60–61.

18. Cott, *Pipers,* 27.

19. Peter Neumeyer, "E. B. White," in Silvey, *Children's Books,* 676–77.

20. Scott Elledge, *E. B. White: A Biography* (New York: W. W. Norton & Co., 1984), 299.

21. Ibid., 293–95; Gerald Weales, "The Designs of E. B. White," *New York Times* (24 May 1970), as reprinted in Miriam Hoffman and Eva Samuels, *Authors and Illustrators of Children's Books: Writings on Their Lives and Works* (New York: R. R. Bowker Co., 1972), 409.

22. E. B. White, *Charlotte's Web* (New York: Harper & Row, 1952), 16, 183; John Griffith, "*Charlotte's Web:* A Lonely Fantasy of Love," *Children's Literature* 8 (1980): 111.

23. Griffith, ibid., 115–16.

24. Sonia Landes, "E. B. White's *Charlotte's Web:* Caught in the Web," in Perry Nodelman, ed., *Touchstones,* vol. 1 (West Layfayette, IN: ChLA Publishers, 1985), 270–72; Elledge, *E. B. White,* 300–301.

25. Theodore Roszak, *The Making of a Counterculture* (New York: Doubleday, 1969).

26. Strickland, "Baby Boom," in Hawes, *American Childhood,* 552–57; Boyer, *Enduring Vision,* 990–93.

27. Donelson, *Literature for Today's,* 553.

28. Sheila Egoff, *Thursday's Child: Trends and Patterns in Contemporary Children's Literature* (Chicago: American Library Association, 1981), 67, 70.

29. Ibid., 68, 160.

30. David Rees, *Painted Desert, Green Shade: Essays on Contemporary Fiction for Children and Young Adults* (Boston: The Horn Book, 1984), 126–37; Silvey, *Children's Books,* 308–9.

31. James T. Henke, "Six Characters in Search of the Family: The Novels of Paul Zindel," *Annual of the Modern Language Group on Children's Literature* 5 (1976): 130–33; Joan McGrath, "Paul Zindel," in Tracy Chevalier, ed., *Twentieth Century Children's Writers* (Chicago: St. James Press, 1989), 1079.

32. McGrath, ibid.; Katrin Tchana, "Paul Zindel," in Silvey, *Children's Books,* 711.

33. Egoff, *Thursday's Child*, 70–71; Henke, "Six Actors," 134–39; David Rees, *The Marble in the Water: Essays on Contemporary Writers of Fiction for Children and Young Adults* (Boston: The Horn Book, 1980), 25–35.
34. Michael Cart, *From Romance to Realism: 50 Years of Growth and Change in Young Adult Literature* (New York: HarperCollins, 1996), 63–64; Jack Forman, "Young Adult Novels," in Silvey, *Children's Books*, 703–705; Egoff, *Thursday's Child*, 44–45. Quotation from Donelson, *Literature for Today's*, 89.
35. Zena Sutherland, "Judy Blume," in Silvey, *Children's Books*, 66–67.
36. Cart, *From Romance to Realism*, 72.
37. Virginia L. Wolf, "Harriet the Spy: Milestone, Masterpiece?" *Children's Literature Annual of the Modern Language Association Seminar on Children's Literature* 4 (1975): 120; Egoff, *Thursday's Child*, 33, 34; Peter D. Sieruta, "Louise Fitzhugh," in Silvey, *Children's Books*, 243–44.
38. Virginia L. Wolf, "A Novel of Children's Liberation," *Children's Literature Annual of the Modern Language Association Group on Children's Literature* 5 (1976): 270–72.
39. Sutherland, "Judy Blume," 66–67; R. A. Siegel, "Are You There God? It's Me, Me, ME!": Judy Blume's Self-Absorbed Narrators," *Lion and the Unicorn* 2 (Fall 1978): 72–77. For a very negative assessment of Blume, see Rees, "Not Even for a One-Night Stand," in *Marble in the Water*, 173–83.
40. Sutherland, ibid.; Siegel, "Are You There," 72–77; Wolf, "Children's Liberation," 271.
41. Peter D. Sieruta, "M. E. Kerr," in Silvey, *Children's Books*, 369–71; Egoff, *Thursday's Child*, 73–74; Sally Holtze, "Norma Klein," in Silvey, *Children's Books*, 375.
42. Peter D. Sieruta, "Bill and Vera Cleaver," in Silvey, *Children's Books*, 147–48; John Rowe Townsend, "Vera and Bill Cleaver," *Horn Book Magazine* 55.5 (October 1979): 505–13.
43. Sharon L. Dussel, "Profile: Mildred D. Taylor," *Language Arts* 58.5 (May 1981): 599; Chevalier, *Twentieth Century*, 951–52; Sallie H. Holtze, "Mildred Taylor," in Silvey, *Children's Books*, 638–39. See also Rees, *Marble in the Water*, 108–12.
44. Boyer, *Enduring Vision*, 1014–16; Constance Curry, *Silver Rights* (Chapel Hill, N.C.: Algonquin Press, 1995).
45. Boyer, *Enduring Vision*, 1047; George C. Herring, *America's Longest War: The United States and Vietnam, 1950–1975*, 2d ed. (New York: Alfred E. Knopf, 1986).
46. Herring, ibid., 274–81.
47. Egoff, *Thursday's Child*, 169; Caroline Hunt, "World War II as Metaphor in Young Adult Fiction, 1968–1978," *The ALAN Review* 20.1 (Fall 1992): 23.

48. Hunt, ibid., 24–25; Hunt, "U. S. Children's Books about the World War II Period: From Isolationism to Internationalism, 1940–1990," *The Lion and the Unicorn* 18.2 (December 1994): 203; Sheila Egoff, "Precepts and Pleasures: Changing Emphases in the Writing and Criticism of Children's Literature," in Egoff, ed., *Only Connect* (New York: Oxford University Press, 1969), 436.

49. Rhoada Wald, "Realism in Children's Literature," *Language Arts* 52 (October 1975): 938; Scott O'Dell, "Scott O'Dell," in Miriam Hoffman and Eva Samuels, *Authors and Illustrators of Children's Books: Writings on Their Lives and Works* (New York: R. R. Bowker Co., 1972), 343–47; Perry Nodelman, "A Second Look: *Sing Down the Moon*," *Horn Book* 60.1, 94–98; Egoff, *Thursday's Child*, 171.

50. Zena Sutherland, "Paula Fox," in Silvey, *Children's Books*, 251–52; Egoff, ibid., 170–71.

51. Sharon Bell Mathis, "*The Slave Dancer* Is an Insult to Black Children," and Binnie Tate, "Racism and Distortions Pervade *The Slave Dancer*," in Donnarae MacCann and Gloria Woodard, eds., *Cultural Conformity in Books for Children: Further Readings in Racism* (Metuchen, N.J.: Scarecrow Press, 1977), 146–53.

52. William Blackburn, "Madeleine L'Engle's *A Wrinkle in Time*: Seeking the Original Face," in Nodelman, *Touchstones*, 123–31; Nancy-Lou Patterson, "Angel and Psychopomp in Madeleine L'Engle's 'Wind' Trilogy," *Children's Literature in Education* 14.4 (Winter 1983): 195–203.

53. Egoff, *Thursday's Child*, 150–51; Hamilton quote in Rees, *Painted Desert*, 168–69.

54. Cart, *Romance to Realism*, 24, 98–100, 105.

55. Cott, *Pipers*, 96–105, 119; Silvey, *Children's Books*, 626–27.

56. Maurice Sendak, *Where the Wild Things Are* (New York: Harper & Row, 1963).

57. Cott, *Pipers*, 43.

58. John Cech, "Maurice Sendak," in Silvey, *Children's Books*, 584–88; Geraldine DeLuca, "Exploring the Levels of Childhood: The Allegorical Sensibility of Maurice Sendak," *Children's Literature*, 12 (1984): 4.

59. Julius Lester and George Wood, "Black and White: An Exchange," in Donnarae MacCann and Gloria Woodard, eds., *The Black American in Books for Children* (Metuchen, N.J.: Scarecrow Press, 1972), 29.

60. Judith Thompson and Gloria Woodard, "Black Perspective in Books for Children," in MacCann, ibid., 16.

61. Rees, *Painted Desert*, 170, 173–76; Townsend, *Soundings*, 100–101; Silvey, *Children's Books*, 627–28.

62. Silvey, ibid., 133, 460.

63. Boyer, *Enduring Vision*, 1018–19, 1072.

64. Ibid., 1071–72.

65. Arthur M. Schlesinger Jr., *The Disuniting of America; Reflections on a Multicultural Society* (New York: W. W. Norton & Co., 1992), 43.

66. Michael Cart, *From Romance to Realism: 50 Years of Growth and Change in Young Adult Literature* (New York: HarperCollins, 1996), 112–15.

67. Yolen as quoted in Cart, *Romance to Realism,* 115; Kay Vandergrift, "A Feminist Perspective on Multicultural Children's Literature in the Middle Years of the Twentieth Century," *Library Trends* 41.3 (Winter 1993): 356.

68. Vandergrift, "Feminist Perspective," 369–71.

69. Peter Hunt, ed., *Children's Literature: An Illustrated History* (New York: Oxford University Press, 1995), 308; Mildred Lee, "Chinese-American Books for Children," in Silvey, *Children's Books,* 133–35; Jennifer M. Brabander, "Japanese-American Children's Books," in Silvey, 350–52.

70. Silvey, ibid., 307, 613–15; Council on Interracial Books for Children, "Chicano Culture in Children's Literature: Stereotypes, Distortions, and Omissions," and "Fiction: Parade of Stereotypes," in MacCann, *Cultural Conformity,* 55–59, 60–64; Cart, *Romance to Realism,* 124–25.

71. James Finn Garner, *Politically Correct Bedtime Stories: Modern Tales for Our Life and Times* (New York: Macmillan, 1994), x, 1–4.

72. Marion Dane Bauer, "Sexism and the World of Children's Books," *Horn Book* 69.5 (September 1993): 580.

73. Mem Fox, "The Gender Agenda between the Lines in Children's Fiction," *Language Arts* 70 (February 1993): 84.

Epilogue

1. Jacqueline Trescott, "Black Author Laments Lack of Kids' Books," *Washington Post,* reprinted in *Memphis Commercial Appeal* (5 December 1991): C1, 3.

2. "Not So Quiet on the Set," *Publisher's Weekly* 242 (14 August 1995): 25–27.

3. Jerry Griswold, "The Disappearance of Children's Literature (or Children's Literature as Nostalgia) in the United States in the Late Twentieth Century," in Sandra L. Beckett, ed., *Reflections of Change: Children's Literature Since 1945* (Westport, Conn.: Greenwood Press, 1997), 37; "Varied Performances," *Publisher's Weekly* 242 (11 September 1995): 32; Jim Milliot, "Looking Down the Road to 2000," *Publisher's Weekly* 243 (23 September, 1996): 30.

4. Milliot, ibid.; Judith Rosen, "They're Everywhere You Look," *Publisher's Weekly* 244 (21 July, 1997): 121–22.

5. "Page Turners," *Forbes* 155 (8 May, 1995): 131.

6. Michael Cart, *From Romance to Realism: 50 Years of Growth and Change in Young Adult Literature* (New York: HarperCollins, 1996), 10–11.

7. Neil Postman, *The Disappearance of Childhood* (New York: Delacourt Press, 1982); Marie Winn, *Children without Childhood* (New York: Pantheon Books, 1983); David Elkind, *The Hurried Child* (Reading, Mass.: Addison-Wesley Publishers, 1981; revised, 1988).

8. Jerry Griswold, "The Disappearance of Children's Literature," in Beckett, ed., *Reflections of Change,* 35–41.

9. William J. Bennett, ed., *Book of Virtues: A Treasury of Great Moral Stories* (New York: Simon & Schuster, 1993); E. D. Hirsch Jr., *Cultural Literacy: What Every American Needs to Know* (Boston: Houghton Mifflin Company, 1987).

Bibliographic Essay

General Texts and Reference Works

This study depends heavily on recent United States social history, particularly the history of childhood in America. The comprehensive text I found consistently helpful is Paul S. Boyer et al., *The Enduring Vision: A History of the American People,* vols. 1 and 2, 2d ed. (Lexington, Mass.: D. C. Heath & Co., 1993); the text is now in a 3d edition (1996). In addition, Lois W. Banner's *Women in Modern America,* 2d ed. (San Diego: Harcourt Brace Jovanovich, 1984), is a useful supplement. No comprehensive history of childhood in America has yet been written. The best guide to the literature available is Joseph M. Hawes and N. Ray Hiner, eds., *American Childhood: A Research Guide and Historical Handbook* (Westport, Conn.: Greenwood Press, 1985), which contains informational and bibliographic essays on various time periods in American history as well as two essays on the history of children's literature. John Cleverly and D. C. Phillips develop a theory of constructions of childhood in *Visions of Childhood: Influential Models from Locke to Spock,* rev. ed. (New York: Teachers' College Press, 1986); though not limited to American thought, they are particularly helpful in understanding the influence of the Enlightenment on educational principles.

Most texts on children's literature tend to consider works from a thematic or critical perspective rather than from a historical one. I found Cornelia Meigs, Anne Thaxter Eaton, Elizabeth Nesbitt, and Ruth Hill Viguers, *A Critical History of Children's Literature,* rev. ed. (New York: Macmillan and Co., 1969), useful in isolating important authors and for assessing the literary merit of their individual works. The most recent history of children's literature in the English-speaking world is Peter Hunt, ed., *History of Children's Literature* (London: Oxford University Press, 1995). British scholar Gillian Avery has compiled the best recent history of American children's books in *Behold the Child: American Children and Their Books, 1621–1922* (Balti-

more: Johns Hopkins University Press, 1994). Her study, which compares
American and British literature, ends in 1922. Both Hunt's and Avery's works
contain many excellent illustrations. Books for older children and teens
receive comprehensive discussion and critical assessment in Kenneth L.
Donelson and Alleen Pace Nilsen, *Literature for Today's Young Adult,* 3d ed.
(Glenview, Ill.: Scott, Foresman & Co., 1989). Mary Lystad brings a unique
approach to the study of children's literature; using a random sampling of
some one thousand children's books in the Library of Congress, she has quan-
tified their attention to various themes in *From Dr. Mather to Dr. Seuss: 200
Years of American Books for Children* (Boston: G. K. Hall, 1980). A later
work uses the same data to examine the books for particular social values in
At Home in America, as Seen through Its Books for Children (Cambridge,
Mass.: Schenkman Publishing Co., 1984). Neither work is very detailed.
James H. Fraser, ed., *Society and Children's Literature* (Boston: David R.
Godine, 1978), includes papers presented at a children's literature conference
at Simmons College in 1976 and spans literature from several centuries.

Locating critical studies of authors and their works is made easier by several finding aids: Virginia L. White and Emerita S. Schulte, *Books about Children's Books: An Annotated Bibliography* (Newark, Del.: International Reading Association, 1979); Suzanne Rahn, *Children's Literature: An Annotated
Bibliography of the History and Criticism* (New York: Garland, 1981); and
Linnea Hendrickson, *Children's Literature: A Guide to the Criticism* (Boston:
G. K. Hall, 1987). The latter is indexed by authors' name, book title, and
subject, as is Serenna F. Day's *Horn Book Index, 1824–1989* (Phoenix: Oryx
Press, 1990).

Biographical information about authors, as well as critical comments
about their works, can be found in any number of reference works. The mul-
tivolume *Dictionary of Literary Biography* (Detroit: Gale Research Co., 1983,
1985, 1986) allows for lengthy articles on particular authors. Volume 22,
edited by John Cech, covers American children's writers from 1900 to 1960;
volume 42, edited by Glenn E. Estes, covers American writers for children
before 1900; and volume 61 covers American writers for children since 1960.
Anita Silvey, ed., *Children's Books and Their Creators* (Boston: Houghton-
Mifflin, 1995), and Jane Bingham, ed., *Writers for Children: Critical Studies
of Major Authors* (New York: Scribner's, 1987), contain succinct and helpful
critical evaluations in one-volume formats.

Chapter 1: The Sinful Child, 1690–1810

The most interesting general social history of colonial America is Jack P.
Greene, *Pursuits of Happiness: The Social Development of Early Modern
British Colonies and the Formation of American Culture* (Chapel Hill: University of North Carolina, 1988). Social historians continue to debate the construction of childhood in the American colonies; the preponderance of

research concentrates on New England. John Demos, *A Little Common-wealth: Family Life in Plymouth Colony* (New York: Oxford University Press, 1970), marks a good beginning point for an investigation of the child's role in colonial culture. Philip Greven presents hundreds of primary accounts of child-rearing practices in *The Protestant Temperament: Patterns of Child-Rearing, Religious Experience, and the Self in Early America* (New York: Alfred A. Knopf, 1977). By examining clothing, furniture, paintings, and other material culture, Karin Calvert draws some intriguing conclusions about colonial children in *Children in the House: Material Culture of Early Childhood, 1600–1900* (Boston: Northeastern University Press, 1992). To assess how children learned to read and how prevalent literacy was in the British colonies, see James Axtell, *The School upon a Hill: Education and Society in Colonial New England* (New York: W. W. Norton, 1974), and Kenneth A. Lockridge, *Literacy in Colonial New England: An Enquiry into the Social Context of Literacy in the Early Modern West* (New York: W. W. Norton, 1974). Jennifer Monaghan provides a necessary corrective to Axtell's and Lockridge's assumptions by examining female literacy in "Literacy Instruction and Gender in Colonial New England," *American Quarterly* 40.1 (March 1988): 18–41. Richard D. Brown provides helpful information about how culture is appropriated in oral cultures in *Knowledge Is Power: The Diffusion of Information in Early America, 1700–1865* (New York: Oxford University Press, 1989).

Information on childhood in the Chesapeake and southern colonies remains sparse. Mary Stephenson has compiled a report entitled "Child-Life in Virginia: Eighteenth Century and Early Nineteenth Century," drawn from any archival evidence at Colonial Williamsburg; it was published in the Colonial Williamsburg Foundation Research Report Collection in 1969. Also concentrating on the eighteenth century, Daniel Blake Smith profiled the roles of southern family members in *Inside the Great House: Planter Family Life in Eighteenth-Century Chesapeake Society* (Ithaca, N.Y.: Cornell University Press, 1980). All the research available through the early 1980s is evaluated by Ross W. Beales Jr. in "The Child in Seventeenth-Century America," in Hawes and Hiner, *American Childhood*, 15–56.

Information on which British books were imported into the colonies can be found in " 'Child's Play? Children's Books in Early America,' an Exhibition from the Collections of the Colonial Williamsburg Foundation for the 22nd Congress of the International Board on Books for Young People" (Williamsburg, 1990), and Rosalie V. Halsey, *Forgotten Books of the American Nursery: A History of the Development of the American Story-Book* (Boston: Charles Goodspeed & Co., 1911; rpt., Detroit: Singing Tree Press, 1969). A bibliographic survey, with helpful data about American publishers, has been compiled by the collector A.S.W. Rosenbach, *Early American Children's Books* (1933; rpt., New York: Kraus Reprint Corp., 1966). A similar listing of early books but limited to those printed in America is D'Alte

Aldridge Welch, *A Bibliography of American Children's Books Printed Prior to 1821* (Worcester, Mass.: American Antiquarian Society, 1972).

Critical evaluations of the purposes of early didactic literature has been evaluated by William Sloane in *Children's Books in England and America in the Seventeenth Century* (New York: King's Crown Press of Columbia University, 1955), and Monica Kiefer, *American Children through Their Books, 1700–1835* (Philadelphia: University of Pennsylvania Press, 1948). Elizabeth A. Francis has a survey entitled "American Children's Literature, 1646–1880," in Hawes and Hiner, *American Childhood*, 185–233. Gail S. Murray utilizes the imported books to examine messages about responsible citizenship in "Rational Thought and Republican Virtues: Children's Literature, 1789–1820," *Journal of the Early Republic* 8 (Summer 1988): 159–77.

For specific information on the *New England Primer* and its evolution over a century and a half, see Paul Leicester Ford, ed., *The "New England Primer": A History of Its Origin and Development* (New York: Dodd, Mead, & Co., 1897). Samuel F. Pickering Jr. has a perceptive and detailed study of John Newbery and his impact on writing for children in *Moral Instruction and Fiction for Children, 1747–1820* (Athens: University of Georgia Press, 1993). To link Newbery's ideas about children to Enlightenment philosophy, consult James Axtell, ed., *The Educational Writings of John Locke* (Cambridge: Cambridge University Press, 1968).

Chapter 2: Virtues for the Little Republican, 1790–1850

Helpful studies of United States society and culture in the post-Revolutionary era include Jean H. Baker, *Affairs of Party: The Political Culture of Northern Democrats in the Mid-Nineteenth Century* (Ithaca, N.Y.: Cornell University Press, 1983) and Lorraine Smith Pangle and Thomas L. Pangle, *The Learning of Liberty: The Educational Ideas of the American Founders* (Lawrence: University of Kansas Press, 1993). The Pangles concentrate on philosophical ideas; the more practical educational proposals of these same men can be found in E. Jennifer Monaghan, *A Common Heritage: Noah Webster's Blue-Back Speller* (Hamden, Conn.: Archon Press, 1983) and David Freeman Hawke, *Benjamin Rush, Revolutionary Gadfly* (Indianapolis: Bobbs, Merrill Co., 1984). Jean V. Matthews examines a broad range of literary, legal, and fine arts accomplishments in *Toward a New Society: American Thought and Culture, 1800–1830* (Boston: Twayne Publishers, 1991).

Society shaped children and childhood through a sustained effort to create a public school system, as first elaborated by Rush Welter, *Popular Education and Democratic Thought in America* (New York: Columbia University Press, 1962). Magisterial in its comprehensiveness is Lawrence A. Cremin's classic, *American Education: The Colonial Experience, 1607–1783* (New York: Harper & Row, 1970). How moral culture was transmitted through public schools is examined by B. Edward McClellan, *Schools and the Shaping of Character: Moral Education in America* (Bloomington: Indiana University, 1992) and Ruth Elston, *Guardians of Tradition: American Schoolbooks of the Nineteenth Century* (Lincoln: University of Nebraska Press, 1964). Elston takes particular care to illustrate the social and cultural content of these textbooks. Similarly, Harvey C. Minnich thoroughly analyzes the cultural messages of the McGuffey readers in *William Holmes McGuffey and His Readers* (Detroit: Gale Research Co., 1975).

Jacqueline S. Reinier has written the only history of American childhood during this critical era; she demonstrates how the teaching of republican virtue was supplanted by an emphasis on the development of Protestant moral character in *From Virtue to Character: American Childhood, 1775–1850* (New York: Twayne Publishers, 1996). Anne Scott MacLeod has written a thorough analysis of children's books from this period, arguing that didactic instruction replaced the moral authority of Puritanism in *A Moral Tale: Children's Fiction and American Culture, 1820–1860* (Hamden, Conn.: Archon Books, 1975). Female didactic writers translated the British nursery tales into an American mode, thus helping to sustain gender roles and domesticity in the early republic. For example, see Sarah Robbins, "Lessons for Children and Teaching Mothers: Mrs. Barbauld's Primer for the Textual Construction of Middle-Class Domestic Pedagogy," *The Lion and the Unicorn* 17 (1993): 135–51, and Judith St. John, "Mrs. Trimmer, Guardian of Education," *Horn Book* 46 (February 1970): 20–25. Carolyn L. Karcher has two perceptive works on the cultural influence of these female writers: "Reconceiving Nineteenth-Century American Literature: The Challenge of Women Writers," *American Literature* 64.4 (December 1994): 781–93 and *The First Woman in the Republic: A Cultural Biography of Lydia Maria Child* (Durham, S.C.: Duke University Press, 1994).

The other principal children's authors of this period are Parson Weems and Peter Parley. The editorial notes historian Marcus Cunliffe supplies to *The Life of Washington by Mason L. Weems* (Cambridge, Mass.: Belknap Press, 1962) are superb for understanding the importance of turning Washington into a moral leader. Peter Parley's "memoirs" were published posthumously by his sons as Samuel G. Goodrich, *Peter Parley's Own Story: From the Personal Narrative of the Late Samuel S. Goodrich* (New York: Sheldon & Co., 1864). Additional information on this early writer is found in Helen S. Canfield, "Peter Parley," *Horn Book Magazine* 46 (April 1970): 135–41; (June 1970): 274–82; (August 1970): 412–18.

One must assess the rather dull and formulaic books produced by the Sunday School Union after 1825 because they were so widely distributed and read. Background on the movement itself can be found in Ann M. Boylan, *Sunday School: The Formation of an American Institution, 1790–1880* (New Haven, Conn.: Yale University Press, 1988), while insight into the structure and gendering of many of these texts has been considered in two articles by

Joanna Gillespie, "Schooling through Fiction," *Children's Literature* 14 (1986): 61–81 and "An Almost Irresistible Enginery: Five Decades of Nineteenth-century Methodist Sunday School Library Books," *Phaedrus* (1980): 5–12. The best sources of information on the emergence of juvenile magazines is R. Gordon Kelly's classic *Mother Was a Lady: Self and Society in Selected American Children's Periodicals* (Westport, Conn.: Greenwood Press, 1974). Two essays are helpful for assessing how much children's authors incorporated awareness of the various social reform efforts in the antebellum period: John C. Crandall, "Patriotism and Humanitarian Reform in Children's Literature, 1825–1860," *American Quarterly* 21 (Spring 1969): 3–17 and Holly Keller, "Juvenile Antislavery Narrative and Notions of Childhood," *Children's Literature* 24 (1996): 99.

Chapter 3: Good Girls, Bad Boys, 1850–1890

Ann Douglas examines the influence of clergy and Protestant women in cultural formation in *The Feminization of American Culture* (New York: Alfred A. Knopf, 1979). Karen Halttunen's *Confidence Men and Painted Women* (New Haven, Conn.: Yale University Press, 1982) helps explain how the middle class came to exert behavioral hegemony during America's population boom of the late nineteenth century, and "The Reality of the Rags to Riches 'Myth,' " in Herbert Gutman's *Work, Culture and Society: Working-Class and Social History* (New York: Vintage Books, 1976) describes the reality of upward mobility in several U.S. locations. Reading habits and the market for dime novels is explored by Michael Denning in *Mechanic Accents: Dime Novels and Working-Class Culture in America* (New York: Verso Press, 1987). John Tebbel has followed the important expansion of publishing in *A History of Book Publishing in the United States,* vol. 1, 1630–1865 (New York: R. R. Bowker, 1972). For the history of childhood in this period, see Barbara Finklestein, "Casting Networks of Good Influence: The Reconstruction of Childhood in the United States, 1790–1870," and Priscilla Clement, "The City and the Child," in Hawes and Hiner, *American Childhood.*

Just as children's literature came into its own after 1850, critical studies of these works are plentiful. A symposium held at the University of Illinois produced a collection of essays edited by Selma K. Richardson, *Research about Nineteenth-Century Children and Books,* that contains several useful essays. Anne Scott MacLeod, a premier scholar of the history of children's literature, collected many of her penetrating essays on nineteenth- and twentieth-century children's literature in *American Childhood* (Athens: University of Georgia Press, 1994). Another superb collection that uses Freudian critical theory to interpret the canonical nineteenth-century texts in readable and often humorous essays is Jerry Griswold, *Audacious Kids: Coming of Age in America's Classic Children's Books* (New York: Oxford University Press,

1992). An equally insightful and sophisticated survey limited to girls' fiction is Shirley Foster and Judy Simons, *What Katy Read: Feminist Re-Readings of "Classic" Stories for Girls* (Iowa City: University of Iowa Press, 1995). Claudia Nelson and Lynne Vallone, eds., have compiled a collection of essays on girls' fiction in both Great Britain and the United States entitled *The Girls' Own: Cultural Histories of the Anglo-American Girl, 1830–1915* (: University of Georgia Press, 1994). Two essays by Ann Trensky bring clarity to the gender distinctions that developed by mid-century: "The Bad Boy in Nineteenth Century American Fiction," *Georgia Review* 27.4 (Winter 1973): 503–17 and "The Saintly Child in Nineteenth-Century American Fiction," *Prospects* 1 (1975): 389–413.

My own thinking about the social construction of childhood and how literature assists in that task has been shaped by the pioneering work of historian Bernard Wishy in *The Child and the Republic: The Dawn of Modern American Child Nurture* (Philadelphia: University of Pennsylvania Press, 1968) and the more recent work of Jane Tompkins in *Sensational Designs: The Cultural Work of American Fiction, 1790–1860* (New York: Oxford University Press, 1985). I found several studies on particular authors most helpful. John B. Boles, "Jacob Abbott and the Rollo Books: New England Culture for Children," *Journal of Popular Culture* 4 (Winter 1972): 507–28 discusses the popularity and cultural messages of the Rollo books. For books by Samuel Clemens, see Patrick Hearn, *The Annotated Huckleberry Finn* (New York: C. N. Potter, 1981); James S. Leonard, Thomas A. Tenney, and Thadious M. Davis, eds., *Satire or Evasion? Black Perspectives on Huckleberry Finn* (Durham, S.C.: Duke University Press, 1992); and Shelley Fisher Fishkin, *Was Huck Black? Mark Twain and African-American Voices* (New York: Oxford University Press, 1993). The best biography of Horatio Alger is Gary Scharnhorst, *The Lost Life of Horatio Alger Jr.* (Bloomington: Indiana University Press, 1985), but the best analysis of Alger's cultural work can be found in Carol Nackenoff, *The Fictional Republic: Horatio Alger and American Political Discourse* (New York: Oxford University Press, 1994). Also very insightful are Michael Zuckerman, "The Nursery Tales of Horatio Alger," *American Quarterly* 24 (May 1972): 191–209 and Daniel T. Rodgers, *The Work Ethic in Industrial America, 1850–1920* (Chicago: University of Chicago Press, 1974); the latter has an excellent chapter on Alger's works. The critical studies of Louisa May Alcott and her place in the literary canon are voluminous. Most useful in terms of her contribution to girls' culture is Elizabeth Lennox Keysar's brilliant *Whispers in the Dark: The Fiction of Louisa May Alcott* (Knoxville: University of Tennessee Press, 1993); Beverly Lyon Clark, "A Portrait of the Artist as a Little Woman," *Children's Literature* 17 (1989): 81–97; Madeleine B. Stern, ed., *Critical Essays on Louisa May Alcott* (Boston: G. K. Hall, 1984); and Angela M. Estes and Kathleen Margaret Lant, "Dismembering the Text: The Horror of Louisa May Alcott's *Little Women*," *Children's Literature* 17, (1989): 98–123.

For juvenile periodicals, see the definitive work by R. Gordon Kelly mentioned previously. The southern nationalism of the 1850s prompted some interest in "southern books for southern children." A 1956 Ph.D. dissertation covers that subject in some detail: Sarah Law Kennerly, "Confederate Juvenile Imprints: Children's Books and Periodicals Published in the Confederate States of America (Ph.D. diss., University of Michigan, 1956).

Chapter 4: Child Consumer, 1880–1920

A useful study for understanding the gendered nature of late Victorian culture is Martha Banta, *Imaging American Women: Idea and Ideals in Cultural History* (New York: Columbia University Press, 1987), read along with Sheila Rothman's study of the complexities of expanded role definitions, *Woman's Proper Place: A History of Changing Ideals and Practices, 1870 to Present* (New York: Basic Books, 1978). Rosalind Rosenberg profiles the first generation of professional women in *Beyond Separate Spheres: Intellectual Roots of Modern Feminism* (New Haven, Conn.: Yale University Press, 1982). Lawrence W. Levine's pathbreaking study *Highbrow/Lowbrow: The Emergence of Cultural Hierarchy in America* (Cambridge: Harvard University Press, 1988) brings clarity to the dispute between the professional "experts" on children's literature and the buying public.

Trends in public education, particularly the expansion of the high school, are covered by Lawrence Cremin, *The History of Education: The Metropolitan Experience, 1876–1980* (New York: Harper & Row, 1988) and the more critical study by David Nasaw, *Schooled to Order: A Social History of Public Schooling in the United States* (New York: Oxford University Press, 1979). John Tebbel continues his *History of Book Publishing in the United States,* vol. 2, *1865–1919* (New York: R. R. Bowker, 1972), which can be read in conjunction with Dennis Thomison, *The History and Development of the American Library Association, 1876–1957* (Chicago: American Library Association, 1978). Again, no history of American childhood exists for this period, but a thoughtful overview of existing scholarship is Ronald D. Cohen, "Child-Saving and Progressivism, 1885–1915," in Hawes and Hiner, *American Childhood,* 273–310. To date, the most thoughtful analysis of the redefinition of childhood in this period can be found in the work of sociologist Viviana A. Zelizer, *Pricing the Priceless Child: The Changing social Value of Children* (Princeton, N.J.: Princeton University Press, 1994; originally published by Basic Books, 1985). She uses the fluctuating settlements awarded to parents in cases of the accidental deaths of their children to trace the evolution of a child's worth from its economic contribution to its emotional value to the family.

Books and authors covered in this chapter receive critical evaluations in several significant essays found in three collections already mentioned: MacLeod, *American Childhood,* Griswold, *Audacious Kids,* and Nelson and

Vallone, *The Girls' Own*. Sallie Allen McNall's essay "American Children's Literature, 1880–Present," in Hawes and Hiner, *American Childhood*, 377–414, should also be consulted, although it is more bibliographical than analytical.

The series books that made their appearance about 1900, seen as harbingers of a new popular culture in America, have prompted much serious scholarship. Comprehensive overviews include Carol Billman, *The Secret of the Stratemeyer Syndicate* (New York: Ungar Publishing Co., 1986) and Deidre Johnson, *Edward Stratemeyer and the Stratemeyer Syndicate* (New York: Twayne Publishers, 1993). Less thorough but with some interesting insights into popular culture is Faye Riter Kensinger, *Children of the Series and How They Grew* (Bowling Green, Ohio: Bowling Green State University Press, 1987). Two essays that utilize some of the lesser-known series books in their analysis of what these books meant to their readers are Jane Smith, "Plucky Little Ladies and Stout-Hearted Chums: Serial Novels for Girls, 1900–1920," *Prospects: An Annual of American Cultural Studies* 3 (1977): 155–74 and Walter Evans, "The All-American Boys: A Study of Boys' Sports Fiction," *Journal of Popular Culture* 6 (1972): 104–21. Critics of the Syndicate books receive a comprehensive discussion in Peter A. Sonderbergh, "The Stratemeyer Syndicate: Educators and the Juvenile Series Book, 1900–1973," *Journal of Popular Culture* 7.4 (Spring 1974): 864–72. The avid series book enthusiast can get the various authors straightened out by using either Deidre Johnson, ed., *Stratemeyer Pseudonyms and Series Books: An Annotated Checklist of Startemeyer and Stratemeyer Syndicate Publications* (Westport, Conn.: Greenwood Press, 1980) or *Girls' Series Books: A Checklist of Hardback Books Published 1900–1975*, compiled by the Children's Literature Research Collections at the University of Minnesota Library (1978).

Roger W. Cummins provides a thorough investigation of the whimsical Brownies in *Humorous but Wholesome: A History of Palmer Cox and the Brownies* (Watkins Glen, N.Y.: Century House Americana, 1973). An excellent beginning point for information on both Frank Baum and the Oz books is Michael Patrick Hearn's *The Annotated Wizard of Oz* (New York: Clarkson N. Potter, 1973). The first scholars to suggest Oz's cultural implications were Martin Gardiner and Russel Nye, in *The Wizard of Oz and Who He Was* (East Lansing: Michigan State University Press, 1957). Since then, popular-culture scholars have dissected this American novel from several angles. Henry M. Littlefield reads it as a "parable of populism," the subtitle of his article "The Wizard of Oz," *American Quarterly* 16.1 (1964): 47–58. Two political scientists provide a bit of a different spin, still focused on contemporary politics, in "William Jennings Bryan on the Yellow Brick Road," *Journal of American Culture* 16.4 (Winter 1993): 59–63. See also the more psychological interpretation in Griswold, *Audacious Kids*.

Other studies on particular authors that proved useful are Sue Lynn McGuire, "The Little Colonel: A Phenomenon in Popular Literary Culture,"

Register of the Kentucky Historical Society (Spring 1991): 121–46 and Phyllis Bixler Koppes, "Tradition and the Individual Talent of Frances Hodgson Burnett: A Generic Analysis of *Little Lord Fauntleroy, A Little Princess,* and *The Secret Garden," Children's Literature* 7 (1978): 191–207. Ann Thwaite has written a perceptive biography of Burnett entitled *Waiting for the Party: The Life of Frances Hodgson Burnett* (New York: Scribner's, 1974).

Chapter 5: Race and Ethnicity, 1850–1930

For African-American history after emancipation, see Lawrence W. Levine, *Black Culture and Black Consciousness: Afro-American Folk Thought from Slavery to Freedom* (New York: Oxford University Press, 1977) and Paula Giddings, *When and Where I Enter: The Impact of Black Women on Race and Sex in America* (New York: Bantam Books, 1984). Analysis of the evolution of white racial attitudes is found in George Fredrickson, *The Black Image in the White Mind: The Debate on Afro-American Character and Destiny, 1817–1914* (New York: Harper & Row, 1971) and Leonard P. Curry, *The Free Black in Urban America, 1800–1850* (Chicago: University of Chicago Press, 1981). Two collections of essays bring the debate over stereotyping in children's literature to the fore, including Donnarae MacCann and Gloria Woodard, eds., *The Black American in Books for Children: Readings in Racism,* 2d ed. (Metuchen, N.J.: Scarecrow Press, 1989) and Leonard, Tenney, and Davis, eds., *Satire or Evasion?,* essays on the racial implications of *Huckleberry Finn.* Shelley Fisker Fishkin brings a new question to the table in *Was Huck Black? Mark Twain and African-American Voices* (New York: Oxford University Press, 1993).

Much discussion about *Uncle Tom's Cabin* and the reactions it created is found in Joan D. Hedrick, *Harriet Beecher Stowe: A Life* (New York: Oxford University Press, 1994). The debate is over whether Joel Chandler Harris perpetuated myths of the Old South or attempted to honor black culture in his retold folktales. Bruce Bixley has collected many pertinent arguments in *Critical Essays on Joel Chandler Harris* (Boston: G. K. Hall, 1981). He has also edited a bibliographic guide to all the writings on Harris, including some by Samuel Clemens, in *Joel Chandler Harris: A Reference Guide* (Boston: G. K. Hall, 1978). The most recent scholarship argues that Harris sympathized with the plight of the freed black family; see Wayne Mixon, "The Ultimate Irrelevance of Race: Joel Chandler Harris and Uncle Remus in Their Time," *Journal of Southern History* 56.3 (August 1990): 457–80.

The earliest critical analysis of minority stereotyping in children's literature is Dorothy Broderick, *The Image of the Black in Children's Fiction* (New York: R. R. Bowker Co., 1973). A broader analysis of stereotyping, which includes some superficial discussion of children's literature, is a 1984 dissertation by John Denis Mercier, "The Evolution of the Black Image in White Consciousness, 1976–1954: A Popular Culture Perspective" (University of

Pennsylvania). Violet Joyce Harris made a thorough study of W.E.B. Du Bois's "The Brownies' Book: Challenge to the Selective Tradition in Children's Literature" (Ph.D. diss., University of Georgia, 1986). Using stories of southern white children to teach racial boundaries is the theme of John Scott Wilson's "Race and Manners for Southern Girls and Boys: The 'Miss Minerva' Books and Race Relations in a Southern Children's Series," which appeared in *Journal of American Culture* 17.3 (Fall 1994): 69–74. Annie Fellows Johnston accomplished the same task; her work is assessed in "The Little Colonel: A Phenomenon in Popular Literary Culture," *Register of the Kentucky Historical Society* 89 (1991): 121–46. Holly Keller has a thoroughly researched article entitled "Juvenile Antislavery Narrative and Notions of Childhood," *Children's Literature* 24 (1996): 86–100. Phyliss J. Yuill's *Little Black Sambo: A Closer Look* (New York: Council on Interracial Books for Children, 1976) peels back several layers of interpretation of that children's classic.

Far less attention has been paid to ethnic minorities in American children's literature. See J. Frederick MacDonald, " 'The Foreigner' in Juvenile Series Fiction, 1900–1945," *Journal of Popular Culture* 81.3 (Winter 1974): 534–44 and also Fred Erisman's essay "Regionalism in American Children's Literature," in Fraser, *Society and Children's Literature*.

Chapter 6: Idealized Realism, 1920–1945

For insight into American social history from 1920 to 1945, see William E. Leuchtenburg's classic study *The Perils of Prosperity, 1914–1932* (Chicago: University of Chicago Press, 1958). On women, see the notes for chapter 4, as well as Estelle B. Freedman, "The New Woman: Changing Views of Women in the 1920s," *Journal of American History* 61 (1974): 372–93. The vibrancy of the Harlem Renaissance is portrayed in David L. Lewis, *When Harlem Was in Vogue* (New York: Alfred A. Knopf, 1981).

For the history of children in this period, see Hamilton Cravens, "Child-Saving in the Age of Professionalism, 1915–1930," and Leroy Ashby, "Partial Promises and Semi-Visible Youths: The Depression and World War II," both in Hawes and Hiner, *American Childhood*. More recently, Elliott West has compiled a brief history of childhood in this century with attention to child health, law, entertainment, and work in *Growing Up in Twentieth-Century America: A History and Reference Guide* (Westport, Conn.: Greenwood Press, 1996). Joseph M. Hawes has a detailed study entitled *Children between the Wars: American Childhood, 1920–1940* (New York: Twayne, forthcoming). William M. Tuttle Jr. solicited thousands of reminiscences from those who experienced World War II as a child to construct a critical child's-eye view of the homefront entitled *Daddy's Gone to War: The Second World War in the Lives of America's Children* (New York: Oxford University Press, 1993). The growing recognition of adolescence is scrutinized by John Modell in *Into One's Own: From Youth to Adulthood in the United States, 1920–1975* (Berkeley: University of California Press, 1989).

Several important authors are profiled in a collection of essays by the prominent critic John Rowe Townsend, *A Sense of Story: Essays on Contemporary Writers for Children* (Philadelphia: J. B. Lippincott, 1971). Author and critic Perry Nodelman served as editor for another collection of essays on books considered to have made a significant contribution to children's literature. The collection is called *Touchstones: Reflections on the Best in Children's Literature*, vol. 1 (West Lafayette, IN: ChLA Publishers, 1985). Anita Silvey, ed., *Children's Books and Their Creators* (Boston: Houghton-Mifflin, 1995) is a one-volume encyclopedia of twentieth-century authors and subjects within children's literature; the essays are uniformly rich in content.

The prolific writing of Laura Ingalls Wilder, and how much that work was reconstructed by her daughter Rose Lane, has been the subject of investigation for a number of scholars. Early evaluations such as Elizabeth Segal's "Laura Ingalls Wilder's America: An Unflinching Assessment," *Children's Literature in Education* 8.2 (Summer 1977): 63–70 have been revised by such studies as Rosa Ann Moore, "The Little House Books: Rose Colored Classics," *Children's Literature* 7 (1978): 7–16 and Anita Clair Fellman, "Laura Ingalls Wilder and Rose Wilder Lane: The Politics of a Mother-Daughter Relationship," *Signs* 15.3 (Spring 1990): 535–61; both Moore and Fellman credit Lane with literarily and politically shaping Little House books. Substantiating their findings in a scholarly assessment of the Rose Lane's career is William Holtz, *The Ghost in the Little House: A Life of Rose Wilder Lane* (Columbia: University of Missouri Press, 1993). Two recent explorations of Wilder's political and cultural agenda were published in *Children's Literature* 24 (1996). Anita Clair Fellman authored " 'Don't Expect to Depend on Anybody Else': The Frontier as Portrayed in the Little House Books (101–16) and Suzanne Rahn's "What Really Happens in the Little Town on the Prairie" (117–26). A thoughtful comparison of two frontier protagonists is the theme of Susan Maher's "Laura Ingalls and Caddie Woodlawn: Daughters of a Border Space," *The Owl and the Unicorn* 18.2 (December 1994): 130–42.

Two essays that explore the popularity of Eleanor Estes are Louisa Smith, "Eleanor Estes' *The Moffats*: Through Colored Glass," in Perry Nodelman, ed., *Touchstones*, vol. 1 (West Layfayette, IN: ChLA Publishers, 1985), 64–70 and "Eleanor Estes: A Study in Versatility," *Elementary English* 45 (May 1968): 553–57. Elizabeth Enright's works are favorably reviewed by Caroline Hunt in "Elizabeth Enright and the Family Story," *The Lion and the Unicorn* 14.2 (December 1990): 16–29. Lois Lenski's research into regional culture is explored by Lois Kuznets in "Fiction, Faction, and Formula in the Regional Novels of Lois Lenski," *Proceedings of the Children's Literature Association* 9 (1982): 96–106. The uniqueness of Florence Crannell Means's presentation of minority protagonists before nonwhite heroes were at all common is explored in a fine essay by Suzanne Rahn, "Rediscovering Florence Crannell Means," *The Lion and the Unicorn* 11 (1987): 98–115. Both of these authors and others are analyzed in Kay E. Vandergrift, "A Feminist Perspective on Multicultural Children's Literature in the Middle Years of the Twentieth Century," *Library Trends* 41.3 (Winter 1993): 354–77.

Series books found a bigger niche with the advent of the most popular girl hero of all time, Nancy Drew. The first serious investigation of this phenomenon was Bobbie Ann Mason, *The Girl Sleuth: A Feminist Guide* (Old Westbury, N.Y.: Feminist Press, 1975), an impressionistic, provocative study of several of the female series heroes. The two studies of the Stratemeyer Syndicate by Billman and Johnson, cited in the notes for chapter 4, continue to be useful for the post-1920 period. Essays from a recent conference for Nancy Drew enthusiasts, writers, and scholars appeared in a special edition of *The Lion and the Unicorn,* 18.1 (June 1994). Expanded versions of some of these papers have been collected by Carolyn Stewart Dyer and Nancy Tillman Romalov, eds., *Rediscovering Nancy Drew* (Iowa City: University of Iowa Press, 1995). In addition, Kenneth Donelson examines the revisions in the series books during the 1950s in "Nancy, Tom, and Assorted Friends in the Stratemeyer Syndicate Then and Now," *Children's Literature* 7 (1978): 17–44, and Nancy Romalov provides a detailed analysis of one kind of series book in "Mobile Heroines: Early Twentieth-Century Girls' Automobile Series," *Journal of Popular Culture* 28 (Spring 1995): 231–43. Sherrie A. Inness edited a collection of essays that appeared too late to utilize in this study, *Nancy Drew and Company: Culture, Gender, and Girls' Series* (Bowling Green, Ohio: Bowling Green State University Press, 1997).

Information about the portrayals of ethnic minorities, particularly African- Americans, can be found in the essays in MacCann and Woodard, *Racism and Sexism* (previously cited) and in Broderick, *Image of the Black American.* MacCann and Woodard have also edited *Cultural Conformity in Books for Children: Further Readings in Racism* (Metuchen, N.J.: Scarecrow Press, 1977).

Christopher Collier, American historian and author of children's books, provides a penetrating analysis of *Johnny Tremain* in "Johnny and Sam: Old and New Approaches to the American Revolution," *Hornbook* 52 (April 1976): 132–38, which can be read in conjunction with Caroline C. Hunt, "U.S. Children's Books about the World War II Period: From Isolationism to Internationalism, 1940–1990," *The Lion and the Unicorn* 18.2 (December 1994): 190–208. Donelson and Nilsen explore books for older children and teens in "From the Safety of Romance to the Beginning of Realism," in their text *Literature for Today's Young Adult,* 499–531.

Chapter 7: Child Liberation, 1950–1980

The culture of the Cold War has received a penetrating analysis by Elaine Tyler May in *Homeward Bound: American Families in the Cold War Era*

(New York: Basic Books, 1988) and by Landon Jones, *Great Expectations: America and the Baby Boom Generation* (New York: Ballantine, 1980). Susan Strasser explains how society invented new tasks for women in *Never Done: A History of American Housework* (New York: Pantheon Books, 1982). Michael Harrington's *The Other America* (New York: Macmillan, 1962) was the first to document the underside of the 1950s' affluent consumer culture. For a broader view of American social history since 1950, see William Chafe, *The Unfinished Journey: America Since World War II* (New York: Oxford University Press, 1986).

Many excellent surveys of the civil rights movement exist; I have emphasized those that give precedence to the grassroots movements, such as Jo Ann Robinson, *The Montgomery Bus Boycott and the Women Who Made It* (Knoxville: University of Tennessee Press, 1987); John Dittmer, *Local People: The Struggle for Civil Rights in Mississippi* (Urbana: University of Illinois Press, 1994); and Claybourne Carson, *In Struggle: SNCC and the Black Awakening of the 1960s* (Cambridge: Harvard University Press, 1981). For the impact of the Vietnam conflict on American society, consult Thomas Powers, *The War at Home: Vietnam and the American People, 1964–1968* (New York: Grossman Publishers, 1973).

This history of childhood since 1950 is thoroughly explored in chapters 3 and 4 of West, *Growing Up*, as well as in two essays in Hawes and Hiner, *American Childhood:* Charles E. Strickland and Andrew M. Ambrose, "The Baby Boom, Prosperity, and the Changing Worlds of Children" (533–86) and Elizabeth Donovan, "The Age of Narcissism, 1960–1982," (587–618). The rise of young adult books as a separate literary category is explored in Donelson and Nilsen, *Literature for Today's Young Adults,* chapters 1 and 15 especially. Writings by and about contemporary authors can be found in Miriam Hoffman and Eva Samuels, *Authors and Illustrators of Children's Books: Writings on Their Lives and Works* (New York: R. R. Bowker Co., 1972). The *Touchstones* collection edited by Perry Nodelman and the one-volume encyclopedia edited by Anita Silvey, described in the listings for chapter 6, are valuable resources for this chapter as well.

Writer Jonathan Cott explores the lives and writings of three authors profiled in this chapter, Theodor Geisel, William Steig, and Maurice Sendak, in *Pipers at the Gates of Dawn: The Wisdom of Children's Literature* (New York: Random House, 1981). Also helpful was Geraldine DeLuca, "Exploring the Levels of Childhood: The Allegorical Sensibility of Maurice Sendak," *Children's Literature* 12 (1984): 3–24. A definitive biography, *E. B. White: A Biography* (New York: W. W. Norton & Co., 1984), by Scott Elledge, relates the labored writing of *Charlotte's Web*.

Sheila Egoff, a Canadian specialist in children's literature, has written the most comprehensive and critical survey of books of the 1960s and 1970s in *Thursday's Child: Trends and Patterns in Contemporary Children's Literature* (Chicago: American Library Association, 1981). British critic David Rees has published two collections of essays on major contemporary American authors. He dislikes most of them, but he also provides knowledgeable insight into the authors' styles and themes. See *The Marble in the Water: Essays on Contemporary Writers of Fiction for Children and Young Adults* (Boston: The Horn Book, 1980) and *Painted Desert, Green Shade: Essays on Contemporary Fiction for Children and Young Adults* (Boston: The Horn Book, 1984). Michael Cart concentrates only on young adult literature but brings his survey up to the present in *From Romance to Realism: 50 Years of Growth and Change in Young Adult Literature* (New York: HarperCollins, 1996). In a very short but cogent essay, Anne Scott MacLeod covers much of the same territory without analyzing particular books: "The Journey Inward: Adolescent Literature in America, 1949–1995," in Sandra L. Beckett, ed., *Reflections of Change: Children's Literature Since 1945* (Westport, Conn.: Greenwood Press, 1997), 125–29. In that same volume, Jerry Griswold sees the popularity of children's books in the 1990s as a reflection of adult nostalgia for a simpler era in "The Disappearance of Children's Literature (or Children's Literature as Nostalgia) in the United States in the Late Twentieth Century," 35–41. Professor Kay Vandergrift, "A Feminist Perspective on Multicultural Children's Literature in the Middle Years of the Twentieth Century," *Library Trends* 41.3 (Winter 1993): 354–77 analyzes early contributions to multicultural awareness in children's literature.

Epilogue

Current information on publishing trends is best garnered from *Publisher's Weekly;* book review columns in major daily newspapers; journals such as *Horn Book* magazine, *Lion and the Unicorn,* and *Children's Literature;* and the annual of the Modern Language Association Division on Children's Literature and the Children's Literature Association, published by Yale University Press. The Children's Literature Association also publishes the ChLA Quarterly (Battle Creek, Mich.: ChLA).

Index

The Author

The author is an assistant professor of American history at Rhodes College, where she teaches courses in early America and the history of childhood. Professor Murray, who received her Ph.D. in 1991 from the University of Memphis, is the author of "Charity within the Bounds of Race and Class: Female Benevolence in the Old South," *South Carolina Historical Magazine* 96.1 (1995), "Rational Thought and Republican Virtue: Children's Literature from 1789 to 1820," *Journal of the Early Republic* 8.2 (1988), and the forthcoming "Childhood and Religion," in *Childhood and Southern History,* edited by Ted Ownby, University of Mississippi Press.

The Editors

Joseph M. Hawes is professor of history at the University of Memphis. His most recent books are *The Children's Rights Movement: A History of Advocacy and Protection* (Twayne, 1991) and *American Children between the Wars, 1920–1940* (Twayne, 1998).

N. Ray Hiner is Chancellors' Club Teaching Professor of History and Education at the University of Kansas. He has published widely on the history of children and education in the United States and is coeditor (with Joseph M. Hawes) of *Growing Up in America* (1985), *American Childhood* (1985), and *Children in Historical Perspective* (1991). He is currently writing a book on children in the life and thought of Cotton Mather.

DATE DUE

PUERTO RICAN PERSPECTIVES

Edited, with an Introduction

by

EDWARD MAPP

The Scarecrow Press, Inc.
Metuchen, N. J.   1974

Royalties on this book are being donated to
The Experimental & Bilingual Institute, Inc.

301.45168729
M297p
1974

Library of Congress Cataloging in Publication Data

Mapp, Edward.
    Puerto Rican perspectives.

    1. Puerto Ricans in the United States--
Addresses, essays, lectures. I. Title.
E184.P85M36   301.45'16'87295073   73-20175
ISBN 0-8108-0691-6

DEDICATED
TO
BLACK AND PUERTO RICAN
UNITY

FOREWORD

by Congressman Herman Badillo

Puerto Ricans constitute the newest major ethnic or cultural group in the continental United States. Even though our people have lived in mainland cities and towns for over one hundred years, the story of the Puerto Rican American really only began with the large migration of people from the island to the mainland which began in the 1930's.

In the forty years during which there has been a major influx of Puerto Ricans into the United States, our community has made numerous and significant contributions to the quality and character of American life--in education, the arts, sports, public affairs and government. However, the Puerto Rican has, until just recently, generally been relegated to second-class citizenship and has had to struggle against seemingly insurmountable odds. Unlike other immigrants of earlier years, Puerto Ricans are already United States citizens. Nevertheless, they are often denied the full advantages of such status and have experienced the greatest difficulty in being assimilated into the American manner of life.

The Puerto Rican seeks nothing more than what other immigrant groups have secured. Our community is actively seeking economic security and independence; full access to educational and social institutions; equal opportunities in employment, housing, education and health services; the enjoyment of basic human rights and freedoms and equal protection and treatment under the law.

Puerto Ricans are not only resourceful and energetic but are very proud of a tradition of taking the initiative ourselves and achieving our goals through self-help efforts. In a wide variety of areas the Boricua works to achieve equality and fair treatment for his fellow compadre and himself. Through various grassroots programs Puerto Ricans are beginning to compete on an equal basis with other groups.

v

For far too long Puerto Ricans have been strangers in their own land. This era hopefully appears to be ending as more Puerto Rican men and women enter professional careers and multiply the contributions to American society. An increasing number are starting to move into the middle class and into suburban communities.

Nevertheless, a great deal more needs to be done to secure fair and equitable treatment for the mainland Puerto Ricans and to insure that full and equal opportunities are open to them. As there develops a greater awareness and appreciation of our community's potential and capabilities, as well as our rich cultural heritage and proud history, both by Puerto Ricans and other Americans alike, the progress and accomplishments revealed in the following pages will certainly grow and increase. By viewing the Puerto Rican community through the diverse perspectives in this book, the reader will hopefully achieve a better understanding of the Puerto Rican community.

TABLE OF CONTENTS

vii

INTRODUCTION

A book entitled <u>Puerto Rican Perspectives</u> would be a presumptuous or foolhardy undertaking for one man (particularly one who is not Puerto Rican) because there is no such thing as <u>a</u> single Puerto Rican perspective.

Most of the essays included in this volume were written by Puerto Ricans who are or have been involved in seeking solutions to the problems confronting Puerto Ricans in mainland United States.

In selecting the essays, I have not attempted to articulate a unified point of view nor to stimulate controversy for its own sake. A broad spectrum of opinion is presented. The essays range from the formal research-type piece to the informal "rap" on paper.

Each essay has been included under one of four sections on the basis of the writer's major emphasis.

The first section of the book deals with "Education." There is considerable controversy among the educational community as to the relevancy of the bilingual program. Some educators contend that it does not work; others feel that it is merely an appeasement to Hispanic parent groups who want the emphasis to be on Spanish rather than English.

Attempts to recruit bilingual employees have enjoyed limited success because there are insufficient bilingual education programs to produce the needed work force. In his essay, Benjamin Pacheco states, "If language-acquisition is not coupled with learning about the culture inherent in the words, then no real language-learning has taken place." In a pluralistic society, ethnic minorities should be allowed to develop and maintain their own cultural heritage. ASPIRA acted recently as plaintiff in a class action suit against the New York City Board of Education for its failure to provide adequate bilingual educational programs for the more than 100,000 predominantly Spanish speaking students in the public school system.

1

The May 1973 community school board elections in
New York City could be heralded as the first totally bilingual
election process in the history of a major city in the United
States.   Petitions for candidates, ballots, and registration
materials were available in Spanish and English.   Heretofore,
the rights of non-English speaking Puerto Ricans to cast a
knowledgeable ballot had been effectively denied.   Luis
Fuentes, Superintendent of Manhattan's Community School
District 1, was a key figure in the election.   In his essay,
Fuentes writes, "We must be aware that the institutions
within our communities do not now belong to us, " a statement supported by other events.   A recent attempt to com-
pile a directory of Spanish-surnamed librarians, a potentially
useful reference resource, was opposed by the teachers'
union on the basis that it was an ethnic survey which could
be used to select school personnel using the criterion of
ethnicity.

One can only wonder how personnel affirmative action
programs are to be executed if ethnic data is not to be
gathered.   Writing about affirmative action at The City University of New York (CUNY), Frank Negrón states, "To
insert the false question of quotas into the situation serves
to obscure the injustice perpetrated against oppressed groups
by releasing a smokescreen of emotionally charged words. "
The Puerto Rican community has been a strong supporter of
CUNY but will probably want to reevaluate its position unless
affirmative action becomes not merely policy but actual
practice at the University.

Alexander Vazquez presents a documented study of
the alienation of Puerto Rican students in the public schools
of Philadelphia.   Vazquez refers to the "powerlessness, "
"meaninglessness" and "normlessness" which contribute to
the alienation of these children.   He too advocates bilingualism as one method of improving the lot of Philadelphia's
Puerto Rican youngsters.

In 1969, militant Puerto Rican youths demanded the
creation of Puerto Rican studies programs in the colleges.
The growing interest in Puerto Rican studies in the United
States is a welcome development.   In his essay, Richard
Rivera provides a sensible and thoughtful rationale for these
programs.

Problems emanating from inadequate educational
systems spill over into other areas.   The book's second

section, "The Arts," includes an essay by Luis Quero-
Chiesa, who writes poignantly of the anguish of the expatriate writer: "Before him rises the wall of the English
language isolating him from the American literary life."
He stresses the point that the writer can be either discouraged or stimulated by the vicissitudes of life.

Jaimé Ruiz-Escobar, himself an expatriate writer,
shares his vision of the Puerto Rican theatrical scene.
His is an essay of great energy with alternating rays of
anger and admiration for the artists about whom he writes.
It is a summary of significant theatrical currents in Puerto
Rico.   He attempts to examine Puerto Rican playwrights,
evaluating their continuing social concerns as well as their
artistic development as dramatists.   Ruiz-Escobar is dedicated to the values of his people and to the richness of
their drama.

In considering the writer and dramatist one must not
forget or minimize the power of non-print media.   The motion picture industry has been as responsible as anything
else for stereotyping the Puerto Rican.   When Puerto Rican
children see their people depicted as they are in films, their
minds become injured in ways we can never know.   The
essay which I have contributed to this book is a brief examination of the portrayal of Puerto Ricans in motion pictures,
seen from my perspective as film researcher.

Along similar lines, Marifé-Hernández takes a penetrating look in her provocative essay at the relationship of
television to the Puerto Rican community.

The third section has as its theme, "The Community,"
a vital force in the life of the Puerto Rican.   Churches,
libraries, police precincts, each in their own way determine
the quality of life within the Puerto Rican community.

Puerto Ricans could become powerful allies of law
enforcement, if and when they are convinced that equal
justice will protect their rights.   A recent report from the
New York City Board of Correction said, "Not only are
many Hispanic defendants enmeshed in a system from which
they are partially or totally alienated, but language barriers
may limit their access to important services."   It is
axiomatic that Spanish speaking people often experience
arrest, prosecution and disposition of their cases without
fully understanding what is happening to them.   John Vazquez

and Charles Bahn in their essay explore the attitudes of
Puerto Ricans toward the police. The authors state: "The
policeman as an instrument of constraint and as a representative service to support a given set of institutions in
the dominant society is often perceived as an obstacle to
movement and adjustment by the Puerto Rican community."

A number of highly successful library programs for
Spanish speaking people are threatened by President Nixon's
cuts in the 1973/74 federal budget. This is occurring at a
time when libraries throughout the United States are awakening to the need for Spanish speaking librarians to bridge the
gap which separates libraries from various ethnic groups
such as Puerto Ricans. For Puerto Ricans, librarianship
remains a little explored avenue of public service. Yet
Puerto Rican librarians are needed in libraries that serve
Puerto Rican people, if our institutions are even partially to
reflect our communities. By virtue of ethnic rapport,
Puerto Rican librarians should be better qualified to inform
people of the Puerto Rican community about the services
libraries can provide. In two different essays, Puerto
Rican librarians speak out about the significance of libraries
for Puerto Ricans. José Betancourt treats the subject from
an historical perspective; Lillian López and Pura Belpré use
the autobiographical approach.

Taking a look at another important institution, the
church, one remembers that half of the 1.8 million Catholics
in the Archdiocese of New York are Hispanic; more young
seminarians than ever before are studying Spanish; the
church has appointed its first cardinal of Puerto Rican
descent, Luis Aponte Martinez. Yet the church has been
criticized. Charges have been made by the Cristianos
Hispano Americanos Pro Justicia (Spanish-American Christians
for Justice) that the Archdiocese of New York has neglected
its Puerto Rican and other Hispanic parishioners. Against
this backdrop, Rev. Antonio Stevens-Arroyo provides an
overview of the meaning for Puerto Ricans of church and
religion.

A fourth and final section of the book deals with
"The Individual." Four Puerto Ricans, two women and two
men, give their impressions of what it means to be a Puerto
Rican. Celia Vice describes in a very personal way the
obstacles and difficulties encountered in the pursuit of success. Humberto Cintrón, Luis Mercado and Amalia Betanzos write on alienation, identity and professionalism,

respectively.   Each in his own way has something special
to say.

All the essays have been collected and edited by a
black man in the belief that there must be effective coalition
between blacks and Puerto Ricans if either is to achieve
success.   Both groups would do well to remember that
Puerto Rican history is an amalgamation of Spanish and
African culture.   Neither Puerto Rican nor black can afford
the luxury of petty antagonisms and divisiveness--not while
discrimination, unemployment, poverty, substandard housing
and unequal education remain the common enemy.

The diverse points of view presented in the collection
are very personal and the editor neither accepts responsibility for any statements made nor necessarily subscribes
to all ideas expressed herein.   It is earnestly hoped that
this volume, to which the authors have so cooperatively contributed, will be not only a unique resource of ideas and
credos unavailable elsewhere but also a significant aid to
the greater understanding of aspects of the Puerto Rican
experience.

Edward Mapp

June 1973

PART I

PERSPECTIVES FROM EDUCATION

CHAPTER 1

A POSITIVE VIEW OF BILINGUALISM

Benjamin Pacheco

The American myth has it that European immigrants came to this country, readily learned the English language and moved up the ladder of success. Students of education have fervently supported this premise. In an anti-intellectual and profoundly undemocratic fashion it has been urged that, since English is the official language of America, there is no rationale in public education for instruction at any level in the student's vernacular. Thus, belief in the concept of the "melting pot" has obscured and distorted the history of the American migrant.

The English language was one of many languages brought here by the colonial powers. During the 19th century there were bilingual schools in several states. In fact, prior to World War I there was little organized pressure in the United States to impose English as the sole language in communities settled by recent immigrants from Europe. The exceptions to this attitude were the black slaves from Africa and many Indian tribes. In the field of education the period from 1838 to 1848 presents a historical breakthrough for bilingual education. A law enacted in Ohio in 1839 stated that "In any district where the directors keep an English school and do not have the branches taught in German, it shall be lawful for youth in such districts who desire to learn in the German language, to attend a district German school."[1]

This directive, which was intended to be permissive for the state, became mandatory for Cincinnati under an 1840 law: "It shall be the duty of the Board of Trustees and visitors of Common Schools to see that some duly qualified teachers are hired for the instruction of such youth as desire to learn the German language or the German and

8

English languages together. "[2]   Cincinnati became famous
for its bilingual schools, which existed until 1917. Missouri's
Superintendent of Public Instruction complained in his report
for 1887-1888 that in a large number of districts of the
State, the classes were not taught in English.   To his dismay, some teachers were barely able to speak English.

In Wisconsin and in the Territory of Dakota similar
conditions prevailed.   The Dakota Territorial Board of Education in its 1886-1888 report noted that "Some instances
came to the attention of the board where the teacher was
not even able to speak the English language and nothing could
be done about it, as the foreign element was so strong that
they not only controlled the schools, but the election of the
county superintendent also. "[3]   How relevant to the contemporary educational scene!

In 1887 Colorado passed a law permitting the bilingual school, and in 1872 an Oregon law even permitted
monolingual German public schools.   In 1874 and 1882 bilingual schools were established which were comparable to
those of Cincinnati.   These schools prided themselves on
their achievements in language maintenance, bicultural education, and minority rights.

Bilingual education declined as anti-German and anti-
foreign sentiments flourished in the United States.   Legislation was enacted which forbade the teaching of languages
other than English in all schools, public or nonpublic, day
schools or supplementary, to pupils below grades eight or
nine.   The current high level of interest in bilingual education in the United States comes after a long period during
which the maintenance of any language but English was
counter to public policy and popular attitude.   A resurgence
of interest in bilingual education occurred with the increased
political activity of "non-white" and non-English speaking
minority groups in the last decade and a half.   The notion
of a pluralistic society is becoming more accepted in the
United States.   The facade that enabled America to pretend
that it was culturally monistic is being discarded.

In 1967, bills were introduced in Congress to amend
the Elementary and Secondary Education Act of 1965 to provide for bilingual education programs.   The amendment,
known as the Bilingual Education Act, was passed.   The
Act is "designed to meet specific education needs of children
3 to 18 years of age who have limited English-speaking

ability and come from environments where the dominant
language is other than English." The passage of the Act
represents a change in the philosophy of American education, from a rejection of foreign languages to an acceptance
of them as valuable resources and necessary mediums of
instruction.

The Search for a Definition

There is a lack of definition of the term bilingualism.
The Bilingual Education Act of 1967 defines bilingual education as "the use of two languages, one of which is English,
as mediums of instruction." Some authors define bilingualism as exposure to two languages. Others use the term
bilingualism to mean the learning of two languages at the
same time from birth. It is also used where a second
language has been acquired after the establishment of the
native language. In parts of the United States, in the southwest and to a large extent in New York City, "bilingual" is
loosely used to refer to students with Spanish surnames,
whether they know two languages or not. A. Bruce Gaarder
provides us with a working definition of bilingual education:
"The concurrent use of two languages as media of instruction
for a child in a given school in any or all of the school curriculum except the actual study of the languages themselves."[4] Gaarder goes on to say that ordinary foreign
language teaching is not bilingual education.

William F. Mackey recommends the Dual Medium
Equal Maintenance (DEM) for bilingual schools.[5] This
system is characterized by equal treatment of the two languages. The focus is to give equal chance to both languages
in all domains, in order to create balanced bilinguals. A
distinction must be made between the content of education
(information, concept development, etc.) and the linguistic
vehicle of education. Students with less competence in
English than monolingual English-speaking children will probably become retarded in their school work to the extent of
their deficiency in English if English is the sole medium of
instruction. On the other hand, the bilingual child's development of concepts and acquisition of other experience
and information could proceed at a normal rate if the
vernacular were used as a medium of instruction. He
learns concepts in his course work and English as a second
language course.

There is no need for the same subjects to be taught in two languages, and concepts do not have to be developed a second time in the second language. New labels are provided in the second language course. A student who learns history or science in Spanish will have English terms or labels for the same concept taught during the English as a Second Language course as partial content for the lesson.

A Story of Success

Six or seven thousand Puerto Rican high school graduates migrate to the mainland annually. Approximately 19,000 Puerto Rican high school students graduate from the public schools of New York City every year. Although The City University of New York (CUNY) has an open admissions policy, the Puerto Rican student is handicapped when he enters the university. The migrant high school graduate does not know the English language, whereas the New Yorker of Puerto Rican background has not learned sufficient Spanish and is grossly deficient in English.

In the spring of 1970, Kingsborough Community College of CUNY initiated a bilingual program in an attempt to reme-dy this "language problem." After two and a half years, this program is one of the most successful in the nation. The program is designed to provide college-level instruction to Puerto Rican high school graduates who have a limited knowl-edge of English. Students take college courses in Spanish for credit, while learning to speak, read, and write English. The objectives of the program include:

a) providing opportunities for post-secondary educa-tion to Puerto Rican and other Spanish-speaking New Yorkers;
b) offering instruction which will further the educa-tional goals of the student and increase his ability to adjust within the framework of American society;
c) meeting both objectives with an awareness of the distinctiveness and value of the student's language and culture, and their importance in maintaining a viable identity within the Puerto Rican community in New York.

The Kingsborough Community College Institute of Bi-lingual Studies is the oldest continuous bilingual program in operation in The City University of New York.

The original program was designed with the intent of qualifying students for graduation in three years. However, under intensive counseling, the first graduates were awarded their Associate degrees in June 1972 in two and a half years. The average graduate had a B level of achievement.

Eighty percent of the June graduates were accepted by the University of Hartford (Conn.) in a teacher-education program. This program will permit students to complete their Bachelor's degree in one year, including summers. One hundred percent of the graduating students went on to senior colleges.

The bilingual students at Kingsborough come from societies which are tradition-oriented. They are mostly Puerto Ricans and come from very poor families. They value education but lack the skills to compete successfully in the academic world. At the Institute, they are given the motivation, as well as the tools, to become the professionals of the Puerto Rican migrant generation. The value of learning the English language is stressed because, without it, they cannot achieve their objectives nor cope with the socio-economic demands of this country.

There is evidence which commends bilingual programs as one of the ways for improving the education of Puerto Rican and other Spanish-speaking groups on the mainland. Besides the learning of two languages, the Institute of Bilingual Studies gives its students access to two cultures. It is important that this be recognized because most people tend to think that learning a new language means merely acquiring new words and their meanings. However, it goes far beyond this. If language-acquisition is not coupled with learning about the culture inherent in the words, then no real language-learning has taken place.

Perhaps the greatest effect that the Bilingual Institute has had is that it has created an atmosphere of respect and recognition for people of different nationalities and for their cultures and their languages. It has also helped to mollify the "culture shock" which is so often the experience of any migrant entering a foreign land.

Notes

1. Fishman, Joshua. "American Heritage: Language Maintenance in the Classroom," Center Forum, published by Center for Urban Education. Vol. 4, no. 1 (September 1969), p. 18.

2. Ibid., p. 18.

3. Ibid., p. 19.

4. John, Vera P. and Horner, Vivian M. Early Childhood Bilingual Education. New York: The Modern Language Association of America, 1971, p. 186.

5. Ibid., p. 186.

CHAPTER 2

PUERTO RICAN CHILDREN AND
THE NEW YORK CITY PUBLIC SCHOOLS

Luis Fuentes

Author Paul Goodman wrote a few years ago: "I have
heard the [New York City school] system described as a tor-
pid dinosaur in a cold swamp; one lights a fire under her but
produces very little motion; and she soon settles back."[1]
That is what has happened to those of us who in 1967-68 lit
a fire named the community control movement. Its outcome
was the decentralization law and, as always, the law distorted
the objectives of the movement and so-called compromise legislation contained the seeds of the destruction of our movement for change. Those of us who have been with this struggle for years resisted this law in the legislature and, when
it passed, boycotted its implementation. But time is the great
asset of legislation and now, three years later, the only way
to re-light the fire of our movement is to get inside this law
and point out the massive, gaping holes in it.

It passes the obligation for the education of elementary
and junior high children from the Central Board to 31 Community Boards. Yet these community boards exercise no
power over their district teaching personnel, no right to hire
and fire, nor even a clear right to transfer or evaluate.
These rights are contractual and are negotiated between the
professional unions and a central board the membership of which
was largely selected with the approval of these very unions.
Consequently, community boards have become agents of contracts negotiated by others. Since the passage of the law,
such powers as control of maintenance and food contracts,
which were supposed to devolve to community boards, have
remained in the main with the Central Board of Education.

Consequently, handed negotiated contracts and stripped
of vital fiscal powers, decentralized school boards are phan-
toms. They are charged with enormous responsibilities (the
education of all elementary and junior high children) but have

14

few visible powers and prerogatives. Their chief power, the
selection of principals, would also have proven largely mean-
ingless had not the courts in the Chance decision proclaimed
the Principal's examination a discriminatory one. This has
freed Community Boards to hire state certified principals and
given them the ability to recruit competent minority leaders.
Clearly, education has stepped into a new neo-colonial stage
where a local group with invisible powers absorbs the brunt
of the community's anger.

It is in the face of these enormous perils that we in
District 1 are taking the offensive. We are not willing to
pose as overseers for junkie production lines. We intend to
take on those who are really running our schools. We intend
to force out in the open the paradoxes in the decentralization
legislation by exercising genuine power and fighting for its
legality. We speak to the needs of the poor we represent,
and representing people whose children are massively cheated
by this school system means that we will speak with anger
and sometimes act with impatience. We will not be used to
explain away the glaring deficiencies of this system. In this
way, we have become in District 1 the very special enemies
of the forces who profit from this system.

I want to concentrate my attention on an analysis of
those forces. I don't want my discussion of these forces to
be distorted. I am not anti-union. But I firmly believe that
the current leadership of the unions bears no relationship to
the historic and decent impulse of the working man to organize. One union is an association of supervisors, namely the
principals and bureaucrats who have historically been the core
of this system. It is in fact a union for management. The
other, a teachers' union, was born in part out of widespread
dissatisfaction with the National Education Association, which
remains the largest teacher organization in America. Earlier
opposition between the two groups was suddenly transformed
into a firm alliance when supervisors' and teachers' organizations perceived a common foe--Black and Puerto Rican parents and community. Not once, since 1968, have these organizations opposed each other. A supposedly workers' union
is thus in complete alliance with a management association;
nothing promotes white solidarity like a couple of black and
brown faces. Yes! The Issues that have united these natural
opposites are purely racial--roughly one percent of the city's
professional staff is Puerto Rican, six to seven percent Black.

These jobs are attracting enormous salaries. Pupil

populations are declining and the rate of school budget growth
is also slowing; thus new positions are not opening up. Indeed in District 1, we have lost 170 teaching positions due to
budget cuts in the last three years. We are losing annually
almost precisely the same number of positions as are vacated
by retiring or otherwise departing teachers. This is a description of a virtually static employment situation. There is
no room for change, unless room is made. The professional
unions perceive their basic responsibility as the protection of
their memberships, regardless of competence in their current
jobs. They recognize that with parent and community control
would come the demand for more minority professionals.
Therefore, together, these groups have combined to resist
both parent-community control and the slightest openings to
minority professionals. They are attempting to lock the present incumbents of professional positions into those jobs. The
result is to freeze the present ethnic distributions of jobs
and to set up a constant war of nerves between the minority
community and the professional unions.

        I recognize that a principal ingredient in the establish-
ment of these enmities between union and community is the
folks up top--the political and economic structure which in
the face of dramatic educational needs constantly comes up
with empty palms. They have created a scarcity of resources
and pitted the forces who must live with these schools against
each other. Community and union should be allied, should be
pressing together for concerted government support of education. Nonetheless, this union leadership has irrevocably
chosen the path of cooperating with those in government and
business who manipulate and dominate this society. This
union leadership has consistently made war on the minority
community. They destroyed Ocean Hill-Brownsville and then
in Albany wrote that destruction into law.

        Their contracts speak to abysmally selfish concerns.
The budget figures for the current Board of Education fiscal
year document the devastation these contracts are causing.
This year's total city budget increased by $220 million, yet
every school district in the city sustained serious cuts.
Where did the increase go? One hundred million dollars went
to cover the fringe benefit costs of the last union and custo-
dial contracts, and another $50 million for the fringe benefit
costs of the new contract; but the real impact of the fringe
benefit costs of the new contract will be felt in coming years.
With the additional costs of debt service and annualizing new
salary costs, there was absolutely no money left for the

schools. So District 1 suffered a $500,000 cut in instruction-
al services, and was faced with increasing personnel costs
across the board.

Even worse is the top-heavy nature of the latest salary
increases. The beginning teachers' salary went up by only
$100; but the increase at the top of the scale was over $4,000.
The union's seniority provisions and its adamant opposition to
any fair method of evaluating a teacher's competence, combined with this payoff for the top of the scale, demonstrate
that the union has selected a portion of its own membership
to favor and another portion to abandon. The new teachers
who are being abandoned at the bargaining table are the few
Blacks, Puerto Ricans and creative young Whites that we have
managed to recruit.

It would cost me at least $6,000 and two and a half
years to rid my district of even one incompetent teacher, and
then it would mean that other children in some other district
may suffer with him. This stranglehold must be broken.
Teachers need unions, but their union should ally them with
parents and students rather than subordinate the interests of
education to the preservation of all job holders at inflated
costs. We need a union that recognizes that teachers are not
assembly-line workers. They are now paid fully professional
salaries, and they must meet fully professional standards,
rather than resist the establishment of all standards.

There is one issue that perhaps demonstrates best the
total opposition of these unions to any positive change: bilingual education. I am a superintendent selected by a community whose school district consists of 73 percent Puerto
Rican youngsters, 15 percent Black, 8 percent Chinese and
the remainder are Jewish, Polish, Ukranian, Indian and Italian. Eighty-five percent of these youngsters, by the time
they reach the eighth grade, are three to four years behind
grade level in reading. There are those who call these statistics a sign of failure; but if 85 percent of the products of
any industry shared a basic characteristic, we would assume
that it was the intention of the industry to mark its products
with that characteristic. The 15 percent of the products not
so marked with this characteristic would be the ones considered deviant. Thus, one could conclude that the 15 percent of the children in my district who graduate from our
schools able to read at their grade level are deviant, and that
the system is 85 percent successful.

There is no great mystery to these statistics. There
are 2,000 children in District 1 who speak no English at all,
4,000 speak it so hesitantly that they cannot be understood.
Understood by whom? By their teachers. When I came to
District 1, there were over 800 regular teachers in the 20
schools of our district. Six spoke Spanish. One spoke Chinese. Our teachers and students can't even talk to each
other.

My district, in the lower East Side of Manhattan, is
illustrative of a broader series of facts. Let's look at some
numbers to learn something about Puerto Rican youngsters in
the city of New York. Recently, the New York Times reported that on the same day that the stock market for the
first time passed the 1000 mark, the New York regional office of the Department of Labor released some startling unemployment figures: 40 percent of the city's Puerto Rican
males, aged 18 to 25, were unemployed, the highest of any
ethnic group in the city. Keep in mind that the unemployment
figures apply only to those seeking work, and that many young
Puerto Ricans by their early twenties have already stopped
trying. Fifty-three percent of the city's Puerto Rican student
population drop out of school; 26 percent of the state's narcotics addicts under treatment are Puerto Rican, and 82 percent of the Puerto Rican addicts are school dropouts. That
is why Puerto Rican parents have come to view their schools
as junkie production lines, since statistically they produce almost twice as many junkies as literates. The 1970 NYC
school census identified 117,469 Spanish-dominant non-English-
speaking pupils. Although 25 percent of the city's student
population is Puerto Rican, less than one percent of its professional staff is Puerto Rican. There is roughly one Puerto
Rican teacher for every 300 Puerto Rican students in New
York District 1 schools, isolating the Puerto Rican child from
his own culture, background and language.

Puerto Rican children are entering school at all ages
and grade levels; some start kindergarten and first grade and
some move to the city when they're older. A child's initial
school experience should, as the New York State Education
Department has argued, "capitalize on his home language and
culture." Instead, in New York schools, from the beginning,
the child is abused culturally and lingually.

If I say to the teachers, "Look, we have to have
schools that can begin by talking the same language as our
children, so your choice is to learn the language or some of

you will have to go," I get this response: I set up classes
in Spanish and Chinese, and two dozen out of 800 teachers
take them. The rest talk job security and get their union
and its powerful media friends to get me tried in a formal
Board of Education hearing as a racist.

I say that bilingual education is the issue without a
liberal position. The union opposes it because its membership is unwilling or unable to undertake it. The maintenance
of current job holders in their positions, regardless of the
high illiteracy, is the union's stern position. My position is
bilingualism, now, in the New York public schools, on as
massive a basis as possible. It may mean that some people
will lose their jobs if they refuse to learn the language.
When the union resists bilingualism it unmistakably prefers
massive illiteracy to the replacement of any of its current
membership with new teachers who may be able to communicate.

This is an example of what I mean by the sabotage of
children. This is what I mean by the union transformation
of our school system into an unbending public works project.
We grind out jobs. We dispense salaries. We help keep the
economy fluid in Queens and the suburban counties. The
schools exist for the people who work in them. The system
churns on, an adult world living off children's needs but meeting the adult needs of the people who run it. Thus one can
say that the New York public system is the most successful
in the world; that is, it pays the highest number of teachers
the highest annual salaries. That has become its purpose.

Our actions are based on a single premise: the unions
run these schools on the basis of what is best for their membership; it is time for the community to run these schools on
the basis of what is best for its children. We are not talking nationalism or ethnic quotas. We are advocating the sensible imposition of new priorities. Schools are for children
and the jobs should be filled by those who can offer something to children. It is clear, after Forest Hills and Canar-
sie, that we in the Black and Puerto Rican communities must
be our own answer to our problems. But we must be aware
that the institutions within our communities do not now belong
to us. They don't because they mean too much in profits to
others. Only struggle and perseverance will bring our institutions home to us.

Note

1. Goodman, Paul. People or Personnel; Decentralizing and
    the Mixed System. New York: Random House,
    c. 1965. p. 53.

CHAPTER 3

WHY PUERTO RICAN STUDENTS
DROP OUT OF SCHOOL:
AN EXPLORATORY ANALYSIS

Alexander Vazquez

Bertrand Russell once wrote, "Education as a rule is
the strongest force on the side of what exists and against fundamental change. "[1] Fromm, in the same vein, says, "Its
(education's) aim is primarily to give the individual the knowledge he needs in order to function in an industrialized civilization, and to form his character into the mold which is needed: ambitious and competitive, yet cooperative within certain
limits; respectful of authority, yet desirably independent as
some report cards have it; friendly, yet not deeply attached
to anybody or anything. "[2] It seems that our complex educational system in the United States acts much like a statisti-
cian who applies a Chi-square test to determine "goodness of
fit" of a previously determined sample of some population.
The significant difference lies in the use of seemingly less
empirical methodology on the part of the educational system
in measuring the "goodness of fit" of a student. Expected by
the pedagogical policy makers is a unilateral compliance on
the part of students to this method of measurement. When
this does not occur, it is the student who "flunks," not the
system or policy. There are reasons why this does not happen among most Puerto Ricans in the Philadelphia school system.

Philadelphia was the home of 71,200 Spanish-speaking
people as of September 1, 1969. Of these, the reliable esti-
mate of Puerto Ricans is 65,000.[3] The median age of the
Puerto Rican population in New York is between 20.5 and 21
years.[4] There is no reason to assume that it is any higher
than this in Philadelphia if it can be hypothesized that the pattern of emigration from Puerto Rico to New York in the late
1940's and early 1950's was repeated in Philadelphia in the
decade from 1960 to 1970. We therefore have a community,
one-half of whose members are under twenty-one. Although

21

no accurate breakdown of Puerto Rican children of school age
(i. e. , above 6 to 7 years of age) exists, it is safe to say
that the number of Puerto Rican children of school age is
much higher than 7,021, the figure given by the Board of Education for Spanish-speaking students in the public school system.   The parochial school enrollment for Puerto Ricans is
negligible.   Such data is not compiled by the Diocesan Board
of Education.   The Puerto Rican population of Philadelphia
constitutes roughly three percent of the total population, but
only two percent of total elementary and high school enrollment is Puerto Rican.   At best, therefore, only 67 percent
of the universe of eligible Puerto Rican students is even enrolled in the public school system.   This, coupled with a dropout rate of 65 percent among Puerto Rican students, [5] presents a dismal picture for the educational future of Philadelphia's most alienated community, the Puerto Rican students.

I. ALIENATION

Alienation is a major contributor to the dropout situation among Puerto Rican students in Philadelphia. Durkheim
defined this sociological phenomenon as "...the lack of harmony between desires and the means of achieving those desires.   If the desires of the individual are insatiable or the
means for achieving goals are not available, alienation is a
result. "[6] Merton defines alienation in stronger terms, actually using the word "conflict. " He says it is "...(1) the
conflict of the individual with societal goals, or (2) that the
goals are acceptable to him but that conventional means are
not accessible. "[7]

Manifestation of alienation takes four forms. Powerlessness is "the expectancy or probability held by the individual that his own behavior cannot determine the occurrence
outcomes or reinforcements he seeks. A significant dimension of the problem is that power has to be taken. It cannot
be given. Moe Chusid said it best when he was discussing
the Puerto Ricans in Chelsea, on Manhattan's west side. He
said they were the majority group. He gave them every opportunity possible to take leadership, but in the final analysis
they had to take power. He couldn't give it to them. "[8]
Meaninglessness is defined as "...the individual's ability to
understand the events in which he is engaged...an individual
is alienated in the sense of meaninglessness when he cannot
answer the question: 'What should I believe?'" Normlessness, well known as Durkheim's anomie concept, "...indi-

cates conflict between conceived and operant values, since there are two types of normlessness: first, when there is confusion over what the norms are; and, second, when the society actively enforces operant norms which are in opposition to the conceived norms of the society. " Finally, isolation, or self-estrangement, "...is used in the sense of the individual withdrawing from the power of society...the individual who wishes to become an isolate simply withdraws. "[9]

A) Powerlessness

Involvement of Puerto Ricans in line (decision-policy making) functions rather than in staff (advisory) functions is a myth for the Puerto Ricans of Philadelphia. This is true not just in education, but in politics and economics as well. Education, however, offers the most glaring examples of this lack of power.

In 1971, there were no Puerto Rican principals or vice-principals in the entire system. There can therefore be no candidates for District Superintendentships. At the Board of Education there are approximately four or five Puerto Rican professional employees, none of whom works at a policy-making level. According to "Criteria for Review of Proposals" for funds under Title VII of the Elementary and Secondary Education Act, a proposal must show how it "Provides for involvement of other cultural and educational resources in program planning and operation, including parents of children who will receive bilingual instruction. "[10] The "Preliminary Proposal for a Multi-Faceted Program of Education Services for the Spanish Speaking Community in Philadelphia" cites nine civic organizations as having "...been involved in the planning of the bilingual school. "[11]

In attempting to ascertain the actual amount of Puerto Rican participation in the cited organizations, a different impression emerges. The existence of the Fairhill Community Council, the Fairhill Civic League, and the Potter Civic League was news to the Assistant Director of the Regional Office of the Commonwealth of Puerto Rico, to two Social Workers at Nationalities Services Center in Philadelphia, and to the Bilingual Specialist of the Office of Intergroup Relations at the Board of Education. The Potter-Thomas Home and School Association and the Potter Civic League appear to be one and the same. No one I asked knows what the constituency of the Puerto Rican Bilingual Employees Association

is. Finally, there seems to be no such organization as the
Spanish Speaking Student Community Action Committee at
Temple University.

It was further discovered that this conglomeration of
organizations was brought about by the Director of the Office
of Foreign Languages for the purpose of planning the Bilingual
School. The constituency of these groups may be known by
the person who actually wrote the proposal, the Director of
the Office of Foreign Languages, but there is no open communication between this author and the Director of the Office
of Foreign Languages due to the basic philosophical disagree-
ment between us on how best to educate the Puerto Rican
student, and the information seems not to be available on a
first-hand basis.

At this writing, the group no longer seems to exist.
According to Ralph Franco, the aforementioned Bilingual Specialist, only seventeen Puerto Ricans served as part of this
group out of a total of forty-seven members. In the final
analysis, the Puerto Ricans of Philadelphia do not feel that
they can change policies affecting them. Hence, "it is probably impossible for a youth who is a member of a group
which is powerless to grow to maturity without some trauma
to the perception of himself because of the compromised position of his group in the community."

It behooves educational facilities, such as those of
Philadelphia, to make policy changes which will help the Puerto
Ricans take power, not only in programs of bilingual educa-
tion but in all educational programs where they are affected.

B) Meaninglessness

"What should I believe?" This, in effect, is what
Puerto Rican students ask themselves when confronted with
the unrealistic attitudes of education towards them.

It is most difficult to supply data on the meaninglessness of education to Puerto Rican students. An abstract concept such as this is often expressed in terms of lack of power or role models. It can be stated, however, that education
is not seen as a means to a richer and fuller life. Whether
Puerto Ricans present an eighth grade education or a high
school diploma, many believe they will still wind up in factories. This idea is enforced by some counselors who en-

courage Puerto Rican students to sidetrack themselves into
non-college preparatory, vocational training in high school.
This policy enforces the concept in the mind of the student
that, indeed, academic education is unrealistic, not only in
his own eyes but in the counselor's as well.

I am reminded of two examples of girls who wanted to
apply to a college but were discouraged quite insistently by
counselors. One girl was told to enlist in the WACS. Another was encouraged to take a secretarial course so that she
could go to work right after finishing high school. Both girls
are now doing quite well at Temple and expect to graduate
soon. In effect, the counselor is answering the question,
"What should I believe?" by saying, "Believe that you are not
intelligent enough for college and try making a living."

The almost complete absence of role models in the
Puerto Rican community or in the schools further enforces
the idea of meaninglessness. The student sees no one like
himself in upper echelon levels of educational responsibility.
This must mean that, to people like him, education doesn't
mean very much. If one visits most schools in District Five,
other than Potter-Thomas, the "pilot" school, one sees an
almost total lack of Puerto Rican heritage displayed in the
halls or throughout the building. (District Five has the largest concentration of Puerto Ricans in the City of Philadelphia,
hence, the highest concentration of students.) Although there
are exceptions, they are just that--exceptions. The rule
seems to be to emphasize white culture. Puerto Rican culture is generally emphasized only in those schools where special bilingual programs have been funded. In visiting schools
throughout Districts Five, Two and Three, this investigator
repeatedly found this to be the case.

All these manifestations of negative enforcement make
it difficult for the student to connect present scholarship performance with future economic or personal gain. Few pre-
cedents in the form of role models, cultural reinforcements,
or teacher-counselor encouragements are being set as a matter of policy. Why not, therefore, follow the footsteps of
big brother or sister into the menial labor market? Here,
at least, a direct connection between work and pay, however
meager, can be made.

C) Normlessness

Meaninglessness and normlessness are related aspects
of alienation, "...except that in normlessness the individual's
concrete relationship to these norms has broken down. "[12]
Biculturalism is the form of normlessness most prevalent
among Puerto Rican students. On one side the student is expected to conform to a majority cultural pattern, but on the
other he is forced to remain segregated and any attempt on
his part to participate in the majority community is often re-
buffed as an "invasion. "[13] The melting pot theory teaches
that American society can become unity. The Puerto Rican
child's differences from other children teach him he is not a
part of this oneness. His mother tells him he is a citizen.
However, he does not speak English in school like other citizens. His culture is different and encouraged by his mother,
who has only the Puerto Rican culture to transmit to her
child. The schools, however, transmit an American culture
and insist it to be the right one, and implicitly, if not explicitly, devalue his uniqueness.

This disparagement of being different, or treating
Puerto Ricans as "foreign," is seen to be more pronounced
when we examine who runs the programs now in operation for
Puerto Ricans. Every program administered by the Board
of Education for Puerto Ricans is run by the Office of Foreign Languages. Extending this further, we can see that peoples who speak Spanish as a first language are considered foreigners by the Board of Education. (Remember that Spanish
was spoken in the Americas before any other Romance language
and before English, a Germanic tongue. Further, there are
perhaps as many as fifteen million American citizens who
consider Spanish their native, first language. Spanish is not
a foreign language, nor are the citizens who speak it as a
first language foreigners.) This is probably not a universal
truth, but whether it is or not remains irrelevant when we
see that most Puerto Ricans believe it is true.

Normlessness, or anomie, establishes a relationship
between opportunities and aspirations. In a bicultural atmosphere a child may conceivably have two sets of opportunities
and aspirations to strive for. These are mutually exclusive
by nature. What the Puerto Rican child has enforced in the
home is not similar to what is enforced in school, and vice
versa.

It is, again, difficult to divorce the rhetoric from the

concrete examples. It has repeatedly been established, however, that the lower the social class, the lower the aspiration
level, and usually the lower the education level. [14] It has
been established that the Puerto Ricans are of the lowest
class in Philadelphia, exhibiting lower family incomes than
any racial, ethnic or national group. We can safely say,
therefore, that the Puerto Ricans experience the highest degree of normlessness of any racial, ethnic, or national group
in Philadelphia. As long as programs for Puerto Ricans are
run by those whose norms are non-Puerto Rican oriented,
anomie in the Puerto Rican student will continue.

As one concrete example of normlessness, I can recall
the student at a high school in District Two who was given a
test translated into Spanish. The only trouble was that she
had been taught the material on which the test was based in
English. Consequently, she failed the test. Although she
might have possessed the aspirations to pass the examination,
the opportunity, through conscious school policy, was not
given her.

D) Isolation and Self-Estrangement

Isolation and self-estrangement are physically manifested in the school system. In 1971, I conducted a series
of lectures on "The Educational Difficulties of the Puerto Ricans of Philadelphia." These lectures were conducted at William Penn High School, not one of the schools where any
demonstration projects in bilingual education were then being
carried out. The practice in this school seemed to be to
place the Puerto Rican students together so that the more
proficient in English could translate for the less proficient.
This results in two deficiencies. For one thing, sixteen and
seventeen year old high school students are acting in the de
facto capacity of teachers. It is these students who are di-
gesting and translating subject matter for those whose only
deficiency as far as understanding material goes is that they
only speak one language. Can it, therefore, be construed
that the policy of the school system toward Spanish-speaking
Puerto Rican students is to supply them with lower quality
education than is considered normal? Secondly, actual, physical isolation from other students, the placing of Puerto Ricans together with an all or mostly black setting, acts as a
separation from the power of the classroom society.

The following statement easily applies to the Puerto

Rican student in school if we think of his relationship to the
teachers and other students:

> Social life is thus somewhat atomized. On the one
> side stands the individual--highly self-conscious and
> unique, calculating his future with little reference
> to community norms and understandings, oriented
> outward toward a confusing world, a world inter-
> preted for him by...[someone]...he can neither
> control nor check up on. On the other side stand
> the great mass organizations...centrally controlled
> by officials and an active minority, as distinct from
> the rank-and-file as the media of mass communica-
> tion. [15]

II.   ADAPTATION TO ALIENATION

Five means of adapting to alienation are available.
Conformity "assumes that most of the members of the society
feel that their needs for satisfaction are being met." Innovation emphasizes goals "to the detriment of an emphasis on
means." In ritualism, "the individual has...lowered his aspirations with regard to the pecuniary goals of the society...."
Retreatism "is the mode of adaptation whereby the individual
completely withdraws his support from the norms of society...." Finally, rebellion, not really a form of adaptation,
"...is rather an attempt by the 'out-group' to establish their
structures as the conventional ones by supplanting those of
the 'in-group'."[16]

In Philadelphia, the most applicable means of adaptation, as far as the Puerto Rican dropout is concerned, are
innovation, ritualism, and retreatism. It is obvious that the
dropout does not feel he is getting satisfaction from society.
Up to this writing, no really vehement, rebellious group,
such as Chicago's and New York's Young Lords, exists among
the Puerto Ricans of Philadelphia.

The form of innovation most popular among Puerto
Rican dropouts is crime. This is illustrated by a Puerto
Rican youth gang operating in the area served by the Hart-
ranft Community Corporation. The Stars are, for the most
part, high school dropouts, most of whom now do nothing.

Ritualism is manifest in patterns the dropouts move
into.   Both boys and girls initially find some kind of menial

work in factories or supermarkets.   Girls will usually marry
and/or have children, or fall into an accepted pattern of serial monogamy.   Boys employing this form of adaptation will
keep a menial job or go from one to another.   They will
never make much money, but this was not expected in the
first place.   However, they will cull some self respect from
the fact that they have a job--any job.   Although the Puerto
Ricans have the highest unemployment rate in the city for any
group, most of the employed are probably ritualistically so.
It is safe to say that the non-Puerto Rican majority prefers
to have Puerto Ricans manifest ritualism as a means of adaptation more than any other.

        Retreatism is the form of adaptation which is em-
ployed by the dropout just before he drops out.   He simply
comes to school once in a while; he is physically present but
no longer taking part in the class, if he ever did.   He drops
out psychologically before he withdraws physically from the
scene.   Outside of school, most Puerto Ricans do not adopt
this form of adaptation, because the kind of strength it takes
to be both a part of a society and an outsider is drained
from the individual in making the other two more appropriate
adaptations.   However, there seems to be some spotty evidence to indicate that some young Puerto Ricans are becoming drug-addicted as a means of retreating from society.

III.   POLICY ISSUES

        My purpose has been to discuss the relationship among
the educational system's policy toward Puerto Ricans, the re-
sultant alienation among Puerto Ricans, and their consequent
high dropout rate.   The following are some issues of policy
which might be considered in an attempt to combat this alienation.

A) Research

        Among the most glaring deficiencies is the lack of
hard data on the Puerto Ricans of Philadelphia.   The Philadelphia Board of Education must make it its policy to com-
pile statistical, empirical data of all kinds, but specifically
data related to the reasons why Puerto Ricans drop out of the
public schools.   It is difficult, if not impossible, to plan for
a population one knows nothing of.

B) Create an Office of Bilingual Affairs

The Office of Foreign Languages was originally designed to devise and administer foreign language courses to
students in the public schools. It has since become the clear-
ing-house for Puerto Rican education affairs of every kind for
the school system. Since this function is apparently necessary, let there be a separate office established for it. This
office would be headed and staffed primarily by members of
the population it is meant to serve. Creation of this office
would also free the Office of Foreign Languages to perform
the duties for which it was originally designed.

C) Creation of an "Orientation School"

The common public school is ill-equipped to teach the
newly arrived Puerto Rican child the "client task" of the public school student. A school such as I propose would perform this function, as well as process the students according
to age and grade level, before the alienation process begins
to take hold. Although the argument can be made that this
school would promote segregation, it could be argued that the
period of time it would take to so process a child need not
be lengthy. Also, the purpose of the school would be to better integrate such children into the school system at their required paces.

D) Recruit and Train Puerto Rican College Graduates for Line Positions Within the School System

At present, there are no Puerto Ricans in line positions within the organization of the Board of Education, although the Institute for Advanced Administrative Development
expects to have several Puerto Rican line administrators
trained and certified by the middle of 1973. Placing Puerto
Ricans in line positions would have the desired effect of creating role models for Puerto Ricans and making subordinate
teachers more sensitive to the needs of their Puerto Rican
students. The entry of Puerto Ricans into executive positions
of public service, particularly education, will eventually be
followed by their entry into other fields and the mainstream
of life in Philadelphia.

E) Revision of Counseling Techniques

It should not be a function of counselors to discourage a student's aspirations, regardless of how inappropriate these seem to the counselor. My experience has been that the correlation between school performance and attainable aspirations must include other variables not empirically measurable by the counselor.

F) Appointment of a Puerto Rican to the Board of Education

In order to bring the aforementioned policy changes to the highest level of the school hierarchy, a member of the Puerto Rican community must be represented on the Board of Education. This would have the effect of placing the Puerto Ricans in a priority position in education, a position rightfully theirs but sorely neglected.

It is fully recognized that this is a policy change in which the Board itself does not have complete authority. The Board can, however, lobby at the level necessary to make this change if it is impressed with the need to do so. It is the job of the school superintendent and his deputies, associates and assistants to make this case.

CONCLUSION

I have attempted to show that alienation, as I have defined it, underlies many policy issues in education affecting Puerto Ricans. Alienation is a major cause for the dropout situation among Puerto Ricans. Their means of adaptation are conducive to a cyclical state of events in which alienation will continue to rear its four separate, ugly heads unless policy is devised to stop it. I have attempted briefly to indicate several definite courses of action, in the light of current conditions, which might guide and determine present and future decisions. Unless policy changes are discussed and adopted, conditions for the Puerto Ricans in education will progressively deteriorate.

Notes

1. Egner, R., and Denonn, L. The Basic Writings of Bertrand Russell. New York: Simon and Schuster, 1961.

2. Fromm, Erich. The Sane Society. New York: Holt,
    Rinehart and Winston, 1965. p. 299.

3. Charles Unanue Associates. The Spanish Speaking Mar-
    ket in the United States. New York, January 2, 1970.
    (Unpublished market study). Exhibit III. Information
    on estimates was culled from telephone conversations
    with Mr. Unanue, personal contacts with Mr. Luis
    Diaz-Carlo of the Puerto Rican Forum in New York
    City, and personal contact with the Philadelphia Puer-
    to Rican community.
        It must be stated here that one of the unavoidable
    deficiencies of any paper on Philadelphia's Puerto Ri-
    can community today is the lack of empirical data on
    the Puerto Rican population.

4. New York State Commission on Human Rights. The Puer-
    to Ricans of New York State. August, 1970.

5. Direct communication with Dr. Bernard C. Watson, Dep-
    uty Superintendent of Policy and Planning, in an inter-
    view for the Community Relations Service, United
    States Department of Justice, August, 1969.

6. Besag, Frank P. Alienation and Education. Buffalo,
    1966. p. 12.

7. Ibid., p. 14.

8. Dodson, Dan, "Education and the Powerless," in: Harry
    Passow, Miriam Goldberg, Abraham J. Tannenbaum,
    eds. Education of the Disadvantaged. New York: Holt,
    Rinehart and Winston, 1967. p. 64-65.

9. Besag, p. 30-32.

10. Manual for Project Applicants and Grantees, Feb. 24,
    1969. Bilingual Education Program. Title VII, Ele-
    mentary and Secondary Education Act of 1965, as
    amended. p. 8.

11. School District of Philadelphia, "Preliminary Proposal
    for a Multi-Faceted Program of Educational Services
    for the Spanish Speaking Community in Philadelphia."
    Dec. 18, 1968. p. 11-12.

12. Besag, p. 31.

13. Bullock, Paul, and Singleton, Robert, "The Minority
    Child and the Schools," in: John Curtis Gowan and
    George D. Demos. The Disadvantaged and Potential
    Dropout. Illinois: C. C. Thomas, 1966. p. 120.

14. Wilson, Alan B. , "Residential Segregation of Social
    Classes and Aspirations of High School Boys," in Pas-
    sow et al. , p. 260ff.

15. Wilensky, Harold L. and Lebeaux, Charles N. Industrial
    Society and Social Welfare. New York: Free Pr. ,
    1965. p. 120.

16. Besag, p. 18-24.

CHAPTER 4

A CASE FOR
PUERTO RICAN STUDIES PROGRAMS

Richard Rivera

The trend in many universities in the United States today is toward so-called ethnic studies. Probably reacting
more to group pressures than to academic and social commit-
ments, university administrators, with few exceptions, do not
seem to be totally committed to the success of these programs, many of which are characterized by differences in
philosophy, priorities, courses offered, staff recruited, and
funding. Apparently, success in this field is due more to
student and staff commitment than to university cooperation.
The public at large also seems to view these programs as
further concessions to radical minority groups. Rather than
analyze a program's academic validity and potential, many
people prefer viewing it as just so much "academic welfare."

This essay discusses some reasons why Puerto Rican
Studies Programs in New York City are not only needed but
are academically valid. We must look for these reasons in
the political, economic and socio-cultural situation of the
Puerto Rican community, born in New York and in Puerto
Rico. Any further development of these programs must necessarily depend upon this tripartite situation.

Perhaps what Preston Wilcox, a former Columbia University professor of education, has said about Black Studies
may also be applied to Puerto Rican Studies: "Black Studies
is that body of experience and knowledge that Blacks have had
to summon in order to learn how to survive within a society
that is stacked against them."[1] This does not imply a sterile
listing of Black or Puerto Rican achievements. On the contrary, as Eduardo Seda-Bonilla, a former Chairman of the
Puerto Rican Studies Department at Hunter College, characterizes it, this is a dynamic and creative process wherein
Puerto Ricans and other socially marginal groups, like the
Black community, American Indians, and Chicanos, participate

34

in "discovering, revitalizing and respecting their own cultural
values as a reference point from which to create their own
cultural identity, which is different from that of the Anglo-
Saxon. "[2] This is a process of self-discovery and analysis,
and also of trying to understand the U.S. society in which we
live.

Puerto Rican Studies have as their purpose the reas-
sertion of the Puerto Rican identity within the culturally standardized U.S. society which is eroding the Puerto Rican's self-
image and esteem. This is the spirit in which students and
educators clamored for ethnic studies, and it is the criterion
upon which to measure their success or failure. Their ob-
jective, according to Seda-Bonilla, is to "revindicate those
groups in the population which have been rejected by the Melting Pot, and to mold a cultural identity and framework which
respects and encourages cultural differences as being socially
healthy instead of degrading and stigmatizing them. "[3]

Clearly, the economic, social and educational forces
operating within the U.S. have been and still appear to be
"stacked against" the Puerto Rican today, and are continuing
to erode the self-image and esteem of many Puerto Ricans.
Andres Torres offers some valuable information in a study he
conducted for Aspira entitled "Puerto Rican Employment in
New York City. "[4]

Mr. Torres found that in New York City, where approximately 1.1 million of the total 1.6 million Puerto Ricans
in the U.S. live, "the median income for Puerto Rican families (which tend to be generally larger than American families)
is about $5,000 a year, " but if we consider Puerto Rican
families which live in poverty neighborhoods, we find that
"half of all Puerto Rican families in New York City are sub-
sisting on incomes of less than $5,000 annually. " This is in
a city "where a moderate family budget (in 1970) has been
determined to be $11,000-$12,000 a year for a family of
four.... " Additionally, Mr. Torres states that "the great
majority of Puerto Ricans who were unattached to families
had less than $5,000 in income; two-thirds had less than
$4,000. "[5]

Similarly, while New York City's consumer price index, the best indicator of the cost of living for families, increased at a rate of 3.2 percent annually from 1960-1969,
the median Puerto Rican family income rose at a rate of only
2.5 percent annually.

According to the Bureau of Labor Statistics, the weekly gross, pre-tax income for 50 percent of all Puerto Rican workers (who work at least 35 hours a week) in the U. S. is less than $100.

As of March, 1971, the unemployment rate among Puerto Rican workers in the U. S. was 10 percent. But this rate is probably much higher if we consider those who have become frustrated looking for a job and have given up looking, those who cannot work because of health reasons, and those who are underemployed (work less than 35 hours a week). According to the U. S. Department of Labor: "Any thinking about unemployment in terms of 3.2 percent or 4 percent just leaves the slums out. The situation there is that few have a decent job, up to a third are unable to earn a living, and between 10 and 20 percent of those who ought to be working are not working at all. "[6]

The employment patterns within the general Puerto Rican community do not promise a better future. In a study published in May, 1971, the U. S. Department of Labor found that approximately 64 percent of the Puerto Rican male labor force in New York City and 66 percent of the female labor force were involved in semiskilled blue collar and service work. These are precisely the employment categories that the New York City job market will least demand in the near future. The New York City Board of Education reported in 1971 that, "although Puerto Rican students comprise less than 19 percent of high school student enrollment, they account for 33.6 percent of enrollment in vocational schools. Puerto Ricans comprise, on the other hand, only 15.8 percent of the academic high school population. "[7] Schools, then, are channeling Puerto Rican students into economically and socially less rewarding areas.

Although a great many Puerto Ricans put their faith in education as a way of getting out of this situation, there is ample evidence that schools are not offering Puerto Ricans an alternative to poverty and unemployment. In a study entitled ".... and Others, " G. Ramsay Liem has documented the underachievement of Puerto Rican children within New York City public schools. [8]

Mr. Liem discovered that the reading comprehension scores for New York City public schools get progressively worse as students advance through the system. While they are in the second grade, New York City school children com-

pare favorably with the national reading norm; however, by
the fifth and eighth grades, they fall below the national norm.
Significantly, schools in Manhattan, the Bronx and Brooklyn
(where most Black and Puerto Rican children live) score lower than schools in Queens and Richmond. Four school districts in Brooklyn, which have the borough's highest percent
of white, middle-class students, enable that borough to achieve
higher reading scores than schools in Manhattan and the
Bronx. Nevertheless, even schools in Queens and Richmond,
although they don't fall below national norms, show a slippage
in reading scores as children advance in grades.

Searching further, Mr. Liem found that schools with
the heaviest concentration of Black and Puerto Rican students
in New York City fell below city and national norms in reading achievement, while schools with the heaviest concentrations of white children fared much better. For example, 70
percent of second grade Puerto Rican children in these
schools fell below their grade norm; in the fifth grade, 82
percent of these children fell below grade norm; and 81 percent of the eighth graders read below grade level. The children in predominantly white schools in New York City fared
relatively better: 22 percent of the second graders, 34 percent of the fifth graders, and 35 percent of the eighth graders
fell below their grade levels in reading.

As Mr. Liem concludes, in New York City "...... all
children are not benefiting equally from the educational system. Puerto Ricans and Blacks are being shortchanged by
the schools and, as a result, are not achieving up to par."

Characteristically, the greatest percentage of least experienced teachers (29-41 percent had from one to three years
of experience) work in poverty areas where books, supplies,
and advanced teaching materials are hardest to find. So the
children who are achieving at the lowest levels are being
"taught" by relatively inexperienced personnel.

According to the Board of Education, overcrowding is
characteristic of all New York City schools and all children
suffer its effects; however, in Manhattan, where schools are
generally the least overcrowded, those districts with the highest percentage of Black and Puerto Rican students have the
highest rate of overcrowding (schools used beyond capacity).

On a city-wide basis, non-English (NE) speaking students seem to have an especially difficult time. Approximate-

ly 160,185 pupils (one out of every seven children) do not
speak English in New York City's public school system. Fifty-
eight percent of these children are Puerto Rican, according to
the New York State Board of Regents, and approximately another 15 percent are also Hispanic.

Nevertheless, as of March, 1969, there could be found
no instance where the percentage of Puerto Rican employees
was equivalent to the percentage of Puerto Rican students in
the school population. This means that in no employment
category (principals, assistant principals, teachers in charge,
department chairmen, school lunch employees, etc.) were people of Puerto Rican background (or other Hispanic people) employed in proportion to their numbers in New York City
schools. As a matter of fact, compared to Philadelphia, Los
Angeles, Chicago and Detroit, New York is the city where
Puerto Rican teachers are most under-represented. While
close to 22 percent of the students in New York City's public
school system were Puerto Rican (1969-1970), only 0.6 percent of its teachers were of Puerto Rican background.

The Board of Education does not offer "scientific data"
on the student dropout rate in New York City. Only qualified estimates are available; these are obtained by computing
the "attrition rate" of a given graduating class; that is, by
comparing the difference between the size of a graduating
class with its enrollment four years earlier.

Using this as our guide, we find that New York City
public high schools lost 36 percent of their students between
1963 and 1967. According to Liem, the attrition rate between 1966 and 1970 was 38 percent for the city at large.
Significantly, there seems to exist a direct relationship between an increase in dropout rates and an increase in Black
and Puerto Rican students: the greater the Black and Puerto
Rican population a school has, the greater is its dropout rate.
Mr. Liem suggests that the majority of these students who
leave school are Black or Puerto Rican and that apparently
"schools are selectively more responsive to White students. "

Attempts to attribute dropout rates to transfers into
parochial schools or migration are not convincing. On the
contrary, a study conducted by HARYOU finds that "failure to
achieve [is] the major reason given by New York City dropouts for leaving school. "[9]

Nor does it seem valid to blame the students totally

for their underachievement. Holt, Silberman, Dennison and
a host of other educators and researchers have eloquently
demonstrated how schools fail in their task of educating our
children. Additionally, researchers at the University of Michigan who "followed the progress of a group of high school
students... concluded that those who dropped out were all capable and motivated when they began their educational careers.
Their failure was seen as a result of middle-class, American
high schools whose academic programs are stacked against
minority group students. "[10] In this connection, we may repeat what Luis Nieves Falcon, a professor of Puerto Rican
Studies at Brooklyn College, has said about the school system
in Puerto Rico: "The school system forces him [the student]
out and contributes to develop in him a feeling of inadequacy
and negative self-image, to make him more likely to manifest
intense personal problems, to accept escapist solutions to this
condition of personal disadvantage; and to blunt his capacity
to figure out the systematic causes that put him into that condition which effectively limits his own potential to overcome
his social situation. "[11]

     The Puerto Rican student who drops out of school has
nothing to "drop into" except low wages, unemployment, un-
deremployment or sub-employment. Some are driven to
drugs, petty thievery, or more serious crimes. Many decide
to return to Puerto Rico, but there they find widespread unemployment (12.8-33 percent, depending on how you compute
your figures; but either way it means no jobs without an education, and even then, the economic structure is prohibitive);
poverty (25 percent of Puerto Rican families earn less than
$500 yearly), and more often than not, social rejection. Hav-
ing grown up in New York (or lived here for 10-20 years), a
"Niuyorrican" may not speak Spanish very well, or else will
speak it differently; his social habits won't fit, or he may dislike Americans, in which case he will either be stereotyped
as a radical or simply and contemptibly as a "Niuyorrican";
in short, a misfit. As Manuel Maldonado-Denis points out in
his valuable study, Puerto Rico: A Socio-Historic Interpretation, Puerto Ricans born and raised in the United States have
been viewed by island groups as not being "Puerto Rican
enough. "[12] Certainly, this will disappear as we all recognize
the historical and social forces that created this situation.
Discriminated against and "out of it" in New York, and different in Puerto Rico, the New York-born Puerto Rican may find
himself culturally and psychologically nowhere.

     This is an especially crucial point within the Puerto

Rican community, and one that has attracted the attention of
many of our working-class and professional people. We must
go beyond the cold statistics on employment, income, dropouts, drug addiction and crime, and find their underlying
causes and effects. Why can't a New York-born Puerto Rican fit into the Island's life? Why, in many cases, isn't he
accepted by his own people? Are we disintegrating socially?
Why has Puerto Rico shown the highest suicide rate among
the Catholic countries of the Western Hemisphere and the
fifth largest rate among all countries of the Western Hemisphere? Why such high rates of drug addiction? Why the apparent popularity of revivalist-type religions within our community? Why is there a relatively sudden rise in mental illnesses within our community?

Eduardo Seda-Bonilla, Eugenio Fernandez Mendez,
Germán de Granda, Manuel Maldonado-Denis, and Luis Nieves
Falcon, among other Puerto Rican anthropologists, linguists,
political scientists and sociologists, have dealt exhaustively
with these questions and in a manner reflecting the urgency
they hold for us.

These writers agree that the essence of a culture is
not quantitative (e.g. the number of heroes or intellectuals,
the number of attractive buildings, the typical architecture,
sculpture, paintings and music) but qualitative. A people's
artistic production, for example, is a reflection of certain
shared values and knowledge, and of a unique way of inter-
preting the world and the events around them. It is the expression of their essence as a distinct group in society. We
must see culture as the underlying values and understandings
which a generation learns, internalizes and transmits to future generations.

The Puerto Rican's cultural reference point is under
attack in the United States where he is stereotyped racially
(a term which lacks scientific validity). He is therefore expected to act in a certain way, has limited access to the
benefits a society may have to offer, and is effectively cana-
lized into those social roles which the existing power groups
choose for him. Correspondingly, his value as an individual
and the value of his culture are either denied or belittled.

In a 1960 study entitled "Anomie and the Quest for
Community: The Formation of Sects among Puerto Ricans of
New York," Renato Poblete, S. J. and Thomas F. O'Dea
studied this process of "cultural erosion" within the Puerto

Rican community in New York City and, among other things,
tried to define the process and its results: 1) the "breakdown
of those social structures [family, church, schools, government, the community Plaza tradition, etc.] in which the individual found personal and psychological security" and 2) the
"loss of consensus or general agreement among the standards
and norms that previously provided the normative orientations
and existential definitions in terms of which individual and
group life was meaningful."[13] The result of this situation is
a feeling of anomie or disorientation in which a person has
nothing to "hold on to," has nowhere to go, no one to turn to.

Viewed in this manner, crime, drug addiction, suicide,
mental illness, escapism, family disorganization, etc., within
the Puerto Rican community seem more comprehensible. Social, cultural and economic disorganization and discrimination
have effectively kept the Puerto Rican as a marginal personality within U.S. society, and many of us have blamed ourselves
for failing to make it in what is billed as the land of opportunity and the land of the free. Consequently, our self-image
and esteem have suffered, with the resulting tragedy that we
fail to see a way out of the situation.

It is irrelevant to say that U.S. society is an especially cruel, brutal and exploitative one. It is potentially neither
more nor less cruel than past colonial societies; rather, it is
today's standard bearer of the historical tradition of colonialism and imperialism. The tragic fact is that the military,
economic, social, political, and psychological tools of destruction, domination, and subjugation at its disposal are more refined and efficient today than ever before. And, as Gordon
K. Lewis has pointed out in his excellent book on Puerto
Rico: "Modern America has not discovered, any more than
did classical Rome, the art of reconciling subordinate nations
to its rule; nor has it found a way to reconcile the subordination with the democratic content of the American creed."[14]
The inherent contradictions between democracy and colonialism, as well as between social equality and racism, lead to
the kinds of situations that Puerto Ricans, Blacks, Chicanos,
American Indians and other minority groups find themselves
in today.

Recognizing the failure of our overcrowded, traditional
and misunderstanding schools and the economic system to include Puerto Ricans justly in the distribution of society's
benefits, Puerto Rican students began their fight for Puerto
Rican Studies in the late 1960's. This effort reflects the new

consciousness within our community in its attempt to reassert
and reconstruct our group identity and purpose in the U.S.
A similar effort is gaining momentum in Puerto Rico as the
renewed influence and attraction of the Independence forces on
the island suggests.   Mutual understanding, unity and a concerted effort at eliminating the obstacles that face us are our
goals.

All this obviously implies the emergence of a new educational philosophy and role for universities in contemporary
society.   The House of Studies (Casa de Estudios) concept
which would isolate schools, students and instructors from
the realities of poverty, discrimination, exploitation, colonialism, etc., is irrelevant in today's world.   Schools do not
exist in a vacuum; they are not oases.   Students and professors alike are Society.   In this context, it is more relevant
and intellectually productive to define, articulate and attempt
solutions to social realities in a classroom rather than on a
battlefield.   Instructors' and students' ideas and beliefs should
find their way into the educational process openly through dialogue and debate, not through a facade of objectivity.

Evaluating Puerto Rican Studies Programs in New York
with these criteria in mind, we see that they are not only
academically valid but also pedagogically advanced.   They
have correctly interpreted (and are therefore in a better position to deal with) the increased intellectual and social demands which contemporary society makes of us.   Since they
are not tied down by tradition they are also in a more flexible position in terms of future expansion and courses offered.

Given the nature of Puerto Rican Studies Programs,
their rationale, and the forces that resulted in their creation,
we can see the possibility of a creative trend in curriculum
expansion.   As Antioch (Ohio, Washington), Northeastern and
Rutgers Law Schools have done (Antioch's education college
has also done this), Puerto Rican Studies Programs can develop out-of-classroom components.   Whether it be through
arrangements with professional and/or community groups,
with other university departments, or through independent programs, Puerto Rican Studies Departments can offer students
first-hand experience with the problems faced by our community in New York City.   Most students in these departments have experienced and continue to experience the potentially destructive nature of U.S. life for Puerto Ricans.   This
experience should be applied and not wasted.   Community political action (court action, tenant-landlord relations, law co-

operatives, consumer education, help with welfare process, political pressure and action based on community needs, political education); economic action (cooperative movement, job bank, Puerto Rican-owned and controlled businesses); educational action (neighborhood mini-schools, day care centers, tutoring); medical action (medical co-ops, medical examinations, x-ray services, vaccinations, child care, visits to sick and/or elderly Puerto Rican men and women)--these and many other activities would not only offer an ample range of experience for Puerto Rican students but would also practically attack many of the problems which governmental and business societies create and refuse to deal with. Controlled, organized and operated by Puerto Ricans, these programs should not become "tourist attractions," but on-going and flexible components of Puerto Rican Studies Programs. Nor should they be viewed as liberal attempts to ameliorate an exploitative society's problems in order to free it for more abuse. In addition to their academic value, these programs have as their purpose political education, social and economic revindication, group identity and, most important, personal intellectual liberation. In no way is it to be viewed or used as an assimilationist program nor as a substitute for traditional political activity. Consequently, definite criteria, course descriptions, objectives, and supervision should be formulated. A clear philosophy is essential, and both students and faculty should be involved.

Perhaps more significant than the extent, shape, or form of this suggestion is its underlying principle: all-inclusive participation of the Puerto Rican Community in shaping and determining its own future, creating its own ideology which is suited to its distinct needs and experiences, and assuring that needed action does take place.

Notes

1. Johnson, Thomas, "Educators Find Black Studies Are Changing Higher Education," The New York Times, June 4, 1972.

2. Seda-Bonilla, Eduardo, "Estudios Etnicos, Pluralismo Cultural y Poder," Ninth Latin American Sociological Congress (November, 1969). (Mimeographed).

3. Ibid.

4. Torres, Andres. Puerto Rican Employment in New York City. New York: Aspira, Inc., June, 1972.

5. Ibid.

6. Ibid.

7. Ibid.

8. Liem, G. Ramsay. .... and Others. New York: Aspira, Inc., January 9, 1971.

9. Ibid.

10. Ibid.

11. Nieves Falcon, Luis, "Social Class and Power Structure in Puerto Rican Society," Revista del Instituto de Estudios Puertorriqueños del Brooklyn College, Vol. 1 (Spring 1971).

12. Maldonado-Denis, Manuel. Puerto Rico: A Socio-Historic Interpretation. New York: Random House, 1972.

13. Poblete, Renato, S. J. and Thomas F. O'Dea, "Anomie and the Quest for Community: The Formation of Sects among Puerto Ricans of New York," The American Catholic Sociological Review, New York, 1960, p. 18-36.

14. Lewis, Gordon K. Puerto Rico: Freedom and Power in the Caribbean. New York: Harper Torchbooks, 1968.

CHAPTER 5

AFFIRMATIVE ACTION IN HIGHER EDUCATION

Frank Negrón

       The 1972 Staff Report of the United States Commission on Civil Rights reveals that the number of college graduates within the Puerto Rican Community is very small. It indicated that in 1960, nine-tenths of one percent of Puerto Ricans 25 years of age and older graduated from college. Over the next ten years, the percentage changed slightly. Estimates indicate that in 1970, only 1.5 percent of the Puerto Rican population in New York City had received a college education. When compared to figures of other groups (12.3 percent for whites and 6 percent for non-whites), the percentage of the Puerto Rican population receiving a college education is minuscule.

       The Puerto Rican Community has been categorized as the ethnic group with the lowest socio-economic status in this region. Since it is at the bottom of the socio-economic scale, the major opportunity for achieving a level of higher education is through The City University of New York (CUNY).

       Special programs, namely, College Discovery and SEEK have been instrumental in increasing the number of Puerto Rican students in the University.

       The 1972 Ethnic Census of CUNY students showed 13,563 Puerto Rican undergraduates and 3,538 "Other Spanish Surnamed Americans." For the Puerto Ricans this is an increase from 5,425 in 1969--the year prior to Open Admissions.

       The University has made an all-out effort to find and recruit qualified Puerto Ricans for faculty positions. In 1972, the rate of increase in the hiring of Puerto Ricans on the instructional level was 33.6 percent (from 247 to 330). This compares with an 18.5 percent increase for Blacks; 23.3 percent for Orientals, and 18.7 percent for other Spanish-speak-

ing personnel.   The rate of increase for employment of women was 10.9 percent, more than twice that of men.

        Puerto Ricans are well represented on the Board of
Higher Education and on the Central Staff of CUNY.   Among
them is the Chairman of the Board and two other members.
The Central Staff members are: the Director of the University Affirmative Action Program, the Executive Assistant to
the Chancellor, and the Director of College Discovery.   One
of the college presidents is also Puerto Rican.

        The university has also established a Center for Puer-
to Rican Studies and Research at the Graduate School and University Center.   This program is directed by a distinguished
Puerto Rican political scientist.   The Center's principal goals
are to provide for the development and coordination of resources for new and established Puerto Rican programs; to
organize and direct research on relevant issues for the Puerto Rican studies programs and the communities they serve;
to develop the facilities and resources for the training of students and faculty; and to establish effective means of communication and coordination between the Puerto Rican community
and CUNY.

        Despite the success that it has experienced in imple-
menting Presidential Executive Orders Nos. 11246, 11375,
The City University of New York is constantly under attack
for what has been labeled as its "plan to impose ethnic quotas"
in the hiring of faculty.   In my experience as the Director of
the City University Affirmative Action Program Office, I can
categorically state that the charge of quota imposition is, at
best, unfounded.

        Newly committed to serving all of New York City's
population, CUNY has adopted Open Admissions as its enrollment policy.   This policy has not only had a major effect in
increasing the enrollment of black, Puerto Rican and other
third world youths, but has surprisingly also had an even
greater effect on the admission of white (blue-collar) working-
class students.   At the same time, female students have been
pressing for curriculum changes which would begin to meet
their needs.   This changing student body has encountered a
faculty which is just short of lily-white and the upper strata
of which is also overwhelmingly male.

        Not surprisingly, this situation has generated demands
for changes in the composition of the faculty.   Students, fac-

ulty, and others concerned with education have claimed that
sufficient efforts have not been made to hire, retain, or advance women and members of minority groups. (Anyone familiar with college hiring practices knows of their dependence
on informal "contacts," thus perpetuating the established character of a faculty.)

The Affirmative Action Program emerged from this
matrix of forces. To redress the circumstances of a faculty
de facto restricted to white males, this program advocated
that strong efforts be taken to recruit new faculty from the
ranks of women and minority groups.

Although at no point was it advocated that unqualified
persons should be hired or that quotas be applied to the hiring of groups already well represented on the faculty, precisely those claims are still being made by the opponents of
the plan. In fact, it was asserted that CUNY was about to
permit the implementation of "reverse racism" (a mixed metaphor if ever there was one, since oppressed racial groups
hardly have the power to practice discrimination against their
oppressors). It seems to me that it is, instead, (white) racism which (1) overlooks the fact that the Affirmative Action
Program is designed for the hiring of women as well as
blacks, Puerto Ricans, and third world people; and (2) suggests that to attempt to hire minority group members is probably to lower the quality of the faculty. In fact, it may be
necessary to re-evaluate this term "quality." Is a faculty
dominated by white males a high-quality faculty even though
it teaches, by force of its own example, that to be intelligent
and respected is to be white and male?

Furthermore, to insert the false question of quotas into the situation serves to obscure the injustice perpetrated
against oppressed groups by releasing a smokescreen of emotionally charged words. The logic of this argument is that
anyone's drive for justice and equality invades the privilege of
others and is, therefore, to be resisted.

The utilization of quotas is an inappropriate means for
eliminating social wrongs. The idea of quotas says that the
proportions of the different kinds of people making up a community be the guide for determining the proportion of such
people to be employed or to be given opportunities in the institutions of that community. Some people think of quotas as
a way of compensating those who have suffered as a result of
past discrimination. While I agree that such compensation is

justified, I think that a quota system is a poor way to carry
out such compensation. While there is seemingly a short-
term advantage of such a policy for those who have suffered
from discrimination, I believe that the use of quotas is a bad
policy whose evils outweigh its desirable consequences. My
reasons are as follows:

(1) It is an impractical program which, if employed on
a large social scale, would require extensive surveys, bureaucratic enforcement, and legal entangle-
ments.

(2) It is unclear what the grounds should be for determining the kinds of people making up a community
in order to create the basis for quota proportions.
For example, should Armenians demand one percent
of all jobs and college admissions if they compose
one percent of the population? Should similar
claims be advanced by those who are over six feet
tall? Those with red hair?

(3) There is a problem about which "community" should
be used as the basis for quota proportions. Should
an agency of New York City hire 20 percent Puerto
Ricans because they make up 20 percent of New
York's population or should it hire only 2 percent
Puerto Ricans since they make up only two percent
of the national population?

(4) Many people who are discriminated against lose out
because of quotas in areas where they have achieved
success. Thus, the rationale to give male applicants
preference to female applicants for teaching jobs
would be solely on the grounds of sex, because the
overwhelming number of teachers are women.

(5) Though the use of quotas may be well intentioned,
there is such a long history of its employment to
keep minority groups from achieving social advancement that it should always be regarded with suspicion.

(6) The adoption of a quota policy would harden the tendency of people to think of themselves as members
of exclusive competitive groups, and runs counter to
the ideal of an integrated society.

Finally, the adoption of a quota system would be in violation of the right of individuals who apply for jobs, promotions, educational opportunities, etc. to be considered on their individual merits and qualifications. While many so-called merit systems have been fraudulent fronts for maintaining existing patterns of discrimination, this is no reason for abandoning the idea that one's right to certain opportunities is to be determined by individual merit.

Although satisfied with its past accomplishments, CUNY is determined to continue its equal employment opportunity policy of recruiting, employing, retaining, and promoting employees without regard to sex, age, race, national origin, color, or creed.

The Affirmative Action Program for the first time has opened up middle and high level positions to Puerto Rican applicants. While in the past all positions in the private and public sectors were filled by persons having the same racial and similar cultural background as the person doing the hiring, now almost all employers are obligated to advertise the availability of a position to the Puerto Rican community, to attempt to recruit Puerto Ricans and, most important, to hire the Puerto Rican if he is the best qualified applicant. While equal employment laws have been on the books in New York State for decades, the Affirmative Action Program may actually enforce these rights for the first time. In the past, the Puerto Rican might justifiably have felt that even if he obtained the necessary training and education, he would still be denied a respectable employment opportunity. Affirmative Action now offers the promise that qualified Puerto Ricans will, in practice, be able to obtain positions commensurate with their ability. This is not the time for Puerto Ricans to ignore or ridicule the Affirmative Action Program as another federal boondoggle, or as empty rhetoric, but to obtain the necessary qualifications for and to seek out the positions which we believe Affirmative Action has finally opened up.

PART II

PERSPECTIVES FROM THE ARTS

CHAPTER 6

TELEVISION AND THE PUERTO RICAN

Marifé Hernández

  The Puerto Rican Community in New York has been
shaped and influenced by television more than any other group
in our City. Puerto Ricans arrived in New York at the same
time that commercial television was beginning to produce heroes and collect fans. The more than 50,000 Puerto Ricans
who landed yearly at the old Idlewild Airport from the late
40's through the late 50's rapidly joined the Television Fan
Club.

  Television meant all kinds of important and marvelous
things to those Puerto Rican families trying to establish a
home base in East 112th Street and Lexington Avenue in 1952.
Television was about the only way Puerto Ricans in those
early days could have any pleasant or positive contact with
the mainstream of American life. All other glimpses into
New York life were difficult for the Puerto Rican migrant.
Work, when you were lucky enough to find it, meant days in
steaming hotel kitchens or dress factories. Communication
meant taking orders. Home was a room meant for two and
used by 10 people, all with the same problems--no English,
no money, nothing to look forward to, and too proud to look
back. But, if you could afford one of those gleaming television sets, at three dollars a week forever, you could get a
glimpse of Milton Berle, the Lone Ranger, pretty ladies and
the golden milkshake--all the reasons for which you had come
to New York anyway.

  Maybe you couldn't get all this beauty right away, but
television assured you it was there--if not for you, then for
your children. The American Dream was sold to the Puerto
Ricans in New York via television. They didn't understand
English well enough to question it, but they saw enough to
stay and bring hundreds of thousands more like them in their
tow. If Juan could somehow become John, just like on T.V.,
the rewards would be forthcoming. A whole generation of

Puerto Rican babies was then born with names like Milton,
George Washington, Nelson, Elizabeth and Jane. Two generations were by then on the waiting list for the Dream.

Then, suddenly, that same television that had meant
escape and dreams for the early Puerto Rican migrants, in
turn discovered its newest customers--the Puerto Ricans.

Television was not the only member of the media to
find sexy and sensational tales in the Puerto Rican community.
By the early 1960's, every major magazine, newspaper and
television station in the New York metropolitan area had done
a series or at least a feature story on the Puerto Ricans.
Whether you read about the gang wars between Puerto Rican
youths, saw the pictures of those thin, dark haired Puerto
Rican girls dressed in skimpy summer dresses in twenty degree winter weather in magazines, or witnessed the rats and
dirt in a Puerto Rican home courtesy of a T.V. screen--
Puerto Ricans had become the ghetto stars of New York media. Of course, all these scoops and horror stories were
written by non-Puerto Ricans after a three-hour session in a
Puerto Rican neighborhood. Apparently, that was all it took
to make a journalist an expert on the Puerto Rican scene in
the 1960's.

So these experts of New York's broadcasting and newspaper world created the Puerto Rican image for the non-Puerto Ricans. What are Puerto Ricans like? What are they all
about? Very simple. Most New Yorkers know the answer;
they either saw it on T.V. or read it somewhere. Puerto
Ricans are a loud, greasy bunch of lazy bums, welfare cases
at best, addicts and criminals at worst.

Surely, this was all a long time ago, way back in the
1950's and 1960's, before words like Black Power, Ethnic
Pride and Community Control restructured the American vernacular. By now, New Yorkers are so secure in their lack
of prejudices and the Black community has softened liberals
to such an extent that to be Puerto Rican might even become
chic this year. To top it all, the Federal Communications
Commission guarantees communities access to the media.

The government can legislate and liberals can exorcize,
but the media are basically news carriers. The American
media are convinced that the American public is a bloodthirsty race with a keen appetite for tragedy. Television programming and newspaper reporting can perhaps be positive in

an international vein; when it comes to domestic consumption,
they go for the jugular. So here we are, in the 1970's and
the Puerto Rican junkie, prostitute and criminal continue making headlines. Only now, it isn't called discriminatory reporting; the Puerto Ricans are now the victims of reform
journalism, crusading to expose the gory hell of Puerto Rican life in New York, expecting the shock to provide the cure.

      There is a lot of poverty, crime, discrimination and
injustice in the Puerto Rican community of the 1970's. The
media can be a powerful help to the Puerto Rican Community
in seeking redress and remedy from government and institutions. There are many cases of Puerto Rican children wrongly classified as retarded, of Puerto Rican social service
agencies denied funds, and of non-English-speaking Puerto Rican students being deprived of bilingual instruction, and the
right television or press coverage can persuade the responsible official or department to change a policy. Everybody
agrees on the power of the media. To a group such as the
Puerto Rican community, whose own power base is very small
and rests largely with a small group of its own elected officials, the media assume an even greater importance as a
power vehicle to champion Puerto Rican causes.

      There is another story about the Puerto Ricans in New
York that needs telling and showing. It's a success story,
and because the media haven't bothered with it, Puerto Ricans
themselves sometimes doubt it and lose sight of it. It is the
impressive story of a poorly-educated migrant community, in
an alien and sometimes hostile environment, that in twenty-
five years stands ready to contribute impressive people to
every field of endeavor in this nation. Impressive men and
women because they can be judged by the American standards
of efficiency and professionalism and, at the same time, have
not lost the warmth, honor, love, rhythm, passion and poetry
that is their own heritage. These impressive Puerto Ricans
are building theater companies, travel agencies, dance companies, printing shops and merchant associations. They are
leading school boards, planning boards and political campaigns.
Their ranks are daily growing through work, study and guts.
These very special Puerto Rican New Yorkers are almost a
complete unknown to the non-Puerto Rican New York mainstream. I'm not talking of an elite group in the making. I'm
talking about a majority of the Puerto Rican community that
is dedicated to bringing along those of its members not on
board.

Does media crusading have to be negative? Don't you
do better after you've had a success, no matter how small?
Well, the Puerto Rican community needs to learn of its success to insure their continuance. And the rest of New York
needs to be shown the disparity between the media image and
the real image of the Puerto Rican New Yorkers to realize
the stupidity and irony of many of its attitudes and actions
towards Puerto Ricans.

Who is doing most of the reporting on the Puerto Rican community today? From NBC to the New York Post, by
way of WPIX (where I hold forth), you will find a group of
reporters, writers and producers known as the token Puerto
Rican or the House P.R.--pick your label. Every television
station and newspaper has one. It's the media's way of saying to the Puerto Rican community: "Look, we've hired one
of your own people, so we've done our job." The token Puerto Ricans, besides pacifying the Puerto Rican community, are
also supposed to show that minorities are making brilliant
careers in communications and that all sides of the American
picture have access to airwaves and print. But the Puerto
Rican community is not ecstatic and those House Puerto Ricans are not making great inroads in the media.

One of the reasons for the type of coverage given to
the Puerto Rican community and the small numbers of Puerto
Ricans working in communications is the hard and real fact
that there are no Puerto Ricans in serious policy-making positions in television, radio, newspapers or magazines. Even
the newly created job of Director of Community Affairs in a
television station is not held by one single Puerto Rican in
the City of New York. Puerto Ricans are looked upon by television executives and newspaper editors as exotic experiments
in community media participation; good to cover their own
ethnic stories and necessary to adorn their employers' fair
employment records. They are still not looked upon as just
good, bad or indifferent writers, editors, producers, modera-
tors or newscasters, without a racial or nationality bias.

The media provide a very special field of employment.
Intelligence or training does not necessarily produce a great
or even average writer or newsman. And the number of jobs
available is pitifully small. But whether magic talent is present or not, young Puerto Ricans will have much more of a
chance of getting a job in communications if they have specialized training. A college degree in communications, television,
broadcasting, journalism or film-making is already one big

step in the right direction. Any college degree at all is a
big help in a career in the media--but, already, we are talking about a very small number of young Puerto Ricans. Twen-
ty-five percent of New York City's public school students are
Puerto Rican, yet less than five percent of The City University of New York's enrollment is Puerto Rican. So, until
more Puerto Ricans get those college degrees, more special
training programs in media should be set up in the New York
City area to train non-college students in intensive three- or
four-month courses. These programs should prepare the student for immediate employment in the media, and job placement should be part of the program's goal. There is only
one such course now in the New York metropolitan area--the
Summer Media Program at Columbia University.

A second alternative to a college degree in communications would be, of course, on-the-job training. This type of
training is particularly applicable in television, where learning
by doing is a must in spite of any degrees earned. No television station in New York City has at this time a full-time
program to train Puerto Ricans in the different jobs available
in the field, especially those jobs that don't require union
membership. WNET, Channel 13, has a partial training program for minorities, but its status is delicate as it depends
on fund raising for its existence. This program also does
not guarantee jobs within the station for those who successfully
complete the training course.

If stations should help create a pool of talent among
New York's Puerto Rican community, unions must begin to
help young Puerto Ricans enter their ranks. In the more than
four years that I have been working in New York television, I
have not worked with a single Puerto Rican cameraman, lighting director, stagehand, associate director, director, video
consultant, editor or engineer.

How are television stations and television unions going
to begin really opening doors to Puerto Ricans rather than
just teasing them with the hope of being the front office Puerto Rican? There are just three ways. Community pressure,
political pressure and legal pressure. I've already mentioned
the Puerto Rican's limited but growing political clout. And,
after all, how willing are politicians to pit themselves against
that media that they so desperately need? Community pressure needs to be much more extensively explored by the Puerto Ricans. A Committee of Puerto Ricans for Responsive
Media, for example, with a broad-gauged membership, even

including some non-Puerto Rican power centers, might be the
way to begin fruitful discussions with this city's media. Le-
gally, Puerto Ricans have recently established the Puerto Rican Legal Defense Fund, modeled after the NAACP Legal Defense Fund.   Perhaps, a legal review of media opportunities
for Puerto Ricans both in unions and station employment,
might be in order.

There is no question that New York City's media have
opened some doors for Puerto Ricans in the last five years.
From newspapers to television stations, to unions, those doors
have been opened just enough to comply with the law but not
enough to matter.   The media will not change of their own accord.   It is now up to the Puerto Rican Community.

CHAPTER 7

PUERTO RICANS IN AMERICAN FILMS:
PELICULAS SIN PERSONAJES

Edward Mapp

The Puerto Rican in American films is mostly shadow
and little substance. He might be a boy in Central Park in
The Out of Towners, a prisoner in Fuzz, or a soldier in The
Dirty Dozen, rarely emerging from the background of films
in which others are major characters.

Early in 1951, the eminent Puerto Rican actor, José
Ferrer, received Hollywood's highest accolade, the Academy
of Motion Picture Arts and Sciences award for the best performance by an actor in a leading role. Although the official
announcement of the award occurred at a presentation ceremony in California, Señor Ferrer actually received his "Oscar" from Luis Muñoz Marin, then Governor of Puerto Rico,
in a triumphant one-day visit to the Island. Only hours after
accepting the coveted statuette, Ferrer presented it to the
University of Puerto Rico as a permanent trophy. Acknowledging his ethnic heritage, Ferrer said, "I want to express
my pride as a Puerto Rican and as a man for the effort that
the Puerto Ricans are making in the face of the most adverse
circumstances, determined not to be defeated either by scarcity or illness nor to be dominated by hatred or envy."[1] The
actor's eloquent remarks would have carried even greater
significance had he won the award for portraying a heroic
Puerto Rican figure instead of the flamboyant fictional Frenchman, Cyrano de Bergerac. Borrowing a phrase from Cyrano,
Ferrer referred to holding high and unsullied "my plume,"
perhaps not fully realizing, himself, how difficult that task
would be. In the years since Ferrer's signal achievement,
the incidence of positive Hispanic characterizations in films
has been rare, and those often portrayed by "gringos." The
casting of Peter O'Toole as the Man of La Mancha is a conspicuous example of this trend.

When Puerto Ricans do appear in American motion

58

pictures, they are frequently portrayed in a demeaning manner. Witness the stereotypical presentation of Puerto Ricans in a film such as Popi, which starred Alan Arkin in the title role. Popi, a Puerto Rican widower in New York, is determined to remove his two young sons from the unwholesome environment of the ghetto slum in which they reside. One can accept the notion of a desperate man terrified by the junkies, muggers, thieves and street gangs of Spanish Harlem, but try to find a "Boricua padre" who would even contemplate casting his beloved "hijos" adrift in a rowboat on the treacherous Atlantic Ocean with some fantastic scheme to have them rescued and adopted as Cuban refugees. Seeing this apparently religious Puerto Rican parent attempt suicide by drowning was as difficult to swallow as it was for Popi to down the Miami surf. This is not to suggest that the film was bereft of truth about some facets of Puerto Rican life in the tenements of New York. The life-sized mannequin propped up by the window, the pre-recorded barking dog, the multiple door locks have the ring of truth about inner city survival. There is the foraging at a hotel banquet for remnants and morsels which can be brought home as a treat for the "niños." There are the unsuccessful efforts to conceal his sexual relationship with a mistress (Rita Moreno) in the next apartment from the eyes of two very "hip" little fellows. Regretfully, Arkin's accent as Popi is part Spanish, part Yiddish--a further challenge to credulity. Popi is no one's reality, least of all the Puerto Rican's.

Films which deal with school themes tend to be less reluctant to recognize the presence of Puerto Ricans. An unfortunate corollary of such recognition is that most youngsters in such films are characterized as problem Puerto Ricans. As early as 1955, Rafael Campos appeared as the Puerto Rican class clown of a vocational high school English class in the movie Blackboard Jungle. At that time Campos was the "token" for roles involving young Chicanos, Puerto Ricans and Apaches. Hollywood recognized no ethnic or cultural distinctions among these groups. It is common knowledge that Puerto Ricans imbue in their youngsters a respect and reverence for authority, education and educators. Yet, in Blackboard Jungle, Campos, as Pete Morales, a Puerto Rican boy, helps disrupt the classroom discipline of a sympathetic and patient teacher. Not content with this negative image, Morales is held up for derision by his classmates because of his thick accent and his excessive and indiscriminate use of a single expletive. The film would have us believe that Morales is not intelligent enough to know when he is being mocked. Odd-

ly enough, with a non-stereotype portrayal by Sidney Poitier
as a student with leadership capability, blacks fared better
than Puerto Ricans in Blackboard Jungle.

The Puerto Rican is again seen as student in Up the
Down Staircase (aren't there any Puerto Rican teachers?)
but this time he is portrayed with dignity by José Rodriguez.
José had been reticent in Miss Barrett's English class until
she decided to simulate a courtroom trial as enrichment of a
literature selection. José was assigned the role of judge and
emerged from his cocoon with an unexpected fervor. The
class and the teacher were overwhelmed not only by the cos-
tume José managed to acquire for the occasion but by his
surprisingly authoritative manner. "I'm the judge and you
gotta listen," he announces.

In stark contrast is the role of Aníbal, the young Puerto Rican in Frank and Eleanor Perry's film, Last Summer.
Aníbal, portrayed by Ernest Gonzalez, experiences complete
humiliation at the hands of some corrupt post-pubescent
WASPs who are out for a season of fun on Fire Island. Aníbal comes out from New York City to keep a computer-ar-
ranged blind date with Rhoda. He does not complain when
Rhoda brings her three friends along on the date. Slowly and
insidiously, the cruel quartet begin to ridicule Aníbal, deliberately calling him Annabelle, getting him drunk, sticking
him with the check and finally abandoning him to a gang of
hoodlums who beat him unmercifully. His pathetic cry,
"Ayúdeme, por Dios," goes unanswered by those whom he
guilelessly assumed were "amigos." Movie script-writers
seem to attribute innocence to Puerto Ricans as eagerly as
they once attributed indolence to blacks.

Almost as vulnerable as Aníbal is Jesus Ortiz as played
by Jaime Sanchez in The Pawnbroker. Although the Jewish
pawnbroker rejects the proffered friendship and admiration of
Ortiz, the Puerto Rican youth's warmth and spirit remain intact. He promises his "madre," no more stealing, peddling
or numbers. Ortiz is resolved to make something of himself.
He beseeches the pawnbroker to teach him the secrets of the
trade. As apprentice to the pawnbroker, he will learn a business and therein gain security and respectability. Despite his
ambition and goals, the film stresses the Puerto Rican's inability to be punctual. Twenty minutes late for work one day,
he tells his employer, "I'm gonna be here practically early
on Monday." Score one for another stereotype. In his eagerness to assimilate, Ortiz admonishes his mother to speak Eng-

lish, not Spanish.   Misguided by the embittered pawnbroker
to believe that money is everything, Ortiz flirts with crime
in a moment of disillusionment.   During a robbery which he
made possible, Ortiz is slain in a courageous attempt to protect the pawnbroker.   American films have a proclivity for
offering up third world people as sacrifices for the salvation
of whites.   Another discordant note in this film involves the
girl friend of Ortiz, a black prostitute who happens to be un-
selfishly devoted to him.   An aspiring young Puerto Rican
who lives with his mother and wears a crucifix might use the
services of a prostitute but is highly unlikely to acknowledge
her as his girl friend.

Juano Hernandez, the distinguished Puerto Rican actor
who forged a screen career in Hollywood portraying black
Americans, contributes a small but memorable characterization to The Pawnbroker.   He is seen as a pathetic and lonely
customer of the pawn shop.

An Elvis Presley movie is an unlikely place to find
realism and his Change of Habit proved no exception.   The
film is about a guitar-playing physician (Elvis) and some female medical assistants (would you believe nuns on loan from
a convent?) who try to solve the problems of an urban ghetto
population.   One of their problems is Julio Hernandez, a
stuttering, emotionally ill Puerto Rican teenager.   When Julio
isn't stealing an icon from the local church or attempting the
rape of a nun (Mary Tyler Moore, no less), he is uttering
pseudo "macho" lines such as "My knife make me big man."
Implicit in the film's conclusion is that Julio will receive
psychiatric care, speech therapy and possibly a jail sentence,
not necessarily in that order.

Further linking Puerto Ricans with crime and imprison-
ment, a producer had the insensitivity to film The Honeymoon
Killers, based upon the actual criminal alliance of Raymond
Fernandez and Martha Beck in the lonely hearts murders for
which they were executed in 1951.   The real tragedy of such
a film which depicts a Puerto Rican as criminal lies in its
imbalance.   Bonnie and Clyde is counterbalanced by numerous
positive film images of whites but no such redress exists for
negative film images of Puerto Ricans.

Puerto Rico is sometimes evident in American films
even when Puerto Ricans are not.   The action-filled conclusion of a Mafia melodrama entitled Stiletto was shot on the
Island of Puerto Rico with historic El Morro used as the set-

ting of an exciting chase sequence. Twentieth Century Fox
shot locations for its film Che! in Puerto Rico because of the
similarity to Cuban landscapes. Many of the guerilla warfare
scenes in Che! were photographed in a Puerto Rican rain
forest.

West Side Story, winner of no less than ten academy
awards including an "Oscar" as best film of 1961, represents
the summit of Puerto Rican prominence in motion pictures.
Told in Romeo and Juliet fashion, West Side Story is essentially the drama of a Puerto Rican girl who falls in love with
a Polish boy, despite the open hostility of their respective
ethnic groups. Ever faithful to fantasy, Hollywood engaged
Natalie Wood, an actress of Russian descent, to play Maria,
the Puerto Rican heroine. Perhaps as a concession to reality, it cast Rita Moreno, a Puerto Rican actress, in the lesser role of Anita, spitfire-confidante of Maria. Miss Moreno
played the role with zest and perception, earning an "Oscar"
as best actress in a supporting role. Previously Miss Moreno
had enacted minor roles in Hollywood films in which she merely had to flare her nostrils, gnash her teeth and look spirited.
West Side Story came not a moment too soon for this talented
Puerto Rican actress, who was losing patience with stereotypical dialogue of the "Yankee pig, you stole my people's
gold" variety. West Side Story must be applauded for its fine
musical score, brilliant photography, imaginative choreogra-
phy and overdue recognition of the presence of Puerto Ricans
in New York City. The film also takes cognizance of the
strong familial bonds which exist even within uprooted Puerto
Rican families. Unhappy about a Polish boy's interest in
Maria, Bernardo warns him, "You keep away from my sister.
Don't you know we are a family people!"[2] The film's positive aspects end there!

Some of the song lyrics denigrate Puerto Rico, allud-
ing to it as an island of tropic diseases, bullets, over-popula-
tion, inadequate roads, no electricity and hundreds of people
in one room. One line actually asks, "what have they got
there to keep clean?" The Puerto Rican gang members and
their girl friends are costumed in gaudy attire in keeping with
still another myth. As a rather sheltered and parochial Puerto Rican girl, Maria seems almost too eager for intercultural
romance. With names like Leonard Bernstein, Robert Wise,
Ernest Lehman, Arthur Laurents and Leonard Robbins heading up the venture, there should be little surprise at the lack
of an authentic Puerto Rican perspective. Yet even the casting of Rita Moreno as the Puerto Rican Anita represents pro-

gress of a kind. Her performance and its subsequent recognition tells motion picture audiences that Puerto Ricans do exist and that they too have value.

No one knows with certainty what the future holds but it does not look too bright, if Badge 373 is a prognosticator. Independence for Puerto Rico is one theme of this film, recently shot on location in New York City. In the story, Felipe Luciano plays a young Puerto Rican, who is helping to send arms to a revolutionary faction in Puerto Rico. The film depicts the Puerto Rican as prostitute, racketeer, crooked policeman and junkie. While it is true that other ethnic groups are portrayed negatively in Badge 373, a greater frequency of appearances for them permits a balance of more positive screen images. The Puerto Rican is seen so seldom in motion pictures that each and every characterization counts a great deal.

José Torres makes the valid point that talented Puerto Rican script writers and well-to-do Puerto Rican investors can do much to provide movie audiences with satisfactory films about Puerto Ricans. [3]

The portrayal of Puerto Ricans in films of the past surely entitles them to a brighter future. It is time for humane and honest films about Puerto Ricans. The potential and possibility are there. It only remains to be realized.

Notes

1. The New York Times, April 16, 1951, p. 20.

2. Fitzpatrick, Joseph P. Puerto Rican Americans The Meaning of Migration to the Mainland. N.J.: Prentice-Hall, 1971, p. 99.

3. Torres, José. "Badge 373," New York Post, September 1, 1973, p. 26.

CHAPTER 8

THE ANGUISH OF THE EXPATRIATE WRITER

Luis Quero-Chiesa

The problems of the writer who is forced to live and create away from his original environment, in the midst of a milieu which is adverse to his way of thinking and acting, is as old as the art of writing. But it is not any less anguishing in the twentieth century. Through the years we have seen our Puerto Rican and other Hispanic intellectuals arrive at these shores: young writers, veterans of the pen, poets burning with that strange fever which produces the creating delirium. Yet we have seen many of them cool down, sink slowly but inexorably into the turmoil of the vulgar, popularized and commercial life, dilute themselves in conformity, become paralyzed with frustration, and, in short, die as writers.

When Spain was the point that attracted us, the Puerto Rican or Hispanic American intellectual who migrated to the mother country incorporated himself harmoniously and naturally to the Spanish literary movement and continued his work in a favorable cultural climate. Thus, we were in this atmosphere able to produce there many major writers, including Garcilaso de la Vega, Antonio Corton, Salvador Canales, Eugenio Maria de Hostos, and others.

But what happens to the Puerto Rican or Hispanic intellectual who comes to this country? He has to face a cultural conflict so serious that it becomes a matter of life and death to him as an artist. Before him rises the wall of the English language, isolating him from the American literary life. The Anglo-Saxon tradition shakes his sensibility with a new scale of cultural values in which the pragmatic prevails. Those ideals that he had learned to venerate--even when they did not always have validity in reality--are here relegated to the last order of priority or even to oblivion. Honor, romanticism, the Latin sense of family unity, the hierarchy of intellectual life compared with other priorities are here al-

most laughable concepts which belong more to the stage than
to actual life. The confusion that this change in values produces in the writer's mind is naturally transmitted to his
work. His work usually suffers, for it seems that it is only
when the writer is at peace with himself and with the milieu
--and this has nothing to do with personal happiness or un-
happiness--that the mysterious essences of literary creation
can flow freely from his brain.

There are still other obstacles of material character
which the Hispanic intellectual must overcome when he arrives in this country: the exhausting demands of time and
energy of the convulsive American society; the scanty opportunities offered to the Hispanic writer in his profession; the
thin intellectual atmosphere which prevails in the Spanish-
speaking community; the scarcity of literary journals, the
astronomical costs of book publishing.

Faced with these obstacles the writer can always look
for refuge in cynicism, lose faith in everything including himself, and continue to talk about the book he is working on until death arrives. This is exactly what many of them do.
Others prefer to come to grips with the environment. They
know that the Hispanic culture is their strongest bulwark.
They entrench themselves in it. Frequently they latch on to
some native motif, such as liberty, folklore or popular ty-
pology. This kind of literature about the idealized motherland with its romantic-nationalistic accent is usually provincial in character and often embodies chauvinism and an exul-
tation of the picturesque. But even this has some literary
merit.

Thus, if the hostility of the new environment pushes
the intellectual towards his own roots, in that measure it can
render him a great service. But because American life exerts such subjugating influences over the individual, soon
these two polarizing forces tend to neutralize each other.
When this happens, a neutral grey spreads over the mind and
a great animal peace envelops the individual. Then, no mature work can be expected from him: he has entered the
peaceable limbo of mediocrity.

Fortunately, however, the true writer knows only one
kind of peace: the desperate peace of the hours of creation
when he faces himself and that provocative, torturing thing
which is the empty sheet of paper. It appears that the age-
old axiom, that the only way to overcome barriers to writing

is by the act of writing, is certainly true for the expatriate
writer.   It is always easiest to work from a basis of what
one knows best.   Thus, when destiny removes the writer
from his origins and transplants him into a strange environment, imposing on him the infinite vicissitudes of spiritual
exile, he must still write.   Conscious of this, a handful of
our intellectuals keep on writing, expressing truth and beauty,
as it is given to them to see it, through the written word.

There is also the possibility that the expatriate writer,
by remaining loyal to his own roots, can discover new dimen-
sions of them on alien soil.   He might discover, as did
Shakespeare, that "one must leave home in order to learn
what it is that he has left. "   It is altogether possible that
one day he might return, but unless he goes into the world,
he will not appreciate fully his own beginnings.

The writer, in a creative attitude, when inspiration
flows harmoniously because he and his environment are in
perfect affinity, becomes an illuminated human being, capable
of transcending reality and penetrating into the deepest meaning of persons and things.   But when he is able to accomplish all this in a foreign milieu where everything is alien to
his nature, he becomes, in addition to a writer, something
of a hero.   And as such he deserves our admiration and respect.

CHAPTER 9

THE PLAYWRIGHT AND THE PUERTO RICAN THEATRE

Jaimé Ruiz-Escobar

It would be ambitious and arrogant to try to cover within this essay the experiences I have lived-suffered-enjoyed on the Puerto Rican stage throughout the past twenty years of my existence. It would also be obscene and ridiculous to attempt to cover within ten or twelve pages the history of the Puerto Rican theatre during the same length of time; especially when during these past twenty years the best of our dramatic works have been produced and have been maintained.

Also, a series of talented histrionic forces has come forth to elevate the stature of our laboring-artistic class to unexpected social-political-intellectual levels. All this has been achieved, but we must not forget the gamut of stiff shams (natives as well as foreigners) who have been engaged in the shameful and ugly game of sheer mediocrity, constantly slapping our public with a conspicuous cluster of disrespectful and mediocre performances sponsored by soap labels, popularity contests, bankers and advertising figures. These have always had, of course, the "generous" backing of the Lions, Rotary, Exchange, "Civicas," Chambers of Commerce, El Deportivo, Boy and Girl Scouts of America and thousands of additional clubs.

This essay is also non-inclusive of the outstanding personalities who in the past have written about the Puerto Rican theatre. Nor is it my intention to offer an essay of praises, pandering and hornblowing to those figures who have worked, interestedly or otherwise, in the artistic panorama of Puerto Rico throughout its history. Therefore, it will not serve as a sort of micronite filter through which these figures can placidly smoke the fumes of their popularity while they masturbate their intellectual egos.

The only goal of this work is to offer personal com-

ments about what my eyes have seen during these two decades
and my reactions, no less personal, to what I have seen and
lived.

The essay is thus divided in two parts: the playwright
in the first place, not because he is most important, but because plays have to be written first before they can be presented; and secondly, the actor. When speaking of playwright
and actor, I am talking directly of the theatre, not in any
way of television or films. Puerto Rican television (in content, not in talent or technical personnel) is a syrup of ram-
pant mediocrity, empty and insulting. About film nothing can
yet be said because not one film has been realized which can
be called Puerto Rican which may have some possibilities.
I can only point out the quality in some of the films which
were once prepared by the Education of the Community Com-
pany--very good pictures which are sleeping the dream of the
lilies inside the same cans where they were placed from the
start, and which have never been given the opportunity to be
seen by a broad audience.

Among the playwrights who have seen and reseen their
works on stage during the last twenty years, we can only
mention a few. If some names are omitted, we do it quite
intentionally--we will not, therefore, have to apologize later.

René Marquéz is without doubt the best known, most
prolific and most valued of the Puerto Rican playwrights. His
works have been presented in and out of Puerto Rico with notable success. His theatre oscillates between pure realism,
as in La Carreta [The Ox-Cart], his best known work a melodrama which faithfully portrays a part of our history, and the
surrealism of Los Soles Truncos [The Truncated Suns], an
extraordinary play; and reaches even the avant-garde committed theatre with Carnaval Adentro, Carnaval Afuera. The
majority of his works are an accusation of the colonial yoke
strangling his--our--Patria. This is the reason why so many
of his works have not yet been presented. René, nevertheless, has much abused the theatrical allegory and has painted
political situations which have reached the public via another
type of theatre, as he so masterfully did in Carnaval Adentro,
Carnaval Afuera, which was presented by Casa Las Américas
in Cuba. But these have remained mutilated because he has
reached for the Bible to paint situations which would hurt the
flesh of the people but which need a theatre more openly committed: a theatre of truths, without patches.

Luis Rafael Sánchez is, to my way of thinking, the most hopeful promise (already a reality) of our theatrical world. In just a few years he has developed a magnificent theatrical output which each day surpasses what came before. From his college days until today, Wico has offered us a continuous and eager search for what is true and real in the Puerto Rican situation. His is a vibrant theatre that takes in ideas from native folklore to the red-hot theme of politics and colonial life. La Pasión Según Antígona Perez is perhaps one of his best works, although we must not fail to mention Los Angeles Se Han Fatigado, La Hiel Nuestra de Cada Día, Sol Trece Interior and, what is to my way of thinking his best work, which still has not been shown: Pa de Catre. His theatrical production is not limited to these few works, but they are examples of a theatre full of poetry and reality, of a new technique which illuminates the conscience of the reader, who sees through his works a Puerto Rico crushed, taken, and abused by foreign powers.

Gerard Paul Marín is an honest and profound dramatist who has removed himself from the Puerto Rican scene the last few years, but whose footprints are indelibly written in the history of our theatre. Al Principio La Noche Era Serena and Al Final de la Calle are excellent examples of his magnificent theatrical production. We know that he is continuing to write; we know that he has a group of new works, and we are only waiting for him to put them on the stage. Puerto Rico has need for writers like Gerard Paul Marín.

Francisco Arriví is one of the most prolific Puerto Rican dramatists. He is the Director of the Theatre Section of The Institute of Puerto Rican Culture and the creator of the Puerto Rican Theatre Festival. This agency, a little strait-laced and ambivalent, has been responsible for popularizing the native theatre, and, although in the hands of a small group of privileged people, has been able to offer a rather panoramic view of our theatrical production. Vegigantes, Club de Solteros, María Soledad, Caso de Muerto en Vida and innumerable other plays comprise the great theatrical production of Paco Arriví, who has been a real force within the Puerto Rican theatrical scene. He has not lived off but for the theatre of the captive island.

Emilio S. Belaval belongs to past generations, really past. His works do not offer anything new. He was until a few years ago a high-ranking figure in the Puerto Rican Theatre Festivals. Don Emilio died recently.

Manuel Mendez Ballester, better as a novelist than a
dramatist, maintained his place of honor in Puerto Rican
theatre for many years.   (Hey, these guys never ever wanted
to leave.) Don Manuel Mendez Ballester gave us some great
moments in his works, however half-heartedly.   La Invasión
was the most recent of his plays that we saw.   Just at the
end of the performance, as the actor Juan Carlos Santa Cruz
cried (changing the author's line from "long live Puerto Rico")
"long live free Puerto Rico," he jumped out of his seat in
such a way as to transform the play into a comedy instead of
a drama.   But I do not want to appear a sceptic; Manuel
Mendez Ballester is an honest dramatist who goes as far as
his ideals will let him.

Luis Rechani Agrait is "Mi Señoria." And that is
enough.

Myrna Casas is one of the new talents of the Puerto
Rican theatre.   She has been an actress, a playwright and a
director.   Within these fields she has developed with professional majesty.   Obviously the inertia and unproductiveness
of the University Theatre has locked her in a labyrinth of ob-
scurity and stagnation.   We already know of her talent, but
not of her new theatrical creations.   Her theatre of the ab-
surd seems to us of praiseworthy quality: Absurdos en Soledad, La Trampa and Eugenia Victoria Herrera are eloquent
proofs of her unique talent.   We are hopefully awaiting more
from Myrna Casas.

On the other hand, new faces have appeared, new
young writers who bring hope to the Puerto Rican theatre.
Theirs are minds that are neither alienated nor compromised
by the Establishment; they raise a closed fist--the left one,
of course.   They have said: "That's enough," and have begun to move.   We do not want to give the impression that a
panacea is at hand, to presume that these young men will be
the paladins of the new Puerto Rican theatre, much less claim
that the dramatists mentioned previously are merely fragments
of the past.   René Marquéz, Luis Rafael Sanchez, Gerard
Paul Marin, Paco Arriví, Myrna Casas and others still have
much to offer.   Their works are a faithful example of their
true value as committed writers who in one way or another
have always been on guard, prepared to denounce social and
political abuses.   They are an indispensable part of our theatre today.   But these young writers, this new blood is very
much needed in Puerto Rico.   Breaking through the old writers' stranglehold on the Puerto Rican Theatre Festival has

been a major achievement, and we have to be grateful for the
decision of the Puerto Rican Institute of Culture for including
new talent in this kind of theatrical endeavor.

Whatever the motives were for this change of direction
on the part of the Establishment, here we have some new
dramatists, some brilliant, others mediocre, whose works
thus far we have only read, not seen, except for La Descom-
posición de César Sánchez, by the actor, poet, dramatist and
militant leftist, Walter Rodríguez. It seemed to us to be a
great work, perhaps the best one in the 1973 Puerto Rican
Theatre Festival--a good play, with great acting, fine technique and excellent direction by Jose Luis Ramos. Walter
Rodríguez has, in his own words, a double duty to his coun-
try--as a writer and as a man, these two fused in a single
ideal: the struggle for the independence of Puerto Rico.

Jaime Carrero is another young playwright who has
developed in the last few years. His Pipo Subway Doesn't
Know How to Laugh is a well-made play of social protest and,
as directed by Pablo Cabrera, a remarkable production.
Without Flag, the second of his plays we have seen, has a
strong theme and good possibilities, but the author seems to
lose track of his original intention; indeed, the play could
easily be called With Flag. But Jaime Carrero has talent
and we expect bigger things from this young dramatist.

Lylel Gonzalez is not a new writer. He had to wait
a couple of decades to see the production of one of his plays
in Puerto Rico. Finally, during the 1973 Puerto Rican Theatre Festival, he saw his Culebra USA staged. The subject of
this play--the suffering island of Culebra, the cruel abuse of
its people by the American Navy which uses its land and wa-
ters as the target for constant bombardment--is a theme that
demands total commitment on the part of the author. Gonzalez is only half-committed and the play suffers. But he
has written a lot and we expect to see more presentations of
his work in the future.

Juan Torres Alonso is a poet who in his prize-winning
first play, The Window (First Theatre Prize from Ateneo de
Puerto Rico in 1972), gives us a positive glimpse of his future productions. Here is a fresh theatre of socio-political
protest, as deadly as a bayonet.

Antonio Ramírez Córdova is an unknown writer who,
following the example of the black American Theatre, has

been writing very terse, brief plays. We have read his works
and 5:PM seemed to us his best play.

Collective theatre has been offered by some young
Puerto Rican groups in the last few years. They meet to
discuss and argue, offering ideas and opinions, improvising
the work that later the director will shape into a full-blown
play. This is collective process of give and take that, guided
by the director, does not end until opening day.

This new approach began when Lydia M. Gonzalez and
Jorge Cordova presented Condado P. M., or The New Life a
few years ago. This play opened a cycle of collective theatre presentations focusing on Colonial Puerto Rico and condemning, with savage wit, the alienation suffered by the Puerto Rican in his degrading world. Plays like Gloria La Boli-
tera, also presented by this group, deal compassionately with
the problems of the poor while angrily denouncing the causes
behind them.

Other groups that have had success working collective-
ly are Grupo Anamu and Grupo Morivivi. Anamu staged Pre-
ciosa y Otras Tonadas que no Llegaron al Hit Parade for the
First Festival of Latin American Theatre, directed by Pablo
Cabrera. Grupo Morivivi, founded by José Luis Ramos and
María Quiñones, is the youngest of these groups but it has already presented two well-received productions. The second
of these plays, Leon Arriba, Leon Abajo, was presented earlier this year. As directed by actor Miguel Angel Suarez, it
is a pointedly funny fable intended for the enjoyment of "all
children under eighty years old. "

There are other more orthodox companies which appear regularly on the Puerto Rican stage. Among them are
Compania de Sandra Rivera; El Cemí; Compañia de Lucy Boscana; Producciones Cisne, de Jossie Perez and Myrna Casas;
Producciones Maíto Fernández; and Compania La Mascara,
directed by Helena Montalbán.

Singular mention must be made of La Compania Teatro
del Sesenta. In our judgment, this is the most professional
and best organized of all the theatrical companies in Puerto
Rico in the last years. Founded by Fernando Aguilu and Dean
Zayas (one of the best Puerto Rican directors), this young
group of people have given themselves fully to their work.
They operate their own theatre and there are no stars, so
that often one finds the principals of one production working

the lights and selling tickets for the next. Their long and
varied list of hits attest to the correctness of their methods.

As we have noted, to be a Puerto Rican actor demands
utmost flexibility, and for little reward. If he wants to work
at all, the actor must be able to jump from committed, collective theatre to the inane placebo of some "vanity production, " to a hastily put together, badly translated "Broadway
hit. " The Puerto Rican actor lives cornered and hungry. He
rehearses and performs for fourteen weeks and earns $250,
and this only if the box-office allows; if it does not, he is
lucky if he is paid for transportation.

It is a truism that in Puerto Rico the best paid actors
are the foreigners. While the same could be said of almost
every field, the native actor is further jeopardized as he
serves his art. The committed actor who dares to bring
theatre to the poor people in the streets of the ever-present
slums becomes a "marked man," the target of petty harass-
ments by the colonial government, tagged as a "trouble-
maker" by those in power, who control the scarce profitable
acting jobs.

But it must be pointed out that the members of this
artist-worker class do not seem to expect any reward other
than the struggle and the eventual victory that will make it
all worthwhile. Independence! To the new Puerto Rican ac-
tor-artist director that is no longer a dream and he lives
dedicated to take to his people the one message: "Wake up!"

To mention all the great and good actors and directors
one has seen in twenty years would be an impossible task.
But we could not end without at least a sampler of the wealth
of talent our sad island has produced despite everything. Directors like Victoria Espinosa, Pablo Cabrera, and Dean
Zayas are artists who have been able to transcend limited resources through their inventive imaginations.

Actors like Miguel Angel Suarez, Jacobo Morales,
Lucy Boscana, Braulio Castillo, and Luz Minerva Rodriguez
are gigantic presences who, through the breadth of their repertoire, need bow to no one.

And in New York (Oh, my poor divided country!),
where nothing changes for us but the weather, Pedro Santaliz
with his Poor Theater of America, Miriam Colon with her
Puerto Rican Traveling Theater, Carla Pinza, Estrellita Ar-

tau, and Roberto Rodriguez are all trying to thaw out relevancy for our people from these uncrying towers of ice.

The path of the Puerto Rican playwright and actor is
not an easy one. Only a clear conscience determines his
speed; whether it will be the sluggishness of mediocrity and
submission, or the swiftness of the daring, who shouts
"Enough!" and forges a future that is hopeful and Puerto Rican, for that is his only task. And he knows with others,
that "the present is struggle but the future is ours."

PART III

PERSPECTIVES FROM THE COMMUNITY

CHAPTER 10

SELF-HELP EFFORTS
IN THE PUERTO RICAN COMMUNITY

Jacinto Marrero

...To every man his chance, to every man, regardless of his birth, his shining, golden opportunity --
to every man the right to live, to work, to be himself, and to become whatever thing his manhood and
his vision can combine to make him--this, seeker,
is the promise of America. --Thomas Wolfe[1]

On Tuesday, May 23, 1972, the National Conference of
Christians and Jews, Inc. sponsored an all day Conference in
cooperation with the Puerto Rican Forum, the Puerto Rican
Educators Association, the Grand Council of Hispanics in Public Service, the Puerto Rican Family Institute, the Puerto
Rican Community Development Project, ASPIRA and the Society of Puerto Rican Bilingual Teachers in School and Community Relations. The Conference addressed itself to the
"Self-Help Efforts in the Puerto Rican Community."

This day-long seminar was engineered by NCCJ as
part of its 1972 Brotherhood Commitment Emphasis on the
Spanish Speaking Americans. NCCJ took the initiative in trying to highlight the difficulties and aspirations of Puerto Ricans on the mainland as well as their contributions to the nation. Congressman Herman Badillo, the keynoter, as well
as Dr. Pascual Sanchez, co-chairman of the 1972 Brotherhood Commitment, spoke on the need to come to grips with
the special problems of the Puerto Rican community. This
educational venture brought together 300 participants who
dealt with the dynamics of the Puerto Rican perspective in
education, housing, economic development, culture, politics,
health and welfare, mass media, the administration of justice
and ethnic group relations. Distinguished Puerto Ricans such
as Dr. Antero Lacot, Judge Cesar Quinones, Cándido de
León, Blanca Cedeno, Hector Vazquez, Tina Ramirez, Marifé
Hernández and Adolfina Montes gave leadership to the panels.

What transpired at this conference tells the story of the plight
of the Puerto Ricans on the mainland as well as what sometimes seem to be insurmountable obstacles which make the
road to self-help such a frustrating experience. The following excerpts from some of the panels dramatize "where it's
at" as far as the Puerto Rican community is concerned:

There are Puerto Ricans living in every state of the
union, with the greatest concentration in New York City where
the population has grown, according to the U.S. Census, from
612,000 in 1960 to 800,000 in 1970. The Puerto Rican community disagrees with these figures because of the discrepancy
with health district and school records. In 1960, 87 percent
of the Puerto Ricans lived in housing built before 1939. Forty
percent of the Puerto Rican households at that time were in
substandard and dilapidated structures. A visit to the South
Bronx, Williamsburg, East Harlem and the Lower East Side
will show that the situation remains the same. Public housing alone cannot do the job of relieving substandard housing,
but every effort has to be made to make public housing responsive to the needs of the Puerto Rican community. The
question is: "How can any poor community help itself?" The
Puerto Rican community is not aggressive and does not demand its rights--that's one problem; and the politicians tend
to respond to the pressures of militant communities. The
Puerto Rican must be heard and must be included in the plans
and development of the communities they reside in. Due to
the lack of Puerto Rican personnel in governmental agencies,
including the Housing Authority, although 21 percent of all
the families living in public housing are Puerto Rican, there
is very little bilingual personnel to service them.

Home ownership should be promoted and improved; bilingual programs should be established. Between 1950 and
1960, the construction of Lincoln Center eliminated 9,000
families. Their civil rights were abrogated and they were
not given an opportunity to return. Instead, housing was built
for the middle class--strangers to the community.

Since so few Puerto Ricans complete their schooling,
how can they develop their own areas without displacing the
people? The community development must be made by the
people. The decision should be theirs in terms of design,
the number of units, etc.

The South Bronx covers 24 acres of land and has the
largest concentration of poor people in the nation; two-thirds

are on welfare, or without means of support. The South
Bronx is different from other communities in that it does not
have a broad economic base. The South Bronx is losing its
stable families. Good planning means no relocation. Such
relocation as is necessary should be available right in the
area until the new housing becomes available.

The South Bronx has 400,000 people and the unemployment rate is twice the national rate. About five percent who
are in the middle class category are employed in poverty programs or in government. Currently, all new construction is
public housing with the exception of Woodstock Terrace. The
South Bronx is steadily losing its solid families, both Puerto
Rican and Black. How can the community help rehabilitate
the "undesirable" families in a self-help type program?

The following recommendations were submitted by the
Housing Workshop:

1. All Housing managers should be bilingual.

2. Puerto Ricans should be represented on the community planning commission and also on all local
   planning boards. The Borough President makes
   the appointments and he should have the approval
   of the community before he makes any appointments.

3. More Puerto Ricans should be given the opportunity
   to work in the construction field.

4. Minority businesses should be given more sub-con-
   tracts in order to get more experience, and develop
   a "track" record.

5. Con Edison should change its practice of estimating
   its bills and hire people from the community who
   are not afraid to go into the ghetto areas to read
   meters.

Some additional problems faced by Puerto Ricans in
the pursuit of health care have included: low-incomes, which
makes it difficult for them to purchase services; the language
barrier for health professionals who do not know how to communicate with the Spanish-speaking patients; and the attitudes
toward newcomers, a factor that has real impact on the quality of services offered.

One of the problems for Puerto Ricans, very evident today, is the result of the discrimination of past years. Puerto Ricans are paying the price of this discrimination in that their community suffers from a lack of health professionals of all kinds, including doctors, nurses and administrators.

Puerto Ricans have had a real problem in improving health care in their communities because of the absence of a large power bloc that would press City Hall for improved services. As a result, services are of poor quality in Puerto Rican neighborhoods, where one of the major problems is the absence of health care. This means that the hospital emergency room is now the primary provider of health services.

There is a broad range of health problems: absence of preventive health care, infant mortality, maternal death rates, absence of services for adolescents, broad drug abuse, problems around family planning and abortion, asthma, anemia, etc.

German Maisonet, a medical student, revealed the racism implicit in the counseling process that in no way encouraged him in applying for medical school. He was, in fact, discouraged from applying, not informed of financial resources, and not told of special scholarship programs. Mr. Maisonet suggested that the admission of minority students into medical schools is not an expression of commitment but rather one of compliance. Once admitted into school, money for tuition, books and equipment is a genuine problem. Even more acute are the personal pressures facing minority medical students in an institution and a community not at all interested in their welfare.

Jose Morales, Jr. suggested that the very sponsorship of the NCCJ conference by a series of Puerto Rican organizations was an indication of strength in the Puerto Rican community. The theme is self-help through Puerto Rican organizations--organized, led and geared to serve Puerto Ricans.

This great network of Puerto Rican community service, civic, social, religious, and recreational groups is concerned with:

1. Maintaining the Puerto Rican identity, culture, and language.

2. Maintaining a common identity with the Puerto Ricans in Puerto Rico.

3. Rejecting any form of American racism that would divide Puerto Ricans within their own families or from other minorities in the nation.

4. Remaining the most effective vehicle for the achievement of service objectives to this community.

Mr. Morales pointed out that a network of service agencies had been developed with no assistance from the social work community or social work education. Social work education, in particular, has been bankrupt, producing no sizeable numbers of Puerto Rican social workers, with no curriculum content involving Puerto Ricans, and with little or no Puerto Rican faculty in the various metropolitan area social work schools--and all of this within a setting in which close to one out of every seven New Yorkers is a Puerto Rican or a Spanish-speaking person.

Summary of Findings

1. The municipal hospitals must be strengthened as providers of health care to the poor, many of whom are Puerto Ricans. Affiliation contracts with voluntary hospitals and medical schools should permit the municipal hospitals to provide much needed services.

2. Consumer involvement is the key to accountability. There have been criticisms of the health system, of the affiliation contracts with municipal hospitals, of the health policies of voluntary agencies, and the health practices of privately managed health centers and medical schools. Involvement of the beneficiaries of service from neighborhoods and communities served by these institutions can immeasurably aid the public interest.

3. Puerto Ricans in New York City have special health needs and, as such, require special planning and funding of special programs to deal with these needs. Puerto Ricans have been shut out of policy-making positions in private health agencies and voluntary health complexes and have been blocked from entrance into medical training institutions. Puerto Ricans and non-Puerto Ricans can join in urging that these institutions undertake appropriate planning, involve Puerto Ri-

cans as policy-makers and providers, and improve medical
services for all consumers.

4. In the social welfare field, the task is the same--
recognition that Puerto Rican agencies are essential to the
general welfare of this community; that resources must be
made available for their work; that social work schools must
net greater numbers of Puerto Ricans, must revamp their
curriculum and recruit Puerto Rican faculty; and that Puerto
Rican consumers must join other community residents in the
governing bodies of social welfare agencies throughout the
City.

The trials we face today will be overcome but it will
take dedication and hard work.   As proud American citizens
of Puerto Rican heritage we can't accept the choice offered
by those who say to us, assimilate or starve.   We can keep
our Puerto Rican cultural profile and at the same time contribute to the main stream in all fields of endeavor, if the
doors of opportunity are open to us.   By the same token, we
must see to it that we get "ourselves together," searching
for new horizons by emancipation from our own "hang ups."
It is not enough to put the blame on the establishment.   The
Puerto Rican institutions ought to articulate their programs
for more effective functioning and cooperative work.   The
strong tradition of humane individualism should not impede
the process of institutional articulation which is so vital to
the very survival of the Puerto Rican Community.

Former Governor Roberto Sanchez Vilella uttered the
following words before his alma mater, Ohio State University:
"We--in Puerto Rico--stand at the threshold of development
and success... a demi-developed society.   The alternative to
stop is no longer ours.   We are already beyond the point of
refusal.   If we put on the brakes, we are going to crash.
And so we must continue, to improve, to alter, to succeed."[2]
This message is just as valid today as it was in March, 1966.
The mainland Puerto Rican community is here to stay looking
ahead with hope.   What future do Puerto Ricans have on the
United States mainland?   Former Governor Luis Muñoz Marin
of Puerto Rico made this prophecy: "The great engines of
creative energy in people are hope and pride.... If you can
find the touchstones to spur hope and pride you will unleash
their creative capacities and energies, and a new dynamism
will enter into their lives before which even stubborn obstacles will fall."[3]

Notes

1. Wolfe, Thomas. You Can't Go Home Again. New York:
   Harper, 1940, p. 508.

2. Wagenheim, Kal. Puerto Rico: A Profile. New York:
   Praeger, 1971, p. 9.

3. Klopf, Gordon J. and Laster, Israel. Integrating the
   Urban School. New York: Teachers College Press,
   1963.

CHAPTER 11

REMINISCENCES OF
TWO TURNED-ON LIBRARIANS

Lillian López, with Pura Belpré

In 1935, my mother, Eva, came to New York with her
two youngest daughters, Lillian and Elva. Her eldest daughter,
Evelina, had been sent ahead. The family did not travel together because there wasn't enough money for all to travel at
once. My mother's sister, Vicenta, who had come to New York
in 1922, was paying the traveling expenses and with her meager
salary she was willing to help her sister bring up her three
daughters. When we came to New York, the country was in the
midst of a depression and if things were bad on the mainland,
they were worse in Puerto Rico.

Two months after we arrived my mother was able to
get a job at the place where my aunt worked. If it were
known that the two were sisters, my mother would not have
been hired. It was a miserable menial job, but with the
$12.40 a week she earned for six days, eight hours a day,
and sometimes half a day on Sundays, she was able to keep
her family together. When we grew up, Mamí used to tell
us how afraid she had been of losing her job, getting sick,
and of many other fears. But all her actions in dealing with
life showed her to be a brave and courageous woman. She
was not only beautiful physically, but also spiritually. She
gave us her moral strength, her compassion and generosity
towards everyone. We had very little of material things, but
whatever we had she was always willing to share with the less
fortunate. All children were her children. When I look back,
I remember that we were always involved in helping someone
with his problems. Mamí was very curious and interested
in the whole world. She read the newspapers and any books
that she could get her hands on. She always found a little
time to read. She was a woman who was always informed on
what was going on in the world.

During those years when my sisters and I were growing up in Spanish Harlem (El Barrio) the Puerto Rican com-

munity was much smaller. It was easier to know or know
about practically everybody. I remember how proud the community was of the position Pura Belpré had in the Library.
I never met Pura when I went to the neighborhood library,
but my older sister, Evelina, remembers going to her story
hour and she remembers that Pura was so beautiful and
sparkling that all the swains in the community were in love
with her. I did not meet Pura until years later when I became a trainee at the New York Public Library.

My mother's biggest dream was that her three daughters would get their high school diplomas and perhaps college,
and have better jobs than she had had. As we graduated
from high school, we each went to work in an office. Later
on, we all decided we needed more education and we followed
our interests. I was the first one to get a college degree
and a masters. Mami would have been in seventh heaven if
she had lived to see Evelina, her eldest child, get awarded
a doctorate from a Catholic university for her humanitarianism.

When I finished high school, against the advice of my
teachers, counselor, relatives and friends, I went to work instead of going on to college. Everyone who knew me said I
was college material and I should go on with my education.
It was a nice thing to say, but to go to college you need more
than intelligence. You need food, shelter, clothing and money
for books and other expenses. There weren't too many
scholarships available and if there were, I didn't know about
them. I had graduated with an academic diploma which did
not prepare me for anything but to continue my education.
But I was good with figures and I had an excellent memory.
Given the chance, I could learn almost anything. I managed
to get a job in an exclusive men's haberdashery and in a
short time I rose from stock clerk to be head of one of the
departments. While I was very young I had to deal with people who were much older and who had been working there
much longer, but I was able to cope with the situation. It
became a very interesting job for me because with my knowledge of Spanish I was called on frequently to serve as an in-
terpreter and I met many interesting people from all over the
Spanish-speaking world. It also made me very popular with
the sales force because they knew I would help them make the
sales. Wherever I have worked my knowledge of Spanish has
helped me move ahead and get better jobs. I think the best
thing that my mother did for us was that she did not let us
lose our maternal tongue or our identification with our culture

and our community.

While I was doing well at my job, I always felt that I
was missing something, so I began to toy with the idea of
going to college. I knew I would have to work and study part-
time. What finally gave me the push was that men I had
trained were getting better salaries than I was. When I discovered this, I confronted my supervisor with it and he said,
"Well, they are men and they have to support a family. " So
I said, "I am glad that you think they should make more
money because they have to support a family, but I am a woman and I have more responsibilities at the job than they
have, so I should be earning more. " I never got any satisfaction because the company didn't see it the way I saw it.
It was a "man's world" as far as they were concerned, so I
left. I applied at Hunter College, took the college entrance
examination and was accepted. I knew that I would have to
work to support myself, so I enrolled for three courses at
night. I got a job doing bookkeeping. From there on, if a
job interfered with my school schedule, I left it and got another one. As I became more interested in getting my degree, I increased my courses and changed to daytime study
and worked part-time. From general office work I had
worked myself up to bookkeeper, and in college I studied accounting because I thought I would stay in the business field.

When I graduated from Hunter College I didn't have a
clear idea of what I would like to do. I made a list of professions which seemed interesting. They were all in the public service area. I investigated them but I still didn't seem
to find what I wanted. I knew that I needed a Masters degree, but in what?

Most of my life I had used the public library extensively both for recreational and educational material. I used
to say to fellow students when we were using the reference
room on the third floor at 42nd Street that if I ever made
two million dollars I would give one to the Library. So when
I was trying to find the field I should go into, my friends
used to say, "Why don't you become a librarian? You are
always reading, so you should enjoy working in the library. "
And I would answer, "Oh, librarians don't get much pay and
I don't want to continue being poor. "

One day while I was waiting to be interviewed at the
placement office in Hunter College, I looked through the magazine rack and found a tiny pamphlet on librarianship. It

aroused my curiosity, so I visited the Information Desk at the
42nd Street Library, where they gave me the last pamphlet
they had left on becoming a librarian. Someone had used the
pamphlet and cut out most of the information, but I had the
address of the American Library Association. I wrote to
them and I received quite a bit of information. I also wrote
to the Special Libraries Association.

I tackled this interest as if I were going to write a
thesis. I looked at it from all angles, and I found out that
any experience, any interest, is useful in librarianship. You
can specialize in whatever field of knowledge you are interested in, such as art, music, films, education, history, etc.
In the public library you can specialize in serving whatever
age level--adults, young adults, children--you feel best suited
for working with.

Since I knew that besides liking books I liked to be involved with people, I decided I would like to work in a public
library, but I was not sure about the age level I wanted to
specialize in. I liked them all. Through all the information
I had gathered, I found out about the library schools in the
metropolitan area and about the trainee program whereby you
could work in a library while studying either part-time or
full-time. I applied at Columbia University's School of Library Science, and on the same day was scheduled to take
the graduate record examination I applied at the New York
Public Library for a trainee position.

I was afraid that an established and conservative institution like the New York Public Library would not hire me.
My family had always been involved in the community and in
labor movement activities. My last three years of employment had been with Local 1199 and when they had their initial
drive to organize the hospital workers, I had been very much
involved in the strike, not only on work time but also on
volunteer time. I had worked on the material which had to
be printed in Spanish for the recruits and had talked to many
of the recruits to explain the union to them.

My misgivings were unfounded. The person who interviewed me was delighted with my experience and she gave
me the red carpet treatment. She was so excited with my
wanting to become a librarian and work for the New York
Public Library that she called the next person who had to interview me, right while I was there, and raved about my
qualifications. When I had the second interview, this person

was just as delighted with my qualifications and I had the feeling that I would get the position. She said I would have to
wait a while but they would call me, and two weeks later they
did. I was very frank with the person who called and I said
that before I started the new job, I would like to take a short
vacation, since once I started school and the new position I
would not be able to take any time off. She agreed with me
and said that as long as I was ready to start on July 1st it
would be all right. The years since July 1, 1960 have been
thirteen wonderful years, full of varied and exciting experiences. Everything has not been what I would have liked it to
be, but it has certainly been worthwhile. I began working at
the Frances Martin Library, across from the Bronx campus
of New York University. It was a great place to start: the
building was pretty new, with modern architecture, a tremendous book collection, a dedicated and well-trained staff, a
marvelous supervisor and a varied and demanding public.

It wasn't until I began working at the library that I
found out that I should have applied to more than one library
school. It never entered my mind that I could be rejected.
But when I heard the stories of people who had been denied
admission, I began to have my doubts. It was with much
trepidation and anxiety that I waited to hear from Columbia.
If they did not accept me, I would have to apply to another
school and it would mean that I could not start school until
the following semester. As a trainee I was not earning much
and increments depended on being accepted at library school
and how fast I accumulated credits. Columbia waited until
the last possible minute to inform me that I was accepted.
I worked full-time and went to school part-time and I was
permitted to take only six credits. At that rate it would take
me three years to get my degree, so I decided to go to
school during the summer in order to earn the degree in two
years. They were two grueling years, but they were worth
the effort.

As I advanced in school, my responsibilities in the library increased. I learned everything that I could about
working in a library, from the bottom up. I found the work
fascinating and realized that all my previous experience was
useful. In a public library you work with everyone who
comes into the library, regardless of sex, age, religion or
ethnic background. Everyone is welcomed and the variety of
exchange makes the work very exciting. At the beginning, I
thought I would specialize in children's work, so I was able
to gain a good deal of experience working with children and

young adults. When I eventually made my choice, I chose to
work with adults because it was the area which led to advancement quicker and because, if the child is going to get
all the help possible at home, the adults have to be informed
about all the services a library can give. Nowadays, it
doesn't make any difference which group you specialize in;
you can advance as quickly in any specialty. But I have
never regretted my choice--it was the right one for me.

It was while working as a trainee in a children's room
that I met Pura Belpré. I knew of her because some of my
relatives were part of the same social group and because, as
the first Puerto Rican librarian in the New York Public Library, she had made all the Puerto Rican community very
proud of her and was known by everyone. Pura was delighted
to meet me. She thought I would follow in her footsteps, but
I chose a different specialty. She was disappointed, but realized that each one of us has to do what we are best suited
for. Before I continue, I'll let Pura tell her story.

> It was at the Countee Cullen Branch of the New
> York Public Library where I found my profession.
> We had recently arrived in New York. One day my
> younger sister and I set out to find a library where
> she could find material for a book report she had
> to do for her English class at Julia Richman High
> School. A policeman pointed out the way to us.
> As we entered the reading room, I noticed the li-
> brarian, Miss Allen, later Mrs. Latimer, moving
> slowly among the crowded room, helping teenagers.
> As I watched them the thoughts of my friends in
> the island made me feel lonely for the first time.
> I thought, 'If I could do what this lady is doing for
> the rest of my life, I would be the happiest person
> on earth.
>
> That wish was granted through the vision of Ernes-
> tine Rose, the branch librarian who, noticing a
> 'Bodega' (grocery store) and a 'Barbería' (barber
> shop) suddenly appearing in the community, thought
> that the best thing to do was to secure the services
> of a Spanish-speaking assistant. One of the read-
> ers at the branch was a Puerto Rican teacher. To
> him she confided her thoughts. He said, 'I have
> just the person you need. ' So home he came to of-
> fer the job to my recently married sister. 'No, '
> said her husband, 'My wife is not going to work. '

My sister said to me, 'Why don't you go and try it.
You might like it. ' So I did, liked it, and a wonderful new world opened for me: reading clubs,
story telling, picture book hours.

Training through the branches gave me the grand
opportunity, not only to achieve craftsmanship but,
what was much better, meet the people who made
the melting pot of America.   At that time the New
York Public Library had its own library school.
So there I went for further training.   There were
no seminars at that time, the library assistants
progressed by a series of examinations for 1st,
2nd and 3rd grade positions.   I was already a second grade assistant when I entered the library
school.   It was here where I wrote my first Puerto
Rican folktale, for an assignment in a story telling
course.   Years after that a former library school
classmate, while freelancing, had a request for a
manuscript similar to the Peter Rabbit books.   The
request was from Frederick Warne.   She asked me
for my manuscript of Perez and Martina.   The
President had the vision and courage, considering
that by America's standards in 1932 it did not have
a happy ending, to publish it.   It has been a popular book ever since, and is now available in Spanish, too.

Library vision and effort to serve the Spanish-
speaking community settling in southwest Harlem
brought me from Seward Park to the 115th Street
branch as first assistant to Maria Cimino and Spanish assistant to the branch librarian.   It was like
a renaissance of Latin American life centered
around the library.   The pressure of adult work
and children's work made it necessary to decide
which of the two services I preferred.   I chose
children's work, and a second Puerto Rican, this
time a high school teacher, entered the library system.   The 115th Street branch became the cultural
center for the Latin American community, the largest at that time in the city of New York.

Reading clubs, conferences and book lists were all
developed in the adult department, while reading,
dramatics, and puppetry clubs flourished in the
children's room.   Spanish story hours at the branch

and at community centers opened doors to a Spanish
community to whom library service had been completely unknown. The feast of the 'Three Kings'
Day, January 6th, became a yearly celebration.

Communities have a way of changing, and the Latin
community was no exception. In order to provide
better service, I was transferred to branches in the
neighborhood where they settled. The last branch
I was assigned to was Aguilar, where the Puerto
Ricans were outnumbering the once Italian residents.
Casita Maria, Union settlement, Boy's Clubs were
places where library programs were arranged for
children, mothers' clubs, and staff members. Summer story hours in parks, play streets and community centers, in the Museum of the City of New
York and churches kept the staff busy. The adult
room developed a magnificent Spanish book collection, while the children's room began a Spanish
reference collection which is still in existence.
Aguilar had been noted for its dramatic clubs for
children; now Spanish clubs as well as puppetry
clubs developed. The programs were given for the
children and parents as well as for the community
in general.

In 1943, I got married, took a year's leave to
travel with my husband, Clarence Cameron White,
musicologist, violinist and composer. In 1945 I resigned to continue traveling. In between, I began
to write the Puerto Rican folktales that, through
the vision of Anne Carroll Moore and Mary Gould
Davis, I had been permitted to tell both in English
and Spanish provided I told the children the stories
might someday become a book. The Tiger and the
Rabbit and Other Tales fulfilled that promise.

In 1961, upon the death of my husband, the New
York Public Library wrote to ask if I was going to
return to Puerto Rico, or would work here, and if
the latter, to give them the first chance. I returned to work part-time as Spanish children's specialist, working from the Office of Children's Services. In that position I resumed the work I used
to do at the branches, only now I did it all over
Manhattan and the Bronx. It was in reality a library special project, which years later was to be-

come the springboard for the South Bronx Project.

With the birth of the South Bronx Project, I became
one of its children's specialists, under the administration of Lillian López, and surrounded by the enthusiasm of a dedicated staff. The library went
out to meet a neighborhood in great need of what
the Project had to offer. The sudden interest in
bilingualism opened new doors and found the Project ready. Story telling in Spanish and in English
at day care centers, mini-seminars for PTA groups
and paraprofessionals, puppet shows and talks to
school librarians at staff meetings are among the
many programs the Project carries out in the South
Bronx. Time for retiring caught up with me, but
a month later I was back at the South Bronx Project to conduct a puppetry workshop for the puppet
theater we had ordered for the Project. The staff
took to the South Bronx, giving puppet shows in libraries, schools, streets, community centers, empty lots and churches. All programs were bilingual.
Story telling with puppets at day care centers is a
special feature and a popular request. My work
for the Project since I retired is one day a week,
or seven hours.

To have lived long enough to see the pioneering library work flourish into a full bilingual library project is something to behold. To see it become a
permanent part of the library system would be the
complete fulfillment of a dream.

Before I take up where Pura left off, let me continue
with the development of my career. As soon as I graduated
from Columbia, I was assigned as acting assistant branch librarian to Miss Hisako Yamashita, the branch librarian at
the Sedgwick Library. In the two years I had worked in the
library, I had not wasted my time. I had learned all I could.
It had been my fortunate experience to have worked with
supervisors who cared and who wanted me to become an excellent librarian and to advance as rapidly as possible in my
career. When I started working at Sedgwick, Miss Yamashita asked me to make a list of all the duties I had performed in the library. When she saw the list she said,
"Well, it looks as if the only thing you haven't done is run
your own branch." We worked together for two years and
she did everything possible to give me supervisory experience.

A year after graduation, having completed the necessary in-
service seminars and because I had worked two years as a
full-time trainee, I was promoted to senior librarian, which
meant I was no longer "acting" but actually assistant branch
librarian. I had also specialized in adult work.

After two years at Sedgwick I thought I should go to
a larger branch where I would be able to work more with the
adults and be able to do some programming. The only programs I was able to schedule at Sedgwick had been reading
aloud to the pre-school children. I applied for a position at
the Fordham Library Center where I was accepted for the
position of assistant branch librarian. Since this is a library
center, it has a large staff with a principal librarian in
charge, a supervising librarian as the first assistant, and a
senior adult specialist as the second assistant; which meant
I was in charge when the two top people were out. At the
time it seemed to me that whenever there was a problem I
was in charge. This was the largest library I had worked
in and the biggest staff which sometimes was under my supervision. It was not like the small and large neighborhood
branches where I had cut my teeth; it was an experience that
would prepare me for the future. I enjoyed working with the
public and, as in every branch that I worked in, my Spanish
was very useful. When Spanish-speaking residents came in
and met with difficulty because they didn't speak English, I
was always there to assure them that they did not need to
feel ashamed because of their lack of English when they spoke
a beautiful language which they had every right to be proud
of. Before coming to Fordham, whenever I worked in the
children's room and because of readers' needs, I would switch
from English to Spanish. The children would be fascinated
and they would follow me around to see how many times I
would change from Spanish to English or vice versa. How
proud and happy the Spanish-speaking children were!

Working in another children's room, I remember Cerita,
a black child who used to come to the Morrisania library two
or three times a week. One day she ran from one end of the
room to the other where I was helping some children. Her
beautiful eyes flashing, keeping back those tears which were
very close to overflowing, she put her hand in mine and said,
"Miss López, I know that you do not believe what they are
accusing me of." The words she used were not important,
what I remember was the way she put her hand in mine. She
was confident that I was a friend and that I would believe
what she said. It seemed that the clerks at the desk ac-

cused her of keeping some books out too long. This, I knew, could not be true. This child was always haunting me for books. She was always in the library, bringing books back and taking others out. So I explained to the clerks that there must be some mistake.

The two words, love and trust, are among the most beautiful in the English language. When you serve with sincerity, people are going to trust you regardless of your ethnic background. A child can always tell when you are sincere.

I have advanced very quickly in my career. Whenever I was due for a promotion, I got it. I was very lucky with my supervisors. They always took an interest in my career and they were quick to point out to me when an in-service seminar was being offered and that I should apply and not leave it for later.

From the Fordham Library Center I want to the Kingsbridge Library as the assistant branch librarian. This is a busy large neighborhood branch in the Riverdale area of the Bronx. Here, again, was a different type of public from that using the other libraries where I had worked. At this branch, because the branch librarian had many outside activities connected with library work, I found that I was in charge most of the time. My previous experience was very helpful in this situation. The public was demanding, some snobbish and some a delight to serve. It was a book-oriented public. As well-to-do as this neighborhood was, I had school classes of adults who were learning English. Many of those in the class were servants, but there were also professionals who had to learn English so that they could pursue their careers. While at Kingsbridge I completed my in-service seminar for supervising librarian. I could not apply for a position for supervisor right away because I did not have all the service time that was required, so my name did not go on the eligibility list for supervisor. When my previous supervisor, Miss Phyllis Tinkler, saw the list, she was very upset because my name wasn't there. As soon as I called her and explained what the problem was she felt better. When I became eligible, I applied for the position at the Hamilton Grange branch, a library in Central Harlem. This branch was unlike any place that I had worked in so far. I chose it because I had lived in Spanish Harlem for many years and I thought I would enjoy working in Harlem. I did; the few months I spent in Hamilton Grange were very happy and re-

warding months. The public liked me and I liked them.   I
also had a very cooperative and understanding staff.

When Pura heard that I had been made supervising librarian, she was very happy.   She kept telling everyone,
"Oh! She is the first Puerto Rican to advance to such a high
position in the New York Public Library. "

From that position I became the Administrator of the
South Bronx Project.   This position was equivalent to principal librarian, and after five and a half years with the Project
I moved on to become Coordinator of Special Services for the
New York Public Library.   From what Pura has said and
what I have found out, we still need many more Puerto Ricans and other Spanish-speaking librarians, if we are to meet
the needs of our people for adequate library service.

The New York Public Library has tried to fill this
need, first by having Pura Belpré, and then by instituting the
South Bronx Project, a program directed at the needs of the
Spanish-speaking community in the South Bronx.   The aims
have been to establish communication with the community,
make the community aware of library services, and buy relevant material for nine branch libraries in the South Bronx.
The material is in Spanish and English or is bilingual.   It
can be in book form, pamphlets, newspapers, magazines,
records, films, posters, or cassettes.   In whatever form or
language it comes, we buy it if it meets the needs of the
community.   We give all types of programs in which the community is interested, and they take place where groups meet.
We help the group keep its cultural pride and identity.   The
success of the program is due to the fact that a Puerto Rican
librarian was given a chance to develop it.   All Project staff
is bilingual.

A position was created where a non-librarian with a
B. A. and community experience would work part of the day
in the community, taking the library outside its walls.   This
program involves nine branch libraries in the Bronx where a
large number of Puerto Ricans and other Spanish-speaking
people live.   The community Liaison Assistant, as this position is called, added a new dimension to the library and it
brought a great deal of help and joy to our sadly over-looked
community.   Using the experience that Pura Belpré had gained
in working with children in Harlem and the Bronx, we expanded services to include all age groups from 0-99, all ethnic groups in the community, and all kinds of groups such as

schools, both private and public, from elementary through
the university, religious groups, civic, social, political, and
parents' groups. Programs in English or Spanish, or bilingual programs, are given both in and outside the library,
in playgrounds, schools, empty lots, streets, sidewalks,
parks, community centers, churches--anywhere where a group
meets, the Project travels to it. We do a great deal of work
with the day care centers, the headstart groups and the senior citizens; we present programs on story telling, reading
aloud, puppet shows, films, book talks, music, poetry, drama,
dance, consumer education, information on narcotics, venere-
al diseases, prenatal care, family planning; and programs
dealing with the cultural heritage of Puerto Ricans and other
Spanish-speaking groups. We have cooperated and collaborated
with all groups in the community and have either done programs alone or with other groups. The family program, built
around a significant event in our history, with a speaker,
poetry and music, has proven to be very popular. Local
talent has been very useful for our programming.

The emphasis is on the Spanish-speaking but the community is mixed, so we help whoever needs it--Black, Jew,
Irish, Italian or Greek, anyone from any country, of any
race, religion or sex. The staff works with any group in the
community regardless of its affiliations, political, social,
civic, religious, educational, etc.

People in the ghetto are not supposed to care about
much beyond their own problems. Commedia dell'Arte, performed by a group of New York University students, was as
well received as a play by the Soul and Latin theater group
or a play in Spanish by the Spanish players. The Project
staff not only tries to help people understand their lives better; it also tries to broaden their horizons by not underes-
timating their ability to appreciate the better things in life.
That's why we try to offer a variety of programs with all the
arts represented. This is a federally funded project. We
realize that the whole city needs the services we have been
offering in the South Bronx. That's why an Office of Special
Services was created to coordinate all the specially federally
funded programs under the supervision of one person. This
is now my responsibility.

From reading Pura Belpré's comments it is clear that
she has been very happy in her library career. In helping
and serving our people and others with whom she comes in
contact, she has found satisfaction and the reward of knowing

that she has given a little happiness and hope to others.
Through the library she has spread the knowledge of our folktales and folklore.

I have also found my library career fulfilling, satisfying and rewarding but I will not be completely satisfied or
have my dream fulfilled until there is a library where any
Puerto Rican or other Spanish-speaking person can go and
find whatever information he needs in Spanish, and a Spanish-
speaking staff who can take care of his needs.

Pura, I, and all the others who have worked on the
Project have contributed a little bit to our community, but we
realize that there is so much more to be done. In any field
of public service we have to be thoroughly involved, and it
is no less so in the library field. Such total involvement and
the opportunity to see that the community gets its due have
made all the work, frustrations and sacrifices worth the
struggle. I have found satisfaction in meeting the challenges
of the past and I am ready to meet the challenges of the future. I hope that more Puerto Ricans and Hispanic individuals will follow Pura and me in selecting librarianship as a
career.

CHAPTER 12

LIBRARY SERVICE TO PUERTO RICANS:
AN OVERVIEW

José A. Betancourt

Libraries under the Spanish Government

Books for the people were considered by the Spanish colonial authorities to be akin to inflammable or explosive substances which it was not safe to introduce freely. From their point of view they were right, and so books and printing materials were subjected to the payment of high import duties and a series of annoying formalities, among which passing the political and ecclesiastical censors was the most formidable.

The result among the poor classes of natives was complete illiteracy. A pall of profound ignorance hung over the island and, although the revival of letters in the seventeenth century was taking place in Western Europe, no part of this was permitted to reach the Spanish colonies. The ruling class, every one of whom came from the Peninsula, kept what books they possessed to themselves. All learning, except such as it was considered safe to import, was forbidden to the people. Under these conditions, it is not unexpected that the idea of founding public libraries did not germinate in the minds of the more intelligent among the Puerto Ricans until the middle of the nineteenth century; although other colonies that had left the guidance of the mother country had progressed further intellectually.

There were, however, in the capital, collegiate libraries as early as the sixteenth century. The first of these was founded by the Dominican friars in their convent; it contained works on art, literature, and theology. The next was founded in the episcopal palace by Bishop Don Bernardo de Valbuena, poet and author of a pastoral novel entitled The Golden Age. The library, together with that of the Dominicans, and the respective episcopal and conventual archives

97

were burned by the Hollanders during the siege of San Juan
in 1625. In 1832, Bishop Pedro Gutierrez de Coz founded
the San Juan Conciliar Seminary, establishing a library in
connection with it; this library remained functioning up to
around 1900.

A library of a semi-public character was founded by
royal order on June 19, 1831. This was shortly after the
installation of the Audencia in San Juan. It was a large and
valuable collection of books on juridical subjects which remained under the care of a salaried librarian until 1899, by
which time it was amalgamated with the library of the college
of lawyers--itself a rich collection of works on jurisprudence,
but for the exclusive use of professional men. The years
1830-1850 were a period of intellectual activity in Puerto Rico.
The Spanish governor, Juan de la Pezuela, toward the close
of his term of government, founded the Royal Academy of
Belles Lettres, an institution of literary and pedagogical character, with the functions of a normal school. This academy
had a modest library. By 1860 the school was closed and
the library passed into the possession of the Economic Society
of Friends of the Country. This, and the library of the
Royal Academy, which the Society had also acquired, formed
a small but excellent nucleus, and with the income from the
public subscription of 1884, it was able to stock its library
with many of the best standard works of the time in Spanish
and French. Thus was opened to Puerto Ricans of all classes
the door of the first long wished-for public library.

From the time it was opened until the beginning of the
war--1889, when it was closed--this was a center of enlightenment for the laboring classes of the capital. During the
transition period, the books were transferred from one local-
ity to another and in the process the best works disappeared.
The island's first civil governor, Charles H. Allen, at the
suggestion of the Commissioner of Education, rescued the remainder and made them the nucleus of the first American
Free Library.

Another Puerto Rican public library was opened by
Don Ramon Santaella in 1880, in the basement of the Town
Hall. It began with 400 volumes. In 1876, the Puerto Rican
Atheneum Library was established. Its collection of books,
consisting mainly of Spanish and French literature, was an
important one, both in number and quality. It was enriched
later on by the accession of books from the library of the extinct Society of Friends of the Country. The library was

opened only to members of the Atheneum and their friends.

Another library with a small select collection was the one at the Casino Español, founded in 1871. It had a comfortable reading room and its collection of books and periodicals, it was said, was one of the richest and most varied in the island. The Spanish Public Works Department possessed another valuable collection of books, mostly on technical and scientific subjects. Books from other libraries, in other than technical subjects, were added to the collection, bringing the total to 1,544 volumes, most in excellent condition.

Besides these libraries of public and collegiate character, there were some private collections of books in the principal towns of the island. One of the most important was that of Don Fernández Juncos of San Juan. His collection contained 15,000 volumes, including classic works, preceptive literature, and works on social and economic sciences.

The opening of the first library of public character in the capital brought a desire for intellectual improvement throughout the island. The municipality of Ponce founded a library in 1894 which contained 809 bound volumes and 669 pamphlets in English, German, French and Spanish, many of them duplicates. There was a municipal appropriation of 350 pesos yearly for library purposes, but it was stopped in 1898. The other municipality feeling the need of a library was Mayagüez. Here the public library was founded in 1872. It contained over 5,000 volumes and had a small archeological and natural history museum attached to it. Other small towns throughout the island followed the example of the big cities and established reading rooms to meet the intellectual needs that were arising.

Libraries under The American Government

After the American occupation in 1898, four more public libraries were established. Two were exclusively Spanish: one of these was the Circulating Scholastic Library of Yauco, established a month later under the auspices of a citizen of the town. Of the other two libraries, one was largely English--The Pedagogical Library, established under the auspices of the Commissioner of Education; the other, the San Juan Free Library, to which Mr. Andrew Carnegie gave $100,000, was polyglot.

In 1903 the Insular Library was established in San Juan. The name of this institution was changed officially to Carnegie Library, it was transferred to the building given to the people of Puerto Rico by the Carnegie Foundation of the United States. The library was administered by a board of trustees appointed by the Governor of Puerto Rico with the approval of the Senate. In 1940, with the authorization of the Legislative Assembly, the Biblioteca Hostos (Hostos Library) was established in Santurce. In 1949 the Agripino Roig Library was opened in Humacao, and in 1948, the Bookmobile Library (Biblioteca Rodante de San Juan) was established.

With the reorganization of the government in 1950, the board of trustees of the Carnegie Library was eliminated and the functions of the library were transferred to the Secretary of Public Instruction of Puerto Rico. From that time until now, library services in Puerto Rico have been under the Department of Public Education.

Public Libraries After 1950

It was in 1956 that library services within the Department of Education were officially established. After 1956, the number of bookmobiles was increased to eight and other libraries had been opened in different towns of the island. Another development taking place at this time was the establishment of libraries in public housing. But this division of the Department of Education was not only concerned with public libraries; it also offered help to institutions in matters concerning library service.

Besides bookmobile service to towns where libraries are not established, the public library administration has a system to serve those parts of the country which the bookmobile cannot reach. This program is called "Biblioteca Rural Viajera" (Rural Traveling Library). Specially made wooden boxes are sent to different communities. These boxes, when opened, form the shelves of the library. Each collection of this kind contains 100 to 150 volumes. All the books are classified and the readers are provided with a catalog. The library is installed in the house of the person in charge of the "library," in community centers, or in the schools of the community. The person in charge of each unit is not a librarian but an interested resident of the community who is trained to serve the people using these libraries. As of 1961, there were 189 of these libraries.

By 1961 there were seven public libraries serving in
Puerto Rico: 1. Biblioteca Carnegie; 2. Biblioteca Eugenio
María De Hostos; 3. Biblioteca Agripino Roig; 4. Biblioteca
Público-Escolar de la Escuela Superior Central; 5. Biblioteca
Pública de Viequez; 6. Biblioteca Pública de Orocovis; 7.
Biblioteca Pública de Jayuya. In the period covering the
years 1959-1960 these libraries circulated 85,885 volumes.
The acquisitions figure for the same period was 48,764 vol-
umes.

The University Libraries

The main library of the University of Puerto Rico contains more than 650,000 volumes. Over 30,000 volumes are
in the open stacks and the Reserve Section. The library
also has a special collection for Puerto Rican Literature (La
Colección Puertorriqueña), which includes more than 40,000
items on Puerto Rico. The Zenobia and Juan Ramón Jimenez
Room, another important collection in the library, contains
books, periodicals, manuscripts, furniture and personal objects donated to the library by the Spanish poet Juan Ramón
Jimenez. Of special interest are the Nobel Prize Medal for
Liberature and the Diploma awarded to the poet in 1956.

Besides the main library there are five departmental
libraries serving the main campus: the Library of the Faculty of Natural Sciences; the Social Sciences Library; the Phar-
macy Library; the Library of the College of Law; and the
Gerardo Sellés Solás Memorial Collection serving the School
of Education. As part of the University of Puerto Rico there
are two other campuses in which the Library of the School of
Medicine and the Library of the College of Agriculture and
Mechanical Arts are located.

Biblioteca Regional Del Caribe Y Norte-Sur

This library started in 1946 as the library of the Caribbean Commission located in Trinidad. In 1961 the commission was dissolved and the Organization for the Caribbean was
created. This new organization had its headquarters in Puerto Rico along with the Regional Library for the Caribbean.
In 1965 the organization stopped functioning. It was decided
that the library would stay as a unit serving the Caribbean,
and the government of Puerto Rico decided to keep the library
on the island. During 1965-1971 the library was administered

by the Economic Development Corporation of the Caribbean.
After 1971 it came under the Centro Norte-Sur, an agency of
the Government of Puerto Rico under the Department of State.

Libraries Servicing Puerto Ricans in New York City

Libraries in New York City are very much involved in
the community and they are constantly programming to meet
the demands and expectations of the people they serve. The
main goal is to bring to Puerto Rican readers the enormous
library resources which are sometimes unknown to many of
them. At the Queens Borough Public Library, evening lectures and tours are offered to groups that are not familiar
with the library, especially Spanish-speaking people in the
Borough. After the lectures, many became part of the library community. The New York Public Library regularly
publishes bibliographies to help the Spanish-speaking reader,
such as Libros en Español; An Annotated List of Children's
Books in Spanish. Another bibliography is Puerto Rico;
Puerto Rican Authors--a Sampling of Books Available in Spanish.

The libraries of The City University are also aware of
the need for special programs and acquisitions to meet the
constantly growing demands of the Spanish-speaking community.
In 1970 the Open Admissions Program started in The City University brought to its libraries and librarians a true challenge. Under this program, students who previously could
not come to college will now find a place in one of the colleges of the University. The Open Admissions student will
come into college, most likely, with a weaker high school
record and with an over-all education not as good as the top
students of high schools in the City. Open Admissions has
brought into The City University of New York the Puerto Rican who could not otherwise afford an education. To meet
this challenge, libraries throughout the University have initiated special orientation classes, individual contacts with interested students, and credit courses in library techniques
to welcome the non-library-oriented student and to make his
adjustment to college a little bit easier.

The best example of a higher concentration of Puerto
Ricans in a particular college within The City University is
Eugenio Maria de Hostos Community College in the South
Bronx. Its student body is roughly 40 percent Puerto Ricans,
40 percent Blacks and 20 percent other ethnic groups. The

college concentrates on health careers and offers a high percentage of its courses in Spanish and English. This bilingual
education is a unique characteristic of Hostos and requires
special attention from the library, particularly in the acquisition of materials. When other CUNY colleges usually do not
purchase non-fiction in Spanish, Hostos has to purchase in
both languages for all subjects. The most rewarding effort
comes from the instruction of library techniques to students
who have not had much access to libraries in the past. Lectures have been instituted on use of the library, both in Spanish and English. These lectures and personal contacts have
brought the student into the library, and every day more and
more students are making use of its resources. Librarians
are always available to individual students who may have special needs. Because Hostos serves such a large number of
Puerto Rican students and because the curriculum in Puerto
Rican Studies is quite extensive, the library's policy is to
purchase two copies of all Puerto Rican publications. This,
of course, includes papers from the Island. The Puerto Rican Collection of the Hostos College is one of the best in The
City University.

CHAPTER 13

THE POLICE AS VIEWED BY
NEW YORK CITY PUERTO RICANS

John Vazquez and Charles Bahn

An attitude is an orientation or a predisposition to behave in a particular way towards a person, situation, object
or idea. Generally speaking, attitudes are likes and dislikes,
attractions and repulsions, interests and apathies.

In sociological terms, an attitude is a state of mind
toward a social object and also a concrete representation of
culture.

A common feature in definitions of the term attitude
is preparation or readiness for a response. [1] In other words,
an attitude predisposes the individual to respond and determines the direction that response will take. An attitude is
not a behavior, but a precondition of behavior.

It is through experiences that attitudes are formed and
therefore it is through experiences that they are changed. It
is experiences that tend to direct an individual towards or
away from certain classes of objects. Human beings often
reflect their attitudes in the forms of opinions, because opinions are a verbal expression of attitudes. [2]

The Puerto Rican and the police attitudes are based in
part on each group's experience with the other. For example,
the Puerto Rican's attitude is influenced by a cultural view
that the policeman's job is to be responsible for controlling
criminality. When the uniformed officer begins to move people from one place in the street to another, he therefore en-
genders hostility.

Niederhoffer describes a police attitude that is sometimes manifested in the movement of people on the street.
He states that an "anti-intraception attitude is an attitude
which easily leads to a devaluation of the human and an over-

104

evaluation of the physical object: when it is most extreme, human beings are looked upon as if they were physical objects to be coldly manipulated. "[3] In other words, the human beings become cattle to be moved from one location to another by a herder or cowboy (policeman).

In the handling of people on the street, of course, the police actually require the cooperation and respect of the citizenry. [4] In the ghetto, the policeman does not have them.

Bayley and Mendelsohn found that even though minority group members call for assistance as frequently as the dominant group, minority members are less likely than the dominant group to talk over a problem with the police. In fact, the study revealed that among Denver's two minority communities (both in poor contact with the police), the Spanish-speaking related less to the police than the Blacks, despite arrest figures which demonstrate that a larger proportion of the Blacks and Spanish-named population was in trouble with the police than were members of the dominant community. The authors found that minority group members have more difficulties that could be discussed with the police; however, proportionally fewer do so. [5] What Bayley and Mendelsohn conclude is that, regardless of the number of contacts, the policeman is viewed as an alien and not as an integral part of the minority group community. In urban America today, the policeman is seen as a symbol of coercive authority and this perception is highly magnified by the minority group member.

Since police officers are human beings, and contemporary urban society is what it is, they are also likely to have been influenced by prevailing patterns of prejudice. Most policemen are white and lower middle class; they have had few close associations with minority group members and have difficulty in telling specific minority sub-groups apart. This puts a burden not only on the police but on minority group members. No one likes to be questioned or suspected by the police, especially a minority group member, and if a policeman has difficulty in recognizing significant differences, it is likely that innocent people may be perceived as suspects.

In addition to those barriers to harmonious relationship between the policeman and the Puerto Rican that derive from realistic specific experiences, there are other, more subtle factors also at work. The police, as the visible symbols of the larger society and its regulatory machinery, bear

the brunt of all of the frustration, anger, and pain caused by
the inadequacies and inefficiencies of the full range of governmental agencies. Thus, the migrant who is bilked by a dishonest storekeeper or swindled by an exploitative employer
may see the policeman as an accomplice to these injustices.
It is easier to focus anger and bad feeling on the policeman
because he dispenses no rewards and is identifiable and visible.   The full range of suppressed and repressed hostility
against society that must accompany poverty and dependence
are also often focused on the policeman.

In the studies of the "Personality in the Depression, "
Runquist and Sletto used a scale which measured attitudes towards the law.   They ascertained that a respondent's negative attitude towards the law was closely related to an over-
all poor adjustment to his social situation.   It was also found
that there was a positive correlation between poor or negative
attitudes towards the law and such conditions as a broken
home, unemployment, and recent migration to the city.   The
latter is closely related to the Puerto Rican in New York
City ghettos. [6]   The reliability and validity of the preceding
findings are substantiated by those of Westley and Gauntly in
which minority status was found to have a probable correlation with an unfavorable attitude towards the police. [7]

Since members of a culture share common experiences,
histories, and destinies, they provide grounds for the development of attitudes that are characteristic of the culture.   New
York Puerto Ricans share street encounters with police in
their neighborhoods, as well as a host of other factors of
common destiny, centering around problems of unemployment,
poverty and dependence.   Therefore, the first step in discussing perceptions is to identify the attitudes that derive
from these commonalities.

What are the significant elements of common history
and destiny of New York Puerto Ricans?   As described above,
they come primarily from rural backgrounds, have a lower
median age, are less educated, are relegated to the bottom
of the economic ladder and have a larger proportion of women than men in their population.   Each of the demographic
variables can be presumed to shape common experiences that
give rise to shared attitudes.

Rural background fosters negative attitudes in two
ways.   The first is that unfamiliarity with urban life makes
for inappropriate behavior and expectations with regard to the

police.   The second is that the difficulties and frustrations
of adjustment to another culture are exacerbated by the task
of adjustment to urban life.   Repressed hostility is therefore
more likely to surface than in the case of an urban-born migrant better able to cope with the city.

        Younger Puerto Ricans have greater contact with the
police, in school and on the street (where they spend their
free and leisure hours), and at the same time they are taught
to expect fair treatment.   However, police often must inter-
fere with some control and keep recreational activities in
check.

        Because of the mutually negative perceptions and mis-
perceptions of the Puerto Rican and the police, additional
contact serves to buttress negative attitudes.   Consequently,
with increased assimilation (often accompanied by rising expectations), perceptions of the police become increasingly
negative.   From these factors, then, we can suggest the following hypotheses to be tested: (1) a rural-born Puerto Rican is more negative toward the police than an urban-born
Puerto Rican; (2) a younger Puerto Rican is more negative
towards the police than an older Puerto Rican; and (3) the
perception of the police by the Puerto Rican becomes more
negative with acculturation and approximate assimilation.   Of
course, being Puerto Rican, in and of itself, does not mean
automatic negativism towards the police.   The assumption is
that an individual Puerto Rican subject to given conditions
will respond to those conditions.   In other words, the Puerto
Rican is influenced by his surroundings and by his background.

Methods and Procedures

        The instruments identified to measure perception and
attitudes, in testing the preceding hypotheses, were the Thematic Apperception Test (TAT), the Semantic Differential (SD),
and a structured interview (SI).

        The TAT materials developed for this study consisted
of four sheets containing semi-structured ambiguous pictures
in black and white.   These pictures depicted various scenes
in which some type of interaction between a policeman and
another is suggested.   The subjects were asked to make up
a story for each picture, telling what led up to the event
shown in the picture; to describe what was happening at the
moment and what were the characters' feeling and thinking;

and finally, giving the outcome.

Following the administration of the Thematic Apperception Test, the Semantic Differential was administered.
The Semantic Differential, as indicated above, is a standardized, quantified method for measuring the connotations of a
given concept for the individual. Every concept is ranked on
a 7-point scale as being more closely related to one or the
other of a pair of opposites, e.g., 1 = negative, 4 = neutral
or ambivalent, and 7 = positive. For every concept a series
of bi-polar adjectives are employed. In this study a series
of 24 bi-polar adjectives were used covering three major factors: evaluative, good-bad; potency or strength, strong-weak,
large-small; and activity, fast-slow, sharp-dull. The concept
here used was "the policeman." It should be noted that the
evaluative factor is often the most conspicuous and accounts
for the largest percentage of total variance. [8]

The final instrument administered was the structured
interview. A series of six open-ended questions on police-
community relationships were asked as they related to the
Puerto Rican community in New York City.

Sample Definition

The instruments described were administered to a
sample of 323 New York City Puerto Ricans from four of the
five boroughs, with the major concentration from the three
boroughs most heavily populated by Puerto Ricans; Brooklyn,
the Bronx, and Manhattan. The fourth borough represented
was Queens. In 1966 the Public Health Service estimated
that New York City had a population 841,000 (11.2 of the
total population) Puerto Ricans and they were distributed as
follows: Manhattan 186,000 (12.5 percent); the Bronx 305,000
(23.5 percent); Brooklyn 319,500 (12.5 percent); Queens and
Richmond had insufficient data. [9] The Public Health Service
estimates that in 1966 the median age for all Puerto Ricans
in New York City was 19.1; the males equaled 17.4, and the
females 21.5. [10] It should be noted that the bulk of the Puerto Rican population is in this segment.

As can be noted, the proportions of the age groups in
the sample do not correspond to those in the population as
indicated by the Population Health Survey. This discrepancy
is due to the fact that the sample sources, Puerto Rican organizations, are comprised primarily of individuals in the

TABLE I

Age Groups in Population
and in Study Sample*

	# in Pop.	(%)	# in Sample	(%)
5 - 14	228.0	31.9	49	15.4
15 - 24	150.0	21.0	150	47.0
25 - 44	210.5	29.5	84	26
45 - 64	101.0	14.2	36	11
64 +	23.5	03.4	0	0
	713	100%	319	

*All numbers are in the thousands

middle age brackets, with a heavy concentration in the 15-24
age category. Thus, sample proportions are more in agreement with the current estimates of the median age of the
Puerto Rican population in New York City.

To obtain the sample for the study, a list was partially developed, and partially obtained from the anti-poverty
agency known as the Puerto Rican Community Development
Project, which supplied a list of Puerto Rican organizations
presently operating throughout the city. The other half of the
list was developed by the investigator, who has been working
within the Puerto Rican Community for more than six years.
From the final list, organizations throughout New York City
were contacted and group interviews were administered during
a two and one-half month period.

Overall Findings

Data for the sample of 323 New York City Puerto Ricans was treated in terms of five variables: sex, age, employment status, education, and major residence.

FINDINGS

MEAN TEST SCORES BY GROUPS

Variable	Thematic Apperception Test	Semantic Differential	Structured Interview
Sex			
Male	4.03	101.18	9.73
Female	2.87	107	10.28
t	2.32*	2.09*	1.96*
Age			
5 - 14	3.33	114.53	10.92
15 - 24	2.91	104.81	9.67
25 - 44	3.04	98.61	10.07
45 - 64	3.58	105.94	10.67
Employment			
Unemployed	3.22	108.82	10.38
Employed	3.51	90.89	8.81
t	not significant	4.28**	5.17**
Education			
0 - 6	4.30	105.75	10.76
7 - 9	2.02	106.81	9.99
10 - 12	3.89	104.68	9.84
F significant at the .01 level	NO	YES	YES

Major Residence   No significant difference

Discussion

The test results revealed that Puerto Rican females viewed the police in New York City more positively than Puerto Rican males. Those in the 5-14 and 45-64 year old groups were more positive in their perception of the police than those in the 15-24 and 25-44 year old groups. An unanticipated finding was that the unemployed Puerto Rican perceived the police in a more positive light than did the employed Puerto Rican. The findings also revealed that those with a limited formal education were more positive towards police than those with a higher grade of formal education completed. Those with an 0-6th grade education were more positive than those with a 7-9th or 10-11th year high school education. It was ascertained that the major residence variable had no bearing on the Puerto Rican's perception of the police in New York City.

Four of the variables tested revealed significant findings. The sex variable findings indicated that perception of police by men were more negative than were those of women, as measured by the semantic differential and the structured interview. However, in terms of Thematic Apperception Test results, males were more positive. This positive male reaction to the TAT pictures might be attributed to the fact that the pictures were primarily composed of males. The identification factor may well have influenced subjects to respond positively to the events illustrated. Their reaction might represent a fear of being labeled "bad." Note that all the subjects are members of a minority group (Puerto Ricans) and have all the group attributes. Among these attributes are feelings of oppression and inferiority. [11]

The Semantic Differential and structured interview may be less restricting and threatening than the TAT. Both tests permit the subject to answer with a degree of objectivity, which might account for the men's negative response on the TAT. On the other hand, the women's positive responses may be attributed to other factors. For example, women view policemen as authoritative and protective. (This is particularly true because of women's fears.) As a protective instrument of society the policeman is expected to either allay or alleviate fears. If we assume that females have more fears than males, it follows that they have more positive views of the police role.

Pressey and Kuhlen noted that certain fears are more

characteristic of females than males. They stipulated that
with increased age these fears decreased more rapidly for
males than females, and that throughout the life-cycle female
fears tend to increase. Some of these fears are directly related to the policeman on the street, i. e. , "going down a
dark street, being followed on the street, noises in the night,
etc. " Note that these fears can be allayed or alleviated by
an officer of the law. [12]

We can infer that the Puerto Rican female's fears are
somewhat more intensive. Whether first or second generation, her initial socialization process has been in a Puerto
Rican home. Coming from an island which is still primarily
rural does not allow for rapid urban acculturation. The
Puerto Rican female has been primarily socialized as a domestic, provincialized person; not as an active participant in
the community. In New York City, life is primarily secular
and urban. It is a port of entry and an industrial, commercial center. More social interaction can occur in a super-
market aisle than in an entire small town in Puerto Rico.
Puerto Rico's economic development has not yet eliminated
its provincial patterns of living. Therefore, we can reason-
ably assume that female fears are more prevalent than males.

The age variable also yielded significant differences.
But these differences were obtained by two of the three instruments administered: the Semantic Differential and the
structured interview. The TAT did not yield significant differences. This might be attributed to limited understanding
of the language, leading to inability to write a comprehensive
story or possible fear of revealing their identification with
those in the picture. However, the other two instruments revealed meaningful findings. With the administration of the
Semantic Differential it was found that the 5-14 year age
groups differed significantly from the other age categories.

The 5-14 age group perceived the police more positively than any other of the groups. This positive perception can
be attributed to several factors. The 5-14 year old might
have limited contacts with the police. Except in extreme
cases, direct contact with the police is likely to be limited.
In other words, child-police confrontations and relations are
not a daily occurrence. (Restrictions possibly, but arrest is
unlikely). During this period in life, dependency is prevalent.
The policeman is seen as a protector, he stops traffic, he
symbolizes "big daddy. " He is often revered, respected, and
admired. His uniform and shining shield attract the malle-

able, impressionable youngster. A positive perception may
be related to a dependent role. In adolescence, another factor might be image ambivalence. A Puerto Rican youth who
is going through his identity socialization process in a Puerto
Rican home might find it difficult to identify with or develop
an image of a policeman--a policeman with a different language, culture, and societal background. His personification
might be nebulous and vague. His confusion might lead him
to view the policeman either positively or negatively. The
specific determination will depend on his dependency need
level or on his contacts with police.

        The socialization process of the Puerto Rican child is
geared toward learning to view a law enforcement agent in a
positive sense. The Puerto Rican parent in teaching right
from wrong, in inculcating moral values, employs warnings
and advice which are often accompanied by slaps and an authoritative tone of voice. The philosophy here is that in order to be good, children must be punished. Beating, repri-
manding, withdrawing privileges (or a combination of these)
are used as disciplinary measures. Castigos (punishments)
involve restructuring the child's activity. [13] Restrictiveness,
familiarity with authoritative figures and reprimands are all
part of the Puerto Rican youngsters' socialization process.
This phase of the initial socialization process might account
for the 5-14 year old group being more positive toward the
police than the older age categories; the 5-14 year old are
close to initial socialization process.

        The 15-24 year old group perceives the police more
negatively than does the 5-14 year old group. This negative
perception might be related to their role and status in our
society. In our society the 15-24 year old group faces problems of ego-diffusion and ego-identity. This is a period of
transition from adolescence to adulthood, from dependence to
independence; its focus is on a secondary socialization. A
transition takes place from an emphasis on the primary institution to an emphasis on the secondary institution.

        In the secondary socialization process self-control,
self-discipline, and self-sustenance are emphasized. The
preceding are all attributes of adulthood, independency and
maturity. The transition from adolescence to adulthood is
often accompanied by many anxieties. The transition introduces many pressures, enough for those of the dominant society, but a multiplicity for a newcomer. The Puerto Rican
in New York City in this age group is to a great extent a

newcomer. It should be noted that the bulk of Puerto Rican
migration was after World War II and the bulk of the Puerto
Rican population falls within the age group under discussion.
This group is still undergoing an acculturation process. This
acculturation process is still on a community association level;
but not at all group structural levels. Elena Padilla comments on Puerto Ricans born or reared in New York City and
their participation in neighborhood cliques compared to all
kinds of individuals. These cliques do not concentrate on
either Puerto Rican culture or society. The orientation is
towards being American and identifying with the dominant society. [14]

The Puerto Rican in the 15-24 year old group is not
only facing the pressure and anxieties of transition but an acculturation process which is restrictive in many cases. In
order to acculturate he might find it necessary to speak his
native tongue less, thus diminishing his powers of communication. The inability to communicate fully is frustrating and
might contribute to under-employment or unemployment. Low
income leads to a limited choice of residence; thus the Puerto Rican is often a resident of substandard housing. The
Puerto Rican is constantly facing challenges in his environment. The 15-24 year old Puerto Rican is in a stage of life
that necessitates direction and the setting of realistic goals
and aspirations. The Puerto Rican's wants and desires are
not markedly different from those of any other newcomer.
However, the ethos is different. New York City is in a state
of change and of constant flux; the Puerto Rican is caught up
in a civil rights movement that is unfamiliar to him. The
15-24 year old is being initiated into a secondary socialization process that is confusing and unfamiliar to New York
City's secondary institutions.

The 25-44 year old group views the police more negatively than any other group. This might be attributed to the
fact that they have undergone transition with all its frustrations and anxieties. They may have faced and possibly still
face restrictions because of their minority group status.
This group is experiencing all the attributes of its marginal
status--aggressiveness, hostility, etc. [15] Another reason for
negative perception might be frequent, frustrating contact with
either the police or other secondary institutions. The necessity for gainful employment might suggest under-employment
for a newcomer. The 25-44 year old group might see their
aspirations diminished because of their minority group status.
Their limitations might be attributed to the dominant society

and all its institutions. One of these visible institutions is
the law enforcer, the oppressor, known as the policeman.

The 45-64 year old group is like the 5-14 year old
group; their perception is less negative than the 15-44 year
olds. This less negative view might be attributed to a less
active role in the community. This age is primarily composed of pre-war Puerto Ricans who experienced less auto-
mation, tension, and turmoil in New York City. Little or
no skills did not necessarily mean under- or unemployment
to this group. Therefore, their frustrations and limitations
were not as extensive as for the other age groups. According to Kantrowitz, the older Puerto Rican has overcome many
of the disadvantages of the younger Puerto Rican, e. g., the
lag in the upper white collar job is minimized. The older
Puerto Rican had less difficulty in getting blue collar positions. [16]

The employment status variable revealed significant
differences in terms of the semantic differential and the
structured interview mean scores. The TAT score revealed
no significant differences and we might attribute this to a
limited ability to communicate, and possibly to a poor understanding of the instructions. What is striking is that the unemployed Puerto Rican perceived the police more positively
than the employed Puerto Rican. The more positive perception of the unemployed might be related to their dependent
role. This group might be dependent on a secondary institution for sustenance. They might have responded more positively in fear of losing their only means of income. This
group might see the police as part of the Establishment, not
in any way detached from the over-all system of government.
An unemployed person might feel that expressing negative
feelings towards any part of the system will limit the opportunity of ever getting or receiving gainful employment. It
should be noted that the sample is composed of more females
(204) than males (119). In our earlier discussion it was stipulated that females perceived the police more positively than
males. This, in conjunction with the fact that most of the
females might have been unemployed, can be another explanation for these findings.

In the area of completed education levels it was found
that in terms of the TAT, a significant difference existed between mean scores. Those in the 0-6th grade school level
perceived the police more positively than those in the 7-9th
grade school level and the 10-11th high school level of educa-

tion. This might suggest that those of the 0-6th grade school
level are more dependent, because limited education can be
correlated with unemployment. A poor formal education may
lead to a limited field of contact; thus a limitation in conflicts and in possible attrition with secondary institutions.
The same would hold true for those in the 7-9th grade school
education level, even though the 7-9th grade school respondents were more negative than the 0-6th grade school respondents. The high school respondents in the 10-11th high school
level were closer to the 0-6th grade school respondents in
their perception of the police. Note that the TAT yields significant findings in the area of the education variable, possibly suggesting that this instrument is more useful in this area
than in others. The Semantic Differential did not yield any
significant difference for this variable. However, the structured interview revealed a significant difference between the
0-6th grade school respondents and those in the 10-11 high
school respondents. Again the 0-6th grade school respondents
were more positive in the perception of the police than the
10-11 high school respondents. The reasons here might be
similar to those of the 5-14 and 15-24 age categories.

        The overall findings do reveal one thing: there exists
a gap between the Puerto Rican community and the police in
New York City.

        The Puerto Rican's alienation from the police or any
other representative of the public services has its origin in
the element of time. According to C. Wright Mills, Clarence
Senior, and Rose K. Goldsen, "movement of the Puerto Ricans according to the classic pattern of assimilation is slowed
up or hampered by (1) the facts that the Puerto Ricans--men
and women, white or black--are occupationally restricted, and
that they enter a social order with a declining rate of upward
mobility, so that they have less chance than previous migrants
to be exposed to the American culture while on the way up;
(2) the fact that two-thirds of the migrants are, by mainland
standards, black, and thus cannot rise as easily or as far as
people of white stock, and may thus presumably develop less
motivation to fit themselves into the lower levels of a world
of color and caste; (3) the fact that among the migrants there
are more women than men [which happens to be congruent to
our sample] and that women have less opportunity to become
exposed to any culture outside their households, the house-
wives among them because their range of social circulation
is so limited, the working women because they are, and are
likely to remain, concentrated occupationally."[17]

The Puerto Rican's late entry into a post-industrial society has engendered an atypical situation of marginality. His journey from accommodation to assimilation must occur in a technological and automated environment. He must adjust from an agricultural, rural, socio-psychological type of thinking to an urban technologically-oriented type of thinking. The transition is slow and all obstacles are viewed with suspicion and hostility. The policeman as an instrument of constraint and as a representative service to support a given set of institutions in the dominant society is often perceived as an obstacle to movement and adjustment by the Puerto Rican community.

The Puerto Rican is aware of how important law enforcement and the role of the police officer are in creating and maintaining social order. On the other hand, the police are sensitive to the role of social control in considerations of general welfare and social survival. Their orientation and public relations devices focus on the fact that they protect life, property, prevent crime, detect and arrest violations of laws, enforce laws and ordinances, and safeguard the rights of all individuals. [18]

Notes

1. Gordon W. Allport, "Attitude," Readings in Attitude, Theory and Measurement, ed. Martin Fishbein. New York: John Wiley & Sons, 1967, p. 1-13.

2. Ibid., p. 431.

3. Arthur Niederhoffer, Behind the Shield. Anchor Books Edition. New York: Doubleday Company, 1969, p. 125.

4. Jerome H. Skolnick, Justice Without Trial. New York: John Wiley & Sons, Inc., 1967, p. 87.

5. David H. Bayley and Harold Mendelsohn, Minorities and the Police. New York: Free Press, 1968, p. 64-66.

6. John P. Clark and Eugene P. Winninger, "The Attitude of Juveniles Toward the Legal Institution," Journal of Criminal Law, Criminology and Police Science, v. 55 (1964), p. 482.

7. Ibid.

8. Anne Anastasi, Psychological Testing. 3rd ed. New
    York: Macmillan, 1968, p. 534-5.

9. Leonard S. Kogan and M. J. Wantman, Population Health
    Survey. New York: Center of Social Research, 1968,
    Table IV, p. 5.

10. Ibid., Table VIII, p. 8.

11. George E. Simpson and J. Milton Yinger, Racial and Cul-
    tural Minorities: An Analysis of Prejudice and Dis-
    crimination. New York: Harper and Row, Inc., 1965,
    p. 143.

12. Sidney L. Pressey and Raymond G. Kuhlen, Psychologi-
    cal Development Through the Life Span. New York:
    Harper & Row, 1957, p. 344.

13. Elena Padilla, Up From Puerto Rico. New York: Co-
    lumbia University Press, 1958, p. 183-4.

14. Ibid., p. 185.

15. Ibid.

16. Nathan Kantrowitz, "Social Mobility of Puerto Ricans,"
    International Migration Review, v. 2, no. 5, Spring
    1968, p. 67-69.

17. C. Wright Mills, Clarence Senior, and Rose Kohn Gold-
    sen, The Puerto Rican Journey. New York: Harper,
    1950.

18. J. Edgar Hoover, Should You Go Into Law Enforcement?
    New York: New York Life Insurance Company, 1961,
    p. 5.

CHAPTER 14

RELIGION AND THE PUERTO RICANS IN NEW YORK

Rev. Antonio M. Stevens-Arroyo, CP

The Puerto Ricans in New York City are Puerto Ricans. Thus, any consideration of their religion must begin on that island where for centuries belief and custom fashioned the religious response of the Puerto Ricans who were to come to New York. Interwoven into the fabric of life here and hereafter are three components of religion: the intellectual, the social and the individual. The intellectual element is contained in doctrines and teachings; the social element is measured by customs and cult; and the realm of mystical experience is individual. All three elements and their unique balance in New York are the subject of this essay.

Criollo Catholicism

It is generally accepted that Puerto Rico is a Catholic nation. This is true, but the Catholicism of Puerto Ricans is unique. History converted the prosperous colony of San Juan de Borinquen, as the Island was known in the 16th century, into a lonely military base. One Spanish governor characterized life on the island as "dancing, drink and dice." The scarcity of clergy and control of the Church by the Spanish Crown did little to ameliorate the situation. According to Old World criteria, Puerto Rican Catholicism was of inferior intellectual formation, with undue amounts of superstition in popular devotion.

Four hundred years of Spanish imperialism had made Puerto Rican Catholicism a religion of the town. The people in the hill-country, or barrios, remote from contact with the parish priest, had developed complicated sets of customs to substitute for the absence of a religious leader. Syncretic elements entered the practice of the Catholic faith. For instance, Puerto Ricans respond to crisis by often using herbs in a variety of ways to combat evil spirits, sickness or bad

119

luck. Botánicas, the stores where such magical remedies
are sold, are everywhere, as is the healer or "curandero"
who applies the herbs, usually for a fee. This "curanderismo"
seems based upon the healing arts of the now extinct Arawak
Indians. The African influence has not created its own religion in Puerto Rico like the Voodoo in Haiti or Santería in
Cuba. Nonetheless, many elements of popular belief and
practice come from African sources.

Protestantism

        Protestantism was present in Puerto Rico in the 19th
century, but in a limited way and with little effect. The
American invasion in 1898, however, and the subsequent take-
over of Puerto Rican society gave the Protestantism of North
America a brief but spectacular ascendency on the Island.
Free-thinkers and Masons who had struggled against the Spanish establishment identified with Protestant ideals of individual
liberty, and in some cases allowed this to manifest an anti-
Catholic bias. The Great Depression of 1929, however, dried
up the funds for the social programs which had given Protestantism a wide base of popular support. Moreover the Catholic Church began importing large numbers of priests and
sisters to initiate their own programs, and there was besides
a general reaction to the Americanizing trend of established
Protestantism with its Puritan ethic, its coldness, and most
especially, its imposition of the English language.

        Puerto Rican customs, such as the wearing of medals,
was considered incompatible with the new religion of the
"Yankees. " The great devotion to the rosary and the cult of
the Virgin Mary had created a cultural form called "rosario
cantao. " Puerto Ricans made vows and undertook severe
penances to obtain favors from the saints. Without clergy,
they depended on home altars for worship and manifested
their belief in the omnipresence of the supernatural by frequent exclamations such as "¡Ay Bendito!" and "¡Ave María
Purísima!" These folk religion practices did not find a comfortable home in the mentality of the North American missionaries, especially the Protestants. And some Puerto Ricans
turned to another religion.

Pentecostalism

Pentecostalism has become the largest and fastest
growing of Puerto Rican churches. Pentecostalism is especially dominant among rural Puerto Ricans who move from
the barrios into or near the big city. In the rupture of traditional patterns of life and structures in the countryside,
many of the jíbaros, or mountain men, are attracted to Pentecostalism with its strong social bonds. Pentecostalism,
which includes some of the Churches of God and the Seventh
Day Adventists, is different from Protestantism, since it is
primarily a literal and fundamentalist return to biblical
Christianity, compatible with a variety of doctrinal tenets,
including those of Catholicism. Most especially, the importance given religious experience reinforces the desire for in-
timacy with the supernatural that Puerto Ricans manifest.

Religion in New York City: The Beginnings

When the "Great Migration" of Puerto Ricans to New
York City began in 1946, Pentecostalism became the great
proselytizer of the newcomers. A survey in 1949 showed
that 50 percent of Puerto Ricans married in New York that
year were united in Protestant ceremonies, as contrasted
with only 14.3 percent in Puerto Rico, while 27 percent
sought Catholic ceremonies in the City and 61.4 percent in
Puerto Rico. About 70 percent or more of the Protestant
churches referred to can be considered Pentecostal. In other
words, a great number of Puerto Ricans in New York were
leaving the Catholic religion to be married in Protestant ceremonies.

The most interesting, if not the most representative
of the Pentecostal Churches is the one founded by Juanita
García Peraza, known as "Mita" by her followers. Basing
her ministry upon a healing experience when sick in a hospital, she dedicated her life in 1940 to the preaching of the
Gospel. Filled with the Spirit of God, she spoke of the Father, whom she called not just "Padre," but "Papá." Her
disciples believed she was the incarnation of the Spirit in our
times, just as Jesus was in His. Thus she was called "La
Diosa"--"The Goddess." Her preaching was supplemented by
varied activities and a number of cooperatives which gave
considerable benefits to those disciples who had shares in the
enterprise. The main temple of "Mita" in New York's West
Side, however, has no cooperatives. And this is a salient

point of Pentecostalism among the Puerto Ricans of New York:
it is not oriented toward life in the city but is, rather, a
means of escaping the cultural and social aimlessness that
many Puerto Ricans experience in the transition to the big
city.   O'Dea and Poblete, in a survey in 1962, discovered a
significant drop in Pentecostal membership among second generation Puerto Ricans.   According to their study, once oriented towards city life, a significant percentage of Puerto Ricans leave the Pentecostal sects for the more established
churches, both Protestant and Catholic.   Nonetheless, about
15 percent of Puerto Ricans in New York are affiliated with
Pentecostal churches.

Protestantism in the City

The Protestant religions in New York have not at-
tracted large numbers of Puerto Ricans to their churches.
It is estimated that about 10 percent belong to the established
Protestant Parish and the Good Neighbor Church, which have
reached many Puerto Ricans.   While not always "making"
Protestants, the Protestant churches have influenced Puerto
Ricans in New York, to the extent that they form the most
Protestant of all Latin American groups.

The Rev. David Wilkerson, author of the book, The
Cross and the Switchblade, established his famous program
of Teen Challenge in Brooklyn.   The Rev. Wilkerson left his
parsonage in Philipsburg, Pa., to dedicate himself to work
among the Puerto Rican youth of New York, specifically those
addicted to drugs.   He had spectacular results in some cases,
and significant conversion in many.   Again, it is important to
recognize that the total and felt surrender to Christ has provided the basis for a Puerto Rican religious experience in the
special crisis situation of New York.

Puerto Rican clergy among the Protestant churches
are a visible and powerful force in most civic associations
and events.   The admirable work of the Reverends Caraballo
and Tanon in the correctional system is especially noteworthy.
The abundance of Puerto Ricans in the clergy is a significant
evidence of the vitality of the Protestant churches, and an advantage not shared by the Catholic church.   Nonetheless,
Puerto Rican Protestants are sectarians within sects, and
some of them, such as the Rev. Cotto and the Rev. Dario
Colón, struggle within their own denominations for Puerto Rican programs.   Piri Thomas, author of Down These Mean

Streets, dedicated his second book to the struggle to be a
Protestant Puerto Rican within a North American Protestant
Church.   And it is significant that the North American Pentecostal Churches, in 1955, refused the petition of affiliation
by the Puerto Rican Pentecostals.

Puerto Rican Catholics and the New York Church

        Before the Great Migration, the needs of Puerto Ri-
cans in the city were lumped together with the spiritual care
of other Spanish-speaking Catholics such as the Cubans and
Spaniards.   The parish of Our Lady of Guadalupe, Esperanza
Church in West Harlem, and St. Peter's in Brooklyn were
viewed as steps towards eventual assimilation.   These were
not parishes based on the people in the neighborhood, but
special language chapels for those who were unable to understand services at the regular parish churches.   La Milagrosa
and Holy Agony were added later on to serve the Puerto Ricans, but in the same pattern of national chapel.   Social
needs were in a separate category, attended to by Casita
María, founded in El Barrio in 1934, and inspired by the heroic work of the Trinitarian and Puerto Rican nun, Sister
Carmelita.   Father Walter Janer, S.J., did similar work
later on from Nativity Mission Center in Lower Manhattan.

        Shortly after his arrival in New York, Francis Cardi-
nal Spellman decided upon a significant change in this policy.
In 1939 he turned over the parish of St. Cecilia in El Barrio
to the Redemptorist priests from Puerto Rico.   He reasoned
that in a church with so many Puerto Ricans, it would be better to offer them the full services of the Archdiocese without
segregation according to language.   Moreover, since the Re-
demptorists Fathers had been working among the Puerto Ricans on the island for many years, he felt they could best
serve the newcomers from the island, just as Italian priests
had done for the Italians in New York and the Slovak priests
for Slovaks, etc.   Unfortunately for this strategy, the Re-
demptorists were not Puerto Ricans but North Americans,
scarcely different from other New York City clergy, except
that they had learned another language.

The Spanish-Speaking Apostolate Office

        In 1953 Cardinal Spellman recognized the inadequacy
of his first plan and founded the Office of Spanish Catholic

Action, which later came to be called the Office of the Spanish-Speaking Apostolate. Meanwhile, on the West Side of
Manhattan, that inquisitive and challenging genius, the Yugo-
slavian-born Archdiocesan priest, Iván Illich, was forging a
new awareness of mission. "Why expect the Puerto Rican
people to become like us?", he reasoned, "It is we who must
become like them. " He suggested a new approach, rejecting
the role of Americanizer and encouraging the Church to restore what had been religious practice in Puerto Rico. This
idea, coupled to the sound sociology of the Fordham Jesuit,
Joseph F. Fitzpatrick, produced the San Juan Fiesta in 1953,
a celebration which publicly embraced the style of religious
practice in Puerto Rico. On the Island, each town celebrates
the feast day of the patron saint with week-long festivities,
culminating in a public procession and a solemn mass at
which the dignitaries of the town join with the faithful as wor-
shippers. The basis for success of Puerto Rican religious
customs such as this is the close identification of the Puerto
Rican with the person of the saint or the Virgin. Whereas
the North American generally thinks of religion as an intellec-
tually-held set of doctrines, membership in societies and
faithful attendance at services, the Latin places his religious
loyalty upon friendship with a person, his family commitment
and participation in a culture with religious values larger
than the individual's whim. For New York, St. John the
Baptist was chosen because he is the patron of all of Puerto
Rico. Open as it was to these personalistic values, the San
Juan Fiesta could not help but create response. After a two-
year stay on the Fordham campus with overflow attendance,
it was relocated in 1956 to Downing Stadium on Randall's Island, where it once drew crowds of upwards of 70,000 people
on the last Sunday of June for religious drama, festivity and
liturgy.

Msgr. Illich's idea was solidified by the foundation of
the Institute of Intercultural Communications in 1957. Mrs.
Encarnación Padilla de Armas, a woman of no mean accomplishments and a fierce Catholic, described to the Cardinal
the growing gap between Puerto Ricans in New York and the
religion of their traditions. Cardinal Spellman then directed
Msgr. Illich, with Fr. Fitzpatrick, to develop programs of
language training and acculturalization. Significant numbers,
and eventually the majority, of priest candidates and many
religious sisters took this training, which was offered during
the summer at the Catholic University of Puerto Rico's campus in Ponce.

By 1959 significant progress had been made in re-
claiming the loyalty of the Puerto Ricans in New York to the
Catholic Church.   Comparing the same marriage statistics as
in the 1949 survey, 41 percent of Puerto Ricans in New York
City were being married in Catholic ceremonies in 1959,
where before it had been 27 percent.   The Protestant share
of the total dropped from 50 to 38 percent.

The Cursillo Movement:
Puerto Ricanization in New York

In 1960, the Cursillo came to New York.   Begun in
Spain, this movement consists of an intensive four-day living
experience, in which groups of men or women separate themselves from their homes and live in Christian community.
During those four days a well-planned and methodical series
of conferences is arranged for participants and, by means of
discussion and group dynamics, the traditional doctrines of
Catholicism are translated into everyday language.

Between the two centers of San José in Manhattan's
West Side and San Pablo in Brooklyn, some 15,000 Puerto
Rican men and women have learned as adults the elements of
their religion.   Much of the success of the Cursillo can be
placed upon the element of mystical experience.   The emotion
in the Cursillo and the feeling of total self-giving are the
springboards of greater religious involvement.   Moreover,
the Cursillo started a process of Puerto Ricanization within
the Catholic Church.   The emphasis of the Cursillo is upon
the role of the layman, and many of the talks and the organization of the movement are dependent upon non-clergy who
perform the duties traditionally assigned to priests.   The
Cursillo thus had two principal effects: first, it gave intellectual support to religious customs and mystic experience,
which had long been the most visible elements of Puerto Rican Catholicism; and, second, it introduced Puerto Ricans
into leadership roles within the Catholic Church, so that today the Cursillo Movement in New York is Puerto Rican.

Summer in the City

Coupled with the development of lay leaders, the Catholic Church itself underwent profound changes by reason of
the II Vatican Council.   In 1964, Msgr. Robert Fox was
named to head the Spanish Office.   His interest in the social

dimension of Christianity, a ready army of like-minded clergy
and nuns trained by Msgr. Illich, and the need for local-
level involvement in the War on Poverty launched a new crusade called "Summer in the City." Msgr. Fox directed large-
scale programs which focused on the cultural values of the
minority groups and gave "white liberals" an opportunity to
recognize that their mission was one of service, not of Amer-
icanization. For the Puerto Rican Catholics, it meant that
the authority figures of religion, the priests and nuns, were
returning responsibility to Puerto Ricans. Moreover, many
of these same clergy and religious were leaving the practice
of the traditional ministry, thus creating a special urgency
for Puerto Rican laymen and laywomen to assume responsibilities of leadership.

When Cardinal Spellman died he left a Catholic Church
in New York that showed great vitality at top-level planning,
enjoyed an increasingly smooth Puerto Ricanization process,
unparalleled prestige in the secular community, a seminary
with minority vocations, and lay leadership of great promise.
However, his successor, Cardinal Cooke, faced the difficult
task of replacing Msgr. Fox, who left the Chancery Office
to the disappointment of many liberal priests in the parishes.

The successor, Father Robert Stern, came to the Spanish Office in 1969. He developed a magnificent set of blueprints which emphasized movements rather than organizations,
in order to carry out the new models of religion being proposed by Msgr. Fox, Msgr. Illich, and the grassroots clergy.
He developed Archdiocesan-wide programs for Spanish families
and for youth. He sought new means of financial support,
such as independent funding. He invited Puerto Rican priests
who belonged to religious orders to assume prominent roles
in his programs. He initiated ecumenical cooperation, con-
solidated the energies of the area dioceses, created the
groundwork for a Greater Metropolitan Council, and eventually
obtained a representative for this region in the Washington
Office of the United States Catholic Conference. Later, in
1972, a national meeting was held to organize a strategy for
all Spanish-speaking Catholics of the United States, and Father Stern had a large share of the responsibility. Most importantly, he formed a Committee of Coordinators which discussed and developed policy in a democratic way.

Unfortunately, Father Stern's imaginative thinking was
not always communicated through the network of Chancery directors. Moreover, his blueprints infringed on other pro-

grams, such as the Language Institute--the year-round version of Ponce's training--which by now was directed by the
only Puerto Rican priest of the New York Archdiocese, Father Peter Ensenat.

In December of 1972, Father Stern resigned from the
Spanish Office after a series of confrontations with his superiors, including the Cardinal. Some of the lay people who had
worked on the Committee of Coordinators did not wish to relinquish their leadership roles, and independently of the Spanish Office and clerical supervision, in 1973 formed a liberal
Catholic pressure group called "Hispanic-American Christians
for Justice." Thus, even in the Catholic Church, the most
hierarchical of churches, Puerto Ricans are organized to promote their own special programs.

The Diaconate Program

Meanwhile, the Brooklyn Diocese, under Bishop Francis Magavero, developed an effective coalition of Chancery-
based planning under Father John O'Brien and grassroots initiative led by Father Brian Karvelis of Transfiguration Church.
Besides the Cursillo for teenagers, Brooklyn offers a plan
for the permanent diaconate. Under this plan, Puerto Rican
married men will be ordained to the ministry, not as priests
but as deacons. This is the logical conclusion to the Puerto
Ricanization of the Church. And it is interesting that the
Brooklyn Diocese, which had often followed the larger and
more prestigious New York Archdiocese, is now asserting an
initiative of its own in the Spanish-speaking Apostolate.

Overview for the Seventies

Religion among the Puerto Ricans of New York follows
no clear pattern of growth. Generally, the clergy must be
considered progressive, involved in a wide range of meaningful programs. Occasionally one finds overt prejudice, usually on the part of a pastor or sometimes in other Puerto Ricans who have opted for assimilation to American ways and
look down on their own heritage. Nonetheless, in very few
places within the world of organized religion can one find the
sort of mystical experience legitimately sought by Puerto Ricans. The Cursillo Movement has had significant problems
in retaining leaders once the Cursillo fervor has worn off,
and the deacon program has still not been fully realized. In-

creasingly, the need for Puerto Rican leadership from within
the ranks of the hierarchy becomes evident, and the lack of
unity among the various civic organizations cries out for a
strong voice of moral leadership.   It is not at all clear
whether such appointments of Puerto Rican bishops, either
Protestant or Catholic, will be forthcoming.

In the meantime, Puerto Rican-sponsored organizations
fill this need by seeking chaplains.   The Puerto Rican Folklore Festival, for instance, which is celebrated annually in
Central Park, has a Puerto Rican folk mass and, in 1971 and
1972, had a larger attendance than the San Juan Fiesta which
was run from the Archdiocesan Chancery.

Puerto Ricans in New York, especially those of the
new generation born state-side, sometimes called "Neoricans,"
continue to be faithful to religious customs such as baptism.
By that sacrament, which is traditionally celebrated with
great solemnity, the child gains godparents, and his mother
and father gain a new relationship called "compadrazgo. "
This relationship, especially common among Puerto Ricans,
in effect extends a brother-sister relationship outside the
natural family.   So strong is the respect for the compadres,
and so lasting is this tradition, that many young Puerto Ricans who neither marry in a religious ceremony nor practice
in any Church, will seek baptism for their children.

Yet they also continue the practice of the asabache,
which is a black piece of wood, usually in the shape of an
arm, meant to protect the child from the evil eye.   Apparently, the inner contradiction of one religion counterposed with
another is not important to the practice of Puerto Ricans in
New York.   With this flexibility and because the disintegration of traditional structures occurs at precisely the moment
of Puerto Rican emergence, new forms of religion and religious practice must be expected for the seventies: spiritism
is one of them.

Spiritism

Spiritism, or the practice of communication with spiritual forces, has always been present in Puerto Rico in one
form or another.   It is estimated that some five percent of
Puerto Ricans profess Spiritism as a religion, but many,
many more Puerto Ricans believe in and drift towards Spir-
itist circles.   The reaction of young Puerto Ricans in New

York to the impersonalism of the city is increasingly a search of mystical experience. Wedded as they are to their Puerto Rican culture, they look to Spiritism rather than to the Orient for the answer to this spiritual desire. And because it is not a total religious system, Spiritism supplies the need without imposing restrictive obligations on marriage, sex, diversion, etc. Coupled with the political activism of growing numbers of Puerto Ricans, Spiritism may well become a religious force in New York.

Without doubt, organized religion is in trouble unless it responds by allowing Puerto Ricans to exercise authority within the structures. If not, Puerto Ricans are quite capable of creating their own forms of religion, as they have continually done throughout history, while maintaining a uniquely strong faith in God, His son Jesus Christ, and the Holy Spirit present in the world.

Suggested Bibliography

Fitzpatrick, Joseph P. Puerto Rican Americans: The Meaning of Migration to the Mainland. Englewood Cliffs, N.J.: Prentice Hall, 1971.

_____. "Intermarriage of Puerto Ricans in New York," American Journal of Sociology, Jan. 1966.

Moore, Donald T. Puerto Rico Para Cristo. Cuernavaca: Sondeos, 1969.

O'Dea, Thomas F. and Renato Poblete, S.J. "Anomie and the Quest for Community: The Formation of Sects among the Puerto Ricans in New York," American Catholic Sociological Review, Vol. 21 (Spring, 1960).

Ribes Tovar, Federico. El Libro Puertorriqueño de Nueva York. New York: Plus Ultra Publishers, 1970. Vol. II.

Steward, Julian, ed. People of Puerto Rico, A Study of Social Anthropology. Champaign, Ill.: University of Illinois Press, 1957.

Wagenheim, Kal. Puerto Rico: A Profile. New York: Praeger, 1970.

Wakefield, Dan. Island in the City, the World of Spanish
     Harlem. Boston: Houghton Mifflin, 1959.

Wilkerson, David R. The Cross and the Switchblade. New
     York: Pyramid Publishers, 1963.

Yurchenko, Henrietta. ¡Hablamos! Puerto Ricans Speak.
     New York: Praeger, 1971.

PART IV

PERSPECTIVES FROM THE INDIVIDUAL

CHAPTER 15

THE PUERTO RICAN WOMAN IN BUSINESS

Celia Vice

The history of the Puerto Rican professional in America may appear to be a repetition of the history of previous ethnic groups. There would be chapters on the struggle of obtaining a college education, difficulties in financing a business and meeting its overhead, and the dreams of owning a home far from the cities' slums. Yet, the story is quite different in many ways. Unlike other groups, the Puerto Rican comes to these shores as a citizen of the United States, supposedly with all the privileges of a native born. Since World War 1, the Puerto Rican has fought the wars under the flag of the United States, although many were residents of the Island and had never set foot on the mainland. His mother, like countless North American mothers, has cried and suffered the loss of a son killed in battle. The Puerto Rican comes with some knowledge of the English language, because for a long time English was a required subject in Puerto Rican schools; thus he has been in contact with "Americanos" in one form or another. He has become familiar with American-made products because this is what is most available in his home town.

If his family, like mine, came prior to the depression years, he had immediately to try to forget his Island and begin to learn English because there were few Spanish-speaking people in the city at that time. He had to take whatever job was available in order to survive, and with this, become accustomed to a completely new life, with no warm breezes, no beautiful and clean sandy beaches around him, no delicious fruits or the chorus of the Coqui lulling him to sleep; but most of all there were few accommodating neighbors. Peculiar to this ethnic migration, the Puerto Rican cannot forget his Island. The many vicissitudes crowding his daily living cannot erase the pleasant thought of, someday, soon, returning home. So then, why did he come?

Before the second World War, many of the people who
came to the United States were just searching for position
and wealth, although most were economically well-to-do, living comfortably in the Island.   There were those who came
for adventure, others for political reasons, and still others
who followed a close relative whom they missed.   The latter
was the reason for my parents' trip to America and, for my
family as well as for others, the dream of returning home
became dimmer and dimmer as months and years passed.
The young always seem to adapt themselves much more easily, though.   They make friends in school, and in the process
forget their Spanish.   General complications of city living
gradually overshadow the Puerto Rican dream of success in
America.   The Puerto Rican feels it is impossible to return
while his children are enjoying their education.   It had not
been easy for him but, he ponders, this is "the land of opportunity" and his children will do great things and have much
more comfortable lives.   Like so many other newcomers, the
Puerto Rican believes that this is the land of free enterprise,
where a man can start by selling a stick of gum for a penny
and eventually acquire a million dollar business.   Surely, he
thinks, there are many good examples of men and women
who have succeeded, although they began with relatively nothing!   The children will have a chance.

When I was a child growing up in Brooklyn, I had
these same dreams and I sensed that my parents held some
for me, too.   My first was to be a missionary nun, but this
soon died when I learned that I had to contribute a considerable dowry to the convent for my training.   My first business
venture, at ten years of age, was making and selling jelly
apples in front of my stoop at 124 Gold Street.   The neighborhood was Italian and Slavic (Polish, Russian, Lithuanian).
I learned how to say "dieshinsenti," or what I thought meant
ten cents in Polish.   I believe it was a marvelous experience,
although I did not collect too many dimes, for everyone was
poor and I allowed too much credit.

Years later, as a teenager, living in Williamsburg, I
would walk along Tompkins Ave. and peer into the windows
of the real estate offices, wondering how it would feel to own
a beautiful office, to really be able to help people.   Looking
back, I believe that I was not thinking merely of the money-
making end, but of owning a place where people would be
confidently helped with their problems.   At 15, I volunteered
to help a family friend, Juan Martinez, who owned a business
brokerage and travel agency.   For a long time, I did not re-

ceive any compensation for my work, nor did I expect any.
I was content with being there and learning.   After I began
full-time employment in a Chinese export-import firm, I continued to work nightly for Mr. Martinez.   One day, he decided to return to Puerto Rico and sell the office for $2,000.
Naturally, I was interested, but all I had was $100 in the
bank.   My Uncle Raymond heard about the sale and promptly
lent me the money.   I suddenly became a business woman.
The contents of the office were not worth the amount, but I
thought the opportunity to continue an ongoing business was.

When I obtained my real estate and insurance brokers'
licenses, I realized that I was probably the only Puerto Rican
woman in Brooklyn in this particular field.   There was a reluctance on the part of men to transact business with a young,
inexperienced woman.   It was a traumatic experience for
businessmen to have to deal with a woman, and a Puerto Rican woman at that!   This was their field, and I had no right
to encroach on their territory.   I decided that if I was to be
successful, I had to gain the confidence of the property owners as well as of other brokers.   I was sure that I could not
tell any potential customer immediately that I was the owner
of the business, so, whenever a broker or a landlord came
into the office asking to see "the Boss," I would say, "I'm
sorry, the Boss is out.   I'm the secretary, perhaps I can
help you?"   Well, the Boss was always out and, in despera-
tion, the broker or landlord was forced to negotiate with me.
They would list the property and I would show it to prospec-
tive buyers.   Finally, when the transaction was being closed,
I would appear at the lawyer's office with my client and there
I would have to reveal my true position.   They would not believe me but would offer me a "nice gift" in place of the required commission.   I would have to show them my license
and, even then, a menial percentage of the commission would
be offered.

Luckily, I had already established myself in the community and this was an asset both to the brokers and the owners.   My office was quickly becoming a sort of unofficial
center where anyone could come in with a problem, seek information, make a phone call, or just drop by to chat.   With
each transaction, property owners gained more confidence in
my clients as well as in my ability; soon, they were helping
me in many ways by teaching me the intricacies of the business, such as what to look for in a house, contracts, etc.
Most of the brokers and property owners were Jewish, the
predominant group in the middle forties.   Many of these home

owners began moving from the area but they did not want to
sell to just anyone, for they still had friends living on the
same block.   I was able to provide them with good neighbors;
95 percent were Puerto Ricans, Cubans and Dominicans who
had recently arrived in the country.   They were hard-working
and honest people.

I have often heard it said that you cannot make money
if you are honest.   This is hogwash.   I never allowed a client to enter into a transaction if I knew that there was something wrong with the house I was selling him.   The client
would be told of any problems beforehand, and it was up to
him to decide.   Many times, I would discover some terrible
condition which was not visible to the client, and I would inform him about it and its cost of repair before he purchased
the house.   I also began to match houses with clients; I really believe that the selection of a home is almost like the selection of a mate.   What may be good and beautiful for one
may be bad and ugly for another.

The families that have purchased homes from me have
remained my friends.   I am constantly invited to weddings,
baptisms, funerals and birth announcements.   I am still kept
abreast of the sad and happy events in the lives of these families.   The hours at the office were long, but I was able to
repay my Uncle Raymond after one year.   I loved this business because it gave me great satisfaction to see recently arrived families, accustomed to living in their own homes, get
settled once again.   It was a joyous occasion when they moved
into their homes.   In spite of the fact that the houses were
old, they were in good condition and, most important, reason-
ably priced.   Most of these houses had been occupied by the
original owners, and they were concerned to get a good buyer
who could pay the mortgage and who would improve the property.   This my clients did; they were poor, but they pooled
all the families' earnings and all their abilities to improve
the property, thereby increasing its value.   In some way, I
felt I was contributing to the happiness of these new home-
owners and I vowed that no one would take advantage of them
while I could come to their aid.   I considered my clients as
my friends, and I felt responsible for their welfare; I had
acquired a grave obligation.   My friends, these people who
had just sold their homes in the Island to invest all their savings on a home in Brooklyn, could not and would not be cheated as far as I was concerned.   In addition to selling the
home, I would service my clients with insurance and help
them with the countless other problems pertaining to real es-

tate ownership, including personal problems.

In obtaining insurance, I encountered many problems because of the reluctance of insurance companies to insure the new home-owners. The frustrations of selling insurance in a neighborhood where companies regarded the residents as "undesirable risks" were heavy. I was told many times to stop selling insurance to "those creeps Gonzalez, Rodriguez, Colons." "Why do you sell to these people?" they would ask, not knowing that I also was one of "those creeps." I deliberately withheld from them that I was Puerto Rican. I would argue that these people were honest, hardworking and reliable and that, furthermore, their money was just as good as anyone else's. I realized that if I said I was Puerto Rican, the insurance would be cancelled for some reason or another and then I would not be able to help my friends. I was usually able to convince the companies, but it always drained me to do so. Once I had established myself as a responsible broker, and my clients had proven to be trustworthy enough for the companies to accept their money, it was no longer necessary to hide my identity as a Puerto Rican. If this appears cowardly, it certainly was not. It involved much humiliation, and required self-denial and discipline, but my goal was to service my friends. Selling insurance in the city of New York was frustrating--indeed, it still is--but at that time, there were no assigned risk plans and few banks were willing to finance premiums. When I mentioned to the insurance companies that they were discriminating, they would find ways to cancel the policy. At one time, a representative of the State Insurance Department told me, as a friend and in a friendly manner of course, that I was jeopardizing my own license if I persisted in protesting about discrimination. Insurance companies, he said, would create problems for me and it was difficult to win. Because of this, I disliked this portion of the business intensely. This frustration, I concluded, was harmful to health and spirit! Financially, the insurance business was the best. Every year, renewals would come automatically. After many years, there is a continuous flow of income which one worked for only once. Yet I could never forget my initial aggravation.

Being a Puerto Rican woman in business creates additional problems. When you take a visual survey of your neighborhood and you see so much need--housing, jobs, education--and such lack of orientation, you cannot close your office at five o'clock, go home, relax and forget your day's experiences. You find your working days overlapping into the

community and its problems.   Making money is not enough.
Giving your children material things, which you lacked as a
child, is not enough.   When one reads the health statistics in
poverty neighborhoods and is shocked by the high infant mortality, and children dying or crippled from lead poisoning after eating plaster off the walls in their tenement apartments;
when children are not learning how to read or write in school
and are dropping out, resigning mentally and physically before
they are 12; when drug addiction becomes a way of life with
the youth and no solution seems probable; when all the people
around you are part of yourself, Puerto Ricans, Americans
by citizenship--then, surely, you cannot continue to take their
money and not return some dividends to them.   Naturally, if
you are still struggling to maintain a business and cannot
give monetary contributions, you have at least to give your
time and energy to this community.   Many times, this is
much more valuable than money.

The Puerto Rican woman in business is demanding in
that she will not be satisfied with being a career woman; she
will also want children and try to lead a normal life as a
woman.   She is demanding because her neighbor's child may
be her children's friend.   One way to assure a better neighborhood for her own offspring is to be concerned about the
welfare of other children.   The people outside your establishment and home also deserve care.   Unlike many other merchants and professionals who earn their livelihood in these
neighborhoods but live elsewhere, we remain here, we live
here, our children go to neighborhood schools, and day and
night we are confronted with the problems of the community.
We are the pulse of the community.

I joined the Brooklyn Real Estate Board and the Bushwick Real Estate Board, thinking that it would help me service my clients and give me more knowledge of the business.
The members were fine people, but I could not keep up with
their activities.   The monthly meetings were friendly enough
but golf outings, from which women were excluded, were high
among the favorite interests of these groups.   I believe there
were only one or two women present at meetings, and they
certainly "kept their place. "   I wasn't particularly interested
in golf, but here I saw an outright form of what was considered elimination, or what could be more appropriately
called discrimination.   This organization was strictly male-
orientated, for although women were permitted to become
members they were prevented from participation in various
important functions.   I have never felt uneasy or different

among businessmen, but I am sensitive to vibrations which
relay that I am considered insignificant. I'm certain that
this organization has changed a little, but knowing the strong
male leadership they have, I doubt whether the change is
very significant.

The Bushwick Real Estate Board was somewhat different, in that women participated as actively as men. While I
was a member, I learned much more than I had expected,
there was a female president, and more comradeship among
the members.

Adults are in the habit of asking young people what
they want to be when they grow up, or what they want to
achieve in life. Those who make these inquiries--and I have
found myself asking the same question--should have learned
through experience that one may study for a particular career
but that fate or circumstances may lead one into another.
The reason I discuss this is that many people become discouraged once they fail in some undertaking. What is wrong
with trying again?

As a Puerto Rican woman in business, with a family,
many responsibilities, and doubts as to whether the business
is truly progressing, it is logical not to waste too much time
in deciding whether to keep the business or not, whether to
sell it and begin anew. The decision is not easy, because
any change always causes expense, and the longer one pro-
crastinates, the more difficult it becomes to make a decision.
Evaluate your resources, capital, etc., and make the choice
quickly.

I have recounted some of my experiences in business
and, in this way, perhaps, have related the experiences of
others in similar situations. Admittedly, I have strayed somewhat in my career; on the other hand, maybe I have not; perhaps it has all been relevant. I began aspiring to a religious
life and since then, I have worked in an artificial flower factory, in a Chinese export-import firm (metallurgists), in a
Wall Street export firm; in real estate, insurance, travel, a
youth program, a manpower center, public relations; as vice-
president of an organization dedicated to the development of
the Brooklyn Navy Yard into an industrial complex, and finally as President of Puerto Rican Heritage Publications, Inc.
for the past three years. The diversity of jobs was beneficial
to me, I believe, as "on the job training" for my present position. I have met each challenge with enthusiasm, eagerness

and dedication. I have set goals for each position, not only
to produce for my employer but also to accomplish an adequate degree of satisfaction. To receive a salary and do only the work required of me has never been my goal; I must
perform well in a field that I consider constructive.

Apart from teaching, nursing, secretarial and a few
other professions, women must compete strongly with the
male. The irony is that many women do not want to compete
with anyone; they just expect equality. During the time I was
Director of JOIN (Job Orientation in Neighborhoods), no other
woman occupied a senior position in that agency. I was fortunate to be related to such a project and be among a group
of officers who were not just appointees collecting high salaries. The administration included individuals of every nationality, race and religious conviction, and they felt strongly
about the clients they serviced. We were peers. Unfortunately, some of those working in my center found it difficult
to adjust themselves to a female supervisor. One of the psychologists, for instance, confessed to me upon my arrival
that he would never take orders from a woman. I reasoned
with him, stressing the importance of team work, but he was
far too stubborn and insecure to listen. I pitied him. He
contrived problems and complained to our superiors, but they
were not deceived and soon he resigned. I felt thoroughly fulfilled in this agency because the results of our efforts were
so visible. JOIN was the first youth program in the city
geared to meet the problems of high school dropouts. Efforts
were rewarding because the majority of the youth being served
responded. My position was a challenging one because it was
the first opportunity I had to supervise a large staff, most of
whom possessed outstanding qualifications in education, social
work, dedication and experience. Several of these people
now hold important positions in government, colleges and
other institutions.

As the Director of a manpower program, although I
felt knowledgeable and confident, the problems, familiar to
us all, were seemingly insurmountable. What do you do when
thousands of men and women desperately come searching for
jobs and there are none available? What do you tell an unskilled, healthy and eager family man who also has a language difficulty? How many times must you tell him to return before he senses the hopeless expression on your face?
How can you keep your staff interviewers and counselors
from becoming discouraged themselves and revealing their
hopelessness to their clients? What programs in training, in

adult education, can you offer that will assure your client a
job? I could not see much of a solution, given the present
system. These questions were being asked while I was Director of Manpower at Williamsburg Community Corporation,
shortly after JOIN was merged with this Corporation. Of
course, some people were helped, but I believed that cooperation had to extend much closer to industry and the professional in the neighborhoods where these unfortunate people live.

While working as Public Relations Director at the Williamsburg Community Corporation and later at the Puerto Rican Community Development Project, I began to envision the
most rewarding profession for women. Public relations covers so many facets of daily living; it is invigorating, fascinating and exciting work, for there are no routine assignments.
You must keep abreast of all types of news, since everything
affects your agency or firm. One learns to speak on virtually any subject. If one likes to write, it provides the opportunity, whether in the form of a newsletter or a press release. It was in this field that I decided to focus my attention on what I am now doing. During this time I realized the
importance of the fact that the world knew extremely little of
the Puerto Rican, and that the Puerto Rican himself was also
unaware of his cultural roots. This revelation forced me to
seek hungrily for books dealing with Puerto Rico. I would
often be asked by people from other agencies and by teachers
to provide literature on the customs, attire, legal tender,
food, etc. of the Puerto Rican. Circumstances, fate or
God's will then gave me a new assignment.

I began to work as Vice President of CLICK (Commerce, Labor, Industry Corporation of Kings), the organization that is developing the Brooklyn Navy Yard as an industrial complex. This was a completely new experience and
certainly a challenge. The Brooklyn Navy Yard was a booming place prior to the end of World War II. Thousands of
men and some women were employed in this yard where the
famous ship "Monitor" was built. On its dry docks, large
cranes hovered above the construction of one of the largest
tankers ever built in the United States. It was an impressive sight. The enormously large, empty buildings with long
stairs and the quaint homes, still occupied by Navy officers,
all blended to make the Yard a small town. The setting was
different, but the problems and concerns were not.

My responsibility as Vice President was to supervise
various divisions of the Corporation such as the Employment

Center, Department of Economic Development, Day Care Center and Medical Center. I was the only female officer in the Corporation and it was soon apparent that a woman and a Puerto Rican in that executive position was not a welcome addition to the firm. Of course, no one said anything, but the forgetfulness of other executives who excluded me from various important meetings was an obvious indication. That I was so involved in community matters was a detriment in the eyes of some of the executives, although it should have been seen as an asset, for after all, the organization was formed to help combat the unemployment problem in the surrounding areas. Occasionally, I inquired about certain information which I felt was important to the community and I would be abruptly warned that my extreme interest in certain information might also be deemed harmful. If I opened my mouth, I might get away with it because I was a woman, but what would I accomplish? I'm not equipped to comment on whether Puerto Ricans lack political power in Brooklyn or commitment to any political group, or whether these were men who felt obligated to political bosses and were caught in a trap, and whose only recourse was to remain silent, collect their pay checks and erase their consciences; but I believe that the situation must have been as frustrating for them as it was for me. There were exceptions, of course, but few of them were in positions to create drastic change.

Union negotiations at CLICK were interesting and revealing. The first time I went to one of these meetings, there was an unusual silence and I wondered what was wrong. Perhaps, I thought, the previous meeting had left some scars? I finally learned that my presence, the presence of a woman, was what provoked the obvious discomfort. The silence persisted for only a short while, but eventually I became uneasy myself. One of my colleagues later informed me that it was not necessary for me to be present at these meetings, but I wanted to learn. After all, the discussions involved workers in the corporation and the Yard's companies whose future relied on the results of these meetings. In one instance, I was surprised to learn that one company based in the Yard had negotiated a contract with a union which stipulated certain hourly wages and that the workers, for years, had been receiving much less. This situation existed long before the company entered the Yard. The workers themselves were not even aware of this or of their rights as Union members. Then, I questioned why a Labor Consultant, hired to serve several hours a week, had earned $7,000 after only two months. This money could have been used constructively to benefit the workers.

Perhaps, I thought, being a woman is a handicap in
such a business, for she is much more sensitive to such injustice. At CLICK, I was able to utilize my experiences in
manpower, in public relations and in business. One of the
purposes of the organization was to encourage small minority
businesses into the Yard. This seemed an ideal opportunity
for local people to enter the world of business, but it was a
rather disastrous failure. The small businessman had difficulty in obtaining licenses, permits and capital. What was
considered small business to the government was big business
to these people, and for some who applied for space, it
proved to be quite an experience. To those at CLICK who
were concerned, it was also disheartening. I did not find the
work difficult or strange, only disillusioning at times, because of the failures of the Agency. Some of these were due
to poor direction and administration, others to unfortunate
circumstances that were sometimes beyond the control of those
in the organization, and some arose from the fact that this
was a new concept being tried out for the first time in Brooklyn. Although I was working unceasingly and was making a
fairly good salary, I felt that I was not, personally, accom-
plishing much. I sometimes felt like the circus bear performing atop a barrel, making it move around and around,
moving unceasingly but remaining on the same spot. Perhaps
I was too eager for things to happen. Here you had to contend with Washington's approval of this and that, with the
city, with the companies already established in the Yard,
their problems, and the process of normal business negotiations. I decided to resign and venture into something which
I felt sure would be beneficial to many people and would enable me to support my family and myself.

I had already decided that the only way for me to obtain satisfaction in my work and support myself and my children was to have my own business. I had been in business
before and had been successful, but now I wanted much more.
I wanted to feel that I was contributing to a great cause.
Time was growing short. I had long been aware that most
Americans, including many Puerto Ricans, did not know anything about Puerto Rico, although its people are American
citizens. Many think that Puerto Ricans have no history, no
heritage, no great talents. When searching for books throughout the city, I was dismayed at their scarcity. What was
more natural than to start Puerto Rican Heritage Publications!

Puerto Rican Heritage Publications proved to be just what was needed to fill the gap. To promote anything you first need capital, extensive knowledge of the merchandise and a good location. All I had was enthusiasm, "coraje" (anger), determination, and a realization that this was the thing I wanted to do more than anything else in the world. This was the kind of business to which I would be happy to devote the rest of my life. I would be able to promote and project all that Puerto Rico had to offer, and there was so much! My previous experiences in business did not include the buying of merchandise, but I soon learned. In the previous business I did not have to invest much. Here I would have to invest a great deal, and space was vital. For the location I decided upon my own two-family home. For financing, I went to the nearest bank and to the Small Business Administration office. I felt like the small business man trying to get into the Yard. It was difficult and risky enough to start this business, but it became more so when I applied for a loan at SBA. The trips back and forth between SBA offices and the bank were enough to discourage anyone. I was told that I had no experience in this type of business, that I had to work at least six months for a publishing house, that I had to have plenty of orders before I could be granted any consideration. My first interviewer told me that he did not believe women should be in business! My enthusiasm and determination kept me going and I vowed that I would continue, barring God's will, regardless of what happened. It took almost eighteen months to convince everyone that I was serious and capable enough to handle this business.

I visited Puerto Rico often, searching for authors and publishers. I scanned every bookstore, discovering hidden treasures, and confirming my opinion that they should be shared with those in the mainland. There are bookstores on the mainland that sell Puerto Rican books but not one is Puerto Rican-owned and exclusively dedicated to the promotion of Puerto Rican educational materials. In fact, there is none even in Puerto Rico! The only place in Puerto Rico where you can find books exclusively by Puerto Rican authors is at the Society of Puerto Rican Writers and Poets, a non-profit organization whose president is Miss Isabel Cuchi Coll. Isabel is a noted writer and the grandaughter of the illustrious Puerto Rican, Cayetano Coll y Toste. Isabel has helped me a great deal and has introduced me to many of the important writers of Puerto Rico. She lived in New York for over fifteen years and then returned to the Island.

I wondered why there were no other businesses of this type anywhere, and then I found out. Ninety-nine percent of all the books of Puerto Rico are not published or printed in Puerto Rico, but in Spain, Mexico, Argentina, Venezuela or other Latin countries. Book printing costs are high, almost as high in Puerto Rico as in the States. Very small editions are made, sometimes 1000 or 2000 copies which are quickly sold. Just when people are beginning to know about the book it is out of print; in the meantime, you have it listed in your new catalogue. Rapid changes in prices are another problem: one month a book may be listed at $3, the next it may have increased to $5.

The first year in business we mailed out 30,000 catalogues to universities, colleges, schools, libraries and other institutions throughout the United States. The response was terrific. It was evident that many people, many educators, want to learn about Puerto Rico and Puerto Ricans. I learned that there are Puerto Ricans scattered throughout the United States in remote places, who sometimes barely know where the Island is situated. One of the first letters I received was from a Puerto Rican who had been living in Ogden, Utah since he was a very young boy. He had not eaten Puerto Rican food or read a newspaper or book dealing with Puerto Rico for over twenty years. When he discovered our catalogue he was thrilled and wrote immediately. He said he was "hungry" for information about Puerto Rico; it was as though he had been stranded on a desert island and had just returned to civilization.

While searching for books in Puerto Rico I traveled to many small towns, and there met several Santeros from whom I learned about the folk art, "santeria." Santeria began in the 16th century, and later became much admired and collected. The Santeros carved wooden Saints for their religious ceremonies and beliefs and, for a very long time, every home had either a set of the Three Kings or some statuette. The Santeros are generally country folk with little or no training or formal education, but with a distinct talent for carving. I began to buy Santos and other types of wood carvings each time I made a trip to the Island. I also discovered many other crafts which were beautiful and unique. Strange that I had never seen any of these in the souvenir shops in Old San Juan and in El Condado? Strange also was the fact that when I searched closely, I found many articles marked "Puerto Rico" which were not made in Puerto Rico and visibly displayed the country of origin in the back! This was an out-

rage, particularly when beautiful native crafts are hidden
from the tourist or the Puerto Rican visiting the Island and
returning to the mainland with nothing to remind him of home.
There are wonderful artists who are struggling for recognition, whose art is beautiful and should be admired and purchased. I was able to find prints, reproductions and origi-
nals of their work, and prints and reproductions, too, of old
masters such as Campeche, Oller, Atiles and Pou.

Puerto Rican Heritage Publications, Inc. is now well
known throughout the country and in Puerto Rico, but the hill
is still steep. Climbing it is not such a great hardship, I
find, because I am walking together with thousands of young
people who are discovering their heritage. Puerto Rican
Heritage still has problems of upkeep, collections, working
capital, but the interest, enthusiasm and love for what I am
doing has not waned. Each time I see the respect and love
in the faces of the young people and many adults when they
visit PRH, I am compensated anew. My goals at PRH, at
first mainly the dissemination of Puerto Rican educational materials, now have broadened. I would like to see more people buying books by Puerto Rican authors--they have so much
to offer. I would like to see more tourists and Puerto Ricans return to the mainland from Puerto Rico with souvenirs,
art and crafts that are truly Puerto Rican and not made somewhere else. I would like to see a permanent boycott of the
thousands of items which are dumped in the Island from all
over the world while Artesanos and other Puerto Rican craftsmen live miserable lives because they have no outlet for their
inspirations. I would only excuse the souvenir shop owners
if they gave the Puerto Rican craftsmen priority in their purchases. I would like to see more Puerto Rican actors, sing-
ers and other performers given the opportunity to present
their talents at the big hotels. I would like to see more
Puerto Rican food being sold at the hotels and fancy restau-
rants. I would like to see more bilingual schools where every
Puerto Rican child will be taught the language of his parents
and his grandparents.

If the Puerto Rican professional would realize the importance of preserving her language, customs, and heritage,
and would help, each in her own way, she would feel much
more fulfilled. If she has children, she cannot overlook her
compatriotas who are in need, because her children must
learn to carry on the mission to preserve all that is Puerto
Rican. Her children must see her efforts and will learn from

them.   The world must know us through our talents and our
heritage.

Adelante, Boricua!

CHAPTER 16

THE PUERTO RICAN PROFESSIONAL IN AMERICA

Amalia Betanzos

From the beginning of American history, men and women from many lands have come to its shores seeking a panacea--a cure-all for whatever has ailed them in their native lands. Be it inadequate housing, insufficient food and clothing, religious persecution, or what have you--America is the answer. The land of opportunity!

These people, at first strangers to one another, become neighbors by working together, by facing endless problems cooperatively, by building communities, by uniting in civic, religious, labor and many other groups to work for their common good. Needless to say, the Puerto Ricans in America are such a people. Yet, like so many immigrants before him, prior to admittance into the mainstream of American life the Puerto Rican had to disprove innumerable fallacies and stereotypes, circulated by ethnocentrics eager to discredit him: all are illiterates...dirty...subject to congenital tropical diseases...few can obtain gainful employment... high tensioned, low motivated people...serious delinquency problems...create slums...mark of the Puerto Rican heritage is the switchblade.

If fighting against such bigotry and rising above it successfully suggests a supernatural cause, then a miracle it is, for the fight of the Puerto Rican professional to gain acceptance has been a two-fold monumental task: first, to gain approbation as a human being, and secondly, to receive recognition for his professional credentials.

Puerto Ricans, whether native or through parentage, come from a culture in which strong emphasis is placed on education and on cooperative effort to improve conditions. As a result of these factors and an innate drive to "make good" in the "Promised Land," Puerto Rican professionals are being assimilated into the life of the city and America,

147

in general, faster than any other group. Demographer Donald
J. Bogue of the University of Chicago has stated:

> The educational attainment, income, and occupational
> level of second-generation Puerto Ricans is clearly
> superior.... In fact, although the evidence is skimpy,
> it suggests that Puerto Ricans may become assimi-
> lated as fast as the Italians, the Polish, and the
> Czechs have.... [1]

The emergence of the Puerto Rican professional in
America has been long coming. No longer can a people solely boast of screen actors, orchestra leaders and athletes as
their contribution to America. But in this time of personal
awareness and cultural pride, we must render special com-
mendation to the countless Puerto Ricans who are leaving
their mark in contemporary American history. There are
numerous Puerto Rican policemen and welfare workers, teachers and social workers, office workers and independent businessmen, doctors and lawyers, psychologists and counselors;
Puerto Ricans have also joined the ranks of the "politicos."
We have state legislators, city magistrates, assemblymen,
congressmen, judges. Closer to home, the expertise of the
Puerto Rican professional is to be found in the hierarchy of
many New York City super-agencies and private foundations--
Youth Service Agency, Relocation, Manpower, Department of
Corrections, Human Rights Commission, the Board of Higher
Education, Economic Development Administration, The Ford
Foundation, and The New York Urban Coalition, to name a
few. Puerto Rican professionals have also been at the core
of their own self-development programs--the Puerto Rican
Community Development Project, The Puerto Rican Forum,
The Puerto Rican Association for Community Affairs, Aspira,
Instituto de Puerto Rico, etc. --all committed to the total
growth of the Puerto Rican.

The quest of the Puerto Rican does not end here, however. In fact, acceptance of the Puerto Rican as a professional in America is only the beginning of a mission. We
must, as a people, dedicate ourselves to the preservation of
our Spanish cultural heritage, as well as to the absorption of
the best of the American culture. We must continue to encourage our compatriots in their pursuit of higher education.
And, if we are to maintain the warmth, vitality, friendliness,
hospitality, and artistic expression inherent to our "Borinquen," we must, above all, preserve our sense of dignity and

worth as individuals.

Note

1. Bogue, Donald J. <u>The Population of the United States.</u>
    New York: Free Press, 1959, p. 372.

CHAPTER 17

A PUERTO RICAN AMERICAN SPEAKS*

Luis Mercado

We Puerto Ricans belong to a large family of people having a common identity, language, and heritage. We deserve to be considered on the basis of our unique story as a people whose culture is not less than the Anglo-American. We simply are, with no claims of superiority, nor any wish to be considered inferior, to any of the peoples living in the U.S.A.

For hundreds of years Puerto Rico and Puerto Ricans have been linked to other countries through language, history, politics, economics, culture, colonialism, imperialism, war, and peace.

The Indians of Puerto Rico, our Tainos, spoke a language that contained words found in language throughout the world today. Some of the words are:

Indian	English
hamaca	hammock
tobaco	tobacco
hurakán	hurricane

Our ancestors studied in Spain, France and Italy. They lived in exile in Caracas, New York City, Paris, Valparaiso (Chile) and made contributions to the systems of education in the Dominican Republic and Chile. Our forefathers died for freedom in Cuba and joined Simón Bolívar in the liberation movement that brought independence for many of the Latin American nations.

---

*Reprinted by permission of J. B. Lippincott Company from The Search for Identity: Modern American History, by John Edward Wiltz, c. 1973.

Men from all nations have made great contributions to the history and culture of Puerto Rico. The man who saved us from losing our language was Manuel Fernandez Juncos, who came from Spain. He translated from English new textbooks that were required by the Americans after they occupied Puerto Rico in 1898. Our cultural hero, Pablo Casals, was a Republican exile from Spain. His mother was Puerto Rican.

Other great men are the American Matias Brugman, the Dominican Bauren and the Venezuelan Manuel Rojas, who were part of the leadership of our aborted revolution, El Grito de Lares (1868). It is interesting to note that the New Poor Theatre of America, directed by Pedro Santaliz, has presented (1972) in New York City a play adapted from various writings by Puerto Rican authors and poets called "El Grito en el Tiempo," a dramatic collage about the Lares uprising.

Rafael Hernandez, world-famous composer, and Jose de Diego, inspirational poet and patriot, were born in Aguadilla; Arecibo was home to Luis Muñoz-Rivera, first premier of the short-lived autonomous State of Puerto Rico (1898). Betances, an abolitionist and the man considered by many to be the "father" of Puerto Rico, was born in Cabo Rojo. This was also the birthplace of a legendary figure, the pirate Cofresi, as well as that of the famous horsethief, "The Eagle." Rio Cañas in the Mayaguez is the birthplace of Eugenio Maria De Hostos, our greatest educator. There is a housing project named after him on West 91st Street in New York City.

The culture of Puerto Rico is the result of a historical process completely different from that of mainland U. S. A. Puerto Ricans have learned to know American culture and civilization, but we do not accept many of its principles. Our goal should be to stimulate interest in our mainland Puerto Ricans as well as in other Americans to learn Spanish and study Puerto Rico's contributions as a people, culture, and civilization, and resist those forces that seek to deny and negate our cultural and historical heritage.

Puerto Rico is the homeland of Puerto Ricans, a people whose first or native language is Spanish. Puerto Rico is a mountainous, beautiful island, 100 miles long by 36 miles wide, with almost three million people. It is part of the Greater Antilles in the Caribbean Sea, 1,600 miles southeast of New York City.

About one and a half million Puerto Ricans living on the mainland are concentrated mainly in urban areas in the northeastern part of the U.S.A. There are about a million people of Puerto Rican descent living in the metropolitan area of New York City.

Puerto Ricans are a proud, angry, and misunderstood people. We have been uprooted from our traditional way of life. We have been cast up on the shores of urban white America. Puerto Ricans on the mainland and on our island have lost those bench-marks, those reference points, by which a person defines his relationship to others.

Our challenge is based on the process of becoming a new people. Who are we? What are we? Where do we belong in racist white colonial America? For the last one hundred years Puerto Ricans in Puerto Rico have struggled to resolve these questions of identity. They still remain to be solved. The dilemma of our modern world catches Puerto Ricans in the squeeze of always becoming and never being.

The writer Gordon Lewis feels that the personality of Puerto Ricans has been shaped by their search for identity. This, he believes, leads them to turn inward to repressed feeling and not outward to remedial action.

The great Puerto Rican migration occurred at the end of World War II. It is comparable to the waves of immigrants of Irish, Polish, Swedish, German, Slavic, Chinese, Jewish, Japanese, Italian, Mexican, and Cuban people. The important difference is that Puerto Ricans migrated here at a time when the "melting pot" idea of forcible assimilation was beginning to lose its intensity and hold upon the American way of life.

Puerto Ricans must have the benefits of the new sociopolitical force, cultural pluralism. Cultural pluralism emphasizes the importance of permitting and encouraging people to retain their culture in a new environment. This enables second and third generations to make a transition into the mainstream of American life. Good examples of this trend are the neighborhood areas in New York City of El Barrio in Manhattan, the South Bronx, the Lower East Side, and Williamsburg in Brooklyn. Puerto Ricans make great efforts to preserve a genuine respect for their own culture. Cultural conflict occurs as Puerto Ricans enter the arena of employment and housing and enroll children in public schools.

Puerto Ricans are American citizens because of the Jones Act of 1917. The island of Puerto Rico was ceded by Spain to the United States on December 10, 1898, by the Treaty of Paris as part payment of the cost of the American-initiated imperialistic Spanish-American War. Thus the U.S.A. ended the one year old Puerto Rican Commonwealth and imposed colonial rule. Puerto Rico was governed through the U.S. Department of Interior and the U.S. Navy and Army Departments. The ruling officials usually were men who strongly reflected the plantation mentality, customs, and folk-ways of the Deep South, with its preoccupation with race, class, and religion.

Puerto Rico has had the longest unbroken stretch of colonial rule, 400 years under Spain and 74 years under the U.S.A., of any land in the world. From 1898 to 1917 the peoples living in Puerto Rico were "things." They did not have citizenship. They were not Spanish or American citizens. They were natives, forcibly colonized and made to act as puppets of the Anglo-Saxon conquerors. English became the official language, the traditional agricultural patterns were destroyed, and southern U.S. landowners bought up great chunks of Puerto Rico and created a sugar colony protected by U.S. quotas. This was also the plan carried out in Cuba and the Philippines, the other parts of the payment by the Spanish losers to the American winners of the War of 1898.

The granting of U.S. citizenship enabled Puerto Ricans to move freely to mainland United States after 1917. The granting of Commonwealth status in 1951, as a result of the loosening of the bonds of world-wide colonialism after World War II, the rapid economic development, changing religious condition, and the growth of nationalism in Puerto Rico as reflected by the growth of influence of the "Third World," have contributed to the challenges facing our people in main-land United States.

The key challenges are:

1. The breaking down of the solidarity of the Puerto Rican community and weakening of its ability to combat stereotypes of Puerto Ricans--caused by the pressures of the colonial ideology of melting pot assimilation.

2. The difficulties imposed by a society which identi-fies and places human beings by color and race.

3. Difficulties brought about by religious identification.

4. The psychological nearness and the reality of easy physical return to Puerto Rico via jet. (Puerto Rico is three and a half hours and $50 away.)

5. Employment and job market recessions.

6. Public schools and the need for bilingual education.

7. The political status of the island of Puerto Rico (commonwealth, statehood, or independence).

8. Problems of housing, public welfare, drug abuse, mental illness, and lack of political representation in the city, state, and federal governments.

9. Nationalism, militancy, and the rise of youth groups such as the Young Lords.

Some dangerous stereotypes reflecting the process or sweeping generalizations against Puerto Ricans are:

Stereotype 1: Puerto Ricans cause slums.
   Answer: City slums were here long before Puerto Ricans arrived. Slums are the result of years of neglect and failure by government and the public in planning our neighborhoods.

Stereotype 2: Everybody knows Puerto Ricans drink too much.
   Answer: Who is everybody? Excessive drinking can be found in many groups, and alcoholism is recognized as a social disease. Alcoholics require treatment to help them overcome the need to drink.

Stereotype 3: Puerto Ricans are always getting arrested. You always see their pictures and stories in the newspapers or on television.
   Answer: Crimes are committed by people of all backgrounds. They are not related to any one group. Many people look at television and read newspapers because these offer sensational stories. This leads to false generalizations about crime and nationality.

Stereotype 4: Why should Puerto Ricans vote? They don't

speak English.

Answer: Puerto Ricans are citizens whether or not they speak English. They have the same responsibilities and enjoy the same rights as other citizens.

Stereotype 5: My brother was in the army in Vietnam. He says all Puerto Rican soldiers had easy soft jobs away from the fighting.

Answer: How does the army assign men to combat units? Do you believe assignments are made on the basis of ethnic backgrounds? During the Korean War, Puerto Rican soldiers suffered six times the casualty rate of mainland American soldiers.

Stereotype 6: Puerto Ricans are poor politicians. They aren't as good as us. They never get elected to public office.

Answer: Puerto Ricans have taken an effective part in political life. Puerto Ricans run the Commonwealth government of Puerto Rico with an elected governor and an elected House of Representatives and a Senate. In New York City Herman Badillo is the first elected congressman; Manny Ramos, Luis Nine, and Robert Garcia are New York State assemblymen; Manual Gomez, Felipe Torres, and Gilberto Ramirez are judges.

Stereotype 7: Puerto Ricans come to New York City or elsewhere to go on public assistance (welfare).

Answer: New York City Department of Welfare reports show that 85-95 percent of the Puerto Rican population is employed. During periods of prosperity 5-6 percent are unemployed.

Stereotype 8: All Puerto Ricans are black.

Answer: Some are, some are not. The U.S. Census classifies the people of Puerto Rico as 79.7 percent white, and 20.13 percent nonwhite. Census figures show that fewer nonwhites come to the U.S. from Puerto Rico than whites. What might be some of the reasons for this?

In recent years an increasing number of Puerto Ricans have returned to their island homeland. Some found that they

could not live in mainland society and still retain their pride
in being Puerto Ricans. Others have gone back in order to
have their children educated in Puerto Rico.

Education is one of the major problems of Puerto Ricans. In 1970, testimony before the Select Committee on
Equal Educational Opportunity stated:

> Our schools have failed. Our schools are damaged.
> Our Puerto Rican children are being destroyed.
> The opportunities must be taken by Puerto Rican
> people to defend our children. The New York City
> educational system is guilty of complicity in a pro-
> cess which has destroyed the self-image and iden-
> tity of hundreds of thousands of our children.

Bilingual education (learning in Spanish and English) is
a part of the solution to the deplorable mainland public school
situation. As an example, in New York City today only 5,000
students out of a total of 105,000 elementary students who
need bilingual education are receiving it in our public schools.
The issue in bilingual education is whether we should hold on
to our familiar friendly culture or abandon family history,
tradition, pride, and respect. Americans need to support
our efforts to preserve our life-style and heritage and recognize our necessity not to ape theirs. We must fight to preserve our cultural trappings, our old ways. Support of bilingual education by all ethnics can be the basis for a new
alliance that can revitalize public education.

My alliance with black educators and the NAACP, leading to the overthrow of the supervisory examination system
in public education in New York City, has been a success.
However, Puerto Rican educational leaders initially considered
it to be a futile gesture. Yet, because of our legal victories
in the federal courts, the year 1971-72 saw the assignment of
17 Puerto Rican public school principals where before there
had been but three. Of course, there are over 1,000 public
schools in New York City, from elementary through high
school.

In the past 15 years the emphasis has shifted in American society from culture to power and the politics of con-
frontation, the development of multiple protest strategies.
Typical of these is the action-oriented movement of the anti-
poverty programs. The strategy of organizing resources
around common interests and alliances tends to reduce the

cultural glue needed for the strengthening of Puerto Rican identity. Power depends upon the group. The rise of the militant youth group, the Young Lords, came as a result of the move away from civil rights and integration into first black and then ethnic power.

In the political turmoil of urban areas, the loss of family cultural values becomes a source of great tension and identity conflicts for Puerto Ricans. The militancy of young Puerto Rican groups creates severe tensions between them and their parents. The sense of identity that youth are finding in a common cause can alienate segments of the Puerto Rican community. Perhaps this is already happening.

Puerto Ricans need a national movement combining and utilizing the potential of a greater population base. The lack of organized national protest movements seems to be a result of migration patterns. Aspira is attempting to become a national urban group. However, the concentration of Puerto Ricans in eastern states, largely in a few cities, has tied us into local situations. Both language and culture can lead to a national alliance of Hispanic peoples in the United States. The Chicanos (Mexican Americans) and the Puerto Ricans formed a successful alliance in 1968 with respect to federal aid for public bilingual education. In recent months there have been attempts to form an alliance with the Chicanos around a National Spanish Bilingual TV program. The geographic distance separating Puerto Ricans from Mexican Americans and the question of whether the rural migrant Mexican will assimilate with urban Puerto Ricans create barriers and difficulties. The rise of ethnic groups throughout the country and our mutual interests can be used to organize and change the nature of anti-democratic, exploitative, imperialistic American society.

CHAPTER 18

ACROSS THIRD AVENUE: FREEDOM

Humberto Cintrón

Third Avenue. As far as the eye could see, the cobblestone street was saddled by a great, black, spider-like iron monster called the "Third Ave. El. " It cast a checkerboard shadow, alternating with shafts of sunlight like a huge web draped across the wide boulevard waiting for unsuspecting victims. I remember sitting on the curb, staring across to the east side of the street, the ominous, forboding presence of the "El" weighing on my 8-year-old mind and giving more substance to the taboo that Third Avenue was for the Puerto Rican kid in East Harlem.

Across that no man's land was an unknown world filled with exotic delights and adventures not accessible to me except through hearsay. Somewhere beyond was Jefferson Park and an olympic-sized swimming pool; the Italian festival of Our Lady of Mt. Carmel, complete with ferris wheel, merry-go-round, pizza pies, cotton candy, multi-flavored ices, and fireworks; there were a live market, fishing piers that extended into the East River, and the Boys Club. That I knew of for certain. The things I didn't know about were endless. My imagination soared as I sat watching the red and gold trolleys rattle along on the shiny silver tracks embedded in the cobblestones and listened to the roar and clatter of the iron horse overhead, spattering sparks into the air.

The traffic wasn't so heavy, and the traffic light was no different from any other. Red meant "stop, " green meant "go. " And there wasn't any barbed wire or solid wall or alligator-filled moat or any other physical obstacle to keep me sitting on the curb day-dreaming while other people came and went, oblivious to my vicarious meanderings. None of that. The fact is, with my P. F. 's I could probably beat nearly anyone across and back.

No, the barrier wasn't one my wiry body couldn't run

under, over or through. The barrier was inside my head.
Not that it wasn't real. It was real. But it had gotten inside my head the same way the knowledge of Jefferson Pool
and the Boys Club had gotten there--through hearsay: stories,
rumors, and countless tales that fill the ether, the "stuff" of
which tradition is made, transmitted from one person to another over time and distance. It was accepted fact without
ever having been experienced. It was self-fulfilling.

Puerto Ricans were not to cross Third Avenue; that
was Italian territory. Period.

Even Danny--"Italian Junior" we called him then--to
this day among my closest and most trusted friends, more a
brother than a friend, could not offer a solution.

Beyond Third Avenue you risked your life. It was a
challenge I grew up with. Over the years the Third Avenue
"barrier" appears to have crumbled under the steady flow of
Puerto Ricans into "El Barrio" and Italians out of East Harlem. Not without a good measure of violence and heartache
and bloodshed. Yet although the "Third Avenue El" and the
trolleys no longer run on Third Avenue, and although the
movement of Puerto Ricans in and around New York seems,
on the surface, to have overcome the "barrier," no such
thing has ever happened. The wall of "unwelcome" flourishes.
As always it is invisible. It came to us through tradition,
through institutional behavior--it is the life-style of America.
It can be traced back through the various ebbs and flows of
waves and waves of immigrants who were nursed on an institutional inferiority syndrome which required them to cast
away their cultural values in order to assume the American
identity.

Nor am I suggesting that his behavior was peculiar to
Italians in East Harlem. No such luck--had it been that way
it would be easy to deal with. No, they learned it here, as
a result of their experience as newcomers. And others had
learned it before them, and they in turn learned from their
predecessors. That's what tradition is. That's how social
institutions are built.

In those days I never questioned the pennies dropped
into the church basket or the coins for the poor box that mom
gave us ritually on Sunday, though our table seldom saw a
chicken or a pork chop. That too was tradition.

In the midst of the roar of bricks launched from a
rooftop and zip gun blasts in the night, we were learning in
school that George Washington never told a lie; Abraham Lincoln freed slaves; and every child in America could grow to
be president.   We learned it all by rote ("Four score and
seven years ago our forefathers brought forth upon this continent
a new nation conceived in liberty and dedicated to the propo-
sition that all men are created equal. . . . . ").   Those words
reverberated through my mind on many occasions; while I
heaved a garbage can down hard and heavy on some bastard
who I'd knocked to the ground before he got to me; and when
I rolled in the gutter tasting blood and dirt while someone's
booted foot dug deep into my ribs and spine.

But I never grew up bitter.

I grew up hauling blocks of ice up five flights for the
little old Italian lady who lived next door; and running every
conceivable kind of errand for anybody who needed it; and
translating for Mrs. Rivera and Mr. Gonzalez to the teacher,
insurance agent, welfare investigator, cop, landlord, nurse,
truant officer, etc, etc, etc.   "What a good boy you have,
Maria," all the neighbors said.   And I was.

And I grew up getting my ass kicked and kicking the
next guy's ass up and down the streets of El Barrio.

"That's a bad dude, Chino," the reputation went.   And
I was.

I grew up knowing that cruelty and violence and deceit
were all part of the personal repertoire of social tools that
I needed to be armed with to fend off the merchants of hypocrisy that rule and govern and perpetuate the "traditions" that
make America "great."   In the vernacular of contemporary
American thought it all comes under the category of "being
realistic."

The idea was never to unleash your weapons until the
showdown came.   The "good guy," after all, never drew his
gun first in the movies.   But when he did, look out.

A strange ethic when you look at it.   In order to be
the "good guy" you had to be able to do all the things that
characterized the "bad guy" better than they did.   Simplistic?
Probably so--it's also what the Watergate mess appears to
be about.   A self-righteous hypocrisy that led some people

to think that they, being the "good guys," could use any
means necessary to insure that they could continue to be the
"good guys."

Bullshit.

But it's the American way and it's the system that has
been perpetuated in institution after institution, from the
church to the Mafia; from government to revolutionary movements; from the suburbs to the central city.   From corporations to united funds.

I'm not going to judge it.   After all, even the "Watergate" came to light; and there may be a remedy for that mess;
and someone may say, "It was that same system that weeded
out the imperfections and developed a solution"; and certainly
the traditions and institutions in America seek to resolve the
problems they confront.

I won't disagree with that.

But history has taught me that the institution which is
a solution to one problem quickly becomes, itself, the next
problem for which a solution must be found.   So it is with
churches and armies and police and museums and corporations
and labor unions and newspapers and commissions.

"Third Avenue" has been with me all my life and I
suspect it will be with all Puerto Ricans all of their lives,
in one form or another.   And it affected and will continue to
affect every experience of any significance in my lifetime.

It was there in the military when, after four years as
an instructor and "Guided Missiles Expert," I was discharged
A/2C.

It was there in college, which required seven years
and three dropouts to complete.

It was there in Mississippi when we started "freedom
schools" to achieve "equal" education.

It was still there in "El Barrio" during the rent strike
days and community action days when the anti-poverty program raised hopes and generated dreams of self-help, only
to be ground into the dust of yesterday's rhetoric.

And it lived on with the experimental school districts
and the struggles for "community control" and the vain attempts to wrest control in a neighborhood shared politically
by legislators from other communities but served by none.

It was there when the publishers sent rejection slip
after rejection slip and I finally had to raise the bucks to
publish my book myself.

It's still there now, when every instrument of mass
communications--print and electronic--chooses to ignore the
Puerto Rican editorially; or carefully selects the images it
presents, thus helping to perpetuate stereotypical negativism
or promote a token Puerto Rican personality while systematically denying employment and opportunities to Puerto Ricans
exclusive of the mail room. In New York City today you can
count on the fingers of your hands the number of Puerto Ricans employed in a professional capacity in all the major
television, radio and print media combined.

I suppose I'll always sit on the curb somewhere, staring in the Third avenues of the world, wanting to belong.
And I suppose too that I'll venture forth into that unknown,
seeking and probing and discovering. And I expect too that
I'll always have my pennies for the poor box, eager to serve
and be "good" in what is likely to be a quixotic adventure.
But one thing you can count on as absolutely certain:

"Third Avenue" was not and will not be a deterrent to
joining the struggle and doing the things that need to be done
--or, better said, trying to do what needs to be done.   It
certainly can not deter me from choosing to put on my P. F.'s
and running under, over or through it.

CONTRIBUTORS

CHARLES BAHN is Professor of Psychology, John Jay College of Criminal Justice of The City University of New York. He is Director of Research, ASPIRA, Inc. and Research Consultant, Puerto Rican Forum, Inc. He has been a consultant to many organizations and a contributor to numerous professional publications.

PURA BELPRÉ is a Children's Specialist with the South Bronx Library Project. She has been a Children's Librarian at the New York Public Library. Miss Belpré is widely known for her children's books, Santiago (Warne), Oté (Pantheon), Tiger and the Rabbit (Lippincott), among others. She is a member of the Institute of Puerto Rico.

JOSÉ BETANCOURT is Assistant Professor in the Library at Eugenio Maria de Hostos Community College, The City University of New York. He has served on the library staff at Brooklyn College and Queensborough Public Library. He is currently organizing a library for the Center for Puerto Rican Studies and Research, The City University of New York.

AMALIA BETANZOS is Commissioner of the Youth Services Agency. She has also served the City of New York as Executive Director of the Puerto Rican Community Development Project; Deputy Administrator/Commissioner of the Housing and Development Administration; Assistant/Executive Secretary to the Mayor.

HUMBERTO CINTRÓN is Executive Producer of the television program "Realidades," seen on Channel 13 in New York. Mr. Cintrón was awarded a silver medal by the International TV and Film Festival of N.Y. for "No Orphans for Tia" (NBC-TV). He is the author of Frankie Cristo, a novel published by Vantage Press.

LUIS FUENTES is Superintendent of Community School District 1, Manhattan. His controversial and stormy tenure there has been widely publicized by the press. Mr. Fuentes claims the distinction of being the first Puerto Rican principal in a New York City public school.

MARIFÉ HERNÁNDEZ is Producer and Moderator, Community Affairs Programming for WPIX-TV (Channel 11 in New York), which telecasts her program "Puerto Rican New Yorker." Ms. Hernández is Chairman, Institute of Contemporary Hispanic Arts, and serves as Member of the Board of Directors of ASPIRA and the Puerto Rican Family Institute.

LILLIAN LÓPEZ is Coordinator of Special Services at The New York Public Library. Much of her professional career has been spent in libraries serving Spanish-speaking communities. Her article describing "The South Bronx Project" appeared in the March 1970 Wilson Library Bulletin.

EDWARD MAPP is Professor and Chairman at New York City Community College and a member of its Puerto Rican Studies Committee on Appointments. He was the Faculty Senate's liaison to The City University Affirmative Action Committee. Dr. Mapp is author of Blacks in American Films (Scarecrow Press) among other publications.

JACINTO MARRERO is Executive Director, New Jersey Region, The National Conference of Christians and Jews. He was previously Director of the Brooklyn Region. Mr. Marrero has been a teacher in Puerto Rico and New York. He is an active participant in numerous civic and community organizations.

LUIS MERCADO is Community Principal, P.S. 75, Manhattan. He has been Project Director for "Building Bilingual Bridges" and Director of Puerto Rican Studies at Fordham University. As plaintiff, with support from the NAACP's legal defense fund, Mr. Mercado challenged the system for hiring public school principals as being discriminatory.

FRANK NEGRON is Director of The City University of New York Affirmative Action Program. His previous appointments include Asst. Director, Center for Urban Education; Deputy Commissioner, Mayor's Office of Education Affairs; Executive Director of ASPIRA of America, Inc. Mr. Negron coordinated the first National Hearings on Equal Educational Opportunity for Puerto Ricans before the U.S.

Senate Select Committee.   He is active in numerous community organizations.

BENJAMIN PACHECO is Associate Professor of Sociology and
Director, Institute of Bilingual Studies at Kingsborough
Community College.   He was a secondary school teacher
of history in Puerto Rico and an instructor in Education of
the Puerto Rican child at Herbert Lehman College.

LUIS QUERO-CHIESA was elected Chairman, New York City
Board of Higher Education in 1971.   He has been Presi-
dent, Institute of Puerto Rico, New York City; Vice Presi-
dent, Puerto Rican Culture Center, New York City, and
Member, Institute of Hispanic Culture (Madrid).   Mr.
Quero-Chiesa is an artist and author.

RICHARD RIVERA is an instructor of Puerto Rican Studies
at College Adapter Program and at New York City Community College.   He has taught in the schools of Puerto
Rico and New York City.   Mr. Rivera has been accepted
as a law school student at Rutgers--The State University,
New Jersey.

JAIME RUIZ-ESCOBAR is Instructor in the Puerto Rican
Studies Program at New York City Community College.
He has taught for the Puerto Rican Development Project
and at the University of Puerto Rico.   Ruiz-Escobar is the
author of numerous plays, short stories and poems and
has been producer/actor on television in Puerto Rico.

ANTONIO STEVENS-ARROYO is Adjunct Assistant Professor,
Hostos Community College, Bronx.   He is Chaplain of the
Puerto Rican Folklore Festival.   Father Stevens-Arroyo
was coordinator of the Spanish Youth Ministry, Archdiocese
of New York.   He has been a television producer, music
composer and author of several articles.

ALEXANDER VAZQUEZ is Coordinator of Industrial Technical Programs, Division of Continuing Education, New York
City Community College.   He has held appointments with
the New York University Graduate School of Social Work,
Bronx Community College, and the Philadelphia School District Office of Policy Planning and Development.

JOHN VAZQUEZ is Assistant Professor of Sociology at New
York City Community College and part-time faculty member in the School of Education at Fordham University.   He

was Director of Puerto Rican Studies at N. Y. C. C. C. and
Research Associate for ASPIRA.   Mr. Vazquez has written
articles on Puerto Rican cultural topics.   •

CELIA VÍCE is President of Puerto Rican Heritage Publica-
  tions, Inc.   Among her previous appointments are Vice
  President, CLICK; Director of Public Relations for the
  Puerto Rican Community Development Project; Commission-
  er, New York City Commission on Human Rights.   Mrs.
  Vice has received many awards from civic, social and ed-
  ucational organizations.   She was Grand Marshal of the
  Puerto Rican Day Parade in 1960.

INDEX

Affirmative Action 2, 45-49
Aguilu, Fernando 72
Alienation 3, 22, 28-31
Anomie 22, 26, 40, 41
Aponte Martinez, Cardinal Luis 4
Arriví, Francisco 69-70
Asabache 128
ASPIRA 1, 35, 76, 148, 157

Badge 373 63
Badillo, Herman v, 76, 155
Barrio, el 83, 123, 152, 159-61
Belavel, Emilio S. 69
Belpré, Pura 84, 88-91, 94-96
Betances, Ramón C. 151
Biculturalism 26, 152
Bilingual Education 1, 2, 8-12, 17, 19, 23-25, 27, 54,
    103, 145, 154, 156-57
Black Studies 34
Blackboard Jungle 59-60
Blacks 5, 15, 17, 37, 41, 102, 105, 156
Bogue, Donald J. 148
Boscana, Lucy 73
Bronx (South) 77, 78, 91, 94, 95, 102, 152
Brooklyn Navy Yard 138, 140-42

Cabrera, Pablo 71-73
Campos, Rafael 59
Carrero, Jaime 71
Casals, Pablo 151
Casas, Myrna 70, 72
Catholic church 4, 40, 123, 126
Change of Habit 61
City University of New York, The (CUNY) 2, 11, 45-47, 49,
    56, 102
  Open Admission Policy 11, 46, 102, 103
Colon, Miriam 73

170